Foundational Issues in Linguistic Theory

Current Studies in Linguistics
Samuel Jay Keyser, general editor

A complete list of books published in the Current Studies in Linguistics series appears at the back of this book.

Foundational Issues in Linguistic Theory

Essays in Honor of Jean-Roger Vergnaud

edited by Robert Freidin, Carlos P. Otero, and Maria Luisa Zubizarreta

The MIT Press
Cambridge, Massachusetts
London, England

MIT Press books may be purchased at special quantity discounts for business or sales promotional use. For information, please e-mail special_sales@mitpress.mit.edu or write to Special Sales Department, The MIT Press, 55 Hayward Street, Cambridge, MA 02142.

This book was set in Times New Roman and Syntax on 3B2 by Asco Typesetters, Hong Kong and was printed and bound in the United States of America.

Library of Congress Cataloging-in-Publication Data

Foundational issues in linguistic theory : essays in honor of Jean-Roger Vergnaud / edited by Robert Freidin, Carlos P. Otero, and Maria Luisa Zubizarreta.
    p.   cm. — (Current studies in linguistics)
Includes bibliographical references and index.
ISBN 978-0-262-06278-7 (hardcover : alk. paper) — ISBN 978-0-262-56233-1 (pbk. : alk. paper)
1. Linguistics. I. Vergnaud, Jean-Roger. II. Freidin, Robert. III. Otero, Carlos Peregrín
1930– IV. Zubizarreta, Maria Luisa.
P125.F68   2008
410—dc22   2007041007

10   9   8   7   6   5   4   3   2   1

Contents

Jean-Roger and Paul Gauguin Have a Chat   vii
Samuel Jay Keyser

Introduction   ix
Robert Freidin, David Michaels, Carlos P. Otero, and Maria Luisa
Zubizarreta

I   Syntax   1

1   Letter to Noam Chomsky and Howard Lasnik on "Filters and Control," April 17,
       1977   3
       Jean-Roger Vergnaud

2   On the Development of Case Theory: Triumphs and Challenges   17
       Howard Lasnik

3   Uninterpretable Features Are Incompatible in Morphology with Other Minimalist
       Postulates   43
       M. Rita Manzini and Leonardo M. Savoia

4   Parallel Nominal and Verbal Projections   73
       Karine Megerdoomian

5   Clause Structure and the Syntax of Verbless Sentences   105
       Elabbas Benmamoun

6   On Phases   133
       Noam Chomsky

7   Phasal Agreement and Reconstruction   167
       Alain Rouveret

8   Superiority, Reconstruction, and Islands   197
     Cedric Boeckx and Norbert Hornstein

9   Identity Avoidance: OCP Effects in Swiss Relatives   227
     Henk van Riemsdijk

10   Ellipsis and Missing Objects   251
     Joseph Aoun and Yen-hui Audrey Li

11   Tokenism and Identity in Anaphora   275
     Edwin Williams

12   Some Preliminary Comparative Remarks on French and Italian Definite Articles   291
     Richard S. Kayne

II   Phonology   323

13   Reduplication   325
     Morris Halle

14   The Logic of Contrast   359
     B. Elan Dresher

     Index   381

Jean-Roger and Paul Gauguin Have a Chat

Samuel Jay Keyser

D'où venons-nous?
Why ask such questions, vieille peau?
What does it matter
where we came from?

Où allons nous?
What does it matter? If the next stop
and the last stop are the same stop,
either way one has to get off.

Qui sommes-nous?
Now that's more like it, old skin.
Like your fine Maori cup,
we can get a handle on that.

Jean-Roger Vergnaud. Photograph by Antonio Nava.

Introduction

Robert Freidin, David Michaels, Carlos P. Otero, and Maria Luisa Zubizarreta

Part I: Syntax

Jean-Roger Vergnaud's work in linguistics has always been concerned with foundational issues. His 1974 MIT PhD dissertation on French restrictive relative clauses was one of the first studies to argue against a matching analysis, which involved deletion under identity within the relative clause, and to propose instead a promotion analysis under which the element modified by the relative clause is raised into an empty head. Now, decades later, this proposal (in a somewhat modified form) has become the standard analysis for the derivation of relative clauses. Moreover, the analysis of relative clauses, movement, and deletion continue to be central topics of current research, as illustrated in several chapters in this book.

One of the most important breakthroughs in the development of the principles-and-parameters framework occurs in an until recently unpublished letter from Jean-Roger Vergnaud to Noam Chomsky and Howard Lasnik regarding the first draft of their 1977 paper "Filters and Control" (the letter appears in chapter 1 of this book).[1] To account for certain properties of infinitival constructions in English, Chomsky and Lasnik had proposed the following surface filter (1):

(1) *$[_\alpha$NP *to* VP], unless α is adjacent to and in the domain of
    a. [−N] (adjunct)
    b. [+V] φ

(1) applies to indexed NPs—that is, to lexical (phonetically realized, hence overt) NPs and trace, but not to PRO. Vergnaud suggests replacing (1) with a filter concerning the licensing of "Governed Case" (as opposed to nominative and genitive), which he suggests "looks very much like a principle of UG." He assumes that NPs are assigned abstract Case, even when Case has no overt morphological realization. Vergnaud explores two alternative theories, one in which only phonetically realized (i.e., overt) NPs are marked for Case and another that includes traces.[2] This constitutes the first proposal of a UG principle to be formulated in terms of Case and

government and leads directly to the formulation of the more general Case Filter (Chomsky 1980). The realization that concepts of Case and government, which Vergnaud's letter brought into focus, lay at the foundation of UG principles opened up extremely fruitful lines of research, still ongoing.[3] Vergnaud, in collaboration with Alain Rouveret (1980), the following year introduced the analysis that passive participles, being adjectival in character, do not assign structural Case to their NP complements,[4] which has become standard in the analysis of Case. They also proposed extending these concepts to binding theory; see their Case Island Condition, an attempt to generalize Chomsky's Nominative Island Condition (1980).[5] In *Dépendances et niveaux de représentation en syntaxe* (1985) Vergnaud recasts his earlier work on French syntax from the perspective of the principles-and-parameters framework, which had developed over the past decade, including a presentation of a formal theory of Case. The fundamental importance of Case in syntactic theory is amply demonstrated in several chapters that follow.

Starting with Vergnaud's fundamental insight that notions of Case and government were deeply embedded in the principles of UG, Lasnik's "On the Development of Case Theory: Triumphs and Challenges" (chapter 2) provides a critical overview of the major landmarks in the twenty-nine-year evolution of Case theory. Vergnaud's original formulation of a Case principle is primarily concerned with the distribution of phonetically realized NP in the subject position of an infinitival clause. As Lasnik notes, Chomsky's formulation of the Case Filter in "On Binding" (written in 1978, published in 1980) generalizes to the phonetically realized NP complements of [+N] categories (i.e., N and A), which had become a problem with the advent of X-bar theory, requiring the apparently ad hoc solution of an *of*-insertion transformation in English. Case theory explains the existence of such rules as well as the distribution of phonetically realized subjects in infinitival clauses.

Case theory involves several interrelated foundational issues, stated here as the following questions:

1. How does Case enter a derivation?
2. What is the precise formulation of the Case Filter?
3. At what level (or levels) of representation does the Case Filter apply?

Lasnik's discussion touches on all three, but is primarily concerned with the latter two.

Initially, it was assumed that Case was assigned to NPs on the basis of the structural configuration in which they appeared. In chapter 4 of Chomsky 1995, an alternative was proposed whereby Case was assigned in the lexicon and then licensed on the basis of structural configuration when the lexical items are inserted in a derivation. More recent analyses (starting with Chomsky 2000 and including Chomsky's contribution to this book) postulate that Case features enter a derivation unvalued and are then valued by syntactic configuration, a variant of the Case-assignment analysis.

Whether Case is assigned or licensed, the question remains: on what basis? Initially, it was assumed that Case was assigned under government by a Case-assigning lexical head (e.g., V and P). However, nominative Case did not fit because it was clearly connected to a functional head I(nflection) and involved agreement, as illustrated in the inflected infinitive construction in Portuguese (see Quicoli 1996 and the works cited there for detailed discussion). With Pollock's (1989) development of clause structure analysis and Chomsky's (1991) revisions, it became possible to re-analyze the basic head government cases of Case assignment[6] as the result of more abstract Spec-head relations where the head was a functional element involving agreement, as has been proposed under the Minimalist Program.[7]

The precise formulation of the Case Filter depends on what syntactic objects are subject to it, which in turn bears on the question of what level(s) of representation it applies to. The initial formulations of the Case Filter, both Chomsky's and Vergnaud's, apply solely to phonetically realized NPs, hence not to empty categories (e.g., trace and PRO). However, as demonstrated in Lasnik and Freidin 1981, relative clauses in which the relative pronoun is not phonetically realized (i.e., deleted or null) provide evidence that the Case Filter must apply to the *wh*-trace in the infinitival subject position.[8] As Lasnik notes, this undermines treating the Case Filter as a PF filter.

An alternative treatment of the Case Filter as involving phenomena at LF is instantiated in the visibility analysis.[9] Basically, Case makes arguments visible for θ-role assignment. A Caseless argument cannot be assigned a θ-role and therefore violates the θ-Criterion at LF. Under this analysis the empirical effects of the Case Filter are derived by the independently motivated θ-Criterion and therefore there is no need to actually postulate a Case Filter holding at LF. However, there are three problems with this analysis, as Lasnik notes. First, the empty category PRO, which had been assumed to occupy a Caseless position, functions as an argument with a θ-role. This problem is resolved under Chomsky and Lasnik's (1993) proposal that PRO is marked with a null Case. The second problem concerns the analysis of expletives, which bear no θ-role and yet cannot occur in a Caseless position. Lasnik discusses how Chomsky's analysis of *there*-replacement by the associate resolves part of the problem, leaving the question of expletive *it* open. The third problem concerns clausal arguments, which have standardly been assumed not to be Case-marked. Lasnik discusses some evidence that suggests that certain clauses may well be marked for abstract Case.

From the beginning (i.e., Chomsky's *Logical Structure of Linguistic Theory* 1955/ 1956) and thus roughly twenty years before the advent of modern Case theory, the interaction between morphology and syntax has been a central focus of transformational grammar and continues as a fundamental focus of syntactic theory today. Manzini and Savoia's "Uninterpretable Features Are Incompatible in Morphology with Other Minimalist Postulates" (chapter 3) explores a radical reevaluation of the view that both morphological and syntactic structures are constructed from the same set of categories. Based on earlier work, beginning in 2001, Manzini and Savoia argue that to account for clitic variation across Romance dialects (specifically Italian and Swiss), it is necessary to redefine the standard morphological feature set {person, number, gender, case}.[10] For them both syntax and morphology should be built on syntactic categories such as N(ominal class), Q(uantification), and D(efiniteness), rather than on the traditional ϕ-features and Case. In their view, linguistic structures are articulated by the merger of lexical elements that project such categories both at the phrase (syntactic) level and at the word (morphological) level, a redefinition motivated in part by the need to attain explanatory adequacy in morphology—that is, to preserve basic minimalist principles such the Inclusiveness Condition (what they call "projection from the lexicon") and the prohibition against comparison of derivations/representations or mechanisms of equivalent power.

In their chapter, Manzini and Savoia concentrate on the redefinition of the feature set, drawing together arguments concerning the ϕ-features and arguments concerning the Case system presented in their previous work in connection with various specific problems relating in particular to the clitic set and agreement. Their discussion here revolves around the issue of structural Case. They argue against the standard notion of Case as a relational feature on the assumption that features of the lexicon can encode only "bona fide lexical properties," never relational ones. Thus nominative Case is a reflection of a D(efiniteness) feature, in contrast to accusative Case, which associates with the N(ominal class) feature. They go on to point out that there is a natural hierarchy of these features, reflected in the structure of DPs where $D > Q > N$ and mirrored in clauses where nominative clitics precede datives (associated with Q), which in turn precede accusatives.

Their approach to agreement and Case departs radically from Chomsky's minimalist proposals by rejecting the assumption that agreement inflections of the verb are "uninterpretable" at the interface levels and that the Case feature is a reflex of agreement in ϕ-features (Chomsky 2001). In fact they consider the notion of "uninterpretable feature" (which includes the device of having unvalued features) to be contrary to the minimalist assumption that linguistic representations contain only arrangements of elements that already exist in the lexicon. The innovations they propose for Case and ϕ-features leave us without the formal means for implementing the minimalist rule of Agree as envisaged by Chomsky (1995, 2000, 2001). However, they argue that generative grammars allow for a different conception of Agree, whereby the agreement between two nominal categories both introduced by Merge allows for their coreference. Following earlier work, they propose that this interpretive construal of Agree, independently needed for anaphora, is to be extended to verb agreement.

The morphological underpinnings of syntactic structure is also a major focus of Karine Megerdoomian's "Parallel Nominal and Verbal Projections" (chapter 4), which investigates syntactic and semantic correspondences between the nominal and verbal domains that are manifested in the morphological properties of Case and agreement in several languages (including Finnish, Scots Gaelic, and Eastern Armenian). Building on unpublished work of Jean-Roger Vergnaud,[11] Megerdoomian proposes that nominal and verbal phrases are composed of a fixed set of primitive elements consisting of a root, a category feature, and functional features of aspect and reference. The former functional feature is associated with an interpretation denoting "boundedness" and the latter with an interpretation concerning "instantiation." Both nominal and verbal phrases are assumed to have a Larsonian shell structure with a vP-shell and nP-shell above the VP and NP, respectively.

In the nominal domain, "boundedness" is expressed in the Num(ber) projection; Num merges with NP and provides information regarding cardinality or specific quantity. In the verbal domain, "boundedness" is expressed as verbal aspect in an Asp(ect) projection, where Asp, which merges with VP, provides information regarding the telicity of the event expressed in the predicate. In the nominal domain, the referential feature "instantiation" is realized in the D projection, where D merges with nP attributing to the DP a "specific" interpretation. In the verbal domain, this feature is realized in the Agr projection, where Agr merges with vP and manifests agreement. A nominal phrase is interpreted as an argument of the verb when the primitive elements in the nominal domain enter into a specifier-of relation with their verbal counterparts in the verbal domain. These specifier relations result from matching the corresponding feature in the parallel nominal and verbal domain. The resulting interpretation and Case marking depend on the level of structure in which the Case-checking relation is established.

For example, in languages like Finnish and Scottish Gaelic the Num projection of the nominal internal argument enters into a checking relation with the Asp projection in the verbal domain. In that configuration, Case is correlated with specific quantity. As illustrated by the Finnish examples in (2), Acc Case correlates with a bounded interpretation and Partitive with an unbounded interpretation:

(2) a. Hän   kirjoitt-i   kirjeet   Bounded
       He/she write-PAST/M/3SG letters-ACC
       'He wrote the letters.'
    b. Hän   kirjoitt-i   kirje-i-tä   Unbounded
       He/she write-PAST/M/3SG letter-PL-PART
       i. 'He wrote letters.'
       ii. 'He was writing (the) letters.'

In contrast, in Eastern Armenian the Case on the (underlying) object is correlated with specificity. Whether the object is Case-marked and specific, as in (3), or non-Case-marked and nonspecific, as in (4), the event is interpreted as telic.

(3) a.   Sirun-ə   mi hat' xndzor-ə mi jam-um k'er-av
          Sirun-NOM one CL apple-ACC one hour-LOC eat-AOR/3SG
          'Sirun ate one of the apples in an hour.'

   b. #Sirun-ə   mi hat' xndzor-ə mi jam k'er-av
          Sirun-NOM one CL apple-ACC one hour eat-AOR/3SG
          '# Sirun ate one of the apples for an hour.'

(4) a.   Sirun-ə   mi jam-um mi hat' xndzor k'er-av
          Sirun-NOM one hour-LOC one CL apple   eat-AOR/3SG
          'Sirun ate an apple in an hour.'

   b. #Sirun-ə   mi jam mi hat' xndzor k'er-av
          Sirun-NOM one hour one CL apple   eat-AOR/3SG
          '# Sirun ate an apple for an hour.'

The difference between the two languages is accounted for by the fact that in the Finnish-type language, Acc Case is checked when the Num P (which correlates with a specific quantity interpretation in the nominal domain) enters into a Spec-head relation with Asp (in the verbal domain). On the other hand, in the Eastern Armenian–type language, Acc Case is checked when DP (which manifests the specific interpretation in the nominal domain) enters into a Spec-head relation with Agr (in the verbal domain). Furthermore, a non-Case-marked N in Armenian (which correlates with a nonspecific interpretation) is merged with its counterpart in the verbal domain, namely V, and hence lower on the verbal projection. The proposed framework thus captures directly the observed one-to-one relations between corresponding nominal and verbal features and provides additional support for the analysis of structural case as a product of checking relations.

   Elabbas Benmamoun's "Clause Structure and the Syntax of Verbless Sentences" (chapter 5) addresses a key issue in the theory of clause structure that also engages the syntax/morphology interface—namely, whether both the categories T(ense) and V(erb) are universally projected elements in every clause, focusing on the nature of the dependency between T and V. Benmamoun sharpens the analysis of the syntactic composition of Tense and, in so doing, provides evidence for the independence of syntax and morphology (in the sense that morphology does not drive the syntax, in contrast to much current work).

   Based on the study of so-called verbless sentences in Arabic, Benmamoun argues that while T is universally projected, the category V is not. This proposal contrasts with that of Grimshaw 1991, in which functional categories are considered extended projections of lexical categories; hence, the presence of the former is contingent on the presence of the latter. Benmamoun proposes that T is categorially defined in terms of a feature D (nominal) and an optional feature V (verbal), a proposal compatible with well-known research in semantics, which has shown that Tense functions as a pronominal element (see Partee 1973, 1984). More precisely, Benmamoun suggests that past tense is specified for both D- and V-features, while present tense is specified for a D-feature only. The argument is based on the distribution of the Arabic negative *ma-š* in sentences with past-tense verbs and in sentences with present-tense verbs in Arabic dialects. A crucial paradigm is given in (5–7).

(5) Omar ma-katab-š   ig-gawaab
    Omar ma-wrote-NEG the-letter
    'Omar didn't write the letter.'

(6) mi-š   biyiktib
    NEG-NEG writing
    'He isn't writing.'

(7) ?ana mi-š   taalib
    I   NEG-NEG student
    'I am not a student.'

As shown in (5), *ma-* with the past tense must appear as a proclitic on the verb (which is taken as evidence that V is attracted to T in the past tense due to its V specification), and -*š* occurs as an enclitic. With the present tense, in contrast, the negative *mi-š* occurs as a unit preceding the verb, as in (6). Predictably, the negative *mi-š* also surfaces as a unit in verbless sentences preceding an adjectival or nominal predicate, as illustrated in (7), where the negative precedes a predicate nominal.

Benmamoun cites evidence from Hebrew as further support for distinguishing the categorial specification of past and present tense. In Hebrew a verbal copula *haya* is obligatory in the past and future tenses in the absence of a lexical verb. This contrasts with the present tense, where a pronominal element that agrees with the subject in number and gender (but not person) occurs between the subject and the adjectival or nominal predicate. Benmamoun argues that this pronominal element is a nominal copula. The dependency between T and V is thus contingent on the categorial specification of T rather than on its morphological status (contra Baker 2003), and furthermore the existence of V in copular constructions is dependent on the feature composition of T (contra Grimshaw 1991).

In Noam Chomsky's "On Phases" (chapter 6) we encounter a shift of focus to very general questions of language design, abstracting away from considerations of the empirical basis, which constitute an important aspect of the previous studies. In this paper he continues to explore the "strong minimalist thesis" (SMT) "that language is an optimal solution to interface conditions that FL [the faculty of language] must satisfy," a thesis that developed within the principles-and-parameters framework of generative grammar over the past decade. Work on the SMT opens the possibility of achieving principled explanation—that is, beyond explanatory adequacy. However, as Chomsky notes, the SMT is not expected to hold completely but rather, as a reasonable research strategy, is taken as a starting point in order to evaluate where it fails and where potentially it succeeds.

Efficient computation, which lies at the core of the SMT, requires the restriction of computational resources. To this end, Chomsky proposes that Merge constitutes the sole computational operation in narrow syntax (from the lexicon to the C-I interface).[12] Unbounded Merge (or its equivalent) is required to account for "discrete infinity consisting of hierarchically organized objects," the basic property of language. In addition there are further limitations on Merge. To begin with, it applies to just two syntactic objects (SO) at a time. Next, Chomsky postulates a No Tampering Condition (NTC) so that Merge cannot make internal changes to the SOs to which it applies. The copy theory of movement follows as a consequence, since leaving an empty category via movement would violate the NTC. It also follows that Merge joins SOs at their edges. The Inclusiveness Condition (IC; see Chomsky 1995 for the original formulation) provides a third limitation on the effects of Merge (or any other operation that creates structure). Under this condition there can be no additional structure in syntactic representations beyond what exists in the lexicon, therefore no indices, bar levels for categories, or traces (i.e., special empty categories linked to displaced constituents).[13]

Merge comes in two varieties, external merge (EM), which joins two previously independent SOs, and internal merge (IM), which operates on a single SO by taking a copy of some part of it and joining the copy to the edge of the SO. IM is driven by edge features (EF) of lexical items (LIs).[14] In this chapter Chomsky generalizes the EF analysis so that EM is also driven by EFs. Thus, the merger of a head and its complement occurs because of an EF the head has. According to Chomsky, excluding IM would require a stipulation and thus IM comes for free. Therefore it is not an imperfection of the computational system for human language as previously considered.

Merge creates set-membership relations. Chomsky suggests that there may be only one other syntactic relation, probe/goal, based on Agree, where unvalued features of a probe are matched to valued features of a goal and then deleted. If correct, then the c-command relation is dispensable under the SMT.[15]

In addition to restricting computational resources, efficient computation requires minimization of computations. This is achieved (primarily) through the theory of phases, SOs that are transferred to the two interfaces at various points in a derivation. This renders the construction of classical D- and S-structure impossible. As in earlier work (Chomsky 2000, 2001), CP and v*P (where v* designates the functional head for transitive and experiencer constructions) are identified as phases. Crucially, T is not a phase head—in particular, T is not the probe that induces A-movement; rather, the phase head C has both an EF and an Agree feature (AF), the latter being inherited by T.[16] Chomsky discusses some empirical motivation for this analysis from subject-condition phenomena.

Under this analysis the phase head contains the relevant unvalued (hence uninterpretable) features that drive the computation. EFs and AFs of a probe can apply in any order or simultaneously. A goal with no unvalued features blocks Agree (intervention), which holds for both A and A′ chains.[17] Computation is further restricted by the Phase Impenetrability Condition (PIC): once the unvalued features of the probe have been valued and eliminated, the phase head becomes inert; when the phase transfers to the two interfaces at S/O, its components cease to be accessible to further computation. Transfer applies cyclically, thereby limiting the space for computation at any given stage of the derivation and thus aiding minimization.

This study constitutes an important development of Chomsky's analysis of phases in pursuing a theory of language in line with the SMT. As with Chomsky's previous writings on the minimalist program, "On Phases" operates at a very high level of abstraction. Much of the chapter is quite speculative and many of the proposals remain to be spelled out in detail, both formally and in terms of empirical consequences. Nonetheless, this chapter makes a creditable case for the plausibility of the SMT by highlighting the fundamental issues to be addressed and offering intriguing avenues to explore.

The phasal analysis of syntactic derivations is explored in Alain Rouveret's "Phasal Agreement and Reconstruction" (chapter 7), dealing with reconstruction and successive cyclicity effects, which are standardly assumed to be properties that result from syntactic movement operations. Rouveret proposes instead a non-movement analysis of resumptive pronouns in Celtic relative clauses in which these properties are derived under a phasal analysis of Agree. This analysis yields two significant implications: (1) successive cyclicity effects are not the exclusive property of movement derivations, and (2) the correlation of movement with reconstruction effects is not absolute.[18] Thus under a phasal analysis, Move and Agree can exhibit similar effects.

The Celtic languages exhibit two types of relativization strategies: one that involves a gap and another that involves a resumptive pronoun linked to the relative complementizer (RC). The resumptive pronoun strategy for relative clauses (in Welsh and Irish) applies in contexts where movement is not an option. Rouveret proposes that the relation between the RC and the relativization site is established via Agree in a cyclic fashion, where the relevant cyclic domains are defined in terms of phases, and the heads of the intervening phases bear the relevant RC features to be checked. The φ-features in the relativization site get spelled out as a resumptive pronoun precisely in those cases in which the φ-features are not accessible to the edge of the phase—that is, for the objects of prepositions and, in Welsh, for embedded subjects and objects as well. He also shows that relatives with a gap exhibit full reconstruction effects, while relatives that involve a resumptive pronoun exhibit partial reconstruction effects; more precisely, the former but not the latter give rise to Principle C effects.

On the other hand, relatives with a resumptive pronoun do exhibit reconstruction effects with respect to pronominal binding and lexical anaphora. Following Freidin and Vergnaud (2001) and Sauerland (2000, 2004), Rouveret goes on to argue that resumptive pronouns are definite descriptions that may include either a D with a full NP antecedent (8a) or just the N without any complement or adjunct (1b):

(8) a. Pron = $[_{DP}$ D $[_{NP}$ N DP]]
     b. Pron = $[_{DP}$ D $[_{NP}$ N]]

While the option in (8b) allows relatives with resumptive pronouns to escape Principle C effects, the option in (8a) can account for the cases of pronominal binding and anaphoric binding. He also shows that the only relevant site for "reconstruction" is the relativization site (and not the intermediate COMPs), which he takes to constitute further evidence in favor of the nonmovement analysis of relatives with resumptive pronouns in Celtic.

As in Rouveret's chapter, the impact of the analysis of resumptive pronouns on syntactic theory constitutes the main empirical focus of Cedric Boeckx and Norbert Hornstein's "Superiority, Reconstruction, and Islands" (chapter 8). Their chapter is centrally concerned with how an analysis of resumptive pronouns in Lebanese Arabic multiple-*wh* constructions (as discussed in Aoun and Li 2003) affects current central assumptions within the minimalist program. These constructions demonstrate both reconstruction and superiority effects—with, however, an asymmetry concerning island contexts. Aoun and Li argue that the analysis of these constructions shows that the two core minimalist assumptions employed to account for superiority and reconstruction phenomena are incompatible. In this chapter, Boeckx and Hornstein examine Aoun and Li's analysis and claims, and offer an alternative solution.

While resumptive pronouns can occur both inside and outside islands, reconstruction effects occur only with those pronouns that are outside islands.

(9) ?ayya taalib min   tulaab-a$_i$ fakkarto   ?'nno k'll m$\it{ì}$allme$_i$
    which student among students-her thought.2PL. that every teacher.FS
    ħatna?-ii
    will.3FS.choose-him
    'Which of her$_i$ students did you think that every teacher$_i$ would choose (him)'

(10) *ʔayya taalib min   tulaab-a$_i$ ʔ'nbasatto laʔinno k'll miʿallme$_i$
     which student among students-her pleased.2PL because every teacher.FS
     ħatnaʔ-ii
     will.3FS.choose-him
     'Which of her$_i$ students were you pleased because every teacher$_i$ would
     choose (him)'

Thus the quantified NP subject of the complement clause can bind the pronoun contained in the fronted *wh*-phrase in (9) where the resumptive pronoun occurs in a nonisland context, while this binding cannot occur in (10) where the resumptive pronoun
occurs in an island—hence the absence of reconstruction effects for such pronouns
inside islands. In contrast, superiority effects obtain in multiple-*wh* constructions
with resumptive pronouns regardless of whether the pronoun occurs outside or inside
an island (cf. (11b) vs. (12b)).

(11) a. miin ʔannaʿto-u   yzuur miin
         who persuaded.2PL-him to-visit who
         'Who did you persuade (him) to visit who?'
     b. *miin ʔannaʿto   miin yzuur-u
         who persuaded.2PL who to-visit-him
         'Who did you persuade who to visit (him)?'

(12) a. miin ʔ'nbasatto laʔinno saami ʕarraf-o   ʕa-miin
         who pleased.2PL because Sami introduced-him to-whom
         'Who were you pleased because Sami introduced (him) to whom?'
     b. *miin ʔenbasatto laʔinno saami ʕarraf   miin ʕal-e
         who pleased.2PL because Sami introduced whom to-him
         'Who were you pleased because Sami introduced who to him?'

Assuming that these constructions involve *wh*-movement to the edge of the clause,
superiority holds even when the launching is expressed at PF as a resumptive pronoun. Aoun and Li contend that the lack of reconstruction effects in islands can be
accounted for if the resumptive pronoun in the island is not derived from a copy of
the *wh*-phrase it is anaphoric on—in contrast to the resumptive pronoun in a nonisland context, which they claim is derived from a full copy of its associated
wh-phrase. However, if this analysis is correct, then the superiority effects involving
multiple-*wh* constructions with a resumptive pronoun in an island context cannot be
explained on current minimalist assumptions. Therefore the copy theory of movement, which follows from the Inclusiveness Condition (Chomsky 1995), must be incompatible with the minimal link analysis of superiority (via either shortest move or
attract).

An account of these constructions appears to require a modification of core assumptions. As Boeckx and Hornstein discuss, if the movement analysis of superiority effects is retained, then the analysis of reconstruction as an effect of the copy theory of movement must be revised. Alternatively, if the prohibition against movement out of islands is retained to explain the lack of reconstruction effects in island contexts, then superiority effects cannot be viewed as a result of economy of movement. Aoun and Li opt for the second approach, while Boeckx and Hornstein argue for the former. They review the Aoun and Li solution and their arguments against the alternative they do not adopt and then elaborate a several-step argument for this alternative. In brief, they propose that the resumptive pronoun and its antecedent form an antiagreement chain when the pronoun is inside an island. They deny that the lack of a reconstruction effect entails the absence of movement and instead propose that the lack of reconstruction in islands is linked to the antiagreement nature of the chain formed. Thus, outside an island, a resumptive pronoun forms an agreement chain, which allows reconstruction effects.

The role of deletion in the analysis of syntactic structure has a long and rich history in generative grammar. To the extent that deletion plays a substantial role in determining PF representations but seems largely irrelevant for determining LF representations, the deletion operation appears to occur in a derivation following Spell-Out in what might be considered the phonological part of a derivation. Nonetheless, deletion depends on some notion of structural correspondence and is therefore strongly linked to the purely syntactic portion of a derivation. Thus deletion provides a window on the syntax/phonology interface. Given that certain requirements of the LF interface drive various aspects of a syntactic derivation, we might ask whether there are also requirements of the PF interface that also drive parts of the syntactic derivation. Henk van Riemsdijk's "Identity Avoidance: OCP Effects in Swiss Relatives" (chapter 9) provides one case study, in which he revisits syntactic problems raised by headed relatives in Swiss German that he first studied in 1989.

In this chapter, van Riemsdijk examines the properties of a range of headed relative-clause constructions in Swiss German, which he divides into three major subclasses: resumptive relative clauses involving either a silent resumptive clitic or a locally accessible resumptive pronoun in situ, "aboutness" relative clauses that lack any visible correlative element, and locative relative clauses involving either an expletive or nonexpletive locative operator. He proposes that resumptive pronouns in Swiss relative clauses manifest cliticlike behavior and as such can be adjoined to a $C°$-position. If that $C°$-position is adjacent to the head of the relative clause, the resulting configuration licenses the deletion of the resumptive pronoun *wo*, which is phonetically identical to the obligatory head C in headed relative clauses. In this case deletion by haplology appears to be absolutely obligatory. Clitic movement, normally optional, must apply here to feed deletion. This account allows van Riemsdijk to reduce his typology of headed relative clause constructions to two main subgroups, resumptives and locatives, and to reanalyze locally accessible resumptive pronouns in situ as another instance of a locative with an expletive operator.

Van Riemsdijk concludes that the true generalization underlying this analysis of headed relatives in Swiss German appears to be the annihilation of the correlative element either by haplology or the Avoid Pronoun Principle (Chomsky 1981a). This is what he calls the "kamikaze conspiracy." A further ingredient of this conspiracy is the Doubly Filled COMP Filter (Chomsky and Lasnik 1977) to the extent that it requires the deletion of any phonetically realized element that moves into the local proximity of a phonetically realized $C°$. Van Riemsdijk suggests that this filter constitutes a "syntactic reflex" of the Obligatory Contour Principle (OCP) in phonology, which accounts for haplology. He further suggests that the case of headed relative clauses in Swiss German demonstrates a generalized OCP in operation, including both haplology and the DFC filter—hence *XX. Van Riemsdijk goes on to speculate about how *XX might relate to more general properties of biological/physical design.

Ellipsis phenomena in natural language, involving instances of meaning without sound as they do, constitute a special challenge for any theory of grammar. Obviously the interpretation of ellipsis constructions requires the presence of some covert structure on which the appropriate interpretation is based. The fundamental question for a theory of ellipsis is how this structure is constructed. Within generative grammar, two distinct major proposals have been suggested: (1) a PF deletion approach, where the ellipsis results from the deletion of a fully specified construct (i.e., containing lexical items, including their phonetic features) in forming PF, and (2) an interpretive approach, where the ellipsis site contains a lexically empty categorial structure whose interpretation is derived from a corresponding structure that contains lexical material. See Williams 1977 for a comparison of the two approaches and an argument for the latter.

Joseph Aoun and Yen-hui Audrey Li's "Ellipsis and Missing Objects" (chapter 10) argues in favor of the interpretive approach, based on data from Mandarin Chinese. Their chapter considers two types of elliptical constructions in Chinese: the Aux-construction, where ellipsis occurs after an auxiliary in the second conjunct (*subject* + *Aux* + ____), as illustrated in (12), and the V-construction, where the ellipsis involves a missing object (*subject* + *V* + ____), as illustrated in (13).

(13) wo yao tanwang ta   san-ci;   wo baba ye   yao.
      I   will visit   him three times my father also will
      'I will visit him three times; my father will (visit him three times), too.'

(14) Ming hen xihuan ni gei ta   de liwu. Han ye hen xihuan.
     Ming very like   you give him De gift   Han also very like
     'Ming likes the gift you gave to him; Han also likes (the gift you gave to Han/
     Ming).'

The elided material in the Aux-construction is a VP, whereas in a V-construction it is
a DP. The V-construction does not allow for the ellipsis of adverbials, as illustrated
in (15).

(15) a. wo jian-guo ta   san-ci;   tamen ye jian-guo ____.
        I   see-ASP him three times they   also see-ASP
        (tamen zhi jian-guo yi-ci).
        (they   only see-ASP one-time)
        'I have seen him three times; they have seen (him), too. (They only saw
        (him) once.)'

Using data like (15), Aoun and Li propose that ellipsis is governed by the following
generalization:

(16) Subcategorization requirement on null categories
     a. If a head is subcategorized for a phrase E, E must be present in the
        syntactic structure.
     b. An E can be generated as null (without lexical materials) only in
        subcategorized positions.

Part (b) accounts for the absence of null adverbials in the V-construction. Under a
PF-deletion approach, this requirement is unexpected—especially given that the
notions of complement versus adverbial (adjunct) are syntactic and therefore presumably not part of the PF vocabulary. In further support of the interpretive approach,
Aoun and Li go on to suggest that in relative clauses containing null VPs the object
of the null VP is invisible to syntactic processes, which in turn suggests that it is lexically empty. They also consider a well-formedness condition on empty elements
(on their visibility) involving Case that accounts for a parametric difference between
Chinese and English where the V-construction is possible in the former, but not the
latter.

   The key to understanding how ellipsis works in natural language is rooted in the
conditions under which ellipsis, whether via deletion or interpretation, can occur. Although it is obvious that some principle of correspondence requires that the ellipsis
site must match some other overtly realized structure in the sentence, the nature of
the matching remains a focus of debate. More recent proposals (e.g., Merchant
2001) have moved away from a stricter identity constraint to a relatively looser parallelism requirement. Edwin Williams's chapter "Tokenism and Identity in Anaphora" (chapter 11) provides a new perspective on this fundamental issue.

Williams argues that the stronger identity constraint is indeed the right formulation for the correspondence principle governing ellipsis phenomena. To this end, he reviews three empirical arguments for a weaker parallelism condition involving antecedent contained deletion, sloppily bound pronouns, and inverse scope constructions like (17) (from Hirschbuhler 1982):

(17) A Canadian flag stood in front of every embassy and an American flag did too.

where the QP *every embassy* has scope over the two indefinite subjects.

Regarding the first case, antecedent contained deletion, Williams argues against a movement analysis (e.g., Fox 2002) on the grounds that some cases "clearly do not require overt extraposition" and furthermore that a parallelism condition on which the movement analysis is based is too weak to account for the failure of ellipsis in (18) and other constructions.

(18) *I saw several pictures of a man who you did.

The problem according to Williams is a lack of relation between the relative clause and the nuclear scope of the quantifier. Ellipsis requires a relation between them, which he designates as the Principle of Tokenism (19).

(19) x and y count as the same variable if they define predicates that are the restrictor and nuclear scope arguments of the same token of the same quantifier.

This principle establishes the identity relation required for ellipsis, which in turn allows us to maintain the stronger identity requirement, dropping the weaker parallelism constraint. Williams extends this analysis to the sloppily bound pronoun and inverse scope constructions that have been used to support parallelism over identity.

Richard S. Kayne's "Some Preliminary Comparative Remarks on French and Italian Definite Articles" (chapter 12) concerns parametric variation within the nominal domain. In this study he demonstrates that crosslinguistic variation across a variety of nominal constructions can be linked to a single parameter—in this case, the presence versus absence of an overt determiner in French versus Italian. His analysis depends crucially on the DP hypothesis and remnant movement, and therefore provides empirical support for both.

Three structures in French and Italian are compared: superlatives, *which*-phrases with a silent N, and mass nouns/partitives. In French and Italian, superlatives (like APs in general) are postnominal, but they differ in that a definite article *le* immediately precedes French *plus*, whereas Italian *più* is not preceded by a definite article.

(20) L'étudiant *le* plus intelligent est Jean.   French
        'The student the most intelligent is Jean.'

(21) Lo studente più intelligente è Gianni.   Italian

In French, but not Italian, *which*-phrases with a silent N are preceded by the definite determiner.

(22) *Le*quel as-tu vu?   French
    'The which have you seen?'

(23) Quale hai visto?   Italian

In Italian, "bare" plurals/mass nouns are possible, but not in French. In the French counterpart of the Italian "bare" plurals and mass nouns, the grammatical formative *de* 'of' must occur with the noun. And, furthermore, French has a definite article, where Italian does not. (The two properties are partially independent, as shown by Piedmontese, which has *de* but not a definite article.) Compare (24) and (25).

(24) a. Jean achetait *des* livres. (*des* = de + les)   French
      'Jean bought (was buying) books.'
   b. Jean buvait *de la* bière.
      'Jean drank beer.'

(25) a. Gianni comprava libri.   Italian
      'Gianni bought books.'
   b. Gianni beveva birra.
      'Gianni drank beer.'

Kayne proposes that in all of the above cases, the structures involve a definite D, with a filled specifier, and that the differences between the two languages can be reduced to whether or not D is pronounced. In the case of the French superlative in (20), the structure and derivation are as shown in (26).

(26) a. [$_{CP}$ C [$_{SC}$ [$_{DP}$ l'étudiant] [$_{AP}$ plus intelligent]]]
   b. [$_{CP}$ [$_{AP}$ plus intelligent]$_i$ C [$_{SC}$ [$_{DP}$ l'étudiant] t$_i$]]]
   c. [$_{DP}$ le [$_{CP}$ [$_{AP}$ plus intelligent]$_i$ C [$_{SC}$ [$_{DP}$ l'étudiant] t$_i$]]]]
   d. [$_{DP}$ [$_{SC}$ [l'étudiant] t$_i$]$_j$ *le* [[plus intelligent]$_i$ C t$_j$]]

Starting with a small clause CP in (26a), the predicate AP is preposed to Spec-CP in (26b), followed by the merger of the determiner *le* to form DP in (26c) and then the preposing of the small clause remnant to Spec-DP in (26d)—thereby giving the observed word order.

   The derivation of the Italian superlative in (21) is exactly the same with the difference that D has no phonetic features. Thus, superlatives in French and Italian are both DPs with the same structure, as shown in (27) and (28), but with the difference that the head of the DP is pronounced in French but not in Italian.

(27) [$_{DP}$ [$_{SC}$ [$_{DP}$ l'étudiant] t$_i$]$_j$ *le* [$_{CP}$ [$_{AP}$ plus intelligent]$_i$ C t$_j$]]   French

(28) [$_{DP}$ [$_{SC}$ [$_{DP}$ lo studente] t$_i$]$_j$ *D* [$_{CP}$ [$_{AP}$ più intelligente]$_i$ C t$_j$]]   Italian

The *wh*-phrases in (22) and (23) have the structures in (29) and (30), respectively, where unpronounced N has moved to the Spec of D. Again, the difference between the two languages is reduced to whether or not D is pronounced.

(29) [$_{DP}$ [$_{Spec}$ N$_i$] *le* [quel t$_i$ . . .]]

(30) [$_{DP}$ [$_{Spec}$ N$_i$] *D* [quale t$_i$ . . .]]

The bare plural/mass nouns in (24) are partitive structures, in which the presence of *de* is related to the presence of an unpronounced noun akin to overt nouns like *number*, *amount*, and *quantity*, as shown in (31).

(31) a. . . . NUMBER de les livres
     b. . . . AMOUNT de la bière

On the other hand, the bare plurals/mass nouns in (24–25) consist of an unpronounced NUMBER/AMOUNT noun situated in Spec of D (presumably via movement).

(32) a. [$_{DP}$ [$_{Spec}$ NUMBER] *D* [libri]]
     b. [$_{DP}$ [$_{Spec}$ AMOUNT] *D* [birra]]

The Italian constructs in (32) thus correspond to the parallel constructs in (28) and (30) in Italian. In all three, D in Italian remains unpronounced in the presence of a filled Spec of D. The absence of constructs like those in (32) in French is related to the absence of forms like (28) and (30) in this language. In other words, in French, D must be pronounced in the presence of a filled Spec of D.

Part II: Phonology

Vergnaud's contributions to phonology take a definite syntactic turn. *An Essay on Stress* (1987), his most extensive writing on phonology, coauthored with Morris Halle, focuses on the most syntactic of phonological processes. In the *Essay*, stress placement applies to strings that are organized into hierarchical metrical constituents whose boundedness is determined by parameters. The Halle and Vergnaud analysis proposes a recoverability condition for constituent structure that involves head location and the direction of government, transformations that move constituent boundaries, and cyclic stress rules (as in Chomsky and Halle's *The Sound Pattern of English* (*SPE*), with some modification). The *Essay* develops a position intermediate between the then standard version of metrical theory and the treeless grid theory of Alan Prince and others. It retains the view that strings are hierarchically organized into metrical constituents, but departs from the standard view by placing narrow restrictions on types of constituents. It also assigns a central role to metrical grids and thereby moves in the direction of the treeless theories. The difference between the *Essay*'s approach and the principles-and-parameters approach in syntax is that phonological rules are linearly ordered in the *Essay*, while they are not ordered in syntax.

Vergnaud's first published work on a principles-and-parameters approach to phonology—that is, without recourse to a language-specific rule component—is developed in "The Internal Structure of Phonological Elements: A Theory of Charm and Government" (1985), coauthored with Jonathan Kaye and Jean Lowenstamm. Vergnaud and his coauthors characterize this paper as part of an ongoing research program that "incorporates the view that phonology is to be regarded as a system of universal principles defining the class of human phonological systems." They further construe this work as a continuation of the line of research in *SPE* that concerns a theory of markedness (see also Kean 1975, 1979). The article gives a general introduction to their theory of phonological representations involving segments and feature tiers and then applies the theory to the vowel system of Kpokolo, an eastern Kru language.

In Vergnaud's subsequent work, "Constituent Structure and Government in Phonology" (1990), also with Kaye and Lowenstamm, phonological representations are also determined by universal principles and processes. The article addresses the notion "possible syllable" in terms of phonological government. It explicitly calls for a syntax of phonological expressions in the study of syntagmatic relations holding between phonological units. And while the authors allow for certain differences between syntax and phonology, such as the recursivity of syntactic categories, but not of phonological categories, their focus is on the similarities between syntax and phonology in terms of constituent structure and government, as well as a derivational approach that conforms to the cyclic principle. They point out that if syntax and phonology are governed by the same underlying principles, the notion that language involves unique properties of mind is strengthened. Here, Vergnaud and his coauthors show a concern for issues of language and mind, which unified generative phonology and syntax in the time of *SPE*.

Thus Vergnaud's work in phonology keeps abreast of the developments in syntactic theory, moving from rule-based systems to the principles-and-parameters approach, and its goals are very much in the mainstream of transformational grammar. Given the divergence of the research program in phonology from that in syntax since *SPE*, Vergnaud's approach is unique in its focus on the reunification of these two fields. His most recent work in phonology, "On a Certain Notion of 'Occurrence': The Source of Metrical Structure, and of Much More" (2003), goes deeper in this direction with a proposal that the notion of "occurrence" constitutes a shared foundational concept for both phonology and syntax. The exploration of foundational questions, so typical of Vergnaud's work, is amply demonstrated in the following two chapters on phonology.

Morris Halle's "Reduplication" (chapter 13) takes a new approach to the descriptive problems of reduplication. Incorporating ideas of Raimy (2000) and Frampton (2004), it develops an explicit formalism to account in a unified way for the different kinds of reduplicative systems described in the literature. Halle concludes that there are only three kinds of reduplication: simple, partial, and augmented. Simple reduplication copies a single sequence of segments in a word. Partial and augmented reduplication are instances of simple reduplication—that is, copying of a single sequence of segments—with deletions (partial reduplication) or additions (augmented reduplication) at the edges of the copied strings. Halle develops a system where brackets are inserted around a segment sequence by readjustment rules linked to a morpheme (say, plural) that might otherwise be phonetically null. In simple reduplication, the bracketed sequence is copied and the brackets erased. In partial reduplication, bracket insertion proceeds as in the simple case with the addition of an internal distinctive bracket that marks an initial or terminal substring of the full reduplication for deletion. In augmented reduplication, once again an internal distinctive bracket marks an initial or terminal subsequence of the full reduplication for repetition outside of the full reduplicated string. All of this is quite straightforward: mark a string in a morphological context with appropriate bracketings, and rearrange the bracketed sequence according to universal rules. What is extraordinary in Halle's account is how reduplications that superficially appear not to be instances of any of the three types are shown to result from applications of one or more of the three basic bracketings, sometimes interacting with other rules of the phonology or morphology. For example, in the treatment of the preterit in Attic Greek, partial reduplication interacts with prefixation and vowel contraction.

Proceeding from simple to complex cases, Halle reviews an extensive literature on reduplication in a variety of languages and demonstrates how the various transformations of segment sequences observed in the literature on reduplication resolve in each case into the proposed formalism for simple, partial, or augmented reduplication, or into combinations of two or three of them. A surprising discovery along the way is that an account of metathesis is implicit in the formalism for partial reduplication. For example, if both the initial and final segments are marked for partial reduplication, then AB becomes ABAB by full reduplication, BAB by partial reduplication (deletion) of the initial segment, and BA by partial reduplication (deletion) of the final segment; the result BA is the metathesis of AB. Halle shows how the many cases of metathesis studied in Hume 2004 receive a unified account under the rule for partial reduplication, and how metathesis, so conceived, interacts with the other kinds of reduplication. In this chapter, Halle gives a unified account of a great variety of instances of reduplication and metathesis, many of which are not in the least transparent on the surface, but are made derivationally transparent in an elegant formal account.

B. Elan Dresher's "The Logic of Contrast" (chapter 14) explores the notion of contrast in phonology. Contrasting feature specifications are a common part of phonological inventory construction, but the way they are determined is often not clear. Dresher gives a formal account of two competing approaches to determining contrast, showing how one fails because it cannot be counted on to differentiate the phonemes in a language and how the other succeeds not only in differentiating the phonemes, but in clarifying some issues in underspecification theory. (This is a theory in which certain features are unvalued in lexical entries and filled in by phonological rule.) The failed approach starts with the full specification of phonemes in an inventory. Any specifications that are predictable from the others are redundant, and only nonredundant features are contrastive in lexical representations. Thus, for the features voice and nasal and the phonemes /p/, /b/, and /m/, since nasals are always voiced, [−nasal] is redundant given [−voice] for /p/, and [+voice] is redundant given [+nasal] for /m/. Dresher calls this the Full Specification (FS) approach. He shows, however, that the mutual redundancy of voice and nasality for an inventory /p, m/ leaves the segments with no nonredundant features, and thus fails to differentiate the phonemes. The successful approach to determining contrast involves a hierarchical ordering of phonological features. Given the two features voice and nasal, and the three segments /p/, /b/, and /m/, if voice is ordered before nasal, then /p/ contrasts with /b, m/ for voice, and nasal is only contrastive in the voiced set /b, m/. If, on the other hand, nasal is ordered before voice, then /m/ contrasts with /p, b/ for nasal, and voice is only contrastive in the nonnasal set /p, b/. Dresher calls this the Contrastive Hierarchy (CH) approach and argues that the FS approach cannot determine contrast in every case, whereas the CH approach can.

He points out that these two approaches to contrast have been used implicitly or explicitly in phonological analyses from the beginnings of distinctive feature theory. In actual practice, either approach or both approaches might be applied in the same work. Jakobson, Fant, and Halle (1952) and Jakobson and Halle (1956), for example, set out the CH approach in which feature specifications are either contrastive or redundant depending on their position in a particular hierarchy. Trubetzkoy (1969), however, in analyzing the inventory of French consonants, uses what appears to be FS to determine that for the dental nasal /n/ voicing and occlusion are predictable and hence not contrastive, but uses what appears to be CH in deciding that place distinguishes /p, b/ from /f, v/ rather than continuance, thus setting up the hierarchical order place before continuance. Trubetzkoy gives as his reason for the hierarchy that the degree to which a segment is continuant is tied to its place of articulation.

Dresher explores the uses of contrast in the generative phonology literature, with interesting results. For example, he argues that Kiparsky's (1985) theory of structure preservation in phonology is based on a wrong analogy to Emonds's (1976) theory of the same name in syntax, since in syntax there are phrase structure rules that set out the structure to be preserved by transformations, but in phonology there are no comparable structure-assigning rules that subsequent phonological rules have to preserve. However, in a CH approach to determining contrast, something approaching structure preservation might be constructed. The example Dresher uses involves the features sonorant and voice. In Russian, voicing assimilations neither affect sonorants nor are triggered by them. Obstruents, on the other hand, both trigger and are affected by voicing assimilation. If sonorant is ordered before voice in determining contrast, then voice will not be distinctive for sonorants in underived lexical representations. Something akin to structure preservation might then constrain rule-derived representations in the lexical phonology from specifying voice in sonorant segments. Thus, the problem for Kiparsky's theory of structure preservation, as Dresher sees it, is the lack of a formal approach for determining contrast in phoneme inventories. He goes on to show that this same lack of an explicit formal approach to determining contrast underlies the inconsistencies in underspecification theory criticized in Steriade 1995 and Kirchner 1997. These inconsistencies are generally the result of the lack of a formal theory for distinguishing contrastive and redundant feature specifications. The CH approach provides a principled means for determining contrast and thus avoids the inconsistencies in underspecification theory. Dresher's chapter points up the importance of making explicit the formal underpinnings of any linguistic analysis, especially in the case of a commonly held but vaguely defined notion, such as contrast in phonology.

Notes

1. Vergnaud's letter is also included in Freidin and Lasnik 2006.

2. The letter also contains an alternative approach to the *that*-trace filter of Chomsky and Lasnik 1977 as well as a few remarks on various passages in the original manuscript.

3. As Chomsky notes in his contribution to this volume, this letter was "one major stimulus to the development of the M[inimalist]P[rogram]."

4. See Chomsky 1981b, note 48.

5. Their paper was written in 1978 and published in 1980 in the same issue of *Linguistic Inquiry* that contained Chomsky's "On Binding." They formulated the Case Island Condition as follows:

(i) An anaphor *x* must have an antecedent in the minimal binding domain containing the element that assigns its Case to *x*.

6. That is, verbal object and subject of an infinitival complement of an exceptional Case-marking verb.

7. The analysis allows us to dispense with head government and hence with complicated definitions of government. Note however that while this analysis generalizes across nominative

and accusative/objective Case, it remains unclear how it applies in the case of prepositional objects and the subjects of infinitival clauses with a *for* complementizer.

8. Note that Vergnaud also suggests that *wh*-trace be subject to his Case Filter in the second theory he proposes.

9. The original proposal is attributed to Aoun 1979.

10. This chapter is but a small sample of their comprehensive study of a wide range of Italian dialects (examining hundreds of systems), a substantial part of which has recently appeared in Italian, including full sets of data (up to ten pages of examples for each major pattern). This chapter draws together arguments concerning the φ-feature set and the case system presented in four earlier papers from 2001 to 2005 in connection with various specific problems relating in particular to the clitic set and agreement. See Manzini and Savoia 2005, a three-volume work adding up to close to 2,500 pages.

11. Vergnaud's proposals are incorporated into an unpublished monograph (in collaboration with Martin Prinzhorn) titled "Some Explanatory Avatars of Conceptual Necessity: Elements of UG" (2005–2006).

12. The other portion of the derivation, from Spell-Out (S/O) to the S-M interface, involves deletion as well.

13. The copy theory of movement also follows from the IC. Thus, there appears to be some intrinsic connection between it and the NTC. Chomsky does not comment on this.

14. EFs seem like a generalization of the EPP property of clauses, though Chomsky does not identify them as such.

15. Chomsky speculates that binding theory involves Agree (i.e., probe/goal) rather than c-command (see Reuland 2001). This would, of course, require a radical reformulation of much of syntactic theory of the past thirty years.

16. This generalizes to v*, where the AF is inherited by V. Chomsky notes that inheritance constitutes a "narrow violation" of the NTC, but suggests that it might nonetheless be compatible with the SMT.

17. In this chapter Chomsky proposes a derivational account of the A/A′ distinction with respect to chains.

18. See Boeckx and Hornstein's contribution in chapter 8 of this book for a similar conclusion.

References

Aoun, J. 1979. On government, Case-marking, and clitic placement. Unpublished ms., MIT.

Aoun, J., and A. Li. 2003. *Essays on the Representational and Derivational Nature of Grammar: The Diversity of Wh-Constructions*. Cambridge, MA: MIT Press.

Baker, M. 2003. *Lexical Categories: Verbs, Nouns, and Adjectives*. Cambridge: Cambridge University Press.

Chomsky, N. 1955/1956. *The Logical Structure of Linguistic Theory*. New York: Plenum. 1975.

Chomsky, N. 1980. On binding. *Linguistic Inquiry* 11:1–46.

Chomsky, N. 1981a. *Lectures on Government and Binding*. Dordrecht: Foris.

Chomsky, N. 1981b. Principles and parameters in syntactic theory. In N. Hornstein and D. Lightfoot, eds., *Explanation in Linguistics: The Logical Problem of Language Acquisition*, 32–75. New York: Longman.

Chomsky, N. 1991. Some notes on economy of derivation and representation. In R. Freidin, ed., *Principles and Parameters in Comparative Grammar*, 417–454. Cambridge, Mass.: MIT Press. (Reprinted in N. Chomsky, *The Minimalist Program*, 129–166. Cambridge, Mass.: MIT Press, 1995.)

Chomsky, N. 1995. *The Minimalist Program*. Cambridge, Mass.: MIT Press.

Chomsky, N. 2000. Minimalist inquiries: The framework. In R. Martin, D. Michaels, and J. Uriagereka, eds., *Step by Step*, 89–155. Cambridge, Mass.: MIT Press.

Chomsky, N. 2001. Derivation by phase. In M. Kenstowicz, ed., *Ken Hale: A Life in Language*, 1–52. Cambridge, Mass.: MIT Press.

Chomsky, N., and M. Halle. 1968. *The Sound Pattern of English*. New York: Harper and Row.

Chomsky, N., and H. Lasnik. 1977. Filters and control. *Linguistic Inquiry* 8:425–504.

Chomsky, N., and H. Lasnik. 1993. The theory of Principles and Parameters. In J. Jacobs, A. von Stechow, W. Sternefeld, and T. Vennemann, eds., *Syntax: An International Handbook of Contemporary Research*. Berlin: de Gruyter. (Reprinted in N. Chomsky, *The Minimalist Program*, 13–127. Cambridge, Mass.: MIT Press, 1995.)

Emonds, J. 1976. *A Transformational Approach to English Syntax: Root, Structure-Preserving, and Local Transformations*. New York: Academic Press.

Fox, D. 2002. Antecedent Contained Deletion and the Copy Theory of Movement. *Linguistic Inquiry* 33:63–95.

Frampton, J. 2004. Distributed reduplication. Unpublished ms., Northeastern University.

Freidin, R., and H. Lasnik. 2006. *Syntax: Critical Concepts in Linguistics*. 6 vols. London: Taylor & Francis.

Freidin, R., and J.-R. Vergnaud. 2001. Exquisite connections: Some remarks on the evolution of linguistic theory. *Lingua* 111:639–666.

Grimshaw, J. 1991. Extended projections. Unpublished ms., Rutgers University.

Halle, M., and J.-R. Vergnaud. 1987. *An Essay on Stress*. Cambridge, Mass.: MIT Press.

Hirschbuhler, P. 1982. VP Deletion and Across-the-Board Quantifier Scope. In J. Pustejovsky and P. Sells, eds., *Proceedings of NELS 12*. Amherst: GLSA, University of Massachusetts.

Hume, E. 2004. The indeterminacy/attestation model of metathesis. *Language* 80:203–237.

Jakobson, R., G. Fant, and M. Halle. 1952. *Preliminaries to Speech Analysis*. MIT Acoustics Laboratory, Technical Report, No. 13. (Reissued by MIT Press, Cambridge, Mass., 1976.)

Jakobson, R., and M. Halle. 1956. *Fundamentals of Language*. The Hague: Mouton.

Kaye, J., J. Lowenstamm, and J.-R. Vergnaud. 1985. The internal structure of phonological elements: A theory of charm and government. *Phonology Yearbook* 2:305–328.

Kaye, J., J. Lowenstamm, and J.-R. Vergnaud. 1990. Constituent structure and government in phonology. *Phonology* 7:193–231.

Kean, M.-L. 1975. *The Theory of Markedness in Generative Grammar*. Doctoral dissertation, MIT.

Kean, M.-L. 1979. On a theory of markedness: Some general considerations and a case in point. *Social Sciences Research Report* 41. Irvine: UC Irvine.

Kiparsky, P. 1985. Some consequences of lexical phonology. *Phonology Yearbook* 2:85–138.

Kirchner, R. 1997. Contrastiveness and faithfulness. *Phonology* 14:83–111.

Lasnik, H., and R. Freidin. 1981. Core grammar, Case theory, and markedness. In A. Beletti, L. Brandi, and L. Rizzi, eds., *Theory of Markedness in Generative Grammar*, 407–421. Pisa: Scuola Normale Superiore. (Reprinted in H. Lasnik, *Essays on Restrictiveness and Learnability*, 172–183. Dordrecht: Kluwer, 1990. Also in R. Freidin, *Generative Grammar: Theory and Its History*, 101–112, 2007. London: Routledge.)

Manzini, M. R., and L. M. Savoia. 2005. *I dialetti italiani e romanci: Morfosintassi generativa.* 3 vols. Alessandria: Edizioni dell'Orso.

Merchant, J. 2001. *The Syntax of Silence: Sluicing, Islands, and the Theory of Ellipsis.* Oxford: Oxford University Press.

Partee, B. 1973. Some structural analogies between tenses and pronouns. *Journal of Philosophy* 70(18):601–609.

Partee, B. 1984. Nominal and temporal anaphora. *Linguistics and Philosophy* 7:243–286.

Pollock, J.-Y. 1989. Verb movement, Universal Grammar, and the structure of IP. *Linguistic Inquiry* 20:365–424.

Quicoli, A. C. 1996. Inflection and parametric variation: Portuguese and Spanish. In R. Freidin, ed., *Current Issues in Comparative Grammar*, 46–80. Dordrecht: Kluwer.

Raimy, E. 2000. *The Morphology and Phonology of Reduplication.* Berlin: Mouton-deGruyter.

Reuland, E. J. 2001. Primitives of Binding. *Linguistic Inquiry* 32(3):439–492.

Riemsdijk, Henk C. van. 1989. Swiss relatives. In D. Jaspers, W. Klooster, Y. Putseys, and P. Seuren, eds., *Sentential Complementation and the Lexicon: Studies in Honor of Wim De Geest*, 343–354. Dordrecht: Foris.

Riemsdijk, Henk C. van. 1998. Syntactic feature magnetism: The endocentricity and distribution of projections. *Journal of Comparative Germanic Linguistics* 2:1–48.

Rouveret, A., and J.-R. Vergnaud. 1980. Specifying reference to the subject: French causatives and conditions on representations. *Linguistic Inquiry* 11:97–202.

Sauerland, U. 2000. The content of pronouns: Evidence from Focus. In T. Matthews and B. Jackson, eds., *Proceedings of SALT 10*. Ithaca, NY: CLC Publications, Cornell University.

Sauerland, U. 2004. The silent content of bound variable pronouns. In K. Johnson, ed., *Topics in Ellipsis.* Oxford: Oxford University Press.

Steriade, D. 1995. Underspecification and markedness. In J. Goldsmith ed., *Handbook of Phonology*, 114–174. Oxford: Blackwell.

Trubetzkoy, N. S. 1969. *Principles of Phonology.* Berkeley: University of California Press.

Vergnaud, J.-R. 1974. *French Relative Clauses.* Doctoral dissertation, MIT.

Vergnaud, J.-R. 1985. *Dépendances et Niveaux de Représentation en Syntaxe.* Amsterdam: J. Benjamins.

Vergnaud, J.-R. 2003. On a certain notion of "occurrence": The source of metrical structure, and of much more. In S. Ploch, ed., *Living on the Edge*, 599–632. Berlin: Mouton de Gruyter.

Williams, E. 1977. Discourse and logical form. *Linguistic Inquiry* 8:101–139.

Syntax

1 Letter to Noam Chomsky and Howard Lasnik on "Filters and Control," April 17, 1977

Jean-Roger Vergnaud

Dear Howard, Dear Noam,

I got your paper, three weeks ago. It is quite exciting. I believe I have some ideas to communicate to you now. They may not be that well organized, but they bear on what you discuss. I shall use the following notation: (FC,x), where *x* is a number, will refer to your paper; for example, (FC,3) refers to the examples of (3) in your paper; on the other hand, such formulae as (V, x), where *x* is a number, will refer to this letter. Let's begin. First, I shall discuss your filter (FC,93) (or (FC,93'), or (FC,107), or (FC,[155]).[1]

Concerning Filter (FC,93)

I believe that this filter could be replaced by a filter that governs the distribution of certain kinds of NPs. Here is what I have in mind. Let's assume that English has three Cases: the Subject Case, which is the Case of subjects in tensed clauses; the Genitive Case (cf. *Mary's book*, *hers*, *yours*, *mine*, etc.); the Governed Case, which is the case of complements of verbs and of prepositions, among others (cf. *Mary saw him, Mary gave him a book, Mary talked to him, a book by him*, etc.). Case inflectional morphology is quite poor, of course. Often, oppositions are neutralized. With full NPs, only the Genitive Case is marked; the Subject Case and the Governed Case are morphologically identical. It is in the system of pronouns that case morphology is the richest (cf. *I*, *me*, *mine*; *you*, *yours*; *he*, *him*, *his*; etc.). But, even with pronouns, forms are often morphologically ambiguous: for example, *which* stands for the Subject Case as well as for the Governed Case; *whom* may be realized as *who* when it is not adjacent to a preposition (with dialectal variations); etc. Now, a characteristic property of infinival construction is that, in such constructions, the subject is in the Governed Case:

(1) a. We'd prefer for *him* to leave.
    b. It is illegal for *him* to leave.

   c. We found a man for *him* to speak to.

   d. For *him* to leave would be unfortunate.

Well, I shall hypothesize that the distribution of infinitival constructions of the form *NP to VP* follows from the distribution of NPs in the Governed Case. Specifically, let's posit the following filter:

(2) A structure of the form $\ldots [_a \ldots NP \ldots] \ldots$, where NP is in the Governed Case and α is the first branching node above NP, is ungrammatical unless (i) α is the domain of $[-N]$ or (ii) α is adjacent to and in the domain of $[-N]$.

Note that the forms in your note 97 are OK by filter (V,2) if we assume that the grammar contains the following PS-rules:

$V' \rightarrow V \,(NP)(NP)$

$V' \rightarrow V \,(NP) \,(Predicate)$

Filter (V,2) looks very much like a principle of UG. Now, there are two alternative theories that are compatible with (V,2), which we will examine in turn.

Theory AI

Within AI, only NPs that are phonologically realized are marked for Case: Case marking does not apply to traces (and, in general, to phonologically empty NPs; this situation is not to be confused with the one in which Case marking applies to traces, but the Case marker for a phonologically empty NP is the zero morpheme $\varnothing$; the latter situation characterizes theory AII, which we will discuss below). Now, if we assume that in a structure of the form *V adjunct NP*, *V* and *NP* are not sisters, then, within AI, we can dispense with filter (FC,[154])[2] [because] the latter filter follows from (V,2) (we will not go into any detail here, but it is easy to see that there exists a natural set of assumptions under which this is true). Thus, your paradigm (FC,150, 152, {153}, [153])[3] follows from (V,2) because a trace is not marked for Case and this is not subject to filter (V,2). Note that within AI, case b of (FC,[133]) (*John$_i$ is certain* ($\varnothing$) *NP$_i$ to win*) does not raise any particular problem. Thus, we can dispense with rule (FC,135)[4] (or, correspondingly, with subcondition (FC,[155b])). We turn now to infinitival relative clauses. From filter (V,2), it follows that a structure of the form $\ldots [_{COMP}$ *wh*-phrase$]$ NP *to* VP$\ldots$, where the *wh*-phrase and the NP are phonologically nonempty, is out (note that the exceptions in (V,2) mention $[-N]$ and not $[-N]^i$, where *i* refers to the number of bars; that is, they require the presence of *terminal* $[-N]$ nodes in the neighborhood of the NP under consideration). In that way, we account for the ungrammaticality of (FC,100c, 101c).[5] From filter (V,2), it follows that a structure of the form $[_{NP}$ NP $[_{S'} [_{COMP}$ e$]$ $[_S$ NP *to* VP$]]]$, where the two NPs are phonologically nonempty, is out. In that way we account for the ungrammaticality of (FC,101d).[6] From filter (V,2), it follows that a structure of the form [$_{NP}$ NP [$_{S'}$ [$_{COMP}$ *wh*-NP]...]], where the head of the relative construction and the *wh*-phrase are phonologically nonempty and the *wh*-phrase is in the Governed Case, is out. In that way, we account for the ungrammaticality of (FC,101c, 105c, 121c).[7] Note that (FC,101b, 105d, 121d, 122c)[8] are permitted by the filter (V,2). In particular, (FC,105d) does not raise any special problem for AI. There is a problem, though. Filter (V,2) stars the following constructions:

(3) a. A woman who(m) you should see
    b. A woman who(m) you should talk to

These forms are perfectly grammatical, though. Thus, they contrast with the constructions below:

(4) a. A woman who(m) to see
    b. A woman who(m) to talk to

In order to accommodate (3), I shall add the additional exception (iii) to (V,5), which is the "unless" condition of (V,2):

(5) Unless   (i)   α is the domain of [−N].
             (ii) α is adjacent to and in the domain of [−N].
             (iii) α is the domain of −WH.

Consider now, for example, (V,3a). Since the rule −WH → *that* (your rule (FC,84b) is optional, one of the surface structures corresponding to the relative clause in (V,3a) is

(6) [$_{S'}$ [$_{COMP}$ *who(m)* −WH] [$_S$ *you should see*]]

Now, I shall modify your filter (FC,53)[9] as follows:

(7) *[$_{COMP}$ *wh*-phrase K] where K is a nonnull terminal string (that is, K has a nonnull phonological representation)

I shall assume that ±WH is a nonterminal. Then, (V,6) is permitted by (V,7) as well as by (V,5). QED. Idem for (V,3b). Of course, we may wonder what (V,5iii) means. Well, suppose we define *branching node* as follows:

(8) A node *f* is branching iff it immediately dominates ...*g*...*h*..., where *g* and *h* dominate terminal strings.

By definition (V,8), *COMP* in (V,6) is not a branching node. Then, the first branching node above *who(m)* in (V,6) is S′. And a in (V,5) is S′. Similarly, the domain of −WH in (V,6) is S′. Thus, it seems that (V,5iii) is an "effect" of the Propositional Island condition. Maybe we could factor it out. I don't see how. Actually, the following forms are highly relevant:

(9) a. The question who to talk to
    b. The question who we should talk to

If the forms in (V,9) are both ungrammatical, then we do not have to change the above analysis. Suppose now that (V,9a,b) are both grammatical. Then, we should add the additional exception (V,10) to (V,5)

(10) α is the domain of $+$WH

The fact that the subject of an infinitival interrogative can (actually must) be controlled shows that positions in the domain of a $+$WH COMP are not in general "opaque" to anaphoric connections outside S′. And we are left with no interpretation for (V,10). Suppose now that (V,9a) is out and (V,9b) is OK. Then it is the tensed-S condition (strictly speaking) that is relevant, and we have to modify (V,5) accordingly. I don't know how to do it. Note that if we want (V,8) and the considerations that follow (V,8) to apply to Middle English, we might have to modify (V,8) (depending on what the facts are): we might simply replace (V,8) with a statement that stipulates that COMP is not branching, period.

Note that, within the preceding analysis, we do not have any account of the ungrammaticality of (FC,129c) (*who is it illegal (for) t to leave (t the trace of who)). Well, I shall assume that the ungrammaticality of (FC,129c) has to do with the nondeletability of for. In the paragraph that follows (FC,128), you say that you "will overlook these special properties [namely, the properties of lexical items that require, allow, or preclude the presence of for—JRV], which are, so far as we know, of no particular interest." Well, it is not obvious that you are right. Suppose we distinguish two complementizers for: for_1 which bears the feature $[-N]$, and for_2, which is a "pure" complementizer and which does not bear the feature $[-N]$. for_2 can delete freely by (FC,52),[10] but for_1 cannot: recoverability of deletion prevents the deletion of for_1 in that case, because for_1 contains some lexical material, namely the feature $[-N]$. We will say that adjectives are subcategorized for for_1, that prefer in certain idiolects is subcategorized for for_1, that want takes freely for_1 or for_2 (there is a filter that is specific to want, namely *want for), etc. I shall assume that EQUI is the following rule:

(11) for PROself $\rightarrow$ $\varnothing$, where the domain of for is S′

Note that, with this formulation of EQUI, for_1 can be deleted by EQUI (because the rule explicitly mentions for). Which is very good because the following is grammatical:

(12) It would be illegal to leave now.

Of course, there are consequences for Ozark English, which I shall not pursue here. I turn now to a discussion of an alternative theory.

Theory AII

Within AII, Case marking applies to the traces that are left by *wh*-movement as well as to the NPs that are phonologically realized. Of course, the Case marker of a trace is phonologically empty. Now, in order to account for (FC,150b, 152b, 152d, 153),[11] we have to add the additional exception (V,13) to (V,5):

(13) α is adjacent to and in the domain of verb + adjunct.

We can no longer dispense with filter (FC,[154]) (because of the paradigm (FC,150, 152, 153)[12]). Within AII, as within AI, case b of (FC,127) does not raise any particular problem: we can dispense with rule (FC,135) (or, correspondingly, with subcondition (FC,[155b])).[13] Within AII, (FC,129c)[14] is perfectly straightforward; we do not have to distinguish two complementizers *for*. The discussion of (V,3, 9) remains unchanged. Similarly, the discussion of infinitival relative clauses remains unchanged, except for case (FC,103–105)[15] (relativization of the subject of the infinitival): the base phrase marker

A man [COMP for] [S who to fix the sink]

is not a deep structure within AII, because (FC,105d) is out by filter (V,2) (since the subject of the relative clause is a trace left by *wh*-movement in surface structure, and, thus, is marked for case in surface structure). Well, what is the source for *a man to fix the sink*, then? I shall assume that the latter construction is derived from

(14) A man [COMP for] [S PRO-self to fix the sink]

In (V,14), a rule of control will relate the reflexive and the head of the relative construction. Thus, the structure of *a man to fix the sink* is analogous to the structure of *a man fixing the sink* (with a relative clause participle).

That ends my discussion of filter (FC,93). Myself, I would choose theory AI over theory AII. I am willing to agree that what I propose is very close to being a notational variant of what you propose. However, I think that filter (V,2) (revised to (V,5)) is likely to be a principle of UG. I turn now to filter (FC,85).

Concerning Filter (FC,85)

I repeat this filter below:

*[±WH t...], except in the context: [NP NP ____]

Here, I would like to show that (FC,85) can be replaced by a more "natural" filter. Basically, I will develop and "amplify" some remarks of yours in the third paragraph of p. 39 in your paper.[16] There you write: "Jointly, these two provisos guarantee that in simple one-clause structures the subject of a verb is indicated 'locally'—either by the verbal inflection, the head of a relative, or the actual subject in place (perhaps separated from the verb by an adverb or parenthetical). Note that this observation does not extend to multiclause structures, because of (68)[17] [=(FC,85)] itself." Well, I think it would be nice if "this observation could extend to multiclause structures," and if the constraint formalized as (FC,85) could be made to follow from it. I shall assume that we are dealing here with a property of tensed clauses. Now, what characterizes the verb of a tensed clause is that it has to *agree* with its subject. I'll try to show that the constraint formalized as (FC,85) is simply the following constraint:

(15) The element that governs the person and number inflection of the verb must be indicated locally.

I shall proceed as follows. First, I shall revise filter (FC,53)[18] (or (V,7)) to (16):

(16) [$_{\text{COMP}}$ C K], where C is a category (which may be empty—that is, which may dominate the identity element e) and K is the (nonnull) phonological representation of some complementizer.

In particular, in (V,16), C may be the trace left by COMP-to-COMP movement. Now, I shall posit the following filter:

(17) SD: ...[$_\alpha$ V...]...
     SC: *, unless the next NP to the right or to the left of α is the NP that governs the person and number inflection of V

I shall assume that (V,17) is subject to the usual conditions, among them A/A and the tensed-S condition. By A/A, α in (V,17) must be taken to be the highest node x such that V is the leftmost terminal string dominated by α. By the tensed-S condition, α must be chosen in such a way that all the categories dominated by α are c-commanded by the lowest Tense that c-commands V. I shall assume that the tensed-S condition takes precedence over A/A; in other words, the maximal value that α can take in (V,17) is S_V, where S_V is the lowest S that dominates V. Consider now the following structures:

(18) a. Who$_i$ do you think [$_{\text{COMP}}$ NP$_i$ that][$_{S_1}$ NP$_i$ saw Bill]
     b. Who$_i$ do you think [$_{\text{COMP}}$ that][$_{S_1}$ NP$_i$ saw Bill]

(V,18b) is derived from (V,18a) by deletion of the category NP$_i$ in COMP (by rule (FC,52)[19]). (V,18a) is out by filter (V,16). (V,18b) is out by filter (V,17): by A/A, we must take α in (V,17) to be S_1 if V is *saw*; but then the closest NP on the left of α is *you*; it is not the NP that governs the person and number inflection of *saw*. In that way, we have accounted for the ungrammaticality of *who do you think that saw Bill*. Consider now the form

(19) Who do you think saw Bill?

One of the surface structures that underlies (V,19) is

(20) Who$_i$ do you think [$_{COMP}$ NP$_i$][$_{S_1}$ NP$_i$ saw Bill]

Clearly, (V,20) is well-formed by (V,16). It is also well-formed by (V,17): in (V,20), we must take $\alpha = S_1$ if V is *saw* (the tensed-S condition and A/A); now, the NP immediately to the left of S_1 is the trace NP$_i$ dominated by COMP; but NP$_i$ is the NP that governs the person and number inflection of *saw*. In that way, we have accounted for the grammaticality of (V,19). Note that the forms in your note 53 do not raise any particular problem for my analysis. It is easy to see that the grammaticality of *the man that saw Bill* follows from our rules and filters: I do not have to add any special subcondition to filter (V,17) to account for this construction. Now, what about the generalization in (FC,71)?[20] Well, suppose that (V,17) or some variant of (V,17), depending on word order, belongs to the stock of filters that are provided as options by UG; that is, the form of (V,17) is given by UG, but a particular language may "elect" to have (V,17), or not to have it. Suppose, in addition, that every language contains a rule of subject deletion (which, of course, is optional):

(21) Delete a subject.

That is, (V,21) belongs to UG. (V,21) is subject to recoverability of deletion. In particular, the subject must be empty. Thus, there is no rule of subject-pronoun deletion; cases where "subject-pronoun deletion" is said to have applied actually are cases where lexical insertion failed to apply. Now, if a language has filter (V,17), rule (V,21) cannot apply to delete free subject-NPs (i.e., unbound subject-NPs). But, necessarily, a free NP is lexically specified. Consider English, for example. Consider the following surface structure:

(22) NP$_1$ left

(V,22) is not well-formed (the corresponding LF has a free variable in the subject position). Now, if NP$_1$ deletes by (V,21), the resulting structure is ill-formed, because English has the filter (V,17) (this is valid under some reasonable interpretation of (V,17); the "unless" condition of the SC of (V,17) should actually read: "unless there exists at least one NP in the construction and the next NP to the right ..."). In that way, we have accounted for the ungrammaticality of *left*. Similarly for *think that left*. Now, consider Spanish. Corresponding to (V,22), we have

(23) NP$_1$ partio

(V,23) is ill-formed for the same reason (V,22) is ill-formed. Now, since Spanish does not have filter (V,17), NP1 in (V,23) can be deleted freely by (V,21): the output will not be starred. Similarly for *creo que partio*. To conclude: if a language does not have filter (V,17), it displays the phenomenon labeled "subject-pronoun deletion" (cf. Spanish); if a language has the filter (V,17), it does not have "subject-pronoun deletion" (cf. English). In other words:

(24) Not filter (V,17) ≡ "Subject-pronoun deletion"

which is the generalization in (FC,71). Now, how does a child know whether a language has filter (V,17) or not? Well, he uses the equivalence in (V,24); the existence of "subject-pronoun deletion" is easy to detect (obviously). I shall assume that UG contains some principle that leads to postulating filter (V,17) as the "unmarked case" unless there is specific evidence to the contrary. I hope all this is not too circular. I presume that the likelihood of a given language having filter (V,17) is inversely proportional to the richness of the verbal inflectional morphology.

Now, what about Joan [Bresnan]'s examples, which I repeat below:

(25) a. It's in these villages that are found the best examples of this cuisine.
     b. It's in these villages that we all believe can be found the best examples of this cuisine.
     c. *It's in these villages that we all believe that can be found the best examples of this cuisine.

Frankly, I have some doubts about the relevancy of these examples. Note that the French analogue of (V,25c) is OK. But French has filter (V,17). Of course, French has a much freer rule of Stylistic Inversion. The French analogue of (V,25b) is

(26) C'est dans ces villages que nous croyons tous peuvent être trouvés les formes les meilleures de cette cuisine.

For (V,26) to be grammatical, *nous croyons tous* (*we all believe*) must be interpreted as a parenthetical (under this interpretation, it should be "bracketed" by commas; thus, strictly speaking, (V,26) is ungrammatical); this is so because French lacks a rule of free complementizer-deletion. Actually, it looks like *we all believe* in (V,25b) should also be interpreted as a parenthetical. I think that the following examples are not grammatical:

(27) a. It's in these villages that Mary, but not Peter, believes can be found the best examples of this cuisine.
     b. It's in these villages that you think that Mary believes can be found the best examples of this cuisine.
     c. It's in these villages that, I believe, Mary believes can be found the best examples of this cuisine.

Compare with

(28) a. It's in these villages that Mary, but not Peter, believes the best examples of this cuisine can be found.
     b. It's in these villages that you think that Mary believes the best examples of this cuisine can be found.
     c. It's in these villages that, I believe, Mary believes the best examples of this cuisine can be found.

Now, my theory makes different empirical predictions from yours, of course. For example, it predicts that in Middle English the form *who do you think that saw Bill* was grammatical. Well, this could be verified, but it cannot be falsified. A dream. Well, actually, there is a variety of French in which such forms as (V,29) below are grammatical:

(29) L'homme *avec qui que* Pierre a parlé vient de partir.

That is, the variety of French under consideration lacks the filter (V,16). My intuition is that in this variety of French, such forms as (V,30) are grammatical:

(30) Qui crois-tu qu'est parti hier?

Well, there might be some "noise," due to the fact that in this variety of French *qui* may be realized as *que* when it is exhaustively dominated by COMP.

Note that my reasoning on examples (V,21) to (V,24) goes through whether the language under consideration has filter (V,16) or not.

Now, there are some consequences for your appendix III. Actually, I don't really understand what you say at the bottom of p. 103. In the last paragraph on p. 103, you consider a dialect that lacks the **for-to* filter, but has the **for-for* filter. You seem to imply that this is equivalent to saying that (FC,213) is grammatical and (FC,214), ungrammatical.[21] In addition, the dialect you discuss accepts (FC,216) but not (FC,217).[22] Then you say that one cannot appeal to the **for-to* filter to block (FC,217), because the dialect lacks this filter. But why not say that the dialect actually has the **for-to* filter, but that this filter is restricted to the complementizer *for* (this is what you propose in the next-to-last paragraph of p. 103)? In other words, I don't understand the difference between (FC,213) and (FC,216).

A last remark concerning filter (V,17). In Latin, a past participle or a future participle in an infinitival declarative agrees in case, gender, and number with the subject, as it does in finite declaratives. Cf. *constat Romanos esse victos* "it is certain that the Romans were defeated." Clearly, this a case of Subject-Predicate agreement, and not a case of Subject-Verb agreement. The verb itself (*esse* in the above example) does not agree.

That ends my substantive comments.

Some scattered remarks:

• Your example (34c), p. 22, would be excluded by Superiority, assuming Strict Cyclicity (but maybe you want the latter to follow from something else).

• Concerning A/A and your filter (93),[23] pp. 52–53: if one takes your proposal literally here (you say: "Under the conventions just outlined, no construction will be submitted to the filter for analysis if it is properly contained within another construction analyzable in terms of the structural condition"), then the following should be grammatical (or am I mistaken?): *a man to expect that Mary will give a book which to read to*; compare with *a man to expect that Mary will give a book to*. I presume that the difficulty would be solved if the NP in the SD of the filter were to bear an anaphoric index (modulo the right conventions).

• I presume that your example (149d), p. 74, is blocked (redundantly) by *it*-insertion (your rule (60)).[24]

• I don't understand the development at the top of p. 77; in the input to the filter, PRO does not bear any index (since the filter does not apply to the output of rules of construal, but to the output of deletion rules, which themselves apply to surface structure).

• Concerning *wh*-deletion, p. 32, you say that the *wh*-word in restrictive relatives has no semantic content, whereas in appositives and in questions it does have semantic content. Well, this could interact with some proposals by Edwin [Williams] and by [Ivan] Sag concerning VP-deletion; consider the following paradigm:

(31) a. The man who Mary tried to visit and couldn't
     b. The man who Mary tried to visit and she couldn't
     c. The man who Mary tried to visit and she couldn't visit

(32) a. John, who Mary tried to visit, but couldn't
     b. John, who Mary tried to visit, but who she couldn't
     c. John, who Mary tried to visit, but who she couldn't visit

In (V,31), we have restrictive relatives and in (V,32), appositives. I am assuming that (V,31b) and (V,32b) are ungrammatical. Now, to account for the ungrammaticality of (V,32b), Edwin and Sag rely on the hypothesis that the *wh*-word in (V,32) is a quantifier binding a variable: then, the LF corresponding to the null VP in (V,32b) contains a variable that is bound by the "wrong" *wh*-word, and the form is out. It seems natural to expect, within Edwin's (and Sag's) framework, that the same explanation will hold for (V,31b). Note that the *wh*-word of a free relative deletes freely only in comparative constructions; see the contrast:

(33) a. John eats more than Mary eats.
     b. *John eats Mary eats.

(V,33a) and (V,33b) are derived by COMP-deletion from (V,34a) and (V,34b), respectively:

(34) a. John eats more than what Mary eats.
     b. John eats what Mary eats.

• Finally, J. Emonds mentions the following paradigm (personal communication):

(35) a. A man to whom to explain my problem
     b. A man to expect that I can explain my problem to
     c. *A man to whom to expect that I can explain my problem

I believe we have a similar paradigm with infinitival indirect questions:

(36) a. I wonder to whom to give this book.
     b. I wonder who to expect that Mary will give this book to.
     c. *I wonder to whom to expect that Mary will give this book.

That's it; comments welcome.

As ever,
Jean-Roger

Notes

1. The Vergnaud letter was a commentary, solicited by Chomsky and Lasnik, on the manuscript version of "Filters and Control." The published version of the paper (*Linguistic Inquiry* 8, 425–504 (1977)) unfortunately does not incorporate any of Vergnaud's excellent suggestions because there was an accidental delay in sending the manuscript to him. His response was very prompt at that point, but by then, the paper had already gone to the printer.

This and all other notes have been added by the editors. The notes give the examples and constraints as formulated in the published version. Example numbers in square brackets indicate numbers in the published version that had changed from the manuscript version. Numbers in braces indicate examples in the manuscript that did not appear in the published version.

(93) *[$_\alpha$ NP to VP] unless α is adjacent to and in the domain of a verb or *for*

(93′) *[$_\alpha$ NP to VP] unless α is adjacent to and in the domain of [−N]

(107) *[$_\alpha$ NP to VP] unless α is adjacent to and in the domain of [−N] or $\alpha = $ NP

(155) *[$_\alpha$ NP to VP] unless α is adjacent to and in the domain of
      a. [−N] (adjunct)
      b. [+V] $\varnothing$

2. (154) *[V adjunct NP], NP lexical

3. (150) a. *John believes sincerely [Bill to be the best man]
         b. Who$_i$ does John believe sincerely [t$_i$ to be the best man]
         c. *NP was proven conclusively [John to be the best man]
         d. John$_i$ was proven conclusively [t$_i$ to be the best man]
         e. John$_i$ was proven to us [t$_i$ to be the best man]
         f. John$_i$ seems to us [t$_i$ to be the best man]

   (152) a. We want very much [*(for) John to win]
         b. Who$_i$ do you want very much [t$_i$ to win]
         c. We'd prefer most of all [*(for) John to be the candidate]
         d. Who$_i$ would you prefer most of all [t$_i$ to be the candidate]

   {153} a. A kid is here [t to play with you]
         b. A man is at the front door [t to fix the sink]

   (153) a. *I believe sincerely John.
         b. *I like very much John.

4. (135) $\varnothing \rightarrow [-N]$ in the context $[+V]$ ____

5. (100c) A topic [$_{COMP}$ on which] [$_S$ Bill to work t]   Deletion of *for*

  (101c) A topic [$_{COMP}$ which] [$_S$ Bill to work on t]   Deletion of *for*

6. (101d) A topic [$_{COMP}$ e] [$_S$ Bill to work on t]   Deletion of both phrases

7. (105c) A man [$_{COMP}$ who] [$_S$ t to fix the sink]   Deletion of *for*

  (121c) A topic [$_{COMP}$ which] [to work on t]   Deletion of *for*

8. (101b) A topic [$_{COMP}$ for] [$_S$ Bill to work on t]   Deletion of *wh*-phrase

  (105d) A man [$_{COMP}$ e] [$_S$ t to fix the sink]   Deletion of both phrases

  (121d) A topic [$_{COMP}$ e] [$_S$ to work on t]   Deletion of both phrases

  (122d) A topic [$_{COMP}$ on which] [to work t]   Deletion of *for*

9. (53) *[$_{COMP}$ *wh*-phrase ϕ], $\phi \neq$ e

10. (52) In the domain of COMP, delete [$_\alpha$ ϕ], where α is an arbitrary category and ϕ an arbitrary structure.

11. See next note.

12. (150) a. *John believes sincerely [Bill to be the best man]
      b. Who$_i$ does John believe sincerely [t$_i$ to be the best man]
      c. *NP was proven conclusively [John to be the best man]
      d. John$_i$ was proven conclusively [t$_i$ to be the best man]
      e. John$_i$ was proven to us [t$_i$ to be the best man]
      f. John$_i$ seems to us [t$_i$ to be the best man]

  (152) a. We want very much [*(for) John to win]
      b. Who$_i$ do you want very much [t$_i$ to win]
      c. We'd prefer most of all [*(for) John to be the candidate]
      d. Who$_i$ would you prefer most of all [t$_i$ to be the candidate]

  (153) See note 3.

13. (127b) NP is certain ϕ John to leave.

  (135)   See note 4.

  (155b) See note 1.

14. (129c) *Who$_i$ is it illegal (for) t$_i$ to leave?

15. (103) A man [$_{COMP}$ for] [$_S$ who to fix the sink]

  (104) A man [$_{COMP}$ who$_i$ for] [$_S$ t$_i$ to fix the sink]

  (105) [The four possible outcomes from (104)—RF/HL]
      a. A man [$_{COMP}$ who$_i$ for] [$_S$ t$_i$ to fix the sink] (= (104))
      b. A man [$_{COMP}$ for] [$_S$ t to fix the sink]   Deletion of *wh*-phrase
      c. A man [$_{COMP}$ who$_i$] [$_S$ t$_i$ to fix the sink]   Deletion of *for*
      d. A man [$_{COMP}$ e] [$_S$ t to fix the sink]   Deletion of both phrases

16. In the third full paragraph after example (74).

17. {68} *[that [$_{NP}$ e]], except in the context [$_{NP}$ NP ____ ...]

    (68) *[$_{S'}$ that [$_{NP}$ e]...], unless S' or its trace is in the context [$_{NP}$ NP ____ ...]

18. (53) See note 9.

19. (52) See note 10.

20. (71) The filter (68) is valid for all languages that do not have a rule of subject-pronoun deletion, and only these.

21. (213) Who$_i$ are you going to try for t$_i$ to VP

    (214) Who$_i$ are you going to try for [for t$_i$ to VP]

22. (216) Who does she long for t [to win]

    (217) Who would it bother you [for t to win]

23. See note 1.

24. (149d) *Bill$_i$ is eager [(for) t$_i$ to win]

    (60)   Insert it in the position of NP in

$$
\text{NP V* (A) (PP) } [_{S'} \left\{ \begin{array}{l} \text{for} \\ \text{that} \\ -\text{WH} \end{array} \right\} \text{S] } (\text{V*} = \text{be, seem,} \ldots)
$$

2 On the Development of Case Theory: Triumphs and Challenges

Howard Lasnik

X-bar theory, introduced in Chomsky 1970, constituted a major step toward explanatory adequacy, dramatically limiting the range of possible phrase structure rules. As with most explanatory advances, the resulting theory encounters serious descriptive problems. In the present instance, the major virtue of X-bar theory—the generalization of the phrase structure schema—immediately encountered empirical problems. For one, N and A, unlike V and P, did not seem to take NP complements:

(1) a. Prove the theorem
    b. *Proof the theorem

(2) a. Resent Harry
    b. *Resentful Harry

Since *prove* has a nominal and since the X-bar theory says that the complement system is general, and since *prove* by its semantic nature takes an NP complement, we would expect *proof* to take an NP as well. As is well known, this gap is completely general.

To account for this paradigmatic gap, Chomsky (1970) proposed an obligatory rule that inserts *of* between N or A and NP:

(3) Of-*insertion rule*

$$\varnothing \Rightarrow \text{of} \left/ \left\{ \begin{array}{c} N \\ A \end{array} \right\} \underline{\quad} NP \right.$$

Or, in terms of the feature system of the mid-1970s:

(4) $\varnothing \Rightarrow \text{of}/[+N] \underline{\quad} NP$

This described the facts, but it raised two questions: Why should there be such a rule, and why should it be obligatory?

Clausal complementation created similar descriptive problems. Given underlyingly distinct finite and infinitival complements, and optional subject raising, we might have expected both (5a) and (5b) to be acceptable, but only the first of these is.

(5) a.   It is likely [that Mary will solve the problem]
    b.   *It is likely [Mary to solve the problem]

In place of (5b), we find the raising analogue:

(6) Mary is likely to solve the problem.

Jean-Roger Vergnaud, in the personal letter to Noam Chomsky and me in early 1977 that is reprinted in chapter 1 of this book, was concerned with a class of phenomena related to this one. Vergnaud's now very familiar basic idea was that even languages like English with very little overt case morphology pattern with richly inflected languages in providing characteristic positions in which NPs with particular cases occur. Vergnaud's formulation, highly reminiscent of modern Case theory (particular in its "checking" formulation), is as follows:

(7) English has three cases: Subject Case, Genitive Case, "Governed Case" ("the case of complements of verbs and of prepositions").

(8) The restrictions on subjects of infinitivals can follow from a general filter limiting the distribution of NPs in the Governed Case.

Vergnaud offered two possible versions of the filter, both involving a structural relation discussed by Chomsky and Lasnik (1977) that is very close to "government" (which is how I will render it here):

(9) a.   A structure containing an NP in the Governed Case is ungrammatical unless that NP is governed by [−N].
    b.   A structure containing an NP in the Governed Case is ungrammatical unless that NP is adjacent to and governed by [−N].

Chomsky (1980) built a theory of abstract case ("Case") around Vergnaud's insights, a fundamental step in the launching of the Government-Binding Theory. Chomsky's initial formulation began with the following suggestion: "Suppose we think of Case as an abstract marking associated with certain constructions, a property that rarely has phonetic effects in English but must be assigned to every lexical NP" (p. 24). Thus, we have at S-structure, Case-assignment rules and a Case Filter excluding NPs lacking Case:[1]

(10) *Case assignment*
     a. NP is oblique when governed by P and certain marked verbs.
     b. NP is objective when governed by V.
     c. NP is nominative when governed by Tense.

(11) *Case Filter*
     Lexical NPs (i.e., those with a lexical head) must have Case
     *N, where N has no Case.

(11) is essentially a morphophonological requirement, though assumed at this point in the development of the theory to hold of S-structure. Note that it presupposes that Case "percolates" from NP to its head N. Given this system, the obligatoriness of *of*-insertion and of raising is directly accounted for. In either instance, failure to perform the relevant operation yields a structure in violation of (11). Similarly accounted for is the unacceptability of a passive verb with a (surface) NP complement, as in (12), under the proposal of Chomsky and Lasnik 1977 that a passive verb is a neutralized verb/adjective, hence [+V] with no specification for [N]:

(12) *It was believed Mary

Compare a clausal complement, predictably acceptable, given the formulation in (11):

(13) It was believed that John won the race.

The restriction of the Case Filter to *lexical* (i.e., phonologically realized) NPs was, of course, crucial. One obvious indication that this is so is the acceptability of the alternative version of (12) with movement:

(14) Mary was believed *t*

Given trace theory, (14) does have an NP in exactly the non-Case position occupied by *Mary* in (12), namely, the trace of *Mary*. Thus, if the trace of NP-movement were subject to the filter, passive and raising structures would always be ungrammatical. An extension of this idea, developed by Chomsky (1981), is that Case is not a property of individual members of a movement A-chain but rather is a property of the entire A-chain. The Case Filter then becomes a requirement on A-chains. It is then not germane to ask whether the trace of *Mary* in (14) obeys the Case Filter; the chain (*Mary*, *t*) has (nominative) Case, thus satisfying the Case requirement.

However, it is still true that PRO can occur in a position where lexical NP cannot—as the subject of (certain) infinitival clauses—and this time there is no relevant chain:

(15) a. Susan tried [PRO to solve the problem]
     b. *Susan tried [John to solve the problem]

We are thus still left with the lexical versus nonlexical distinction.

Chomsky (1980) noted one potential problem for this lexical versus nonlexical basis for Case theory. At S-structure, *wh*-NPs are typically not in any of the positions enumerated in (10), yet the resulting sentences are well-formed. Further, if the *wh*-NP originates in a non-Case position, the result is ill-formed. The following constitute a representative minimal pair:

(16) a. Who does it seem [__ is a nice fellow]
     b. *Who does it seem [__ to be a nice fellow]

To deal with this, Chomsky resorted to a complication. Specifically, (10) is replicated internal to the rule of *wh*-movement:

(17) *Move α for wh*
    −Assign Case under (10)
    −Adjoin α to COMP (coindexing by convention)

Now the moved *wh*-phrase has the Case that it received prior to moving. Given all of this, we have the following a priori plausible taxonomy:

(18) *NPs that obey the Case Filter*   *NPs that ignore the Case Filter*
    Lexical NPs (including *Wh* ones)   PRO
    Expletives   (A-traces)

This taxonomy makes sense since Case is treated as essentially morphophonological, and the NPs (or A-chains) that fall under its purview are morphophonologically realized—they have phonetic content.

The system seemed to work, in that it did handle contrasts like that in (16). But it was awfully cumbersome and redundant, in that all of Case assignment is replicated in the *wh*-movement rule. There is a rather straightforward way to eliminate the redundancy. Davis (1984) proposed that Case assignment not be limited to S-structure in the general situation, but rather be an anywhere process. Whenever in the course of a derivation an NP finds itself in a Case position, Case is assigned. If that has not happened by S-structure, (11) will rule out the resulting structure, just as in Chomsky's approach. However, in the 1979 Pisa GLOW meeting presentation that became Lasnik and Freidin 1981, it was pointed out that Chomsky's (17) does not cover all of the relevant facts (and the same is true of Davis's improved version). Note first that, unsurprisingly, the paradigm in (16) is replicated with relative clauses:

(19) a.   I talked to the man [who [it seems [__ is a nice fellow]]]
     b. *I talked to the man [who [it seems [__ to be a nice fellow]]]

There is no special difficulty here; we already know that *who* is subject to the Case Filter. The difficulty arises in consideration of the other forms that a relative clause can take in English. As is well known, alongside relative clauses with overt *wh*-operator, there are relative clauses with just the complementizer *that*,[2] and those with nothing at all:

(20) a. I talked to the man [who [you met __]]
     b. I talked to the man [that [you met __]]
     c. I talked to the man [[you met __]]

There is thus the basis for a clear experiment. Alongside the unacceptable (19b), we should, under the Chomsky 1980 analysis, find acceptable analogues with the other two relative-clause types, those lacking relative pronouns. However, as Lasnik and Freidin (1981) pointed out, the examples are uniformly unacceptable:

(21) a. *I talked to the man [who [it seems [__ to be a nice fellow]]]
     b. *   that
     c. * $\emptyset$

The finite versions are clearly better:

(22) a. I talked to the man [who [it seems [__ is a nice fellow]]]
     b.   that
     c. ? $\emptyset$

Lasnik and Freidin (1981) therefore concluded that, contrary to expectation, the *trace* of *wh*-movement is subject to the Case Filter. They reformulated (11) as (23).

(23) *NP, where NP is lexical or the trace of WH, and has no Case.

Chomsky (1981, 175) accepts this conclusion and gives the following formulation:

(24) *[$_{NP}$ α] if α has no Case and α contains a phonetic matrix or is a variable.

Chomsky observes that in this respect, as in certain others, NP variables (i.e., traces of *wh*-movement of an NP) behave like names, for example, with respect to anaphoric possibility. As observed in Wasow 1972, and developed by Chomsky 1976, Freidin and Lasnik 1981, and Chomsky 1981, variables and names show identical effects with respect to what became Condition C of the binding theory in Chomsky 1981:

(25) a. *He$_i$ said Mary likes John$_i$
     b. *He$_i$ said John$_i$ likes Mary

(26) a. *Who$_i$ did he$_i$ say Mary likes t_i
     b. *Who$_i$ did he$_i$ say t_i likes Mary

Given all of this, the PF motivation for the Case Filter is evidently gone. Chomsky proposes instead an LF motivation, attributing the basic idea to Aoun (1979). In particular, Chomsky (1981, 331 ff.) proposes reducing the Case Filter to the θ-criterion. Case renders an argument (chain) visible for θ-role assignment. A Caseless argument will violate the θ-criterion. An immediate problem arises with PRO, as in (15), which was assumed not to have Case. Thus, we wind up with the following disjunction (Chomsky's (18) on p. 334):

(27) Suppose that the position P is marked with the θ-role R and $C = (\alpha_1, \ldots, \alpha_n)$ is a chain. Then C is assigned R by P if and only if for some i, α_i is in position P and C has Case or is headed by PRO.

Clearly the disjunction is a problem. Chomsky and Lasnik (1993, 561) eventually suggested a way of assimilating PRO to other arguments: "PRO, like other arguments, has Case, but a Case different from the familiar ones: nominative, accusative, etc. From the point of view of interpretation, we might regard PRO as a 'minimal' NP argument, lacking independent phonetic, referential or other properties. Accordingly, let us say that it is the sole NP that can bear null Case (though it may have other Cases as well, in nonstandard conditions that we will not review here)." Chomsky and Lasnik proposed that null Case is licensed by nonfinite Infl, but that is not quite precise. As shown by Lasnik (1993) and Martin (1996), following Stowell (1982), there is a crucial distinction between the Infl in raising and ECM constructions and that in Control configurations. It is only the latter that licenses null Case.

In addition to the conceptual simplification provided by the hypothesis that PRO is Case-marked, there is also an empirical argument presented by Chomsky and Lasnik, based on the overwhelming generalization that A-movement from a Case-checking position is barred. This prohibition has been stated in various ways over the years, including the following:

"Movement is a kind of 'last resort.' An NP is moved only when this is required . . . in order to escape a violation of some principle [such as] the Case filter." (Chomsky 1986, 143)

We must "prevent a nominal phrase that has already satisfied the Case Filter from raising further to do so again in a higher position." (Chomsky 1995b, 280)

"A visible Case feature . . . makes [a] feature bundle or constituent available for 'A-movement.' Once Case is checked off, no further [A-]movement is possible." (Lasnik 1995b, 16)

"If uninterpretable features serve to implement operations, we expect that it is structural Case that enables the closest goal G to select P(G) to satisfy EPP by Merge. Thus, if structural Case has already been checked (deleted), the phrase P(G) is 'frozen in place,' unable to move further to satisfy EPP in a higher position. More generally, uninterpretable features render the goal active, able to implement an operation: to select a phrase for Merge (pied-piping) or to delete the probe." (Chomsky 2000, 123)

What Chomsky and Lasnik observed is that this same prohibition seems to be in force for PRO, as illustrated by the following examples:

(28) a. *We want PRO to strike t [that the problems are insoluble]
      b. *We want PRO to seem to t [that the problems are insoluble]

Compare:

(29) a. *We want John to strike t [that the problems are insoluble]
      b. *We want John to seem to t [that the problems are insoluble]

Note that subject of the complement of *want* is a position where PRO is normally permitted.

(30) We want PRO to solve the problem

But it cannot arrive in that position from a Case position. This is fairly straight-forward if PRO is fundamentally like *John* with respect to Case requirements, but mysterious otherwise.

There are still two related problems with this θ-theoretic approach to Case. First, with respect to Case, pleonastic nominal expressions seem to have exactly the same distribution as referential ones:

(31) a. *Susan tried [it to rain]
     b. *Susan tried [it to appear [that Mary is a genius]]
     c. *Susan tried [there to be an investigation]

(32) a. *It is likely [it to rain]
     b. *It is likely [it to appear [that Mary is a genius]]
     c. *It is likely [there to be an investigation]

(33) a. *My belief [it to be raining]
     b. *My belief [it to appear [that Mary is a genius]]
     c. *My belief [there to be an investigation]

In each instance, pleonastic *it* or *there* is no better in a Caseless position than a referential expression would be:

(34) a. *Susan tried [Mary to win the race]
     b. *It is likely [Mary to solve the problem]
     c. *My belief [Mary to be a genius]

Another (possibly complementary) problem is that clauses are often arguments, hence requiring θ-roles, yet they can (sometimes) appear in Caseless positions:

(35) a. My proof **[that 2+2=4]**   cf. *My proof **the theorem**
     b. It was proved **[that Mary is a genius]**   cf. *It was proved **the theorem**

With respect to pleonastics, there are two classes, according to Chomsky. First, there is weather *it*, which Chomsky argues is not truly a pleonastic, but is, rather, a "quasi-argument," patterning with arguments. Chomsky's evidence for this is that PRO, normally an argument, can be controlled by weather *it*, as in (36).

(36) It often rains after PRO snowing

There is further supporting evidence. The subject of *try* is a strongly argumental position. Yet it is reasonably acceptable, on observing a quickly darkening sky, to utter (37).

(37) It's trying to rain.

This is in sharp contrast to the behavior of a true expletive:

(38) *It's trying to seem that Mary is a genius.

As for the apparent Case requirement of true pleonastics, Chomsky proposes that this follows from the association between these items and their "associates," forming a θ-chain. The pleonastic then requires Case, so that its clausal associate (in the instance of *it*) or its nominal one (in the instance of *there*) will be visible, under the assumption that the surface position of the associate is not a Case position. This kind of approach is often called "Case transmission." Note that this does not address (35a), with a clausal complement to a noun, and no associated expletive in a Case position. I return to this problem.

Chomsky (1986) offers a more elegant version of Case transmission (though, somewhat curiously, only for *there*). In particular, under the assumption that *be* is not a Case licensor, the proposal is that in the LF component the associate of *there* literally replaces it, as schematized in (39).

(39) a. There is [a man in the room]   S-structure
      b. A man is [t in the room]   LF

Now there is no need for transmission. After the movement, the associate is in its characteristic Case position—Spec of Infl. Further, the peculiar agreement displayed by existential constructions, as seen in (40), is now rationalized.[3]

(40) a. There is a man in the room.
      b. There are men in the room.

The LFs show standard agreement configurations:

(41) a. A man is t in the room
      b. Men are t in the room

This has an extremely significant consequence that Chomsky did not explicitly comment on. Prior to this development, there was no observable difference between two potential theories of Case—Case assignment and Case checking. The former was presented by Chomsky (1981) (though with the acknowledgment that little was at stake). The latter is more in the spirit of Vergnaud's original proposal. But once appropriate Case configurations can be created in covert syntax, Case assignment is excluded as a possibility (at least in languages that display overt case morphology). Given the GB organization of the grammar, an LF operation cannot have PF consequences. Thus, NPs must have Case all along. The Case then must be *checked*—certified as appropriate—rather than *assigned*. Given the *there*-replacement analysis, checking is at the level of LF. To the extent that this analysis is successful, it provides additional reason for rejecting the morphological version of the Case Filter in favor of the Visibility approach. At this point, we have the following revised taxonomy:

(42) *Items that obey the Case Filter*   *Items that ignore the Case Filter*
        Argumental lexical NPs   Expletives
        PRO   (NP traces)
        WH-trace
        Argumental clauses
        (sometimes via transmission)

The Case transmission configuration, now reduced to a Spec-head relation by hypothesis (at least for *there*), had actually been one of four distinct structural Case configurations, the other three being standard Spec-head (nominative), head-complement (accusative), and "exceptional" government across IP (ECM). It was one of the great early minimalist achievements to reduce all of these to Spec-head. Structural nominative is licensed[4] in the Spec-head relation with the functional head $Agr_{S(ubject)}$-Tense created by the raising of Tense to Agr_S.[5] Structural accusative Case, on the other hand, is licensed under government by V. In fact, these two distinct relations were often incorporated under a general notion of government. But in the spirit of the minimalist approach, one would prefer to avoid appeal to such arbitrary syntactic relations, and, following Chomsky 1991 and 1993, to base the theory on core primitive relations, in particular those provided by X'-theory. Given this, the relevant relation licensing accusative Case is the head-complement relation.

Consider now "exceptional Case marking" as in (43).

(43) John believes Mary to be intelligent.

In this instance, the licensing takes place in a relation not statable in X'-terms at all, requiring the rather complicated notion "government" and additionally requiring that IP, exceptionally among maximal projections, is not a barrier to government. Assuming that raising to object position is not an available operation,[6] the "exceptional" Case licensing in (43) must be reduced to a Spec-head relation. Derivation (44) provides a way to instantiate this, in terms of the Chomsky 1991 development of the Pollock 1989 split-Infl hypothesis. The movement of NP is assumed to be covert, since in PF, the ECM subject follows the verb.

(44)

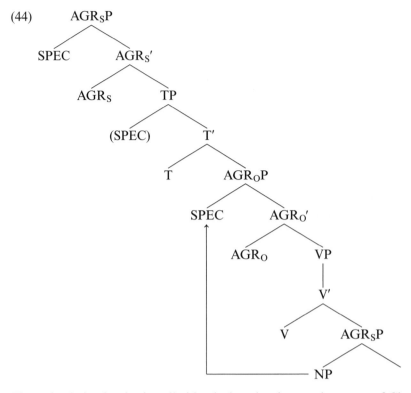

Thus, the derivation is virtually identical to the *there*-replacement of Chomsky 1986. Further, once we posit raising to Spec of Agr$_O$ for ECM subjects, there is no reason not to do the same for simple direct objects. Then, as suggested by Chomsky, we can reduce all structural Case licensing to one and the same configuration: Spec-(functional) head, a large step toward simplicity and symmetry in the system.

Lasnik and Saito 1991, developing observations and arguments of Postal 1974, presented evidence for this sort of raising approach. One relevant phenomenon involves the distribution of reciprocal expressions. Note that (45) is not significantly worse than (46).

(45) ?The DA proved [the defendants to be guilty] during each other's trials.

(46) ?The DA accused the defendants during each other's trials.

They both are considerably better than (47), the finite counterpart of (45).

(47) ?*The DA proved [that the defendants were guilty] during each other's trials.

Given usual assumptions, the antecedent of a reciprocal must c-command the reciprocal. But an embedded subject does not c-command an adverbial in the matrix clause. This indicates that at the point in the derivation relevant to the licensing of reciprocals, or anaphors in general, the structure of (45) has changed in such a way that the position of *the defendants* is comparable to what it is in (46). Further, as also observed by Lasnik and Saito, the direct object in the relevant paradigms is itself possibly not high enough to c-command into an adverbial adjunct. The LF theory of Case outlined above solves both problems at once: both an object and an ECM subject raise to Spec of Agr_O.

Negative polarity item licensing is also known to display asymmetries characteristic of c-command determined relations. Thus, a negative subject of a simple sentence can license *any* in the object, but not vice versa:

(48) No one saw anything.

(49) *Anyone saw nothing.

Further, a negative object can, to a reasonably acceptable extent, license *any* in an adverbial:

(50) The DA accused none of the defendants during any of the trials.

Now notice that to roughly the same extent, a negative subject of an infinitival can license *any* in an adverbial attached to the higher VP.

(51) ?The DA proved [none of the defendants to be guilty] during any of the trials.

This is in rather sharp contrast to a corresponding finite complement:

(52) ?*The DA proved [that none of the defendants were guilty] during any of the trials.

Once again, there is reason to believe that at the relevant level of representation, the subject of the infinitival complement is approximately as high in the structure as an NP complement would be, and that is higher than the base position of the NP complement.

At this point, a surprising problem arises. The model for the covert raising to Case position analysis is the Chomsky 1986 *there*-replacement. However, as pointed out by Lasnik and Saito, in ECM configurations, the associate of *there* exhibits none of the "high" behavior of argumental ECM subjects, even though under *there*-replacement, the LFs in the following pairs should be identical:

(53) a. The DA proved [two men to have been at the scene] during each other's trials.
       b. *The DA proved [there to have been two men at the scene] during each other's trials.

(54) a. The DA proved [no one to be at the scene] during any of the trials.
       b. *The DA proved [there to be no one at the scene] during any of the trials.

Den Dikken (1995) makes the same point for standard raising configurations, with examples like the following, involving Condition A and bound variable anaphora:

(55) a. Some applicants seem to each other to be eligible for the job.
     b. *There seem to each other to be some applicants eligible for the job.

(56) a. No applicant seems to his interviewer to be eligible for the job.
     b. *There seems to his interviewer to be no applicant eligible for the job.

There is one argument that seems to go in the other direction. Uriagereka (1988) observes that in the following example, the reciprocal can successfully take the associate as its antecedent, which is unexpected on the assumption that the position of complements is lower than that of adjuncts.

(57) There arrived two knights on each other's horses.

Uriagereka explicitly argues that LF expletive replacement, as in Chomsky 1986, is involved here. But, as shown just above, there are very strong reasons for doubting such derivations as a source of new binding possibilities. This near paradox is rather straightforwardly resolvable. Suppose that the associate of *there* does raise, but not all the way to the position of *there*. In particular, the raising to Spec of Agr_O already posited for transitive and simple ECM constructions could also be a possibility for existential constructions, as hinted by Lasnik and Saito 1991. This would correctly distinguish between Uriagereka's acceptable example and the unacceptable ones of Lasnik and Saito and den Dikken. However, now notice, that this suggests that the Case of the associate of *there* is licensed independent of *there* itself. In fact, Belletti 1988 provides strong arguments that *be* (along with unaccusative verbs) is a Case licensor (licensing a Case that Belletti calls partitive). Lasnik 1992 and 1995a present additional evidence for Belletti's position. See also Boskovic 1997 and 2002.

Once we accept that *there* does require Case in its own right, it is reasonable to conclude that pleonastic *it* does as well. This then tends to implicate some version of the morphological approach to the Case Filter, as opposed to the θ-theoretic Visibility one that succeeded it. In some respects, this is a positive conclusion, since clauses are often arguments, but, as observed above, can occur in a variety of Caseless positions. One such configuration is (35b), repeated as (58).

(58) It was proved **[that Mary is a genius]**

Case transmission, now rejected, might have handled this. But Case transmission never had anything to say about clausal complements to nouns or adjectives, as in (59), repeated from (35a).

(59) My proof **[that 2+2=4]**

Visibility would incorrectly exclude (59). An idea of Stowell 1981 provides one possible way out of the problem presented by examples like (59). Stowell argued that, contrary to appearances, nouns simply do not take finite clausal complements at all.[7] Rather, the apparent complements are actually appositives. Then, from the perspective of Visibility, it would be irrelevant for (59) that nouns are not Case licensors. However, this would not cover the full range of relevant phenomena. Stowell showed that apparent infinitival complements to nouns pass all his complement tests that the finite ones fail. From the perspective of the present discussion, then, an example like the following is still deeply problematic for Visibility:

(60) Jack's attempt **[PRO to finish on time]**

Clauses, whether thematic complements or not, do not need Case.

   Boskovic 1995, following Kitagawa 1986, points out one interesting class of exceptions to this conclusion. In particular, the following generalization (Boskovic's (17)) obtains:

(61) Although clauses can appear in Caseless positions they need Case when they function as subjects.

Kitagawa gives the following examples (compare with *That John loves Mary is surprising*):

(62) a. ??I believe [[that John loves Mary] to be surprising]
   b. *It is likely [[that John loves Mary] to be surprising]
   c. *It was believed [[that John loves Mary] to be surprising]

To these, we could add the following contrast:

(63) a. ?My belief [that [[that John loves Mary] is surprising]]
   b. *My belief [[that John loves Mary] to be surprising]

Both Kitagawa and Boskovic propose that a CP can optionally be a nominal expression. One way of instantiating this is to say that the C head of CP optionally has nominal features. As Boskovic observes, this paradigm casts further doubt on a θ-theoretic approach to Case, since there is no clear thematic difference between nominal and nonnominal clauses. I will abstract away from the full details of the analysis of these facts. One possibility (definitely not the one Boskovic advocates) is that only an NP (or DP; I continue to use the label NP for ease of exposition) can satisfy the EPP, so a purely CP clause could not move to Spec of IP at all. A nominal CP would then, like other nominals, have to obey the Case Filter, yielding the result that a CP in Spec of IP will invariably require Case. A CP not in Spec of IP will "optionally" require Case, depending on whether its head is selected with nominal features or not.

   The assumption of optional nominal status of CP can address another problem as well. Suppose that a Case assigner must assign its Case (i.e., a Case checker must check its Case), a requirement sometimes referred to as the Inverse Case Filter. The problem raised by this requirement involves verbs that can freely take nominal expressions or clauses as their complement, as exemplified in (64).

(64) a. Mary believes [your story]
     b. Mary believes [that John is a genius]

If clauses don't bear Case, (64b) would violate the Inverse Case Filter. But, as we have seen, they do not necessarily bear Case. Boskovic's proposal is a neat way of resolving the near contradiction. At this point, though, it might be good to take a step back to examine the Inverse Case Filter. To the best of my knowledge, it was first proposed by Fukui and Speas (1986), mainly to deduce the effects of the EPP (a research goal currently still being intensely pursued). The reasoning went like this: if Spec of (finite) IP is not filled (either by movement or by insertion of an expletive), finite Infl will be unable to assign its nominative Case, under the assumption of Fukui and Speas that Infl can assign Case only to its Spec. If the Case Filter is "symmetrized," this failure will rule out examples like (65), rendering the EPP superfluous.

(65) a. *__ seems that Mary is a genius
     b. *__ has been a man in the room

   EPP in a nonfinite clause does not completely fall under such an analysis. For ECM contexts, Fukui and Speas propose that filling the Spec of IP is necessary so that the matrix verb can assign its accusative Case (under government; if the embedded subject, or passivized object, were VP internal, VP would act as a barrier to government). This is already not without difficulties, as discussed above. Successive cyclic A-movement, as in (66), is still more difficult.

(66) Mary is believed [t'' to be likely [t' to be chosen t]]

The movement to matrix subject position can be assumed to be Case-driven, but not the movements to t' or t''. If we assume that the sole driving force for A-movement is Case, we are led to a global conception of economy of derivation, as discussed by Chomsky (1995a). In particular, we would be led to the conclusion that a specific instance of movement need not immediately result in the checking of a feature. Rather, it need only be a necessary step in a sequence of movements that ultimately result in the required checking configuration. For Chomsky (1995a) the intermediate steps in a successive cyclic A-movement derivation are licensed in this way. A more local, Markovian, conception of economy implicates the EPP. If each Infl, finite or not, has an EPP requirement, then (assuming a bottom-up structure-building mechanism) as soon as Infl is introduced into the structure, that EPP requirement will have to be satisfied. No "look-ahead" will be needed. And now notice that if the EPP is required completely independent of the Inverse Case Filter, it is the latter, rather than the former, that might be rendered superfluous. This is a significant enough issue that it is worth examining whether A-movement is, in fact, successive cyclic. Chomsky (1981, 44–45) presents an empirical argument for intermediate A-traces, hence, for successive cyclic A-movement. He observes that (67) is acceptable, indicating that Condition A is satisfied.

(67) They are likely [t' to appear to each other [t to be happy]]

Based on this, he argues for intermediate traces (hence, for successive cyclic movement). His line of reasoning is as follows: "The GF-$\bar{\theta}$ filled by medial traces such as t' . . . may . . . be relevant to LF; for example in the sentence [(67)], . . . where the medial trace serves as the antecedent of *each other*, which requires an antecedent in the same clause in such sentences in accordance with binding theory." Interestingly, though, it does not seem that the antecedent must be in the same clause, given the binding theory in Chomsky 1981 (or those in Chomsky 1973 and 1986 for that matter). Consider the Chomsky 1981 formulation:

(68) β is a governing category for α if and only if β is the minimal category containing α, a governor of α, and a SUBJECT accessible to α.

(69) SUBJECT = AGR in a finite clause; NP of S in an infinitival; . . .

(70) γ is accessible to α iff α is in the c-command domain of γ and . . .

If there is a trace in the intermediate clause then that clause is the governing category (GC) of *each other*. But that is no argument that there is such a trace. Suppose there were none. Then the intermediate clause, lacking a SUBJECT, would not be the GC, and Condition A would, correctly, be satisfied with *they* as the binder of *each other*. Thus, there is no argument here for successive cyclicity of A-movement.[8]

I have just shown that Chomsky's argument for successive cyclicity does not go through on standard formulations of the binding domain for anaphors. Chomsky's argument relied on a clause-mate condition, but those formulations do not require that an antecedent of an anaphor be a clause-mate in the crucial cases. However, in Lasnik 2002 and 2003, I argued that clause-mate is, in fact, the correct characterization, as argued much earlier by Postal 1966 and 1974, and generally assumed until Chomsky 1973. My argument was initially based on a very interesting verb-particle construction first discussed by Kayne 1985 and later analyzed by Johnson 1991 in terms relevant to the present discussion. Johnson provided an insightful account of examples like (71) involving overt raising of the ECM subject *John*.

(71) Mary made John out to be a fool.

Both Kayne and Johnson convincingly treat (71) as an infinitival counterpart of (72).

(72) Mary made out that John is a fool.

Very plausibly, *John* in (71) has overtly raised into the matrix clause. Now consider that for many speakers, the raising seen in (71) is optional. For those speakers, (73) is an acceptable alternative to (71).

(73) Mary made out John to be a fool.

This time, plausibly *John* has remained in the embedded clause, and in Lasnik 2002 and 2003, I provided evidence that this is so. Now note that an anaphor on the upstream side of *out* is much better than one on the downstream side, with antecedent in the matrix clause:

(74) a. Jack made himself out to be honest.
     b. *Jack made out himself to be honest.

(75) a. They made each other out to be dishonest.
     b. *They made out each other to be dishonest.

None of the standard formulations of the notion governing category predict the disparity between the (a) and (b) versions of these examples, but a clause-mate formulation would. In each of the (b) examples, the anaphor is separated from its antecedent by the boundary of the infinitival clause, while in the (a) examples, no clause boundary of any sort intervenes. It must be acknowledged that there is an interfering factor: Verb-particle-NP order with reflexives and reciprocals is somewhat degraded even with only one clause, as in (76)–(77).

(76) ?Jack called up himself.

(77) ?They called up each other.

However, the deviance is less severe than that seen in ECM instances like (74b)–(75b). Thus, the argument for the clause-mate condition stands.

Given the clause-mate requirement on anaphors, examples like the following, attributed to Danny Fox, via David Pesetsky, in Castillo, Drury, and Grohmann 1999, argue for successive cyclic A-movement:

(78) John appears to Mary [to seem to himself/*herself [to be the best candidate]]

In the absence of successive cyclic movement, *himself* would incorrectly be predicted to violate Condition A, and, on fairly standard assumptions, *herself* to be in conformity.

A similar, though somewhat less direct, argument can be constructed based on Condition B. Examples (79)–(80) display familiar Condition B effects.

(79) *John$_i$ injured him$_i$

(80) *John$_i$ believes him$_i$ to be a genius

As would be expected, (79) remains unacceptable under VP ellipsis:

(81) *Mary injured him$_i$ and John$_i$ did too

What is not expected is that (80) is substantially improved under VP ellipsis:

(82) ?Mary believes him$_i$ to be a genius and John$_i$ does too

How is it that deletion, which I take to be a PF process following Ross 1969, Chomsky and Lasnik 1993, and Lasnik 1999b, among others, remediates a presumably semantic violation? Suppose that in addition to their properties with respect to anaphora, the pronouns under consideration also have a morphosyntactic requirement, in particular that as weak pronouns they must cliticize onto the verb, as suggested by Oehrle 1976, based on data like that presented by Chomsky 1955:

(83) The detective brought John in.

(84) The detective brought in John.

(85) The detective brought him in.

(86) *The detective brought in him.

If the relevant structural configuration for Condition B is based on the notion clause-mate, an account of the ellipsis paradigm presents itself. In particular, it is not actually the Condition B violation (presumably an LF effect) in (80) that is repaired by ellipsis in (82). Rather, it is failure to cliticize (a PF violation) that is repaired (by PF deletion).[9] And without cliticization, the pronoun can remain in the lower clause (if, as argued in Lasnik 1999a and 2001, "subject raising" in these constructions is generally optional). On the other hand, in (81), the pronoun and its antecedent are clause-mates independent of cliticization, so there is no possibility of "repair" of the Condition B violation by ellipsis. Given the clause-mate character of Condition B, (87) constitutes evidence for successive cyclic movement, because *John* must have moved through the intermediate Spec of IP to yield the observed obviation. *John* in its surface position is not a clause-mate of *him*.

(87) *John$_i$ is believed [to seem to him$_i$ [to be a genius]]

Given this motivation for the EPP, I will remain agnostic about the Inverse Case Filter.[10] It is worth observing that under the Agree theory of Chomsky (2001), neither the Inverse Case Filter nor even the classic Case Filter ever drives movement. Whatever checking by a head needs to take place can, in fact must, take place prior to movement of an XP to the specifier position of that head, since Agree demands that the Case licensing head (the Probe) c-command the Case licensee (the Goal). Phrasal movement is, then, invariably driven by the EPP. I do continue to assume some version of the classic Case Filter, since its effects are not entirely deducible from the EPP, nor from anything else, as far as I can tell. Thus, the original question is still germane: Exactly what are the items that must obey the filter? The discussion here has led to the following empirically motivated taxonomy, admittedly problematic in that it does not make much sense, though very simple: NP A-chains obey the Case Filter.

(88) *Items that obey the Case Filter*   *Items that ignore the Case Filter*
        Argumental lexical NPs   Clauses (nonnominal)
        PRO   (NP traces)
        WH-traces   Everything else
        Expletives
        Clauses (nominal)

The second fundamental question about the Case Filter also still persists: Exactly where does it have to be satisfied? Is it an LF requirement or a PF one? Conceptually, either can be motivated. But, as seen above, in both instances, the motivations are not without difficulties. I have no definitive way to resolve this issue at the moment. I will, however, end with a new argument suggestive of a PF approach. Postal (1974) discovered a class of verbs that take infinitival complements, but where the subject must (to put it in more modern terminology) be an A′-trace. *Allege* is one of about two dozen that he lists. With these verbs, we find the unacceptable (89) rescued by such operations as topicalization (90).[11]

(89) *I alleged John to be a fool.

(90) ?John, I alleged to be a fool.

Kayne (1984), followed by Boskovic (1997), takes (89) to be a violation of the Case Filter. For Kayne and for Boskovic, A′-movement provides a way of satisfying the Case Filter violation. Unlike standard ECM verbs, *allege*-type verbs are somehow not powerful enough in their Case-checking ability to reach all the way down into the spec of the IP in their complement; the first step of A′-movement brings the relevant DP into close enough proximity for its Case to be checked. The accounts of Kayne and Boskovic differ in many details, but here I will abstract away from the details entirely, and just assume that they are correct that the Case Filter is implicated and that A′-bar movement somehow provides a way that it can be satisfied. Consider now the sequence of sentences in (91).

(91) a. John, I alleged to be a fool.
       b. Mary did ~~[allege John to be a fool]~~ too.

In (91a), we have the aforementioned satisfaction of the Case Filter via A′-movement. (91b) is more interesting. The source must have been as indicated,[12] since it is obvious that topicalization did not take place. (If it had, *John* would be far outside of the deleted VP and would be pronounced.) The question is why *John* in (91b), different from its nonelliptical source, is not ruled out by the Case Filter. Along the lines of Merchant 2001, Lasnik 1995c, and Lasnik 1999b, among others, I suggest that we have here an instance of repair by ellipsis. In particular, a PF process (deletion) is repairing a violation, indicating that the violation is (or would have been) a PF one. Thus, we have some rather surprising evidence that the Case Filter is, in fact, a PF requirement. What it means for items with no phonetic content (PRO, WH-trace) to have to obey a PF requirement is a question I will have to leave for future consideration.

Notes

I am very pleased to be able to contribute a discussion of Case theory to a book celebrating Jean-Roger Vergnaud's many contributions to linguistic theory. The importance of Case for syntactic analysis was, of course, entirely Jean-Roger's discovery. And it is hard to imagine the principles and parameters framework ever being developed without this crucial insight. I would also like to take this opportunity to thank Zeljko Boskovic, Cedric Boeckx, Bob Freidin, and Noam Chomsky for hundreds of hours of discussion with me over the years (or decades) of Case theory and many related matters. Without those discussions, my research would have come to a dead end on many occasions. Finally, I would like to thank Tomohiro Fujii, Bob Freidin, and two reviewers for many penetrating suggestions for improvement of an earlier draft.

1. An alternative conception, more like Vergnaud's, assumes that all NPs are "born" with Case and the Case Filter excludes mismatch between the Case an NP already has and the position in which the NP finds itself. I will return to potential ways of teasing these two conceptions apart. In passing, I note that Chomsky's taxonomy of Case types is a bit of a departure from the classical terminology, under which all cases other than nominative are classified as oblique. I am grateful to Scott Olsson for reminding me of this.

2. As already demonstrated by Jespersen (1927), the *that* introducing a relative clause is, indeed, a complementizer and not a "relative pronoun."

3. The agreement patterns are not always this simple. See Sobin 1997 for an important discussion of agreement when the associate is a coordinate structure.

4. At this point, I intend the term *licensing* as neutral between a mechanism of Case assignment to a previously Caseless NP (as in Chomsky 1980, 1981) and one of "checking," under which an NP is initially inserted into a structure with a Case feature whose appropriateness to its position is later certified. As discussed just above, under some circumstances, an NP is not in a Case position until the LF component, arguing for a checking approach.

5. See Chomsky 1991, developing ideas of Pollock 1989.

6. See Postal 1974 for numerous arguments for raising to object position; Chomsky 1973, 1981, and 1986 for opposing arguments; and McCawley 1988, Postal and Pullum 1988, and Lasnik and Saito 1991 for some discussion of the controversy.

7. See Safir 1985 and Takahashi 1994 for discussion of Stowell's proposal.

8. Bob Freidin points out that I am here assuming that the completely empty subject of the intermediate clause would not count as any kind of SUBJECT. Note that in later developments of the theory, there would be literally no subject at all unless something actually moved into that position.

9. Postal (1974) provides independent evidence that pronominal ECM subjects show the same cliticization behavior as pronominal objects.

10. Boskovic (2002) provides a new argument for the Inverse Case Filter, based on (i) and (ii):

(i) *Mary loves here/there.

(ii) a. Mary loves it here/there.
    b. Mary loves this/that place.

Boskovic reasons that the examples in (i) are perfectly coherent (as demonstrated by (ii)), and are bad just because *here* and *there* cannot bear Case. However, this phenomenon is much more limited than would be expected. The following examples contrast minimally with Boskovic's:

(iii) a.   Mary found/discussed this place.
     b.   *Mary found/discussed here.
     c.   (*)Mary found/discussed it here.
           [Good only on the irrelevant reading where *it* denotes some object.]

(iv) a.   I talked about this place.
    b.   *I talked about here.
    c.   (*)I talked about it here.
          [Good only on the irrelevant reading where *it* denotes some object.]

I leave for future research further investigation of (i) and (ii), but note in passing that Lydia Grebenyova plausibly suggests relating them to

(v) a. I love it when you sing.
    b. I love when you sing.

11. Bob Freidin informs me that for some speakers, *allege* behaves just like *consider*, licensing ECM even when the subject of the infinitival clause has not undergone A′-movement. Needless to say, for such speakers the following argument does not go through. I suspect, though, that for all speakers, at least some verbs on Postal's list pattern as he reports.

12. Two reviewers each suggest alternative sources, which I will briefly consider here. The first alternative relies on the proposal of Merchant 2001 that there is no formal identity requirement for ellipsis, just a purely semantic one. Under this approach to ellipsis, the elided material in (91) could be *allege that John was a fool*, rather than the indicated infinitival. This would then raise no issues of Case licensing. However, there is at least some reason to believe that formal identity is at least to some degree relevant in licensing ellipsis. One such reason is provided by Merchant himself. Active-passive pairs typically do not alternate:

(i) *Someone shot Ben, but I don't know by whom [Ben was shot t]

In the absence of any formal identity condition, it is not immediately clear why ellipsis is not possible here. Merchant proposes that the subject of the active transitive induces relevant entailments that the *by*-phrase does not. This might turn out to be the right direction, but as it stands, it is just a promissory note. There are two other residues of formal identity that could be mentioned here. One is the fact that for many speakers, sloppy identity is disfavored if there is a mismatch of agreement features:

(ii) ??Mary washed her car and John did ~~[wash his car]~~ too

The second is a restriction on VP ellipsis with forms of *be* discussed in Warner 1986 and analyzed in terms relevant to the present discussion in Lasnik 1995d. As illustrated in (iii), finite forms of *be* cannot antecede the infinitive.

(iii) *Mary is a doctor and John will ~~[be a doctor]~~ too

Here again it is hard to see how any semantic identity could be at issue.

The second alternative is based on the observation that while the *allege* class of verbs do not license Case on full DPs, they do, for many speakers, on weak pronouns (perhaps via incorporation):

(iv) I alleged *John/?him to be a fool.

The elided material in (91) could then be *allege him to be a fool*, once again obviating any Case difficulty even without ellipsis. And even accounts of ellipsis demanding formal identity necessarily allow this kind of "vehicle change" in the sense of Fiengo and May 1994. However, Tomo Fujii shows that this kind of account cannot cover all of the relevant data. Consider (v):

(v) His$_i$ mother, John$_i$ alleged to be beautiful. Bill did too.

Fujii observes that sloppy identity is possible here, unexpected if the elided material were simply *allege her to be beautiful*.

Finally, I note that one of the A′-ECM constructions discussed by Kayne is not even potentially amenable to a vehicle change to pronoun analysis. In (vi), a pronoun is no better than a full DP.

(vi) *I assure you John/him to be the best candidate.

Compare (vii).

(vii) I assure you that John is the best candidate.

Here, as with Postal's examples, A′-movement rescues the violation:

(viii) ?John, I assure you to be the best candidate.

Significantly, the VP ellipsis pattern with *allege* can also be replicated:

(ix) ?John, I assure you to be the best candidate. Mary will too.

References

Aoun, Joseph. 1979. On government, Case-marking, and clitic placement. Ms. Cambridge, Mass.: Massachusetts Institute of Technology.

Belletti, Adriana. 1988. The Case of unaccusatives. *Linguistic Inquiry* 19:1–34.

Boskovic, Zeljko. 1995. Case properties of clauses and the Greed principle. *Studia Linguistica* 49:32–53.

Boskovic, Zeljko. 1997. *The syntax of nonfinite complementation: An economy approach.* Cambridge, Mass.: MIT Press.

Boskovic, Zeljko. 2002. A-movement and the EPP. *Syntax* 5:167–218.

Castillo, Juan Carlos, John Drury, and Kleanthes K. Grohmann. 1999. The status of the Merge over Move preference. In *University of Maryland Working Papers in Linguistics* 8:66–104.

Chomsky, Noam. 1955. The logical structure of linguistic theory. Ms. Cambridge, Mass.: Harvard University and MIT. [Revised 1956 version published in part by Plenum, New York, 1975; University of Chicago Press, 1985.]

Chomsky, Noam. 1970. Remarks on nominalization. In *Readings in English transformational grammar*, ed. Roderick A. Jacobs and Peter S. Rosenbaum, 184–221. Waltham, Mass.: Ginn and Co. [Reprinted in Noam Chomsky, *Studies on semantics in generative grammar*, 11–61. The Hague: Mouton, 1972.]

Chomsky, Noam. 1973. Conditions on transformations. In *A festschrift for Morris Halle*, ed. Stephen Anderson and Paul Kiparsky, 232–286. New York: Holt, Rinehart and Winston.

Chomsky, Noam. 1976. Conditions on rules of grammar. *Linguistic Analysis* 2:303–351.

Chomsky, Noam. 1980. On binding. *Linguistic Inquiry* 11:1–46.

Chomsky, Noam. 1981. *Lectures on government and binding*. Dordrecht: Foris.

Chomsky, Noam. 1986. *Knowledge of language*. New York: Praeger.

Chomsky, Noam. 1991. Some notes on economy of derivation and representation. In *Principles and parameters in comparative grammar*, ed. Robert Freidin, 417–454. Cambridge, Mass.: MIT Press. [Reprinted in Noam Chomsky, *The minimalist program*, 129–166. Cambridge, Mass.: MIT Press, 1995.]

Chomsky, Noam. 1993. A minimalist program for linguistic theory. In *The view from Building 20: Essays in linguistics in honor of Sylvain Bromberger*, ed. Kenneth Hale and Samuel J. Keyser, 1–52. Cambridge, Mass.: MIT Press. [Reprinted in Noam Chomsky, *The minimalist program*, 167–217. Cambridge, Mass.: MIT Press, 1995.]

Chomsky, Noam. 1995a. Bare phrase structure. In *Government and binding theory and the minimalist program*, ed. Gert Webelhuth, 383–439. Oxford: Blackwell. [Also in *Evolution and revolution in linguistic theory: Essays in honor of Carlos Otero*, ed. Hector Campos and Paula Kempchinsky. Washington, D.C.: Georgetown University Press.]

Chomsky, Noam. 1995b. Categories and transformations. In *The minimalist program*, 219–394. Cambridge, Mass.: MIT Press.

Chomsky, Noam. 2000. Minimalist inquiries: The framework. In *Step by step: Essays on minimalist syntax in honor of Howard Lasnik*, ed. Roger Martin, David Michaels, and Juan Uriagereka, 89–155. Cambridge, Mass.: MIT Press.

Chomsky, Noam. 2001. Derivation by phase. In *Ken Hale: A life in language*, ed. Michael Kenstowicz, 1–52. Cambridge, Mass.: MIT Press.

Chomsky, Noam, and Howard Lasnik. 1977. Filters and control. *Linguistic Inquiry* 11:425–504. [Reprinted in Howard Lasnik, *Essays on restrictiveness and learnability*, 42–124. Dordrecht: Kluwer, 1990.]

Chomsky, Noam, and Howard Lasnik. 1993. The theory of principles and parameters. In *Syntax: An international handbook of contemporary research*, Vol. 1, ed. Joachim Jacobs, Arnim von Stechow, Wolfgang Sternefeld, and Theo Vennemann, 506–569. Berlin: Walter de

Gruyter. [Reprinted in Noam Chomsky, *The minimalist program*, 13–127. Cambridge, Mass.: MIT Press, 1995.]

Davis, Lori. 1984. *Arguments and expletives*. Doctoral dissertation, University of Connecticut, Storrs.

den Dikken, Marcel. 1995. Binding, expletives, and levels. *Linguistic Inquiry* 26:347–354.

Fiengo, Robert, and Robert May. 1994. *Indices and identity*. Cambridge, Mass.: MIT Press.

Freidin, Robert, and Howard Lasnik. 1981. Disjoint reference and *wh*-trace. *Linguistic Inquiry* 12:39–53. [Reprinted in Howard Lasnik, *Essays on anaphora*, 110–124. Dordrecht: Kluwer, 1989.]

Fukui, Naoki, and Margaret Speas. 1986. Specifiers and projection. In *MIT Working Papers in Linguistics* 8:128–172.

Jespersen, Otto. 1927. *A modern English grammar*. London: George Allen and Unwin.

Johnson, Kyle. 1991. Object positions. *Natural Language and Linguistic Theory* 9:577–636.

Kayne, Richard. 1984. *Connectedness and binary branching*. Dordrecht: Foris.

Kayne, Richard. 1985. Principles of particle constructions. In *Grammatical representation*, ed. Jacqueline Guéron, Hans-Georg Obenauer, and Jean-Yves Pollock, 101–140. Dordrecht: Foris.

Kitagawa, Yoshihisa. 1986. *Subjects in Japanese and English*. Doctoral dissertation, University of Massachusetts, Amherst.

Lasnik, Howard. 1992. Case and expletives: Notes toward a parametric account. *Linguistic Inquiry* 23:381–405.

Lasnik, Howard. 1993. Lectures on minimalist syntax. In *University of Connecticut Occasional Papers in Linguistics* 1. [Reprinted in Howard Lasnik, *Minimalist analysis*, 25–73. Oxford: Blackwell.]

Lasnik, Howard. 1995a. Case and expletives revisited: On Greed and other human failings. *Linguistic Inquiry* 26:615–633. [Reprinted in Howard Lasnik, *Minimalist analysis*, 74–96. Oxford: Blackwell.]

Lasnik, Howard. 1995b. Last resort. In *Minimalism and linguistic theory*, ed. Shosuke Haraguchi and Michio Funaki, 1–32. Tokyo: Hituzi Syobo. [Reprinted in Howard Lasnik, *Minimalist analysis*, 120–150. Oxford: Blackwell, 1999.]

Lasnik, Howard. 1995c. A note on pseudogapping. In *Papers on minimalist syntax, MIT Working Papers in Linguistics* 27:143–163. [Reprinted in Howard Lasnik, *Minimalist analysis*, 151–174. Oxford: Blackwell, 1999.]

Lasnik, Howard. 1995d. Verbal morphology: *Syntactic structures* meets the Minimalist Program. In *Evolution and revolution in linguistic theory: Essays in honor of Carlos Otero*, ed. Héctor Campos and Paula Kempchinsky, 251–275. Washington, D.C.: Georgetown University Press. [Reprinted in Howard Lasnik, *Minimalist analysis*, 97–119. Oxford: Blackwell, 1999.]

Lasnik, Howard. 1999a. Chains of arguments. In *Working minimalism*, ed. Samuel D. Epstein and Norbert Hornstein, 189–215. Cambridge, Mass.: MIT Press. [Reprinted in Howard Lasnik, *Minimalist investigations in linguistic theory*, 139–157. London: Routledge, 2003.]

Lasnik, Howard. 1999b. On feature strength: Three minimalist approaches to overt movement. *Linguistic Inquiry* 30:197–217. [Reprinted in Howard Lasnik, *Minimalist investigations in linguistic theory*, 83–102. London: Routledge, 2003.]

Lasnik, Howard. 2001. Subjects, objects, and the EPP. In *Objects and other subjects: Grammatical functions, functional categories, and configurationality*, ed. William D. Davies and Stanley Dubinsky, 103–121. Dordrecht: Kluwer Academic Publishers.

Lasnik, Howard. 2002. Clause-mate conditions. In *Proceeding of the 2002 International Conference on Korean Linguistics*, 386–393. Seoul: Association for Korean Linguistics.

Lasnik, Howard. 2003. On the Extended Projection Principle. *Studies in Modern Grammar* 31:1–23.

Lasnik, Howard, and Robert Freidin. 1981. Core grammar, Case theory, and markedness. In *Theory of markedness in generative grammar: Proceedings of the 1979 GLOW Conference*, ed. Adriana Belletti, Luciana Brandi, and Luigi Rizzi, 407–421. Scuola Normale Superiore, Pisa. [Reprinted in Howard Lasnik, *Essays on restrictiveness and learnability*, 172–183. Dordrecht: Kluwer, 1990.]

Lasnik, Howard, and Mamoru Saito. 1991. On the subject of infinitives. In *Papers from the 27th Regional Meeting of the Chicago Linguistic Society, Part I: The general session*, ed. Lise M. Dobrin, Lynn Nichols, and Rosa M. Rodriguez, 324–343. Chicago: Chicago Linguistic Society, University of Chicago. [Reprinted in Howard Lasnik, *Minimalist analysis*, 7–24. Oxford: Blackwell, 1999.]

Martin, Roger. 1996. *A minimalist theory of PRO and control*. Doctoral dissertation, University of Connecticut, Storrs.

McCawley, James D. 1988. Review article on Noam Chomsky, *Knowledge of language: Its structure, origin, and use*. *Language* 64:355–365.

Merchant, Jason. 2001. *The syntax of silence: Sluicing, islands, and the theory of ellipsis*. Oxford: Oxford University Press.

Oehrle, Richard. 1976. *The grammatical status of the English dative alternation*. Doctoral dissertation, MIT, Cambridge, Mass.

Pollock, Jean-Yves. 1989. Verb movement, universal grammar, and the structure of IP. *Linguistic Inquiry* 20:365–424.

Postal, Paul M. 1966. A note on understood transitively. *International Journal of American Linguistics* 32:90–93.

Postal, Paul M. 1974. *On raising: One rule of English grammar and its theoretical implications*. Cambridge, Mass.: MIT Press.

Postal, Paul M., and Geoffrey K. Pullum. 1988. Expletive noun phrases in subcategorized positions. *Linguistic Inquiry* 19:635–670.

Ross, John Robert. 1969. Guess who? In *Papers from the Fifth Regional Meeting of the Chicago Linguistic Society*, ed. Robert I. Binnick, Alice Davison, Georgia M. Green, and Jerry L. Morgan, 252–286. Chicago: Chicago Linguistic Society, University of Chicago.

Safir, Kenneth. 1985. *Syntactic chains*. Cambridge: Cambridge University Press.

Sobin, Nicholas. 1997. Agreement, default rules, and grammatical viruses. *Linguistic Inquiry* 28:318–343.

Stowell, Timothy. 1981. *Origins of phrase structure*. Doctoral dissertation, MIT, Cambridge, Mass.

Stowell, Timothy. 1982. The tense of infinitives. *Linguistic Inquiry* 13:561–570.

Takahashi, Daiko. 1994. *Minimality of movement*. Doctoral dissertation, University of Connecticut, Storrs.

Uriagereka, Juan. 1988. *On government*. Doctoral dissertation, University of Connecticut, Storrs.

Warner, Anthony. 1986. Ellipsis conditions and the status of the English copula. In *York Papers in Linguistics* 12:153–172.

Wasow, Thomas. 1972. *Anaphoric relations in English*. Doctoral dissertation, MIT, Cambridge, Mass. [Revised version published as Thomas Wasow, *Anaphora in generative grammar*. Ghent: E. Story-Scientia, 1979.]

3 Uninterpretable Features Are Incompatible in Morphology with Other Minimalist Postulates

M. Rita Manzini and Leonardo M. Savoia

In recent work, Manzini and Savoia (2001, 2002a, 2002b, 2004a, 2004b, 2005, 2007) argue that accounting for variation across Romance dialects, specifically Italian and Swiss ones, requires a reform of the morphological set {person, number, gender, case}. Comparison with the different data set offered by Albanian dialects (Manzini and Savoia 1999, 2003, 2007) confirms this conclusion. In a nutshell, the proposed reform is that syntax and morphology should run on the same categories, namely syntactic categories like N, Q, D, and so on, to the exclusion of the traditional morphological feature set. Thus linguistic structures are articulated by the merger of lexical items that project such categories both at the phrase (syntactic) level and at the word (morphological) level.

To be more precise, such a reform is needed if basic explanatory-adequacy criteria are to be met in morphology, or put differently, if we are to preserve basic minimalist postulates such as projection from the lexicon, or the prohibition against comparison of derivations/representations or mechanisms of equivalent power. In this chapter we will concentrate on the reform of the feature set, drawing together arguments concerning the φ-set and arguments concerning the case system presented by Manzini and Savoia (2002a, 2002b, 2004a, 2004b, 2005, 2007) in connection with various specific problems relating in particular to the clitic set and agreement. We will briefly indicate what we consider to be the basic inadequacies of the classical model at the end of the chapter, in comparing that model with the model sketched here, thus motivating the title of the chapter.

3.1 Plural and Dative

As discussed in Manzini and Savoia 2002a, 2007, Romance dialects may or may not have a lexicalization for the third-person dative belonging to the same l ($d\, j$ etc.) series as the lexicalization for third-person accusatives and nominatives. If they do, in some cases the dative has a morphology different from that of the accusative series, as in the Sardinian dialect of *Làconi* from Manzini and Savoia 2002a, where the accusative is lexicalized as in (1a), while the dative corresponds to (1b).

(1) *Làconi* (Sardinia)
    a. ɖu, ɖa, ɖus,   ɖas
       him, her, them-M, them-F
    b. ɖi,   ɖis
       to him/her, to them

However, in many dialects the dative overlaps with one of the forms of the accusative paradigm; in this case, represented in (2) by the dialect of *Vagli*, again taken from Manzini and Savoia 2002a, the overlapping is generally between the dative and the plural (masculine accusative), to the exclusion of other possible forms of the third-person paradigm.

(2) *Vagli Sopra* (Tuscany)
    a. l,   la, ʝi,   lə
       him, her, them-M, them-F
    b. ʝi
       to him/her/them

Describing the phenomenon in (2) in terms of traditional morphological features yields opaque results. In other words, the coincidence between accusative masculine plural and dative appears to be completely accidental, since there is not a single feature overlap between the two forms. It is in principle possible that this is the correct result and that morphology is a domain of purely accidental variation; however, pursuing an explanatory goal in morphology requires a revision of the relevant set of primitives.[1] In particular, Manzini and Savoia (2002a, 2007) propose that the lexical entry for a clitic form such as *ʝi* of Vagli in (2a) and (2b) is characterized in terms of a quantificational property. This gives rise to two possible readings, namely plurality, as in (2a), and distributivity, which we take to be the proper characterization of "dativity" as in (2b).

To be more precise, clitic pronouns of the form of (1)–(2) are not elementary lexical entries, but correspond to the merger of two separate morphemes, namely an *l/ɖ/ʝ* allomorph, introducing definite reference, and inflectional endings introducing the properties traditionally described in terms of number, gender, and Case. This analysis is particularly transparent for series such as (1) where the invariable *ɖ* base combines with *u, a, i* inflections for masculine accusative, feminine accusative, and (masculine or feminine) dative respectively and with *s* for plural. In this dialect, the *i* ending is therefore specialized for distributivity (i.e., the dative), while plurality is lexicalized by *s*, and *a, u* lexicalize nominal class (i.e., gender), as schematized in the lexicon in (3).

(3) *Làconi*
    ḍ: Definiteness
    a, u: Nominal class
    s: Plurality
    i: Distributivity

Similarly for the Vagli dialect, we assume that the *l*, *j* allomorphs are associated with a definiteness property in their lexical entry. Therefore, the quantificational denotation to which we reduce both plural and dative properties is associated with the *i* inflectional ending, as illustrated in (4). The nominal class (i.e., gender) specifications are *a*, *ə* in this dialect. What is of immediate relevance here is that lexical entries of the type in (3)–(4) have no recourse to the traditional morphological φ-features and case set; on the contrary, the characterization of the different morphemes is transparently related to syntactic categorization at least in the case of Definiteness, D, and Quantification, Q. The nominal-class property will be considered in sections 3.2 and 3.3.[2]

(4) *Vagli Sopra*
    l, ɹ: Definiteness
    a, ə: Nominal class
    i: Quantification

Manzini and Savoia (2002a) argue that the two different readings that the *i* morpheme in (4) gives rise to depend on its different contexts of insertion. To understand the plural interpretation it is sufficient to make reference to the morphological level. Thus we assume that the merger of the *j* definiteness base with the *i* inflection can by itself imply plurality; this can further be restricted to the masculine nominal class, as it is in the Vagli dialect, where the feminine is lexicalized by the nominal-class morpheme *ə*.

By contrast, the dative interpretation can be understood only in connection with the syntactic properties of the clitic. For the sake of simplicity we assume that the surface order of clitics results from hierarchical constraints on their merger directly in the inflectional domain; we exclude therefore that it results from the interaction of the order of arguments within the VP-shell with movement, though nothing hinges on this. Under the assumptions just reviewed, the dative interpretation is obtainable from the quantificational property of *ji* when it projects the Q category in the syntactic hierarchy.[3]

Concretely, consider the simple example in (5) where two *ji* clitics can combine in a dative-accusative cluster. We can see that the dative precedes the accusative from clusters where the accusative is morphologically distinct—that is, *l, la, lə*.

(5) *Vagli Sopra*

    i ɟi   l/   la/   ɟi/ lə ˈða

    he to. him/her/them it-M./it-F./them-M./them-F. gives

    'He gives it/them to him/her/them.'

We assign to sentences of the type in (5) structures like (6), where the higher *ɟi*, corresponding to the so-called dative, projects the Q category in the sentential tree, while this is not the case for the lower *ɟi*, corresponding to the so-called accusative. What is relevant here is that the dative interpretation of the higher *ɟi* depends on its projection of the Q property at the sentential level. At the word level the quantificational denotation of the *i* morpheme simply implies the plurality of the *ɟi* form. It will be noticed that Vagli is a subject clitic language, where the EPP argument is obligatorily lexicalized by a clitic (Brandi and Cordin 1989; Manzini and Savoia 2002b, 2007). In the tree in (6) the category projected by the EPP argument is identified with D, following in essence the intuition of Chomsky 1995, according to which in the inflectional domain of the sentence the subject checks a D-feature. We return to the category projected by the accusative in section 3.3 (for the subject clitic see note 7).

(6) *Vagli Sopra*

The tree in (6) bears no indication as to the labeling of the projections dominating the constituents resulting from Merge. Now, the preceding discussion strictly adheres to the minimalist principle whereby all structure is projected from the lexicon; indeed we have systematically referred to the categorial content being projected by a given lexical item. Thus we have avoided the more traditional, misleading terminology whereby lexical items are inserted under nodes with a given categorial content; in what follows we also say that the lexical item x lexicalizes category y. The adoption of the relevant minimalist postulate excludes the presence in the tree of empty nodes, not corresponding to the insertion of any lexical material. Under a strong construal this assumption may exclude a phrase structure theory of the type proposed by Chomsky (1995), and also Kayne (1994), in which (phonologically) empty heads support a filled Spec. If so, we need a theory where projection from the lexicon entirely abstracts from the Spec-head mechanism. One such theory, which we adopt in Manzini and Savoia 2005, is Starke's (2000); the blank nodes in (6) and in the trees that follow are meant to indicate, however, that any phrase structure theory that has this crucial property will be acceptable for present purposes.

Finally, many scholars (Cinque 1999; Freidin and Vergnaud 2000; Starke 2000) agree on the assumption that categorial hierarchies are stipulated as part of Universal Grammar, though the exact content of the hierarchies may differ greatly. We follow them, in assuming that the hierarchy (7), implied by (6), is a stipulated constraint on the structures created by Merge. At the same time we expect that at least if the hierarchies we introduce are sufficiently simple, they will eventually be derivable on interpretive grounds. Thus if Q and D are a good guess as to the nature of the subject and the indirect object/dative, their ordering is the one familiar from the internal structure of DPs, whereby Definiteness takes wide scope over indefinite Quantification. To be more accurate, in a perspective such as the minimalist one where structures are projected from the lexicon (as opposed to lexical items being inserted into structures), we expect that the relevant interpretive constraints will work by assigning to any structure a rigid interpretation, where for instance two adjacent clitics can instantiate D-Q but cannot conversely instantiate Q-D (within the same string)

(7) [D   [Q   [X   [I

3.2   Nominal Class and Person

In this section we quickly run through the remaining features of the ϕ-set, in order to return to Case in the second part of the chapter. Besides number, the traditional agreement set includes gender and person. Adopting a view independently proposed within generative models (Harris 1991; Di Domenico 1998), we assimilate gender to nominal class. In terms of the reform of morphology sketched above, we predict that nominal class is but the morphological reflex of some independently needed syntactic category. The very term *nominal class*, already adopted in the partial lexicons in (3)–(4), suggests that the relevant category is N.

Motivating such a move requires a preliminary discussion of the syntactic category N. One possible view of N, and of the other lexical categories such as V, takes them to be inherent properties of (uninflected) lexical bases. Thus in English the lexical base *cat* would be associated with the N category as a lexical property, while the lexical base *bring* would be associated with V, and so on. An alternative view, recently revived by Marantz (1997), holds however that *cat* and *bring* are just predicative bases and that syntactic specifications such as N and V are byproducts of the syntactic environment where such predicates appear. The motivation for such a theory is strongest in case of bases such as *play*, which can appear in both N and V syntactic environments while maintaining exactly the same predicative content. The fact that their phonological and semantic interface properties remain constant provides a compelling argument that we are in the presence of a single lexical item. The N or V categorization will then optimally depend on the context of insertion, if we want to avoid an undesirable disjunction in the lexical entry.

Romance languages also abound in predicates that can either surface as a noun or as a verb; one such example is provided by standard Italian (8). The difference with respect to the well-known case of English is that in Italian the predicate stem will be systematically enriched by inflectional morphology; the choice of a lexical base ending in a vowel in (8) makes it clear that it is not syllabic constraints that are at stake. At least in (8b–c), it is evident that the relevant morphology can be sufficient to disambiguate between nominal and verbal contexts.

(8) *Italian*
    a. nause -a
             FSG/3SG
      'nausea/he nauseates'
    b. nause -e
             FPL
      'nauseas'
    c. nause -o
             1SG
      'I nauseate'

We propose that what is known as a noun, for instance in (8b), is produced by the merger of a predicate with a nominal-class morpheme projecting categorial N properties. In structural terms this proposal gives rise to word-internal structures of the type in (9); the position of the predicate inside the word is identified with the ordinary position of predicates inside the sentence (i.e., I). We return to the parallelism between phrase-level and word-level structures that this implies throughout the chapter.

(9) *Italian*

    I   N
  nause   a/e

Applying the same principles we obtain precise structural representations for the clitic series in (3)–(4) as well, as illustrated below for the case of Vagli. We take each clitic to have the same internal structure as a noun such as *nausea* in (9); specifically the definiteness morphemes *l*, *ɟ* serve as the predicative base inserted in I with respect to which the vocalic morphemes *a, ə, i* provide inflectional information. Note that precisely because they provide such information, the latter are inserted in N uniformly in the structures in (10); the fact remains that while *a* and *ə* denote nominal class, *i* has a quantificational denotation, as already indicated in (4). It is important to note that the indications in (4) are meant to specify the intrinsic denotational content of each lexical entry. This content in turn is meant to restrict the occurrences of the relevant entry when the latter is subjected to the combinatorial Merge operation of morphosyntax. However, these restrictions do not simply map an element characterized by a property Z to the position that lexicalizes Z in a higher-order string. Rather the Z property will determine the range of mappings that it is compatible with. This means for instance that the inflectional N position in (10) can equally well be filled by the nominal-class specifications *a*, *ə* and by the quantificational specification *i*.

(10) *Vagli Sopra*

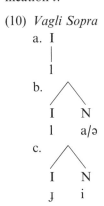

    a. I
       |
       l

    b.
      I   N
      l   a/ə

    c.
      I   N
     ɟ   i

For the sake of explicitness, the nesting of word-internal structures like those in (10) into sentential strings of the type in (6) are provided here in (6′). The minimalist point of view adopted here, whereby syntactic structures are directly projected by the insertion of lexical material, means that there cannot be structures such as (7) produced by the syntactic component, to which lexical material is matched by lexical insertion, as in the Late Insertion model of Distributed Morphology (Halle and Marantz 1993). In other words, one cannot simply insert a clitic in an already given position as a default lexicalization, not presenting any mismatch with the syntactic category. On the contrary, we must be able to show that in each case an internal property of the clitic projects the relevant categorial properties of the sentential string. In (6′) it is evident that the Q position projected by the *ji* is consistent with the fact that the *i* inflection of the *ɟ* head of the clitic is associated with quantificational properties; in this particular case we could equivalently say that it is *ɟ* that projects the relevant categorial properties, since *ɟ* specializes for the *i* inflection. Crucially the same clitic must be able to project the separate X position for accusative clitics. We complete the discussion of this point by reference to the dialect of *Corte* in (17)–(20).

(6′) *Vagli Sopra*

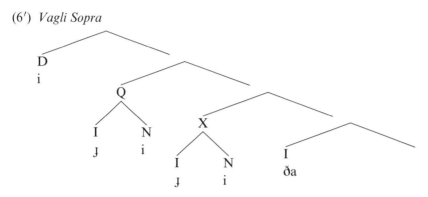

For ease of reference, we may speak of clitic insertion points. By the insertion point of a clitic, we always understand the category that the clitic itself projects on the basis of its internal constituency. For Vagli our provisional list runs along the lines of (10′). (10′) makes the discussion surrounding (6′) graphically evident, in the sense that the properties of the *ji* clitic in (10′) make it compatible with more than one point of insertion, while those of the *l* series make it compatible with the sole accusative position. A more complete elucidation of the schema in (10′) as well as of the structure in (6′) will have to wait for the value of X to be fixed, and will therefore be taken up again in connection with the dialect of Corte below.

(10′) *Vagli Sopra*
    l, la, lə → X
    ʝ(i)   → X, Q

Returning to our main line of discussion, it should be acknowledged that the two preliminary assumptions on which our conclusions are based, namely that nominal class is an adequate rendition of gender, and that there is no primitive lexical category N, could themselves be objected to. The issue of nominal class versus gender reduces to the fact that different morphological endings can imply reference to male or female gender in the case of animates, as in Italian (11). But this kind of fact simply suggests that gender be treated as part of the meaning of nominal class—in other words, as an interpretation of nominal-class morphology.

(11) *Italian*
    a. fidanzato
       fiancé-MSG
    b. fidanzata
       fiancé-FSG

Another problem arising in this connection concerns the notion of agreement wrt gender involving elements of different classes. In (12), for instance, a noun belonging to the (masculine or feminine) *-e* class is matched respectively with a masculine adjective in (a) and a feminine adjective in (b). The interpretive perspective taken above suggests that the -*e* inflection of *docent*- and the -*o,-a* inflections of *brav*- agree in the sense that they are referentially compatible; in this case in fact it is only the adjectival inflection that fixes reference to gender.

(12) *Italian*
    a. docente bravo
       teacher-SG good-MSG
    b. docente brava
       teacher-SG good-FSG

More in general, we would want to conclude that nominal class (i.e., in present terms simply N) subsumes gender in its aspects relevant for the morphosyntax; the notion of gender contains an interpretive residue that contributes to the fixing of denotation at the interface. Other issues concern the treatment of the predicative base as neutral between the V and N categorizations. Though this treatment has been argued for on the basis of predicates that can turn up in both verbal and nominal environments, it may be objected that there are large classes of predicates that can turn up in only one such environment. This can be treated as a straightforward subcategorization problem, certain lexical bases having a denotation compatible only with nominal or verbal properties.

The last remaining feature of the ϕ-set is person. This is suggested as a candidate for reform by much recent literature, showing that first and second person have an altogether different distribution from so-called third person (Davis 1999 on Salish; Déchaine 1999 on Algonquian). The contrast between first/second person and third person—that is, between the speaker/hearer and other referents—is in fact crucial for a series of grammatical processes, which include person splits in ergative Case assignment (Nash 1995 on Georgian) but also in Romance auxiliary choice (Kayne 1993; Cocchi 1995; Manzini and Savoia 1998, 2007). Leaving aside these more complex issues, it is evident that different distribution counts as a powerful argument in terms of distributional analysis for assigning separate categorial status to first/second person on the one hand and third person on the other.[4]

A straightforward example of different distribution is found within the clitic string of Italian. Thus the two examples in (13) involve the same predicate and the same theta-role array, including an animate object and a locative. Since the locative is the same in the two sentences there is no reason to believe that its distribution varies. However, the third-person clitic appears in what we have already identified as the accusative position in the analysis of Vagli in (6)—that is, the position in the string closest to the verb, where it is preceded by the locative as in (13a). By contrast, the first- and second-person clitics appear in a higher position, preceding the locative, as in (13b–c).

(13) *Italian*
    a. Ce lo mando
       there him send-1SG
       'I send him there.'
    b. Ti ci   mando
       you there send-1SG
       'I send you there.'
    c. Mi ci   mandi
       me there send-2SG
       'You send me there.'

Examples such as (13) provide a strong argument in favor of postulating for first/ second person a category P(erson) whose position in the sentential hierarchy is different from that assigned to the accusative.[5] The locative clitic in turn is taken as the representative of a specialized Loc category. As indicated in (14a), the accusative (on whose categorial nature we return in section 3.3) is lower than Loc, while as indicated in (14b), the P clitic is higher.

(14) *Italian*

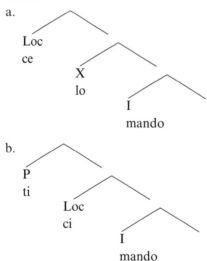

The discussion of P implies that this category is characterized entirely in terms of the denotational properties of speaker/hearer. This characterization is strongly supported by the observation that the distribution of the P clitic is entirely independent of whether its role is that of accusative or dative since in both cases it simply precedes the locative as in (13b–c) and (15) respectively. As expected, it also precedes the accusative, as shown in (15). The relation of P to the argument structure of the verb is then irrelevant for its morphosyntax and is simply derived by interpretive principles at the interface.

(15) *Italian*

    a. Ti ce   lo metto   sopra
       you there it put-1SG over
       'I put it over there (for you).'

    b.

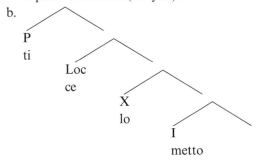

Needless to say, a traditional theory holding that there is a three-valued feature of person can perfectly well separate first/second person from third person by stipulation. Similarly, the natural class formed by first and second person (at the interpretive interface) can be used to ensure that in cases of split they will normally pattern together against the third person. The problem with more traditional theories is therefore not a descriptive but an explanatory one. Indeed it is only in syntactic-categorization terms that we expect the interpretive split to give rise to different distributional properties. In other words, if P is a categorial property we fully expect it to correspond to an autonomous position in the sentence hierarchy, with all of the empirical consequences already noted; these consequences can be stipulated in terms of a first- and second-person feature set but are in no way predicted by it.

3.3   Accusative

With this background concerning the φ-feature set, we can then proceed to Case. The influential work of Rouveret and Vergnaud 1980 as well as Vergnaud 1982, in introducing the Case Filter as a principle of Universal Grammar, required that the notion of Case become independent of its morphological instantiation. Indeed a number of languages do not have morphological Case, or only have it in the pronominal system like English; however, Case must be present as an abstract feature—that is, a feature without PF realization—if the Case Filter that imposes a Case on all noun phrases is to be satisfied. In what follows we attack Case starting precisely with its visible morphological instantiations. But we take the consequences to hold for Case in general—in other words, abstract Case.

Furthermore, according to Chomsky 1986, there are two types of Cases. Inherent cases are associated with a particular thematic specification. Dative would presumably be such a Case, and locative certainly would be. They are Cases in that they evidently satisfy the Case Filter of Rouveret and Vergnaud 1980 and Chomsky 1981; however, they can be reduced to more elementary primitives, that is, θ-roles. By contrast, structural Cases do not match any particular thematic configuration; in particular, nominative can be the Case of both an agent (in the active) and a theme (in the passive). As for accusative, the classical argument in favor of its structural status is Exceptional Case Marking, of which English, as in (16a), is the standard example. Forms of Exceptional Case Marking in which the external argument of an embedded predicate appears as the accusative object of the matrix predicate are found in most languages, though, if we take into account causative predicates such as (16b).

(16) a. I believe him to lie.

   b. *Italian*
       Lo feci   mentire
       him I made lie
       'I made him lie.'

Causative examples such as (16b) are generally assumed to instantiate some form of complex predicate formation; in other words, the accusative does not really correspond to the external argument of the embedded verb, superficially raised to matrix object position. Rather the embedded predicate and the matrix verb form a complex predicate whereby the eternal argument of the embedded predicate is evidently identified with the internal argument of the causative matrix predicate. The exact nature of what is happening is not directly relevant for the present discussion; the point is simply that everybody would accept that the accusative in (16b) is connected to an internal argument specification. Thus causatives are generally avoided as motivation for the structural status of the accusative. The next step is to notice that the original idea of Chomsky 1975 is that in a sentence like (16a), the accusative *him* is the object of the complex predicate *believe-to-lie*. This line of thought of suggests a view of the accusative as inherent Case. Therefore we tentatively eliminate the distinction between inherent and structural Cases in the complement (i.e., nonsubject) set in favor of inherent Case.

In both sections 3.1 and 3.2 we said nothing as to the nature of the accusative position, involved in such representations as (6) or (15). An interesting handle on the question of what categorial properties are projected by the direct object is nevertheless provided by the way so-called accusative Case shows up in those systems that register it morphologically. In Romance, since morphological Case is limited to pronouns, the most relevant languages are those that have subject clitics, including French and Northern Italian dialects. One such dialect, on which Manzini and

Savoia (2004b) remark in passing, is that of *Andràz*, more correctly relabeled here as *Corte* (Manzini and Savoia 2007). In the feminine the nominative and accusative forms of Corte simply overlap, as shown in (17).

(17) *Corte*
    la/le   la/le   klama
    she/they-F her/them-F call-3
    'She calls her/They call her/She calls them/They call them.'

However, in the masculine it is evident that the nominative and accusative forms are systematically distinguished, as shown in (18). Thus in the singular nominative *el* contrasts with accusative *lo*, while in the plural nominative *i* contrasts with accusative *ie*. Remarkably, the system *el* versus *lo* is the one familiar, from French, where nominative accusative pairs take the form *il* versus *le* or *elle* [ɛl] versus *la*.

(18) *Corte*
    el/i   lo/ie   klama
    he/they-M him/them-M call-3
    'He calls him/They call him/He calls them/They call them.'

The system of Corte, like that of French, admits of an interesting description in terms of the theory of the internal structure of nouns presented in section 3.2, as applied to clitics for Vagli in (10). In the system of Corte the feminine clitics consist in all cases of the definiteness base *l* followed by the nominal-class morpheme *a/e*, as indicated in (19a). Consider then the masculine. The accusative singular has the same structure as its feminine counterparts with the *l* base followed by the nominal-class morpheme *o*, as in (19a) again. By contrast, *el* of the nominative clearly lacks nominal-class morphology; we take it to correspond to a lexicalization of an allomorph of the pure base of definiteness *l*—that is, *el*, as in (19b). In the plural the *i* morpheme, to which we impute the same quantificational denotation as in other languages reviewed so far (including Vagli above), lexicalizes the plural without attaching to the *l* base. We can again attribute this pattern, frequently found in Romance dialects, to the denotational properties of *i*. What interests us here is that in the accusative *i* itself acts as the lexical base hosting the nominal-class inflection *e*, as in (19c).

(19) *Corte*

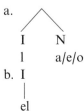

    a.
        I   N
        l   a/e/o
    b. I
       |
      el

c.

In terms of the analysis in (19) the obvious generalization emerges that accusative Case in the Corte language is lexicalized by nominal-class morphology. The comparison with French shows that this apparent syncretism is not casual; the same conclusion is supported by the observation that no system among the hundreds examined by Manzini and Savoia (2005) shows the reverse pattern—that is, the nominative includes a lexicalization of nominal class while the accusative does not. A theory that can only register the coincidence of the two different features of nominal class and accusative Case leaves this same coincidence entirely unexplained. Thus the same general criticisms of traditional morphological theories apply in this case as for the apparent syncretism of dative and plural in section 3.1.

By contrast, within a theory employing the same kind of categorization in the morphology and in the syntax, the hypothesis naturally suggests itself that the coincidence of so-called accusative Case with nominal-class morphology is due to the fact that accusative projects on the sentential tree the same N categorial properties connected at the morphological level with nominal class. In other words, sentences like (18) receive the structure in (20a). Analogously the provisional Vagli structure in (6) is completed as in (20b).

(20) a. *Corte*

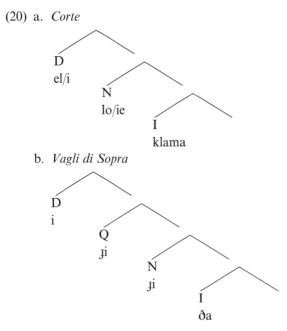

b. *Vagli di Sopra*

On the basis of the preceding discussion, we can further clarify a point that, though it does not advance our main line of discussion, is crucial for understanding the arguments based on cliticization. In light of the proposal in (19), we can specify the insertion points for Corte as in (19′). Recall the discussion of Vagli above, where we stated that it is always an internal property of the clitic that projects the relevant categorial properties of the sentential string. Even the simplified picture in (19′) allows us to see that for the feminine, where *la, le* are the only extant forms, both will insert in either D or N, because of their combination of referential properties (definiteness) and nominal-class properties. What is more relevant for us here is the existence of a double series *el, i* and *lo, ie* in the masculine. The series endowed with a class marker (*o, e*) will be mapped to N, while the other series will be mapped to D.[6]

(19′) *Corte*
    la, le → N, D
    (e)l,i → D
    lo, ie → N

For the dialect of Vagli, we confirm the insertion points in (10′) simply by substituting N for the unspecified X category, as in (10″). In this case the whole series of clitics in (10″) can be inserted in the N position by virtue of the fact that they include in all cases a nominal inflection in N. By virtue of the quantificational denotation of *i* (and of *ɟ* that selects it), on the other hand, the *ɟi* clitic can equally insert in Q.[7]

(10″) *Vagli*
    l, la, lə → N
    ɟ(i)   → N, Q

Before we consider the overall plausibility of this proposal, we introduce what we regard as the most important piece of independent evidence in its favor. In many Romance languages, while the finite verb agrees with the subject in person and number, the perfect participle agrees with the object in number and gender (Burzio 1986; Kayne 1989), as seen in Italian (see (21a)). For the participle embedded under the auxiliary in (21), our treatment of the nominal morphology of Italian, in section 3.2, obviously suggests the structure in (21b), where the nominal-class morpheme, is the N argument of the predicative base.

(21) *Italian*
    a. La hanno   riconosciuta
       her have-3PL recognized-FSG
       'They have recognized her.'
    b.

    I   N
    riconosciut   a

Under the clearcut separation of the morphological (word-level) and syntactic (phrase-level) components that characterizes classical theories, it can only be accidental that agreement with the accusative in Romance languages characterizes a nominal form of the verb (i.e., the participle). In other words, under current theories we might equally expect the reverse system to exist—that is, a system in which it is agreement with the nominative that is uniquely associated with a nominal form of the verb. On the contrary, the present system makes a predictive hypothesis as to the relation between nominal morphology and accusative Case, since so-called accusatives project on the sentential tree the same N categorial properties that are instantiated by nominal-class morphology within the noun. It follows that we expect systems where the object agrees only with the participle, as in (21), but we do not expect systems where the subject agrees only with the participle.

Notice that we have been careful to phrase the relevant generalizations so as not to exclude agreement of the N morphology with D subjects, which is of course found in a language like Italian, with those subjects that are deep objects—that is, that correspond to the internal argument of unaccusative verbs. Further, among the many dialects studied by Manzini and Savoia (2005) there are some where agreement of the perfect participle with the derived subject is found to the exclusion of agreement with the accusative object. But despite the existence of several parametric options, the system described above remains impossible.

To consider a different issue, the fact that in a language like Corte the feminine presents identical forms for nominative and accusative clitic, both endowed with nominal-class properties, is allowed for by our theory, which does not prohibit a match of nominal properties to nominative. In fact, all lexical nouns in Italian behave exactly like this, presenting the same nominal-class ending independently of the position they are associated with.[8] Other languages, where both nominative and accusative are morphologically marked, are equally compatible with our theory or actually support it. Thus in pairs such as *reg-s (rex), reg-e-m* 'king-NOM, king-ACC' of Latin it is evident that the nominative, though overtly marked by *s*, implies the absence of the nominal-class morpheme *e* present on the accusative. In turn, the hypothesis as to agreement with the accusative is compatible with languages where perfectivity provokes the shift from a nominative-accusative to an ergative-absolutive Case system, for instance, Hindi within the Indo-European family, where quite simply the question of agreement of the perfect with the accusative never arises.

A point connected with ergativity is that our hypothesis bears equally on the nature of accusative, and on the nature of N. It will have been noted that categorial properties such as Loc, P, Q, and even D clearly have interpretive content—that is, a content interpreted at the LF interface. In terms of the preceding discussion, the interpretive content of N is that of the internal argument of the predicate; in other words the lexicalization of N, both as an inflection and as a sentential argument, means satisfaction of the internal obligatory argument of the predicate itself.[9] From this perspective what we are saying is that given a predicative base, by adding an internal argument to it in the form of an N inflection, we form what is traditionally known as a noun like (9) or a nominal form of the verb like (20b). In essence then a noun is simply an ergative inflection of a predicate base. By contrast what we call a verb, at least in Italian and similar languages, is a nominative inflection of a predicative base.

It seems to us that the conclusions we have been suggesting represent a step forward with respect to those of Marantz 1997, with which they share the basic idea that noun and verb are the names of morphosyntactic constructs and not of primitive categories. In fact for Marantz 1997, N or V categorization ultimately depends on the merger of the predicate with an *n* or *v* functional category. To the extent that the contrast between the lexical categories N and V is simply restated as a primitive at the level of functional categories, *n* and *v* respectively, Marantz's (1997) theory weakens the initial hypothesis as to the derived nature of N and V. What we pursue here is a stronger solution, since N is by no means the dedicated category for deriving nouns, but rather is an independently needed category, projected in the sentential tree as well, and associated with an independent interface intepretation—that is, that of internal argument.

Next, we can consider the changes that the notion of accusative Case and of Case in general undergoes in the present model. In the conception of Rouveret and Vergnaud 1980, Vergnaud 1982, and Chomsky 1981, the notion of Case is strictly connected with that of government by a Case-assigning head; in other words, it is a relational notion. While issues such as the shift from assignment to checking, and the abandonment of government in favor of sisterhood, have been treated in detail by the minimalist literature, it seems to us that a deeper issue arises. If the minimalist notion of feature is to have a restrictive enough content, features can only encode bona fide lexical properties and not relational ones; it is on these grounds that Chomsky 1995 blocks θ-roles from being encoded as features and θ-role assignment from becoming a matter of feature checking (contra Hornstein 1999; cf. Manzini and Roussou 2000). However, on the same grounds the notion of Case cannot be relational, because otherwise it could not be encoded featurally, nor enter into checking. But if it is not relational, it is not evident what Case may be.

It seems to us that the more often noted anomalies of Case features within the minimalist system, such as their radically uninterpretable nature, are just the way the conceptual difficulty hinted at here surfaces. This difficulty certainly does not escape Chomsky (2001, 2004), to the extent that he again introduces a slight technical modification of the notion of Case. In this version of the model, lexical items are inserted with the relevant range of features, which are however not assigned a value if they are uninterpretable. Hence uninterpretable features are unvalued. Matching of probe and goal means matching of the features independently of their values, whereas Agree is an operation that assigns a value to the unvalued features and sends them to the phonological component, before deleting them from the computation. In this picture it is explicitly said that "structural Case is not a feature of the probe.... Case itself is not matched, but deletes under matching of ϕ-features" (Chomsky 2001, 6). On the one hand, we believe that what Chomsky proposes faces empirical problems, in the sense that there is no necessary correlation in natural languages between morphological agreement and morphological Case. Thus Romance participial clauses display the type of ergative agreement discussed in (21) but overtly lexicalize their subject in the nominative (Belletti 1990); the reverse pattern, where an accusative element agrees with a finite verb, is found for instance in Albanian causatives (Savoia 1989; also reported in Guasti 1993; Manzini and Savoia 2007).

On the other hand, the theoretical picture proposed by Chomsky 2001 is in a sense exactly the one that we are trying to implement here by completely different means, since the only properties that have an independent existence are denotational ones, while Case is but a reflex of them. Indeed the reform of Case provided here, though rejecting Case as a feature, has the effect of eliminating the problem for the featural theory of Case. For, if the preceding discussion is on the right track, the traditional notion of Case with its relational characterization is reduced to a nonrelational notion of the type easily manageable by minimalist theories. To reiterate, in the present view accusative corresponds to nominal-class properties, that is N, being projected on the sentential tree. The only relation they bear to the predicate is the interpretive one of internal argument. Crucially, if we are correct (Manzini and Savoia 2005, 2007), the present system is more flexible than the checking/valuation system of Chomsky and correspondingly better equipped to accommodate language variation.

Finally, we are in a position to complete the hierarchy of nominal positions of the sentence, provisionally introduced in (6), as in (22). The relative order of the various positions is in part justified by some of the examples provided above, such as the relative order of P, Loc, N, while for other aspects of the ordering (as well as for the R position) we refer the reader to Manzini and Savoia (2002a, 2004a, 2005, 2007), who also justify two further theoretical moves. The first is that the same skeleton in (22) can be found not only in sentences, but also in noun phrases. In fact, Q and D are categories first introduced in the literature to account for nominal structures, while others have fairly transparent instantiations (for instance, demonstratives as Loc's). The second step toward unification, and hence simplification, of grammar is that the string in (22), justified in the discussion of the clitic positions in the inflectional domains, characterizes the other domains of the sentence as well. Thus it provides the basic order of arguments in the VP-shell below the inflectional domain as well as in the left periphery above the I domain.

(22) [D [R [Q [P [Loc [N [I

3.4 Nominative

The same kind of treatment that we have proposed in some detail for the accusative has been anticipated for the nominative in section 3.2, where we identified the subject of the sentence with an element projecting a D definiteness property. Again the relational view of the nominative is replaced by a view under which the nominative corresponds to the projection of a bona fide lexical property on the sentential tree—that is, Definiteness.

Our primary reason for returning to the nominative is to provide an argument in favor of one of the key assumptions of the present model, namely the homogeneity of word-level and phrase-level structure. An argument for such an assumption could be obtained if we could show that elements can occasionally be raised from the lower to the higher level (under conventional assumptions about rules of grammar we expect promotion rather than its contrary); in this case we predict of course that a given element will occupy within phrase structure the same position that it normally occupies within morphological structure. In more accurate terminology, we predict that it will project the same categorial properties in both cases.

Now, in the preceding section we have proposed that N is projected both at the word-internal level as nominal-class inflection and at the phrase level as sentential accusative. Manzini and Savoia (2002b, 2004b, 2004a, 2007) analogously propose that D is not only the category projected by the sentential subject but also corresponds to the word-internal category projected by the finite verb inflection, as seen for instance in the representation in (23) for Italian (8c) or for the verbal reading of (8a).

(23) *Italian*

```
      /\
     /  \
    I    D
  nause  a/o
```

The analysis that Manzini and Savoia (2004b, 2007) provide for the phenomenon of mesoclisis in the imperative in Southern Italian dialects uses the positioning of the verb inflection in D of the sentential string, rather than in D internal to the verb. The phenomenon, also known from Caribbean Spanish examples in the Distributed Morphology literature (Halle and Marantz 1993, 1994), is exemplified in (24) with an Albanian dialect spoken in Italy (*Arbëresh*), as reported by Manzini and Savoia (1999, 2007). Sentence (24a) exemplifies the enclitic position of the accusative clitic, following the verb stem and its inflection, while in (24b) it can be seen that the person clitic is inserted between the verb stem and its inflection.

(24) *S. Sofia d'Epiro*
    a. 'zjɔ -ni -ɛ
        wake.up-2pl -him
        'Wake him up!'
    b. 'zjɔ -m -ni
        wake.up-me -2pl
        'Wake me up!'

Under the analysis proposed by Manzini and Savoia (2004b, 2007) for Southern
Italian dialects, in (24b) and similar examples the so-called inflection of the imperative is treated as a subject clitic. In other words, it maintains the D categorization
that it would have inside the verb, but it projects at the sentential level, as in (25);
the empty heads C and I are just mnemonics to help read the representation, since
in the absence of lexical material they are not projected in the sentence. The relevant
assumptions are that the stem of the verb is hosted by a specialized head in the left
periphery of the sentence, namely C_I; the stranded verb inflection occupies the same
position above I that we have adopted for the subject clitic of Vagli in (6). Manzini
and Savoia (2004b, 2007) argue that the high position of the imperative leaves the
syntactic space necessary for the stranding of the agreement inflection, effectively a
subject clitic. The strict hierarchy that characterizes (22) means that the clitic that
appears in between must be hosted by a set of nominal positions in the left periphery,
between C and C_I; thus the one stipulated feature of the construction is precisely that
the P clitic appears in this higher domain rather than in the ordinary inflectional one.

(25) *S. Sofia d'Epiro*

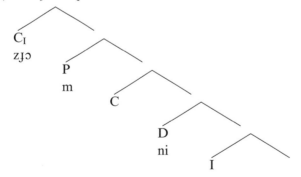

The sentence in (24a) can be accounted for along the same lines, except for the
position of the clitic, which appears in the normal inflectional domain. The split
between P clitics, as in (25), and accusative clitics, as in (26), can be seen as a reflex
of the deeper conceptual split between discourse-anchored and event-anchored (pro)-
nominals that was invoked to assign them separate categories in section 3.2. Thus
what needs to be stipulated about the mesoclisis phenomenon is that clitics whose

reference is directly anchored to the discourse appear in the C domain bound to modal specifications.[10]

(26) *S. Sofia d'Epiro*

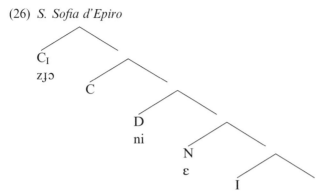

If this account of mesoclisis is on the right track, then the present view of the verb inflection and of subject clitics as projecting the same categorial properties D at two different structural levels receives important confirmation.

3.5   Compatibility with Minimalism

In the preceding sections, we have pointed to specific empirical evidence that suggests abandoning traditional morphological features in favor of syntactic categorization. While this evidence forms an important part of our motivation, overall conceptual considerations also play a role in motivating the present proposals. In particular, our assumptions are compatible with crucial postulates of minimalism, which are possibly violated by alternative models.

One relevant comparison is with Distributed Morphology, with which the present model shares a certain number of postulates, such as the structuring of morphological units by the basic operation of Merge; Distributed Morphology furthermore takes minimalism into account and is largely interested in the same empirical phenomena that are at the core of this chapter. Now, the present grammar is construed so that all structures are projected from lexical material; by contrast Distributed Morphology has recourse to Late Insertion. Similarly, the present theory has no recourse to comparison between derivations or representations, while arguably Distributed Morphology has recourse to mechanisms that have equivalent power, such as Impoverishment. Thus in principle the lexical item that best matches certain terminal specifications is inserted under them; however, phenomena under which underspecified lexical items are inserted require the application of Impoverishment, pruning feature specifications at the interface between syntax and morphology. A rule like Impoverishment is simply not statable in the non-feature-based theory that we put forward. In fact, the elimination of features in favor of absolute categorization means more generally that there can be no underspecification and no default. Thus the present theory turns out to be significantly more restrictive than these competitors.

Manzini and Savoia (2002b, 2002a, 2004a, 2007) deal with some of the empirical implications of these restrictions of the theory. For instance, if Manzini and Savoia (2002a, 2004a, 2007) are correct, absolute categorization of the type proposed here is sufficient to describe a phenomenon such as the Spurious *se* of Spanish for which both Distributed Morphology treatments (Bonet 1995; Harris 1994) and Optimality Theory ones (Grimshaw 1997) crucially use underspecification.

We are aware that the reform of the φ-and-Case set has important implications for the syntax as well. In particular, the elimination of features, with the attending notions of feature value and underspecification, leaves us without the formal means for implementing the minimalist rule of Agree as envisaged by Chomsky 1995, 2000, 2001. However, generative grammars include a different conception of Agree, whereby the agreement between two nominal categories both introduced by Merge allows for their coreference. Following Manzini and Savoia 2002b, 2004b, 2005, 2007, we take it that this interpretive construal of Agree, independently needed for anaphora, can be extended to verb agreement. In other words, the D argument of the verb (its inflection) and the D argument of the sentence agree because they correspond to the same argument slot in the argument calculus at the interface, hence they must corefer.

In general, it seems to us that precisely the conclusion anticipated in our chapter title holds. In other words, while the postulates of the minimalist theory of Chomsky 1995, 2000, 2001, are compatible with one another in the narrow syntax, they cannot be extended to the morphology without one or the other of them being abandoned. In particular, it seems to us that an account of morphological structure consistent with projection from the lexicon and absolute (nonranked) constraints must of necessity abandon the conception of features on which uninterpretability and checking are based. The reverse path is of course in principle possible, and is in fact taken notably by Distributed Morphology. The empirical phenomena sketched above provide a possible ground of comparison between these two (and other) possibilities. In principle, however, it seems to us that abandoning uninterpretability and checking, as we do here, simply means giving up a particular implementation of the grammar. The alternative implies that syntax and morphology, despite their obvious overlap, will not be unifiable, giving rise to substantial (nonminimalist) redundancy in the computational component. Furthermore, we cannot underestimate the consequences for the syntax of allowing powerful mechanisms such as ranking of constraints or ad hoc elimination of lexical information (features) to be hosted in the morphology. For, if a grammatical subcomponent can make use of them, the barrier to using them in the grammar in general obviously disappears.

Notes

The research reported in this chapter has been partially financed through the Programma di ricerca cofinanziato of the MIUR *Categorie linguistiche: Categorie di flessione nominale e verbale (Accordo, Aspetto). Nome e Verbo* for the years 2001–2003, *I sistemi linguistici "speciali" (apprendimento, disturbi) e la variazione tra i sistemi linguistici "normali." Categorie funzionali del nome e del verbo* for the years 2003–2005 and *Strutture ricorsive in sintassi, morfologia e fonologia. Studi sulle varietà romanze, slave e albanesi* for the years 2005–2007.

1. An anonymous reviewer suggests that a perfectly transparent description of the Vagli system can be obtained while holding on to the traditional system of features, if one has recourse to the notion of default, whereby the *ji* clitic of Vagli is the Elsewhere clitic—that is, the default clitic of the system. This observation is correct, presenting a highly relevant and important challenge for the entire line of work pursued here.

Trying to argue against the ultimate opacity of the notion of default on the basis of the empirical data would take up not just a chapter but an entire book. Here we limit oursevelves to a few schematic arguments. First, the dative coinciding with the masculine plural cannot simply be *the* default clitic of the system. Thus *Nociglia* (from Manzini and Savoia 2002a, 2007) has the relevant coincidence of dative and accusative masculine plural on *li* as in (ia) and (ib), but it combines this with the phenomenon whereby in dative-accusative clusters, the specialized dative is replaced by another clitic (in this case coinciding with the partitive and first-person plural *nɛ*) as in (ic). By default theorists' explanations, *nɛ* is the default of the system, but then *li* cannot be.

(i) *Nociglia* (Apulia)
   a. li   'dajɛ   'kwistu
      to him he gives this
      'He gives this to him.'
   b. li   'viʃu
      them-M I see
      'I see them.'
   c. nɛ   lu   'dajɛ
      to him it-M he gives
      'He gives it/them to him.'

The difficulty in (i) can be resolved, by saying for instance that *li* is third-person default and *nɛ* is (overall) default. But more exotic patterns can be found where the default model is impossible as far as we can see. Thus consider *Piobbico* (from Manzini and Savoia 2002a, 2007). The dative in isolation is *i* as in (a), the accusative masculine plural is either *i* or *li* as in (b), and the combination of dative and accusative always turns up in the system as *i li*, as in (c).

(ii) *Piobbico* (Marche)
   a. i   da   kwest
      to him he gives this
      'He gives this to him.'
   b. m   (l)i   da
      to me them-M he gives
      'He gives it/them to me.'

    c. i   li   da
       to him it/them he gives
       'He gives it/them to him.'

Example (iic) requires *li* to be the third-person accusative default. If so the appearence of *i* as an alternative to *li* in (iib) could be explained by saying that *i* is the third-person default. One could even say that *i li* is a combination of a third-person default with a third-person accusative default. But when the defaults begin to combine the situation really is totally opaque from the point of view of explanatory adequacy. Thus for instance why would the accusative default *li* crop up in (iic), if there is no conflict of (third-person) features? And vice versa, if *i* has in effect a subset of the (third-person) specifications of *li*, why do they combine at all?

We chose to illustrate empirical difficulties with independently published evidence not only for ease of reference but also to emphasize that such evidence is not hard to find. But it is not for empirical reasons that we ultimately reject the notion of default—rather for theoretical reasons. It seems to us that default is adopted without discussion in morphological treatments in that it is assumed that this notion has abundant independent motivation elsewhere in grammar. We do not wish to question that there could be a well-defined notion of default in phonology, if it were true for instance that the unmarked value for consonants is voiceless (Trubetzkoj 1949), or more generally that a markedness theory of the type envisaged by *SPE* (Chomsky and Halle 1968) holds. Crucially, however, such notions argued for in the phonological tradition, refer to universal hierarchies. When the notion of markedness is applied to morphological variation of the type considered here, no universal hierarchy could be appealed to. If default is universally set, by definition it need not be learned and no problem arises. But if it is to be learned, then it requires all other values to be set. Thus default may be a well-defined descriptive notion for linguists who have the spread of available evidence in front of them, but it does not represent a realistic model for the internalization of grammar by children learning their language.

Another reason why it seems crucial to us to avoid recourse to default is that the existence of default forms in the lexicon connects to a grammar where lexical insertion is itself governed by Elsewhere conditions, whereby everything else equal, the nondefault form is chosen, while the default form becomes visible where other forms clash, and so on. It seems to us that this amounts to introducing a notion of comparison between representations/derivations into the grammar. Because this argument is explicitly made to some extent by Manzini and Savoia (2002a, 2004a, 2007), we avoid repeating it here (see also the discussion at the beginning of section 3.5).

2. One general question that can be raised about the evidence presented here is that it all comes from a single language family, namely the Romance one, except for some cursory remarks on English or Albanian. This question is implicitly raised by one of our reviewers, who points us to the Serbo-Croatian third-person clitic series in (i), asking whether the same treatment we give Làconi or Vagli is possible for it.

(i) *Serbo-Croatian*
    ACC: ga je ih
    DAT: mu joi im
       him her them

Though we are not in a position (as of now) to provide a morphological analysis for Serbo-Croatian, we would like to point out that many Romance dialects present clitic series where gender, number, and Case select specialized lexical bases. An example of this is Vagli itself when the more complete spread of data in note 7 is considered. Thus at least three bases are present: *eq* for the feminine nominative, *(i)ɟ* for the masculine and *(ə)l* for the accusative. Any basic knowledge of Romance historical syntax will reveal that *q* and *ɟ* are phonological developments of an etymological *l*. However, the relevant process is not alive in the language, so that from the point of view of the internalized grammar, there simply are three different consonantal bases. These admit of an analysis along the lines of note 7.

More in general, it seems to us that in a mentalist approach like the one we are adopting here, we may expect that the same significant range of parametrization is to be expected within a large enough sample of genetically close varieties as within a spread of varieties chosen for their genetic and typological diversity. This is of course up to the fact that a certain type of feature is or is not found within a given language family, so that trivially the distribution or lexicalization of ergative can indeed not be studied in Romance. This is not to say that for instance the same person split that is relevant for ergative Case systems will not turn up in Romance, as in the discussion below.

3. Specifically, we propose that datives instantiate the quantificational property of distributivity. This proposal, inspired by the work of Beghelli and Stowell (1997) concerning the mapping of quantificational interpretations to functional structures, is argued for in Manzini and Savoia 2002a, 2007.

4. Because this chapter is not on the person-features system, we felt no obligation to be even reasonably complete on the history of this topic in linguistics. In particular, an anonymous reviewer points out that Hale (1973) proposes a system whereby first person is [+I, −II] and second person is [−I, +II]. Such a system is indeed close to ours, in the sense that underlying both is the idea that only speaker and hearer are true "person" referents. But then the same is true of a nonformal account such as Benveniste's (1966). Conversely, the binary feature formalization of Hale (1973) does not make his theory directly compatible with ours.

5. In the text we illustrate but one instance in which the person split becomes visible in Romance dialects. There are many other such cases. Thus person determines auxiliary choice in many Central Italian dialects, as mentioned in the text. The anonymous reviewer of note 2 points out that in Serbo-Croatian, the third-person auxiliary *je* follows all argumental clitics, while other forms of the "to be" auxiliary precede them. In the spirit of note 2, we limit ourselves to mentioning that a superficially similar distribution crops up in Calabrian dialects such as *Albidona* in (i).

(i) *Albidona*
    a. ddʒ- u   'ßistə
       I have him seen
       'I saw him.'
    b. l   ε   'ßistə
       him you have/he has seen
       'You/he saw him.'

For Albidona, Manzini and Savoia (2005) propose that the first-person auxiliary is inserted in the C field of the sentence, while the other persons are associated with the ordinary I position, because of what may be called the illocutionary salience of the first person in declarative contexts. In discussing Serbo-Croatian, Boskovic (2001) provides evidence that under deletion *je* is treated like all other forms of the auxiliary, showing in his terms that they all have the same abstract position and all that varies is the position where they are pronounced. In the framework developed for Albidona the equivalent stipulation would be that under Serbo-Croatian deletion, the auxiliary has to be in I for independent reasons.

6. The evidence concerning Corte (referred to as Andràz) in Manzini and Savoia 2004a is richer than the evidence we are able to introduce here, and contains in particular examples like (i); what these show is that the lexicalization of the N position is also computed in reference to the lexicalization of the D position. Thus it may be noted that if D is feminine and hence contains a nominal-class marker, a masculine N element will lack it. For an explanation of this further facet of the problem we refer the reader to Manzini and Savoia 2004a, 2007. Interestingly, it still remains true that *lo* will be found only in N. Furthermore, as we may expect, *i(e)* is also the dative of the system; see Manzini and Savoia 2005.

(i) *Corte*
    la   l/i   'veiga
    she him/them-M sees
    'She sees him/them.'

7. The discussion of Vagli abstracts from the lexicalization of the nominative set, though a subject clitic perforce appears in the example in (5). In a more complete presentation of the data (Manzini and Savoia 2005), it would have been noted that before vowels the masculine subject clitic is *iɟ* as in (ia); a careful transcription of the contexts before consonants would reveal that as in (ib), *i* doubles the following consonant, which means that its lexical entry actually has a consonantal slot following the vowel. Thus the subject clitic for the masculine is actually *iɟ/iC*. Incidentally, (ia) and (ib) taken together show that there is no singular/plural differentiation.

(i) *Vagli Sopra*
    a. iɟ a   dur'mite
       he has slept
       'He slept.'
    b. i   lla/llə   'caməne
       they-M her/them-F call
       'They call them.'

To complete the picture, in subject position the feminine is lexicalized by *əɖ(ə)*. The pattern that emerges is summarized in (ii); this is only slightly simplified, in that it does not take into account the interactions between subject and object clitics of the type alluded to in note 6 and analyzed in Manzini and Savoia 2004a, 2007.

(ii) *Vagli*
     la, lə, l   → N
     ɟ(i)   → N, Q
     iɟ/C, əɖ(ə) → D

Vagli is therefore an interesting dialect where in the feminine the N and D points are lexicalized by two different lexical bases, namely *l* and *ɖ* respectively. In the masculine *iɟ/C* (i.e., an uninflected base) only shows up in D. In N we find the inflected *ɟ(i)* for the plural, while the singular is *l*.

8. The anonymous reviewer of note 1 notices that one not only finds clitics with class markers mapped to the D node (such as *la* of Corte) but also clitics without a class marker mapped

to the N node (like *l* of Vagli). Crucially, the claim we are making is that there will be no (language-particular) grammar in which, given the availability of a clitic such as Corte's *lo*, inclusive of a specialized nominal-class marking, this clitic will serve as a nominative, while the accusative is represented by its bare counterpart such as *el* in Corte. Such a generalization cannot be read as a crosslinguistic prohibition against nominal-class markers in subject position, for which Corte's *la* is an example, as mentioned in the text; nor can it be read as a crosslinguistic prohibition against inserting a bare stem clitic in accusative position, as exemplified by Vagli's *l*. This is because we do not seek to establish a universal principle of mapping, but only a generalization that holds internally to each language. In a domain of variation as widespread and subtle as the one represented by Romance clitics, the importance of even such a partial generalization cannot be underestimated. In itself it is not part of the theory (a principle of it), but it is what the theory should aim at explaining.

9. The anonymous reviewer of note 1 also wonders why the N position could not be coupled with the external role. The answer is of course that association of the N position with the internal argument is an irreducible fact within the present theory. As in all cases where irreducible postulates are encountered, one may legitimately wonder whether one is hitting on a limit of the theory being considered. In reality an inspection of available alternatives will quickly reveal that in one form or another the same postulate is part of all theories within the generative (minimalist) fold. Thus within the theory of Chomsky 1995, in order to achieve the correct match of arguments and θ-roles it is obviously necessary to assign to the first argument merged with the predicate the internal θ-role. Since a verb may have more than one argument slot available at the point of merger, one may ask the same question of the Chomskyan system, namely why the argument is not assigned, say, the external θ-role.

The only aspect under which the present theory and standard generative ones differ is discussed in the text surrounding (16). In other words, it is not the case, as in standard generative theory, that there is an accusative position (say N) definable independently of the internal argument position, which can therefore bear an external θ-role. To put it in still other terms, accusative (or N) is an inherent Case in this system. We would emphasize that for us the issue is an entirely empirical one.

10. An anonymous reviewer notices that imperatives give rise to a whole series of quirky interactions with argumental clitics, quoting in this respect the pattern of Greek whereby the dative-accusative order in declaratives alternates with the accusative-dative order in imperatives (Terzi 1999). Exactly the reverse phenomenon is known to us from Corsican dialects and Western Ligurian ones (close to the Occitan border), as shown in (i) with *Olivetta*, whose (a) example also crops up in Manzini and Savoia 2002a, 2004a, 2007; the (b) example displays the imperative.

(i) *Olivetta S. Michele*
    a. el u/   a/   i/   e/   i/   'duna
       he it-M/ it-F/ them-M/ them-F/ to him gives
       'He gives it/them to him.'
    b. duna- i-   'ru/ 'ra/ 'ri/   're
       give to him it-M/ it-F/ them-M/ them-F
       'Give it/them to him!'

For the analysis of the declarative order in (a) we refer the reader to Manzini and Savoia 2002a, 2004a, 2007. What is relevant here is that in Manzini and Savoia 2005, we note that the reverse order of the imperative in (b) can be obtained if we assume that the clitics arrange themselves according to the rules of the Arbëresh imperatives in (25)–(26), namely the dative in a higher domain and the accusative in a lower one.

Because the Greek pattern reported in the literature is superficially the opposite, no immediate reduction to the present one is possible; however, we expect the same principles to be at work.

References

Beghelli, F., and Stowell, T. 1997. Distributivity and negation: The syntax of *each* and *every*. In A. Szabolcsi, ed., *Ways of Scope Taking*, 71–107. Dordrecht: Kluwer.

Belletti, A. 1990. *Generalized Verb Movement*. Turin: Rosenberg & Sellier.

Benveniste, E. 1966. *Problèmes de linguistique générale*. Paris: Gallimard.

Bonet, E. 1995. Feature structure of Romance clitics. *Natural Language and Linguistic Theory* 13:607–647.

Boskovic, Z. 2001. *On the Nature of the Syntax-Phonology Interface: Cliticization and Related Phenomena*. Amsterdam: North Holland.

Brandi, L., and Cordin, P. 1989. Two Italian dialects and the Null Subject Parameter. In O. Jaeggli and K. Safir, eds., *The Null Subject Parameter*, 111–142. Dordrecht: Reidel.

Burzio, L. 1986. *Italian Syntax*. Dordrecht: Kluwer.

Chomsky, N. 1975. *The Logical Structure of Linguistic Theory*. Cambridge, Mass.: MIT Press.

Chomsky, N. 1981. *Lectures on Government and Binding*. Dordrecht: Foris.

Chomsky, N. 1986. *Knowledge of Language*. New York: Praeger.

Chomsky, N. 1995. *The Minimalist Program*. Cambridge, Mass.: MIT Press.

Chomsky, N. 2000. Minimalist inquiries: The framework. In R. Martin, D. Michaels, and J. Uriagereka, eds., *Step by Step*. Cambridge, Mass.: MIT Press.

Chomsky, N. 2001. Derivation by phase. In M. Kenstowicz, ed., *Ken Hale: A Life in Language*, 1–52. Cambridge, Mass.: MIT Press.

Chomsky, N. 2004. On phases. Unpublished ms., MIT.

Chomsky, N., and Halle, M. 1968. *Sound Patterns of English*. New York: Harper and Row.

Cinque, G. 1999. *Adverbs and Functional Heads: A Cross-Linguistic Perspective*. Oxford: Oxford University Press.

Cocchi, G. 1995. *La selezione dell'ausiliare*. Padua: Unipress.

Davis, H. 1999. Subject inflection in Salish. *UBC Working Papers in Linguistics* 1:181–241.

Déchaine, R.-M. 1999. What Algonquian morphology is really like: Hockett revisited. *MIT Occasional Papers in Linguistics* 17:25–72.

Di Domenico, E. 1998. *Per una teoria del genere grammaticale*. Padua: Unipress.

Freidin, R., and Vergnaud, J.-R. 2000. A presentation of minimalism. Unpublished ms., USC and Princeton University.

Grimshaw, J. 1997. The best clitic: Constraint conflict in morphosyntax. In L. Haegeman, ed., *Elements of Grammar*, 169–196. Dordrecht: Kluwer.

Guasti, M. T. 1993. Causative and perception verbs: A comparative study. Turin: Rosenberg & Sellier.

Hale, K. 1973. Person marking in Walpiri. In S. Anderson and P. Kiparsky, eds., *A Festschrift for Morris Halle*. New York: Holt, Rinehart and Winston.

Halle, M., and Marantz, A. 1993. Distributed morphology and the pieces of inflection. In K. Hale and S. J. Keyser, eds., *The View from Building 20*. Cambridge, Mass.: MIT Press.

Halle, M., and Marantz, A. 1994. Some key features of Distributed Morphology. In A. Carnie, H. Harley, and T. Bures, eds., *MIT Working Papers in Linguistics 21: Papers on Phonology and Morphology*, 275–288.

Harris, J. W. 1991. The exponence of gender in Spanish. *Linguistic Inquiry* 22:27–62.

Harris, J. W. 1994. The syntax-phonology mapping in Catalan and Spanish clitics. In A. Carnie, H. Harley, and T. Bures, eds., *MIT Working Papers in Linguistics 21: Papers on Phonology and Morphology*, 321–353.

Hornstein, N. 1999. Movement and control. *Linguistic Inquiry* 30:69–96.

Kayne, R. 1989. Facets of Romance past participle agreement. In P. Benincà, ed., *Dialect Variation and the Theory of Grammar*. Dordrecht: Foris.

Kayne, R. 1993. Toward a modular theory of auxiliary selection. *Studia Linguistica* 47:3–31.

Kayne, R. 1994. *The Antisymmetry of Syntax*. Cambridge, Mass.: MIT Press.

Manzini, M. R., and Roussou, A. 2000. A minimalist theory of A-movement and control. *Lingua* 110:409–447.

Manzini, M. R., and Savoia, L. M. 1998. Clitics and auxiliary choice in Italian dialects: Their relevance for the person-ergativity split. *Recherches linguistiques de Vincennes* 27:115–138.

Manzini, M. R., and Savoia, L. M. 1999. The syntax of middle-reflexive and object clitics: A case of parametrization in arbëresh dialects. In M. Mandalà, ed., *Studi in onore di Luigi Marlekaj*, 283–328. Bari: Adriatica.

Manzini, M. R., and Savoia, L. M. 2001. The syntax of object clitics: *si* in Italian dialects. In G. Cinque and G. Salvi, eds., *Current Studies in Italian Syntax: Essays to Honour Lorenzo Renzi*, 234–264. Amsterdam: North Holland.

Manzini, M. R., and Savoia, L. M. 2002a. Clitics: Lexicalization patterns of the so-called 3rd person dative. *Catalan Journal of Linguistics* 1:117–155.

Manzini, M. R., and Savoia, L. M. 2002b. Parameters of subject inflection in Italian dialects. In P. Svenonius, ed., *Subjects, Expletives and the EPP*, 157–199. Oxford: Oxford University Press.

Manzini, M. R., and Savoia, L. M. 2003. Participio e infinito nella varietà di Scutari. In Matteo Mandalà, ed., *Cinque secoli di cultura albanese in Sicilia. Atti del XXVIII Convegno Internazionale di Studi Albanesi*, 401–432. Palermo: A. C. Mirror.

Manzini, M. R., and Savoia, L. M. 2004a. Clitics: Cooccurrence and mutual exclusion patterns. In L. Rizzi, ed., *The Structure of CP and IP: The Cartography of Syntactic Structures*, vol. 2, 211–250. New York: Oxford University Press.

Manzini, M. R., and Savoia, L. M. 2004b. The nature of the agreement inflections of the verb. In A. Castro, M. Ferreira, V. Hacquard, and A. P. Salanova, eds., *MIT Working Papers in Linguistics 47: Collected Papers on Romance Syntax*, 149–178.

Manzini, M. R., and Savoia, L. M. 2005. *I dialetti italiani e romanci: Morfosintassi generativa*. Alessandria: Edizioni dell'Orso.

Manzini, M. R., and Savoia, L. M. 2007. *A Unification of Morphology and Syntax: Investigations into Romance and Albanian Dialects*. London: Routledge.

Marantz, A. 1997. No Escape from Syntax: Don't Try Morphological Analysis in the Privacy of Your Own Lexicon. Unpublished ms., MIT.

Nash, L. 1995. *Portée argumentale et marquage casuel dans les langues SOV et dans les langues ergatives: l'example du géorgien*. Thèse de Doctorat, Université de Paris VIII.

Rouveret, A., and Vergnaud, J.-R. 1980. Specifying reference to the subject: French causatives and conditions on representations. *Linguistic Inquiry* 11:97–202.

Savoia, L. M. 1989. Processi morfologici, proprietà di caso e accordo nel causativo arbëresh. *Zjarri* 33:186–293.

Starke, M. 2000. *Move Dissolves into Merge: A Theory of Locality*. Doctoral dissertation, University of Geneva.

Terzi, A. 1999. Clitic combinations, their hosts and their ordering. *Natural Language and Linguistic Theory* 17:85–121.

Trubetzkoj, N. 1949. *Principes de phonologie*. Paris: Klincksieck.

Vergnaud, J.-R. 1982. *Dépendences et niveaux de rèpresentation en syntaxe*. Thèse de Doctorat d'Etat, Université de Paris VII.

4 Parallel Nominal and Verbal Projections

Karine Megerdoomian

4.1 Introduction

The split-vP hypothesis was first proposed by Larson (1988) for capturing the properties of double object constructions. According to this hypothesis, the verbal projection consists of two distinct VP-shells that combine to form the full verbal phrase. More recent work on verbal configurations has extended the split-vP structure, proposing further decomposition of the verb into roots and categorial and functional heads that combine to form the complete verbal element (see Hale and Keyser 1993; Halle and Marantz 1993). At the same time, research on nominal elements has also led to a decomposition of the structure of the noun phrase. The conclusions from these works have led to the introduction of several functional projections within the noun phrase, providing a decomposed structure in which the various nominal elements are represented in distinct syntactic nodes (Abney 1987; Valois 1991; Ritter 1992). In addition, it has been shown that there is a direct correlation between the functional elements in the noun phrase and verb phrase structures, such as Number and Aspect (Travis 1992; Verkuyl 1993; Borer 1994). Yet despite arguments that noun phrases are parallel to verbal clauses in many respects, nouns have generally been treated as less complex than verbal projections, and the functional categories within the noun phrase itself have not played a significant role in establishing relations such as Case and agreement between the nominal and verbal predicates.

In this chapter, I investigate the correlation between the noun phrase and the verb phrase by studying morphological and semantic properties of Case and agreement in several languages. The connection between boundedness (or telicity) and Case marking on direct objects is well documented in the literature. Furthermore, studies on a number of languages have pointed to a direct relation between specific readings and the presence of overt Case morphology on the direct object. Based on these data, I argue that these correspondences can be captured by establishing a direct relation between the functional categories within two parallel nominal and verbal projections. Following ideas developed in Vergnaud 2000, I suggest a framework in which the verbal predicate and nominal phrase each project their own domain in syntax, and Case and agreement are realized when a nominal node enters into a specifier relation with its verbal counterpart. I argue that the two parallel domains can enter into a checking relation at various points in the computation, giving rise to corresponding semantic interpretations as well as Case and agreement morphology. The parallel architecture proposed for nominal and verbal projections straightforwardly captures the direct correspondence between meaning and structure and provides a new perspective on the notion of specifier-head relations.

4.2   Case and Aspect

Literature on Finnish Case marking demonstrates that a clear correspondence exists between verb phrase aspect and accusative Case in this language. Kiparsky (1998) convincingly shows that when the verb phrase receives a bounded aspect reading, the direct object appears with accusative Case; however, when the verbal predicate is unbounded, the object appears with partitive Case. This is illustrated in the following example. In (1a), the object receives accusative Case and the predicate is interpreted as bounded, as shown by its compatibility with the 'in an hour' adverbial. Example (1b), on the other hand, has a partitive object and is interpreted as an unbounded predicate.

(1) a. Matti   luk-i   kirja-t   (tunni-ssa)
         Matti-SG/NOM read-PAST/3SG book-PL-ACC (hour-INESS)
         'Matti read the books (in an hour).'
     b. Matti   luk-i   kirjo-j-a   (tunni-n)
         Matti-SG/NOM read-PAST/3SG book-PL-PART (hour-ACC)
         'Matti read books (for an hour).'

The following example also illustrates the close relation between aspect and Case morphology in Finnish. The direct object in (2a) has accusative Case and the VP is bounded, whereas the partitive Case on the object in (2b) gives rise to an unbounded reading. The object in this example can be interpreted either as an indefinite as in (i) or as a definite object in the progressive reading in (ii), indicating that Case assignment in Finnish does not depend on the strength or definiteness of the object.

(2) a. Hän   kirjoitt-i   kirjeet   Bounded
         He/she write-PAST/m/3SG letters-ACC
         'He wrote the letters.'
     b. Hän   kirjoitt-i   kirje-i-tä   Unbounded
         He/she write-PAST/m/3SG letter-PL-PART
         i.   'He wrote letters.'
         ii. 'He was writing (the) letters.'

In fact, Case assignment in Finnish correlates with what Kiparsky calls *quantitative determinacy*. This notion is equivalent to *quantization* of Krifka 1992 or *specific quantity of A* (+SQA) of Verkuyl 1993. It is used to refer to an object that represents a specific quantity or cardinality, and is closely related to VP aspect. Thus, an event is bounded if the direct object refers to a specific quantity (i.e., is +SQA), as illustrated in the contrast in (3) and (4), repeated from Verkuyl 1993.

(3) a. They ate cheese.   Unbounded
    b. They ate from the cheese.   Unbounded
    c. They ate sandwiches.   Unbounded
    d. They ate three sandwiches.   Bounded
    e. They ate a sandwich.   Bounded

(4) a. He played from Schumann's cello concerto.   Unbounded
    b. He played music.   Unbounded
    c. He played a piece from Schumann's cello concerto.   Bounded
    d. De Machula played the cello concerto by Schumann.   Bounded

In these sentence groups, the verb remains constant, but the choice of the object affects the boundedness of the predicate. Verkuyl argues that the difference in the aspectual interpretations obtained can be explained in terms of quantification or delimitation of mass. Hence the mass noun "cheese" or the bare plural "sandwiches" both refer to an unspecified quantity of cheese or sandwiches (which he represents as −SQA). A noun phrase with a cardinal such as "a sandwich" or "three sandwiches" refers to a specified quantity (+SQA). Definites, of course, are +SQA. A partitive reading such as "from the cheese" refers to an unspecified quantity as opposed to "a piece from Schumann's cello concerto," which expresses a specified quantity. [+SQA] can thus be defined as finite cardinality of a noun.

Finnish VP aspect also depends on the lexical properties of the verb. In order for a predicate to be bounded at the VP level, the verb needs to allow the formation of bounded predicates. Following Ghomeshi and Massam 1994, I will classify these verbs as *result-oriented* since they can emphasize the result of the action they denote.[1] Hence, verbs such as *buy*, *take*, *kill*, *get*, *lose*, and *find*, are result-oriented verbs in Finnish, while verbs such as *love*, *touch*, *kiss*, *seek*, *hate*, *want*, and *doubt* always give rise to unbounded predicates and do not allow accusative Case on the direct object regardless of the quantitative determinacy or cardinality of the noun phrase, as illustrated below:

(5) a.   Anu suutel-i   Esa-a   Unbounded
         Anu kiss-PAST/3SG Esa-PART
         'Anu kissed Esa.'
    b. *Anu suutel-i   Esa-n
         Anu kiss-PAST/3SG Esa-ACC

Table 4.1
Correlation between case and aspect in Finnish

	Verb	Object	vP aspect	Object case	Example
1	+result	+SQA	+bounded	Accusative	*Matti luki kirjat* 'Matti read the books'
2	+result	−SQA	−bounded	Partitive	*Matti luki kirjoja* 'Matti read books'
3	−result	+SQA	−bounded	Partitive	*etsin karhuja* 'I am looking for the bears'
4	−result	−SQA	−bounded	Partitive	*etsin karhuja* 'I am looking for bears'

Table 4.1 correlates with the generalizations proposed in Kiparsky 1998, and shows how the verbal and object properties interact to contribute to the formation of verb phrase aspect in Finnish. If the verb is result-oriented, then it depends on the object properties (i.e., whether it represents a specific quantity) to determine the aspect at the vP level. Thus, a +SQA object will delimit the event (see Tenny 1987; Borer 1994), giving rise to a bounded verb phrase aspect, whereas a −SQA object will form an unbounded event. If the verb is not result-oriented, however, the vP event is always unbounded, regardless of the object properties. Case marking on the object correlates with the boundedness of the predicate.[2]

Ramchand (1993) argues that Scottish Gaelic also provides direct evidence for the correspondence between the aspectual properties of the predicate and the Case assigned on the direct object. In this language, the periphrastic constructions appear with overt aspectual particles that indicate the boundedness of the verb phrase. In addition, the occurrence of these aspectual heads correlates with the Case assigned on the direct object, as shown in the following examples taken from Ramchand 1993:

(6) a. Bha   Calum a'faicinn a'bhalaich.
       Be-PAST Calum *ag* see-VN boy-GEN
       'Calum was seeing the boy.'
    b. Bha   Calum air am balach (a) fhaicinn.
       Be-PAST Calum *air* the boy-DIR 3rd see-VN
       'Calum had seen the boy.'

In Scottish Gaelic, the verbal noun appears with an aspectual particle and a Tense morpheme as discontinuous elements. When the sentence appears with the aspectual head *ag* the object always appears in the genitive Case and is the direct complement of the verbal noun as in (6a). These sentences also represent an unbounded verb phrase, as shown by the compatibility of the *ag* constructions with the adverbial "for two hours" in (7). However, if the sentence contains the aspectual head *air* as in the example in (6b), the object receives the direct Case and it appears in the preverbal position. These particles appear in sentences that are unambiguously bounded (or telic).

(7) Bha   mi   ag ol   leann fad da uair a thide
    Be-PAST I-DIR *ag* drink-VN beer   for two hours
    'I drank beer for two hours.'

In this section, we saw that both Finnish and Scottish Gaelic show a correspondence between the aspect of the predicate and Case marking on direct objects. The type of Case that an object receives correlates directly with the (un)boundedness of the *v*P, which is itself dependent on a combination of the result-orientedness of the verb and the quantitative determination of the NP. In particular, an unbounded predicate can only occur with a partitive Case in Finnish or a genitive in Scottish Gaelic. A bounded predicate, on the other hand, appears with the "strong" Case: accusative in Finnish and direct in Scottish Gaelic. Crucially, the Finnish data discussed clearly showed that the ±SQA properties (or finite cardinality) of the object NP affect the boundedness of the verb phrase.

4.3 Specificity and Agreement

In Eastern Armenian,[3] the overt morpheme ə (/n/ after vowels) is described as the definite article in traditional grammar (see for instance Kozintseva 1995). This can be seen in the examples below where the presence of the schwa (marked as AFF) on the direct object seems to indicate the definiteness of the nominal.

(8) Ara-n   girk'-ə   ayr-ets
    Ara-NOM book-AFF burned
    'Ara burned the book.'

(9) Ara-n   girk' ayr-ets
    Ara-NOM book burned
    'Ara burned a book/books.'

Sentence (8) contains a definite object, which consists of a noun carrying the overt ə morpheme. If the object lacks overt morphology, such as the one illustrated in (9), it is interpreted as an indefinite (*a book*) or as a bare plural (*books*). I will argue, however, that ə is not a marker of definiteness on direct objects, but rather occurs in the context of specific objects and is actually a marker of objective or accusative case.[4]

The fact that the presence of ə does not correlate with definiteness can be seen in the following examples containing quantified indefinite objects. Quantified indefinites consist of a numeral, an optional classifier, and a noun, and may appear with or without overt ə, as shown in (10a) and (10b), respectively.

(10) a. Ara-n   mi girk' ayrets
        Ara-NOM one book burned
        'Ara burned a book.'
     b. Ara-n   mi girk'-ə   ayrets
        Ara-NOM one book-AFF burned
        'Ara burned one book/one of the books.'

In the rest of this section, I will treat the overt ə or *n* morpheme as the manifestation of accusative Case on the object and I will show that, unlike Finnish and Scottish Gaelic, the overt Case in these examples corresponds to the specificity on the object noun.

4.3.1 Case Marking and Interpretation

The correlation between Case marking and the semantic interpretations found on the object NPs has been noted in a number of languages. For instance, Enç (1991) remarked that in Turkish, object NPs with overt accusative Case are always specific, whereas NPs appearing without the accusative Case are obligatorily interpreted as nonspecific. This is illustrated in the Turkish sentences below.

(11) Ali bir piyano-yu kiralamak istiyor.
     Ali one piano-ACC to-rent   wants
     'Ali wants to rent a certain piano.'

(12) Ali bir piyano kiralamak istiyor.
     Ali one piano to-rent   wants
     'Ali wants to rent a (nonspecific) piano.'

As the translations indicate, the Case-marked object in (11) is interpreted as specific: there is a particular piano that Ali wishes to rent. In the case of the indefinite object in (12), however, Ali does not have a particular piano in mind. He wants to rent some piano or other.

Enç (1991) provides a definition for the semantic interpretation of specificity based on the link of the NP to the previously established domain of discourse. If an element is specific, then the link is usually one of inclusion; the referent of the NP is a *subset* of the already established domain of discourse. The sentence in (11), for instance, suggests a context where there are several pianos (say in a showroom), hence the domain of the discourse has been established. When (11) is uttered, the NP *bir piyano-yu* is linked to the previously established referent "pianos," by virtue of being a subset. The object is then interpreted as a specific NP. This preestablished referent domain is not available when (12) is uttered. An important distinction between specific and nonspecific elements is that specificity presupposes existence, whereas nonspecific NPs assert an existence. Diesing (1990) uses a very similar classification for NPs, but she refers to specifics as "presupposed" material and nonspecifics are described as "existential."

Consider the Eastern Armenian sentences in (13). The indefinite object in (13a) does not carry an accusative Case morpheme, and it receives a nonspecific interpretation. This sentence suggests that Ara is trying to catch a horse, any horse will do. The indefinite in (13b), however, bears accusative Case,[5] and it refers to a particular horse that Ara is trying to catch. Hence the indefinite in (13b) receives a strong reading and is interpreted as a specific object.

(13) a. Ara-n ašxat-um e   mi hat dzi bəRni
       Ara-NOM try-IMPF be-PRES/3SG one CL horse catch-Subj/3SG
       'Ara is trying to catch a horse.'
    b. Ara-n ašxat-um e   mi hat dzi-an   bəRni
       Ara-NOM try-IMPF be-PRES/3SG one CL horse-ACC catch-Subj/3SG
       'Ara is trying to catch a horse.'
       → 'There is a horse such that Ara is trying to catch it.'

Accusative Case marking on the quantified indefinites can also mark a partitive reading, as exemplified in the contrast below:

(14) a. katu-n mi mək-an   bəRn-el   e
       cat-NOM one mouse-ACC catch-PERF be-PRES/3SG
       'The cat has caught a mouse/one of the mice.'
    b. katu-n mi muk e   bəRn-el
       cat-NOM one mouse be-PRES/3SG catch-PERF
       'The cat has caught a mouse.'

Suppose a context in which the cat has been chasing some mice for a while. The Case-marked direct object in (14a) would then refer to a mouse from this presupposed set of mice, namely that the cat has caught one of the mice that it had been chasing. Example (14b), on the other hand, does not allow for such a reading; it is about some mouse or other (there is no preestablished set of mice in the discourse).

Example (15) is another example of an NP with a partitive reading. The sentence presupposes a set of books previously introduced in the discourse and it refers to one book out of the set, which has been burned by Ara. This sentence is semantically equivalent to the overtly partitive construction in (16). Note that the partitive construction in (16) also bears the accusative Case. This is expected since by virtue of referring to an element from a previously established set, partitives are interpreted as specific NPs.

(15) Ara-n   mi girk'-ə   ayr-el   e
Ara-NOM one book-ACC burn-PERF be-PRES/3SG
'Ara has burned a book/one of the books.'

(16) Ara-n   gərk-er-its   mek-ə   ayr-el   e
Ara-NOM book-PL-ABL one-ACC burn-PERF be-PRES/3SG
'Ara has burned one of the books.'

Since definites always receive a specific interpretation, we naturally expect definite object NPs to always carry the accusative Case. This expectation is borne out, as illustrated in the following three examples involving proper names, pronouns, and demonstrative NPs, respectively.

(17) Ara-n   Siran-in   hamp'uyr-um e
Ara-NOM Siran-ACC kiss-IMPF   be-PRES/3SG
'Ara is kissing Siran.'

(18) Ara-n   iren   hamp'uyr-um e
Ara-NOM her/him(Acc) kiss-IMPF   be-PRES/3SG
'Ara is kissing her/him.'

(19) Ara-n   ays girk'-ə   kart'ats-el e
Ara-NOM this book-ACC read-PERF be-PRES/3SG
'Ara has read this book.'

Without the accusative Case marking, these sentences are ungrammatical:

(20) *Ara-n   Siran hamp'uyr-um e
Ara-NOM Siran kiss-IMPF   be-PRES/3SG

(21) *Ara-n   ir   hamp'uyr-um e
Ara-NOM her/him(Gen) kiss-IMPF   be-PRES/3SG

(22) *Ara-n   ays girk' kart'ats-el e
Ara-NOM this book read-PERF be-PRES/3SG

Milsark (1977) distinguishes two types of determiners, which he classifies as "weak" and "strong." He observed that weak determiners, but not strong ones, can occur in existential sentences.

(23) There is/are *a/some/a few/many/three* flower(s) in this garden.

(24) *There is/are *the/every/all/most* flower(s) in this garden.

Enç points out that the specific/nonspecific categorization parallels Milsark's distinction between "strong" and "weak" determiners. That is, if an NP contains a strong determiner, it is specific, and if the determiner of the NP is weak, it can be interpreted as either specific (including partitive) or nonspecific. If Eastern Armenian Case marking does in fact correspond to the specificity of the object, the object NPs with strong determiners should always bear overt Case morphology, while those containing weak determiners could appear with or without accusative Case. We have already seen that definite descriptions follow this pattern (examples (17)–(19)). The following sentences further confirm this contrast.

According to Enç (1991), universally quantifying indefinites often behave like specific elements. In Eastern Armenian, the universal quantifiers *amen* (=all) or *amen mi* (lit: all one = each) need to appear within an object NP that has been marked for Case, as illustrated in (25).

(25) a. Yes amen gərk'-er-ə   kart'ats-el em
        I   all   book-PL-ACC read-PERF be-PRES/1SG
        'I have read all the books.'

   b. Yes amen mi girk'-ə   yerku ank'am kart'ats-el em
        I   all one book-ACC two   time   read-PERF be-PRES/1SG
        'I have read each book twice.'

Consider the following sentences containing object NPs with weak determiners. All of the sentences in (26) show the weak readings of the direct object NPs containing the determiners *three*, *a few* (or *several*), and *many*, respectively. None of these objects bears accusative Case. In the corresponding sentences in (27), however, all the direct objects appear with overt Case[6] and they are interpreted as partitives— that is, receive a specific reading.

(26) a. Ays ašakert-ə   yerek' hat girk' e   kart'ats-el
        this student-NOM three CL book be-PRES/3SG read-PERF
        'This student has read three books.'

   b. Ara-n   mi k'ani hat girk' e   aʀ-el
        Ara-NOM one few   CL book be-PRES/3SG buy-PERF
        'Ara has bought a few books.'

   c. Ara-n   šat   girk' e   aʀ-el
        Ara-NOM many book be-PRES/3SG buy-PERF
        'Ara has bought many books.'

(27) a. Ays ašakert-ə   yerek' hat gərk'-er-ə   kart'ats-el e
        this student-NOM three CL book-PL-ACC read-PERF be-PRES/3SG
        'This student has read three of the books.'
        'This student has read the three books.'

   b. Ara-n   mi k'ani hat gərk'-er-ə   art'en kart'ats-el e
        Ara-NOM one few   CL book-PL-ACC already read-PERF be-PRES/3SG
        'Ara has already read a few of the books.'

c. Ara-n   šat   gərk'-er-ə   art'en   kart'ats-el e
Ara-NOM many book-PL-ACC already read-PERF be-PRES/3SG
'Ara has already read many of the books.'
'Ara has already read most of the books.'

Additional evidence for the relation between overt Case morphology and strong interpretation comes from *wh*-elements. Pesetsky (1987) argues that certain *wh*-phrases of the form *which N* are D-linked (or discourse linked). As Enç notes, this notion seems to correspond to specificity reading as described here. As expected, *which N* phrases always carry the accusative Case in object positions in Eastern Armenian, as illustrated in (28). This is in contrast to other *wh*-phrases that behave like the weak determiner NPs, in that they can appear with or without overt Case, as shown in (29).

(28) a.   Ara-n   vor   girk'-ə   kart'-ats
           Ara-NOM which book-ACC read-AOR/3SG
           'Which book did Ara read?'

     b.   *Ara-n   vor   girk' kart'-ats
           Ara-NOM which book read-AOR/3SG

(29) a.   Ara-n   inč   kart'-ats
           Ara-NOM what read-AOR/3SG
           'What did Ara read?'

     b.   Ara-n   inč-ə   kart'-ats
           Ara-NOM what-ACC read-AOR/3SG
           'What did Ara read?' (i.e., 'Which part did Ara read?')

Example (28a) consists of an object in the form of *which N*, which bears the accusative Case. As shown in (28b), the Case is obligatory on this DP. The sentences in (29) also contain *wh*-phrase objects. These *wh*-DPs have the option of appearing with or without the Case morpheme. Example (29a) simply inquires about what Ara is reading. The interpretation is similar to the English question given in the translation. In (29b), the question can be translated as 'which part did Ara read?'. The presupposition is that Ara read something and there is a preestablished domain of referents that the *wh*-DP is linked to. Hence, the accusative Case is forcing a partitive reading, as in 'which one (of the sections/books) did Ara read?'.

The data discussed in this section clearly point to a correlation between Case morphology and the specificity reading of the direct objects in Eastern Armenian. In addition, the objects appearing with the overt Case have been shown to occupy a higher position within the syntactic configuration. In particular, Megerdoomian (2002) shows that bare objects need to remain in the immediately preverbal position, while overtly marked objects do not display such verb-adjacency requirements. This contrast can be seen in the following examples with intervening adverbial elements. As the examples in (30) show, the sentential adverbs *vstah* and *havanabar* are allowed to separate the Case-marked direct object from the main verb.

(30) a. Ara-n   ays girk-ə   *vstah*   kə-kart'a
      Ara-NOM this book-ACC certainly COND-read/3SG
      'Ara will certainly read this book.'

    b. Ara-n   mek'ena-n *havanabar art'en*   ləvats-el   e
      Ara-NOM car-ACC   probably   already wash-PERF be-PRES/3SG
      'Ara has probably already washed the car.'

In contrast, the bare object may not be separated from the verb, as illustrated in (31).

(31) a. *Ara-n   votanavor *vstah*   as-ets
      Ara-NOM poem   certainly say-AOR/3SG
      '*Ara will certainly recite a poem/poems.'

    b. *yerexa-ner-ə hetzaniv *havanabar* kə-k'əš-en
      child-PL-NOM bicycle   probably   COND-ride-3PL
      '*The children will probably ride a bicycle.'

Other constituents, such as instrumentals, locatives, and full prepositional phrases, may also intervene between the Case-marked object and the verb, but are unable to appear between the Caseless (bare or quantified indefinite) object and the verbal element.

That sentential adverbs may separate the Case-marked objects from the verb but are disallowed from appearing between the bare indefinites and the verb clearly suggests that the two object types occupy different structural positions. Furthermore, sentential adverbs have been argued to occupy a position that is high in the clausal structure. These adverbs are considered to be outside of the verbal domain, generally licensed either by the Complementizer or the Inflectional heads (Potsdam 1999). Within a split-*v*P analysis, sentential adverbs occupy a position outside the *v*P node. The fact that these adverbs can appear between the accusative objects and the verb indicates that the overtly Case-marked direct objects are also outside of the *v*P projection. On the other hand, objects without an overt Case morpheme are not allowed to separate from the verb by sentential adverbs and remain in the preverbal position, which is a good indication that the bare indefinites are *v*P-internal arguments. Furthermore, a study of the phrasal stress pattern shows that the indefinites appearing without overt morphology remain internal to the verb phrase, receiving main stress, whereas Case-marked objects are external to the *v*P (see Tamrazian 1994; Megerdoomian 2002). Hence, the different specificity readings observed in this section correlate with distinct object positions: specific objects appear outside the *v*P structure and nonspecific objects are *v*P-internal.

The existence of two distinct structural positions for the direct object that correlate with overt Case marking and specificity readings on the NP have been observed for a number of languages (Mahajan 1990 for Hindi; Enç 1991 for Turkish; Butt 1995 for Urdu; Karimi 1996 and Kahnemuyipour 2004 for Persian). Most of the analyses proposed to capture the relation between nominal specificity and the structural position of the object DP have made use of the Agr$_o$P projection, which is assumed to be a functional node outside the vP domain responsible for Case checking with the direct object.

It should be noted, at this point, that traditionally the animate noun morphology on the direct object is treated as accusative Case in Eastern Armenian, while the ∂/n morpheme has been categorized as an enclitic definite marker. The reason that the schwa is not treated as Case morphology is due to the fact that, although in Eastern Armenian stress usually falls on the last syllable of the morphophonological word, the ∂ morpheme never carries the word-level stress. Hence, it seems that the morpheme appearing on animate nouns is part of the word thus receiving word stress: *dzi-án* (horse-ACC), *Ara-ín* (Ara-ACC), *mart'-ún* (man-ACC). On the other hand, the schwa morpheme and its /n/ allomorph are encliticized onto the word: *gírk'-ə* (book-AFF), *hanrapetut'yún-ə* (republic-AFF), *katú-n* (cat-AFF).

In this chapter, I have shown that both animate accusative case (*in* and its variants) and the ∂/n affix display identical properties in terms of marking specificity on object nouns in Eastern Armenian. The similar behavior of both the *in* morpheme and the ∂ or *n* suffix in Eastern Armenian strongly suggests that the two morphemes are to be treated as overt direct object markers. Furthermore, the lack of word-level stress on the ∂ can easily be explained by the morphophonological properties of Armenian. Recall that if a word ends in a vowel, the *n* morpheme is used on specific objects (32). Vaux (1998) has argued that the underlying form of the "definite determiner" is /n/ and the schwa is an epenthetic vowel inserted between two consonants; /n/ is then deleted if it is not followed by a vowel. Hence in (33a), /n/ is removed leaving only the schwa, while in (33b), /n/ is not deleted since it is followed by the vowel /e/.

(32)   dzu-**n**   ker-a
        pro egg-ACC eat.AOR-1SG
        'I ate the egg.'

(33) a.   girk'-ə   kart'ats-el em
           pro book-ACC read-PERF be-PRES/1SG
           'I have read the book.'

     b.   t'eRt'-ən   el   kart'-ats-i
           pro newspaper-ACC also read-AOR-1SG
           'I also read the newspaper.'

Vaux's analysis therefore suggests that the underlying form of the accusative Case for inanimate direct objects is indeed /n/. I suggest that the insertion of the epenthetic vowel and *n*-deletion take place after word-level stress has applied at PF. Thus, the reason ə never receives word-level stress is due to the fact that the underlying form of the accusative Case is the consonant /n/ and word stress is always applied to the last vowel within the word prior to schwa insertion. If this analysis is on the right track, there is no reason to treat the ə or *n* morpheme as distinct from the animate Case morphemes.

In the next section, the relation between Eastern Armenian Case marking and VP aspect is investigated suggesting that, unlike Finnish, overt accusative Case in Armenian does not correspond to aspectual interpretation of the predicate.

4.3.2 Specified Quantity in Eastern Armenian

One of the most common methods for distinguishing bounded and unbounded predicates is to combine the sentence with the temporal adverbials *in an hour* and *for an hour*. If a predicate is bounded, it will be felicitous when combined with *in an hour*. But since this adverbial requires that the event be terminated or bounded, it cannot occur with an unbounded predicate. On the other hand, *for an hour* is compatible with an unbounded aspect but not with a bounded one. We can apply a similar test to the sentences in Eastern Armenian in order to investigate the effect of the object type on the aspect of the predicate. Consider the example in (34), which contains a definite direct object.

(34) a.   Sirun-ə   xəndzor-ə mi jam-um   ker-av
         Sirun-NOM apple-ACC one hour-LOC eat-AOR/3SG
         'Sirun ate the apple in an hour.'

    b. #Sirun-ə   xəndzor-ə mi jam ker-av
         Sirun-NOM apple-ACC one hour eat-AOR/3SG
         '#Sirun ate the apple for an hour.'

The sentence *Sirun-ə xəndzor-ə ker-av* ('Sirun ate the apple') is felicitous with the *in an hour* adverbial, as shown in (34a). Example (34b), however, gives rise to a forced stretching of the event.[7] These readings suggest that the aspect of this sentence is bounded. In contrast, the example in (35) shows that the sentence *Sirun-ə xəndzor ker-av* ('Sirun ate apples') is unbounded.[8]

(35) a. ?*Sirun-ə   mi jam-um   xəndzor ker-av
         Sirun-NOM one hour-LOC apple   eat-AOR/3SG
         '?*Sirun ate apples in an hour.'

    b.   Sirun-ə   mi jam xəndzor ker-av
         Sirun-NOM one hour apple   eat-AOR/3SG
         'Sirun ate apples for an hour.'

At first sight, these results seem to suggest a correlation between overt Case marking and bounded VP aspect. But recall that Eastern Armenian has two types of quantified indefinites, which may appear with overt accusative Case (specific reading) or without any overt Case morphology (nonspecific reading). The addition of the temporal adverbials to these two constructions shows that both sentences behave as bound predicates.

(36) a. Sirun-ə   mi hat xəndzor-ə mi ǰam-um ker-av
         Sirun-NOM one CL apple-ACC one hour-LOC eat-AOR/3SG
         'Sirun ate one of the apples in an hour.'

    b. #Sirun-ə   mi hat xəndzor-ə mi ǰam ker-av
         Sirun-NOM one CL apple-ACC one hour eat-AOR/3SG
         '#Sirun ate one of the apples for an hour.'

(37) a. Sirun-ə   mi ǰam-um mi hat xəndzor ker-av
         Sirun-NOM one hour-LOC one CL apple   eat-AOR/3SG
         'Sirun ate an apple in an hour.'

    b. #Sirun-ə   mi ǰam mi hat xəndzor ker-av
         Sirun-NOM one hour one CL apple   eat-AOR/3SG
         '#Sirun ate an apple for an hour.'

This is not surprising since, as discussed in section 4.2, the boundedness of the VP is dependent on whether the object denotes a specified quantity. Given that both specific and nonspecific quantified indefinites in Armenian clearly represent a specified quantity, we would expect them to affect verb phrase aspect uniformly. These examples also show that the Case on the objects or their specific/nonspecific interpretation do not seem to correspond to the aspectual properties of the predicate. The following sentences confirm this result.

(38) a. lezvaban-ner-ə yerku šiš   gini-n   mi ǰam-um xəm-ets-in
         linguist-PL-NOM two   bottle wine-ACC one hour-LOC drink-AOR-3PL
         'The linguists drank the two bottles of wine in an hour.'
         'The linguists drank two of the wine bottles in an hour.'

    b. #lezvaban-ner-ə yerku šiš   gini-n   mi ǰam xəm-ets-in
         linguist-PL-NOM two   bottle wine-ACC one hour drink-AOR-3PL
         '#The linguists drank the two bottles of wine for an hour.'
         '#The linguists drank two of the wine bottles for an hour.'

(39) a. lezvaban-ner-ə mi ǰam-um yerku šiš   gini xəm-ets-in
         linguist-PL-NOM one hour-LOC two   bottle wine drink-AOR-3PL
         'The linguists drank two bottles of wine in an hour.'

    b. #lezvaban-ner-ə mi ǰam yerku šiš   gini xəm-ets-in
         linguist-PL-NOM one hour two   bottle wine drink-AOR-3PL
         '#The linguists drank two bottles of wine for an hour.'

The object in (38) carries an accusative Case whereas the object in (39) is bare. Both sentences are compatible with the *in an hour* adverbial, and they both give rise to a forced stretching with the *for an hour* adverb (i.e., the linguists were drinking two bottles of wine for the period of an hour). The main distinction between the two sentences is that the object in (38) refers to two specific bottles of wine (or definite ones as in *the two bottles of wine*) whereas (39) is about two nonspecific wine bottles.

It is not necessary that the wine be completely consumed under this interpretation. But as the examples below indicate, either quantified indefinite could be used in a completed event (forced by the verb *verčatsnel* 'finish') with similar results. These data show that the presence or absence of Case (and specific/nonspecific interpretation) does not correspond to completion or resultativity either.

(40) a. Ara-n   yerku hat garejur-ə mi jam-um xəm-ets
       Ara-NOM two   CL beer-ACC one hour-LOC drink-AOR/3SG
       verč-a-ts-r-ets
       finish-INCH-CAUS-ASP-AOR/3SG
       'Ara drank up the two beers/two of the beers in an hour.'
   b. Ara-n   mi jam-um   yerku hat garejur xəm-ets
       Ara-NOM one hour-LOC two   CL beer   drink-AOR/3SG
       verč-a-ts-r-ets
       finish-INCH-CAUS-ASP-AOR/3SG
       'Ara drank up two beers in an hour.'

Based on these results, I conclude that Case morphology does not correlate with aspect in Eastern Armenian. Instead, the aspectual interpretations obtained correspond to the object's "quantitative determination" following Kiparsky 1998 or ±SQA ("specified quantity of A") according to Verkuyl 1993, as was discussed in section 4.2.

4.4 Parallel Nominal and Verbal Domains

4.4.1 Functional Projections in DP

The data discussed in the previous sections have pointed to a connection between verbal aspect and the finite cardinality (±SQA) properties of the direct object. In Finnish and Scottish Gaelic the resulting (un)boundedness of the predicate is overtly marked through Case on the direct object, whereas in Eastern Armenian this relation is not overtly observed. On the other hand, Eastern Armenian and a number of other languages, such as Turkish, Hindi, Persian, and Urdu, display a direct correspondence between specificity readings on the direct object and a vP-external position such as Agr$_o$P, a structural position above vP posited in Chomsky 1995 and responsible for object-verb agreement as well as accusative Case checking. In fact, in Hindi the case on the specific object co-occurs with agreement on the verb (Mahajan 1990), suggesting a connection between nominal specificity and verbal agreement in these languages. In the rest of this section, I will show how a decomposed structure for the noun phrase can allow us to capture Case morphology in the languages studied, as well as the observed correspondences between verbal and nominal features.

Distinguishing the two notions of [±SQA] and specificity is crucial in order to account for the distinct domains in which the cardinality of the NP and its specificity play a role, given that there seems to be a close relation between the cardinality of the NP (or ±SQA) and aspect while specificity does not seem to contribute to any aspectual reading in the predicate. I therefore propose to separate the information provided by specificity and cardinality into distinct syntactic nodes within the noun phrase structure. This would allow us to capture the direct correlation between cardinality and verb phrase aspect as well as the close relation between nominal specificity and a higher argument projection within the extended verb phrase structure.

Much current research on nominal elements has, in fact, argued that the structure of the noun phrase should reflect the structure of the verb phrase. This approach has led to the introduction of several functional projections within the NP/DP, providing a decomposed structure in which the various nominal elements are represented in distinct syntactic nodes (Abney 1987; Tang 1990; Valois 1991; Ritter 1992; Bhatta-charya 1999; Borer 2000; among others). In addition, it has been argued that there is a direct correspondence between the functional elements in the Noun Phrase and Verb Phrase. Travis (1992), for instance, shows that the Number Phrase projection argued for in Ritter (1992) behaves similarly to Aspect Phrase. Based on a semantic correlation between Progressive aspect and plural number in English and morphological similarities marking aspect and number in Tagalog, Travis (1992) argues for the correspondence of the Number and Aspect functional heads and provides two parallel verbal and nominal structures in which NumP corresponds to AspP. Travis's analysis confirms the Eastern Armenian and Finnish data discussed in this chapter that point to a close relation between cardinality of the argument NP and aspect of the verb phrase.

In addition, the mass/count distinction in nominals discussed in Chierchia 1998 has been correlated with the atelicity/telicity distinction (i.e., the boundedness properties) of verbs. Borer (2001) argues that all nominals are listed as mass in the lexicon (her Encyclopedia) and they only receive a count interpretation in the context of a "count" structure. Hence, unless provided with more structure, the default interpretation of N^o is mass. Likewise, the default interpretation of a V^o is atelic or unbounded and can become telic or bounded only when it appears in the context of an aspectual structure. Thus, all these approaches draw parallels between a Number projection on the nominal structure and an Asp head in the verbal domain.

Specificity, on the other hand, is usually associated with the DP projection. A definite argument is interpreted as specific by virtue of appearing with an overt determiner in D. Bare indefinites and mass nouns lack a determiner and are considered nonspecific NPs. Quantified indefinites that do not have a specific reading in Armenian would also be analyzed as lacking the D projection. However, quantified indefinites in these languages may also carry a specific interpretation, as shown for Eastern Armenian in section 4.3.1 I suggest that, in these cases, the specific reading is obtained when the DP projection is headed by a null determiner (see Karimi 1996 and Ghomeshi 2001 for similar proposals positing a null determiner head in Persian). No D head is projected, however, in the case of nonspecific quantified indefinites.

Based on these conclusions and following Travis 1992, I propose the syntactic structure for the noun phrase illustrated in (41).

(41)

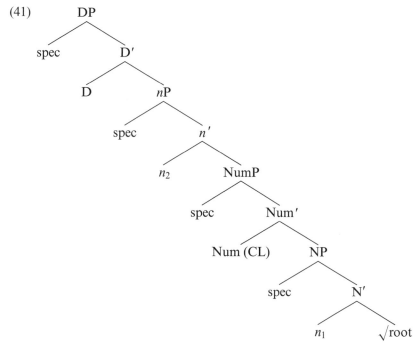

The information about the cardinality of the nominal phrase is expressed in the NumP projection, where Num stands for *Number* and CL for *Classifier*. When NumP is projected, the noun phrase receives a specified quantity or +SQA interpretation. Note that in this configuration, the classifier does not project a separate head since in Eastern Armenian and Persian the classifier is optional with count nouns and can only appear if a number is already present. Similarly, Bhattacharya (1999) argues for a fused head in Bangla consisting of a number or quantifier that marks cardinality, and a classifier.

The *n*P projection has been proposed by several researchers (Valois 1996, Bhattacharya 1999 for Bangla possessors, and Travis 1992 for gerundive *Poss-ing* structures) and parallels the *v*P-shell configuration used in recent syntactic approaches. The noun phrase is thus formed when a root element combines with the functional nominal features represented in the structure in (41).

The resulting noun phrase configuration parallels the decomposed structure of the verbal predicate and its nodes correspond to the features represented in the *v*P structure. Yet the connection between the nominal features and the verbal domain has always been established through a Spec-head relation where the whole noun phrase appears in the specifier position of the relevant verbal head, and the inner nodes or features of the NP play absolutely no role. For instance, to capture the direct correlation between aspectual boundedness of the *v*P and the cardinality or "quantitative specification" of the NP, a number of analyses have been proposed establishing a Spec-head relation between the direct object and the Asp head of the verb phrase. Hence, Borer (1994) proposes that a bounded aspect obtains when a quantitatively specific noun phrase appears in the specifier position of Aspect Phrase. The aspect of the verbal event is "delimited" or "measured out" when the [Spec,AspP] position is occupied and the boundedness information in the verb phrase is then marked in Aspect Phrase. Similarly, Mahajan (1990) captures the Hindi data by proposing that accusative Case obtains when the specific object DP moves to the [Spec,Agr$_o$P] position, thus establishing a Spec-head relation with the Agr$_o$P projection. None of these approaches, however, make explicit use of the internal features of the NP in order to establish the Spec-head relation with the relevant verbal head.

In this chapter, I argue that in order to capture the close relations between the nominal and verbal features in establishing Case relations in languages such as Eastern Armenian and Finnish, the relevant corresponding features of the two nominal and verbal domains are to appear in a direct one-to-one relationship, as schematized in (42).

(42)

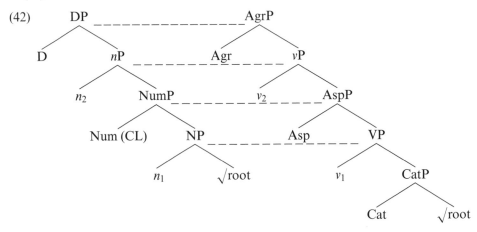

In current approaches, when a Spec-head relation is established between a noun phrase and a verbal head, it is assumed that only the relevant features of the nominal and verbal elements are checked against each other. The configuration in (42), however, allows us to explicitly capture the direct correspondences between parallel features in the noun phrase and verb phrase. In particular, we are now able to represent the parallel contributions of nominal and verbal features in the formation of the correspondences on verb phrase aspect and object-verb agreement. Hence, in this structure, the notion of "boundedness" is represented by Number in the nominal domain and by Aspect in the verbal component, and the notion of "specificity" is represented by the Determiner projection in the nominal structure and by the Agreement phrase in the verbal domain.

The parallel architecture of nominal and verbal domains proposed here is reminiscent of the computational system developed in Vergnaud 2000 as well as Vergnaud and Zubizarreta 2001, which is presented in the following section.

4.4.2   Primitive Assemblies of Constituent Structure

In the framework developed in Vergnaud and Zubizarreta 2001, the syntactic structure consists of right-branching trees that consist of a fixed set of primitive features, as shown in (43).

(43) $F_n\ F_{n-1}\dots F_2\ F_1$

These features are the same for all categories. Hence, the same feature underlies the notion that represents "mass/count" for nominal categories as well as the notion denoting "aspect" for verbal categories. Similarly, the abstract feature of "instantiation" (what I referred to as "specificity" in the previous section) is manifested by D in the nominal domain and by T for the verbal category. The hypothesis that all categories have the same underlying features is referred to as the Extended X-bar Principle and is described as below in Vergnaud and Zubizarreta 2001:

(44) *Extended X-bar Principle*
      Every cognitive (semantic) category is analyzed in terms of a fixed set of
      features common to all categories.

The features in (43) form an ordered list of primitive syntactic elements where F_1 is the head denoting the *root*, F_2 is the feature representing *categories* such as Noun or Verb, F_3 is the *aspect* or *classifier* feature, while F_n is manifested as determiner or tense and denotes the notion of *instantiation*.

These uniformly branching trees constitute parallel primitive assemblies. The goal of the computational system is to reduce the abstract features of the nominal and verbal assemblies to single strings by projecting them into a single linear axis. This is accomplished when a matching relation is established between the two unibranching trees by forming a one-to-one link between corresponding features. The grammatical relation *specifier-of* arises from the association of the two equivalent primitive assemblies. In this configuration, the abstract feature for "mass/count" in the nominal assembly is associated with the "aspect" feature in a matching verbal assembly. This specifier-of relation is schematized in the feature pairs in (45):

(45) $([F_3\ F_2\ F_1]_N, [F_3\ F_2\ F_1]_V) = (F_{3N}, F_{3V})\ (F_{2N}, F_{2V})\ (F_{1N}, F_{1V})$

In the formal framework in Vergnaud and Zubizarreta 2001, Agreement morphology is then an instance of a specifier-of relation realized as the matching of equivalent features across the N and V categories.

The specifier-of relation is one of the operations available to two parallel unibranching trees and is defined by the *distributive product* in (46).

(46) $[F_1 \ldots F_i \ldots F_n] \otimes [G_1 \ldots G_i \ldots G_n] \overset{def}{=} F_i \approx G_i,\ F_i$ precedes G_{i+1},
       $i = 1, \ldots, n-1$

In addition, two primitive unibranching assemblies may also combine to form an *extended assembly*, as illustrated in (47). In this operation, a primitive assembly combines with another by identifying the tail of one assembly with the head of the other.

(47) $[F_1\ F_2 \ldots F_i \ldots F_{n-1}\ F_n] * [G_1\ G_2 \ldots G_i \ldots G_{n-1}\ G_n] = [F_1 \ldots F_{n-1}\ H$
       $G_2 \ldots G_n]$ where $H = F_n = G_1$

This operation is used, for instance, to compose the verbal constituent structure by combining the verbal category with the complementizer category (or "proposition"). Similarly, a noun category can combine with a pronominal category to provide the "point of view". The node at which the two primitive assemblies combine creates a boundary condition for the syntactic code.

In the next section, I provide an analysis for the relation between object Case and semantic interpretation in Armenian and Finnish by adopting a syntactic structure consisting of parallel primitive assemblies as in the framework of Vergnaud and Zubizarreta 2001.

4.5   Checking Relations and Structural Case

Adopting Vergnaud and Zubizarreta 2001, I suggest that nominal and verbal predicates are composed of a fixed set of primitive elements consisting of a root, a category feature, and features denoting *boundedness* and *instantiation*. These features give rise to slightly different interpretations depending on the domain in which they are realized. Hence, the feature representing boundedness corresponds to aspect in the temporal or verbal domain and to the classifier or count system in the physical or nominal domain. The suggested unibranching configurations are illustrated in (48), where *n* represents an entity and *v* denotes an event.

(48) *v*P

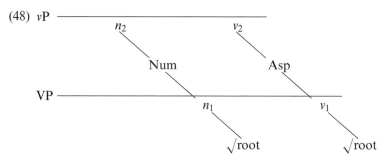

According to this proposal, the mass noun would consist of a root element, similar to the notion of root in Distributed Morphology (Halle and Marantz 1993), combined with the categorial feature n_1. This level of the structure corresponds to the bare noun in Eastern Armenian. If the nominal structure combines with the Num feature specifying its cardinality, the noun formed has a "count" reading. A parallel structure is formed in the verbal domain as shown. I claim that the noun phrase is interpreted as an argument of the verb when the primitive elements in the nominal structure form a specifier-of relation with their verbal counterparts, as discussed in section 4.4.2. The resulting interpretation and Case marking depend on the level in the structure at which the checking relation is formed.

Recall from the discussion of Eastern Armenian that a bare noun argument, which lacks specificity and cardinality features, needs to remain low in the verb phrase. These constructions give rise to unbounded verb phrase aspect. In these instances, the root $+ n_1$ configuration in the nominal domain enters into a specifier-of relation with the corresponding verbal elements. Since the $n_1 - v_1$ relation is the highest checking level in the construction, aspect remains unbounded and the bare noun appears low within the *v*P structure. In the case of quantified indefinites, however, the highest specifier-of relation is formed between the nodes Num and Asp. Note that the presence of the Num feature in the nominal domain modifies the mass interpretation and forms a count noun argument or a nominal with a specified cardinality. The presence of the Aspect node on the verbal domain provides what I have referred to as "result-orientedness" of the event. It is only when the two corresponding nodes enter into a checking relation, thus merging the temporal and physical worlds, that a bounded verb phrase aspect is obtained. In other words, by the establishment of the specifier-of relation between Num and Asp nodes, the physical domain delimits the temporal domain by providing a final endpoint or a measure for the event (see Verkuyl 1993).

Both unibranching assemblies may undergo a "direct product" in the sense of Vergnaud and Zubizarreta 2001 to form an extended assembly. I claim that the domain corresponding to tense, agreement, and higher aspectual features is combined with the *v*P domain through this operation. This extended assembly provides the temporal instantiation to the underlying event. Similarly, the nominal domain can be extended to include the physical instantiation of the entity (i.e., specificity) within the structure, as illustrated in (49).[9]

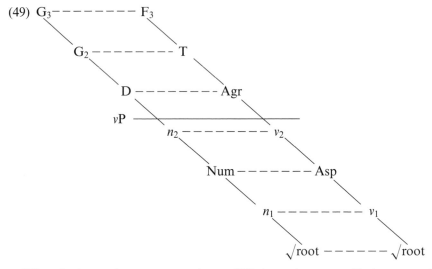

(49)

When the internal argument projects a DP, it receives a specific interpretation and the head D enters into a relation with the Agr node. Note that in the framework proposed by Vergnaud and Zubizarreta (2001), the "instantiation" feature is represented by Determiner (D) on the nominal structure and by Tense (T) rather than Agr in the verbal unibranching tree. However, the data discussed here suggest that specificity features of the noun correlate with verbal agreement features. This is overtly marked by agreement on the verb in Hindi in the presence of the specific object. Based on data from argument alternations, valency, and attachment of modifiers, Larson (2003) has also proposed that, contrary to the common view, DP is not analogous to TP but rather corresponds to the VP structure. On the other hand, Sportiche (1999) argues that the D head is external to the domain of the VP. These results may then suggest that the notion of "instantiation" that corresponds to D (the marker of specificity and definiteness) in the nominal domain should correspond to a verbal node that appears outside the VP, yet is distinct from T. Given the data from Eastern Armenian, Persian, Turkish, and Hindi, I propose that Agr (a node responsible for instantiating verbal agreement) is in fact the verbal counterpart of nominal D.[10] Furthermore, the interpretation of the specific objects in Eastern Armenian as external to the vP domain rests on the fact that the highest level at which a checking relation is formed—that is, between D and Agr—occurs outside of the vP.[11]

I propose that Case assignment in languages such as Eastern Armenian and Finnish is simply the overt realization of a specifier-of relation between nominal and verbal domains. In Finnish, accusative Case is expressed on the object as a result of the checking correspondence between Num and Asp nodes. It is, however, the specifier-of relation between D and Agr features that is expressed as an accusative Case on the noun in Eastern Armenian (and as overt object agreement on the verb in Hindi).[12] In other words, the node at which Case is realized is treated as a parameter of the language. The proposed framework captures the correlation between cardinality and aspect, it accounts for Case marking in Finnish (which relates to the feature of *boundedness*) and object Case in Eastern Armenian (which relates to the notion of *instantiation*). This model thus explains the close relation of structure and interpretation in the noun phrase by establishing explicit correspondences with the verbal predicate.

4.6 Subjects

The subject in Eastern Armenian can also be marked with *ə* or *n*, as illustrated below:

(50) a. Aram-ə   senyak-um nəst-atz namak er   gər-um
        Aram-NOM room-LOC sit-PART letter   was write-IMPF
        'Aram was sitting in the room, writing a letter.'
        (Lit: 'Aram, sitting in the room, was writing a letter.')
     b. harevan-ner-ə   mer hamar xmičk en ber-el
        neighbor-PL-NOM our for   drink are bring-PERF
        'The neighbors have brought us drinks.'
     c. katu-n   norits muk   e vors-um
        cat-NOM again mouse is hunt-IMPF
        'The cat is hunting mice again.'

The fact that the *ə/n* allomorph can appear on subjects may seem to be strong evidence against the treatment of these morphemes as accusative Case markers. However, a closer investigation of subjects in Eastern Armenian shows that overt morphology corresponds with specificity interpretation on subjects of unaccusative verbs but not of transitives. In addition, while subjects of unaccusatives may occupy a position within the *v*P structure on a par with the direct object, transitive subjects are external to the *v*P domain and display distinct Case-assignment possibilities. The data in fact are in accordance with a structural analysis of the overt morphology as has been proposed in this chapter, since there is a direct correlation between the structural position occupied by the argument and the manifestation of *ə/n* on the subject.

In her study of specificity in Standard Western Armenian, Sigler (1997) noticed that with verbs that are arguably unaccusative or passive, the presence of overt morphology correlates with specificity. This is illustrated for Eastern Armenian in the contrast between (51) and (52). In (51), the subject appears without an overt morpheme and is interpreted as nonspecific. In (52), however, the overt morphology on the subject correlates with a specific reading.[13]

(51) a. mart' e gal-is
　　　　man is come-IMPF
　　　　'People are coming/Someone is coming.'
　　 b. bak-um gulpa-ner en čor-an-um
　　　　yard-LOC sock-PL　 are dry-INCH-PERF
　　　　'(Some) socks are drying in the yard.'

(52) a. mart'-ə　 gal-is　　 e
　　　　man-NOM come-IMPF is
　　　　'The man is coming.'
　　　　'Her husband is coming.'
　　 b. mi gulpa-n čor-ats-el　　e
　　　　one sock-NOM dry-AOR-PERF is
　　　　'One (specific) sock has dried.'
　　　　'One of the socks has dried.'

The presence of overt morphology also correlates with the structural position of the subject. The subjects in (51) remain within the verb phrase and receive the main phrasal stress as indicated by the *be* auxiliary enclitic, which always appears on the constituent carrying the most prominent stress in the clause (Tamrazian 1994). In addition, these subjects cannot be separated from the verb by intervening adverbial elements (53a). The subjects in (52), on the other hand, do not receive main stress and intervening adverbials are allowed (53b).

(53) a. ?*mart' e havanabar gal-u
　　　　　man is probably   come-FUT
　　　　　'*Someone will probably come.'
　　 b. 　mart'-ə　 havanabar gal-u　　 e
　　　　　man-NOM probably   come-FUT is
　　　　　'The man is probably coming.'
　　　　　'Her husband is probably coming.'

Thus, subjects of unaccusatives and passives that do not receive overt morphology occupy a position within the verb phrase and are interpreted as nonspecific. If the subject appears with overt morphology, however, it is specific and is external to the *v*P domain. These properties parallel those of the direct object discussed in previous sections, suggesting that the D head of specific unaccusative subjects establishes a relation with the Agr head of the verbal domain.[14] The relation is then marked on the noun as overt morphology. This parallel behavior is not surprising since subjects of unaccusatives and direct objects both occupy the internal argument position (see Perlmutter 1978; Williams 1981).

Additional support for the D-Agr relation can be found in the agreement properties of unaccusative and passive subjects. If the noun phrase lacks overt morphology, subject agreement is optional for unaccusative or passive verbs, as shown in the following examples.

(54) a. aysor baqdad-um   hing hat zinvor e meʀ-el
today Baghdad-LOC five CL soldier is die-PERF
'Five soldiers have died in Baghdad today.'

 b. vaxenalu   dzayn-er e ləs-v-um
frightening voice-PL is hear-PASS-IMPF
'I hear frightening voices.' (Lit: Frightening voices is being heard.')

When the subject is specific and carries overt case, the agreement is obligatory.

(55) a. aysor baqdad-um   hing hat zinvor-ner-ə   meʀ-el en/*e
today Baghdad-LOC five CL soldier-PL-NOM die-PERF are/*is
'The five soldiers have died in Baghdad today.'
'Five of the soldiers have died in Baghdad today.'

 b. norits ayt vaxenalu dzayn-er-ə   ləs-v-um   en/*e
again that frightening voice-PL-NOM hear-PASS-IMPF are/*is
'I hear those frightening voices again.' (Lit: Those frightening voices are being heard again.')

Subjects of transitive or unergative verbs, which are considered external arguments, differ from subjects of unaccusatives and passives in several ways. Subjects of transitives and unergatives cannot appear as bare arguments (56), they do not receive the phrasal stress as shown by the positioning of the auxiliary clitic (57), and subject-verb agreement is always obligatory in these cases.

(56) a. *mart' e tzitzaq-um
man is laugh-IMPF
'*A man/Someone is laughing.'

 b. *yerexa mijat e span-um p'oqots-um
child   insect is kill-IMPF street-LOC
'*A kid is killing insects in the street.'

(57) a. mart'-ə   tzitzaq-um e
man-NOM laugh-IMPF is
'The man is laughing.'

 b. yerexa-n mijat e span-um p'oqots-um
child-NOM insect is kill-IMPF street-LOC
'The kid is killing insects in the street.'

To refer to a nonspecific agent, the quantified indefinite is used, which can also refer to a specific nominal. But crucially, unlike the subject of unaccusatives and passives, the quantified indefinite noun phrase used as a transitive subject never carries
overt morphology, showing that the presence of *ə* or *n* does not correlate with specificity in this instance. The subjects in (58) are ambiguous between a nonspecific and a
specific reading. Note that these Caseless quantified indefinites, unlike the quantified
indefinites used in object or unaccusative subject capacity, occupy a position outside
of the *v*P domain since they do not receive the main clausal stress and can be separated from the verb.

(58) a. sərah-um mi mart' bartsər dzayn-ov tzitzaq-um er
        hall-LOC one man loud   voice-INST laugh-IMPF was
        'In the hall, someone/a man was laughing loudly.'
     b. mi bəjišk indz as-ets vor hima karoq em tun   gən-al
        one doctor me   say-AOR that now able am home go-INF
        'Some/A doctor told me that I can go home now.'

This preliminary study of subjects in Eastern Armenian seems to provide further
support for the main argument put forth in this chapter, namely that overt morphology on the nominal argument corresponds to a structural relation established between the verbal and nominal domains. The data presented here provide evidence
for the distinct positions of internal and external arguments and their correlation
with overt Case marking, showing that subject and object internal arguments display
parallel behavior and contrast with the properties of the external argument. Thus in
Eastern Armenian, overt morphology appears on the internal argument DP that has
established a structural correspondence with the Agr node in the verbal domain. The
examination of the external argument further showed that the *ə* or *n* morpheme is
not simply a marker of specificity in Eastern Armenian and thus can be treated as a
Case marker.[15] Although the properties of the subject in this language need to be
investigated in depth in order to determine the position at which nominative Case is
assigned and its semantic contribution to the external argument, the facts presented
in this section seem to confirm the claim that overt Case morphology is the manifestation of a structural relation. More specifically, Case is the overt realization of the
correspondence established between the verbal and nominal domains in the syntax.

   In the framework presented in this chapter, structural Case is not treated as an
uninterpretable feature of a noun phrase that needs to be checked by LF, nor is it
represented as a functional projection in the syntax. Instead, Case appears as the result of a checking relation between nominal and verbal structures. Hence, Case assignment and also verbal agreement are simply the overt realization of a checking
mechanism between the verbal and nominal domains, and are not listed with the lexical entry. The position that a Case-marked object occupies or its correlation with

certain semantic readings is a byproduct of the checking mechanism and is not a property of the case morpheme. Furthermore, I suggest that languages can be distinguished based on the structural position at which accusative Case (or marked object Case) is realized. In Finnish and Scottish Gaelic, the projection node at which the checking relation is overtly realized on the argument is the node corresponding to the feature "boundedness," hence the close relation between Case, cardinality (Num), and aspect (Asp) observed in these languages. In Eastern Armenian, Persian, Turkish, and other languages of this group, the checking relation is realized on the object at the higher node denoting "instantiation" (D/Agr), resulting in a correlation between Case and specificity and in the case of Hindi, with verbal agreement as well. I assume that certain languages have a default object Case that is realized at the level at which $n_1 - v_1$ form a checking relation and the default Case in Finnish is the partitive. Hence, a direct object in this language receives the partitive Case marking unless the nominal Num and verbal Asp nodes enter into a specifier-of relation.

In addition, the examination of nominative Case marking on subjects in Eastern Armenian showed that the presence of overt Case on the internal argument correlates with specificity, while overt Case on the external argument does not exhibit such a relation. These results suggest that (nominative) Case does not always correspond to the same semantic role on the noun phrase but rather depends on the configurational relation between the verbal and nominal domains.

This approach then predicts that Case assignment is a postsyntactic phenomenon since overt Case is realized after all syntactic projections and checking relations have been formed. Object Case morphology is overtly expressed in languages based on the resulting syntactic configurations and on the correspondences composed between parallel primitive assemblies.

4.7   Conclusion

The investigation of Case marking in Eastern Armenian and Finnish led to the formalization of a correspondence of universal primitive features that are shared by both the nominal and verbal domains. Hence, aspect and cardinality are two different facets of the same feature, namely *boundedness*. Similarly, the feature *instantiation* is interpreted as agreement on the verbal side and as specificity in the nominal domain. It was argued that these parallel features could not be easily accounted for within the current framework of tree structures and Spec-head relations, and it was therefore suggested that a natural extension for the generalizations observed was to adopt a framework in which the corresponding nominal and verbal features are represented as parallel configurations. I presented the framework developed in Vergnaud and Zubizarreta 2001, whereby predicate composition takes place by the various combinations of Primitive Assemblies and by checking relations formed between parallel verbal and nominal domains. It was proposed that the close connection be-tween Case marking and semantic interpretation can be derived from the syntactic configuration resulting from the relations formed between corresponding nodes with-in these parallel domains.

The framework provided allows us to directly capture the one-to-one relation of corresponding nominal and verbal features observed in the literature. This analysis further suggests that Case marking in the languages discussed is dependent on a lan-guage-specific parameter that overtly manifests either the *boundedness* feature (e.g., Finnish and Scottish Gaelic) or the *instantiation* feature (e.g., Eastern Armenian, Per-sian, Turkish, Urdu, or Hindi). How this parameter is determined remains an open question.

Acknowledgments

I would like to thank two anonymous reviewers for their valuable suggestions on an earlier version of this chapter. The ideas presented here have benefited greatly from discussions with Jan Amtrup, Hagit Borer, Lina Choueiri, Arsalan Kahnemuyipour, Jean-Roger Vergnaud, and Maria Luisa Zubizarreta. All remaining errors are natu-rally mine.

Notes

1. Kiparsky refers to these verbs as *intrinsically bounded* verbs.

2. For further details on Finnish verb phrase aspect and its correlation with Case marking, see Kiparsky 1998.

3. This chapter is concerned mainly with the Armenian dialect spoken in Iran. Most of the discussion, however, also applies to Standard Eastern Armenian.

4. The overt morphemes *ə* and *n* also occur on subject NPs and have sometimes been treated as the nominative Case in these instances. Based on Standard Western Armenian data, Sigler (1997) has argued that their presence on subjects also correlates with the specificity of the noun phrase, and therefore treats *ə* and *n* as specificity markers. In section 4.6 I will show that this generalization does not hold for Eastern Armenian.

5. The suffix *-an* is one of the forms used in Eastern Armenian for animate objects, while *ə* or *n* appears on inanimate direct objects.

6. The plural marker on the direct objects in the examples in (27) is obligatory with specific readings but is usually omitted in the nonspecific interpretations of the object. A similar phe-nomenon exists in Persian (Karimi 1989; Ghomeshi 2001); also see Sigler 1997 for a discussion of plural marking and specificity in Western Armenian.

7. Following Verkuyl 1993, I use # to mark a stretched or iterative interpretation.

8. Note that the judgment on this sentence refers to a bare plural reading on the object since (35a) would be quite acceptable if the bare indefinite *xəndzor* is interpreted as 'an apple'

(which denotes a specified quantity) in this context. If the reading of the bare plural 'apples' is forced, however, the distinction in judgment between (35a) and (35b) becomes more significant, as shown. When the object is a mass noun, the judgment in the presence of an 'in an hour' adverbial is clearer: *katun mi ǰamum kat' xəmets 'The cat drank milk in an hour'.

9. I will leave the higher nodes represented by G_2, G_3, and F_3 undefined since they do not enter the discussion in this chapter.

10. Another possibility is that *Instantiation* could be licensed for the internal argument when nominal D and verbal Agr establish a relation, but it is licensed for the external argument at a higher node in the verbal structure such as T. This is only speculation at this point, but it may explain why several verbal levels have been equated with nominal D in the literature.

11. For now, I assume following Travis 1992 and other sources that n_2 and v_2 will form a relation as well, but I do not have any evidence for such a relation in the data dicussed here.

12. Why overt morphology is manifested in some languages on the nominal (e.g., object Case in Eastern Armenian and Finnish) rather than on the verb (e.g., agreement in Hindi or aspect in Slavic languages) remains an open question.

13. Note that for subjects there is no animacy distinction; both animate and inanimate subjects receive the ∂/n morpheme.

14. Whether the specific subject DP further moves to the T level is not discussed here and requires further investigation. One possible analysis would be that nominal D forms a relation with Agr_s rather than Agr_o.

15. Interestingly, Kiparsky (1998) points out that partitive case in Finnish also appears on subjects. In these instances, however, partitive case does not correspond to the aspectual behavior of the verb phrase or clause but instead only marks the nominal properties of boundedness; hence bare plurals and mass nouns receive partitive case in subject position and cardinally marked (+SQA) subjects receive nominative case. He also notes that the partitive can only appear on subjects of *presentational* verbs (e.g., *kuolla* 'die', *ilmaantua* 'appear', *kasvaa* 'grow', *kukkia* 'blossom'); all other verb categories require a nominative case on the subject.

References

Abney, Steven P. 1987. *English Noun Phrase in Its Sentential Aspect*. Doctoral dissertation, MIT.

Bhattacharya, Tanmoy. 1999. Specificity in the Bangla DP. In *Yearbook of South Asian Languages and Linguistics*, vol. 2. London: Sage.

Borer, Hagit. 1994. The Projection of Arguments. In E. Benedicto and J. Runner, eds., *Occasional Papers in Linguistics 17*, 19–48. Amherst: GLSA, University of Massachussetts.

Borer, Hagit. 2000. The Forming, the Formation, and the Form of Nominals. Unpublished ms., University of Southern California.

Borer, Hagit. 2001. Plurals as Classifiers. Paper presented at MIT; unpublished ms., University of Southern California, March 16.

Butt, Miriam. 1995. *The Structure of Complex Predicates in Urdu*. Dissertations in Linguistics. Stanford, CA: CSLI Publications.

Chierchia, Gennaro. 1998. Plurality of Mass Nouns and the Notion of "Semantic Parameter." In Susan Rothstein, ed., *Events and Grammar*, 53–103. Amsterdam: Kluwer Academic Publishers.

Chomsky, Noam. 1995. *The Minimalist Program*. Cambridge, Mass.: MIT Press.

Diesing, Molly. 1990. *Indefinites*. Cambridge, Mass.: MIT Press.

Enç, Murvet. 1991. The Semantics of Specificity. *Linguistic Inquiry*, 22:1–25.

Ghomeshi, Jila. 2001. What Does Plural Marking in Persian Tell Us about Definiteness? Lecture presented at *New Trends in Linguistics Workshop*, Tehran, May 27–29.

Ghomeshi, Jila, and Diane Massam. 1994. Lexical/Syntactic Relations without Projections. *Linguistic Analysis*, 23(3–4):175–217.

Hale, Kenneth, and Samuel Jay Keyser. 1993. On Argument Structure and the Lexical Expression of Syntactic Relations. In Kenneth Hale and Samuel Jay Keyser, eds., *The View from Building 20: Essays in Linguistics in Honor of Sylvain Bromberger*, 53–110. Cambridge, Mass.: MIT Press.

Halle, Morris, and Alec Marantz. 1993. Distributed Morphology and the Pieces of Inection. In Kenneth Hale and Samuel Jay Keyser, eds., *The View from Building 20: Essays in Linguistics in Honor of Sylvain Bromberger*, 111–176. Cambridge, Mass.: MIT Press.

Kahnemuyipour, Arsalan. 2004. *The Syntax of Sentential Stress*. Doctoral dissertation, University of Toronto.

Karimi, Simin. 1989. *Aspects of Persian Syntax, Specificity, and the Theory of Grammar*. Doctoral dissertation, University of Washington.

Karimi, Simin. 1996. Case and Specificity: Persian *Râ* Revisited. *Linguistic Analysis*, 26:174–194.

Kiparsky, Paul. 1998. Partitive Case and Aspect. In Miriam Butt and Wilhelm Geuder, eds., *The Projection of Arguments*. Stanford, Calif.: CSLI Publications.

Kozintseva, Natalia. 1995. *Modern Eastern Armenian*. Languages of the World, vol. 22. Munich: Lincom Europa.

Krifka, Manfred. 1992. Thematic Relations as Links between Nominal Reference and Temporal Constitution. In Ivan Sag and Anna Szabolcsi, eds., *Lexical Matters*. Stanford, Calif.: CSLI Publications.

Larson, Richard. 1988. On the Double Object Construction. *Linguistic Inquiry*, 19:335–391.

Larson, Richard. 2003. The Projection of DP. Paper presented at University of Southern California, October 15.

Mahajan, Anoop. 1990. *The A/A-Bar Distinction and Movement Theory*. Doctoral dissertation, MIT.

Megerdoomian, Karine. 2002. *Beyond Words and Phrases: A Unified Theory of Predicate Composition*. Doctoral dissertation, University of Southern California.

Milsark, Gary. 1977. Toward an Explanation of Certain Peculiarities of the Existential Construction in English. *Linguistic Analysis*, 3:1–29.

Perlmutter, David. 1978. Impersonal Passives and the Unaccusative Hypothesis. In *Proceedings of the Annual Meeting of the Berkeley Linguistics Society*, vol. 4, 157–189.

Pesetsky, David. 1987. Wh-in-Situ: Movement and Unselective Binding. In Eric J. Reuland and Alice G. B. ter Meulen, eds., *The Representation of (In)definites.* Cambridge, Mass.: MIT Press.

Potsdam, Eric. 1999. A Syntax for Adverbs. In *Proceedings of WECOL 98.* Fresno: California State University.

Ramchand, Gillian C. 1993. Verbal Nouns and Event Structure in Scottish Gaelic. In Utpal Lahiri and Adam Wyner, eds., *Salt III,* 162–181. Ithaca, N.Y.: Cornell University Press.

Ritter, Elizabeth. 1992. Cross-Linguistic Evidence for Number Phrase. *Canadian Journal of Linguistics/Revue Canadienne de Linguistique,* 37(2):197–218, June.

Sigler, Michele. 1997. *Specificity and Agreement in Standard Western Armenian.* Doctoral dissertation, MIT.

Sportiche, Dominique. 1999. Reconstruction, Constituency and Morphology. GLOW presentation, Berlin.

Tamrazian, Armine. 1994. *The Syntax of Armenian: Chains and the Auxiliary.* Doctoral dissertation, University College London.

Tang, C.-C. J. 1990. A Note on the DP Analysis of the Chinese NP. *Linguistics,* 28:337–354.

Tenny, Carol. 1987. *Grammaticalizing Aspect and Affectedness.* Doctoral dissertation, MIT,

Travis, Lisa. 1992. Inner Tense with NPs: The Position of Number. In *1992 Annual Conference of the Canadian Linguistics Association,* 329–345. Toronto: University of Toronto Working Papers in Linguistics.

Valois, Daniel. 1991. *The Internal Syntax of DP.* Doctoral dissertation, University of California, Los Angeles.

Valois, Daniel. 1996. On the Structure of the French DP. *Canadian Journal of Linguistics/Revue Canadienne de Linguistique,* 41(4):349–375.

Vaux, Bert. 1998. *The Phonology of Armenian.* Oxford: Oxford University Press.

Vergnaud, Jean-Roger. 2000. Primitive Aspects of the Syntactic Code. Paper presented at *Determiners and Pronouns* Colloquium, CNRS/Université Paris 8. Paris, France, October 5–6.

Vergnaud, Jean-Roger, and Maria-Luisa Zubizarreta. 2001. Derivation and Constituent Structure. Unpublished ms., University of Southern California, April.

Verkuyl, Henk K. 1993. *A Theory of Aspectuality: The Interaction between Temporal and Atemporal Structure.* New York: Cambridge University Press.

Williams, Edwin. 1981. Argument Structure and Morphology. *Linguistic Review,* 1:81–114.

5 Clause Structure and the Syntax of Verbless Sentences

Elabbas Benmamoun

5.1 Introduction

Variation in clause structure is one of the important issues in linguistic theory, because it tests our conceptions of Universal Grammar and the extent to which it may account for linguistic variation. This chapter deals specifically with the issue of whether the categories of tense and verb are projected universally as part of a universal clause structure schema (Cinque 1999). It also deals with the nature of the widely attested codependency between tense and verbs, particularly with whether the dependency is morphological or syntactic. I will use the so-called verbless sentences in Arabic (and Hebrew) as a test case to argue that tense is universally projected but does not necessarily need to co-occur particularly with a verbal head.[1] I will provide empirical arguments for the projection of a syntactic tense node and against the projection of a verbal node (VP). This naturally leads to a number of central questions that will be the focus of this chapter. First, if there is a tense node, what is its feature structure? It is usually claimed that tense is intimately related to the verb. This idea is captured in three ways, by assuming that (1) tense is morphologically dependent on the verb, (2) tense is specified for a verbal feature (Chomsky 1995), or (3) tense is an extended projection of the verb (Grimshaw 1991). Second, how do we account for the obvious variation between languages and also within the same language where a verb cannot be projected in some contexts but must be projected in other contexts? I will argue that the two questions are related and can receive an adequate answer if we zero in on the nature of the functional category *tense* and its categorical feature *structure*. The proposal is consistent with the idea that the syntax of natural language and locus of variation are to a large extent due to the interaction between functional and lexical categories.

5.2   Arguments for a Tense Projection in Verbless Sentences

In both Arabic[2] and Hebrew, an independent present-tense sentence may overtly consist only of a subject and a nonverbal predicate.[3] The predicate can be a noun phrase (1a, 2a), an adjective phrase (1b, 2b), or a prepositional phrase (1c, 2c).

(1) a. ʕumar muʕəllim   MA
         Omar teacher
         'Omar is a teacher.'
     b. ḍ-ḍar   kbira
         the-house big
         'The house is big.'
     c. lə-ktab   fuq l-məktəb
         the-book on the-desk
         'The book is on the desk.'

(2) a. dani more   ba-universita   Hebrew
         Dani teacher in-the-university
         'Dani is a teacher at the university.'
     b. dani nexmad ad meod
         Dani nice   very
         'Dani is very nice.'
     c. dani al ha-gag
         Dani on the-roof
         'Dani is on the roof.'

These types of constructions, which are by no means restricted to Arabic and Hebrew,[4] raise questions about clause structure.[5] The standard assumption is that independent sentences usually consist of a lexical layer and a functional layer that minimally contains a temporal projection (TP) and a clause typing projection (CP). Within minimalism, the functional layer is instrumental in accounting for various cases of displacement such as NP movement and *wh*-movement, the distribution of expletives, Case, and agreement (Chomsky 1995, 2000, 2001). Thus, in English, for example, assuming that the subject in (3) is generated lower than the modal, the fact that it surfaces preceding the modal is attributed to a property of T that requires that it have a specifier. Moreover, T, which also enters into an agreement relation with the subject, checks/deletes the Case feature of the latter, which is considered non-interpretable.

(3) John may read the book.

Similarly, in (4) the displacement of the *wh*-complement from within the lexical VP projection is attributed to some property of the functional category C (complementizer). While it is not clear what this property is (a *wh*-feature that needs to be checked or just an EPP feature of C that requires it to have a specifier on a par with T), the crucial point for us is that the displacement of the *wh*-complement is driven by a functional category.

(4) What did Mary read?

Similar questions can be reproduced in the context of verbless sentences. Thus, the subject of a verbless sentence can be nominative, as is clearly the case in Standard Arabic where Case is morphologically marked.

(5) a. ʕaliy-un muʕallimun   SA
       Ali-NOM teacher
       'Ali is a teacher.'
    b. al-ɣurfat-u   kabiiratun
       the-room-NOM big
       'The room is big.'
    c. l-kitaab-u   ʕalaa l-maktabi
       the-book-NOM on   the-desk
       'The book is on the desk.'

It is easy to show that the nominative Case on the subject in (5) is structural rather than the default nominative usually assigned to topicalized and left-dislocated elements binding resumptive pronouns. Thus, the subject gets nominative Case in the context of the expletive that precedes it in (6).

(6) hunaaka ṭaalib-un   fii l-bayti   SA
    there   student-NOM in the-house
    'There is a student in the house.'

The subject *Taalibun* in (6) is clearly not topicalized or left dislocated, and so its Case must be checked by a functional category. In Arabic, as in many other languages, structural nominative Case, as opposed to default Case, usually occurs in the context of finite clauses. It is, therefore, reasonable to assume that it is due to the presence of the functional category tense that checks it.

Moreover, the presence of the expletive in (6) also argues for a functional category above the lexical layer in verbless sentences. The standard analysis of expletives is that they fulfill a requirement of the functional category T.[6] That is, the distribution of expletives has to do with the syntax of the functional layer rather than the lexical layer. Thus, the dominant view within the principles-and-parameters framework is that the presence of the expletive *there* in (7) is due to some property of the tense projection.

(7) There is a student in the garden.

If this analysis of expletives is correct, then we have an additional argument for the functional category tense in the verbless sentence in (6) where there is both a nominal expletive and an argument NP.

One additional argument for the functional category tense comes from the movement of the subject from within the lexical/thematic layer. This movement is clearly shown in the context of sentential negation where the subject must precede the sentential negative.

(8) a. ʕumar maši muʕəllim   MA
       Omar not   teacher
       'Omar is not a teacher.'
    b. d-dar   maši kbira
       the-house not   big
       'The house is big.'
    c. lə-ktab   maši fuq l-məktəb
       the-book not   on the-desk
       'The book is on the desk.'

Assuming that sentential negation in Arabic is generated between the TP and VP (Benmamoun 2000, below), the fact that the subject must precede it can easily be captured by movement of the subject from within the lexical domain to a functional layer. The movement in question is obligatory, as shown by the ungrammaticality of the sentences in (9), where the subject remains in a position lower than negation, hence lower than TP.

(9) a. *maši ʕumar muʕəllim   MA
       not   Omar teacher
       'Omar is not a teacher.'
    b. *maši d-dar   kbira
       not   the-house big
       'The house is big.'
    c. *maši lə-ktab   fuq l-məktəb
       not   the-book on the-desk
       'The book is on the desk.'

Obligatory NP movement in languages such as English is usually associated with properties of T such as the need to check the Case of the subject or to have a specifier. Given that the movement in (8) affects NPs with nominative Case, it would be more principled to also attribute it to the presence of the category tense above the lexical/thematic layer in verbless sentences.

With respect to the category C, there is also strong evidence that it is present in verbless sentences. For example, *wh*-movement targets the left periphery of verbless sentences as it does in the context of sentences containing verbal predicates.

(10) a. fiin ʕumar   MA
        where Omar
        'Where is Omar?'
     b. mʕa men   nadya
        with whom Nadia
        'Who is Nadia with?'

Moroccan Arabic questions obligatorily deploy the *wh*-movement option. Assuming that *wh*-movement targets the specifier of CP, there must then be a functional category C in verbless sentences. In fact, this is trivially shown by the fact that embedded verbless sentences can be headed by complementizers.

(11) sməʕt bəlli ʕumar f-ḍ-ḍar   MA
     I heard that Omar in-the-house
     'I heard that Omar is at home.'

Interestingly, the complementizer *bəlli* occurs only in the context of finite complement clauses. Nonfinite complement clauses in Moroccan Arabic are headed by the particle *baš* (12a) or no particle at all (12b). Similarly in Standard Arabic, finite complement clauses are headed by the Case-assigning complementizer *ʔanna/ ʔinna*, while nonfinite complement clauses are headed by *ʔan*.

(12) a. rfəd   baš yži   MA
        refused that come
        'He refused to come.'
     b. bɣa   yəmši
        wanted come
        'He wanted to come.'

(13) a. ʔaʕtaqidu ʔanna l-walada mariiḍun   SA
        I believe that the-child sick
        'I believe that the child is sick.'
     b. ʔaraada ʔan   yadrusa
        wanted that/to study

There is a consensus that the presence of C signals the presence of T.[7] Putting aside the issue of how to capture this dependency, the important implication for the present concerns is that verbless sentences headed by complementizers must contain a functional category T.

Finally, verbless sentences headed by a participle with a nominal template (such as *waqəf* in (14)) can be conjoined with sentences with verbal predicates. This follows straightforwardly if the coordination in question is a coordination of clauses headed by functional projections such as TPs rather than lexical projections.

(14) ʕumar waqəf   f-l-baab   w   ʕali ta-ysbaɣ ɦit   MA
     Omar standing at-the-door and Ali ASP-paint the-wall
     'Omar is standing at the door and Ali is painting the wall.'

To sum up this section, I have provided several independent syntactic arguments for a TP projection in verbless sentences.[8] The evidence is based on Case, NP movement, expletives, complementizers, and coordination. Therefore, the structure of the verbless sentences in (1) and (2) is as in (15).[9]

(15)

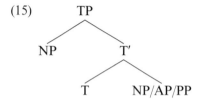

In (15), the lexical layer is headed by a nonverbal predicate, which is in turn dominated by a functional layer headed by tense. The T head of the TP projection contains the tense features and whatever formal features are relevant to checking the nominative Case of the subject and to forcing the movement of the subject from the lexical projection to the specifier of TP. We will explore what those features are in detail below, but before we do that we need to explore another alternative analysis that would posit a VP headed by a null copula in verbless sentences.

5.3 Verbless Sentences Do Not Contain a Verbal Copula

The structure in (15) does not contain any verbal projection, which challenges the standard assumption that in finite full clauses (as opposed to small clauses, for example) the presence of T requires a VP projection. In Chomsky 1995, this is captured through a checking relation between the verb and a verbal noninterpretable feature on T. Under Grimshaw's (1991) extended projection account, this dependency is captured by the assumption that functional projections are extended projections of lexical projections. Under such a system, T (and C) are essentially extended projections of VP. In fact, Grimshaw's account explicitly bars structures such as (15) where T (an extended projection of V) does not take VP. There is no source for TP in that system since there is no VP projection that could give rise to TP (or CP for that matter). A possible solution would be to posit a null verbal copula between the TP projection and the main predicate projection, as illustrated in (16).

(16)

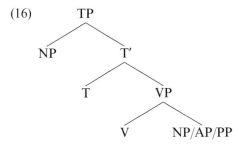

The representation in (16) would then be consistent with the theory that T has a verbal feature that needs to be checked by V. Within Grimshaw's extended projection theory, TP would indeed be an extended projection of the VP headed by the null copula. The only difference between Arabic and Hebrew, on the one hand, and English, on the other, is that the latter has an overt copula in the present tense and the former has a null copula. This is a reasonable alternative and in fact has been proposed in different forms (Bakir 1980; Fassi Fehri 1993). Accordingly, the structure of the so-called verbless sentences is not different from that of their verbal counterparts. That is, they are on a par with sentences containing overt verbal copulas such as the past-tense sentences in (17) and future-tense sentences in (18).

(17) a. ʕumar kan muʕəllim   MA
        Omar was teacher
        'Omar was a teacher.'
     b. dani haya nexmad ad meod   Hebrew
        Dani was nice   very
        'Dani was very nice.'

(18) a. ʕumar ɣadi ykun f-ḍ-ḍar   MA
        Omar will be   in-the-house
        'Omar will be in the house.'
     b. dani yihye more   ba-universita   Hebrew
        Dani be.FUT teacher in-university
        'Dani will be a teacher at the university.'

However, there are many problems with the null copula analysis. First, sentences with a negated verbal copula display both Predicate-Subject or Subject-Predicate orders, as illustrated in (19).[10]

(19) a. ma-kan-š   ʕumar muʕəllim   MA
        NEG-was-NEG Omar teacher
        'Omar was not a teacher.'
     b. ʕumar ma-kan-š   muʕəllim
        Omar NEG-was-NEG teacher
        'Omar was not a teacher.'

In (19a), the copula *kan* containing the negative precedes the subject *ʕumar*, while in (19b), it follows it. By contrast, when there is no overt copula, negation must follow the subject, as shown in (9) above and (20b) below (Berman and Grosu 1976; Jelinek 1981).

(20) a. ʕumar ma-ši   muʕəllim   MA
        Omar NEG-NEG teacher
        'Omar is not a teacher.'
     b. *ma-ši   muʕallim ʕumar
        NEG-NEG teacher   Omar

If there is a null copula it is not clear why it could not merge with negation and move past the subject on a par with the overt verbal copula in (19). The ungrammaticality of (20b) cannot be due to some requirement that negation be supported by a lexical head since the negative can occur by itself, as is the case in (20a).[11]

Second, and related to the first problem, if there is a null copula, its syntax is different from that of the overt copula. The latter blocks movement of the nonverbal predicate to negation, as illustrated in (21b).

(21) a. ʕumar ma-kan-š   muʕəllim   MA
        Omar NEG-was-NEG teacher
        'Omar was not a teacher.'
     b. *ʕumar ma-muʕallim-š   kan
        Omar NEG-teacher-NEG was

In (21b) the nominal predicate *muʕallim* has moved across the verbal copula to merge with negation. This movement, however, is blocked presumably because the predicate moves across the verbal copula *kan*, a movement that violates minimality in the sense of Rizzi 1990.

However, if there is no verbal copula, the nonverbal predicate is allowed to move and merge with negation, as shown by the grammaticality of (22b), which contrasts with (21b).[12]

(22) a. ʕumar ma-ši   muʕəllim   MA
        Omar NEG-NEG teacher
        'Omar is not a teacher.'
     b. ʕumar ma-muʕəllim-š
        Omar NEG-teacher-NEG

The third argument that there is no null verbal copula that heads a VP in verbless sentences comes from the distribution of Case on predicates. Like many other languages, predicates in Standard Arabic can be marked for Case. The Case can be either nominative or accusative depending on the head that the predicate is a complement of (Déchaine 1993). For example, in the context of the past tense (23) the predicate is assigned accusative Case by the copula verb *kaan*.

(23) a. kaana r-ražul-u muʕallim-an   SA
         was   the-man   teacher-ACC
         'The man was a teacher.'
    b. *kaana r-ražul-u muʕallim-un
         was   the-man   teacher-NOM

On the other hand, predicates of verbless sentences carry nominative Case, as illustrated in (24).

(24) a. r-ražul-u   muʕallim-un   SA
         the-man-NOM teacher-NOM
         'The man is a teacher.'
    b. *r-ražul-u   muʕallim-an
         the-man-NOM teacher-ACC

This is problematic if there is a null copula. Clearly, the Case on the predicate is not sensitive to the type of tense of the clause. This is evident from the fact that the future-tense copula also assigns accusative Case to the predicate (25).[13]

(25) a. sa-kuunu r-ražul-u muʕallim-an   SA
         FUT-be   the-man   teacher-ACC
         'The man will be a teacher.'
    b. *sa-yakuunu r-ražul-u muʕallim-un
         FUT-be   the-man teacher-NOM

In addition, in Standard Arabic the negative head *laysa*, which occurs in the present tense, also assigns accusative Case to the predicate (26).

(26) a. laysa r-ražul-u   muʕallim-an   SA
         NEG   the-man-NOM teacher-ACC
         'The man is not a teacher.'
    b. *laysa r-ražul-u   muʕallim-un
         NEG   the-man-NOM teacher-NOM

The same facts obtain the context of the aspectual head *laazaala*, which can also occur in the present tense (27).

(27) a. laazaala muʕallim-an   SA
         still   teacher-ACC
         'He is still a teacher.'
    b. *laazaala muʕallim-un
         still   teacher-NOM

The generalization seems to be that some heads, such as the past-tense and future-tense copula, negation, and aspectual heads, assign accusative Case to the predicate. This generalization does not obtain in the context of the putative null verbal copula where the predicate surfaces with nominative Case. The most reasonable conclusion to draw from these facts is that the copula is not there—that is, verbless sentences are indeed configurationally verbless.

To summarize, while there is syntactic evidence for a functional category tense in verbless sentences, support is lacking for a verbal head that would license it under the checking theory of Chomsky 1995 or Grimshaw's extended projection system. Recall that both systems are set up to capture the dependency between tense and verbs in languages such as English. However, verbless sentences in Arabic and Hebrew do not display such dependency. This raises the question of how to capture the dependency that exists in English and the lack of such dependency in Arabic and Hebrew verbless sentences. In the next section, I will explore in detail the nature of such dependency. I will show that the observed dependency cannot be grounded in the morphology and instead argue that it is categorial features, in the sense of Chomsky 1995, that are critical to whether a sentence should have a verbal head. I will depart, however, from Chomsky 1995 by arguing that a particular tense is not universally specified for the same set of categorial features.

5.4   The Formal Features of the Present Tense

5.4.1   The Categorial Features of Tense
One of the central aspects of the Minimalist Program is the assumption that the syntax of lexical categories, their ordering, displacement, and relationship with other categories, is due to the interaction between formal features on the lexical categories and functional categories. Thus, the displacement of the subject from the VP to TP implicates formal noninterpretable features of tense, such as the EPP and ϕ-features, and formal features of the subject, such as Case and its interpretable ϕ-features. While it is not clear what the exact features are that drive the syntax of functional categories (whether the EPP is a nominal feature of T that requires pairing with a nominal or just a requirement to have an XP in the specifier position), the main idea is that it is formal features that drive the interaction between lexical categories and functional categories.

With respect to the interaction between tense and the verb, the Minimalist Program departed from earlier morphophonologically inspired analyses whereby the dependency between tense and the verb is essentially morphological, stemming from the need of tense to have a lexical host. According to Chomsky 1995, the dependency between tense and the verb is due to a categorial verbal feature of tense that forces it to be paired with the verb. The main reason the pairing of tense and the verb is not grounded in the need of a lexical host for the tense affix is presumably that in English, as opposed to French for example, the two codependent elements are paired covertly (after Spell-Out), even though tense is realized on the verb at PF. This is captured by allowing tense to be generated on the verb and endowing tense with a categorial feature (+V) that can be checked by the verb either overtly or covertly. In English, the verbal categorial feature is checked covertly in the context of main verbs, while in French, it is checked overtly. The use of categorial features to capture the dependency between the verb and tense makes this dependency parallel to the dependency between tense and the subject. Here also, according to Chomsky 1995, tense has a categorial feature (+D) that needs to be paired with a nominal element such as the NP subject. Movement of the subject to check the categorial feature of T can also be overt or covert if it turns out that the subject can remain lower than TP at the point of Spell-Out, as has been argued for VSO languages.[14]

While the dependency between tense and the verb with respect to the categorial feature of the former has not been widely adopted and has, in fact, been abandoned in Chomsky's recent work (2000, 2001), I would like to argue that this idea has empirical merit and should be retained.[15] It will allow us to account for the contrast between the syntax of present-tense and past-tense sentences and also the structure of verbless sentences. However, I argue that languages may differ as to whether a particular tense is specified for the verbal and nominal categorial features. In English, both the present tense and the past tense are specified for such features, hence the movement of the subject to check the nominal feature and the obligatory presence of verbal copulas in both tenses to check the verbal feature. On the other hand, in Arabic, the present tense is not specified for the verbal feature. It is only specified for the nominal feature, which gets checked by the subject. The past tense, by contrast, is specified for both nominal and verbal features.

(28) a. Past [+V, +D]
      b. Present [+D]

This analysis allows us to account for the distribution of the copula. Since the present tense is not specified for a verbal feature, it does not need to be paired with a verbal element. Therefore, the verbal copula is not needed, which yields a representation without a VP, as illustrated in (29).[16]

(29)

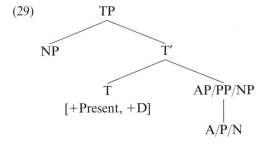

By contrast, the past tense is specified for the verbal feature. In this case, if the main predicate is not verbal, the presence of the verbal copula is forced, as illustrated in (30).

(30)

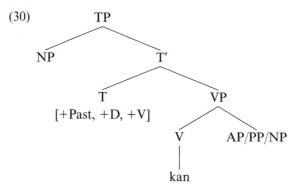

Relying on the verbal categorial feature to account for the structure of verbless sentences does work, but as it is, it appears to be nothing more than a diacritic feature to distinguish these sentences from other sentences that contain verbs that head VP constituents. What we need is independent evidence for the presence of the verbal feature in the past tense and its absence in the present tense. Also, if indeed the present tense is not specified for the categorial verbal feature, then we predict that the syntax of sentences containing verbal predicates in the present tense should not be different from the syntax of verbless sentences. Moreover, the analysis would be strengthened if we can find overt evidence that the T head in the present tense is only specified for the nominal feature. In the following sections, I show that these different types of independent evidence actually exist in Arabic and Hebrew, which in turn supports the present argument in favor of maintaining reliance on categorial features to capture dependencies between tense and predicates (and subjects for that matter).

5.4.2 Sentential Negation and Tense

The syntax of sentential negation in Arabic dialects shows a clear demarcation between verbless sentences and present-tense sentences on the one hand, and past tenses on the other hand. I take this to prove that the differences between them has to do with the feature composition of the functional category tense.

Sentential negation in many Arabic dialects consists of two parts, a proclitic *ma* and an enclitic *š*. In verbless sentences, the two negative particles cliticize onto each other, as illustrated by the following sentence from Egyptian Arabic:

(31) ?ana mi-š   ṭaalib   EA
     I   NEG-NEG student
     'I am not a student.'

In the context of the past-tense verb in Egyptian Arabic, *ma* is realized as a proclitic while *š* is realized as an enclitic:

(32) Omar ma-katab-š   ig-gawaab   EA
     Omar NEG-wrote-NEG the-letter
     'Omar didn't write the letter.'

Most importantly, the two negative particles cannot cliticize onto each other as they do in verbless sentences.

(33) *Omar mi-š   katab ig-gawaab   EA
     Omar NEG-NEG wrote the-letter

Suppose that sentential negation in Egyptian Arabic, and other Arabic dialects (Benmamoun 1992, 2000), heads its own projection between TP and the predicate as illustrated in (34).

(34)

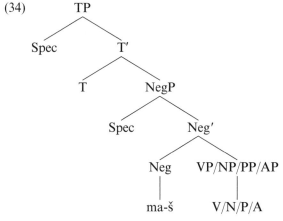

Assuming that the past tense has a [+V] feature that must be overtly paired with a verb, the verb then raises from the VP to T. To obey minimality, the verb must move through the negative rather than across it, hence negation is realized on the verb with *ma* as proclitic and *š* as enclitic. In verbless sentences, by contrast, tense is not [+V] and therefore does not need to be paired with a verbal head. Consequently, the negative particles end up cliticizing onto each other.

Turning to present-tense sentences with verbal predicates, we predict the verb not to have to raise past the negative projection to tense since the latter does not have a verbal feature that needs to be paired/checked by a verbal head. This prediction is correct. In Egyptian Arabic the present tense does not have to merge with negation.[17]

(35) a. ma-biyiktib-š   EA
        NEG-writing-NEG
        'He isn't writing.'

    b. mi-š   biyiktib   EA
       NEG-NEG writing
       'He isn't writing.'

In this respect, present-tense sentences with verbal predicates pattern with verbless sentences rather than past-tense sentences with verbal predicates. This is as predicted; regardless of whether there is a verbal predicate, the tense head of present-tense sentences does not have a verbal categorial feature that forces verb movement. The fact that verbless sentences pattern with present-tense sentences with verbal predicates shows clearly that the pivotal factor is the tense head and its formal features. The tense head in the present tense does not require a verbal head, a generalization that is captured by not specifying it for a verbal categorial feature.

5.4.3 The Morphology of Tense

Another piece of evidence that tense is specified for verbal categorial features comes from the interaction between the past tense and the verb in Standard Arabic in the context of sentential negation. Standard Arabic is peculiar in allowing negation to carry future and past tense (Benmamoun 1992; Ouhalla 1993; Shlonsky 1997).

(36) a. lan   yaktuba   SA
       NEG.FUT write
       'He won't write.'
    b. lam   yaktub
       NEG.PAST write
       'He didn't write.'

In Benmamoun 1992 and 2000, this is captured by arguing that the negative *laa* heads a negative projection between TP and VP that blocks verb movement to tense. The negative instead moves to tense. Interestingly, the tensed negative must be adjacent to the verb.

(37) a. lam   yadrusuu   SA
       NEG.PAST study
       'They didn't study.'
    b. *lam   T-Tullaab-u   yadrusuu
       NEG.PAST the-students-NOM study

This adjacency does not signal morphological merger because two tensed negatives can be conjoined, as illustrated in (38).

(38) lam   wa lan   yaktubuu   SA
     NEG.PAST and NEG.FUT write
     'They did not and will not write.'

The fact that negation can carry tense shows that tense is not required to be affixed to the verb exclusively. The question is what explains the adjacency between the verb and the tensed negation. There must be a reason beyond morphology that requires that negation be adjacent to the negative-carrying tense. The reason could be the categorial verbal feature on T that requires that it be paired with a verb. The adjacency between the tensed negative and verb mirrors the situation in English where, though the verb does not move to tense, the latter must be adjacent to the VP (Bobaljik 1994).

The tensed negative facts make a stronger argument for the present analysis. Suppose we try to account for the distribution of the copula in the present and past tenses by assuming that the present tense does not require a lexical host while the past tense does. This is essentially the alternative that Baker (2003) advances to counter Benmamoun's (2000) analysis in terms of categorial verbal features. Baker puts forward a theory of lexical categories that does not rely on categorial features. Restricting our attention to verbs, Baker (2003, 23) defines verbs as in (39).

(39) X is a verb if and only if X is a lexical category and X has a specifier

The crucial defining factor for verbs, as opposed to nouns for example, is the presence of a specifier. The question then is how to license the subject of nonverbal predicates. To solve this problem Baker introduces a head *Pred* heading projection that dominates the nonverbal predicate. The *Pred* enables the nonverbal predicate to assign a thematic role to the subject.[18]

Turning to Arabic, Baker argues that in past-tense sentences where a verbal copula is obligatory, the structure is as in (40).

(40)

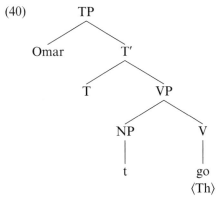

Past tense is an affix that must be supported by a lexical head. Nonverbal predicates should, in principle, be able to support tense. But then they would have to move across the *Pred* head, which must be generated in such contexts to license the specifier/subject. That movement would violate minimality. This explains why a verbal head is obligatory in the past tense.

The present-tense head, on the other hand, is not an affix that requires a host. It is projected but does not need to be supported. The *Pred* head, however, must be projected to license the subject. The structure Baker (2003) proposes for present-tense sentences containing nonverbal predicates is as in (41).

(41)

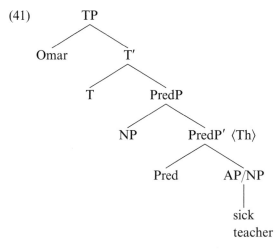

Past-tense sentences whose main predicates are nonverbal contain a *Pred* head to license the subject and a verbal copula to support the past-tense affix (42).

(42)

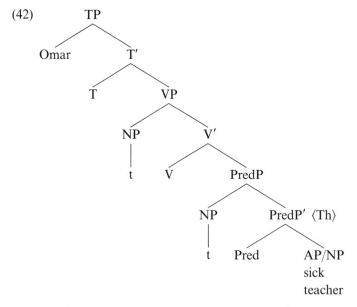

A copula is prevented in the present tense because, by economy of projection, it is superfluous. A sentence that does project it is superseded by a sentence that does not project it (see also Benmamoun 2000).

Putting aside questions about Baker's general claim about the definition of lexical categories since it is not directly relevant to this chapter, what concerns us is whether the alternative analysis that does not rely on categorial features but rather on the morphophonological status of tense to explain whether the latter requires a verbal codependent is empirically more desirable. If we look at the Arabic facts more closely we realize that they do not support Baker's analysis. The facts are, rather, more consistent with an analysis that deploys categorial features.

First, nonverbal predicates can raise and merge with negation, as illustrated in (43b–45b)

(43) a. ʕumar ma-ši   muʕəllim   MA
        Omar NEG-NEG teacher
        'Omar is not a teacher.'
   b. ʕumar ma-muʕəllim-š
        Omar NEG-teacher-NEG
        'Omar is not a teacher.'

(44) a. ʕumar ma-ši   ṭwil   MA
        Omar NEG-NEG tall
        'Omar is not tall.'
   b. ʕumar ma-ṭwil-š
        Omar NEG-tall-NEG
        'Omar is not tall.'

(45) a. ʕumar ma-ši   hna   MA
        Omar NEG-NEG here
        'Omar is not here.'
   b. ʕumar ma-hna-š
        Omar NEG-here-NEG
        'Omar is not here.'

Presumably, the movement of the nonverbal predicates in (43b–45b) is across or through *Pred*. But if that is the case, then it is not clear why they cannot support tense too. One can argue that it is *Pred* that supports negation, but then the question is why can't it support tense too?

Second, recall that in Standard Arabic, negation can support tense (36), contradicting the claim by Baker that tense can only be supported by lexical heads. Even if we loosen the morphological requirement of tense to allow for negation to support it, we would have to explain why the verbal copula is still needed as illustrated in (46) (Moutaouakil 1987).

(46) a. *lam   fii l-bayt   SA
        NEG.PAST in the-house
        'He is not at home.'

b. lam   yakun fii l-bayt
   NEG.PAST be   in the-house
   'He wasn't at home.'

On the other hand, the obligatory presence of the copula even when tense is hosted by negation is straightforwardly explained if the reason is not exclusively affixation but rather a verbal feature of tense.

Third, as shown in Benmamoun 2000, there is actually no morphophonological difference between the past tense and present tense. Both are abstract morphemes with no phonological matrix. The major difference between them is in their agreement affixation patterns.[19] Person agreement is realized as a prefix in the present tense but as a suffix in the past tense. Number, by contrast, is always realized as a suffix.

(47) a. ya-ktub-uu   SA
        3-write-MP
        'They write.'
     b. katab-uu
        wrote-3MP
        'They wrote.'

In Benmamoun 2000, the distribution of person agreement is given a historical explanation that is well grounded in studies of the history of Semitic languages. There, it is shown that person agreement evolved out of a pronominal clitic. The syntactic explanation of how the agreement patterns arose follows easily from the present analysis that relies on whether tense has a verbal categorial feature.[20] In the past tense, the verb always raises to tense in order to check the verbal feature. The pronominal subject remains lower and surfaces as an enclitic, hence the suffixation pattern of the past-tense verb (48).

(48)

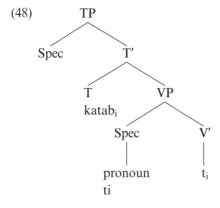

In the present tense, by contrast, the verb does not need to raise to tense because the latter does not have a categorial verbal feature. The verb stays in situ and the pronominal subject ends up as a proclitic, hence the prefixation pattern of the present tense (49).

(49)
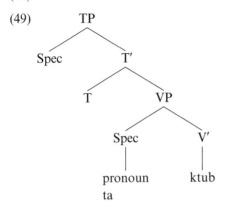

In short, whether tense enters into a dependency relation with a verb depends on its categorial features and is not related to its morphological status as an affix. Of course the codependents might merge and form a single morphological unit (word), but that might be a reflection of a syntactically grounded dependency involving categorial features. The past tense is specified for both nominal and verbal features while the present tense is specified for nominal features only.

The arguments we have discussed so far consist of constructions that show the interaction or lack of interaction between the tense and the verb. There is also evidence that could be taken to show that the categorial features in questions can be morphophonologically realized.

5.4.4   Overt Realization of the Nominal Feature of Tense

Above we saw that the past tense differs from the present tense in having an overt verbal copula. I argued that this contrast has to do with the categorial feature specification of the past and present tenses. Past tense is specified for a verbal categorial feature that must be paired with/checked by a verbal head, hence the obligatory presence of the verbal copula in contexts where the main predicate is not verbal. The present tense, by contrast, is specified only for a nominal feature that is paired with/checked by the subject. Interestingly, in Hebrew there is a head that is not verbal that shows up only in present-tense contexts. This is the so-called pronominal copula discussed in Doron 1986, from which the Hebrew data in this section are taken.[21]

In Hebrew, as in Arabic, a verbal copula, *haya*, is obligatory in the past and future tenses, as illustrated in (50).

(50) a. dani haya nexmad ad meod   Hebrew
      Dani was nice   very
      'Dani was very nice.'
   b. dani yihye more   ba-universita
      Dani will.be teacher in-university
      'Dani will be a teacher at the university.'

In the present tense, however, a pronominal element that agrees with the subject in
number and gender (but not person) may occur, as shown in (51).

(51) a. dani hu more   ba-universita   Hebrew
      Dani he teacher in-the-university
      'Dani is a teacher at the university.'
   b. dani hu nexmad ad meod
      Dani he nice   very
      'Dani is very nice.'
   c. dani hu al ha-gag
      Dani he on the-roof
      'Dani is on the roof.'

In Moroccan Arabic as well, a pronoun may show up in the context of questions
from within verbless sentences.

(52) fin   huwa ʕumar   MA
    where he   Omar
    'Where is Omar?'

Doron (1986) provides convincing arguments that the pronoun in (51) is not a
subject but rather a copular inflectional element. For example, Hebrew adheres to
the highest subject condition whereby the highest extracted subject cannot bind a
resumptive pronoun (Shlonsky 1992), as illustrated in (53).

(53) a. ha-iš   še ohev bananot   Hebrew
      the-man that loves bananas
      'The man who loves bananas.'
   b. *ha-iš   še   hu ohev bananot
      the-man that he loves bananas

The pronominal in Moroccan Arabic in (52) is also clearly not a subject, otherwise it
would end up binding the subject argument that follows it.

    With respect to its syntactic position, the pronoun precedes sentential negation,
which shows that it is higher than the lexical projection of the main predicate.

(54) a. dani lo roce   banana   Hebrew
      Dani not wants banana
      'Dani doesn't want a banana.'

    b. *dani roce lo banana
       Dani wants not banana
    c. dani (hu) lo more
      Dani (he) not more
      'Dani is not a teacher.'
    d. *dani lo hu more
      Dani not he teacher

Doron proposes that the pronominal is the realization of the agreement features of the functional category I. For the present purposes, I will take that to mean that it is a Spell-Out of the nominal categorial feature of tense. I will follow Ritter (1995, 418–421) and Shlonsky (1997, 122) and take the person feature of pronominals to be associated with definiteness, which basically provides the categorial label of the (DP) projection. It is not surprising, then, that the D-feature of tense can be realized by the person feature of a pronoun.

    That the person feature of the pronoun may be an overt realization of the nominal feature of tense may provide a possible explanation for an agreement puzzle that arises in the context of copular constructions. The pronoun that shows up in copular constructions in Hebrew agrees with the subject in number and gender only.[22] Crucially, it does not agree in person. This can be accounted for as follows. Consider the feature structures of the present and past tenses. The present tense is [+D] while the past tense is [+D] and [+V]. As a nominal element the present tense is expected to display the nominal agreement pattern, namely agreement in number and gender, on a par with adjectives and nouns. The past tense, by contrast, is both nominal and verbal. As a verbal element we expect it to display the agreement pattern of verbs, namely agreement in person, number, and gender. In other words, T in the present tense has the tense, categorial, and agreement specification in (55a) while T in the past tense has the tense, categorial, and agreement specification in (55b).

(55) a. *Present tense*   b. *Past tense*
     [+D, Number, Gender]   [+D, +V, Person, Number, Gender]

In other words, the genuine agreement features in the present tense—that is, those involving agreement between T and the subject—are number and gender. The person feature is a realization of the D-feature of the present tense. It is not an agreement feature. Needless to say, this account of agreement in the present and past tenses is a first approximation and is highly tentative.

    To summarize this section, I have proposed to analyze the third-person pronominal that surfaces in the copular constructions in the present tense in Hebrew as a realization of the nominal feature of that tense. If this is on the right track, it provides the clearest evidence for categorial features as part of the feature structure of tense, and probably other functional categories.

5.5   Conclusion

In this chapter, I argued that the functional category tense may be specified for categorial verbal and/or nominal features, partially following Chomsky 1995. Departing from Chomsky 2001, I showed that categorial features can be independently motivated and may even be morphologically realized. While the analysis is not consistent with approaches that assume the necessity of a verbal projection in the context of a tense projection (Grimshaw 1991) or that ground the dependency or lack thereof in the morphology of tense (Baker 2003), it has been able to account for a number of independent facts, the important being the similarities in the syntax of verbless sentences and present-tense sentences containing verbal predicates. Admittedly, the analysis is tentative and in turn raises its own questions, such as whether there are languages where the past tense is nominal only while the present tense is both verbal and nominal. If such cases do not exist, then does that have to do with some semantic aspect of the present and past tenses that is ultimately related to their categorial features? However, if the analysis I provided is correct, we have strong arguments that functional categories are specified for categorial features that drive their interaction with lexical categories. The fact that tense in the majority of cases requires a nominal subject, that the expletive is usually a demonstrative or locative pronoun, and that nonverbal copulas can be realized as pronouns in the present tense, may reflect the nominal nature of tense and perhaps other functional categories. This nominal nature is obscured in cases where tense also has a verbal feature. However, in verbless sentences where tense does not have a verbal feature, the nominal feature of tense is more explicitly manifested.

Notes

1. It is a trivial fact that not all clauses need a verbal head crosslinguistically or even within the same language. The main concern of this chapter, however, is with the syntax of the functional category tense and its formal features. The issue is whether in sentences without verbal predicates the functional category tense, if it is at all projected, has the same set of formal features that drive its syntax in sentences with verbal heads.

2. Data for this chapter come from Egyptian Arabic (EA), Moroccan Arabic (MA), Standard Arabic (SA), and Hebrew.

3. See, among others, Berman and Grosu 1976; Ayoub 1981; Bakir 1979; Jelinek 1981; Eid 1983, 1991; Doron 1986; Moutaouakil 1987; Rapoport 1987; Heggie 1988; Déchaine 1993; Fassi Fehri 1993; Shlonsky 1997; Benmamoun 2000; Greenberg 2002.

4. See Carnie 1995; Massam 2000.

5. Bošković (2001, 103) provides data from Russian that show that the copula can be used in the present tense in the context of homophonous wh-phrases as in (ia).

(i) a. kto   *(est) kto?
       Who is   who
    b. kto   (*est) professor?
       Who is   professor
    c. kto   (*est) Ivan
       Who is   Ivan

Bošković proposes that the copula is inserted in PF to avoid the ban on homophonous sequences of *wh*-phrases. Thanks to an anonymous reviewer for pointing out these facts to me.

6. Again it is not clear what that requirement is. It could be the requirement to have a subject (EPP) or the need for T to check its nominal D-feature by being paired with a nominal category in its Spec.

7. Under various analyses the relation between the complementizer system and finiteness is captured either through selection with C selecting T or by assuming that C contains T or some feature related to T (Pesetsky and Torrego 2001). Under Grimshaw's extended projection account this is captured by restriction on the F value of functional and lexical categories.

8. Verbless sentences, which have a present-tense interpretation, can contain temporal adverbs (Eisele 1988). If temporal adverbs must be anchored to a syntactically projected tense node, then this is additional evidence for a tense projection (Benmamoun 2000).

9. See Jelinek 1981 for Arabic, Doron 1986 for Hebrew, and Carnie 1995 for Irish.

10. Sentential negation in Moroccan Arabic can surface as a "discontinuous" morpheme. See section 5.4.2 for further discussion.

11. One could argue that the reason the negative and null copula do not raise past the subject is because in the present tense the verb does not need to raise to tense, as will be argued below. Therefore, both the negative and the copula remain below the subject. However, verbs (and other predicates) in present-tense sentences merge with negation and can precede the subject, indicating that the merger with negation can occur independently of movement to tense (Benmamoun 2000). For example, in (i) both the VS and SV orders are possible:

(i) a. ʕumar ma-ta-asp-yxdəm-š hna   MA
       Omar NEG-work-NEG   here
       'Omar does not work here.'
    b. ma-ta-asp-yxdəm-š ʕumar hna
       NEG-work-NEG   Omar here
       'Omar does not work here.'

12. One reviewer suggested that the null copula could merge with the predicate and the whole complex may or may not move to negation. The problem with this alternative is that the incorporation of the null copula and the predicate is not independently motivated. Moreover, this merger would have to be restricted to the null copula because all the overt copulas do not merge with the predicate.

13. Notice that we cannot appeal to incorporation whereby the Case of the predicate in the present tense is satisfied through some putative incorporation with a putative null copula. The reason this is not viable is because in the instances where Case has been argued to be satisfied through incorporation, namely noun incorporation discussed in Baker 1988, the incorporated noun does not display the Case-related morphology that it usually displays when it is not incorporated. In Standard Arabic, the predicate does display default nominative Case and other

inflectional markers, which raises doubt about a possible incorporation account. Moreover, the predicate can undergo movement as shown in (10), which is also challenging for an incorporation alternative.

14. However, this is by no means the consensus about VSO orders. For Arabic, Aoun, Benmamoun, and Sportiche (1994, 1999) and Benmamoun (2000) argue that the subject is at least in TP overtly with the verb being in a higher position in VSO order. See McCloskey 1996 for a detailed discussion of the syntax of subjects, including in VSO languages.

15. The main reason the use of verbal categorial features has been abandoned is the uncertainty about whether verb movement is part of narrow syntax (Chomsky 2001). D-features have been retained under some analyses, however.

16. In fact, the copula must be absent, which can be due to economy of projection (see below).

17. Of course, the question remains as to why the verb raises and merges with negation in (35a). The question is actually much broader because nonverbal predicates also can raise and merge with negation, as is evident from (22b).

18. This conflicts with analyses that posit such a category between T and the nonverbal predicate. For example, Bowers (1993) allows it in the context of all predicates.

19. The vowel melodies do not carry temporal information. In fact, it is not even clear that they carry aspectual information. Verbs in the past tense, for example, vary in their vocalic melodies:

(i) a. kataba   SA
      wrote.3MS
      'He wrote.'
   b. laʕiba
      played-3MS
      'He played.'
   c. kabura
      grew.3MS
      'It grew bigger.'

Moreover, agreement does not carry tense. Thus, the negative *laysa* in Standard Arabic has the same agreement affixation pattern as the past tense. Compare the agreement pattern on the verb in (ii) and the negative in (iii).

(ii) a. katab-tu   SA
      wrote.1s
      'I wrote.'
   b. katab-ta
      wrote.2MS
      'You wrote.'

(iii) a. las-tu   SA
       neg-1s
       'Not I.'
    b. las-ta
       neg-2MS
       'Not you.'

20. Another issue relevant to word order is how the nominal feature is checked. Following Alexiadou and Anagnostopoulou 1998, Benmamoun 2000 argues that either agreement on the verb in T or the subject can license/check the nominal feature of T.

21. See also Berman and Grossu 1976; Rapopport 1987; Rothstein 1995; Shlonsky 1997; Greenberg 2002; Falk 2004. The consensus is that the pronominal in (51) is not a subject pronoun but a realization of features of the I/T.

22. Arabic too has a pronominal that surfaces in identificational but not predicational copular constructions. This pronoun also agrees in person and gender only. See Eid 1991 for an extensive discussion of this pronoun and its distribution.

References

Alexiadou, A., and Anagnostopoulou, E. 1998. Parametrizing AGR: Word Order, V-Movement and EPP-Checking. *Natural Language and Linguistic Theory* 16:491–539.

Aoun, J., Benmamoun, E., and Sportiche, D. 1994. Agreement and Conjunction in Some Varieties of Arabic. *Linguistic Inquiry* 25:195–220.

Aoun, J., Benmamoun, E., and Sportiche, D. 1999. Further Remarks on First Conjunct Agreement. *Linguistic Inquiry* 30:669–681.

Ayoub, Georgine. 1981. *Structure de la Phrase en Arabe Standard.* Doctoral dissertation, Université de Paris VII.

Baker, Mark. 2003. *Lexical Categories: Verbs, Nouns, and Adjectives.* Cambridge: Cambridge University Press.

Bakir, Murtadha. 1979. *Aspects of Clause Structure in Arabic.* Doctoral dissertation, Indiana University.

Benmamoun, Elabbas. 1992. *Inflectional and Functional Morphology: Problems of Projection, Representation and Derivation.* Doctoral dissertation, University of Southern California, Los Angeles.

Benmamoun, Elabbas. 2000. *The Feature Structure of Functional Categories: A Comparative Study of Arabic Dialects.* Oxford: Oxford University Press.

Berman, Ruth, and Alexander Grosu. 1976. Aspect of the Copula in Modern Hebrew. In Peter Cole, ed., *Studies in Modern Hebrew Syntax and Semantics.* Amsterdam: North Holland.

Bobaljik, Jonathan. 1994. What Does Adjacency Do? MITWPL 22.

Bošković, Željko. 2001. *On the Nature of the Syntax-Phonology Interface: Cliticization and Related Phenomena.* Amsterdam: North Holland.

Bowers, John. 1993. The Syntax of Predication. *Linguistic Inquiry* 24:591–656.

Carnie, Andrew. 1995. Non-Verbal Predication and Head-Movement. Doctoral dissertation, MIT.

Chomsky, Noam. 1995. *The Minimalist Program.* Cambridge, Mass.: MIT Press.

Chomsky, Noam. 2000. Minimalist Inquires: The Framework. In Roger Martin, David Michaels, and Juan Uriagereka, eds., *Step by Step: Essays on Minimalist Syntax in Honor of Howard Lasnik*, 89–155. Cambridge, Mass.: MIT Press.

Chomsky, Noam. 2001. Derivation by Phase. In Michael Kenstowicz, ed., *Ken Hale: A Life in Language*, 1–52. Cambridge, Mass.: MIT Press.

Cinque, Guglielmo. 1999. *Adverbs and Functional Heads*. Oxford: Oxford University Press.

Déchaine, Rose-Marie. 1993. *Predicates across Categories*. Doctoral dissertation, University of Massachusetts, Amherst.

Doron, Edith. 1986. The Pronominal "Copula" as Agreement Clitic. In H. Borer, ed., *Syntax of Pronominal Clitics*, 313–332. New York: Academic Press.

Eid, Mushira. 1983. The Copula Function of Pronouns. *Lingua* 59:197–207.

Eid, Mushira. 1991. Verbless Sentences in Arabic and Hebrew. In Bernard Comrie and Mushira Eid, eds., *Perspectives on Arabic Linguistics*, vol. 3, 31–61. Amsterdam: John Benjamins.

Eisele, John. 1988. *The Syntax and Semantics of Tense, Aspect, and Time Reference in Cairene Arabic*. Doctoral dissertation, University of Chicago.

Falk, Yehuda. 2004. The Hebrew Present-Tense Copula as a Mixed Category. Unpublished ms., Hebrew University of Jerusalem.

Fassi Fehri, Abdelkader. 1993. *Issues in the Structure of Arabic Clauses and Words*. Dordrecht: Kluwer.

Greenberg, Yael. 2002. The Manifestation of Genericity in the Tense Aspect System of Hebrew Nominal Sentences. In J. Ouhalla and U. Shlonsky, eds., *Themes in Arabic and Hebrew Syntax*, 267–298. Dordrecht: Kluwer.

Grimshaw, Jane. 1991. Extended Projections. Unpublished ms., Rutgers University.

Heggie, Lorie. 1988. *The Syntax of Copular Structures*. Doctoral dissertation, USC, Los Angeles.

Jelinek, Eloise. 1981. *On Defining Categories: Aux and Predicate in Colloquial Arabic*. Doctoral dissertation, University of Arizona.

Massam, Diane. 2000. VSP and VOS: Aspects of Niuean Word Order. In A. Carnie and E. Guilfoyle, eds., *The Syntax of Verb Initial Languages*, 97–116. Oxford: Oxford University Press.

McCloskey, James. 1996. Subjects and Subject Positions. In R. Borsley and I. Roberts, eds., *The Syntax of the Celtic Languages*. Cambridge: Cambridge University Press.

Moutaouakil, Ahmed. 1987. *min qaDaayaa r-raabiT fii l-lugha l-'arabiyya*. 'ocaadh, Casablanca, Morocco.

Ouhalla, Jamal. 1993. Negation, Focus and Tense: The Arabic maa and laa. *Rivista di Linguistica* 5(2):275–300.

Pesetsky, D., and Torrego, E. 2001. T-to-C Movement: Causes and Consequences. In M. Kenstowicz, ed., *Ken Hale: A Life in Language*, 355–426. Cambridge, Mass.: MIT Press.

Pollock, Jean-Yves. 1989. Verb Movement, UG and the Structure of IP. *Linguistic Inquiry* 20:365–424.

Rapoport, Tova. 1987. *Copular, Nominal, and Small Clauses: A Study of Israeli Hebrew*. Doctoral dissertation, MIT.

Ritter, Elizabeth. 1995. On the Syntactic Category of Pronouns and Agreement. *Natural Language and Linguistic Theory* 13:405–443.

Rizzi, Luigi. 1990. *Relativized Minimality*. Cambridge, Mass.: MIT Press.

Rothstein, Susan. 1995. Small Clauses and Copular Constructions. *Syntax and Semantics* 28:27–48.

Shlonsky, Ur. 1992. Resumptive Pronouns as Last Resort. *Linguistic Inquiry* 23:443–468.

Shlonsky, Ur. 1997. *Clause Structure and Word Order in Hebrew and Arabic: An Essay in Comparative Semitic Syntax*. Oxford: Oxford University Press.

6 On Phases

Noam Chomsky

I would like to review some recent and ongoing work in the general framework of the so-called Minimalist Program (MP), which addresses an array of concerns that are a core part of the traditional study of language, assuming a different form within the biolinguistic perspective that began to take shape fifty years ago. I will presuppose familiarity with recent publications, while recalling some conclusions that seem pertinent to proceeding along lines they suggest. One major stimulus to the development of the MP was a personal letter by Jean-Roger Vergnaud in 1977, unpublished until recently but famous in the field, which initiated very extensive and productive inquiries that remain central to the study of language to the present, including the considerations here.[1]

The traditional concerns have to do with the properties that are specific to human language, that is, to the "faculty of language" FL. To borrow Jespersen's formulation eighty years ago, the goal is to unearth "the great principles underlying the grammars of all languages" with the goal of "gaining a deeper insight into the innermost nature of human language and of human thought." The biolinguistic perspective views FL as an "organ of the body," one of many subcomponents of an organism that interact in its normal life. From this perspective, the closest approximation to the informal notion "language" is a state of FL, an I-language. UG is the theory of the initial state of FL, virtually shared; in terms of traditional concerns, the theory of the distinguishing features of human language.

For any such system, we can identify three factors that enter into its growth and development: (1) external data, (2) genetic endowment (for language, the topic of UG), and (3) principles of structural architecture and developmental constraints that are not specific to the organ under investigation, and may be organism-independent. Factor (2) interprets data as linguistic experience, not a trivial matter; it constructs part of what ethologists called the organism's *Umwelt*.[2] And it sets the general course of growth and development within a narrow range. The particular path is determined by experience (among other factors that we can ignore here). The questions arise in principle for any organic system, and have been raised since the early days of modern biology. The only general questions concerning them have to do with feasibility, not legitimacy.

These questions arose in the early days of the biolinguistic perspective, which converged quickly with efforts to develop generative grammar, rooted in different concerns. The matter was brought up in print in the course of critical discussion of prevailing assumptions in the "behavioral sciences": basically, the belief that language, like all behavior, is shaped by association, conditioning, and simple induction, along with "analogy," and perhaps also "general learning procedures" of some unspecified sort. While such notions were understandable "in the context of eighteenth century struggles for scientific naturalism, . . . there is surely no reason today for taking seriously a position that attributes a complex human achievement entirely to months (or at most years) of experience, rather than to millions of years of evolution or to principles of neural organization that may be more deeply grounded in physical law," a stand that would furthermore take humans to be "unique among animals."[3] The three factors, essentially. The issues were not much discussed in public, partly because the third factor was at the remote horizons of inquiry (as commonly in other domains), but also because of the much more urgent concern of justifying even the legitimacy of the generative grammar/biolinguistic amalgam as a way of studying language at a time when even the second factor was considered highly contentious or worse, and it was commonly assumed that languages can "differ from each other without limit and in unpredictable ways,"[4] or could vary at most within limited constraints on patterns and structures.

UG is said to meet the condition of "explanatory adequacy" insofar as it is a true theory of the genetic endowment, and thus, under appropriate idealizations, maps experience to attained I-languages—abstracting here from effects of the third factor. We can regard an explanation of some property of language as *principled*, to the extent that current understanding now reaches, insofar as it can be reduced to the third factor and to conditions that language must meet to be usable at all—specifically, conditions coded in UG that are imposed by organism-internal systems with which FL interacts. Insofar as properties of I-languages can be given a principled explanation, in this sense, we move to a deeper level of explanation, beyond explanatory adequacy.

Though these terms are not used in other domains—say, bee communication, or the mammalian visual system—investigation adopts effectively the same categories. In the study of language as in other domains, it is uncontroversial that search for explanatory adequacy not only does not await achievement of descriptive adequacy, but rather contributes to that goal and even to discovery of the nature of the task, by clarifying the true nature of the object of inquiry (I-language) and of descriptive adequacy. It is no less a truism that the same relation holds between both inquiries and the search for principled explanation.

Concern for principled explanation is often framed in methodological terms as the attempt to keep to simple taxonomies or generative systems without excessive redundancy and other unattractive properties. Sometimes methodological considerations, largely intuitive, can be reframed within the biolinguistic perspective as empirical hypotheses that can be investigated in other domains as well. For computational systems such as language, we naturally hope to discover concepts of computational efficiency that carry us beyond explanatory adequacy, and to investigate how these relate to principles of a more general character that may hold in other domains and for other organisms, and may have deeper explanations.

For reasons that need not be reviewed,[5] the crystallization of the principles-and-parameters (P&P) program removed some serious conceptual barriers to exploring the possibility of principled explanation. Since that time, it has been the subject of extensive inquiry, from various approaches, with sufficient progress and convergence, many researchers have felt, to identify a reasonably integrated subdiscipline that focuses on these issues, the minimalist program MP.[6]

Adopting the P&P framework, I will assume that one element of parameter-setting is assembly of features into lexical items (LIs), which we can take to be atoms for further computation and the locus of parameters, sweeping many complicated and important questions under the rug.

It has been a useful guide for research to consider an extremely far-reaching thesis—the "strong minimalist thesis" SMT—which holds that language is an optimal solution to interface conditions that FL must satisfy; that is, language is an optimal way to link sound and meaning, where these notions are given a technical sense in terms of the interface systems that enter into the use and interpretation of expressions generated by an I-language. If SMT held fully, which no one expects, UG would be restricted to properties imposed by interface conditions. A primary task of the MP is to clarify the notions that enter into SMT and to determine how closely the ideal can be approached. Any departure from SMT—any postulation of descriptive technology that cannot be given a principled explanation—merits close examination, to see if it is really justified. The more fully principled explanation can be achieved, the better we understand the nature of FL; and the better we can formulate, perhaps even constructively investigate, the problem of how FL evolved, apparently appearing quite recently in a small breeding group of which all contemporary humans are descendants, part of a "great leap forward" in human intellectual and moral faculties, as some paleoanthropologists term this development. Evidently, inquiry into evolutionary origins becomes more feasible the less special structure is attributed to UG: that is, the more we can proceed beyond explanatory adequacy.[7]

It is hardly necessary to add that the conditions that enter into principled explanation, in this sense, are only partially understood: we have to learn about the conditions that set the problem in the course of trying to solve it. The research task is

interactive: to clarify the nature of the interfaces and optimal computational principles through investigation of how language satisfies the conditions they impose—
optimally, insofar as SMT holds. This familiar feature of empirical inquiry has long
been taken for granted in the study of the sensorimotor interface (SM). Inquiry into
acoustic and articulatory phonetics takes cues from what has been learned about
phonological features and other such properties in I-language research and seeks
SM correlates, and any discoveries then feed back to refine I-language inquiry. The
same should hold, no less uncontroversially, at the semantic/conceptual-intentional
interface (C-I). And it should also hold for third factor properties. We do not know
a priori, in more than general terms, what are the right ways to optimize, say, neural
networks; empirical inquiry into such matters is interactive in the same ways.

A further question is whether the contribution of the two interfaces to principled
explanation is symmetrical. It is well known that language is in many ways "poorly
designed" for communicative efficiency: apart from such ubiquitous phenomena
as ambiguity, garden paths, and so on, one core property of languages—recursive
embedding with nested dependencies—leads to exponential memory growth and
therefore has to be avoided in language use, giving it something of the character of
paratactic constructions. Languages have various devices to overcome the problems.[8] These devices might be close to or even beyond the SM interface. Some of
them are used to overcome prosodic difficulties, as in familiar examples of the "house
that Jack built" variety. Others yield "rearrangements" near the SM interface that
violate crossing constraints and have other properties that indicate that they are
not operations of the narrow syntax. PP-extraposition is a likely case, to which we
return.[9]

It might be, then, that there is a basic asymmetry in the contribution to "language
design" of the two interface systems: the primary contribution to the structure of
FL may be optimization of mapping to the C-I interface. Such ideas have the flavor
of traditional conceptions of language as in essence a mode of expression of thought,
a notion restated by leading biologists as the proposal that language evolved primarily as a means of "development of abstract or productive thinking" and "in sym-
bolizing, in evoking cognitive images" and "mental creation of possible worlds" for
thought and planning, with communicative needs a secondary factor in language
evolution.[10] If these speculations are on the right track, we would expect to find
that conditions imposed by the C-I interface enter into principled explanation in a
crucial way, while mapping to the SM interface is an ancillary process. If so, we
might discover that SMT is satisfied by phonological systems that violate otherwise
valid principles of computational efficiency, while doing the best they can to satisfy
the problem they face: to map to the SM interface syntactic objects generated by
computations that are "well designed" to satisfy C-I conditions. There is, I think,
empirical evidence that something like that might be correct. But, again, the ques-

tions can only be answered by interactive research in many dimensions. Such questions are worth keeping in mind, even though they are at the periphery of current empirical study.

Suppose we assume SMT to be true, and see how far we can go towards accommodating properties of language, identifying places in the argument where assumptions are introduced that require independent research, and where the quest fails, for now at least.

In the early 1990s, Howard Lasnik and I sketched our best understanding of what UG might be, adopting the familiar EST/Y-model, within the P&P framework (Chomsky and Lasnik 1993). A great deal of work since then, including ours, has been devoted to investigating stipulated components of that model to determine whether the phenomena for which they were designed could be derived by keeping more closely to SMT—or perhaps even better, with richer empirical coverage.

Two linguistic levels are assumed to be indispensable (though it is more than truism): the interface levels that are accessible to SM and C-I. These language-external though organism-internal systems have their own properties, which for present purposes we can assume to be independent of language, suppressing important questions that merit independent inquiry. The EST/Y-model postulated three additional internal levels, each with specific properties: d-structure, s-structure, and LF.[11] Furthermore, each of the five postulated levels is generated by cyclic/compositional operations, which are highly redundant, covering much the same ground. That sharp departure from SMT raised the question whether all of this technology can be reduced to a single cycle, dispensing with all internal levels. An even better result would be that the three internal levels are not only dispensable, but literally unformulable. That seems possible, if we examine more closely the generative procedure that constructs interface representations. I will briefly review (and somewhat restate) the line of argument in earlier papers.

As has long been recognized, the most elementary property of language—and an unusual one in the biological world—is that it is a system of discrete infinity consisting of hierarchically organized objects.[12] The simplest such system is based on an operation that takes *n* syntactic objects (SOs) already formed, and constructs from them a new SO. Call the operation *Merge*. Unbounded Merge or some equivalent (or more complex variant) is unavoidable in a system of hierarchic discrete infinity, so we can assume that it "comes free," in the present context.

Of course, the operation does not "come free" in human evolution. Rather, its emergence was a crucial event, so far without any explanation. Suppose that some ancestor, perhaps about 60,000 years ago, underwent a slight mutation rewiring the brain, yielding unbounded Merge. Then he or she would at once have had available an infinite array of structured expressions for use in thought (planning, interpretation, etc.), gaining selectional advantages transmitted to offspring, capacities that came to dominate, yielding the dramatic and rather sudden changes found in the archeological record. Speculation, of course, as are all such stories, but about the simplest one imaginable, consistent with what little is known, and presupposed in some form (often tacitly) in all speculations about the matter. Since the integration of language precursors into FL together with innovation of unbounded Merge would have been sudden (in evolutionary time), effects of path-dependent evolution and other complexities that underlie the logic of Jacobian "bricolage" might be secondary phenomena, and evolution to a form of FL approaching SMT, not too surprising.

Though study of the evolution of language is in its infancy,[13] consideration of the nature of the problem can be of some help in thinking about the core problems of study of language. It is hardly controversial that FL is a common human possession apart from pathology, to an approximation so close that we can ignore variation. Evidently, study of evolution of language is not concerned with developments since the "great leap forward" and the trek from Africa: say, with the large-scale effects of the Norman Conquest on English. It should be equally uncontroversial that investigation of explanatory adequacy and beyond will try to abstract from such developments to the extent that understanding permits, thus putting to the side many topics of great interest to anyone concerned with language.[14]

Returning to SMT, arguably restriction of computational resources limits n for Merge to two, as Luigi Rizzi suggests, thus yielding the "unambiguous paths" structure postulated by Kayne (1981). There are other conditions that conspire to this conclusion: minimal search within a probe-goal framework, for example. Perhaps also interface conditions: at the SM interface, requirements of linearization, perhaps along the lines of Kayne's LCA; at the C-I interface, conditions of predicate-argument structure and others. Let us assume the limitation to be accurate, at least sufficiently so that we can take it as a good first approximation.

A natural requirement for efficient computation is a "no-tampering condition" (NTC): Merge of X and Y leaves the two SOs unchanged. If so, then Merge of X and Y can be taken to yield the set {X, Y}, the simplest possibility worth considering. Merge cannot break up X or Y, or add new features to them. Therefore Merge is invariably "to the edge" and we also try to establish the "inclusiveness principle," dispensing with bar levels, traces, indices, and similar descriptive technology introduced in the course of derivation of an expression. It seems that this desideratum of efficient computation can also be met within narrow syntax at least, with apparent departures that have a principled explanation; and that it sometimes even yields superior empirical results, in one well-studied case, with regard to reconstruction effects. There is an ample literature on these matters, and I will assume it to be more less on the right track. Note that SMT might be satisfied even where NTC is violated—*if* the violation has a principled explanation in terms of interface conditions (or perhaps some other factor, not considered here). The logic is the same as in the case of the phonological component, already mentioned.

A more complex alternative, consistent with NTC, is that Merge forms the pair $\langle X, Y \rangle$. The underlying issue is whether linear order plays a role in narrow syntax and mapping to C-I, or whether it is restricted to the phonological component, motivated by interface conditions at SM. The latter assumption has guided a good deal of research since Reinhart 1979, and while the issue is far from settled, there seems to me good reason to suppose that the simpler assumption can be sustained: that order does not enter into the generation of the C-I interface, and that syntactic determinants of order fall within the phonological component.

Suppose that a language has the simplest possible lexicon: just one LI, call it "one." Application of Merge to the LI yields{one}, call it "two" Application of Merge to{one}yields{one, {one}}, call it "three." And so on. In effect, Merge applied in this manner yields the successor function. It is straightforward to define addition in terms of Merge(X, Y), and in familiar ways, the rest of arithmetic. The emergence of the arithmetical capacity has been puzzling ever since Alfred Russell Wallace, the co-founder of modern evolutionary theory, observed that the "gigantic development of the mathematical capacity is wholly unexplained by the theory of natural selection, and must be due to some altogether distinct cause," if only because it remained unused. It may, then, have been a side product of some other evolved capacity (not Wallace's conclusion), and it has often been speculated that it may be abstracted from FL by reducing the latter to its bare minimum. Reduction to a single-membered lexicon is a simple way to yield this consequence.[15]

For an LI to be able to enter into a computation, merging with some SO, it must have some property permitting this operation. A property of an LI is called a *feature*, so an LI has a feature that permits it to be merged. Call this the *edge feature* (EF) of the LI. If an LI lacks EF, it can only be a full expression in itself; an interjection. When merged with a syntactic object SO, LI forms {LI, SO}; SO is its *complement*. The fact that Merge iterates without limit is a property at least of LIs—and optimally, only of LIs, as I will assume. EF articulates the fact that Merge is unbounded, that language is a recursive infinite system of a particular kind. What kind? That depends on further specification of EF, which, like any other feature of UG—say, sonorant—has to be defined. Its definition, to which we return, is an empirical hypothesis about the subcategory of recursive infinite systems that language constitutes.

Reliance on iterable Merge as the sole computational operation of narrow syntax eliminates, as unformulable, the notions d- and s-structure, and three of the compositional operations of EST: those that form d-structure and map it to s-structure, and then on to LF. It also revives, in far more elementary terms, the notion of generalized transformation of the earliest work in generative grammar in the 1950s. A great deal of descriptive capacity is lost by this optimal assumption, including all processes and principles associated with d- and s-structure, bar-level distinctions in phrase structure (N versus N', etc.), and much else. Since this descriptive technology has been widely and productively used, it is a significant empirical task to show that it is dispensable—to show, that is, that it was misconceived, and should be abandoned. I will assume that success in this endeavor has been sufficient so that it is reasonable to assume it for our purposes here.

Suppose that X and Y are merged (for expository purposes, think of Y as merged to X). Either Y is not part of X (*external Merge*, EM) or Y is part of X (*internal Merge*, IM).[16] In both cases, Merge yields {X, Y}. IM yields two *copies* of Y in {X, Y}, one external to X, one within X.[17] IM is the operation *Move* under the "copy theory of movement," which is the null hypothesis in this framework, required by strict adherence to the NTC. Unless there is some stipulation to the contrary, which would require sufficient empirical evidence, both kinds of Merge are available for FL and IM creates copies.

If the means of language are fully exploited by the interface systems, in accord with a reasonable interpretation of SMT, then we would expect the two types of Merge to have different effects at the interfaces. At the phonetic interface, they obviously do; IM yields the ubiquitous displacement phenomenon. At the semantic interface, the two types of Merge correlate well with the duality of semantics that has been studied within generative grammar for almost forty years, at first in terms of "deep and surface structure interpretation" (and of course with much earlier roots). To a large extent, EM yields generalized argument structure (θ-roles, the "cartographic" hierarchies,[18] and similar properties); and IM yields discourse-related properties such as old information and specificity, along with scopal effects. The correlation is reasonably close, and perhaps would be found to be perfect if we understood enough—an important research topic.

The two available types of Merge have been treated very differently since the early days of modern generative grammar. But that is a historical residue; we have to ask whether it is accurate. It has always been presupposed without comment that EM comes free: no one has postulated an "EPP property" for EM or stipulated that it satisfies the NTC. IM, in contrast, has been regarded (by me, in particular) as a problematic operation, an "imperfection" of language that has to be postulated as an unexplained property of UG unless it can be motivated in some principled way. The displacement property of natural language is simply a fact: expressions are commonly pronounced in one place and interpreted in others as well. There have been many ideas as to how to capture that fact, transformational operations being one. My own view had always been that the alternatives might turn out to be close to notational variants, and that any decision among them would have to be teased out by subtle empirical evidence. A few years ago, it became clear that this is a misunderstanding. IM (= Move, with the "copy theory") is as free as EM; it can only be blocked by stipulation. The *absence* of the operation would be an imperfection that has to be explained, not its use in deriving expressions. It follows that any alternative device to deal with the displacement property and the duality of semantics requires double stipulation: to ban IM, and to justify the new device. The proposal faces a serious empirical burden of proof, unlike the core (and over time, much refined) principle of transformational grammar.

We thus expect language to use IM rather than other mechanisms that can be devised to express semantic properties apart from generalized argument structure; largely true, it appears, perhaps better than that. Note that this line of argument is an adaptation to the C-I interface of the reasoning familiar at the SM interface, already discussed. Here too, we may regard these observations as an empirical hypothesis about the nature of the C-I system, to be investigated in language-independent terms. The hypothesis is that C-I incorporates a dual semantics, with generalized argument structure as one component, the other being discourse-related and scopal properties. Language seeks to satisfy the duality in the optimal way, EM serving one function and IM the other, avoiding additional means to express these properties.

Each SO generated enters into further computations. Some information about the SO is relevant to these computations. In the best case, a single designated element should contain all the relevant information: the *label* (the item "projected" in X′-theories; the *locus* in the label-free system of Collins 2002). The label selects and is selected in EM, and is the *probe* that seeks a *goal* for operations internal to the SO: Agree or IM. A natural interpretation of the notion "edge" can capture some of the properties of "tucking in" in the sense of Richards 2001, taking the "edge" to be the position as close as possible to the probe—a literal violation of NTC, but arguably a principled one, hence consistent with SMT.

We therefore have two syntactic relations: (A) set-membership, based on Merge, and (B) probe-goal. Assuming composition of relations, (A) yields the notions *term-of* and *dominate*. These seem to be the minimal assumptions about the available relations. If we add "sister-of," then composition will yield c-command and identity (the latter presumably available independently). Whether c-command plays a role within the computation to the C-I interface is an open question. I know of no clear evidence that it does, so will keep to the relations that seem unavoidable, set membership and probe-goal.

It has always been assumed that c-command relations function in Binding Theory BT, which would mean, if the above is correct, that BT is at the outer edge of the C-I interface (as suggested, in essence, in Chomsky and Lasnik 1993). It is not entirely clear, however, that c-command is actually required here, in addition to set-membership and probe-goal. Condition (C) could be formulated as a probe-goal relation, taking the c-commanding pronoun X to be the label of {X, SO}, hence a probe (along lines to which we turn below, though with complications and consequences I will put aside here). As for Condition (A), suppose we adopt the framework of Reuland (2001). Then the most important case is bare subject-oriented reflexives R that satisfy locality conditions, and are thus plausibly to be understood as within the I-language. In a structure of the form {SPEC, {H, ...R...}}, with R c-commanded and bound by SPEC, R could be taken to be the goal probed by H, and thus only indirectly bound by SPEC; hence a case of Agree, not c-command. The crucial empirical test is a structure of the form [H...XP...R], where H and XP agree, XP does not c-command R, and R is in the minimal search domain of the probe H; a sentence of the basic form (1):

(1) It became [[introduced a man] for R (self)]

Here "a man" does not c-command R, but both "a man" and R are goals of the probe that heads the construction. Reuland points out[19] that in an interesting range of such cases the reflexive must have the bare form R, meaning it is in an agreement (probe-goal) relation with H, though not c-commanded by its antecedent XP. If so, then the core case of Condition (A) does not involve c-command, but rather Agree. C-command may turn not to be an operative relation for Condition (A), which would support the view that the only relations are the inescapable ones: set-membership and probe-goal.

I will take over here the probe-goal framework of earlier work, including Ken Hiraiwa's theory of Multiple-Agree.[20] The probe agrees with goals in its domain as far as a goal with no unvalued features, which blocks further search (intervention). In the simplest case of two-membered probe-goal match (say [φ-features]-N), intrinsic features of the goal value those of the probe, and also value the structural Case feature of the goal (in a manner determined by the probe). Generalizing to Multiple-Agree (e.g., probe-[participle sequence]-N), features of the goal (including the structural Case, sometimes visible as in Icelandic) value all matched elements (probe, participles), and the option of raising the goal may or may not be exercised[21]—and if exercised will be all the way to the probe, matters to which we return.

As noted, iterated Merge incorporates the effects of three of the EST/Y-model compositional cycles, while eliminating d- and s-structure. Still unaccounted for are the cyclic/compositional mappings to the phonetic and semantic interfaces. These too are incorporated, and the final internal level LF is eliminated, if at various stages of computation there are Transfer operations: one hands the SO already constructed to the phonological component, which maps it to the SM interface ("Spell-Out"); the other hands SO to the semantic component, which maps it to the C-I interface. Call these SOs *phases*. Thus SMT entails that computation of expressions must be restricted to a single cyclic/compositional process with phases. In the best case, the phases will be the same for both Transfer operations. To my knowledge, there is no compelling evidence to the contrary.[22] Let us assume, then, that the best-case conclusion can be sustained. It is also natural to expect that along with Transfer, all other operations will also apply at the phase level, as determined by the label/probe. That implies that IM should be driven only by phase heads. Empirical evidence to which we return supports this conclusion.

For minimal computation, as soon as the information is transferred it will be forgotten, not accessed in subsequent stages of derivation: the computation will not have to look back at earlier phases as it proceeds, and cyclicity is preserved in a very strong sense.[23] Working that out, we try to formulate a *phase-impenetrability condition* PIC, conforming as closely as possible to SMT. I will again assume that the literature about this is more or less on target (including Chomsky 2001, 2004, and Nissenbaum 2000), though with modifications.[24]

Note that for narrow syntax, probe into an earlier phase will almost always be blocked by intervention effects. One illustration to the contrary is agreement into a lower phase without intervention in experiencer constructions in which the subject is raised (voiding the intervention effect) and agreement holds with the nominative object of the lower phase (Icelandic).[25] It may be, then, that PIC holds only for the mappings to the interface, with the effects for narrow syntax automatic.

The next question is: What are the phases? I will pursue the suggestion in Chomsky 2004 that they are CP and v*P, where C is shorthand for the region that Rizzi (1997) calls the "left periphery," possibly involving feature spread from fewer functional heads (maybe only one); and v* is the functional head associated with full argument structure, transitive and experiencer constructions, and is one of several choices for v, which may furthermore be the element determining that the selected *root* is verbal, along lines discussed by Marantz (1997). Similarities between CP and DP suggest that DP too may be a phase, possibilities explored by Svenonius (2004) and Hiraiwa (2005) among others. I will put that aside here, and keep to the clausal skeleton—avoiding much structure here as well.

It seems problematic for T to fail to define a phase boundary along with C, since on the surface it seems to be T, not C, that is the locus of the φ-features that are involved in the nominative-agreement system, and raising of the external argument subject or unaccusative/passive object to Spec-T. There is, however, antecedent reason to suspect otherwise, confirmed (as we will see) by empirical phenomena. The antecedent reason is that for T, φ-features and Tense appear to be derivative, not inherent: basic tense and also tenselike properties (e.g., irrealis) are determined by C (in which they are inherent: "John left" is past tense whether or not it is embedded) or by the selecting V (also inherent) or perhaps even broader context. In the lexicon, T lacks these features. T manifests the basic tense features if and only if it is selected by C (default agreement aside); if not, it is a raising (or ECM) infinitival, lacking φ-features and basic tense. So it makes sense to assume that Agree and Tense features are inherited from C, the phase head.[26] If C-T agrees with the goal DP, the latter can remain in situ under long-distance Agree, with all uninterpretable features valued; or it can raise as far as Spec-T, at which point it is inactivated, with all features valued, and cannot raise further to Spec-C.[27] We thus derive the A-A' distinction.

There is ample evidence that the A-A' distinction exists.[28] Let's assume it therefore to be a real property of I-language. The device of inheritance establishes the distinction in a simple way, perhaps the simplest way. The mechanism is a narrow violation of NTC. The usual question therefore arises: does it violate SMT? If it does, then the device belongs to UG (perhaps parametrized), lacking a principled explanation. But the crucial role it plays at the C-I interface suggests the usual direction to determine whether it is consistent with SMT though violating NTC. If the C-I interface requires this distinction,[29] then SMT will be satisfied by an optimal device to establish it that violates NTC, and inheritance of features of C by the LI selected by C (namely T) may meet that condition. If so, the violation of NTC still satisfies SMT.

When φ-features appear morphologically at T without tense (or in participles, etc.), they should therefore be regarded as just a morphological effect of agreement, without significance in the syntactic computation.[30] The relative inability of TP to be moved or to appear in isolation without C gives some further reason to suspect that TP only has phaselike characteristics when selected by C, hence derivatively from C, though this is not a criterial property.[31] We turn later to further evidence for these assumptions.

Let's return first to the properties of EF. Suppose that EF permits free Merge to the edge, indefinitely. That yields a certain subcategory of recursive systems: with embedding, a pervasive feature of human language.[32] If an LI α enters a derivation and its EF is not satisfied, the resulting expression will often crash, but not always; say, the expression "No." If EF is minimally satisfied for α, then α has a complement, to which C-I will assign some interpretation; a theta role in some configurations. The predicate-internal subject hypothesis asserts that C-I will also assign a theta role to second EM to v*, that is, to its specifier, the external argument EA. If only phase heads trigger operations (as I will assume), then IM will satisfy EF only for phase heads; apparent exceptions, such as raising to Spec-T, are derivative, via inheritance. Merge can apply freely, yielding expressions interpreted at the interface in many different kinds of ways. They are sometimes called "deviant," but that is only an informal notion. Expressions that are unintelligible at the SM interface may satisfy the most stringent C-I conditions, and conversely. And expressions that are "deviant" are not only often quite normal but even the best way to express some thought; metaphors, to take a standard example, or such evocative expressions as Veblen's "perform leisure." That includes even expressions that crash, often used as literary devices and in informal discourse, with a precise and felicitous interpretation at the interfaces. The only empirical requirement is that SM and C-I assign the interpretations that the expression actually has, including many varieties of "deviance."[33]

The label of an SO must be identifiable with minimal search, by some simple algorithm. Two obvious proposals, carried over from X-bar-theoretic approaches, are (2) and (3):

(2) In {H, α}, H an LI, H is the label.

(3) If α is internally merged to β, forming {α, β} then the label of β is the label of {α, β}.

These principles suffice for virtually every case.[34] Sometimes, however, they conflict. One example is the first step of every derivation, when two LIs merge, so that by (2), either may project. That seems unproblematic, though one of the choices may yield some form of deviance. A more interesting case arises when LI α is internally merged to non-LI β. In this case, (2) yields the conclusion that α is the label, while (3) yields the conclusion that the label of β is the label. Consider, for example, *wh*-movement of the LI *what* to Spec-C, forming (4), *t* a copy of *what*:

(4) What [C [you wrote *t*]]

If C projects, in accord with (3), then (4) can be, for example, the interrogative complement of "wonder" in "I wonder what you wrote." Iatridou, Anagnastopoulou, and Izvorksi (2001) and Donati (2006) point out that *what* may also project, in accord with (2), yielding the free relative object of "I read [what you wrote]," interpreted as a DP headed by *what*. In conformity with (2), that is possible only when the phrase that is moved is a head; there can be no free relative interpretation in "I read [what book you wrote]." Relying on more subtle properties, Donati shows that the same is true for comparatives. Binding Condition (C) might be a case of (2) under EM, with the pronominal Spec becoming the label, hence serving as the probe, as discussed earlier. Note that when *what* is taken to be the label in (4), so is C (for reasons of feature-inheritance by T). That is, the two labels coexist, in accord with a literal interpretation of the labeling algorithm (2)–(3).

The conclusion, then, is that the labeling algorithms apply freely, sometimes producing deviant expressions. The outcome will satisfy the empirical conditions on I-language if these are the interpretations actually assigned.

There must be some way to identify internally merged α with its copy, but not with other items that have the same feature composition: to distinguish, say, "John killed John" or "John sold John to John" (with syntactically unrelated occurrences of *John*), from "John was killed John" (with two copies of the same LI *John*). That is straightforward, satisfying the inclusiveness condition, if within a phase each selection of an LI from the lexicon is a distinct item, so that all relevant identical items are copies. Nothing more than phase-level memory is required to identify these properties at the semantic interface C-I, where the information is required.

It has sometimes been suggested that IM should be eliminated in favor of EM. As noted, that necessitates a stipulation barring IM, and thus requires empirical support.

It also requires some other device to distinguish copies from unrelated occurrences. And it involves additional computation when a phrase that would otherwise be internally merged (moved) has to be generated independently before merger, then somehow identified as a copy; perhaps generated many times, as in successive-cyclic movement. There are other rather severe complications resulting from the cyclic local character of IM, discussed below. I do not see any compensating advantages to this departure from SMT.

Since IM always leaves a copy, thanks to the NTC, and the copies are carried to the semantic interface, we eliminate the lowering operation of reconstruction— though just how reconstruction works is by no means a simple question. What about the phonetic interface? Here two desiderata conflict: (1) ease of processing, and (2) minimization of computation. Processing would be eased if all copies remain. That would eliminate many of the "filler-gap" problems that complicate parsing programs and perceptual theories. But minimization of computation calls for erasure of all but one copy, so that the phonological component can forget about the others; the issue does not arise in the mapping to the semantic interface, where all copies remain without complication.[35] Overwhelmingly, the second desideratum is correct. That provides more evidence that language is "designed" so that mapping to C-I approximates the SMT, with utility for communication only a secondary factor.

If minimization of computation is the driving force in "Spell-Out" of copies, there should be an exception to the conclusion that only one is phonetically realized: namely, when special conditions, such as Lasnik's stranded affix filter, require some residue of the lowest copy to satisfy interface conditions. For evidence supporting that conclusion, see Abels 2001, Bošković 2001, Landau 2004, and Hiraiwa 2002.

For minimal computation, the probe should search the smallest domain to find the goal: its c-command domain. It follows that there should be no m-command, hence no Spec-head relations, except for the special case where the Spec itself can be a probe. That requires considerable rethinking of much important work, particularly on agreement. I think the conclusion is tenable,[36] but it is far from obvious. Without further stipulation, the number of specifiers is unlimited; the specifier-complement distinction itself reduces to first-Merge, second-Merge, and so on. Again, these conclusions, restricting descriptive technology and thus approaching SMT, have to be shown to be empirically viable.

Minimal search is not uniquely defined in XP-YP structures where neither XP nor YP is a head: the "wrong choice" yields island effects. Among the means proposed to identify the right choice are Kayne's connectedness principle and government. Each involves stipulation of mechanisms that depart from SMT, and hence motivates a search for alternatives.

Consider the CED effects discovered by Huang (1982), involving XP-YP structures with island violations under the wrong choice. The adjunct-island subcase follows if an adjunct is not in the search domain of the probe. That in turn follows from the approach to adjuncts in Chomsky 2004, taking them to be entered into the derivation by pair-Merge instead of set-Merge to capture the fundamental asymmetry of adjunction,[37] then simplified to set-Merge at the point of Transfer, thus permitting phonetic linearization and yielding "late-insertion" effects at the semantic interface.

Consider the subject-island subcase. It has been assumed since Huang's discovery of these properties that the surface subject is the island, but there is reason to doubt this assumption. Compare (5) and (6):[38]

(5) a. It was the CAR (not the TRUCK) of which [they found the (driver, picture)]
    b. Of which car did [they find the (driver, picture)?

(6) a. *It was the CAR (not the TRUCK) of which [the (driver, picture) caused a scandal]
    b. *Of which car did [the (driver, picture) cause a scandal]

These are standard examples of the subject-island condition. The interesting case is (7):

(7) a. It was the CAR (not the TRUCK) of which [the (driver, picture) was found]
    b. Of which car was [the (driver, picture) awarded a prize]

These fall together with (5), not (6), though the surface subject is in the same position as in (6). If so, then the effect is determined by the base structures of (7), not the surface structures, in which the distinction between the cases has been effaced by raising of the surface subject from the verb phrase. The relevant base structures are (8):

(8) a. C [T [v [V [the (driver, picture) of which]]]]
    b. C [T [$_\alpha$ [the (driver, picture) of which] [v* [V XP]]]]

In (a) v is unaccusative/passive, so that only (b) but not (a) has the internal phase α. We now have the right distinction,[39] though it remains to explain it.

There are further consequences. One is that T is not the probe that yields A-movement of [*the (driver, picture) of which*] to the Spec-T position in (7) before C is merged: if it were, the required distinction would again be effaced before *wh*-movement. Rather, A- as well as A'-movement must be triggered by probes in C: the probe for *wh*-accesses *which* in its base position in (7), raising *of-which* to Spec-C, while the Agree-probe in C, inherited by T, raises the full DP [*the (driver, picture) of which*] to Spec-T, the two operations proceeding in parallel. It follows further that TP is not a phase; rather CP, as already concluded on other grounds. Other considerations converge towards the same conclusion.

It remains to explain why the probe for *wh*-movement cannot readily access the *wh*-phrase within the external argument of α. That could reduce to a locality condition: *which* in α is embedded in the lower phase, which has already been passed in the derivation. We know that the external argument itself can be accessed in the next higher phase, but there is a cost to extracting something embedded in it—facts to which we return.[40]

Note that in (5), the problem does not arise. In (5), the *wh*-phrase is extracted to the edge of v*P unproblematically, then on to the edge of CP; nothing is extracted from it in the CP phase. In (6), the PP-complement of the subject cannot be extracted in the same way in the v*P phase, because its base position is not in the search domain of the label/probe v*; for the same reason, Spec-to-Spec movement is always impossible. Therefore extraction in (6) would have to be from the base position, distinguishing the cases properly.

We therefore reinforce the conclusion that C has two probes: the edge feature EF that is automatically available for an LI, and an Agree-feature (φ-features). The former attracts the *wh*-phrase to the edge of C, the second attracts the DP, but only as far as T, with which it agrees. These facts raise the usual two questions: *how* (what are the mechanisms?) and *why* (what is the motivation?).

The obvious mechanism is the one already suggested for other reasons: T inherits its Agree feature from C, and then derivatively serves as a probe at the phase level CP. The motivation may trace back to a C-I interface requirement that both arguments and operator-variable structures be available, analogous to the requirement of semantic duality that is satisfied in an optimal way by the A-A′ distinction, as already discussed.

On optimal assumptions, transmission of the Agree feature should be a property of phase-heads in general, not just of C. Hence v* should transmit its Agree feature to V, and probe of an object with structural Case by v* should be able to raise it to Spec-V, a step-by-step analogue to raising to Spec-T by C. That would yield the intriguing but puzzling conclusions about raising of objects to Spec-V, particularly in ECM constructions, but perhaps generally.[41] The evidence is compelling, but has been unclear why such rules should exist: why should objects raise to Spec-V at all, an operation that is even more odd because its effects are not visible, given that V then raises to v*? These strange facts fall into place automatically if the properties of the C-phase hold of phases generally. They thus yield further evidence to support the basic assumptions: C and v* are the phase heads, and their Agree feature is inherited by the LI they select. Futhermore, if the suggestions above about motivation prove to be accurate, the curious phenomenon of raising to Spec-V follows from the C-I requirement that the A-A′ distinction must be observed at the CP-phase, supplemented by third-factor conditions of efficient computation.

As noted earlier, it is tempting to speculate that the resistance to extraction of the complement of C and v* (TP and VP respectively) is traceable to the requirement of feature inheritance from the selecting phase head. Note also that there is still an asymmetry between C-T and v*-V: T can appear without C, but V requires v*. That too would follow if lexical items are roots, with functional elements (v, n, etc.) deter-mining their category, along lines already mentioned.

Another question is whether inheritance is obligatory or optional. For C-T, that raises familiar questions about universality of EPP and about mechanisms of agree-ment. For v*-V, properties of Binding Theory condition (B) indicate that the rule must be obligatory, by the general logic of the clause-mate principles of Postal-Lasnik-Saito. Thus in (9), *him* is necessarily free:

(9) The slave expected [(the picture, the owner) of him] to be somewhere else

The *for-to* analogue, to my ear, allows the bound option more readily, as would be expected. Lasnik, however, has given arguments to the contrary (see Lasnik 2002). The questions are unsettled for both C-T and v*-V.

What is true of (5)–(7) should hold in general for *wh*-questions. Consider the sim-pler cases (10), (11), with indices for expository purposes only:

(10) a. C [T [who [v* [see John]]]]
     b. Who$_i$ [C [who$_j$ [T [who$_k$ v* [see John]]]]]
     c. Who saw John

(11) a. C [T [v [arrive who]]]
     b. Who$_i$ [C [who$_j$ [T [v [arrive who$_k$]]]]]
     c. Who arrived

In (10), in the v*-phase v*-*John* agreement values all uninterpretable features. Turn-ing to the C-phase, both the edge and the Agree feature of C seek the goal *who* in Spec-v*. The Agree feature, inherited by T from C, raises it to Spec-T, while the edge feature of C raises it to Spec-C. The result is (10b). There is a direct relation between *who$_i$* and *who$_k$*, and between *who$_j$* and *who$_k$*, but none between *who$_i$* and *who$_j$*. There are two A-chains in (b): (*who$_j$*, *who$_k$*) and (*who$_k$*). Each A-chain is an ar-gument, with *who$_i$* the operator ranging over the A-chains, interpreted as restricted bound variables.[42] Similarly in (11), with no lower phase, parallel operation of the edge and Agree features of C derives (b) from (a), with the operator *who* in Spec-C and the two A-chain arguments (Spec-T, Complement-V) and (Complement-V).

In both cases the A-chains are invisible, but familiar properties of A-movement (binding, scope, weak crossover, etc.) reveal that there really is a copy in the position *who$_j$* heading the two-membered A-chain, even though it is not pronounced. Thus we have such standard distinctions as in (12):

(12) a. Who was never seen, *who was there never seen
     b. Who$_i$ seems to his$_i$ friends to be preferable, *who$_i$ do you seem to his$_i$ friends to prefer

It has been conventionally assumed that in such constructions as (10), (11), there is an A-chain formed by A-movement of the *wh*-phrase to Spec-T, and an A′-A chain

formed by A′-movement of the subject to Spec-C. There was never any real justification for assuming that there are two chains, a uniform A-chain and a nonuniform A′-
A chain, rather than just one A′-A-A chain formed by successive-cyclic raising of the
wh-phrase to Spec-T and then on to Spec-C. We now see, however, that the intuition
is justified. There is no direct relation between the *wh*-phrase in Spec-C and in Spec-
T, and no reason to suppose that there is a nonuniform chain at all: just the argument A-chains and an operator-argument/variable construction. By the usual
demand of minimal computation, the A-chains contain no pronounced copy.

As matters now stand, constructions of the form (10), (11), can be formed in two
ways: (1) as just described, with the edge feature of C extracting the *wh*-phrase from
its base position, and (2) with the Agree feature of C-T forming the A-chain headed
by Spec-T (who_j in these examples), at which point the edge feature EF of C raises
who_j to Spec-C.[43] Alternative 2 looks suspicious, both because it is redundant, and
because we know that EF of C cannot extract the PP complement from within Spec-
T: if it could, the subject-condition effects would be obviated. It must be, then, that
the Spec-T position is impenetrable to EF, and a far more natural principle would be
that it is simply invisible to EF, hence barring alternative 2 as well. That principle
generalizes the inactivity condition of earlier work, which takes the head of an A-
chain (which always has any uninterpretable features valued) to be invisible to
Agree.[44] A reasonable principle, then, is that an A-chain becomes invisible to further
computation when its uninterpretable features are valued. That will incorporate the
effects of the earlier inactivity condition, restated in terms of phases.[45]

We have been presupposing the informal notions A- and A′-position. For our purposes here, it will suffice to define an A′-position as one that is attracted by an edge
feature of a phase head; hence typically in Spec-C or outer Spec of v*. Others are
A-positions. From this point of view, A- and A′-positions are distinguished not by
their structural status within a phrase marker, but by the manner in which they are
derived. The shift of perspective has many consequences. I will tentatively assume
that it is on the right track. It follows that successive-cyclic A′-movement creates a
uniform A′-chain, no matter where the landing sites are along the way. Intermediate
positions do not induce binding effects or have other A-position properties, whatever
their structural status is.

Let us review some of the properties of the theory of IM. With all operations
driven by the phase head, the only A-chains are completed A-chains with all features
valued, either inherently or by Agree. It follows that "traces" (technically, lower
copies) are invisible, as desired.[46] We also conclude that in A-movement, features
are not valued until the operation is completed; otherwise the operation could not
apply. Suppose PH is a phase head (C or v*) selecting PH_s. Then EF of PH can raise
XP to Spec-PH, but only from its base position. If the Agree feature of PH (inherited
by PH_s) has raised XP to Spec-PH_s, then XP is invisible; it cannot be raised and

nothing can be extracted from it. If, however, EF raises XP to Spec-PH, it no longer heads an A-chain (by definition), and is subject to raising or extraction by a higher EF. Extraction from this A′-position should be on a par with extraction from an external argument, carrying the cost of searching into a phase already passed. Thus (13) should have about the same status as the subject-island violations (6):[47]

(13) Of which car did you wonder [which [(picture, driver)] [caused a scandal]]

Let's look more closely at legitimate application of EF of the phase head PH to XP in its base position, either raising XP to Spec-PH, or raising its complement to Spec-PH as in (5), (7). We know that raising cannot follow long-distance agreement valuing the features of XP, or XP would be invisible, for the reasons just given: its PP-complement could not be extracted, and XP itself could not be raised. Furthermore, XP cannot be raised before agreement, or its Case feature will be unvalued. It follows that the edge and Agree features of PH apply in parallel: EF raises XP or a PP complement within XP to Spec-PH, while agreement values all uninterpretable features and may or may not raise XP to form an A-chain.[48]

We therefore have a rather delicate array of conclusions about the mechanisms of probe-goal relations and IM. They amount to the conclusion that all options are open: the edge and Agree features of the probe can apply in either order, or simultaneously, with only certain choices converging.

What holds for *wh*-movement should extend to A′-movement generally. Suppose that the edge feature of the phase head is indiscriminate: it can seek any goal in its domain, with restrictions (e.g., about remnant movement, proper binding, etc.) determined by other factors.[49] Take, say, Topicalization of DP. EF of a phase head PH can seek any DP in the phase and raise it to Spec-PH. There are no intervention effects, unless we assume that phrases that are to be topicalized have some special mark. That seems superfluous even if feasible, particularly if we adopt Rizzi's approach to the left periphery: what is raised is identified as a topic by the final position it reaches, and any extra specification is redundant. The same should be true for other forms of A′-movement. We need not postulate an uninterpretable feature that induces movement, and can thus overcome a long-standing problem about crash at the lower phase levels in successive-cyclic movement.

Further elaboration depends on how the relevant structures are to be analyzed properly. To mention a few possibilities, suppose that the moved phrase is labeled by an interpretable interrogative *wh*-feature. Then it will have to reach the right position in the left periphery for interpretation, or be associated with such a position by some other operation.[50] Otherwise the expression may converge, but will be interpreted as deviant at the C-I interface. A *wh*-phrase lacking the interpretable interrogative feature, or an empty operator, will yield a structure that converges but will again have no interpretation unless the phrase undergoes A′-movement to the root, constituting a possible predicate or source for a head-raising relative.[51] Note that there should be no superiority effect for multiple *wh*-phrases; any can be targeted for movement. We are led to that conclusion for other reasons as well. Thus suppose that we have *what* in (10) instead of *John*:

(14) C [T [who [v* [see what]]]]

At the lower v* phase the subject *who* does not intervene, so even if uninterpretable *wh*-features are targeted by the edge-feature of v*, *what* can be raised to the edge, voiding any superiority effect. That leaves the problem of explaining the superiority phenomena in the languages in which they appear: English, but apparently not German in simple cases, for example. Standard examples, such as (14), tell us very little, and it is not so simple to find convincing cases.[52]

Do A′-chains function in the manner of A-chains with regard to intervention? The line of argument we are pursuing indicates that they should. That appears to be correct. Consider such constructions as "who did John see," schematically (15):

(15) C [T [John [v* [V who]]]]

Given PIC, at the lower v* phase *who* raises to the edge, so it is accessible to the phase head C. The Agree feature of C-T seeks the subject *John* and raises it to Spec-T, and the edge feature of C seeks the object *who* in the outer Spec of v* and raises it to Spec-C. If T were a phase head, or an independent probe for some other reason (as assumed in earlier work, mine in particular), then raising of subject to Spec-T would be blocked by intervention of the φ-features of *who* in the outer Spec of v*. But since it is not a phase head, and both operations are driven by the phase head C in parallel, the problem does not arise. However, raising of the subject does cross the lower copy of *who* in the A′-position of the outer Spec of v*, that is, the lower copy in the A′-chain (Spec-C, Outer-Spec-v*). A′-chains thus behave in this respect like A-chains: if uniform, only the full chain (equivalently, its head) is the object that intervenes. We therefore have uniform chains—either A-chains or A′-chains— but no mixed chains.[53]

A somewhat more complex illustration similar to (5)–(7) has been discovered in Icelandic.[54] Keeping just to the essence, consider the dative-nominative experiencer construction (16) (e.g., "to-someone seems [the horses are slow]"):

(16) C [T [DAT [v* NOM . . .]]]

If DAT remains in situ, in an expletive construction, it blocks T-Nom agreement, as expected. If Dat is raised to Spec-T, T-Nom agreement is permitted, again as expected: there is no intervening argument. But if DAT is *wh*-moved, it blocks agreement, which is paradoxical since it appears to be the lower copy of an A-chain. The solution suggested by Holmberg-Hroarsdottir (along with several other devices) is that the Dat subject moves to Spec-C, directly, so that the sole A-chain has only one position, its base position, which blocks agreement by intervention. That seems basically right, but it yields new problems, because we do want to have the A-chain (Spec-T, Spec-v*), for reasons already mentioned. The desired result follows, as before, if both operations, A- and A′-movement, are driven by the phase head C. That will leave no relation between Spec-C and Spec-T, but an operator-argument relation between Spec-C and each of the two A-chains, (Spec-T, Spec-v*) and (Spec-v*). The A-chain (Spec-v*) suffices to block T-Nom agreement, by standard intervention; the A-chain (Spec-T, Spec-v*) yields the A-movement effects.

One might explore whether the variation in judgments (see note 54) can be attributed to the timing of the edge and Agree probes.

The examples discussed so far are restricted to two-membered A-chains, as in (5–7), (10–11), (16). Consider now successive-cyclic A-movement.[55] Compare (17) = (6) with (18), in both cases with boldface brackets around the internal phases and the other brackets around TP, and *t* used for the lower copies in the A-chains:

(17) a. *It was the CAR (not the TRUCK) of which [the (driver, picture) [*t* caused a scandal]]

 b. *Of which car did [the (driver, picture) [*t* cause a scandal]]

(18) a. It is the CAR (not the TRUCK) of which [the (driver, picture) is likely [*t* to [*t* cause a scandal]]]

 b. Of which car is [the (driver, picture) likely [*t* to [*t* cause a scandal]]]

In (17), as already discussed, the PP phrase in the EA "the (driver, picture) of which" raises to Spec-C from its base position, and we have the subject-island effect. But in (18), the effect is obviated. These expressions have the status of extraction from object, not subject, as in (5), (7). That follows from the previous conclusions about IM, assuming the (still mysterious) condition EPP, which requires A-movement to pass through Spec-T, with familiar consequences for binding, and possibly reconstruction. One permitted order of operations is this: the Agree feature of C-T raises EA step by step to its final position, and along the way, the edge feature of C extracts the PP complement and raises it to Spec-C, with no deep search required because no phase boundaries are crossed. The parallel operations interweave, again unproblematically.

Note that the same conclusions hold, as expected, for ECM. Thus (19) has the status of (18), not (17):

(19) Of which car did they believe the (driver, picture) to have caused a scandal

It must be, then, that "of which car" is raised from an intermediate position, Spec-T of the ECM infinitival, before it reaches Spec-V, a position analogous to Spec-T in the matrix clause. In Spec-T and Spec-V, all features are valued in the completed A-chain, and its head is invisible, as we have seen.

Reinforcing earlier conclusions, we find that the two searches driven by the phase head operate in parallel, and can even interweave. What yields the subject-island effect, it appears, is search that goes too deeply into a phase already passed, not the difference between base and surface position. The Agree feature of C raises XP to Spec-T (by inheritance), while its edge feature raises XP (or part of it) to Spec-C. The generalized inactivity condition bars extraction from matrix Spec-T (and if fully generalized, raising of full XP from that position). Such constructions as (19) provide an independent reason for ECM-raising to Spec-V. And extraction of complement provides an independent reason, alongside of binding and (perhaps) reconstruction effects, for successive-cyclic A-movement through Spec-T.

Note that raising of the PP-complement is sharply different from extraposition of PP in such constructions. Thus (20) has the same status as extraposition from EA, as in (21), and both are much worse than the (relatively weaker) subject-island effect of (17):

(20) *The (driver, picture) is likely to cause a scandal of the car

(21) *The (driver, picture) caused a scandal of the car

We conclude, then, that despite some superficial similarities, extraposition and A'-movement of PP-complement are entirely different phenomena. Quite possibly, as suggested earlier, PP-extraposition is part of the mapping to the SM interface, hence is part of Spell-Out. If so, it should be restricted to the interior of a phase, thus allowing extraposition from object but not from EA subject.[56]

As discussed elsewhere (Chomsky 2001), the size of phases is in part determined by uninterpretable features. Such features are a striking phenomenon of language that was not recognized to be significant, or even particularly noticed, prior to Vergnaud's original ideas about the role of structural Case (see note 1). The values of these features are redundant, fixed by structural position in the course of derivation. We therefore expect them to be selected from the lexicon unvalued. Since these features have no semantic interpretation, they must be deleted before they reach the semantic interface for the derivation to converge. They must therefore be deleted either before Transfer or as part of Transfer. But these features may have phonetic realization, so they cannot be deleted before transfer to the phonological component. They must therefore be valued at the stage in computation where they are transferred—by definition, at the phase-level—and this must be the same stage for both transfer operations, again supporting the optimal assumption that transfer to both interfaces is at the same stage of derivation. Once valued, the uninterpretable features are deleted by the mapping to the semantic component, and given whatever phonetic properties they have in particular I-languages by the phonological component. The conclusion is supported by the fact that once features are valued, they are indistinguishable from interpretable features and there is no indication of their relation to the interpretable features that match them and assign them their values.[57] Hence they must be transferred at the point where they are valued: again, at the phase level, assuming that all operations apply at this level, as determined by the label.

These observations provide further support for the conclusion that v*P and CP are phases, the locus of determination of structural Case and agreement for object and subject. For subject, the conclusion is based on the assumption that TP is not a phase, for reasons discussed, so that T operates as a probe only derivatively by virtue of its relation to C (similarly, v* and V). A stronger principle would be that phases are exactly the domains in which uninterpretable features are valued, as seems plausible.

There is also morphological evidence that CP, v*P are the phases. Just for these two categories the edge is sometimes morphologically marked in successive-cyclic movement, with the effect of movement through Spec-C sometimes found in the subject-agreement domain, another reason to suspect that T-agreement is derivative from properties of C.[58] These also seem to be the stages that permit parasitic gap constructions; for extensive discussion, based on the assumption that these are phases for A'-movement, see Nissenbaum 2000. There is also evidence for other effects of phases, among them in phonology (Ishihara 2003) and covert movement (Cecchetto 2004), and there is also much further investigation of alternatives and further articulation that I cannot review here.

Phases should, presumably, be as small as possible, to minimize computation after Transfer and to capture as fully as possible the cyclic/compositional character of mappings to the interface. C and v* impose an upper bound, and T is too small, as we have seen. More generally, there are two basic cases to consider:

1. SO cannot be transferred to the SM interface ("spelled out") if it is subsequently going to move.
2. SO cannot be moved to an edge unless it can be spelled out right there, satisfying any uninterpretable features by long-distance Agree.

Case 1 is transparent, unless more complex apparatus is introduced that we would hope to avoid. Case 2 has to be sharpened. It conforms to a fairly general empirical observation that should be captured:

3. In a probe-goal relation, the goal can be spelled out only in situ (under long-distance Agree) or at the probe (under internal Merge).

Standard illustrations are passive/unaccusative in situ or with movement. The goal cannot stop at some intermediate point of the derivation, in particular, at intermediate Spec-T positions through which it must pass in successive-cyclic A-movement (including ECM constructions).[59] In the case of A'-movement, reconstruction effects indicate that the raised goal also passes through internal positions leaving copies that are visible at the semantic interface.[60] These observations tell us something important about the operation of IM: the raised goal must reach the probe by means of local steps, passing through intermediate positions where it leaves copies, but not stopping there to be spelled out.[61] Just how small these local steps are remains to be clarified. For A'-movement, they could turn out to be as small as every category, as proposed more generally on completely different (and long-abandoned) grounds in Chomsky 1986. As noted earlier, there is an exception, which may have principled grounds: inheritance of the features of the phase head by the category it selects, T and V. These properties of IM, which appear to be quite general, add further reason to suppose that operations are at the phase level only, and that inactivation of Spec-T in a tensed clause is a reflex of inheritance of C features.

There are some asymmetries between A- and A'-movement with regard to local steps. One is that the reconstruction effects are far weaker for A-movement (if they exist at all[62]). The only strong argument for local steps for A-movement are those based on binding and (as discussed above) extraction. In the latter case, the argument supports only the option, but not the necessity, of the local step. In both cases the effects hold only at Spec-T, hence fall within the EPP category. Furthermore, there is strong evidence that raising of EA to Spec-T does not pass through intermediate positions (hence presumably that A-movement never does). If there were intermediate positions between the base and surface position in this case (say, at the edge of a participial phrase), then subject-island effects would be obviated, exactly as they are in successive-cyclic (and ECM) raising.[63] These properties remain to be explained.

A consequence of the conclusion that the Agree-feature belongs to C, and to T only derivatively, is that it is in the same region as the left-periphery head for Focus. This conclusion is developed by Miyagawa (2005) to argue that agreement and Focus are two values of the same parameter, with languages varying as to which of them is prominent: φ-features for English-type languages, Focus for Japanese-type languages (including Bantu and others discussed by Baker (2003), whose proposals he adapts). Strengthening ideas on universality of features in Sigurdsson 2004, Miyagawa argues that these functional features are not only present in all languages, but are also phonologically expressed in some fashion. The relevant point here is that if analysis along these lines can be sustained, it provides further indirect evidence to support the conclusion that the phases are CP and v*P, the locus of valuation of uninterpretable features, placing Vergnaud's seminal ideas of twenty-five years ago in a much broader context and carrying the MP some important steps forward.

Let us turn finally to the mysterious property EPP, which has been an annoying problem ever since it was originally formulated to describe the obligatory presence of expletives in subject position of English-type languages if nothing raises to that position. EPP problems are considerably more general, however. Thus, while v typically permits both long-distance agreement and raising, v* does not:[64]

(22) *There will [a student [v* [take the class]]]

Rather generally, it seems, if languages of the relevant typology lack an expletive, the closest noun phrase raises to Spec-T, sometimes with default agreement morphology (or none) on T.[65]

For infinitivals, we may be able to disregard control structures: subject is null so its structural position is uncertain, and they presumably fall under CP structures in any event. That leaves raising/ECM infinitivals. For these, EPP may in part be reducible to the general step-by-step property of IM, already discussed; but only in part, because of the special role of Spec-T in such operations, a residual EPP effect. It also remains to account for EPP in tensed clauses (the C-T category) and the analogous v*-V issues.

It is tempting to ask whether EPP can be reformulated in terms of feature inheritance. Suppose that EF can be inherited from the phase head along with the Agree feature. Not being a phase head, T need have no option for second-Merge by IM, but rather inherits it from C, and by some kind of feature spread, this extends to all T's in the phase.[66] Operations then proceed as before. If there is no accessible NOM, then T will have default morphology, as in Icelandic and the Slavic constructions discussed by Lavine and Freidin; or null morphology, as in Miyagawa's Japanese examples. And there are a few other options.[67] If nothing is raised, then the inherited edge feature of T must be satisfied by EM, necessarily of an expletive since no argument role can be assigned. Possibly reformulation of the EPP properties in such terms might open a way to resolving the problems they raise. If so, it would be a welcome development, another step toward the goals of the MP and the long tradition of inquiry from which it derives.

Notes

I would like to thank Robert Freidin, Samuel Epstein, and Eric Reuland, among others, along with participants in a fall 2004 seminar at MIT, for valuable comments on an earlier draft.

1. Letter, April 17, 1977 (reprinted in chapter 1 of this book); Vergnaud 1985.

2. Obviously, this is an extreme abstraction. Each stage of development, along various paths, contributes to interpretation of data as experience.

3. Chomsky 1965, 59.

4. Joos's (1957) summary of the guiding "Boasian" tradition of American linguistics.

5. For some discussion, see Chomsky 2005.

6. See Brody 1995, Chomsky 1993 and 1995, as well as much subsequent work. For illuminating comment on the general project, see Freidin and Vergnaud 2001. Despite repeated clarification, MP is often taken to be a hypothesis about language or a new approach to language, displacing earlier ones. It is neither. Furthermore, as again repeatedly stressed, the program is theory neutral: whatever one's conception of UG, one can be interested in principled explanation (MP), or not. And if so, essentially the same questions will arise.

7. For some discussion and sources, see Chomsky 2005.

8. See, for example, O'Neil 1977, and sources cited. Also discussion in Miller and Chomsky 1963.

9. See Chomsky 1995, chaps. 4, 7.3. Such considerations suggest that the freezing principle of Wexler and Culicover 1980 should be generalized to immobilization of the full extraposed phrase, within narrow syntax. On apparent counterexamples with semantic consequences (involving "late Merge" and Antecedent-contained-deletion), see Chomsky 2004, suggesting that these are actually generated in situ. For additional evidence in support of this conclusion, see Szczegielniak 2004, showing that raising relatives have the same crucial properties, barring the possibility of QR-style covert raising of the nominal head of the relative clause as proposed in the papers discussed in Chomsky 2004.

10. Nobel laureates Salvador Luria and François Jacob. See Chomsky 2005 for context and sources.

11. Some confusion has been caused by recent use of the term "LF" to refer to the C-I interface itself, thus departing from its definition within EST as the output of (overt and covert) syntactic operations and the input to rules of semantic interpretation that map LF to C-I. I am keeping here to the original sense, within the EST/Y-model. There is no issue beyond terminology.

12. Hierarchy is automatic for recursive operations, conventionally suppressed for those that merely enumerate a sequence of objects.

13. And might not proceed much beyond, some leading evolutionary biologists believe. See particularly Lewontin 1990. His chapter in an updated 1995 edition is no less skeptical about the prospects.

14. Topics that may, however, have bearing on growth of language in the individual, and indirectly even on language evolution. As an example, Yang (2002), adapting ideas of Morris Halle's, has shown that contrary to widely held beliefs, even in such marginal corners of English as irregular verbs, children appear to impose a principled system of generation, assigning the elements to rule-governed categories, thus providing evidence about the role of extralinguistic principles of efficiency in determining the nature of I-languages attained.

15. Dissociations in aphasia and performance, which have been known for many years, tell us little in this regard, contrary to much discussion, because they reflect many different factors. Similarly, dissociation of reading from other language performance has never been taken to entail that there is a "reading faculty" independent of the faculty of language, as Luigi Rizzi observes (personal communication).

16. "Part of" here means "term of," in the technical sense: a term of the SO α is a member of α or of a term of α.

17. There has been much misunderstanding since the copy theory was proposed in Chomsky 1993, modifying earlier conceptions of movement by eliminating trace and indexing in favor of the NTC: that is, leaving the moved element unaffected instead of replacing it by an indexed trace (indexing is now superfluous, under identity). It has sometimes been supposed that a new "copy" is created, then inserted in the position of the moved element—all unnecessary—and an alternative has been proposed in terms of "remerge," which is simply a notation for the copy theory as originally formulated in the most elementary terms.

18. See Cinque 1999, 2002; Rizzi 2004; Belletti 2004.

19. Personal communication. His examples are from Norwegian and Icelandic.

20. Chomsky 2004. See Hiraiwa (2002) for discussion of these and many related questions along lines rather similar to those adopted here. Also Boeckx 2004a.

21. As noted in Chomsky 2004, note 51, generalization to Multiple-Agree overcomes problems in Chomsky 2001 discussed by Frampton et al. (2000), who develop an alternative approach in this and later papers; see Frampton and Guttman 2004 for recent extensions. The same processes hold elsewhere, for example, in Hindi multiple-gender agreement; see Boeckx 2004b and Hiraiwa 2002.

22. The optimal conclusion is, in fact, required, under the theory of adjuncts outlined in Chomsky 2004.

23. On various notions of cyclicity, often confused, see Lasnik (2006). Note that the considerations discussed here suggest a principled explanation for the successive-cyclic property of A'-movement.

24. To mention one, in the analysis developed below we can dispense with the "next higher phase" condition of my earlier papers cited.

25. Another case, brought up by a reviewer (citing Mel'cuk 1988 and Bošković 2005), is agreement into finite clauses in Chukchee.

26. Sometimes the φ-features of C are morphologically expressed, as in the famous West Flemish examples. We leave open the question of how, or whether, expression of the features on C relates to the CP-internal syntax. See Miyagawa (2006) for review of a number of cases.

27. In the framework of Chomsky 2001, "inactivation" of raised DP at Spec-T was attributed to the fact that T is *complete*, with all features specified (unlike participles, lacking person). Those additional assumptions are unnecessary here; only completeness at the phase level has an effect. The earlier assumptions are also refuted by empirical phenomena in various languages, as discussed by Frampton and Guttman (2004) and Nevins (2005), who develop different approaches.

28. See Rizzi (forthcoming) for review, and a much more general context.

29. To pursue the matter, one should ask such questions as whether quantifier-variable notation (as distinct from formally equivalent variable-free systems) is somehow an empirical property of the C-I (thought) systems, analogous to properties of the SM systems. Similar questions arise in other connections: e.g., is the familiar notation for sentential calculus, matching nested embedding in natural language, an empirical property of the C-I system, as distinct from Polish notation? Relative ease of learning and interpretation suggests a positive answer to both questions, which might turn out to bear on language design in interesting ways.

30. See Iatridou 1988 on tenseless T with φ-features in Greek. See also Freidin 2004 for similar conclusions on different grounds.

31. Thus TP cannot be clefted stranding C, and so on. There are proposals to move TP in Kayne's LCA framework, to account for right-most complementizer and other phenomena. See also Rooryck 2000. These operations are unformulable in the present limited framework, at least for tensed CP, and even here do not separate TP from C, leaving TP adjacent to C and in its m-command domain—a notion that also departs from optimal assumptions about minimizing search.

32. Note that we understand Merge(XP, YP) as satisfying EF if one or the other label has EF—say the label of YP, if we think of XP as merged to YP—even if it is not an LI. Thus Merge of external argument to v*P satisfies the EF of v*. NTC requires that Merge in this case too is to the edge.

33. These are the earliest assumptions of generative grammar, in Chomsky (1955) and later work. They still seem to me basically accurate, though the early proposals for assigning a status to expressions were quickly shown to be inadequate.

34. The exceptions are EM of nonheads XP, YP, forming {XP, YP}, as in external argument merger of DP to v*P. The conventional assumption is that the label is v*. A possibility is that either label projects, but only v*-labeling will yield a coherent argument structure at C-I Another possible case is small clauses, if they are headless. A suggestive approach, along the general lines of Moro 2000, is that these structures lack a label and have an inherent instability, so that one of the two members of the small clause must raise.

35. Technically, this statement requires minor qualification: there is processing of each copy in the mapping to the semantic interface. But it is assumed (for good reasons) that these operations are universal, hence in effect instantaneous and costless, unlike the mapping to the phonetic interface, which tolerates substantial variety (again for obvious reasons) and therefore involves language-specific and sometimes complex computations.

36. E.g., Reuland's observations on Condition (A), cited above. For another illustration, see McCloskey 2002, which argues that the form of the complementizer in Irish A′-binding does not depend on Spec-head agreement, as had been supposed, but on how Spec is formed—by EM or IM.

37. For some similar ideas, see Åfarli 1995; Rubin 2003; Safir 1986. A slight modification might be needed, restricting simplification to the Transfer operations themselves, never entering narrow syntax. That depends on whether intervention effects and PIC will bar all other cases.

38. Idealizing the judgments, and keeping to the pied-piping case, to exclude the incomplete constituent effects studied by Kuno (1972). In the oral tradition, including talks of mine, examples have kept to "picture-PP," but that lexical choice introduces extraneous issues because of the ambiguity of the phrase, which can be understood with PP interpreted not as a complement of "picture" but as, in effect, a reduced relative clause (roughly, "I have a picture which is of Boston," contrary to *"I saw a driver who is of the car," "I saw an author who is of the book"). The differences show up elsewhere—for example, in *one*-replacement. Note that there are apparent counterparts to (5) and (6) in extraposition structures, but these diverge sharply, as we will see below, strengthening the conclusion already mentioned that PP-extraposition is not part of narrow syntax.

39. Choice of v* might have an effect. Perhaps "of which books did the authors receive the prize" is more acceptable than (6). If so, difference among theta roles might be relevant, perhaps requiring a deeper analysis of base structures.

40. These considerations suggest a possible independent argument for the predicate-internal subject hypothesis. For some suggestions, on different grounds, about C as the locus of mood and agreement features, see Aygen 2004.

41. See Lasnik and Saito 1991; Lasnik 2003 for further discussion; and for summary of history, back to Postal 1974.

42. Reformulation of application of operations can dispense with chains, if there is some reason to do this. I will keep to the chain notation for expository convenience.

43. As we will see directly, such interweaving of operations is permissible.

44. If in Spec-T, it is already invisible to IM, because of PIC.

45. It remains the case that inherent Case will be visible to Match, inducing interference effects.

46. That would also be true of the trace of a raised DP with quirky Case, adopting earlier assumptions that quirky Case involves a structural Case feature, valued by raising. From the formulation given here, it follows that the quirky-Case head of a nontrivial A-chain should not cause an interference effect. I do not know if it is possible to test this consequence.

47. On such cases, see unpublished work by Esther Torrego, reviewed in Chomsky 1986, 26f.

48. There is nothing problematic about application of features in parallel. It has always been assumed, unproblematically, for probing by φ-features.

49. That should be the case for independent reasons, since EF-probe does not involve feature matching, hence Agree.

50. See among others Pesetsky 1987, Fiengo et al. 1988, Reinhart 1993, and Tsai 1994 on options for *wh*-in-situ languages. For extensive discussion of many related issues, see Cheng and Corver, 2006.

51. For evidence that the two kinds of relatives can coexist, head-raising and head-Merge, see Szczegielniak 2004.

52. See Chomsky 1995, chap. 4, note 69. The basic problem with the standard cases is that the in-situ *wh-phrase* is the prosodic peak, and might have wide scope under a focus interpretation. The problem is compounded by the fact that the pair-list interpretation disappears if stress is shifted, as in "who NEVER saw what"? See Nissenbaum 2000, chap. 3, note 2, for observations on deaccenting, which can be stated in terms of superiority, though it remains to explain them. Standard efforts to account for superiority in terms of locality do not apply, at least in any obvious way. See Pesetsky 2000 on what may be superiority effects in more complex constructions.

53. Notice again that we are again glossing over the question of the precise mechanisms, which can be formulated in various ways, including elimination of chains altogether. The questions are interesting, but do not seem to bear directly on this level of discussion.

54. Hiraiwa (2002, 2005); Holmberg and Hroarsdottir (2003), who observe that not all speakers accept the data they describe.

55. Cases brought up by Sam Epstein, personal communication.

56. Something similar appears to be true with regard to peculiarities of in-situ object in English; see Chomsky 2001.

57. Assuming no resort to extra mechanisms, which can always be devised, but require independent justification.

58. See sources cited in Chomsky 2004, and for further elaboration, several papers in Cheng and Corver, 2006.

59. A long-standing problem, for which a number of devices have been proposed, none really satisfactory. An apparent exception in Icelandic might be related to the fact that transitive expletives are allowed, as discussed elsewhere. For similar conclusions, see Bošković 2002.

60. On interpretive effects, see Legate 2003, and more generally, Fox 2000. On morphologically visible agreement at stages intermediate between probe-goal (whether the goal remains in situ or moves to the probe), see Boeckx 2004b.

61. I am adapting here proposals of Boeckx (2003), based on work by Takahashi (1994), and earlier ideas phrased in terms of a minimal link condition.

62. See Lasnik 2003, chaps. 9, 10; the issue of Freidin-Lebeaux effects that he discusses is not relevant here.

63. John Frampton, personal communication.

64. It has been argued that this property reduces to the requirement that something must evacuate v*P (Alexiadou and Anagnostopoulou 2001). On subject in situ in Icelandic transitive expletive constructions, see Jonas 1995, 1996.

65. See, among others, Lavine and Freidin 2002; Miyagawa 2005. In the present framework, the Lavine-Freidin account has to be slightly revised so that it is C, not v, that assigns the (unexplained) structural accusative case in object position of unaccusative/passive in Slavic.

66. It does not matter whether Agree also spreads, given the revised version of the inactivity condition.

67. An implicit assumption here is that locative inversion in English (e.g., "in the square stood a statue") is to the same position as in sentences with overt subjects ("in the square, there stood a statue"), perhaps with null expletive. That seems to account for the clearest cases and their restrictions (e.g, the lack of V-C movement as in *"did in the square stand a statue"), though problems remain. On languages with clear locative-inversion of DP to subject, see Baker 2003; Miyagawa 2005.

References

Abels, K. 2001. The Predicate Cleft Constructions in Russian. In S. Franks, ed., *Proceedings of FASL* 9.

Åfarli, T. 1995. A Note on the Syntax of Adverbial Phrases. *Norsk Lingvistisk Tidsskrift* 13:23–40.

Alexiadou, A., and E. Anagnostopolou. 2001. The Subject-in-Situ Generalization and the Role of Case in Driving Computations. *Linguistic Inquiry* 32:193–231.

Aygen, G. 2002. *Finiteness, Case and Causal Architecture*. Doctoral dissertation, Harvard University.

Baker, M. 2003. Agreement, Dislocation, and Partial Configurationality. In A. Carnie, H. Harley, and M. Willie, eds., *Formal Approaches to Function in Grammar* (John Benjamins).

Belletti, A., ed. 2004. *Structures and Beyond—The Cartography of Syntactic Structure*, vol. 3 (Oxford).

Boeckx, C. 2003. *Islands and Chains: Resumption as Stranding* (John Benjamins).

Boeckx, C. 2004a. *Bare Syntax*. Unpublished ms., Harvard University.

Boeckx, C. 2004b. Long-Distance Agreement in Hindi: Some Theoretical Implications. *Studia Linguistica* 58(1):1–14.

Bošković, Ž. 2001. *On the Nature of the Syntax-Phonology Interface* (Elsevier).

Bošković, Z. 2002. A-Movement and the EPP. *Syntax* 5:167–218.

Bošković, Z. 2005. On the Locality of Move and Agree: Eliminating the Activation Condition, Generalized EPP, Inverse Case Filter, and the Phase-Impenetrability Condition. Unpublished ms., University of Connecticut. (To appear in *U. Conn Occasional Papers 3*).

Brody, M. 1995. *Lexico-Logical Form: A Radically Minimalist Theory* (MIT).

Cecchetto, C. 2004. Explaining the Locality Conditions of QR: Consequences for the Theory of Phases. Unpublished ms., Milan.

Cheng, L., and N. Corver, eds. 2006. *Wh-Movement on the Move* (MIT).

Chomsky, N. 1955. *Logical Structure of Linguistic Theory*, unpublished ms. Parts of revised 1956 version published in 1975 (Plenum, Chicago).

Chomsky, N. 1965. *Aspects of the Theory of Syntax* (MIT).

Chomsky, N. 1986. *Barriers* (MIT).

Chomsky, N. 1993. A Minimalist Program for Linguistic Theory. In K. Hale and S. J. Keyser, eds., *The View from Building 20: Essays in Linguistics in Honor of Sylvain Bromberger* (MIT).

Chomsky, N. 1995. *The Minimalist Program* (MIT).

Chomsky, N. 2001. Derivation by Phase. In M. Kenstowicz, ed., *Ken Hale: A Life in Language* (MIT).

Chomsky, N. 2004. Beyond Explanatory Adequacy. In A. Belletti, ed., *Structures and Beyond—The Cartography of Syntactic Structure*, vol. 3 (Oxford).

Chomsky, N. 2005. Three Factors in the Language Design. *Linguistic Inquiry* 36:1–22.

Chomsky, N., and H. Lasnik. 1993. The Theory of Principles and Parameters. In J. Jacobs, A. von Stechow, W. Sternefeld, and T. Vennemann, eds., *Syntax: An International Handbook of Contemporary Research* (de Gruyter). Reprinted in N. Chomsky, *The Minimalist Program* (MIT, 1995).

Cinque, G. 1999. *Adverbs and Functional Heads* (Oxford).

Cinque, G., ed. 2002. *Functional Structure in DP and IP—The Cartography of Syntactic Structures*, vol. 1 (Oxford).

Collins, C. 2002. Eliminating Labels. In S. Epstein and D. Seely, *Derivation and Explanation in the Minimalist Program* (Blackwell).

Donati, C. 2006. On *wh*-Head-Movement. In L. Cheng and N. Corver, eds., *Wh-Movement on the Move* (MIT).

Epstein, S., and D. Seely, eds. 2002. *Derivation and Explanation in the Minimalist Program* (Blackwell).

Fiengo, R., C.-T. J. Huang, H. Lasnik, and T. Reinhart. 1988. The Syntax of *wh*-in-Situ. *Proceedings of West Coast Conference on Formal Linguistics* VII, 81–98.

Fox, D. 2000. *Economy and Semantic Interpretation* (MIT).

Frampton, J., and S. Guttman. 2000. Agreement as Feature Sharing. Unpublished ms., Northeastern University.

Frampton, J., and S. Guttman. 2004. How Sentences Grow in the Mind. Unpublished ms., Northeastern University.

Frampton, J., S. Guttman, C. Yang, and J. Legate. 2000. Some Inconsistencies in the DBP Feature Valuation Algorithm. Unpublished ms., Northeastern University.

Freidin, R. 2004. *Syntactic Structures* Redux. *Syntax* 7:100–126.

Freidin, R., and J.-R. Vergnaud. 2001. Exquisite Connections: Some Remarks on the Evolution of Linguistic Theory. *Lingua* 111:639–666.

Hiraiwa, K. 2002. Multiple Agree. 25th GLOW-TiLT workshop, Utrecht.

Hiraiwa, K. 2002. Dimensions of Agreement. In C. Boeckx, ed., *Complex Agreement Systems* (Oxford).

Hiraiwa, K. 2005. *Dimensions of Symmetry in Syntax: Agreement and Clausal Architecture.* Doctoral dissertation, MIT.

Holmberg, A., and T. Hroarsdottir. 2003. Agreement and Movement in Icelandic Raising Constructions. *Lingua* 113:997–1019.

Huang, C.-T. J. 1982. *Logical Relations in Chinese and the Theory of Grammar.* Doctoral dissertation, MIT.

Iatridou, S. 1988. On Nominative Case Assignment and a Few Related Things. Ms., MIT. *MIT Working Papers in Linguistics 19:175–196, Papers on Case and Agreement II* (1993).

Iatridou, S., E. Anagnostopoulou, and R. Izvorksi. 2001. Observations about the Form and Meaning of the Perfect. In M. Kenstowicz, ed., *Ken Hale: A Life in Language* (MIT).

Ishihara, S. 2003. *Intonation and Interface Conditions.* Doctoral dissertation, MIT.

Jonas, D. 1995. *Clause Structure and Verbal Syntax in Scandinavian and English.* Doctoral dissertation, Harvard University.

Jonas, D. 1996. Clause Structure, Expletives, and Verb Movement. In W. Abraham, S. D. Epstein, H. Thrainsson, and C. J.-W. Zwart, eds., *Minimal Ideas* (John Benjamins).

Joos, M., ed. 1957. *Readings in Linguistics* (Washington, DC: American Council of Learned Societies).

Kayne, R. 1981. Unambiguous Paths. In R. May and J. Koster, eds., *Levels of Syntactic Representation* (Reidel).

Kuno, S. 1972. Functional Sentence Perspective. *Linguistic Inquiry* 3:269–320.

Landau, I. 2004. Chain Resolution in Hebrew V(P)-fronting. Unpublished ms., Ben-Gurion.

Lasnik, H. 2002. Clause-mate Conditions Revisited. *Glot International* 6(4), April.

Lasnik, H. 2003. *Minimalist Investigations in Linguistic Theory* (Routledge).

Lasnik, H. 2006. Cyclicity. In L. Cheng and N. Corver, eds., *Wh-Movement on the Move* (MIT).

Lasnik, H., and M. Saito. 1991. On the Subject of Infinitives. In L. Dobrin, L. Nichols, and R. Rodriguez, eds., *Papers from the 27th Regional Meeting of the Chicago Linguistic Society.* Reprinted in H. Lasnik, ed., *Minimalist Analysis* (Blackwell 1999).

Lavine, J., and R. Freidin. 2002. The Subject of Defective T(ense) in Slavic. *Journal of Slavic Linguistics* 10:253–289.

Legate, J. 2003. Some Interface Properties of the Phase. *Linguistic Inquiry* 34:506–516.

Lewontin, R. 1990. The Evolution of Cognition. In D. Osherson and E. Smith, eds., *An Invitation to Cognitive Science: Thinking*, vol. 3 (MIT).

Marantz, Alec. 1997. No Escape from Syntax: Don't Try Morphological Analysis in the Privacy of Your Own Lexicon. In A. Dimitriadis and L. Siegel, eds., *Proceedings of the 21st Annual Penn Linguistics Colloquium: Penn Working Papers in Linguistics* 4:2.

McCloskey, J. 2002. Resumption, Successive Cyclicity, and the Locality of Operations. In S. Epstein and D. Seely, eds., *Derivation and Explanation in the Minimalist Program* (Blackwell).

McGinnis, M., and N. Richards, eds. 2005. *Perspectives on Phases, MIT Working Papers in Linguistics* 49.

Mel'cuk, I. 1988. *Dependency Syntax: Theory and Practice* (SUNY).

Miller, G., and N. Chomsky. 1963. Finitary Models of Language Users. In R. D. Luce, R. Bush, and E. Galanter, eds., *Handbook of Mathematical Psychology*, vol. 2, chap. 13 (Wiley).

Miyagawa, S. 2005. On the EPP. In M. McGinnis and N. Richards, eds., *Perspectives on Phases, MIT Working Papers in Linguistics* 49.

Moro, A. 2000. *Dynamic Antisymmetry: Movement as a Symmetry Breaking Phenomenon* (MIT).

Nevins, A. 2005. Derivations without the Activity Condition. In M. McGinnis and N. Richards, eds., *Perspectives on Phases, MIT Working Papers in Linguistics* 49.

Nissenbaum, J. 2000. *Investigations of Covert Phrase Movement*. Doctoral dissertation, MIT.

O'Neil, W. 1977. Clause Adjunction in Old English. *General Linguistics* 17(4):199–211.

Pesetsky, D. 1987. Wh-in-Situ: Movement and Unselective Binding. In E. Reuland and A. G. B. terMeulen, eds., *The Linguistic Representation of (In)definiteness* (MIT).

Pesetsky, D. 2000. *Phrasal Movement and Its Kin* (MIT).

Postal, P. 1974. *On Raising* (MIT).

Reinhart, T. 1979. The Syntactic Domain of Syntactic Rules. In F. Guenther and S. Schmidt, eds., *Formal Semantics and Pragmatics* (Reidel).

Reinhart, T. 1993. Wh-in-Situ in the Framework of the Minimalist Program. Unpublished ms., Tel Aviv. *Natural Language Semantics* 6:29–56, 1997.

Reuland, E. J. 2001. Primitives of Binding. *Linguistic Inquiry* 32(3):439–492.

Richards, N. 2001. *Movement in Language* (Oxford).

Rizzi, L. 1997. The Fine Structure of the Left Periphery. In L. Haegeman, ed., *Elements of Grammar* (Kluwer). Reprinted in L. Rizzi, *Comparative Syntax and Language Acquisition* (Routledge, 2000).

Rizzi, L., ed. 2004. *The Structure of CP and IP—The Cartography of Syntactic Structures*, vol. 2 (Oxford).

Rizzi, L. 2006. On the Form of Chains: Criterial Positions and ECP Effects. In L. Cheng and N. Corver, eds., *Wh-Movement on the Move* (MIT).

Rooryck, J. 2000. *Configurations of Sentential Complementation* (Routledge).

Rubin, E. 2003. Determining Pair-Merge. *Linguistic Inquiry* 34(4):660–668.

Safir, K. 1986. Relative Clauses in a Theory of Binding and Levels. *Linguistic Inquiry* 17:663–689.

Sigurdsson, H. 2004. Meaningful Silence, Meaningless Sounds. Unpublished ms., Lund.

Svenonius, P. 2004. On the Edge. In D. Adger, C. de Cat, and G. Tsoulas, eds., *Peripheries: Syntactic Edges and Their Effects* (Kluwer).

Szczegielniak, A. 2004. *Relativization and Ellipsis*. Doctoral dissertation, Harvard University. *MIT Occasional Papers in Linguistics*, no. 24, 2005, Cambridge, MA.

Takahashi, D. 1994. *Minimality of Movement*. Doctoral dissertation, University of Connecticut.

Tsai, W.-T. D. 1994. *On Economizing the Theory of A-Bar Dependencies*. Doctoral dissertation, MIT.

Vergnaud, J.-R. 1985. *Dépendance et niveaux de représentation en syntaxe. Lingvisticae Investigationes Supplementa* 13, 1985 (John Benjamins).

Wexler, K., and P. Culicover. 1980. *Formal Principles of Language Acquisition* (MIT).

Yang, C. 2002. *Knowledge and Learning in Natural Language* (Oxford).

7 Phasal Agreement and Reconstruction

Alain Rouveret

7.1 Introduction

Aoun and Li (2003) argue that it is necessary to distinguish several types of restrictive relative constructions, not only across different languages, but also within individual languages. This claim stands in sharp contrast with the position, previously shared by many researchers, that a single analysis should be sufficient to cover the full range of relative phenomena. Basing their analysis on English, Lebanese Arabic, and Chinese, they propose that three strategies are made available by Universal Grammar (UG) to derive relative constructions:

(1) a. Promotion analysis, also labeled head-raising analysis[1]
    b. Matching analysis—that is, *wh*-operator movement analysis
    c. Direct base-generation (no-movement) analysis

The diagnostic properties that support the divide in (1) are reconstruction effects and locality effects. The structures derived via head raising display the full range of reconstruction effects.[2] This corresponds to the expected situation since the moved head originates in the relativization site. The relatives involving operator movement do not show reconstruction effects, since there is no chain relationship between the base-generated head and the *wh*-operator moved to the peripheral position of the relative CP and entering into a predication/agreement relation with the head. Base-generated relatives exhibit no reconstruction effects. As for locality effects, they are observable in the relatives whose derivation involves movement—that is, in those that make use of (1a) or of (1b), but not in those that are directly base-generated.

It will not have escaped the reader's notice that Aoun and Li's typology assigns no specific status to resumptive relatives. The reason is that, in their approach, the gap/resumptive divide is orthogonal to the typology in (1). In Lebanese Arabic, reconstruction effects are found in definite resumptive relatives, provided that the resumptive pronoun is not separated from the head by an island boundary, but not in definite relatives in island contexts nor in indefinite relatives. Aoun, Choueiri, and

Hornstein (2001) take advantage of this contrast to distinguish between "true" resumption—the only strategy available in island contexts—and "apparent" resumption—that involves the presence of a movement chain linking the resumptive and the relative head or the *wh*-phrase.

The primary aim of this study is to motivate a different conception of the articulation between resumption, reconstruction, and locality, taking Celtic relative constructions as a paradigmatic case. It can be summarized as follows:

(2) The derivation of resumptive relatives does not involve any movement of the resumptive pronoun or of a null operator in overt or in covert syntax.

(3) In the structures containing no island boundaries, the dependency between the resumptive pronoun and the head is established through a syntactic process, taking place in narrow syntax.

The position expressed in (2) is the one that has been defended by McCloskey for Irish since the late 1970s (see McCloskey 1979, 1990, 2001, 2002; also Awbery 1977 on Welsh). It implies that a resumptive pronoun in an A'-binding structure is "not created by movement" and should not be identified with a stranded D either, left behind by the A'-movement of the NP complement of a big DP, as Boeckx (2003) has recently proposed.[3] (3) amounts to the claim that resumptive pronouns are not just ordinary pronouns that happen to be A'-bound at LF: narrow syntax is direcly involved in the establishment of resumptive dependencies, which do not result exclusively from an LF interpretive procedure.

Both the movement and the nonmovement analyses must be confronted with the following empirical generalizations, put forth by various authors working within the Government and Binding framework or the Minimalist Program:

(4) a. Welsh resumptive structures display some reconstruction effects in nonisland contexts, but not the full range of reconstruction effects (see Rouveret 2002).

  b. Successive cyclicity effects manifest themselves in Welsh and Irish resumptive relative constructions (see Harlow 1981; McCloskey 1979, 2001, 2002; Rouveret 1994, 2002; Willis 2000).

  c. Subjacency effects are observed in Welsh resumptive relative constructions (see Tallerman 1983). No Subjacency effects can be detected in Irish resumptive relatives (see McCloskey 1990, 2002).

If we try to put (4a–c) into a consistent whole, we are confronted with a paradox. If we take reconstruction to be crucially tied up with movement and assume that in nonisland contexts, (at least some) resumptive structures are derived via head raising, we understand why they display reconstruction effects, but not why they do not exhibit the full range of reconstruction effects. If on the other hand, resumptive constructions instantiate some version of the base-generation strategy, the fact that they display some reconstruction effects and seem to obey Subjacency (in Welsh at least) is unexpected. The asymmetric Subjacency behavior of Welsh and Irish resumptive constructions makes the picture even more complex. I intend to show that this paradox can be conveniently solved within a nonmovement analysis of resumptive structures.

The second goal of this study is to provide the theoretical foundations from which this analysis can be derived. I will argue that Agree is the operation involved in the establishment of nonmovement dependencies in nonisland contexts and that (4b) and (4c) should be viewed as morphological and syntactic reflexes of the phasal character of this operation. As for reconstruction in resumptive structures, it is natural to assume that it is made possible by the material that is lexically represented at the tail of the dependency at the relevant level of the derivation. The analysis of pronouns as definite descriptions with a silent NP part, sketched by Freidin and Vergnaud 2001, paves the way for an elucidation of reconstruction effects in resumptive structures. If it can be maintained, this account has two important implications:

(5) a. Successive cyclicity effects are not an exclusive property of the structures derived by movement.

 b. The correlation between movement and reconstruction should be loosened.[4]

7.2   Phasal Agreement in Resumptive Relatives

7.2.1   Agree and Phases

Two syntactic notions introduced by Chomsky (2000, 2001) will play a prominent role in the analysis developed here:

1. The operation *Agree*, which takes place in narrow syntax between an uninterpretable feature on a head (the Probe) and another instance of the same feature on a head or phrase in its c-command domain (the Goal), which results in the valuation of the uninterpretable feature of the Probe, if the Goal feature itself has a value. *Agree* is a precondition on the operation *Move*.

2. The notion of *phase*, which refers to the stages of the derivation at which the internal parts of syntactic domains cease to be accessible for further syntactic computation, and as such defines both the units appropriate for the successive cyclic displacement of expressions and the domains in which all the requirements of a head must be satisfied. CPs, transitive and unergative vPs, and plausibly DPs are taken to define (strong) phases, but not IPs, nor unaccusative or passive vPs.

A crucial component of the phasal approach is the Phase-Impenetrability Condition stated in (6):

(6) *Phase-Impenetrability Condition (henceforth, PIC)*
 In phase α with head H, the domain of H is not accessible to operations outside α, only H and its edge are accessible to such operations.

(6) yields a very strong cyclicity constraint. As it is formulated, it should be relevant for all the grammatical operations that participate in the formation of dependencies, not only Move, but also Agree. In what follows, I will adopt the claim in (7), which amounts to the null hypothesis if the PIC is adopted, and explore its consequences.

(7) Agree applies phase by phase, in a cyclic fashion.

7.2.2   The Gap/Resumption Divide

In a theory incorporating Agree, the A′-dependency involving the head of a relative clause (or the relative complementizer) and the relativization site in nonisland contexts may result from (i) movement—that is, from Agree followed by Move—or from (ii) base generation combined with Agree, or from (iii) base generation alone. These three options turn out to be instantiated in Welsh, which confirms that several strategies can be used within the same language to derive relative clause constructions (see Rouveret 2002 for data and analysis). The "direct" gap relatives are good candidates for inclusion in class (i).

(8) a. y   llong a   werthodd y   dyn
        the boat REL sold   the man
        'The boat that the man sold'
    b. y   dynion a   ddaeth
        the men   REL came-3SG
        'The men that came'

In the examples in (8), the complementizer *a* coexists with a gap at the position of the variable.[5] They should be contrasted with those in (9), which illustrate the "indirect" resumptive relative construction:

(9) a. y   dyn y soniais amdano
        the man C I-talked about-AGR
        'The man I talked about'
    b. y   dyn y siaradasoch chwi ag   ef
        the man C spoke   you with him
        'The man that you spoke with'
    c. y   dyn yr oedd ei fam   gartref
        the man C was   CL mother at-home
        'The man whose mother was at home'
    d. y   dynion y dywedodd Siôn y darllenasant y   llyfr
        the men   C said   Siôn C read-3PL   the book
        'The men that Siôn said had read the book'
    e. y   dyn y gwn   y gwêl Wyn ef
        the man C I-know C sees Wyn him
        'The man that I know that Wyn sees'

The complementizer *y* coexists with a pronominal element functioning as a resumptive and signaling the relativization site. The pronominal element can itself be an agreement marker on an inflected preposition or on a finite verb (cf. 9a, 9d), an independent pronoun, object of a preposition or of a finite verb (cf. 9b, 9e), or a possessive clitic (cf. 9c). I will assume that the resumptive relatives in (9) illustrate the base generation + Agree option, that is, case (ii), whereas the structures in which the relativization site is included in an island and filled by an "intrusive" pronoun illustrate the pure base-generation option, that is, case (iii).[6]

Since the gap strategy is not available in the structures resorting to the resumptive strategy and vice versa, it must be asked which principle governs the divide between the two. The question can be reformulated as follows: When is Agree followed by Move? And the correct answer appears to be: whenever possible. It does not come as a surprise that a locality restriction is directly involved in the availability of movement. The notion of phase appears to provide a simple characterization of the relevant locality. Examples (8a) and (8b) show that the movement strategy (in fact, the head-raising strategy) is available in Welsh when the term to be relativized is the subject or the object argument of a single-clause structure. By definition, the nominal arguments of the verb either are merged at the edge of the vP-phase or can move to the edge. In a PIC-based phasal approach, the material at the edge of vP is visible from the relative C position.

The resumptive strategy is used in the other situations—when the term to be relativized is not accessible to the relative C. The object of a preposition internal to vP cannot be moved to the edge of vP across the prepositional head. The relativization of nonlocal subjects and objects, illustrated by (9d) and (9e), also falls under this characterization if one assumes that an element α in the position of the pronoun can move out of the complement clause only if it is attracted by the complementizer that heads it. The ungrammaticality of (10a) shows that *y* is not equipped to attract argument DPs. Examples (10b) and (10c) show that Welsh *a* cannot head declarative clauses embedded under relative ones. This precludes the recourse to the movement strategy, because an embedded subject or object is not accessible to the attracting relative complementizer. The Irish data confirm this analysis: contrary to its Welsh equivalent, Irish *a* (= *aL*) can head a declarative embedded in a relative and the movement strategy is available for long-distance relativization; see (11).

(10) a. *y dyn y gwn y gwêl Wyn
         the man that I-know that sees Wyn
     b. *y dyn a wn a wêl Wyn
         the man REL I-know REL sees Wyn
     c. *y dyn y gwn a wêl Wyn
         the man C I-know REL sees Wyn

(11) an t-ainm a   hinnseadh dúinn a   bhí ar an áit
     the name aL was-told   to-us aL was on the place
     'The name that we were told was on the place'

In other words, *a* is tied up with movement in both Welsh and Irish, but its distribution is more restricted in the former than in the latter: in Welsh, the attracting complementizer *a* can only head [+predicative] clauses.[7]

The fact that the higher subject and the higher object are grouped together in direct relativization confirms the relevance of the accessibility of the higher vP edge to movement and shows that in Welsh, the recourse to resumption is barred in the highest object position as well as in the highest subject position. This could indicate that the constraint captured by the Highest Subject Restriction (see McCloskey 1990, among others) is not specific to subjects and could be derived from phase theory.[8]

In conclusion, the notion of phase appears to lead to an adequate characterization of the locality condition underlying the divide between gap relatives and resumptive relatives, a welcome result. Our approach exploits a crucial feature of the theory of phases: the access to the phonological component is cyclic. The reason resumptive pronouns must be spelled out is because the syntactic objects that bear the corresponding φ-features are trapped within vP and have no access to its edge. On the contrary, relativized subjects and direct objects that have access to the vP edge postpone Spell-Out through movement.

7.2.3   How Is the Resumptive Dependency Established?

Let us now make explicit the way the resumptive dependency is established in the syntax. The null hypothesis is that resumptive configurations, like movement structures, require the establishment of a relation between the content of the relativized position and the relative C. I propose (12) as a working hypothesis:

(12) The link between the resumptive pronoun and the periphery results from the operation Agree, triggered by the presence of "active," uninterpretable features on the relative C and on the pronoun.

Contrary to what happens in gap relatives, Agree is not followed by Move in resumptive relatives.[9] Rather, a null operator is merged directly into the highest SpecCP position of the A'-dependency and binds the resumptive pronoun. If one follows the guideline provided by (12), the first step is to determine the feature composition of resumptive C. Assume that when it functions as a relative complementizer, *y* is endowed with uninterpretable φ-features.[10] It also bears a [+definite] feature, which is inseparable from the associated φ-features (and will not be mentioned separately in what follows). A feature [Rel] on C encodes the relative status of the clause; the same feature is found on resumptive pronouns, where it is clearly uninterpretable. Finally, an operator binding the resumptive pronoun must be present in SpecCP.

Since it does not reach this position through movement, it must be directly merged with C. This requirement is encoded by an EPP feature, which can, but need not, be viewed as a property associated with the [Rel] feature. The feature makeup of y is thus as follows:

(13) y is the realization of C bearing the following features:
ϕ-features (uninterpretable)
[Rel] feature (interpretable)
EPP

Given the PIC, the pronoun has no direct access to the CP periphery. Its relation to the relative C must be mediated by v, which must itself be endowed with features in order to function as a probe. Let us provisionally assume that v bears an uninterpretable ϕ-set and an uninterpretable [Rel]-feature. The relevant feature configuration is given in (14) (u-ϕ/u-Rel and i-ϕ/i-Rel stand for uninterpretable and interpretable ϕ-/Rel-features, respectively).

(14) DP [y T [...   v   ...pronoun...]]
           u-ϕ u-ϕ i-ϕ
      i-Rel/EPP   u-Rel   u-Rel

C, v, and the pronoun are all syntactically active because they each bear at least one uninterpretable feature. Agree relations are successively established between the features of the pronoun and those of v, then between the features of v and those of C, whose ultimate effect is to provide the uninterpretable ϕ-features on C and the uninterpretable [Rel] feature on the pronoun with a value. The merger of a null operator with C disposes of the EPP feature.[11] The resulting configuration does not contain any uninterpretable/unvalued feature and satisfies the demands of the interface.

Note that, if only u-ϕ was present on v, the derivation should crash at the lower phase level, when this feature is valued. This is the reason an extra feature is needed on v, which we provisionally identify as [u-Rel]. The characteristic of this feature, which can be referred to as the "activation feature," is that it remains active until the derivation reaches the highest C, where it is valued at last. The same difficulty arises in long-distance dependencies and can be accommodated along similar lines, with the successive cyclic assignment of a value, through Agreement, to the uninterpretable ϕ-features present on each phasal head:

(15) DP [y ...[v   ...[y ...[v   ...[y ...pronoun...]]]]]
     u-ϕ u-ϕ u-ϕ u-ϕ u-ϕ i-ϕ
     i-Rel   u-Rel   u-Rel   u-Rel   u-Rel   u-Rel

If the phasal account of resumptive relatives is on the right track, one can legitimately expect to find morphological manifestations of the agreement relations postulated between the successive phasal heads. Examples like (16), which are only found in written Welsh, confirm this expectation ((16) is discussed by Harlow 1981, 252).

(16) Beth yr ydych chwi yn   ei   ddisgwyl i   mi ei   wneud?
       what C are   you Prog CL expect   for me CL do
       'What do you expect me to do?'

The presence of the lower clitic attached to the verb-noun *wneud* requires no explanation: *ei* functions as a resumptive, spelling out the ɸ-content of the argument position it doubles. The higher clitic, which would be absent in standard Welsh, can only be characterized as an agreement marker recapitulating the ɸ-features of the relativized element. It is safe to analyze it as the morphological reflex of the agreement relation between the matrix v and the phase heads C and v of the subordinate CP.[12] (16) confirms that ɸ-features directly participate in the establishment of the agreement relation involved in the resumptive dependency.

7.3 Resumption and Successive Cyclicity

In the approach adopted here, the successive cyclic character of operations follows from the need to satisfy the requirements of phase heads functioning as probes and to value the uninterpretable features of the goals. Each step involves a different phase head and can thus potentially have a different motivation. This approach is just an extension to nonmovement A′-structures of the phasal analysis of successive cyclic movement developed by Chomsky (2000, 2001), which ties movement to the feature properties of intermediate phase heads. I tried to argue that the same mechanisms are involved in the derivation of nonmovement and movement A′-structures, the only difference being the unavailability of intermediate heads triggering movement in the former. It is clear, however, that the Agree derivation encounters some of the same difficulties as the Agree+Move derivation. In multiclause A′-movement structures, it must be guaranteed that the uninterpretable [wh]-feature of the *wh*-phrase remains active during the whole process. To achieve this result, Chomsky (2000) proposes that an extra P(eripheral) feature is present on intermediate heads and that it can be valued by any A′-phrase that is available, but cannot itself value and delete the activation feature of that phrase, because it is incomplete.

In this section, I will briefly consider some patterns of long-distance resumptive relativization in Irish, which strongly suggest that the P-feature can be dispensed with. As we saw above, Welsh is quite parsimonious concerning the morphology of complementizers, since it uses the same form *y* to introduce resumptive relatives, adjunct relatives, and embedded declarative clauses.[13] The situation is quite different in Irish, which distinguishes between the embedded declarative complementizer *goN* and the nonmovement relative complementizer *aN*.[14]

7.3.1   The Irish Dominant Pattern

The dominant pattern in Irish long-distance resumptive relatives is the one schematized in (17) and exemplified in (18).

(17) *Pattern 1*
DP_i [*aN* . . . [*goN* . . . [*goN* . . . $pron_i$ . . .]]]

(18) postaí ar maoidheamh go   rabh siad sócamhlach agus buan
jobs   *aN* was-claimed *goN* were they comfortable and permanent
'Jobs that were claimed to be comfortable and permanent'

In (17)/(18), the form of C associated with the binding of a resumptive pronoun, *a* (= *aN*), appears in the topmost C-position, while all the lower C-positions are occupied by the neutral declarative complementizer *go* (= *goN*).

Pattern 1 seems to indicate that the resumptive dependency is unbounded, ignores the Cs intervening between the resumptive C, spelled out as *aN*, and the pronoun, and is licensed through anaphoric binding in a single step at LF. I wish to argue that, on the contrary, this pattern provides direct morphological evidence that a feature that is neither the inherently valued φ-set of the resumptive, nor its unvalued A′-feature (the [Rel] feature), is directly involved in the establishment of the resumptive dependency. The possibility that A′-movement structures exploit the presence of a noninherently valued feature, found on the *wh*-phrase as well as on all the intermediate heads, is explored by Nissenbaum (2000), who, interestingly, proposes to identify the "other" feature as [mood], a suggestion that he attributes to Chomsky. This "other" feature on the *wh*-phrase is attracted by the intermediate heads, but left undeleted. It is deleted only at the final landing site.

In Irish, the form of the various complementizers and particles varies along a dimension that traditional grammars identify as the [+past]/[−past] distinction. The resumptive relative complementizer is no exception to this claim, as shown by (19) and (20).

(19) *Tensed complementizers (Christian Brothers 1997)*

Nonpast	*Past*[15]	
go	gur	Default complementizer
a	ar	Resumptive complementizer
an	ar	Interrogative particle

(20) a. fear a gcabhróinn   leis
man *aN* help-COND-1SG with-him
'A man whom I would help'
b. bean   ar   maraíodh   a mac
woman *aN*-PAST kill-IMP-past her son
'A woman whose son was killed'

Note however that if the relevant dimension has to do with the periphery of the
clause, it is more natural to identify it with [mood]. Whether [mood] is inherently
valued (interpretable) or not (uninterpretable) depends on the C that bears it. It is
not inherently valued on the C heading a selected domain—that is, a complement
clause—but it is in nonselected contexts, for example on the C heading the highest
CP in a relative clause construction. It is also plausible to assume that the mood
property is represented on v and that the corresponding [mood] feature is not inherently valued. The tense-mood morphology on finite verbs should be taken as evidence that v is indeed endowed with a [mood]-feature (in each clause, the finite verb
on its way to T transits through v). Finally, I will posit that [mood] is also a property
of the pronominal (and nominal) phrases that must be linked to the periphery. Just
as their being marked for [tense] allows nominal expressions to function as arguments in the inflectional domain (see Pesetsky and Torrego 2001), their being marked
for [mood] allows a subset of them to be linked to the periphery and participate in
A′-relations. This feature makes them eligible for Agreement with the heads that
also have this feature, namely the probes C and v. If this speculation is on the right
track, there is one feature that distinguishes resumptive pronouns from ordinary
third-person pronouns: only the former are specified for [mood]. The relevant structure is the one given in (21):

(21)   *aN* — T — v — *go* — T — v — *pron*
      i-mood u-mood u-mood u-mood u-mood u-mood u-mood
      i-Rel   u-Rel
      u-φ   i-φ

The resumptive dependency associates *aN*, which is endowed with uninterpretable φ-features, and the pronoun, which bears interpretable φ-features. There is no
doubt that in (21), the PIC should prevent any agreement relation from being established between the two φ-sets. A possible way out would consist in assigning an uninterpretable φ-feature to all the phase heads intervening between the two agreeing
objects, as we did in (15). A more interesting solution would start from the observation that the mood dependency in (21) is strictly phasal—[mood] on each phase-
defining head functions as a probe in the phase it heads, then defines a goal in the
next higher phase; the process stops when it encounters a head whose [mood] is
inherently valued; in relative constructions, this head is the topmost relative C.[16]
One could then propose that the reason the first Agree relation involving C and the
pronoun does not have to be phasal is that the second relation implicating C and
resulting in the formation of the [mood]-chain is. In other words, I propose to extend
Richards's Principle of Minimal Compliance, formulated in (22), to Agreement
chains.

(22) *Principle of Minimal Compliance (Richards 1997)*
Once an instance of movement to β has obeyed a constraint on the distance between source and target, other instances of movement to β need not obey this constraint.

In conclusion, we can take the mood marking on each intervening complementizer and finite verb as overtly manifesting the successive cyclic agreement relationships established between the phasal heads C and v.[17] Another way to express this result is to say that in pattern 1, the [Rel]-feature disguises itself as unvalued [mood].

7.3.2 The Second Irish Pattern

McCloskey (2002) identifies additional multiclausal patterns that, although far less common, nevertheless exist in the language. One of them is illustrated in (23)–(24).

(23) *Pattern 2*
$DP_i [aN \dots [aN \dots [aN \dots pron_i \dots]]]$

(24) an bhean a   raibh mé ag   suil a   bhfaighinn uaithi   é
the woman *aN* was   I   PROG hope *aN* I-would-get from-her it
'The woman that I was hoping that I would get it from her'

The complementizer *aN* marks the lowest complement clause, as well as the intermediate ones, as containing a pronominal resumptive dependency. Pattern 2 has thus a "successive character" in the sense that it involves a "distinctive morphosyntactic marking in intermediate positions" (McCloskey 2002, 195). The reiteration of *aN* at each cycle could be taken to reflect the successive cyclic character of A′-movement. But this pattern can also be analyzed as involving the successive cyclic establishment of an Agree relation between the phasal heads involved. The difference with pattern 1 reflects a different choice of features driving the establishment of the dependency.

There is no way to maintain that in pattern 2, the features of *aN* qualify it as a deficient intervener, as Chomsky proposes for the the P-feature in *wh*-movement constructions.[18] In fact, the lowest CP in (24) could define the relative part in a single-clause construction. Yet this CP does not stand in the appropriate environment to function as a relative, since it finds itself in a selected context. Moreover, if the view that null operators do not move is maintained, the relative dependency cannot be complete when the lowest phase is completed since, at this level, the resumptive pronoun is not bound by an A′-antecedent in the specifier of CP. The question is then: How is the resumptive dependency defined? How is it transmitted?

I propose that *aN* is the form taken by C endowed with φ- and mood-features. It is natural to assume that the resumptive complementizer is specified for [mood], since it varies along the [+/−past] dimension. The embedded complementizer *goN* itself is exclusively specified for [mood]. The property that distinguishes pattern 2 from pattern 1 is that ϕ-features are (also) involved in the step-by-step establishment of the resumptive agreement dependency. The relevant feature structure is given in (25):

(25) aN — T — v — aN — T — v — $pron$
  i-mood u-mood u-mood u-mood u-mood u-mood u-mood
   u-ϕ u-ϕ u-ϕ u-ϕ i-ϕ
   i-Rel   u-Rel
   EPP

As pattern 1 demonstrates, however, resumptives, which are also marked for [mood], can at no cost enter into a dependency based on this feature. Resorting to intermediate ϕ-features means that no advantage is taken of the freedom afforded by the Principle of Minimal Compliance. The reason pattern 2 is less common than pattern 1 can thus be traced back to the fact that the recourse to aN in lower clauses is a less economic option, involving more operations.[19]

One should ask at this point whether it is necessary to associate a [Rel] feature with the resumptive goal and with the C probe in (21) and in (25). It could be assumed that [mood] and [ϕ] in patterns 1 and 2, combined with the EPP feature on the "relative" C, are both necessary and sufficient to establish the dependency. [u-mood] on the resumptive pronoun both functions as a "beacon" feature distinguishing the resumptive from the other pronouns present in the relative clause, and as an uninterpretable feature satisfying the Activity Condition. Finally, the [Rel] feature is not needed to distinguish the resumptive complementizer from the embedded declarative one: [u-ϕ] fulfills this function. The existence of pattern 2 confirms that aN is not inherently [i-Rel], since it can head clausal domains that are not contextually identified as nonselected predicative domains. If these considerations are on the right track, representations (21), (25) and (14), (15) should be revised accordingly.

7.4 Which Diagnostic Properties for Movement/Nonmovement?

Let us step back a little and consider what has been accomplished so far. I have shown that the notion of phase, combined with the claim that the dependency-forming featural operation Agree can or cannot be followed by the operation Move, opens the way to a nonmovement analysis of resumptive relative clauses, which provides an elegant account of the successive cyclic effects displayed by these structures. Phase theory, in particular the idea that the access to the interfaces is cyclic, also provides a natural way to explain the gap/resumptive divide.

It may be fruitful at this point to specify how, in current minimalist theorizing, the structures derived by movement and those that exclusively resort to agreement can be empirically distinguished. The question arises because certain properties that were previously considered to provide reliable diagnostics of whether movement has taken place or not can potentially be construed as reflecting constraints on the Agree operation itself.[20] As far as locality conditions are concerned, the division of labor between Agree and Move can be conceived of in either of two ways. A first possibility is to assume that Move obeys conditions that Agree is insensitive to. This is the position developed by Bošković (2005), who claims that Agree is not subject to the PIC and can apply at a distance.[21] If, however, we take the phasal requirement as a general condition on derivations, along the lines of Chomsky 2000, 2001, this requirement should be observed by both operations.[22] Similarly, minimality effects should emerge in the nonmovement structures that exclusively resort to Agree if Agree is governed by a closest c-command requirement, as in Chomsky's (2000) original definition.

As for the strong island conditions, it is generally held that resumptive structures do not obey them, whereas movement structures do. Subjacency would thus be an exclusive property of the constructions derived by movement. The Welsh facts discovered by Tallerman (1983) show that the picture is more complex. In this language, the relation between a resumptive and the relative complementizer cannot cross strong island boundaries. In other words, resumption per se does not remedy strong island violations.

(26) a. ??Dyma'r dyn y   cusanaist ti   'r ddynes a   siaradodd amdano
         here the man that kissed   you the woman REL talked   about-AGR

    b. ??Dyma'r dyn y   cusanaist ti   'r ddynes y   gwn   y   cyfarfu hi
         here the man that kissed   you the woman that I-know that met   her

The status of (26a) improves a lot if the object position of the inflected preposition is filled by an auxiliary pronoun:

(26) c. ?Dyma'r dyn y   cusanaist ti   'r ddynes a   siaradodd amdano   ef
         here the man that kissed   you the woman REL talked   about-AGR him
         'Here is the man that you kissed the woman that talked about him'

(26c) illustrates the third of the three options available to derive relative structures: direct base-generation. To account for the ungrammaticality of (26a) and (26b) and for the contrast between (26a) and (26c), one possibility, immediately compatible with the phasal agreement analysis, would be to take Subjacency effects as deriving from the properties of Agree, rather than from the movement of an (abstract) operator. Either the island-inducing heads cannot participate in phasal agreement, because they are not endowed with the appropriate features (see Rouveret 2002),[23] or they block phasal agreement because they introduce an additional phasal boundary. A variant of the second option would consist in viewing Subjacency effects as reflecting a general property of the derivational cycle. For example, if in a complex DP configuration, both CP and DP define phases, the piece of structure containing the resumptive is not accessible anymore when the derivation reaches the post-DP level. Whatever the correct option, these effects cannot be used to distinguish between movement and nonmovement structures.[24]

The last of the diagnostic properties that are standardly resorted to in order to distinguish movement structures from nonmovement ones is reconstruction. Recent analyses of resumptive constructions have converged on the idea that they indeed display reconstruction effects, as ordinary gap/movement structures do. Significantly, however, they do not display the full range of reconstruction effects: in the general case, Principle C effects are obviated in these constructions. To account for this set of properties, an alternative approach to reconstruction, encompassing resumptive constructions, is required. Once this alternative treatment is made explicit, it appears that reconstruction effects are plainly compatible with a nonmovement analysis of resumption.

7.5 Resumption and Reconstruction

7.5.1 Movement and Reconstruction

The notion of "reconstruction" is both natural and necessary in a theory where traces are silent morphemes of a particular type, as is the case in the Government and Binding framework, but it is redundant in a theory in which the trace left by a movement operation is a copy of the moved element, as proposed by Chomsky (1993) in the first minimalist paper. It is no longer necessary to assume that the nonoperator material is literally reconstructed in the trace position, since the copy is deleted in the PF component (in the case of overt movement), but remains at LF, providing the material for reconstruction.

It is well known, however, that not all binding relations have the same reconstruction properties. Whereas Principle C is systematically checked on a reconstructed structure, the anaphoric relations that invoke Principle A do not seem to force reconstruction at the tail of the chain. This is shown by the following *wh*-interrogative constructions:

(27) *[Which argument of John's father] [did he defend *t*]

(28) a. John wondered [which picture of himself] [Mary saw *t*]
      b. John wondered [which picture of herself] [Mary saw *t*]

Chomsky (1993) shows that the asymmetry between Principle A and Principle C in A′-movement structures can neatly be accounted for within the copy theory of movement, once the following assumptions are made:

(29) Preference Principle: Reconstruction—that is, the representation of the
      restrictor at the tail of the chain—is obligatory if possible.[25]

(30) Principles A and C exclusively apply at LF.[26]

(31) The Principle C requirement does not take precedence over reconstruction and does not motivate a violation of (29).

(32) The satisfaction of Principle A takes precedence over reconstruction and motivates a violation of (29).

My aim in what follows is to determine whether this mode of explanation can be extended to reconstruction effects in resumptive relatives or whether they fall under radically different principles. The first possibility is clearly preferable if tenable. My analysis will thus follow the guidelines in (33)–(34):

(33) "Reconstruction" should not be viewed as a separate process—the term itself should be taken as a convenient descriptive label to refer to some range of phenomena.

(34) Some adjustments at LF are necessary to account for the full complexity of reconstruction phenomena. They should be formulated as preferences, not as absolute requirements.

7.5.2 Reconstruction Effects in Resumptive Relatives

A careful examination of Welsh resumptive relatives shows that these constructions, contrary to gap relatives, do not exhibit the full range of reconstruction effects: they display these effects with respect to pronominal variable binding and anaphoric binding, but not with respect to Principle C. Examples (35), (37), and (38) illustrate this asymmetry.

7.5.2.1 Principle C Principle C effects are obviated in resumptive relatives.

(35) Yn ddiweddar, dygwyd   darlun o Siôn yr   oedd ef wedi ei roddi i Mair
     recently   was-stolen picture of Siôn that was he PERF it give   to Mair
     'Recently was stolen a picture of Siôn that he had given to Mair.'

In (35), the construal of the pronoun *ef* in the relative subject position as coreferent to *Siôn*, a name embedded as a prepositional complement in the relative head, is legitimate. If the antecedent is reconstructed into the position occupied by the resumptive pronoun *ei*, a Principle C violation should arise. Their binding behavior sharply distinguishes resumptive relatives from gap relatives, which clearly display Principle C effects.

(36) Yn ddiweddar, dygwyd   darlun o Siôn a   roddasai i Mair.
     recently   was-stolen picture of Siôn REL had-given to Mair
     'Recently was stolen a picture of Siôn that he had given to Mair.'

In (36), the construal of the subject of *roddasai* as coreferent to *Siôn* is excluded. In this structure derived via head raising, the relativization site contains a copy-trace of the raised head. In the coreferent reading, the occurrence of *Siôn* in the copy-trace is c-commanded by the coreferent null pronominal subject. The resulting ungrammaticality immediately follows from Principle C.

7.5.2.2 Pronominal Binding   Reconstruction effects emerge in constructions such as (37), where a quantifier internal to the relative clause takes scope over a pronoun contained in the nominal antecedent.

(37) Mae gan Siôn farn   ar   ei lyfr y mae pob awdur yn   ei pharchu
     is   with Siôn opinion about his book C is   each author PROG it respect
     'Siôn has an opinion about his book that each author respects.'

For the bound interpretation of the pronoun to be derived, it is necessary to suppose that the expression "opinion about his book" is represented in the relativization site, signaled by the resumptive.[27]

7.5.2.3 Anaphoric Binding   Anaphoric binding may also require the "reconstruction of the antecedent" in the relativization site.

(38) Fe 'm hysbyswyd   am   y   clecs   amdano ei hun y mae Siôn wedi eu
     PRT me was-reported about the gossip about   himself C is   Siôn PERF them
     clywed yn y   cyfarfod
     hear   at the party
     'The gossip about himself that Siôn heard at the party was reported to me.'

For the anaphoric expression *ei hun* to be construed as anaphoric to *Siôn*, it must be c-commanded by its antecedent at LF, which suggests that the expression 'gossip about himself' is lexically represented in the relativization site in this case.[28]

7.5.3   Resumptive Pronouns as Definite Descriptions

In the analysis of reconstruction in resumptive structures, much depends on what we take resumptive pronouns to be: What is their underlying representation? How is their interpretation reflected at LF?

Semanticists dealing with donkey anaphora and related phenomena have claimed that the pronouns occurring in the relevant sentences should be analyzed as "hidden" or "disguised" definite descriptions; see Evans 1980, Heim 1990, and Elbourne 2001. But they insist that pronouns are not totally free to reconstruct their descriptive content and that donkey anaphora (E-type) pronouns may have less hidden content than the corresponding definite descriptions. Sauerland (2000, 2004) extends the E-type characterization to bound pronouns, but he shows that, if bound pronouns can also be hidden definite descriptions, they need not be—they are definite descriptions when focused.

Interestingly, an analysis of personal pronouns as definite descriptions has also been put forth by Freidin and Vergnaud (2001) from an entirely different perspective, since their primary interest was to develop a minimalist account of Principle C. From the set of assumptions they put forth, I will set (39) apart:

(39) *Underlying representation of definite pronouns*
     [$_{DP}$ [+def] ϕ ~~NP~~],
     with ϕ the agreement features of the nominal expression and ~~NP~~ the silent NP-component.

The intention underlying (39) is clear. The Inclusiveness Condition (see Chomsky 1995, 225), which is one of the foundational assumptions of the Minimalist Program, implies that indices are not legitimate elements of syntactic representations and thus that coreference and anaphoric relations should be represented in another way. Representation (39) implies that it is not possible to define a semantic notion of pronoun at LF distinct from that of definite description. When we see a definite pronoun on the surface, we are actually dealing with a definite description, an idea that comes close to assimilating the syntactic and semantic contribution of pronouns to that of definite determiners. On the PF side, a definite pronoun is simply a definite description whose NP-component is not pronounced.

In what follows, I will extend the definite-description analysis to resumptive pronouns and check how far we can go with (39) in the analysis of the reconstruction behavior of resumptive structures. Since (39) is supposed to hold for all pronoun types, the requirement of a formal link between a definite pronoun and its antecedent reflects a general condition on pronoun construal, not a restriction on resumptive pronouns. The property that sets resumptive pronouns apart is that the antecedent that anaphorically binds them is necessarily the relative antecedent. It will appear however that, just as has been observed for other pronoun types, the silent anaphoric NP may have less content than its antecedent and that a preference is involved at LF.

The first property to be dealt with is the obviation of Principle C effects in resumptive relatives, illustrated by (35). The line of research I will follow is that, just as in the case of *wh*-movement structures, the LF rules interpreting resumptive pronouns can yield more than one option. If resumptive pronouns are definite pronouns at LF, the silent NP part must be lexically represented in one form or another at this level. My claim is that this representation can include either the full NP antecedent or just the N without any complement or adjunct, which leaves us with either (40a) or (40b) (I will henceforth represent the couple *[+def]* ϕ as *D*):

(40) a. Pron = [$_{DP}$ D [$_{NP}$ N DP]]
     b. Pron = [$_{DP}$ D N]

For (35), this gives us either (41a) or (41b) (both *darlun* 'picture' and *Siôn* being masculine, D_1 and D_2 in (41a) include the ϕ-matrix [third person, singular, masculine]):

(41) a. ei = [$_{DP}$ D_1 [darlun o [D_2 Siôn]]]
     b. ei = [$_{DP}$ D_1 [darlun]]

It is easy to show that option (40b)/(41b) correctly predicts the absence of Principle C effects in (35). The relative clause contains a second pronoun, *ef*, which bears the grammatical features [third person, singular, masculine, animate], allowing it to be interpreted as *Siôn*. If this option is chosen, the corresponding representation of *ef* is as in (42):

(42) ef = [$_{DP}$ D_2 [Siôn]]

The structural representation of the relative clause thus contains the sequence (43), in which the second pronominal stands in the c-command domain of the first:

(43) ... [$_{DP}$ D_2 [Siôn]] ... [$_{DP}$ D_1 [darlun]] ...

The selection of (40b) thus gives rise to a converging derivation, with no violation of Principle C being involved.

Suppose, however, that (40b) only corresponds to the preferred option at LF. Whenever convergence requires the full NP-component to be active, the preference is overridden. The constructions illustrating the binding of an external pronoun by an internal quantifier are a case in point; consider the well-formedness of (37). The representation associated with the resumptive pronoun *ei* in (37) can only be (44):

(44) ei == [$_{DP}$ D_1 [barn ar [[D_2 awdur] llyfr]]]

The structural representation of the relative clause thus contains the following sequence, in which the quantifier phrase c-commands the definite pronominal expression:

(45) ... [$_{DP}$ pob$_2$ [awdur]] ... [$_{DP}$ D_1 [barn ar [[D_2 awdur]$_3$ llyfr]]] ...

For the bound interpretation of the pronoun to be derived, it is necessary to suppose that the expression "opinion about the author's book" is represented in the relativization site and active at LF. Suppose that, in reference to the Preference Principle proposed for gap/movement structures, we define a second Preference Principle for resumptive structures:

(46) *Preference Principle (for resumptive structures)*
     Given Pron = [$_{DP}$ [+def] ϕ ~~NP~~] a definite pronoun functioning as a
     resumptive, only the [+def]- and ϕ-components of Pron (i.e., D) and the N
     head of the NP-component are syntactically active at LF for interpretive
     purposes.

(46) states that the representation of pronominal definite decriptions should be minimal at LF at the site of the resumptive variable. But this preference only holds up to convergence. It is overridden in (37)/(45). It is also ignored when anaphoric binding imposes the representation of the antecedent in the internal position. The option in which the NP-component of the definite pronominal expression is fully represented at the tail of the chain must be selected in (38). No reconstruction operation is required to introduce the necessary material, since, given (39), it is there from the start.

7.5.4 A Fine-grained Prediction

Another facet of reconstruction in resumptive structures should be discussed at this point: the existence of a correlation between Principle C effects and the possibilities for pronominal binding. This correlation has been brought to light by Lebeaux (1992) for English *wh*-interrogatives and further discussed by Fox (2000). Aoun, Choueiri, and Hornstein (2001) have discovered that the same correlation could be observed in the resumptive structures of Lebanese Arabic. Guilliot (2002) and Rouveret (2002) discuss Breton and Welsh examples supporting the same conclusion: only when a pronoun is construed as bound by a quantifier (and a functional interpretation is derived) do Principle C effects emerge in resumptive constructions. Example (47) confirms that "reconstruction" for pronominal variable binding forces "reconstruction" for Principle C:

(47) barn   yr athro   ar ei mab y   gŵyr ef y   mae pob mam   yn   ei
     opinion the teacher on her son that knows he that is   each mother Prog it
     pharchu
     respect
     'The teacher's opinion of her son that he knows that each mother respects.'

Example (47) can be assigned the distributional reading in which each mother is paired with a different son. However, if one tries to establish a coreference relation between *yr athro* ("the teacher") and *ef* ("he"), the distributive reading becomes impossible. This is so because for this reading to obtain, the relative antecedent must "reconstruct" to the relativization site signaled by the resumptive pronoun. But if it does, a Principle C violation results: after reconstruction, the relativized nominal expression *barn yr athro ar ei mab* ('opinion of the teacher on her son') is c-commanded by the QP *pob mam* ('each mother'), but also by the pronoun coreferent with a DP contained in the reconstructed phrase (*ef*). The fact that resumptive structures display the same correlation as gap structures is elegantly derived in an approach based on (39) and (46). The full NP-component of the resumptive pronoun must be syntactically present and active when a bound pronoun construal is at stake. But if it is, it will give rise to a Principle C violation when a nominal complement of N is construed as coreferent to a c-commanding pronoun. The phenomenon under discussion

strongly suggests that Principle C and the principle responsible for pronominal binding apply at the same level of representation, namely LF.[29]

7.5.5 An Argument against Movement

In all the cases considered so far, "reconstruction" of the head of the relative occurs
in the site occupied by the resumptive in single-clause configurations (cf. pronominal
binding by a quantifier in (37) and anaphoric binding in (38)) as well as in long-
distance structures (cf. pronominal binding in (47)). It must be asked, however,
whether reconstruction can exclusively occur at the tail of the relative dependency
or can take place in other positions. The answer to this question represents an important challenge for the nonmovement analysis of resumption. Recent work by Fox
(2000) and Legate (2003) has established that successive cyclic *wh*-movement leaves
copy-traces at the edge of every intermediate CP- and vP-phase, whose presence is
revealed by the interpretive effects they give rise to. If it turned out that the same reconstruction possibilities are available in intermediate positions in resumptive structures, we would have a clue for analyzing the latter along the same lines as the
former, namely as movement structures. If, on the other hand, it turns out that reconstruction is exclusively possible at the tail of the dependency, the case for movement will be considerably weakened. Consider (48):

(48) barn   yr athro ar ei mab y   gŵyr pob mam y   mae ef yn   ei
     opinion the teacher on her son that knows each mother that is   he PROG it
     chuddio
     conceal
     'The teacher's opinion on her son that each mother knows that he conceals'

Example (48) cannot be given the distributional reading where each mother is paired
with a different son, and at the same time allow the establishment of a coreference
relation between *yr athro* 'the teacher' and *ef* 'he'. In other words, (48) has exactly
the same ungrammatical status as (47), under the coreferent reading. A movement
analysis would wrongly lead us to expect this reading to be available, provided that
the antecedent is lexically represented at LF in a position higher than the one occupied by *ef*, but lower than the one filled by the subject *pob mam* 'each mother'. This
site coincides with the edge of the lower CP-phase. The ungrammaticality of (48)
under the coreferent reading corresponds to the expected situation in the nonmovement account of resumption developed here: it should be traced back to a Principle C
violation.

   In conclusion, careful examination of the data confirms that reconstruction is only
possible at the position of the pronominal variable and that the analysis of resumptive pronouns as definite descriptions, combined with an appropriate definition of the
Preference Principle, suffices to account for the range of possibilities without resort to
movement being necessary.[30]

7.6   Conclusion

The descriptive generalization that emerges from this chapter is that there is no simple correlation between the presence/absence of reconstruction effects in a structure
and the presence of a copy-trace/resumptive element in the relevant clause. Partial
reconstruction effects (excluding Principle C effects) are found in Welsh resumptive
relative clauses. Resumptive constructions also display successive cyclicity effects,
which thus cannot be taken as an exclusive property of the structures containing a
copy-trace either. At a more theoretical level, I hope to have shown that the nonmovement account of resumption developed here represents a viable alternative to
(at least some versions of) the movement analysis of the same phenomenon. Proposals 1–3 subsume this account:

1. The link between the resumptive pronoun and the relative C results from the
phasal establishment of an Agree relation between the two, not from a movement
operation.
2. Resumptive pronouns are definite descriptions with a silent NP part, which is visible and active at LF only.
3. A Preference Principle is necessary at LF to select among the possible LF representations of resumptive definite descriptions, which is different from the one required
to reconfigure movement structures.

By way of a conclusion, I will briefly examine some objections that could be raised
against this account. The first concerns the relation between proposals 1 and 3. From
the fact that reconstruction effects reflect interpretive requirements of the interface
and are evaluated at LF, one could conclude that they are largely independent of
the derivation of the relevant resumptive structures and, as such, do not provide any
argument for or against a nonmovement analysis. In particular, the reconstruction
asymmetry with respect to Principle C should not be taken as a clue that resumptive
relatives and gap relatives should be assigned different derivations. The second objection is a development of the first and is concerned with the status of the Preference
Principle (46). If the reconstruction asymmetry between the two types does not follow from their derivational properties, the task of distinguishing them exclusively
falls upon the Preference Principle. But what is the motivation of this principle?
Why is the preference different in gap and in resumptive structures?

   Let us answer the second objection first. The reason it is necessary to resort to a
preference principle, rather than to an absolute requirement, is empirical: not all
binding relations give rise to reconstruction effects in resumptive constructions. The
reason two different principles are necessary is again strictly empirical and directly
reflects the asymmetric reconstruction behavior of the two relative types with respect
to Principle C. This asymmetry, it seems to me, provides sufficient motivation for the

claim that the principles responsible for the establishment of binding relations treat the variables left by A′-movement differently from the pronominal variables present in resumptive constructions. Recall that the idea underlying (46) is that the reconstruction behavior of resumptive constructions is closely related to the semantics of pronouns.[31] The claim that the LF representation of pronouns can be, but is not always, a maximally developed definite description has been advanced by semanticists dealing with different relations from the ones considered here.

We are now in a position to consider the first objection. The reconstruction asymmetry does not in itself constitute an argument against a movement analysis of resumption.[32] However, in the derivational model adopted here, the operations taking place in narrow syntax directly constrain the range of options available at LF. Under the nonmovement analysis, the material present at the position of the variable at LF is a pronominal definite description, which preferentially reduces to a D-N combination. This structure is precisely what is necessary to account for the absence of Principle C effects. If one adopts the particular version of the movement analysis developed by Boeckx (2003), where the NP part of a big DP is moved and the D part stranded, the content of the variable position will always be a D-NP combination, including the complements of and adjuncts to N. An additional mechanism, different from the Preference Principle (29), will thus be necessary to account for the absence of Principle C effects in resumptive constructions.[33] It was also shown that the nonmovement analysis and the movement analysis of resumption are not predictively equivalent concerning the distribution of reconstruction effects in long-distance relativization. The fact that these constructions do not display interpretive effects that could result from copies being present at the edge of intermediate phases, but exclusively show such effects at the position of the pronominal variable, supports the nonmovement analysis. Recall that one of the major claims of this chapter is that resumptive pronouns are precisely found in positions from which movement, for one reason or another, is not legitimate. Thus the fact that one does not find interpretive effects linked to movement corresponds to the expected situation.

Notes

This chapter has greatly benefited from the insightful comments of Nora Boneh, Bob Borsley, Željko Bošković, Chris Collins, Marcel den Dikken, Bob Freidin, Edwin Williams, and two anonymous reviewers. It also owes much to Jean-Roger Vergnaud, whose stimulating observations, when a preliminary version of this work was presented at USC in October 2003, led to much needed clarification and improvement. I also wish to thank the audiences at USC, CUNY, and Princeton University for their questions and their readiness to argue.

1. The promotion analysis was initially developed by Brame (1968) and Vergnaud (1974) and revived by Kayne (1994) within his Antisymmetry approach to word order and phrase structure.

2. The fact that Condition C reconstruction effects are generally entirely lacking in English *that*-relative clauses, which Aoun and Li derive through head raising, is unexpected in their analysis; see Aoun and Li 2003, 242, note 3.

3. A stranded analysis along similar lines had also been developed by Rouveret (1994) within the principles-and-parameters framework.

4. It has been known since Cinque's (1990) pioneering work on Clitic-Left-Dislocation that some constructions for which a movement derivation is not the obvious choice display some of the properties of movement structures, in particular reconstruction/connectivity effects and strong-island sensitivity. With respect to the latter, Cinque's conclusion is that it is a representational property of A′-chains.

5. For lack of space, we ignore adjunct relatives, which are gap relatives headed by the complementizer *y*, observe the standard conditions on movement, but do not show reconstruction effects. They should be analyzed as involving the movement of a *wh*-operator, deleted through matching; see Rouveret 2002.

6. See example (26c) below. These constructions usually display an "auxiliary" pronoun in the relativization site in doubling contexts (it can be doubled by a clitic or by an agreement marker). This is in sharp contrast with the resumptive structures studied here, where the relativization site, when doubled, is systematically empty. Base-generated structures and resumptive structures are thus morphologically distinguished.

7. Example (10c) shows that the accessibility condition is not the only requirement that must be satisfied for the head-raising strategy to be available. Suppose that the DP subject, a phase itself, is realized in a position internal to the inflectional domain and hence belongs to the highest CP-phase. An element in the specifier of DP should have direct access to the relative C, since no phasal boundary intervenes between the two. The head-raising strategy is thus blocked by some other condition. One possibility is to assume that SpecDP is a scope position and that expressions that have reached a scope position cannot move further; see Bošković 2003 and Rizzi 2004.

8. More precisely, direct objects in single-clause structures are always brought within the reach of movement—that is, at the edge of the vP phase in Welsh. This is not the case in Irish, where the gap strategy and the resumptive strategy are both available for the relativization of local direct objects. This contrast can be taken to show that direct objects systematically shift to the edge of vP in Welsh, but can remain buried within vP in Irish.

9. The preservation of its idiomatic meaning is usually considered to be a reliable clue of whether movement is involved in the derivation of a construction or not. If resumptive relatives are "Agree only" structures and gap relatives are "Agree + Move" configurations, one should observe a difference between the following two sets of examples:

(i) y   fantais   a   gymerodd Mary ar Bill
     the advantage REL took   Mary on Bill

(ii) y   fantais   y   dywedodd John fod Mary wedi ei   chymryd ar Bill
     the advantage that said   John be Mary PERF CL take   on Bill

(iii) y   llun   a   dynnodd Paul o Mary
      the picture REL took   Paul of Mary

(iv) y   llun   y   dywedodd John fod Mary wedi ei   gymryd o 'r digwyddiad
     the picture that said   John be Mary PERF CL take   of the event

Native speakers detect no difference between the gap relatives in (i) and (iii) and the resumptive relatives (ii) and (iv), in part because they have much difficulty in perceiving the idiomatic meaning in gap relatives in the first place.

10. Syntactic evidence in favor of this claim comes from the existence of structures in which a clitic is adjoined to C.

(i) a. y   dyn y 'i   rhoddais (ef)   iddo
        the man C CL I-gave   him/it to-him
        'The man to whom I gave it'
    b. yr amser y   'ch gwelais
        the time   that you I-saw
        'The time when I saw you'

The Unselective Attract Principle proposed by Nash and Rouveret (2002) implies that only a head endowed with φ-features can attract a clitic. In their view, cliticization is a case of "unselective attraction."

11. The analysis in the text presupposes that resumptive relatives enter into the same type of relation with the head as Matching relatives: a predication/agreement relation that is mediated by a null operator directly merged into the specifier of CP. A second possibility, although less plausible, should not be discarded a priori: that in which the specifier of CP is filled not by a null operator, but by the head itself, directly merged with C. In this view, the head stands in the same structural relation with respect to the relative clause as the raised head in gap structures derived by the promotion analysis.

12. There is some similarity between the resumptive pattern illustrated here and the phenomenon of long-distance agreement (LDA) found in Tsez (see Polinsky and Potsdam 2001), and in Innu-aimûn (Algonquian) (see Branigan and MacKenzie 2002), where the verb agrees with the direct object that it selects, but can also agree with a constituent internal to its clausal finite complement (thanks to Marcel den Dikken for pointing out the relevance of these constructions). Example (16) illustrates a similar situation, since the higher verb agrees in φ-features with the resumptive. The Welsh phenomenon is quite restricted, however, since it exclusively occurs in nonfinite complement clauses embedded under relative/interrogative ones (i.e., when an operator-variable relation is involved), and since the agreement exclusively concerns embedded pronominal arguments (this property could reflect the fact that clitic doubling in Welsh is only possible with pronouns, not with DPs). Evidence supporting (or refuting) the account developed here should be provided by languages that both display LDA and resort to resumption in A′-constructions. Cursory inspection indicates that neither Tsez nor Algonquian fulfills this characterization.

13. This form also functions as a declarative particle in *be*-sentences and happens to be homophonous to the definite article.

14. I follow a notational convention introduced by McCloskey 1979: the final N indicates that the relevant complementizer triggers nasal mutation. The complementizer *aN* occurring in monoclausal resumptive relatives is thus distinct from the complementizer *aL* heading head-raising gap relatives, which triggers lenition (soft mutation). All the Irish examples in sections 7.3.1 and 7.3.2 are taken from McCloskey (1979, 2001, 2002).

15. To specify the mutations induced by these various particles, one should write *goN*, *gurL*, *aN*, *arL*…

16. If one adopts Frampton and Gutman's (2001) conception that views Agreement as a feature-sharing process, rather than as an assignment process, once an Agreement link (covaluation) is established between two syntactic objects, the value assigned to a feature F on the first automatically becomes the value of F on the second. Once [mood] on the higher T or v is valued through Agreement with [mood] on the topmost C, all the [mood] features of the chain get similarly valued.

17. The mood marking is also present in nonrelativization declarative contexts. The idea defended here is that relative dependencies take advantage of an independently available, morphologically manifested relation. The relative dependency is parasitic on the mood dependency.

18. The same observation holds for the long-distance movement pattern exemplified in (11).

19. It would be interesting at this point to determine whether the Welsh pattern (15) corresponds to pattern 1, to pattern 2, or constitutes a type in itself. Although the answer is delicate, cliticization data suggest that (15) is the Welsh equivalent of (17). The possibility of infixing a clitic to the relative C in indirect relatives, which has been taken as evidence that it is endowed with an uninterpretable φ-set (see note 10) is not available in embedded declaratives, whether they contain a resumptive pronoun or not:

(i) a. *Gwn   y 'i   gwelodd Wyn
       I-know C CL saw   Wyn
       'I know that Wyn saw him.'
    b. *y   dyn y dywedodd Mair y 'i   rhoddais (ef) iddo
       the man C said   Mair C CL I-gave it   to-him
       'The man to whom Mair said that I gave it.'

This suffices to show that all the occurrences of *y* in (15) do not have the same feature composition. The topmost complementizer is the one that heads resumptive dependencies in the simple-clause cases, while the lower ones should be identified as instances of the default declarative complementizer, introducing complement clauses.

20. This consequence of Agree is also discussed in Adger and Ramchand 2002, 2003 and in Rouveret 2002. Adger and Ramchand develop a semantic Agree-based analysis of Celtic relatives, in which neither gap relatives nor resumptive relatives are derived through movement.

21. This is so because, in Bošković's view, the PIC effects are established at PF, via pronunciation. Agree, which does not affect pronunciation, should not be subject to the PIC.

22. In fact, this requirement is attached to Matching, a precondition on Agree, not to Agree itself (see Chomsky 2000, 122).

23. This suggestion has far-reaching implications that cannot be seriously examined here. One of them, pointed out by den Dikken, is that closely related items such as English *that* and Dutch *dat* should be assigned quite different feature matrices, an unavoidable conclusion if one considers the contrasting Subjacency behavior of the corresponding clauses in the two languages. Another implication concerns the phasal organization of the left periphery in the multilayered conception of the CP area defended by Rizzi (1997).

24. Other possibilities can be explored. A movement approach along the lines of Iatridou's (1991) account of island effects in clitic constructions is developed in Rouveret 1994, but it relies on the claim that empty operators can move, an option rejected here. As for the difference between Welsh and Irish, it could be argued to be only apparent and to reflect a difference

in the pronominal system of the two languages: Welsh morphologically distinguishes syntactically bound pronouns from intrusive ones, Irish does not; see note 6.

25. Fox (2000) reformulates the Preference Principle as an economy condition—not having the restriction part at the tail involves an extra deletion at LF, thus a violation of Economy—and states that it can be overridden in a subset of constructions (namely, Antecedent Contained Deletion structures). See also Sauerland 1998, which proposes an elaborate analysis of nominal expressions in terms of "segments" and claims that it is a property of A'-movement chains that the NP part of a moving DP must be represented in the lowest trace position.

26. In other words, Principles A and C are not anywhere principles. In Lebeaux's (1992) approach, they are, but they differ in that Principle A is a positive condition, whereas Principle C is a negative one: if Principle A is satisfied anywhere during the derivation, its requirement is met; if Principle C is violated anywhere during the derivation, there is no well-formed output.

27. One could ask whether nonresumptive pronouns also give rise to reconstruction effects and, if they do not, why this is so. Chris Collins (personal communication) proposes the following example:

(i) His mother said that every boy likes her.

Although this construction is in part parallel to the relative one that allows the binding of an external pronoun by an internal quantifier, *his mother* cannot reconstruct into *her*. The different behavior of resumptive and nonresumptive pronouns could be traced back to the distinction between A'-dependencies and A-dependencies, which obviously is relevant to movement and to nonmovement structures. The fact that one occurrence of *his mother* is not in the scope of *every* could thus be part of the problem. If this conclusion is correct, (i) should not be better than (ii):

(ii) His mother said that every boy likes Madonna.

28. Example (38) is the transposition into Welsh of one of Bianchi's (1999) examples.

29. In Freidin and Vergnaud's (2001) account, Principle C effects reflect a conflict between the Principle of Phasal Coherence, holding at PF, and the Parallelism Principle on Anaphora, holding at LF. The two principles cannot both be satisfied in the relevant structures. Principle C is thus a strictly syntactic principle, relying on a property of the LF-PF correspondence. This characterization potentially affects the way the various reconstruction phenomena studied in this section should be looked at. It draws the required distinction between Principle C and the other binding principles (Principle A and the principle responsible for pronominal binding) in a very natural way, since, contrary to the former, the latter are exclusively LF principles. I will leave the discussion of Freidin and Vergnaud's proposal for future research.

30. The fact that reconstruction seems to be impossible within islands in Welsh could be traced back to the status of the intrusive pronouns occurring in the relevant structures. One could suggest that they don't fall under characterization (39).

31. In the terms of (46), the representation of pronominal definite descriptions should be minimal at the site of the resumptive variable. Vergnaud (personal communication) observes that this result can be achieved if, by analogy with what Lebeaux (1992) and Chomsky (1993) have proposed to account for the argument-clause/adjunct-clause asymmetry with respect to reconstruction, the complements of N-heads are uniformly treated as adjuncts and, as such, can be

introduced noncyclically and directly adjoined to the nominal head in the head position of the relative clause. Suppose that this option is indeed available. Whenever it is chosen, at no point in the derivation does the offending noun complement finds itself in the context triggering a Principle C violation. Note however that the late adjunction option should be restricted to resumptive structures and not resorted to in movement structures, as shown by the fact that Principle C effects are not obviated in Welsh gap relatives. This state of affairs is expected if the preference relevant for gap structures is the one stated in (29), which goes against the "high" insertion of both complements and adjuncts. Bošković (personal communication) observes that the late adjunction idea, as used here, is at odds with Lebeaux's use of the same hypothesis.

32. It is well known that some constructions standardly taken to be derived by movement do not display Principle C effects under reconstruction. This is true of *that*-relative clauses in English; see Munn 1994 and Citko 2001 for interesting solutions to this puzzle. As observed by one reviewer, the explanation and mechanism devised by these authors could probably be extended to account for the lack of Principle C effects in Welsh resumptive constructions. The parallelism between English movement and Welsh resumption, however, cannot seriously be taken as an argument for the analysis of resumption as movement. Moreover, many languages, including Italian, Norwegian, and Welsh, do display Principle C effects in gap relatives, a fact that would become problematic if the same mechanism was extended to cover all gap structures.

33. It remains to be checked whether the alternative movement analyses of resumption also have to resort to a preference principle of some sort to draw the appropriate distinctions. One case in point is Demirdache's (1991) account in which the resumptive element covertly raises to the relative C. In this case, movement affects an element that has already been spelled out.

References

Adger, David, and Gillian Ramchand. 2002. Phases and interpretability. In K. Megerdoomian and L. A. Bar-el, eds., *WCCFL 20 Proceedings*, 1–14. Somerville, Mass.: Cascadilla Press.

Adger, David, and Gillian Ramchand. 2003. Merge and Move: *Wh*-dependencies revisited. Unpublished ms., Queen Mary, University of London, and Oxford University.

Aoun, Joseph, Lina Choueiri, and Norbert Hornstein. 2001. Resumption, Movement, and Derivational Economy. *Linguistic Inquiry* 32:371–403.

Aoun, Joseph, and Yen-hui Audrey Li. 2003. *Essays on the Representational and Derivational Nature of Grammar: The Diversity of Wh-Constructions*. Cambridge, Mass.: MIT Press.

Awbery, Gwenllian. 1977. A transformational view of Welsh relatives. *The Bulletin of the Board of Celtic Studies* 27:155–206.

Bianchi, Valentina. 1999. *Consequences of Antisymmetry: Headed Relative Clauses*. Berlin: Mouton de Gruyter.

Boeckx, C. 2003. *Islands and Chains: Resumption as Stranding*. Amsterdam: John Benjamins.

Bošković, Željko. 2003. On *wh*-islands and obligatory *wh*-movement contexts in South Slavic. In Cedric Boeckx and Kleanthes Grohmann, eds., *Multiple Wh-Fronting*, 27–50. Amsterdam: John Benjamins.

Bošković, Željko. 2005. On the locality of Move and Agree: Eliminating the Activation Condition, Generalized EPP, Inverse Case Filter, and the Phase-Impenetrability Condition. *UConn Occasional Papers in Linguistics* 3.

Brame, Michael. 1968. A new analysis of the relative clause: Evidence for an interpretive theory. Unpublished ms., MIT.

Branigan, Phil, and Marguerite McKenzie. 2002. Altruism, A'-movement, and object agreement in Innu-aimûn. *Linguistic Inquiry* 33:385–407.

Chomsky, Noam. 1993. A Minimalist Program for linguistic theory. In Ken Hale and Samuel Jay Keyser, eds., *The View from Building 20*, 1–52. Cambridge, Mass.: MIT Press. Also in Noam Chomsky, *The Minimalist Program*. Cambridge, Mass.: MIT Press, 1995.

Chomsky, Noam. 1995. *The Minimalist Program*. Cambridge, Mass.: MIT Press.

Chomsky, Noam. 2000. Minimalist inquiries, the framework. In Roger Martin, David Michaels, and Juan Uriagereka, eds., *Step by Step: Essays on Minimalist Syntax in Honor of Howard Lasnik*, 89–156. Cambridge, Mass.: MIT Press.

Chomsky, Noam. 2001. Derivation by Phase. In Michael Kenstowicz, ed., *Ken Hale: A Life in Language*, 1–52. Cambridge, Mass.: MIT Press.

Christian Brothers. 1997. *New Irish Grammar*. Reprint, Dublin: Fallons.

Cinque, Guglielmo. 1990. *Types of A'-Dependencies*. Cambridge, Mass.: MIT Press.

Citko, Barbara. 2001. Deletion under Identity in relative clauses. *Proceedings of NELS 31*, 131–145. Amherst: GLSA, University of Massachusetts.

Demirdache, Hamida. 1991. *Resumptive Chains in Restrictive Relatives, Appositives, and Dislocation Structures*. Doctoral dissertation, MIT.

Elbourne, Paul. 2001. E-type anaphora as NP-deletion. *Natural Language Semantics* 9:241–288.

Evans, Gareth. 1980. Pronouns. *Linguistic Inquiry* 11:337–362.

Fox, Danny. 2000. *Economy and Semantic Interpretation*. Cambridge, Mass.: MIT Press.

Frampton, John, and Sam Gutmann. 2001. How sentences grow in the mind: Efficient computation in Minimalist Syntax. Unpublished ms., Northeastern University.

Freidin, Robert, and Jean-Roger Vergnaud. 2001. Exquisite connections: Some remarks on the evolution of linguistic theory. *Lingua* 111:639–666.

Guilliot, Nicolas. 2002. *Les trois "R" en breton: Relatives, résomptivité et reconstruction*. DEA de Sciences du Langage, Université de Nantes.

Harlow, Stephen. 1981. Government and Relativization in Celtic. In Franck Heny, ed., *Binding and Filtering*. London: Croom Helm.

Heim, Irene. 1990. E-type pronouns and donkey-anaphora. *Linguistics and Philosophy* 13:137–177.

Iatridou, Sabine. 1991. Clitics and island effects. Unpublished ms., MIT.

Kayne, Richard. 1994. *The Antisymmetry of Syntax*. Cambridge, Mass.: MIT Press.

Lebeaux, David. 1992. Relative clauses, licensing, and the nature of the derivation. In Susan Rothstein and Margaret Speas, eds., *Perspectives on Phrase Structure: Heads and Licensing*, 209–239. Syntax and Semantics 25. San Diego, Calif.: Academic Press.

Legate, Julie Ann. 2003. Some interface properties of the phase. *Linguistic Inquiry* 34:506–516.

McCloskey, James. 1979. *Transformational Syntax and Model Theoretic Semantics: A Case-Study in Modern Irish*. Dordrecht: Reidel.

McCloskey, James. 1990. Resumptive pronouns, A′-binding and levels of representation in Irish. *The Syntax of the Modern Celtic Languages*. Syntax and Semantics 23, 199–248. New York and San Diego: Academic Press.

McCloskey, James. 2001. The morphosyntax of *Wh*-extraction in Irish. *Journal of Linguistics* 37:67–100.

McCloskey, James. 2002. Resumption, successive cyclicity, and the locality of operations. In Samuel David Epstein and Daniel Seely, eds., *Derivation and Explanation in the Minimalist Program*, 184–226. Oxford: Blackwell.

Munn, Alan. 1994. A minimalist account of reconstruction asymmetries. *Proceedings of NELS 24*, 397–410. Amherst: GLSA, University of Massachusetts.

Nash, Lea, and Alain Rouveret. 2002. Cliticization as Unselective Attract. *Catalan Journal of Linguistics* 1:157–199.

Nissenbaum, Jonathan. 2000. *Investigations of Covert Phrase Movement*. Doctoral dissertation, MIT.

Pesetsky, David, and Esther Torrego. 2001. T-to-C movement: Causes and consequences. In Michael Kenstowicz, ed., *Ken Hale: A Life in Language*, 355–426. Cambridge, Mass.: MIT Press.

Polinsky, Maria, and Eric Potsdam. 2001. Long-distance agreement and topic in Tsez. *Natural Language and Linguistic Theory* 19:583–646.

Richards, Norvin. 1997. *What Moves Where in Which Language?* Doctoral dissertation, MIT.

Rizzi, Luigi. 1997. The fine structure of the left-periphery. In Liliane Haegeman, ed., *Elements of Grammar*, 281–337. Dordrecht: Kluwer.

Rizzi, Luigi. 2004. On the form of chains: Criterial positions and ECP effects. Unpublished ms., University of Siena.

Rouveret, Alain. 1994. *Syntaxe du gallois: Principes généraux et typologie*. Paris: CNRS Editions.

Rouveret, Alain. 2002. How are resumptive pronouns linked to the periphery? *Linguistic Variation Yearbook* 2:123–184.

Sauerland, Uli. 1998. *The Meaning of Chains*. Doctoral dissertation, MIT.

Sauerland, Uli. 2000. The content of pronouns: Evidence from Focus. In T. Matthews and B. Jackson, eds., *The Proceedings of SALT 10*. Ithaca, N.Y.: Cornell University, CLC Publications.

Sauerland, Uli. 2004. The silent content of bound variable pronouns. In K. Johnson, ed., *Topics in Ellipsis*. Oxford: Oxford University Press.

Tallerman, Maggie. 1983. Island Constraints in Welsh. *York Papers in Linguistics* 10:197–204.

Vergnaud, Jean-Roger. 1974. *French Relative Clauses*. Doctoral dissertation, MIT.

Willis, David. 2000. On the distribution of resumptive pronouns and *wh*-trace in Welsh. *Journal of Linguistics* 36:531–573.

8 Superiority, Reconstruction, and Islands

Cedric Boeckx and Norbert Hornstein

8.1 A Challenge for Minimalism

The Minimalist Program for Linguistic Theory (Chomsky 1995, 2000, 2001, 2004, 2005) has generated substantial changes in grammatical theory by emphasizing economy, computational efficiency, and simplicity as criteria of explanatory adequacy. This has prompted a reanalysis of earlier results reached during the "Government-Binding" era. Although many aspects of grammar remain to be subjected to a serious minimalist evaluation, several phenomena have been reexamined in interesting ways. Two such phenomena are *superiority* and *reconstruction* effects. They have come to occupy a privileged position within the Minimalist Program because the analyses offered to explain them have rested on constructs reflecting deep minimalist intuitions.

Recently, Aoun and Li (2003) have brought to light some facts from multiple *wh*-constructions in Lebanese Arabic (henceforth, LA) and proposed an analysis for them that suggests that the core minimalist assumptions used to explain superiority and reconstruction are incompatible. In this section we first show why the minimalist approaches to superiority and reconstruction became pillars of the theory. Then we turn to the core facts presented by Aoun and Li as what we think is a genuine empirical and conceptual challenge to standard minimalist assumptions. In subsequent sections we develop various ways minimalism could meet the challenge posed by LA facts, and try to show which ways seem more promising.

8.1.1 Superiority Effects
Superiority effects like (1) are described by (2) (see Chomsky 1973, 246).

(1) a. Who bought what?
    b. *What did who buy?

(2) *Superiority Condition*
   a. No rule can involve X,Y in the structure
      $\ldots X \ldots [\ldots Z \ldots WYV \ldots] \ldots$
      where the rule applies ambiguously to Z and MY, and Z is superior to Y.
   b. The category A is superior to the category B if every major category
      dominating A dominates B as well but not conversely.

The condition in (2) has received several implementations over the years (Cheng
and Demirdash 1990; Ferguson and Groat 1994; Hornstein 1995; Lasnik and Saito
1992; Müller 2002; Pesetsky 1982, 2000; Richards 1997, 2001; among many others).
Recently, the nature of superiority has been illuminated by detailed investigations of
patterns of overt multiple *wh*-fronting in Slavic languages and other language groups
(Rudin 1988; Bošković 1997, 1998, 1999, 2002; Hornstein 1995; Richards 1997, 2001;
Pesetsky 2000; Boeckx and Grohmann 2003; Williams 2003; Grewendorf 2001;
among many others). Bošković, in particular, has argued in a series of important
papers that superiority is an economy condition that requires the *wh*-phrase closest
to the target of movement (typically, C^0) to move first. Accordingly in Bulgarian, a
language that displays multiple *wh*-fronting, the first *wh*-phrase in the *wh*-cluster is
the one whose launch site c-commands the launch sites of the other *wh*-phrases.
This is illustrated in (3) and schematized in (4).

(3) a.   Koj kogo kakvo e pital?
         who whom what   is asked
         'Who asked whom what?'
    b.   Koj kakvo kogo e pital?
    c.   *Kogo kakvo koj e pital?
    d.   *Kakvo kogo koj e pital?
    e.   *Kakvo koj kogo e pital?
    f.   *Kogo koj kakvo e pital?

(4) $[_{CP} \underline{\quad} [_{C^0} [_{IP}$ koj $[_{I^0} [_{VP}$ kakvo V^0 kogo$]]]]]$

The empirical coverage and conceptual appeal of Bošković's proposal have played
an important role, as can be gathered from the numerous contributions supporting
his key insights in Boeckx and Grohmann 2003. The reasons for this are twofold.
First, the sort of economy account that Bošković offers fits neatly with what minimalist guidelines lead us to expect. On this account, superiority is not a primitive
property of Universal Grammar (UG) but rather emerges from a computational
economy condition embodied in the operation Closest Attract. Second, the empirical
coverage is superior to the coverage in GB (see Rudin 1988). By combining theoretical elegance and empirical breadth, this analysis has become a poster child for mini-

malism and its proposals concerning economy and movement have been widely adopted as fixed points within minimalist theory.

8.1.2 Reconstruction Effects

Reconstruction effects are illustrated in sentences like (5). Here the reflexive in the moved phrase, *which picture of himself*, is interpreted not in its overt position but in the position it occupied prior to movement.

(5) Which picture of himself does everyone like?
(Cf. Everyone likes that picture of himself.)

The conventional minimalist analysis of reconstruction effects emerges from the *Inclusiveness Condition* outlined in Chomsky 1993, 1995. Inclusiveness requires that the computational system only manipulate lexical features. Effectively, this forbids adding new kinds of "objects" during the syntactic computation, including devices such as indices and traces. To retrieve the empirical benefits of these GB devices but without their use, Chomsky 1993 revives an idea put forth in Chomsky 1955, where movement is analyzed as a process involving a "copy" operation. This has the effect of leaving a copy of a moved expression in its base position upon displacement. Reconstruction arises if the base copy feeds interpretation. For example, the reflexive *himself* in (5) is licensed under the interpretation of the copy of *which picture of himself* in the thematic position, as illustrated in (6).

(6) Which picture of himself does everyone like ⟨which picture of *himself*⟩?

The copy-theory-based analysis of reconstruction has been widely adopted (Aoun and Benmamoun 1998; Aoun, Choueiri, and Hornstein 2001; Bhatt 2002; Brody 1995; Fox 1999, 2000, 2002; Grohmann 2000; Hornstein 1995; Kim 1998; Lasnik 1999; Merchant 2000; Pesetsky 2000; Rizzi 2001; Romero 1998; Safir 1999; Sauerland 1998, 2004; Sportiche 2003; Witkos 2001; among many others). It too exploits central minimalist intuitions and provides broad empirical coverage. Like the economy condition underlying accounts of Superiority, the link between movement and reconstruction forged by the copy theory of movement is now a central feature of minimalist theory.

8.1.3 Aoun and Li's (2003) Challenge

To understand the force of Aoun and Li's challenge, it is useful to highlight some relevant properties of LA.[1]

LA has three ways of forming interrogative sentences: a fronting-gap strategy of the English type (7), a resumption strategy (8), and a *wh*-in-situ strategy (9).

(7) Miin ʃəft
    who saw.2sg
    'Who did you see?'

(8) Miin ʃəft-o
     who saw.2SG-him
     'Who did you see?'

(9) ʃəft   miin mbeeriħ
     saw.2.SG who yesterday
     'Who did you see yesterday'

As is often the case in such situations, not all strategies are created equal. For instance, the gap strategy is sensitive to islands (Complex NP in (10)), whereas the in-situ and resumption strategies are not ((11)–(12)).[2]

(10) *Miin btaʕrfo   l-mara   yalli ʃeefit   __ bə-l-maTʕam
      who know.2PL the-woman that saw.3FSG   in-the-restaurant
      'Who do you know the woman that saw in the restaurant'

(11) Btaʕrfo   l-mara   yalli ʃeefit   miin bə-l-maTʕam
     know.2PL the-woman that saw.3FSG who in-the-restaurant

(12) Miin btaʕrfo l-mara   yalli ʃeefit-o   bə-l-maTʕam
     who know.2PL the-woman that saw.3FSG-him in-the-restaurant

But resumption is not a strategy confined to islands. LA allows *wh*-phrases to be resumed even in nonisland contexts, as shown in (13).

(13) ʔayya mmasil ʃəft-uu   bə-l-matʕam
     which actor saw.2SG-him in-the-restaurant
     'which actor did you see in the restaurant?'

Aoun and colleagues, however, note an important difference between resumption inside and outside of island contexts (see Aoun and Li 2003; Aoun, Choueiri, and Hornstein 2001). Whereas resumption outside of islands allows for reconstruction, reconstruction inside islands is impossible. Witness the contrast between (14) and (15).

(14) ʔayya taalib min   tulaab-a$_i$ fakkarto   ʔənno kəll mʕallme$_i$
     which student among students-her thought.2PL. that every teacher.FS
     ħatnaʔ-ii
     will.3FS.choose-him
     'Which of her$_i$ students did you think that every teacher$_i$ would choose (him)?'

(15) *ʔayya taalib min   tulaab-a$_i$ ʔənbasatto laʔinno kəll mʕallme$_i$
      which student among students-her pleased.2PL because every teacher.FS
      ħatnaʔ-ii
      will.3FS.choose-him
      'Which of her$_i$ students were you pleased because every teacher$_i$ would choose (him)'

Based on this contrast, Aoun et al. distinguish between "true" and "apparent" resumption. The terms *true* and *apparent* hark back to the original views of resumption (Ross 1967; Perlmutter 1972). True resumption is understood as the absence of a *wh*-chain. It is the only strategy available in island contexts. Apparent resumption involves the presence of a *wh*-chain linking the the resumptive pronoun and the *wh*-operator. One can (slightly misleadingly) understand the resumptive pronoun as a pronounced trace left behind by *wh*-movement. This strategy is available outside islands.

Aoun et al. are now able to capture the reconstruction asymmetry noted above, by tying reconstruction effects to the presence of a copy left by *wh*-movement. Since no *wh*-movement is allowed to take place from within an island, reconstruction in such contexts is impossible.

The logic of Aoun et al.'s proposal is schematized in (16)–(17).

(16) wh-NP . . . [$_{island}$ . . . RP . . .] → no copy of wh → no reconstruction

(17) wh-NP . . . [$_{nonisland}$ . . . RP (= $\langle_{copy}$wh-NP$\rangle$) . . .] → copy of wh → reconstruction

So far Aoun et al.'s conclusion provides rather strong support for the copy-based analysis of reconstruction.

Aoun and Li (2003), however, provide data that makes the picture much more complex. This time the data come from superiority effects. In multiple questions, LA, like English and many other languages, shows superiority effects:

(18) a.　miin ʔannaʕto　　yzuur　miin
　　　　 who persuaded.2PL 3MS.visit who
　　　　 'Who did you persuade to visit who?'
　　 b.　*miin ʔannaʕto　　　miin yzuur
　　　　 who persuaded.2PL. who 3MS.visit
　　　　 'Who did you persuaded who to visit?'

As expected under Aoun et al.'s view on "apparent resumption," superiority effects are found in the context of resumption outside islands, as shown in (19).

(19) a.　miin ʔannaʕto-u　　　yzuur　miin
　　　　 who persuaded.2PL-him to-visit who
　　　　 'Who did you persuade (him) to visit who?'
　　 b.　*miin ʔannaʕto　　　miin yzuur-u
　　　　 who persuaded.2PL who to-visit-him
　　　　 'Who did you persuade who to visit (him)?'

If superiority is analyzed as Closest Attract or Shortest Move, we expect no superiority effects in the context of true resumption (resumption inside islands). However, Aoun and Li show that superiority effects obtain in such contexts.

(20) a. miin ʔənbasatto laʔinno saami ʕarraf-o   ʕa-miin
         who pleased.2PL because Sami introduced-him to-whom
         'Who were you pleased because Sami introduced (him) to whom?'
     b. *miin ʔənbasatto laʔinno saami ʕarraf   miin ʕəl-e
         who pleased.2PL because Sami introduced whom to-him
         'Who were you pleased because Sami introduced who to him?'

So from the point of view of superiority, true and apparent resumption strategies are symmetric: they behave in exactly the same way. But from the point of view of reconstruction, they behave asymmetrically. It seems that our minimalist conceptions of Reconstruction (qua Copying under movement) and Superiority (qua Attract Closest/Shortest Move) are incompatible empirically.

8.2   Aoun and Li's (2003) Analysis

The challenge posed by the reconstruction/superiority asymmetry in LA leaves us with basically two theoretical options:

1. We could hold constant the idea that superiority is always a result of movement. This would force a revision of our conception of islandhood and requires a loosening of the correlation between movement (/copying) and reconstruction.
2. We could maintain the prohibition against movement across islands (and, hence, explain the absence of reconstruction effects in such contexts), and divorce superiority effects from the economy of movement.

Aoun and Li (2003) develop a solution of type 2 to the LA challenge. Specifically, they propose that "chains can be generated either derivationally or representationally. The derivational process is at work when Move applies.... We further argue that minimality constrains all chains" (pp. 3–4). Before examining their proposal in detail, it is useful to note that Aoun and Li reject a solution of type 1 by saying that "one could introduce a distinction between two types of movement rules. The first one (call it *standard movement*) displays reconstruction; the second one (call it *illicit movement*) applies across islands and does not display reconstruction. However, within a minimalist framework, this option is not available since 'islandhood' or minimality is part of the definition of Move" (p. 2). We will return at length to Aoun and Li's rejection of a type 1 solution. But let us first provide the details of their proposal.

Aoun and Li propose that in addition to a condition like Relativized Minimality (in any of its incarnations: Shortest Move, Closest Attract, Minimal Link Condition) constraining the *formation* of chains, there is also a representational condition on chains that is at work when movement is not involved—that is, in cases of true resumption, when an operator is directly generated in SpecCP. The representational process constrains the search for an element that could be bound and function as a variable. Aoun and Li call the representational process the Minimal Match Condition, and define it as in (21).

(21) *Minimal Match Condition*
     An operator must form a chain with the closest XP that it c-commands that contains the same relevant features.

For Minimal Match to work, Aoun and Li have to assume that resumptive pronouns are not just pronouns; they must be pronouns endowed with a [+wh] feature (p. 33).

Aoun and Li note that Minimal Match is distinct from the Minimality Condition on Move in that Minimality on Move imposes a c-command relation on three elements: the target of movement, the moving element, and the (potential) intervener. Minimal Match only constrains two elements. This difference is important, since Minimal Match can rule out cases that "Minimal Move" would be silent on. For instance, Aoun and Li (2003, 20–21) note that cases like (22), illustrated in (23), provide evidence for the superiority of Minimal Match:[3]

(22) *$[_{CP}$ Wh$_1$ ... $[_{IP}$ ... $[_{Island}$ ... wh$_2$ ...] ... RP$_1$]]

(23) *miin fakkarto   laʔinno l-mʕallme   ħikət   maʕ miin ʔənno
       who thought2PL because the-teacher.FSG spoke3SG with who that
       l-mudiira   ħa-təʃħat-o
       the principal.FSG will-3FSG.expel-him
       'Who did you think because the teacher spoke with whom that the principal would expel him?'

In situations like (22), *wh$_2$* and the resumptive pronoun (RP) do not c-command each other, so neither position is closer to the operator position in SpecCP. However, from the point of view of Minimal Match, the sentence can be excluded, because the search for a [+wh] element originating from SpecCP (*Wh$_1$*) first encounters *Wh$_2$* before hitting on the desired variable (RP), in violation of Minimal Match. (Note, crucially, that for Minimal Match to apply, "closest XP" in (21) must be understood as "first XP"—that is, Closeness in this case cannot be understood in terms of c-command, contra Aoun and Li's (2003, 36) claim.) Interestingly, Aoun and Li (2003, 47) note that there is evidence that Minimal Match, in addition to constraining relations across islands, also constrain chains formed by Move (i.e., nonisland contexts). Specifically, they note that the unacceptability of sentences like (24), schematically represented as in (25), falls beyond the scope of Minimal Move (since *wh$_2$* and *t$_1$* are not in a c-command relation), but within the scope of Minimal Match (same situation as in (22)).[4]

(24) *miin fakkarit   l-bənt yalli ʕazamit   miin ʔənno faadi ħa-yiʕzum
     who thought.3FSG the-girl that invited.3FSG who that   Fadi will-invite.3MSG
     'Who did the girl that invited who think that Fadi would invite?'

(25) *[wh$_1$ ... [$_{Island}$ ... wh$_2$ ...] ... t_1 ...]

8.3 Problems with Aoun and Li's (2003) Solution

There are several problems with Aoun and Li's (2003) account. The first concerns the
logic they rely on to dismiss a type 1 solution. They claim that such a solution "is not
available since 'islandhood' or minimality is part of the definition of Move" (p. 2).
However, as Adger and Ramchand (2003, 2) observe,[5]

Given recent approaches to syntax [e.g., Chomsky 2000, 2001], locality effects can no longer be
assumed to be a diagnostic of movement. This is because, in theories like [Chomsky's], the abstract operation Agree, which applies between features of heads in a structure, must itself be
constrained by some theory of locality. The syntactic operation of movement is parasitic on
Agree, so it is not possible to use locality as a diagnostic for whether movement has taken
place.

Furthermore, "islandhood" is not part of the definition of Move. Chomsky's (1995,
296) claim regarding the formulation of the Move operation (which Aoun and Li
adopt) is that "we ... add to the definition of Move [/Attract] the condition ... expressing the M[inimal] L[ink] C[ondition]."

The Minimal Link Condition only subsumes Relativized Minimality effects. As
Rizzi (1990, 1) had originally noted, "The Minimality principle is a *partial* characterization of the locality conditions on movement." Minimality does not extend to cases
of CED-islands, for instance. (See Ochi 1999 for a clear demonstration of this.) But
such islands are the ones involved in the examples Aoun and Li examine to support
their argument.

We conclude that Aoun and Li's argument against a type 1 solution is inconclu-
sive. Furthermore, the specific type 2 solution they develop relies on two overlapping
(see (24) and (25)) yet distinct Minimality conditions: a derivational condition (Minimal Link Condition) and a representational condition (Minimal Match Condition).
This sort of duplication is methodologically unfortunate.

Aoun and Li (2003, 49) are aware of this: "Our [A&L's] approach unfortunately
goes against Brody's (1995) claim that derivations and properties of LF representations duplicate each other and that a parsimonious theory of syntax should dispense
either with representations or with derivations. Grammar seems to contain redun-
dancies." But it is hard to disagree with Brody's (2002, 20) clear statement that "having both [representations and derivations duplicating each other] would weaken the
theory in the sense of increasing the analytic options available ..., hence very strong

arguments would be needed to maintain that both concept-sets are part of the competence theory of syntax." Finally, we would like to point out a problem for Aoun and Li's solution in terms of Minimal Match. It technically requires that resumptive pronouns be treated as pronouns with an extra [+wh] feature. But as Boeckx (2001a, 2003a) observes, in every language studied to date, the morphological, syntactic, and semantic properties of resumptive pronouns are in every respect identical to those of pronouns.[6] In McCloskey's (2002, 192) words,

A remarkable but little commented on property of resumptive pronouns is that they simply *are* pronouns. I know of no report of a language that uses a morphologically or lexically distinct series of pronouns in the resumptive function. If we take this observation to be revealing, there can be no syntactic feature which distinguishes resumptive pronouns from "ordinary" pronouns, and any appeal to such a feature must be construed as, at best, an indication of the limits of understanding.

This statement applies to Aoun and Li's account,[7] and reinforces our conclusion that pursuing another solution to their very interesting empirical challenge is worthwhile.

8.4   A Unified, Movement-Based Approach

As noted at the outset, a type 1 solution requires several nontrivial moves: while it keeps constant the idea that superiority is the result of Relativized Minimality, it requires the formation of chains across (strong) islands and the loosening of the relationship between movement/copying and reconstruction. We think that both consequences are actually necessary and desirable (conceptually and empirically), and in fact, we show below that both have been (implicitly) entertained in the literature.[8]

The argument we develop requires several steps. First, we review prima facie evidence against the idea that antecedent-resumptive pronoun relations are chain/movement relations. Second, we show that the prima facie evidence discussed in the previous subsection, once properly analyzed, turns out to be evidence in favor of a movement-based account. Third, we examine the nature of islands, and adduce evidence independent of resumption that all islands must be seen as violable, or selective. Fourth, we suggest two ways of accounting for the absence of reconstruction despite movement in island contexts.

8.4.1   Step I: "Identity Effects"
Adger and Ramchand (2003, 2) observe, "[Given recent approaches to syntax, Chomsky's 1977 diagnostics[9] for movement as opposed to base-generation in terms of island effects and the presence of a gap no longer hold.] How, then, can we distinguish between the two? The core difference is whether the bottom of the dependency is occupied by a *pro* or a trace. On the assumption that traces are simple copies (Chomsky 1993), we expect to see what we will call *identity effects* in a movement

derivation, but not necessarily in a base-generation derivation." The identity effects Adger and Ramchand have in mind are of two kinds:

1. *Syntactic*: "The syntactic features of the putatively displaced constituent and its trace are exactly the same with respect to selection, agreement and case."
2. *Semantic*: "Idiomatic expressions and reconstruction phenomena."

They provide evidence from languages like Irish and Scottish Gaelic that no identity effects of either kind obtain in the context of resumption. First consider cases of syntactic nonidentity.

(26) *Anti–Person Agreement*
    A   Alec, tusa a   bhfuil an Béarla aige   Irish
    hey Alec you aN is   the English at-him
    'Hey Alec you that know(s) English.'

(27) *Anti–Number Agreement*
    Na daoine a chuirfeadh   isteach ar an phost sin   Irish
    the men   C put-COND-3SG in   for the job   that
    'The men that would apply for that job.'

(28) *Anti–Gender Agreement*
    Dè   a'mhàileid a chuir thu am peann ann   Sc. Gaelic
    which the.bag-FEM C put   you the pen   in-3-MASC
    'Which bag did you put the pen in?'

(29) *Anti–Case Agreement*
    a. Bha   thu a'geàrradh na craoibhe   Sc. Gaelic
       be-PST you cutting   the three-GEN
       'You were cutting the tree.'
    b. Dè   a'chraobh a bha   thu a'geàrradh
       which tree.NOM C be-PST you cutting
       'Which tree were you cutting?'

Turning to "semantic identity," Adger and Ramchand observe the loss of idiomatic reading and the absence of reconstruction under resumption.

(30) a.   Bidh   e a'toirt sop às   gach seid   Sc. Gaelic
         be-FUT he taking wisp from each bundle
         'He's not a very focused person.'
     b.   'S 'ann às   gach seid   a bhitheas e a'toirt sop
         it's   from each bundle C be-FUT   he taking wisp
      * 'He tries his hand at everything'
     OK: 'It's from every bundle that he has taken a wisp.'

(31) 'S toil leam   [[am peann] aige∗ₖ] [a bha   Iainₖ a'sgriobhadh leis]
     liking with me the pen   at him C be-PST Iain writing   with
     'I like his pen that Iain was writing with.'

We disagree with Adger and Ramchand's claim that the lack of identity effects under
resumption argues for a base-generation analysis and against a movement analysis.
In fact, Boeckx (2003a) argues at length that antiagreement under resumption is a
necessary precondition for movement. We briefly sketch the argument in the next
subsection. (For fuller discussion, see Boeckx 2003a.)

8.4.2 Step II: Antiagreement as a Condition on Resumption and Extraction

There is independent evidence that movement is closely related to what is known
in the literature as "antiagreement" effects. Consider the following examples from
Northern Italian dialects:

(32) a. La Maria l' è venuta   Italian
         The Maria she is come
         'Maria came.'
     b. Gli è venuto la Maria
         It is come the Maria
         'Maria came.'
     c. Quante   ragazze gli è venuto con te
         How.many girls   it is come with you
         'How many girls came with you?'
     d. *Quante   ragazze le   sono venute con te
         How.many girls   they are come   with you
     e. Chi hai detto che __ e partito
         Who has said that   is left
         'Who did he say that left?'

Example (32a) shows that preverbal subjects relate to a ϕ-feature matching clitic
(third-person feminine singular). By contrast, postverbal subjects do not (32b), the
clitic bearing default morphology. Examples (32c) and (32d) show that subject extraction requires the use of a nonagreeing clitic. Based on (32c), we can conclude (as
did Rizzi 1982) that in standard Italian examples like (32e), subject extraction takes
place from a postverbal position related to a silent nonagreeing clitic (*pro*), which
obviates the [*that*-trace] effect.

As Boeckx (2008) argues at length, antiagreement is often a prerequisite for successful extraction. Consider the well-known case of so-called *wh*-agreement in Chamorro (Chung 1994, 1998). Verbs in Chamorro are generally marked for person/
number agreement. However, in constructions involving A-bar extraction (i.e., in

the context of *wh*-agreement), normal agreement is replaced with special (*wh*-) mor-phology indicating the grammatical function (subject, object, etc.) of the extracted element.

(33) *Ha*-fa'gasi si   Juan i   Kareta
     3SG-wash   DET Juan DET car
     'Juan washed the car.'

(34) Hayi f*uma*'gasi   i   kareta
     who whɸ[subj].wash DET car
     'Who washed the car.'

Described this way, *wh*-agreement is in fact anti-(regular/"A") agreement.[10] This is precisely the description offered by Boeckx (2003a) for "resumptive chains." Building on an insight of Richards (1997, 2001), Boeckx argues that chains cannot contain two "strong" positions, where "strong position" can be equated with "checking po-sition" for present purposes (for a more precise characterization, see Boeckx 2003a, 2008). As a result of this ban on "chains that are too strong," elements that normally agree ("A"-type agreement, or what Chomsky 2001 calls "complete ɸ-feature agree-ment") must disagree (i.e., "antiagree") in order for them to successfully enter into a checking relation with an A-bar target ("Wh-/A-bar-"agreement).[11]

Boeckx claims that the role of a resumptive pronoun is to take care of "A-style" agreement, freeing the *wh*-phrase from establishing a successful relationship with an A-bar target. To achieve this, Boeckx proposes the following derivation for resump-tive chains:

(35) [Wh [C^0 [...[...[$_{DP}$ RP [⟨Wh⟩]]...]]]]

The resumptive pronoun and its antecedent start off as a big DP constituent, which is split in the course of the derivation in a way very reminiscent of Sportiche's 1988 influential Quantifier-Float stranding analysis. Boeckx argues in order for this "big DP" splitting to take place, the resumptive pronoun and the *wh*-phrase cannot be in an agreement relation (if they match in features, this matching must be seen as accidental). This correctly predicts the instances of anti-identity reviewed above, and accounts for Merchant's (2001, 146) generalization that "no resumptive-binding operator can be case-marked" once Case marking is taken to be a reflex of ("A-")agreement (see Chomsky 2000, 2001).

8.4.3   Step III: The Nature of Islands

Boeckx (2003a) also argues that the derivation in (41) reconciles a movement-based approach to resumption with the absence of island effects in the context of resump-tive chains. Keeping to the intuition expressed there (see Boeckx 2003a for technical details), we view (strong) islands as domains corresponding to exactly those domains that are impervious to "A"-agreement: adjuncts and elements that have already agreed (e.g., displaced subjects). This approach predicts that objects triggering "rich" (ϕ-complete) agreement will also block extraction. Basque examples like (42) show that this prediction is borne out.

(36) *Nori buruzko sortu zitusten aurreko asteko istiluek zurrumurruak
       who about-of create aux   last   week scandals rumors
       'Who have last week's scandals caused [rumors about]?'   Basque

Island effects arise when languages cannot resort to an anti-("A"-)agreement strategy such as resumption.[12]

It is useful at this stage to point out how a "(split) big DP" analysis of resumptive chains incorporates one key point of Aoun and Li's analysis (without inheriting the problems pointed out above): by combining the resumptive pronoun and the *wh*-phrase into one phrase headed by the resumptive pronoun, the pronoun *phrase* contains a *wh*-phrase, and thus qualifies as [+wh].

Another key aspect of the big DP analysis is that even though the presence of the resumptive pronoun frees the *wh*-phrase from A-agreement (and islandhood), it does not void superiority effects. This is because superiority effects, or Minimality effects more generally, are not tied to agreement. This is clear from what Chomsky (2000, 123) calls *defective intervention*.

The latter is best illustrated by means of the following paradigm from Icelandic (the data are taken from Boeckx 2000b, where the agreement facts are discussed at length).[13] As is well known, Quirky subjects fail to trigger agreement on the finite verb (43), despite the fact that they behave for all other purposes as bona fide subjects.

(37) Stelpunum   var   hjálpað
       the girls.DAT.PL.FEM was.3SG helped.NEUTER.SG
       'The girls were helped.'

Yet the presence of a Quirky element inside the internal domain of the agreeing verbal element at the point of Spell-Out ("surface structure") blocks the establishment of an agreement relation between the verb and a nominative element (38), which is otherwise possible (39).

(38) Mér   fannst/*fundust henni   leiDast their
       me.DAT seemed.3SG/3PL her.DAT bore   they.NOM
       'I thought she was bored with them.'

(39) Mér   *virðist/virðast their   vera skemmtilegir
       me.DAT seem.3SG/3PL   they.NOM be interesting
       'It seems to me that they are interesting'

For Chomsky, the Quirky element *henni* in (38) is a defective intervener. It blocks an agreement relation even though it itself lacks the relevant property to trigger agreement in. Boeckx and Jeong (2004) argue, based on a variety of examples, that Minimality effects can be consistently defined at the level of feature matching, not at the level of feature valuation (agreement per se).[14] This means that the presence of a resumptive pronoun freeing the *wh*-phrase from agreement does not eliminate Minimality requirements.

It is again interesting to note that the present proposal incorporates a key component of Aoun and Li's analysis. As we saw above, for them, Minimal Match constrains both chains formed by Move and base-generated chains. In our case we do not need to distinguish between Minimal Move and Minimal Match. We simply have to state that Minimality constrains the first step of syntactic relations (feature matching), which include agreement and nonagreement relations.[15]

To recap, what we have done so far is point to a way to form chains across islands, but nevertheless subject to Minimality effects. We have argued that such chains must be antiagreement chains. The next question to address is why such chains cannot give rise to reconstruction.

8.4.4   Step IV: Copying and Reconstruction

Aoun and Li's argument reviewed in section 8.3 appears to rely on the idea that in the context of islands, movement is banned. Once movement is understood as copying, and reconstruction arises as the result of interpreting a copy left behind by movement (see section 8.1), Aoun and Li's account predicts, correctly, that there will not be any reconstruction effects inside islands. In this section we would like to emphasize the fact that the relationship between movement/copying and reconstruction cannot be taken as a biconditional (contra Sportiche 2003). That is, (40) does not hold:

(40)   a. If movement → reconstruction possible   AND
        b. If no reconstruction ↛ no movement:

In particular, we contend that (40b) is false.[16] To motivate our claim we rely on the absence of reconstruction effects with A-movement, discussed by Lasnik (1999). Consider cases like (41).

(41)   No one is certain to solve the problem.
        *'It is certain that no one will solve the problem.'

We have argued elsewhere (see Boeckx 2000b, 2001b; Hornstein 1999; contra Manzini and Roussou 2000) that antireconstruction effects like (41) cannot be analyzed in terms of nonmovement, since some instances of A-movement (especially movement involving indefinites) reconstruct. If this conclusion is correct, (40b) cannot be right.

Another argument against (40b) comes from the fact that even weak islands, those that permit a significant degree of movement, do not accommodate reconstruction, as witnessed in (42).

(42) a. Which of his$_{1/*2}$ pictures did Bill$_1$ ask me why nobody/everybody$_2$ hated t
     b. Which of his$_{1/*2}$ pictures doesn't Bill$_1$ think that everyone$_2$ liked t

In a similar vein, Bobaljik and Wurmbrand (2005) provide evidence that the lack of reconstruction effect in restructuring contexts in German (and other languages) must be analyzed as an antireconstruction effect in the presence of movement.

(43) ... weil er alle Fenster   vergessen hat [⟨alle Fenster⟩ zu schliessen]
     because he all windows forgotten has   to close
     'Because he forgot to close all the windows'
     (alle Fenster ≫ vergessen; *vergessen ≫ alle Fenster)

To conclude, it appears that whereas reconstruction effects signal movement (/copying), antireconstruction effects do not necessarily signal lack of movement. Crucially, this conclusion is not construction-specific, because data beyond resumption have been provided to support it.

8.4.5   Step V: Accounting for Antireconstruction in the Presence of Movement
There are four classes of analysis that could reconcile a movement-based approach to resumption with the antireconstruction effects noted by Aoun and Li. The first class of analysis would follow in the footsteps of Lasnik (1999), who claims that the absence of reconstruction in situations like (41) is the result of A-movement not leaving copies. Salem (2001) has argued that resumptive chains are formed roughly as in (41),[17] and claimed that the presence of the resumptive pronoun allows for A-bar movement not to leave copies. This would account for the lack of reconstruction effects in island contexts.[18] But as far as we can see, it would make the same prediction in nonisland contexts (unless some proviso is added). This is incorrect, in light of the data discussed in section 8.1.[19] Apart from this empirical difficulty, a Lasnik-inspired account of the lack of reconstruction effects in islands is problematic on conceptual grounds. Under the Minimalist Program, it is not at all clear what it means for movement not to be copying. Although it is common to say that "movement leaves a copy behind," it is actually the copy of an element that moves. That is, copying is a prerequisite of movement. In the absence of a copy, nothing can move. As Lasnik himself observes at the end of his 1999 paper, "How can movement without a trace [copy] possibly be reconciled with a 'bare phrase structure' theory of structure building? A-movement not leaving a trace means that a 'term' in the sense of Chomsky [1995] is eliminated" (p. 209). We think that this is a serious problem

that future research must address before we can adopt it as a solution to the superiority/reconstruction paradox at the heart of the present chapter. A second class of solutions to the superiority/reconstruction paradox would allow for the *wh*-phrase to move to its surface position, but not quite in the way sketched in (35). Iatridou (1995) argues that Clitic Left-Dislocated material, which relates to a clitic in much the same way a *wh*-antecedent relates to a resumptive pronoun, is (or at least can be) base-generated at the edge of an island, and move from there to its surface position. Since it does not move from within the island, no island effect will ensue, and no reconstruction effect within the island. But such an account faces two problems. First, it is not clear how it would account for the superiority effects observed above, unless it imposes a Minimal Match condition very similar to Aoun and Li's.[20] As argued above, we think that this is highly problematic. Second, assuming, as Chomsky (2000) has argued (see also Hornstein 2001; Collins 1997), that each instance of Merge (including external/first merge) must be motivated by feature matching, it is not clear what would be the rationale for merger at the edge of an island.[21] For these reasons we do not find it advantageous to pursue a solution of this type to the problem at hand. A third class of solutions capitalize on the antiagreement condition on resumptive chains discussed above, and claim that antiagreement forces antireconstruction. But why should this be so?

We think that a generalization proposed by Nevins and Anand (2003) might provide a key part of the answer. Their discussion focuses on the following contrast in Hindi:

(44) Kisii Saayer-ne har   ghazal lik^{h}ii   Hindi
      Some poet-ERG every song   write.F-PERF
      'Some poet wrote every song.' (some > every; *every > some)

(45) Koi   Saayer   har   ghazal lik^{h}taa   hai
      Some poet-NOM every song   write.M-IMPF be-PRES
      'Some poet writes every song.' (some > every; every > some)

The generalization Nevins and Anand uncovered is that ergative subjects, which do not trigger agreement on the verb, always take wide scope with respect to an object, whereas nominative subjects, which trigger agreement on the verb, may be outscoped by the object. Contra May 1985, and following Hornstein 1995, 1999, as well as Johnson and Tomioka 1998, they take subject/object scope reversal to refer to a situation where the object c-commands (via movement) a copy of the subject. In other words—and crucially for our purposes—scope reversal requires interpreting a lower copy of the subject chain; that is, it requires reconstruction of the subject. Nevins and Anand argue that the impossibility of scope reversal in (44) indicates that ergative subjects cannot reconstruct.[22] They tie this antireconstruction effect to the absence of subject-verb agreement with ergative subjects and propose the following generalization:

(46) *PEPPER: Pure EPP Eliminates Reconstruction*
    A-movement only for EPP [with no agreement involved] blocks reconstruction.

The essence of PEPPER is that anti-A-agreement results in antireconstruction, which is exactly what we need to reconcile the LA reconstruction facts with a movement-based approach to resumptive chains. (Recall from note 11 that we assume, following Boeckx 2003a, that *wh*-movement takes place for pure EPP/matching reasons in resumptive contexts.) But PEPPER is only a generalization, not an explanation. It is a step forward, though, because it relates our findings concerning LA to an independent set of facts from Hindi. In closing this section we would like to offer some speculation as to why something like PEPPER might hold.

Nevins and Anand conjecture that PEPPER holds because reconstruction (*qua* interpretation of a lower copy) is a last-resort option. Reconstruction takes place if and only if early Spell-Out fails to apply. By early Spell-Out they mean that an element is spelled out (transferred to the interfaces in Chomsky's 2004 terminology) as soon as it contains no uninterpretable features. Taking the ergative case to be inherent (see Woolford 1997), in contrast to the nominative case, we can say that the ergative case will be spelled out early, hence will not be able to reconstruct.

The same could be said of a *wh*-phrase associated with a resumptive pronoun. As noted in section 8.1, LA allows for *wh*-in-situ, so it is plausible to assume that the *wh*-feature on *wh*-phrases is interpretable. And, as we saw above, Merchant 2001 argues that *wh*-antecedents to resumptive pronouns are not Case-marked. So, *wh*-phrases associated with resumptive pronouns do not appear to contain any uninterpretable feature. (If they move, it is for purposes of pure EPP, or as Boeckx 2003a argues, for purposes of *wh*-matching. See note 11; see also Rizzi's 2006 understanding of his Wh-criterion.) Nothing prevents them from being spelled out early.

But notice that the same reasoning predicts the absence of reconstruction effects with resumptive pronouns in nonisland contexts. By focusing on early Spell-Out of *elements*, Nevins and Anand's solution does not take into account the notion of *domain* that may distinguish between islands and nonislands. As an alternative to Nevins and Anand's speculation, we would like to capitalize on the role of agreement in licensing reconstruction. Whereas it may seem odd that an operation based on the valuation of uninterpretable features feeds an interpretive process (such as interpretation of a lower copy), it is not unprecedented. For instance, on the PF side of the grammar, Lobeck 1995 and Saito and Murasugi 1990 have argued on the basis of sentences in (47) that functional heads license deletion of their complements only when they undergo Spec-head agreement.

(47) a.   John's talk was interesting but Bill's ~~talk~~ was boring
    b.   *A single student came to class because the ~~student~~ thought it was
       important

The important point here is that deletion of copies at PF are subject to a licensing mechanism based on agreement. PEPPER can be interpreted in the same way: agreement licenses (in this case) the nondeletion of a lower copy (i.e., it licenses interpretation of that copy). Absence of agreement means absence of licensing, and thus absence of reconstruction. We may think of this licensing condition as follows: agreement is an asymmetric operation in which an element α values an element β. It is the presence of such an asymmetry that allows the LF asymmetry underlying reconstruction ((upper) copy deletion). It is the activation of α for purposes of agreement in syntax that activates α at LF. Crucially, since valuation underlies movement (Chomsky 2000, 2001), the copy that is activated under agreement is the copy that we call "low" after movement has taken place—that is, the copy that undergoes interpretation.[23]

Notice that we have now made a *relation* (the agreement/valuation operation), defined over a certain *domain*, the source of reconstruction.[24] It now becomes possible for us to say that if a domain prohibits an element α from entering into an agreement relation, α will be not be allowed to reconstruct within that domain. This fits our characterization of islands perfectly. As argued above, islands are antiagreement domains. They thereby become antireconstruction domains. This allows us to ban reconstruction for resumptive chains inside islands, but not outside of islands, since in the latter case, no antiagreement is imposed. A fourth type of solution would give a contemporary gloss to the interpretation of islands advanced in Ross 1967. Ross proposed that islands limited chopping rules, rather than movement per se. Speaking anachronistically, he proposed that it is the phonetically null trace that induces island effects, not the movement operation itself. In contemporary terms, we could implement Ross's idea as follows. Departing somewhat from the agreement-based notion of island developed in Boeckx 2001a, 2003a, and sketched above, suppose that what makes an island an island is that it is a linearized structure (along the lines of Uriagereka 1999), and movement that leaves behind a phonetic gap cannot apply to linearized structures. There are various reasons why this might be so. For example, linearization feeds the interfaces and cannot be "undone." If movement leaves behind a phonetically empty expression, then linearization is altered and this is prohibited (see Fox and Pesetsky 2003 for a related idea). This captures (and possibly explains) Ross's idea that chopping rules are blocked inside islands.

We need a few more assumptions to make this concrete. First, linearization proceeds strictly cyclically. Most importantly, a structure A that forms a proper subpart of another structure B cannot be linearized if B has already been linearized. This makes sense if linearization is a rule like any other.[25]

Second, linearization is a precondition for interpretation at both the AP and CI interfaces. It is a standard assumption that linearization is a precondition for AP operations (see Chomsky 1995). That it (or something very like it) is also required for CI processes is more contentious. However, we assume it here.[26]

Third, we assume that the underlying DP plus RP structure that characterizes RP constructions need not be linearized. Of course, unless certain conditions are met, these unlinearized structures will not be interpretable. The relevant conditions make available a loophole that we will exploit in what follows.

Together, these assumptions imply the absence of reconstruction into islands. Consider how.

Movement is only possible in the absence of linearization. Movement from islands is possible only if the source of the movement has not been linearized. However, we have assumed that Islands *are* linearized. So, it must be that though the island *as a whole* has been linearized, *some subpart* has not been. In particular, in accord with the third assumption above, the DP plus RP structure has not been *internally* linearized. Thus, in (48), the constituents of the island have been assigned a linear order though the "RP structure" has not been internally ordered.

(48) ...[$_{island}$ ...[$_{RP}$ DP pronoun]...]...

Technically speaking, this assumption might require that more than terminals linearize. In particular, we are assuming that the following can be implemented: though the whole RP in (48) has been assigned a linear order with respect to the other constituents in (48), the internal constituents of the RP, namely the DP and Pronoun, have not been ordered. Strictly speaking, for what follows, we require that the DP within the RP structure has not been linearized. It is consistent with out proposal that the resumptive pronoun itself has been. Because the DP within the RP has not been linearized, it can move the RP structure. However, so as to provide a stable linearization for the island as a whole, this movement cannot have any impact on the linear order of the other elements within the island, all of which, by assumption, have been assigned a linear position. But this is possible just in case the output of movement leaves behind an element within the RP structure that does not need to be linearized in order to be interpreted at the interfaces and whose properties would not affect the prior linearizations of the other elements. Let's expand this a bit.

Recall that in (48) the RP as a whole has been assigned a linear order with respect to the other elements in the island. More exactly, the resumptive pronoun has been ordered while the DP within the RP structure has not been. Given that linearization is, by assumption, required for interpretation at the interfaces, the DP cannot surface in this position at the interfaces. Thus, it must move. Moving will leave behind a phonetic gap. This gap has all the properties required to allow movement from islands, because it can be "interpreted" without being linearized and will have no effects on prior linearization. Consider why.

The key idea here is for movement to have this null repercussion on linearization because the gap left behind is not subject to linearization requirements. Here we assume, with Chomsky 1995, that traces are not subject to AP linearization since they are phonetically null and so not subject to the LCA. Analogously, Hornstein 2001 suggests that variables (A'-movement traces) are not subject to linearization at LF (scope assignment) because they are scopeless elements. Thus, movement from the RP is allowed just in case what is left behind is phonetically null and whose only semantic contribution is that of a variable. Under these conditions we can fully interpret the island at AP and CI and also not disturb the linearization of the elements in the island.

Note that this blocks "reconstruction." Reconstruction involves not a pure variable but a restricted one and it is the restriction that causes the difficulty. To be interpretable at LF this restriction must be linearized (see the second assumption above). But were it linearized it could not move (Ross's assumption). Moreover, late linearization is not possible because this would violate the strict cycle. Thus, there is no way to linearize the "reconstructed" material and so no way to interpret it if there. Thus, it cannot be there. All that can occur within the RP is a variable that is not restricted—that is, one that will not license reconstruction.

In sum, if linearizations are unalterable and they are necessary for interpretation at both AP and CI, then movement is only allowed if what it "leaves behind" need not be linearized to be interpreted, and that has no impact on the linear or scope properties of the other elements. In short, it must be a phonetically null unrestricted variable.

Note that none of this applies to movement from an RP structure if it is not contained within an island. The reason for this is that unless it is inside an island the larger structure that contains it is only linearized *after* the movement takes place. Thus, even if the elements of the RP have a definite linear order, the movement will not "undo" the order of the larger structure because it has not yet been fixed. As such, we expect reconstruction to be possible if movement is not from an island. As noted, Lebanese Arabic RP structure allows reconstruction when the movement is not from an island.

This proposal, like the solution relying on agreement and licensing, is sketchy. However, if the general line of reasoning can be maintained, then it would be compatible with the facts attested in LA without requiring that movement from islands be prohibited—just the desired conclusion if we wish to understand Superiority in terms of restrictions on movement.

At this point, a solution of type 3 or 4 seems most promising. Hopefully, future research will help us decide which solution is optimal.

8.5   Conclusion

We know of very few problems of the type delineated by Aoun and Li 2003 that have the potential of forcing a serious reconsideration of the central assumptions of current syntactic theory. The LA data brought to light by Aoun and Li touch on the very foundations of the Minimalist Program, hence require serious attention. Our study moves beyond a reply to Aoun and Li's work, and offers the possibility of refining the mechanisms of movement, locality, the syntax-semantics interface, and the hotly debated derivational/representational issue touching the very nature of the syntactic component of the grammar. In the course of this study we have made three claims:

1. Movement across islands is possible (see Boeckx 2003a).
2. The optimal approach to Superiority in terms of Attract Closest/Minimality can be maintained.
3. Reconstruction is more than copying.[27]

All three claims have received independent preliminary motivation, and we feel that they strengthen key aspects of the Minimalist Program, hence, deserve further attention.

Notes

Jean-Roger Vergnaud was one of the first linguists to understand the deep theoretical connection between reconstruction and movement (see, e.g., Vergnaud 1974). The ruminations that follow owe much to his pioneering work. The present chapter also owes much to Joseph Aoun and Audrey Li's seminar work. Although we take issue with some details of their analysis, we would not have been able to begin to think about the issues discussed herein without their insights. Finally, we thank Noam Chomsky, two anonymous reviewers, and audiences at Berkeley, Georgetown, Seoul, and Stony Brook for comments.

1. Here we rely largely on Aoun and Choueiri 1999 and Aoun and Li 2003.

2. Aside from island contexts, Aoun and Choueiri note several asymmetries between the gap strategies and the two other strategies. First, only two types of *wh*-phrases are allowed in the last two strategies: *miin* 'who' and *ʔayya X* 'which X' ((i)–(ii)). The *wh*-phrase corresponding to 'what,' *ʃu*, is impossible in those contexts (iii).

(i) a. Miin/ʔayya mmasil ʃəft-o
       who/which actor   saw.2SG-him
       'Who/which actor did you see'

   b. ʔayya kteeb ʃtarayt-i
      which book bought.2SG-it
      'Which book did you buy?'

(ii) a. ʃəft   ʔayya mmasil mbeeriħ
        saw.2SG which man   yesterday
        'Which actor did you see yesterday?'

b. ʃəft   miin mbeeriħ
   saw.2SG who yesterday
   'Who did you see yesterday?'

(iii) a. *ʃu   ʃtarayt-i
         what bought.2SG-it
         'What did you buy'

     b. *ʃtarayte   ʃu mbeeriħ
        bought.2SG what yesterday
        'What did you buy yesterday?'

Aoun and Choueiri note that the dividing line seems to be provided by the notion of D-linking (Pesetsky 1987). As they show on the basis of carefully defined contexts, *miin* and *ʔayya X*, but not *ʃu*, can be D-linked in Lebanese Arabic. (The D-linking restriction on resumption in interrogatives is one of the robust generalizations one finds in the domain of resumption. For evidence, see Boeckx 2001a, 2003a.)

3. Aoun and Li (2003, 20–21) also claim that situations like (i), illustrated in (ii), also provide evidence for the superiority of Minimal Match, in the absence of c-command between RP and wh_2. But we fail to see why this so. Minimal Match appears to incorrectly rule in (i), because the first matching [+wh] element is the correct one (RP) in this case (unlike in (22)).

(i) *$[_{CP}$ Wh$_1$ ... $[_{IP}$ ... $[_{Island}$ ... RP$_1$ ...] ... wh$_2$]]

(ii) *miin fakkarto   laʔinno l-mʕallme   ħikət   maʕ-o   ʔanno l-mudiira
     who thought2PL because the-teacher.FSG spoke3SG with-him that   the principal.FSG
     ħa-təʃħat   miin
     will-3FSG.expel who
     'Who did you think because the teacher spoke with him that the principal would expel who?'

4. Similar examples have been reported for German by Heck and Müller 2000.

5. A similar point is made throughout in Boeckx 2003a.

6. Semantically, they behave like definite determiners/pronouns, as discussed in Boeckx (2003a, chap. 2). (Boeckx captures this fact by assuming that the resumptive pronoun takes its antecedent as its complement upon first Merge: $[_{DP}$ Res. Pro [Antecedent]]; in effect, a DP structure.)

7. Aoun and Li (2003, 30ff.) try to justify their special treatment of resumptive pronouns by showing that, unlike standard bound pronouns, resumptive pronouns are subject to superiority and Weak Crossover. The relevant examples are given in (i)–(ii) for Weak Crossover and in (iii)–(iv) for superiority.

(i) *[ʔayya təkmiiz min   tlamiiħ-a$_i$]$_k$ xabbarto ʔəmm-o$_k$ ʔanno kəll$_i$ mʕalme
    which student among students-her told.2PL mother-his that   every teacher.FSG
    ħa-təəke   maʕ-o$_k$
    will.3FSG.speak with-him
    'Which of her students did you tell his mother that every teacher will speak with him?'

(ii) [ʔayya təkmiiz min   tlamiiz saamia]$_k$ xabbarto ʔəmm-o$_k$ ʔanno kəll$_i$ mʕalme
    which student among students Samia   told.2PL mother-his that   every teacher.FSG
    ħa-təəki   maʕ-o$_k$
    will.3FSG.speak with-him

'Which of Samia's students did you tell his mother that every teacher will speak with him?'

(iii) *miin$_i$ xabbarto saami ʔənno miin ħa-yexd-o$_i$ ʕa-l-mataar
      who told.2PL Sami that who will-3MSG.take-him to-the-airport
      'Who did you tell Sami that who would take him to the airport?'

(iv) miin$_i$ xabbart-u$_i$ ʔənno miin ħa-yexd-o$_i$ ʕa-l-mataar
      who told.2PL-him that   who will-3MSG.take-him to-the-airport
      'Who did you tell him that who would take him to the airport?'

However, the facts just mentioned are amenable to alternative explanations. The contrast in (i) and (ii) would follow if we assume that *wh*-phrases do not reconstruct (for purposes of scope and binding) below the leftmost resumptive pronoun they are associated with. This makes parsing sense if we assume that a dependency is "discharged" as soon as possible so as to limit the costs of retaining the information online. In (i), reconstruction below the first RP is forced (hence the unacceptability of (i)), whereas in (ii), it is not. The contrast in (iii) and (iv) follows once we realize that the *wh*-phrase in SpecCP may have been attracted from the higher "resumed" position in the matrix clause.

So, it appears that the contrasts above rest not so much on a distinction between resumptive pronouns and bound pronouns, but on the presence of material in (i), absent in (ii), that must reconstruct below a position that defines a lower bound for reconstruction, and on the presence of an additional resumptive pronoun (hence launch site for movement) in (iv), in contrast to (iii).

8. Notice, for example, that much recent work on the island-amnestying effect of sluicing (Merchant 2001; Lasnik 2002) takes movement across islands to be possible.

9. Those diagnostics are adopted, incorrectly we think, in Aoun and Li 2003, 1.

10. Boeckx (2003a, 2008) argues that "successive" cyclic *wh*-agreement markers in Chamorro are in fact instances of anticlausal agreement. Boeckx (2008) also extends antiagreement to phenomena of antipassivization, and of "topic-only" extraction.

11. Boeckx argues that the *wh*-chain is driven, not by a (*wh*-)agreement requirement, but by a *wh*-matching requirement. This is equivalent to saying that the *wh*-movement step is purely driven by EPP considerations. For extensive discussion, see Boeckx 2003a, chap. 3.

12. For a discussion of the variation in antiagreement strategies across languages, and an account of the differences among "*wh*-"agreement languages (Chamorro versus Palauan) when it comes to island (in)sensitivity, see Boeckx 2003a, chap. 3; 2008.

13. For the need to recognize defective intervention effects as a distinct class of constraints, see Boeckx and Lasnik, 2006.

14. On the distinction between feature matching and feature valuation, see Chomsky 2000, 122; Boeckx 2003b, Boeckx and Jeong 2004.

15. An anonymous reviewer wonders how the present approach to resumption can explain the absence of *wh*-island effects on *wh*-movement with resumption in Lebanese Arabic, given that *wh*-islands are, like superiority, a classic case of Relativized Minimality. One can account for the absence of *wh*-island effects with resumption by capitalizing on the fact that generally resumptive pronouns force the *wh*-phrases associated with them to be D-linked (Boeckx 2003a, chap. 2). As Boeckx and Jeong (2004) show, a careful featural analysis of D-linking,

coupled with a version of Relativized Minimality defined over feature classes (Starke 2001; Rizzi 2004; Boeckx 2008), captures the fact that D-linked *wh*-phrases can cross *wh*-islands.

We would like to point out that data like (22) remain problematic for any version of Minimality/Intervention that relies on c-command. A processing explanation may be required for such cases. For an alternative, structural solution, see Müller 2004.

16. We assume that (40a) is true, although see Cecchetto and Chierchia 1998 and references therein for arguments in favor of the need for semantic reconstruction (reconstruction in the absence of movement).

17. Salem focuses on Palestinian Arabic, and takes resumptive pronouns to be agreement clitics.

18. Salem also argues that the lack of copying under movement accounts for the absence of island effects if islands are understood as representational conditions on "traces."

19. In fairness, we note that Salem claims that resumptive chains allow for reconstruction even in island contexts in Palestinian Arabic. This is puzzling under his account, where movement is not accompanied by copying.

20. Alternatively, we may claim, as does Demirdache 1991, that the resumptive pronoun is moving to the *wh*-antecedent. But this would require endowing the resumptive pronoun with a *wh*-feature to motivate movement, which we have argued against above. Furthermore, such an approach would be hard pressed to explain the anti-identity effects discussed at length here. If two elements are "anti-identical," why would they have to be combined with one another?

21. It will not do to say, as McCloskey (2002, 203) does, that merger is licensed by the checking of an EPP feature, because, as Lasnik 2001 has argued, the EPP is not a feature, but a property, a "filled specifier" requirement. The EPP does not say what the matching feature is that allows merger.

22. We note that Nevins and Anand consider several alternative analyses for the contrast in (44) and (45), including the Tense/Aspect difference, and provide compelling reasons for narrowing down the search for a solution to the Case contrast.

23. Miyagawa (2005) appears to have the same intuition, because he notes that the role of agreement in reconstruction licensing is due to the fact that agreement, under Agree, is established with the copy before movement—that is, the copy that is interpreted under reconstruction.

24. This idea is related to Epstein and Seely's 2002 claim (see also Epstein et al. 1998) that syntactic computation and semantic interpretation proceed in parallel, with each syntactic rule application being followed by the application of a semantic rule. Our formulation also has some similarity to the role of SUBJECT in the GB definition of BT-compatibility (Huang 1983).

25. This is compatible with linearization being part of another rule such as Spell-Out, as in Chomsky 2004.

26. See Hornstein 2001 following ideas of Jairo Nunes (personal communication). Hornstein suggests that "LF" linearization should be understood as endowing every element with a scope. Both linearization at PF and "scopification" at LF induce linear orders on phrase structures.

27. See also Fox 2002 and Sauerland 2004, who argue that copies need to be converted prior to interpretation.

References

Adger, David, and Gillian Ramchand. 2003. Merge and Move: Wh-dependencies revisited. Unpublished ms., Queen Mary, University of London, and Oxford University.

Aoun, Joseph, and Elabbas Benmamoun. 1998. Minimality, reconstruction, and PF-movement. *Linguistic Inquiry* 29, 569–597.

Aoun, Joseph, and Lina Choueiri. 1999. Modes of interrogation. Unpublished ms., USC.

Aoun, Joseph, Lina Choueiri, and Norbert Hornstein. 2001. Resumption, movement, and derivational economy. *Linguistic Inquiry* 32, 371–403.

Aoun, Joseph, and Audrey Li. 2003. *Essays on the representational and derivational nature of grammar: The diversity of wh-constructions.* Cambridge, Mass.: MIT Press.

Bhatt, Rajesh. 2002. The raising analysis of relative clauses: Evidence from adjectival modification. *Natural Language Semantics* 10, 43–90.

Bobaljik, Jonathan D., and Susi Wurmbrand. 2005. The domain of agreement. *Natural Language and Linguistic Theory* 23, 809–865.

Boeckx, Cedric. 2000a. A Note on contraction. *Linguistic Inquiry* 31, 357–366.

Boeckx, Cedric. 2000b. Quirky agreement. *Studia Linguistica* 54:354–380.

Boeckx, Cedric. 2001a. Mechanisms of chain formation. Doctoral dissertation, University of Connecticut.

Boeckx, Cedric. 2001b. Scope Reconstruction and A-movement. *Natural Language and Linguistic Theory* 19, 503–548.

Boeckx, Cedric. 2003a. *Islands and chains.* Amsterdam: John Benjamins.

Boeckx, Cedric. 2003b. Symmetries and asymmetries in multiple checking. In *Multiple Wh-fronting*, ed. C. Boeckx and K. K. Grohmann, 17–26. Amsterdam: John Benjamins.

Boeckx, Cedric. 2008. *Bare syntax.* Oxford: Oxford University Press.

Boeckx, Cedric, and Kleanthes K. Grohmann, eds. 2003. *Multiple Wh-fronting.* Amsterdam: John Benjamins.

Boeckx, Cedric, and Youngmi Jeong. 2004. The fine structure of intervention in syntax. In *Issues in Current Linguistic Theory: A Festschrift for Hong Bae Lee*, ed. Chungja Kwon and Wonbin Lee, 83–116. Seoul: Kyungchin.

Boeckx, Cedric, and Howard Lasnik. 2006. Intervention and repair. *Linguistic Inquiry* 37, 150–55.

Bošković, Željko. 1997. *The syntax of non-finite complementation: An economy approach.* Cambridge, Mass.: MIT Press.

Bošković, Željko. 1998. Multiple wh-fronting and economy of derivation. In *Proceedings of WCCFL* 16, 49–63. Stanford University, Stanford, Calif.

Bošković, Željko. 1999. On multiple feature checking: Multiple wh-fronting and multiple head-movement. In *Working minimalism*, ed. S. D. Epstein and N. Hornstein, 159–187. Cambridge, Mass.: MIT Press.

Bošković, Željko. 2002. On multiple wh-fronting. *Linguistic Inquiry* 33, 351–383.

Brody, Michael. 1995. *Lexico-logical form.* Cambridge, Mass.: MIT Press.

Brody, Michael. 2002. On the status of derivations and representations. In *Explanation and derivation in the Minimalist Program*, ed. S. D. Epstein and T. D. Seely, 18–41. Oxford: Blackwell.

Cecchetto, Carlo, and Gennaro Chierchia. 1998. Reconstruction in dislocation constructions and the syntax/semantics interface. In *Proceedings of WCCFL 17*, 132–146. Stanford, Calif.: CLSI.

Cheng, Lisa, and Hamida Demirdash. 1991. Superiority violations. In *MIT Working Papers in Linguistics 13*, 27–46. Cambridge, Mass.: MITWPL.

Chomsky, Noam. 1955. The Logical Structure of Linguistics Theory. Unpublished ms., Harvard University. Published in part, 1975, New York, Plenum.

Chomsky, Noam. 1973. Conditions on transformations. In *A Festschrift for Morris Halle*, ed. S. Anderson and P. Kiparsky, 232–286. New York: Holt, Rinehalt, and Winston.

Chomsky, Noam. 1977. On wh-movement. In *Formal syntax*, ed. P. Culicover, T. Wasow, and A. Akmajian. New York: Academic Press.

Chomsky, Noam. 1993. A minimalist program for linguistic theory. In *The view from Building 20*, ed. K. Hale and S. J. Keyser, 1–52. Cambridge, Mass.: MIT Press.

Chomsky, Noam. 1995. *The Minimalist Program*. Cambridge, Mass.: MIT Press.

Chomsky, Noam. 2000. Minimalist inquiries: The framework. In *Step by step*, ed. R. Martin, D. Michaels, and J. Uriagereka, 89–155. Cambridge, Mass.: MIT Press.

Chomsky, Noam. 2001. Derivation by phase. In *Ken Hale: A life in language*, ed. M. Kenstowicz, 1–50. Cambridge, Mass.: MIT Press.

Chomsky, Noam. 2004. Beyond explanatory adequacy. In *Structures and beyond*, ed. A. Belletti, 104–131. Oxford: Oxford University Press.

Chomsky, Noam. 2005. Three factors in language design. *Linguistic Inquiry* 36, 1–22.

Chung, Sandra. 1994. Wh-agreement and "referentiality" in Chamorro. *Linguistic Inquiry* 25:1–44.

Chung, Sandra. 1998. *The design of agreement*. Chicago: Chicago University Press.

Collins, Chris. 1997. *Local economy*. Cambridge, Mass.: MIT Press.

Demirdache, Hamida. 1991. Resumptive chains in restrictive relatives, appositives, and dislocation structures. Doctoral dissertation, MIT.

Epstein, Samuel D., Erich Groat, Ruriko Kawashima, and Hisatsugu Kitahara. 1998. *The derivation of syntactic relations*. Oxford: Oxford University Press.

Epstein, Samuel D., and T. Daniel Seely. 2002. Rule application as cycles in a level-free syntax. In *Explanation and derivation in the minimalist program*, ed. S. D. Epstein and T. D. Seely, 65–89. Oxford: Blackwell.

Ferguson, Scott, and Erich Groat. 1994. Shortest Move. Unpublished ms., Harvard University.

Fox, Danny. 1999. Reconstruction, binding theory, and the interpretation of chains. *Linguistic Inquiry* 30, 157–196.

Fox, Danny. 2000. *Economy and semantic interpretation*. Cambridge, Mass.: MIT Press and MITWPL.

Fox, Danny. 2002. Antecedent Contained Deletion and the copy theory of movement. *Linguistic Inquiry* 33, 63–96.

Fox, Danny, and David Pesetsky. 2003. Cyclic linearization. Unpublished ms., MIT.

Grewendorf, Gereon. 2001. Multiple wh-fronting. *Linguistic Inquiry* 32, 87–122.

Grohmann, Kleanthes K. 2003. *Prolific peripheries*. Amsterdam: John Benjamins.

Heck, Fabian, and Gereon Müller. 2000. Successive cyclicity, long-distance superiority, and local optimization. In *Proceedings of WCCFL 19*, 218–231. Somerville, Mass.: Cascadilla Press.

Hornstein, Norbert. 1995. *Logical form*. Oxford: Blackwell.

Hornstein, Norbert. 1999. Movement and Control. *Linguistic Inquiry* 30, 64–96.

Hornstein, Norbert. 2001. *Move!* Oxford: Blackwell.

Huang, C. T. James. 1983. A note on the binding theory. *Linguistic Inquiry* 14, 554–561.

Iatridou, Sabine. 1995. Clitic left dislocation and islands. *Penn Working Papers in Linguistics* 2, 11–31.

Johnson, Kyle, and Satoshi Tomioka. 1998. Lowering and mid-size clauses. In *Proceedings of the 1997 Tübingen Workshop*, ed. G. Katz, S. Kim, and H. Winhart, 127–154. University of Tübingen.

Kim, Kwang-sup. 1998. (Anti-)Connectivity. Doctoral dissertation, University of Maryland.

Lasnik, Howard. 1999. Chains of arguments. In *Working minimalism*, ed. S. D. Epstein and N. Hornstein, 189–215. Cambridge, Mass.: MIT Press.

Lasnik, Howard. 2001. A note on the EPP. *Linguistic Inquiry* 32:356–362.

Lasnik, Howard. 2002. When can you save a structure by destroying it? In *Proceedings of NELS 31*, 301–320. University of Massachusetts, Amherst: GLSA.

Lasnik, Howard, and Mamoru Saito. 1992. *Move α*. Cambridge, Mass.: MIT Press.

Lobeck, Anne. 1995. *Ellipsis*. Oxford: Oxford University Press.

Manzini, Maria Rita, and Anna Roussou. 2000. A Minimalist Theory of A-Movement and Control. *Lingua* 110:409–447.

May, Robert. 1985. *Logical form*. Cambridge, Mass.: MIT Press.

McCloskey, James. 2002. Resumption, successive cyclicity, and the locality of operations. In *Explanation and derivation in the Minimalist Program*, ed. S. D. Epstein and T. D. Seely, 184–226. Oxford: Blackwell.

Merchant, Jason. 2000. Economy, the copy theory, and Antecedent Contained Deletion. *Linguistic Inquiry* 31, 566–575.

Merchant, Jason. 2001. *The syntax of silence*. Oxford: Oxford University Press.

Miyagawa, Shigeru. 2005. Unifying agreement and agreement-less languages. Unpublished ms., MIT.

Müller, Gereon. 2002. Order preservation, parallel movement, and the emergence of the unmarked. In *Optimality-Theory syntax*, ed. J. Grimshaw, G. Legendre, and S. Vikner. Cambridge, Mass.: MIT Press.

Müller, Gereon. 2004. Phase impenetrability and wh-intervention. In *Minimality effects in syntax*, ed. A. Stepanov, G. Fanselow, and R. Vogel, 289–325. Berlin: Mouton de Gruyter.

Nevins, Andrew, and Pranav Anand. 2003. Some AGREEment matters: A crosslinguistic generalization on reconstruction and agreement. Paper presented at WCCFL 22.

Ochi, Masao. 1999. Constraints on feature checking. Doctoral dissertation, University of Connecticut.

Perlmutter, David. 1972. Evidence for shadow pronouns in French relativization. In *The Chicago which hunt: Papers from the relative clause festival*, 73–105. Chicago: Chicago Linguistic Society.

Pesetsky, David. 1982. Paths and categories. Doctoral dissertation, MIT.

Pesetsky, David. 1987. Wh–in situ: movement and unselective binding. In *The representation of (in)definiteness*, ed. E. Reuland and A. G. B. ter Meulen, 98–129. Cambridge, Mass.: MIT Press.

Pesetsky, David. 2000. *Phrasal movement and its kin*. Cambridge, Mass.: MIT Press.

Richards, Norvin. 1997. What moves where when in which language? Doctoral dissertation, MIT.

Richards, Norvin. 1999. Featural cyclicity. In *Working minimalism*, ed. S. D. Epstein and N. Hornstein, 127–158. Cambridge, Mass.: MIT Press.

Richards, Norvin. 2001. *Movement in language*. Oxford: Oxford University Press.

Rizzi, Luigi. 1982. *Issues in Italian syntax*. Dordrecht: Foris.

Rizzi, Luigi. 1990. *Relativized Minimality*. Cambridge, Mass.: MIT Press.

Rizzi, Luigi. 2001. Reconstruction, weak island sensitivity, and agreement. In *Semantic interfaces*, ed. C. Cecchetto, G. Chierchia, and M.-T. Guasti, 145–176. Stanford, Calif.: CSLI.

Rizzi, L. 2004. Locality and the left periphery. In *Structures and beyond*, ed. A. Belletti, 223–251. Oxford: Oxford University Press.

Rizzi, L. 2006. On the form of chains: criterial positions and ECP effects. In *WH-movement: Moving On*, ed. L. Cheng and N. Corver, 97–133. Cambridge, Mass.: MIT Press.

Romero, Maribel. 1998. Problems for a semantic account of reconstruction. In *Proceedings of the 1997 Tübingen Workshop*, ed. G. Katz, S. Kim, and H. Winhart, 127–154. University of Tübingen.

Ross, John R. 1967. Constraints on variables in syntax. Doctoral dissertation, MIT. (Published 1986 as *Infinite syntax!* Norwood, N.J.: Ablex.)

Rudin, Catherine. 1988. On multiple wh-questions and multiple wh-fronting. *Natural Language and Linguistic Theory* 6, 445–601.

Safir, Ken. 1999. Vehicle change and reconstruction in A-bar chains. *Linguistic Inquiry* 30, 587–620.

Saito, Mamoru, and Keiko Murasugi. 1990. N'-deletion in Japanese. In *UConn WPL 3*, 86–103.

Salem, Murad. 2001. Resumption. Unpublished ms. Michigan State University, Lansing.

Sauerland, Uli. 1998. The meaning of chains. Doctoral dissertation, MIT.

Sauerland, Uli. 2004. The interpretation of chains. *Natural Language Semantics* 12, 63–127.

Sells, Peter. 1984. Syntax and semantics of resumptive pronouns. Doctoral dissertation, University of Massachusetts, Amherst.

Sportiche, Dominique. 1988. A theory of floating quantifiers and its corollaries for constituent structure. *Linguistic Inquiry* 19:425–449.

Sportiche, Dominique. 2003. Movement, binding, and scope. Unpublished ms., UCLA.

Starke, M. 2001. Move dissolves into merge: A theory of locality. Doctoral dissertation, University of Geneva.

Uriagereka, Juan. 1999. Multiple spell-out. In *Working minimalism*, ed. S. D. Epstein and N. Hornstein, 251–282. Cambridge, Mass.: MIT Press.

Vergnaud, Jean-Roger. 1974. French relative clauses. Doctoral dissertation, MIT.

Williams, Edwin. 2003. *Representation theory*. Cambridge, Mass.: MIT Press.

Witkos, Jacek. 2001. Movement and reconstruction: A comparative analysis. Unpublished ms., University of Maryland.

Woolford, Elen. 1997. Four-way case systems: Ergative, nominative, objective, and accusative. *Natural Language and Linguistic Theory* 15, 181–227.

9 Identity Avoidance: OCP Effects in Swiss Relatives

Henk van Riemsdijk

9.1 General Principles of Design and the Syntax-Phonology Divide

For decades, generative linguists have viewed the internal grammar in terms of the interplay of two types of factors: genetic endowment, generally referred to as Universal Grammar (UG), and experience—that is, exposure to e-language.[1] In recent years this picture has been augmented by a third type of factor: general principles of biological/physical design.[2] This new focus tends to worry those who had been hoping for a rich and articulate UG (see Pinker and Jackendoff 2004), but on the other hand it is fully in line with minimalist thinking. A particularly welcome effect produced by this shift of focus is that we may now reassess the issue of formal similarities and dissimilarities between syntax and phonology. For many years, the dominant view has been that syntax and phonology are fundamentally different.[3] It seems clear that recursion, which is now the main cornerstone on which the genetic uniqueness of "narrow syntax" rests, is not found in phonology, at least not in the pervasive way that it manifests itself in syntax. But general principles of design may very well be active in syntax and phonology in similar ways. Jean-Roger Vergnaud has always been one of the few who have insisted on the importance of exploring the formal connections between the two components of grammar.[4]

The objective of this chapter is to examine the way identity avoidance manifests itself in one particular area of syntax, the syntax of relative clauses in Swiss German. I will try to show that most of what is going on is governed by strategies to avoid or reduce adjacent identical elements. The instrumental factors are a specific version of the Doubly Filled Comp Filter (see Chomsky and Lasnik 1977), and haplological reduction of two adjacent identical morphemes. Section 9.2 constitutes the analytical section, in which the essentials of Swiss German relative clauses are presented.

What I call Identity Avoidance is really what has been known in phonology under the name of "Obligatory Contour Principle" (OCP; see Leben 1973; McCarthy 1986).

Discussions of OCP effects in syntax have remained rather marginal so far,[5] but with the present discussion I hope to emphasize yet again that OCP effects are found in many diverse guises in syntax. More importantly, I will suggest in section 9.3 that Identity Avoidance may well be one of the core principles of physical and, in particular, biological design that are on a par with the more commonly cited examples such as Economy and Locality. A major question that attends the scientific investigation of the way such general design principles manifest themselves in grammar is how linguistic theory can deal with the diversity of their effects and the diverse nature of the devices that grammars exploit to accommodate themselves to these general design constraints. This is not a question that I can answer, but one that I hope to formulate with some clarity.

9.2 Swiss Relatives Revisited

9.2.1 The Analysis in Van Riemsdijk 1989

In Swiss German,[6] headed relative clauses are always introduced by an invariable complementizer *wo*. But, unlike Bavarian and other German dialects (including some of the other Alemannic ones as well as certain varieties of Hessian[7]), *wo* is never preceded by an (overt) *wh*-word or *wh*-phrase.[8] In most cases we find a resumptive pronoun as the representative of the element relativized. This is illustrated in (1).

(1) s   mäitli wo de Leo immer mit *(ere) i's   kino   gaat
     the girl   WO the Leo always with her in-the cinema goes
     'The girl that Leo always goes to the movies with'

The resumptive pronoun in question behaves like a "normal" pronoun, not like a variable in that it is insensitive to island configurations, as shown in (2).

(2) es mäitli wo öpper   wo mit ere i's   kino   gaat zimli mues spine
     a girl   WO someone WO with her in-the cinema goes quite must crazy-be
     'A girl that someone who goes to the movies with her must be quite crazy'

Gaps are only found in the subject and the direct object and, subject to dialect variability, the indirect object position of the top CP layer of the relative clause.[9]

(3) a. es mäitli wo (*si) gëërn i's   kino   gaat
         a girl   WO (she) gladly in-the cinema goes
         'A girl that likes to go to the movies'
     b. es mäitli wo mer (*si) gëërn i's   kino   mitnämed
         a girl   WO we (her) gladly in-the cinema with-take
         'A girl that we like to take along to the movies'

In my earlier article (Van Riemsdijk 1989), I argue that these cases are best accounted for by assuming that these positions are also filled by a resumptive pronoun that behaves like a clitic and is adjoined to C°, putting it in a position where, being locally identified by the head of the relative clause, it can—and due to the Avoid Pronoun Principle (Chomsky 1981) must—be deleted.[10] In support of this analysis, note that clitic movement is clause-bound while *wh*-movement is not. If the gaps in (3) were the result of *wh*-movement, we would expect to find gaps in embedded subject and object positions as well. But we don't. Instead we find resumptive pronouns again.

(4) a. es mäitli wo mer säit das *(si) geërn i's   kino   gaat
     a girl   WO one says that she gladly in-the cinema goes
     'A girl that they say likes to go to the movies'
  b. es mäitli wo niemer cha gläube das mer *(si) geërn i's   kino
     a girl   WO nobody can believe that we   her gladly in-the cinema
     mitnämed
     with-take
     'A girl that nobody can believe we like to take along to the movies'

My original analysis failed to address two important points that I will now turn to in the next two subsections.

9.2.2 Locative Relatives

So far, the conclusion seems to be that *wh*-movement is not involved in the formation of headed relative clauses in Swiss German.[11] There is, however, one type of headed relative clause in which the typical *wh*-movement pattern appears: locative relatives.[12] Example (5) shows that there are gaps.

(5) a. s   huus wo de Hans wont
     the house WO the Hans lives
     'The house where Hans lives'
  b. s   fäscht wo de Hans anegaat
     the party WO the Hans to-goes
     'The party that Hans is going to'

Long-distance dependencies are possible and they have a gap rather than a resumptive pronoun (as opposed to the examples in (4)):

(6) a. s   huus wo mer säit das de Hans wont
     the house WO one says that the Hans lives
     'The house where people say Hans lives'

b. s   fäscht wo i ghöört han das de Hans anegaat
   the party WO I heard have that the Hans to-goes
   'The party that I have heard Hans is going to'

Furthermore, the dependency is island sensitive:

(7) a. *s   huus wo d   behäuptig das de Hans wont nie   bewise worde isch
       the house WO the claim   that the Hans lives never proven been   has
       'The house that the claim that Hans lives there has never been proven'
    b. *s   fäscht wo ich s   mäitli wo mit em Hans anegaat scho   mal troffe
       the party WO I   the girl   who with the Hans to-goes already once met
       han
       have
       'The party that I have already once met the girl who goes there with Hans'

Finally, a resumptive strategy is used in very much the same way as in English to
avoid island violations:

(8) a. s   huus wo d   behäuptig das de Hans deet wont nie   bewise worde
       the house WO the claim   that the Hans there lives never proven been
       isch
       is
       'The house that the claim that Hans lives there has never been proven'
    b. s   fäscht wo ich s   mäitli wo mit em Hans deet anegaat scho   mal
       the party WO I   the girl   WO with the Hans there to-goes already once
       troffe han
       met   have
       'The party that I have already once met the girl who goes there with Hans'

Why should this be so? The key to an understanding of this phenomenon is the fact
that the *wh*-word for locatives is *wo* ('where'). That is, the *wh*-element, in this case, is
phonologically identical to the complementizer *wo*. This, of course, is a haplology effect. In other words, the sequence in (9a) is ruled out, but it can be saved by haplological reduction (9b).

(9) a. *wo wo
    b. wo wo → wo

And of the various strategies that a language can use to prevent such a configuration
from arising, Swiss German uses deletion (rather than, say, substitution). Apparently, it is not impossible for *wh*-movement to be operative in Swiss German
headed relative clauses, as long as it is possible to get rid of the *wh*-word in the
output. This immediately raises the question of why *wh*-movement, overt or covert,

cannot be used in nonlocative relatives. At this point, I make the following preliminary assumptions:

(10) a. In headed relatives, the complementizer *wo* must be (overtly) present.

   b. The Doubly Filled Comp Filter[13] rules out sequences of an overt *wh*-word followed by the complementizer *wo*.

We will return to the details of the analysis in sections 9.2.4 and 9.3.

9.2.3 Aboutness Relatives: Where Is the Variable?

9.2.3.1 What is Aboutness?   Another question raised by the data above is: Where is the variable? This question is prompted by the fact that, apart from locative relatives, there is no evidence for *wh*-movement patterns. Even the resumptive pronouns do not behave like variables in that they have the distribution of normal pronouns. While they might be bound in some way by the head of the relative clause, they are completely impervious to island effects; see (2). The suspicion that the resumptive pronoun does not play a very crucial role is confirmed by additional facts that I had overlooked in my 1989 article: resumptive pronouns are not obligatory, as long as certain semantic aboutness criteria are satisfied. Consider the following examples:

(11) a. Es äuto wo d   stoossstange fëëlt   ghöört nöd uf d   straass
        a car WO the fender   misses belongs not on the street
        'A car that has no fender on it does not belong on the street'

   b. Familie wo de eltischti soon s   gschäft übernimt git's   hüt
      families WO the oldest   son the business over-takes gives-it today
      nöme   vil
      no-longer many
      'Families in which the oldest son takes over the business, there are not many any more today.'

   c. Es drüüeck wo d   sume vo de kwadraat vo de zwäi chürzere siite
      a triangle WO the sum of the squares of the two shorter sides
      gliich grooss isch wie s   kwadraat vo de lengschte siite isch es
      equally large is   as the square   of the longest   side is a
      rächteckigs drüüeck
      right-sided triangle
      'A triangle such that the sum of the squares of the two shorter sides equals the square of the long side is a rectangular triangle.'

What makes these examples acceptable is the aboutness relation that holds between the head and the content of the relative clause. In the cases at hand, this aboutness relation appears to be describable in terms of a kind of part-whole relation—that is, a kind of possessive or locative inclusion relation.

Such apparently variableless relatives are well known from the literature. Take the definition of relative clauses in Grosu 2002, 145:

(12) a. A relative clause is subordinated.
   b. A relative clause includes, at some level of semantic representation, a variable that ultimately gets bound *in some way* by an element of the matrix.

Even this quite flexible definition full of hedges would exclude the examples above, but Grosu does mention some exceptions, including:

(13) a. The mathematical system such that two and two are four is Peano arithmetic.
   b. California-syuu-ga   Nihon yori ooki America-wa   hontooni ooki
      California-state-NOM Japan than big America-Top really   big
      kuni   desu
      country is
      'America, such that the state of California is larger than Japan, is a really big country.'
      (From Kuno 1973, 257, ex. (35b).[14])

Similar facts are found in Chinese and Korean:

(14) a. ta xiu   che-de fangfa
      he repair car-DE method
      'The way in which he fixed the car'
      (From Wu 2000, 95, cited from Ning 1993.)
   b. thayphwung-i cinaka-n   huncek
      typhoon-NOM passed.by-PNE debris
      'The debris that resulted from a typhoon passing by'
      (From Chung and Kim 2003, ex. (37a).)

The Chinese case may not be an exception, according to Wu, but rather similar to examples like (15) in English, where the choice of a very generic, semantically bleached head of a specific type permits the corresponding preposition to be deleted, a deletion normally prohibited because the deletion is irrecoverable.

(15) The place he lives   vs.   The bungalow he lives *(in)
     The day she left   vs.   The interval *(during which) she left
     The way we solved it   vs.   The accuracy *(with which) we solved it
     The reason you came   vs.   The funeral you came *(for)

Regarding the Korean example in (14b), notice that aboutness here seems to be a semantic relation of a somewhat different type. The relationship between the debris and the typhoon's passing by is one of causation, a resultative connection. This is generally not possible in English *such that* relatives, nor in Swiss German relative clauses:

(16) ?*The *wh*-island violation such that a *wh*-phrase is extracted from an indirect question

Instead, English would use a temporal adjunct clause, as in (17).

(17) ?The *wh*-island violation when a *wh*-phrase is extracted from an indirect question

Swiss German works like English here:

(18) *D truur wän/*wo eltere   iri   chind   verlüüred duuret immer lang
     the grief when/WO parents their children lose   lasts always long
     'The grief when parents lose their children always lasts long.'

In the East Asian languages too there is considerable discussion as to whether there is some hidden operator-variable structure involved in relative clause formation. The same question arises for *such that* relatives of the type given in (19a) in English.

(19) a.   A rectangle such that the long sides are twice the length of the short sides
     b.   (#)A circle such that each of the four corners is 90°
     c.   #A circle such that our parrot is whistling the Marseillaise

The gradations in acceptability in (19) strongly suggest that semanticopragmatic factors play an important role in the assessment of aboutness. From that perspective, there does not seem to be any direct semantic pressure to have a variable in the syntax of relative clauses. But this leaves one question entirely unanswered.

If semanticopragmatic aboutness constitutes a sufficient licensing factor for relative clauses, why don't considerations of economy rule out the use of *wh*-movement patterns in relative clauses altogether? More specifically, why does Swiss German jump to the use of *wh*-movement in the one case where it can get away with it—that is, in locative relatives?

Apparently, the pressure to employ operator-variable structures is purely syntactic. But if that is so, where are these operators and variables? Again take the case of English *such that* relatives. A rather simplistic but no less attractive theory would be to say that *such* is indeed the head of a predicate phrase and that the subject and copula are deleted (or silent). The above examples in (19) would then be represented as in (20).

(20) a.   A rectangle ~~which is~~ such that the long sides are twice the length of the short sides

b. (#)A circle ~~which is~~ such that each of the four corners is 90°

c.   #A circle ~~which is~~ such that our parrot is whistling the Marseillaise

The advantage of such an analysis would be that aboutness is reduced to where it belongs: predication. But of course, such an analysis is not available for the whole range of aboutness relatives in Swiss German. Recall that aboutness can essentially be characterized as a part-whole relation. This observation yields two major candidates for the hidden variable: possessive constructions and locative constructions.

9.2.3.2 The Possessive Strategy   First consider possessive constructions. It is interesting to note that Dutch employs the possessive (or genitive) *waarvan* ('where-of', that is, 'of which') where English uses *such that* relatives.[15]

(21) een driehoek waarvan de som van de kwadraten van de twee korte kanten
     a   triangle whereof the sum of the squares   of the two short sides
     even   groot is als het kwadraat van de lange kant noemen we een
     equally big is as the square   of the long side call   we a
     rechthoekige driehoek
     rectangular triangle
     'A triangle such that the sum of the squares of the two short sides equals the square of the long side, we call a rectangular triangle.'

But what about Swiss German? Could the hidden variable be part of a possessive construction? Again consider (11a), repeated here as (22).

(22) Es äuto wo d stoossstange fëëlt   ghöört nöd uf d   straass
     a car WO the fender   misses belongs not on the street
     'A car that has no fender on it does not belong on the street.'

Here the fender is part of the car. The corresponding possessive expression would be:

(23) em   äuto sini stoossstange
     the$_{DAT}$ car its fender

In view of the fact that the article is present in (22), the obvious candidate for covert movement is the possessive adjective *sini*. Or perhaps the possessive adjective plus the possessive dative of the relevant *d-* or *w*-pronoun *dem/wem sini*. But given that Swiss German disallows extraction from possessive structures, this seems quite implausible.[16]

(24) *[Dem   sini]$_i$ fëëlt (d) [e]$_i$ stoossstange
      that-one its   misses (the) fender

Consequently, we discard the possessive analysis. Instead we turn to hidden locatives as a potential source for the variable in aboutness relatives.

9.2.3.3 The Locative Strategy Observe first that this could be an alternative to the *which is* deletion analysis of *such that* relatives:

(25) a. The mathematical system such that two and two are four is Peano
         arithmetic.
      b. The mathematical system such that *in it* two and two are four is Peano
         arithmetic.

But in many cases the locative is obligatory:

(26) a. A country such that you don't feel so good #(in it)
      b. A picture such that #(in it) Rosa has a snake near her

And conversely, sometimes the locative is inappropriate. Example (27) is presumably unfelicitous because the sides are not *in* the triangle. Rather they constitute the triangle.

(27) A triangle such that (#in it) the sum of the squares of the two shorter sides
      equals the square of the long side . . .

Again, these patterns are also found in predicative contexts, supporting our simplistic *which is* deletion analysis for *such that* relatives.

(28) a. The mathematical system ~~which is~~ such that (in it) $2 + 2 = 4$
      b. A country ~~which is~~ such that you don't feel so good #(in it)
      c. A picture ~~which is~~ such that #(in it) Rosa has a snake near her

Nevertheless, hidden locatives may well be the solution for Swiss German. First, observe that German uses a vague adjunct locative where Dutch uses an independent possessive. The triangle example discussed above, for instance, would be translated as follows:

(29) ein Dreieck, bei dem   die Summe der   Quadrate der   beiden kurzen
      a   triangle with which the sum   of-the squares of-the two   short
      Seiten gleich gross ist, wie das Quadrat der   langen Seite
      sides equally big   is as the square of-the long   side

It is important to note that the locative preposition *bei* is ambiguous between a strict and a loose reading. This can be illustrated with the following examples:

(30) a. ein Haus bei dem   eine Garage steht   Meaning (31b) only
          a   house near which a   garage stands
          'A house that has a garage next to it'
      b. ein Haus bei dem   eine Garage fehlt   Meaning (31a) or (31b)
          a   house with which a   garage is-missing
          'A house that does not have a garage'

(31) a. 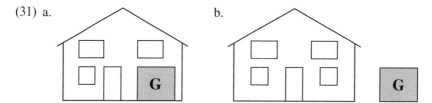 b.

The locative in (29) is of the loose type, typically nonselected. In fact, one may ask whether the meaning is locative at all. Jespersen coined the term "corollary circumstance" to describe absolutives as in *with this weather we had better stay here*, and for all its vagueness, when we consider examples like the following, such a definition seems quite appropriate here.

(32) a. Bei diesem Wetter lohnt es sich nicht, den Rasen zu mähen
        with this   weather pays it REFL not   the lawn to mow
        'With this weather it isn't worth the trouble to mow the lawn.'
     b. Bei einer solchen Farbenpracht muss ja   sogar der Appel verblassen
        with a   such   color-splendor must PRT even the Appel turn-pale
        'With such a splendor of colors, even the Appel must look pale.'

(33) a. ein Wetter, bei dem es sich nicht lohnt, den Rasen zu mähen
     b. eine Farbenpracht, bei der ja sogar der Appel verblassen muss

The adjuncts in question, both the free possessive of Dutch and the adjunct locative in German, might be said to perform a bridge function. This is so because, among other uses, they serve to circumvent island configurations, as in the following examples:[17]

(34) a. Dat is een probleem waarvan ik drie artikelen heb gelezen   Dutch
        that is a   problem of-which I three articles   have read
        waarin   het gewoon wordt verzwegen
        in-which it   simply is   ignored
        'That is a problem such that I have read three articles in which it is simply ignored.'
     b. Das ist ein Problem bei dem ich drei Artikel gelesen habe,   German
        that is a   problem with which I   three articles read   have
        in denen es einfach verschwiegen wird
        in which it simply ignored   is

This means that the adjunct, which I will henceforth refer to as the *bridge adjunct*, can originate higher than the apparent variable in the relative clause, represented by the resumptive pronoun in the above examples.[18] The actual point of origin of the bridge adjunct is sometimes difficult to pin down in view of its vague semantics, but bridge sensitivity shows that it may sometimes originate lower than the topmost CP layer. The following German examples illustrate this. They also show that the adjuncts in question can occur independently of whether a relative clause is involved.

(35) a. Bei diesem Wetter glaube ich nicht, dass es sich lohnt, den Rasen zu
         with this   weather believe I   not   that it REFL pays   the lawn to
         mähen
         mow
         'With this weather I don't believe that it is worth the trouble to mow the lawn.'

    b. #Bei diesem Wetter flüsterte   er, dass es sich nicht lohnt, den Rasen zu
         with this   weather whispered he that it REFL not   pays   the lawn to
         mähen
         mow
         'With this weather he whispered that it isn't worth the trouble to mow the lawn.'

(36) a. ein Wetter bei dem er nicht glaubt, dass es sich lohnt, den Rasen zu
         a   weather with which he not   believes that it REFL pays   the lawn to
         mähen
         mow
         'A weather in which he does not believe that it is worth the trouble to mow the lawn.'

    b. #ein Wetter bei dem er flüsterte,   dass es sich nicht lohnt, den Rasen
         a   weather with which he whispered that it REFL not   pays   the lawn
         zu mähen
         to mow
         'A weather in which he whispered that it isn't worth the trouble to mow the lawn.'

9.2.3.4 Swiss German: The Silent Locative   Returning now to Swiss German, the main generalization that we have established so far is that there is a sharp conflict between two main requirements. First, the Doubly Filled Comp Filter excludes overt *wh*-phrases next to the obligatory relative complementizer *wo*. And second, the only way we can get rid of a *wh*-word in SpecCP is by haplological reduction of *wo wo* to *wo*. A third assumption that plays a crucial role here is that the *wh*-movement strategy must be used whenever it can, perhaps always. This is so because the *wh*-movement pattern in locative relatives is obligatory. If nothing forced *wh*-movement in that case, economy considerations would presumably favor a nonmovement strategy.

At this point, the logical next step is the conjecture in (37).

(37) *Conjecture*

All aboutness relatives, including those with resumptive pronouns, are formed by means of a bridge adjunct; the bridge adjunct in Swiss German is the general locative *wo*; *wo* does not show up overtly because of haplological reduction.

The stipulation about the resumptive pronoun cases (except, of course, those that are local enough to cliticize to $C°$ and then to be deleted, or to be silent) follows from the fact that the apparent resumptive pronouns are island insensitive, as shown in example (2), repeated here as (38).

(38) es mäitli wo öpper   wo mit ere i's   kino   gaat zimli mues spine
     a girl   WO someone WO with her in-the cinema goes quite must crazy-be
     'A girl that someone who goes to the movies with her must be quite crazy'

A final refinement should be taken into account. It is sometimes rather difficult to ascertain whether a certain relative clause involves a true locative or a locative bridge adjunct. This is particularly true for locative pronominals originating inside prepositional phrases.

   In Swiss German locative PPs, the (nonhuman) pronominal object of the preposition often appears as *da* ('there') or *wo* ('where'), preceding the preposition. In addition there is a kind of reduced copy, *dr*, that is cliticized to the preposition, also to its left.

(39) [PP da dr-in] (there (thr-)in) — [PP wo dr-in] (where (thr-)in)
     [PP da dr-aa] (there (thr-)at) — [PP wo dr-aa] (where (thr-)at)
     [PP da dr-uf] (there (thr-)on) — [PP wo dr-on] (where (thr-)on)

Da and *wo* can move independently, stranding the rest of the PP:

(40) Da / Wo   isch s   buech dr-uf gläge?
     There/where is   the book thr-on lain
     'That the book was lying on? / What was the book lying on?'

Correspondingly, we get the following type of relative clauses:

(41) a. de tisch wo s   buech dr-uf gläge isch
        the table WO the book thr-on lain   has
        'The table that the book was lying on'
     b. d schublade wo mer din schmuck dr-ii gläit händ
        the drawer   WO we your jewelry thr-in laid have
        'The drawer that we put your jewelry into'

Presumably these are like locative relatives in that *wo* is moved to SpecCP and then deleted by haplology. Notice, however, that the strong pronominal *da* is often optional, as shown in (42).

(42) a. Mer leged s   buech (da)   dr-uf
      we   put   the book (there) thr-on
      'We put the book on that/it.'
   b. Si läit de schmuck (da)   dr-ii
      she lays the jewelry (there) thr-in
      'She puts the jewelry into that/it.'

This invites the question of whether the examples in (41) could not be analyzed as being on a par with the "weak" variants in (42) and involving a locative bridge adjunct. In other words, there might be two derivations for the examples in (41). That locative bridge adjuncts can co-occur with locative PPs is confirmed by the fact that the (reduced) locative PP can occur inside islands as in example (43), which means that a locative bridge adjunct must be involved. Example (44) shows that *da* in Contrastive Left Dislocation constructions works the same way.

(43) a. S git   götter wo mer sich nöd cha vorstelle das es lüüt   hat wo dr-aa
      it gives gods   WO one REFL not can imagine that it people has WO thr-in
      gläubed
      believe
      'There are gods that you cannot imagine that there are people who believe in them.'
   b. Das isch dëë wald wo ich vil   vründe ha   wo regelmëëssig dr-in gönd
      that is   that forest WO I   many friends have WO regularly   thr-in go
      go spaziere
      to walk
      'That is that forest that I have many friends who regularly go walk in it.'

(44) a. Die götter, *da*   cha mer sich nöd vorstelle das es lüüt   hät wo dr-aa
      those gods, there can one REFL not imagine that it people has WO thr-in
      gläubed
      believe
      'Those gods, you cannot imagine that there are people who believe in them.'
   b. Dëë wald *da*   han ich vil   vründe wo   regelmëëssig dr-in gönd go
      that forest there have I   many friends WO regularly   thr-in go   to
      spaziere
      walk
      'That forest, I have many friends who regularly go walk in it.'

9.2.4 Summary

The picture that has emerged in the preceding discussion is that the rather complex and obscure range of relative clause patterns in Swiss German can be considerably simplified. The main types are given in table (45).

(45) Headed Relative Clauses

| | Aboutness relatives | | Locative relative clauses | |
Resumptive relative clauses				
A	**B**	**C**	**D**	**E**
Fronted and deleted (silent) resumptive clitics	Locally accessible resumptive pronouns in situ	Relative clauses without any visible correlative element	True locative operator moved into Spec,CP and deleted at PF under haplology	Expletive locative operator moved into Spec,CP and deleted at PF under haplology

The arguments presented above suggest that the cases in B and C (the shaded cells) are in reality cases of E. And D and E are both locative relatives involving movement of *wo*. The main generalization to be drawn from this is what I call the Kamikaze Conspiracy.

(46) *The Kamikaze Conspiracy*

Swiss German optimizes those strategies that will result in some correlative element that moves to C° and is then subject to annihilation (by haplology or by Avoid Pronoun).

The main ingredients that fuel this conspiracy are the following:

A. *Wo is obligatory* (in headed relative clauses).
B. The *Doubly Filled COMP Filter* forces the deletion (or silence) of any element that moves to the proximity of C°.
C. *Haplology*: The reduction of *wo wo* to single *wo* favors the optimization of the use of *wo* as a locative bridge adjunct.
D. *Avoid Pronoun* is forced by A and B.
E. Some correlative element, be it a *w*-word or a clitic, must (at some stage of the derivation) occupy a position next to C°; call this element the operator; in other words the presence of an *operator is obligatory*.

It should be kept in mind that the above is an overall description pertaining to headed relative clauses. The situation in headless relatives and in *wh*-questions is quite different. (47) presents a rough summary of how these differ.

(47)

		DFC	
		Spec,CP	C°
A	Headed Relatives		[+REL]
		(*X ≠ Ø)	*wo*
		Spec,CP	C°
B	Headless Relatives		[+REL]
		wh-word	(**wo*)
		Spec,CP	C°
C	Questions		[−REL]
		wh-phrase	(*dass*)

Considerations of space prevent me from illustrating this picture in any detail. There are a few important things to notice. First, recoverability obviously distinguishes A from B and C. Only in headed relatives can the main features of the operator word be recovered. Second, recoverability outweighs the obligatoriness of *wo* in case B. Third, in questions, the complementizer is *dass* (*öb* in yes/no questions), and *dass* may, subject to regional, individual, and stylistic variation, co-occur with the *wh*-phrase.

I take the latter point to be significant. *Wo* is overtly characterized as a complementizer with operator potential by being a *w*-word. *Dass* lacks this property, rightly so since it also, and mainly, serves to introduce declarative complement clauses. What this suggests is that the Doubly Filled COMP Filter (DFC) is sensitive to this difference. This in turn invites the interpretation of the DFC as an identity-avoiding device. That has, in fact, always struck me as the correct interpretation of the DFC because in all Germanic languages, to the extent that they have any DFC effects at all, the DFC filter is completely impervious to verbal elements in C°. In other words, you never get any DFC effects when Verb Second (or Subject Aux Inversion) has moved V into C°.

(48) a. John asked   [who]$_{\text{Spec,CP}}$ [(*that)]$_{\text{C°}}$ Bill saw
    b. [Who]$_{\text{Spec,CP}}$ [did]$_{\text{C°}}$ Bill see?

This suggests to me that the DFC is essentially a syntactic reflex of the Obligatory Contour Principle (OCP), which, in phonology, prohibits adjacent occurrences of identical elements. I will refer to the generalized version of the OCP as Identity Avoidance or *XX. Note that *XX covers both Haplology and the DFC effect in Swiss German relative clauses. But clearly, Haplology applies under strict phonological identity, while the DFC appears to be primarily sensitive to certain syntactic-semantic features such as operatorhood. This, I believe, is what one would expect if Identity Avoidance is a general principle of biological organization: its effect can be detected at both interfaces, PF and LF. The following section pursues this line of thinking.

9.3   Some Speculations about Identity Avoidance

9.3.1   *XX in Grammar and in Nature

The idea that the OCP is active in syntax is not new. Proposals include Van Riemsdijk 1988, 1998a; Grimshaw 1997; Yip 1998; and Ackema 2001.[19] The next question that arises is whether *XX is a principle of narrow syntax or a property holding at the interfaces. The former seems unlikely, while the latter interpretation is more plausible (see the end of the previous section). In principle, nothing precludes the possibility that some property of the interface is unique to human language, but the idea that *XX is a principle of a much more general type imposes itself. First, as noted above, it appears that *XX may be active in different guises both at the PF and at the LF interface. Second, we already know that *XX is operative in phonology proper. Third, *XX may be active within grammar in other ways as well. And finally, there are suggestive indications that *XX is found in many varying domains of nature. Let us look at the latter two ideas in turn.

First, feature cancellation under checking may be seen as an instance of *XX. Note, for example, that, under the copy theory of movement (remerge), there is an apparent problem with respect to checking. If the relevant features are eliminated upon checking, the chain consisting of the remerged element and its copy will not be uniform because the remerged element lacks certain features that the copy still has. Gärtner (2002) proposes to solve this problem by interpreting remerge as multi-dominance (see also Vergnaud 2003). The question still remains as to whether the remerged element and the node against which it is checked are fully identical. *XX would rule this out. And in fact it might be attractive to view feature checking and elimination as a kind of haplological effect. A radical view along these lines is presented in Piattelli-Palmarini and Uriagereka (2004), in which feature checking plus cancellation is compared with the biological mechanism of anti-immune reactions.

Another area of syntax that might be reexamined in the light of *XX is (relativized) minimality (see Rizzi 1990). What the term *relativized* refers to, in fact, is the relative identity of both the element engaged in a dependency relation, and the intervening element.[20] The idea, highly speculative, of course, is that if the element that is moved (or remerged) is identical to an intervening element in some crucial respect (such as being a potential Ā-binder), then the dependency is blocked. And in a graphic interpretation of how such a movement process takes place, there is a virtual intermediate stage at which the two elements in question are also adjacent. The reason I believe this to be another genuine case of *XX is that, if we look closely at the way locality works, it turns out that there is considerable variation from language to language as to which morphosyntactic features produce detectable effects. To give just one example, the [+R]-feature in Dutch produces a strong effect, regardless of the fact that one of the items involved is [+WH] and the other [−WH], as discussed in detail in Van Riemsdijk 1978; conversely, the interaction of two [+WH]-elements of which one is [+R] and the other [−R] produces only a weak effect.[21]

A suggestion like the one by Piattelli-Palmarini and Uriagereka (2004) is obviously largely metaphorical, and they are the first to admit this. But at the same time they say that the idea may well be pursued and could turn out to be more than a metaphor.

This is where we turn to some speculations as to other domains of nature where *XX-effects can be observed:

Magnetism   Likes repulse each other while opposites attract each other. In Van Riemsdijk 1998a, I argue that magnetism is at the core of what governs the distribution of maximal projections (phrases) in the clause.

Covalent bonding   Pursuing a similar idea, this time taken from chemistry, Haeberli (2003) proposes to deal with abstract Case, and, more generally, the EPP mechanism, by means of the idea that the goal and the probe are unstable elements that need to enter into a bonding relationship to form a stable element. One interesting aspect of this idea is that it is similar to the idea that "fusion" by means of reanalysis is one of the standard ways syntax (and phonology) eliminate offending *XX configurations. Such an effect was posited for so-called coherent infinitival complements in German (and Dutch) in earlier work of mine (see Van Riemsdijk 1984).

Antiagreement effects   Essentially, this involves cases in which subject-verb agreement is given up in favor of a disagreement pattern when the subject is involved in an Ā-dependency (see Ouhalla 1993).[22]

Anti-immune reactions   These are as proposed in Piattelli-Palmarini and Uriagereka (2004). See above.

Buffers in DNA sequencing   Adjacent identical sequences in DNA are apparently avoided by the interposition of buffer sequences in nonjunk DNA, while junk-DNA permits large numbers of adjacent identical sequences (see Li 1999).

9.3.2   Violability of Principles of Organization

One of the main problems that we now face is the question of how the actual repercussions of such highly general principles of physical/biological organization in the grammar of specific languages can be insightfully represented.[23] The problem is simple. *XX cannot be omnipotent in grammar. Otherwise, for example, adjacent DPs would presumably be ruled out, and adjacent PPs as well. Equally importantly, we cannot escape the conclusion that the effects of a principle like *XX are somehow parameterized since some languages are more tolerant of *XX configurations than others, and furthermore languages employ different strategies to escape the *XX effect. A good example is the *si si/se se* problem in Romance (see Grimshaw 1997). Standard Italian avoids *si si* by changing the first *si* to *ci*. In the Conegliano dialect of Italian, however, the *si si* sequence survives. In Spanish, on the other hand, the corresponding *se se* is avoided not by substitution but by deletion of one occurrence of *se*. Given that the constraint in question is a general principle of biological organization, it would be absurd to propose that the constraint itself is parameterized. Of course, following the trend of minimalism, we could say that it is the lexical items only that are the locus of the parameters. That would amount to saying that Conegliano *si* has an exception feature, say [−*XX], which exempts it from the effects of the general principle. But that would take us back to a Lakoff-style "theory" of exceptions (see Lakoff 1970), hardly an attractive prospect.

Another approach to this type of problem can be found in optimality-theoretic (OT) syntax. OT deals with parameterized effects of general principles in the following way. The general principle is a predicate and individual applications of the principle constitute the argument of the constraint. In other words, in any given specific language, we might have a multitude of occurrences of the constraint C applied to a (sometimes quite large) list of elements or features: C(F1), C(F2), C(F3), . . . Each of these individuated constraints can be ranked individually with respect to the other constraints in the grammar.[24]

Consider first the DFC. There appear to be (at least) two ways of incorporating the DFC into an OT-based system. The first, exemplified by Keer and Baković 1997, makes use of alignment constraints, in particular SPEC LEFT and HD LEFT. The idea here is that the head (C°) wants to be leftmost in the clause, but the SpecCP also wants to be leftmost. Obviously, the C°-element can only be leftmost if the specifier is null (we are talking about phonetically realized instances of these categories here). Hence, if the ordering of these two constraints is SPEC LEFT ≫ HD LEFT, we get the DFC effect. Languages that do not show any DFC effect adopt the opposite ordering.

The other strategy would be to extend the use of the *XX constraint (see Ackema 2001; Grimshaw 1997). The general constraint *XX must then be relativized to the specific features that trigger the DFC effect in a given language. In Swiss German, for example, we might say that the relative complementizer *wo* has a feature [+OP], meaning that it is an operatorlike complementizer (see the discussion in section 9.2.4). And we are assuming that the *w-/d*-words in SpecCP as well as the clitics adjoined to C° have the status of operator. *XX (OP) will then yield the DFC effect. As discussed above, this second strategy would seem to be preferable, in particular because it accounts for the fact that a C° filled by the finite verb after Verb Second—that is, by a nonoperatorlike element—shows no DFC effect whatsoever. An interesting consequence of adopting *XX (OP) is that apparently the Avoid Pronoun Principle is not needed, at least not to derive the Swiss German relative clause pattern. Hence we can dispense with the corresponding constraint AV PRO here.

Several other constraints are needed to get things to work, but it can be done. The outcome, however, will be rather unsatisfactory, not least because typical interface constraints end up being intermingled, regardless of whether they are of the phonological or the semantic kind.[25] One main conclusion emerges from this short discussion: developing principled and parameterizable ways to incorporate the manifestations of general principles of biological and physical organization into the theory of grammar will constitute a major challenge for generative research in the years ahead.

Notes

1. This chapter is in honor of Jean-Roger Vergnaud, one of the most inspirational minds in modern linguistics. Some of the materials presented here are also discussed in Van Riemsdijk 2003b. I would like to thank audiences in Debrecen, Konstanz, Nijmegen, Utrecht, and Vienna as well as Peter Ackema, Josef Bayer, Cedric Boeckx, Hans Broekhuis, Marcel den Dikken, Joe Emonds, Hubert Haider, Riny Huijbregts, Massimo Piattelli-Palmarini, Martin Prinzhorn, Martin Salzmann, and Edwin Williams, as well as two anonymous reviewers for helpful advice and interesting discussions.

2. See for example Chomsky, 2005.

3. See in particular Bromberger and Halle 1989. Extensive discussion is found in Chomsky 2004. For some dissenting discussion, see Van Riemsdijk 2003a.

4. See for example Kaye, Lowenstamm, and Vergnaud 1990 as well as Vergnaud 2003.

5. See Ackema 2001, to which I return in section 9.3, and Van Riemsdijk 1988, 1998a.

6. I should specify that my data reflects more specifically the dialect of Zürich, which is the one I speak. By and large, however, it appears that the description given here carries over to other Swiss German dialects, and probably to some Alemannic dialects in Austria and Germany as well. For more discussion, see Bader and Penner 1988 as well as Penner and Bader 1995. For a discussion of certain related properties of Swiss German relative clauses that may partly be problematic but are in many ways complementary to my present proposals, see Salzmann 2006.

7. See Bayer 1984 and Pittner 1995. Thanks to Viola Schmitt for enlightening me on Hessian, see Schmitt 2006.

8. Relative pronouns in varieties of German are either *d*-words or *w*-words. It should be noted that headless (free) relatives are entirely different: the relative complementizer *wo* is absent and there is an overt *w*-pronoun.

9. Marginally, gaps are also sometimes found in the indirect object position, at least in some Swiss German dialects. I will not pursue this issue here; see Van Riemsdijk 1989 for further discussion.

10. Such an analysis is inspired by the theory of locally licensed deletions as proposed in Den Besten 1981, later reprinted as Den Besten 1983, 1989.

11. If correct, this conclusion may well have far-reaching consequences for the so-called raising analysis of relative clauses as advocated in Vergnaud 1974, 1985. I will not pursue this angle, however.

12. I first noticed this fact in Van Riemsdijk 1998b.

13. See Chomsky and Lasnik 1977; Bayer 1984, 2004; Pesetsky 1998; and many others.

14. For more discussion on Japanese, see among others Fukui and Takano 2000. For Chinese (below), see also Tsai 1994.

15. One question that arises is whether the possessive *waarvan* could be extracted out of one of the DPs in the relative clause. This seems implausible since the only DPs inside the relative clause are parts of the triangle, not all of it. Hence, the head of the relative clause would, in a sense, be a more plausible source for the possessive. But syntactically there does not seem to be any source for the head inside the relative clause. This again reflects on the raising analysis of relative clauses proposed by Vergnaud 1974, 1985. I will assume that the possessive is an independent possessive adjunct that stands in a possessive relationship with the head of the relative clause. For more discussion of the relative independence of possessives in Dutch, see Van Riemsdijk 1997.

16. It should be noted that the following example is grammatical:

(i) Dem   fëëlt   sini stoossstange
    that-one misses its   fender
    'That one has no fender.'

But the meaning is completely different. In (i) *dem* can only be a demonstrative pronoun referring to a (human) experiencer missing his fender. Hence no extraction is involved in (i).

17. Some speakers of Dutch, including Marcel den Dikken (personal communication), can also use locative bridge adjuncts. When they do, they use the general locative *waar* ('where'), the same choice that I claim Swiss German makes; see below.

18. The use of bridge adjuncts is reminiscent of the appearance of the expletive or placeholder *was* in partial *wh*-movement constructions such as (ii).

(ii) Was glaubst du mit wem Maria getanzt hat?
     what believe you with whom Mary danced has
     'Who do you think Mary danced with?'

If the *was* that shows up in German partial *wh*-movement binds a placeholder variable, as claimed by Dayal (1994, 1996) contra Horváth (1997), then, one might ask, why is it not used in relative clauses? See also the various contributions to Lutz, Müller, and von Stechow 2000, as well as Fanselow 2006.

19. See also Bošković 2002 for interesting ideas on how to use haplology effects at the PF interface to determine which copy in a chain should be spelled out.

20. The interpretation of locality constraints as intervention constraints goes back at least to Wilkins 1977, 1980. Wilkins's way of putting it is that if the intervenor is too similar to the head and the foot of the chain, these are no longer adjacent.

21. For reasons of space, I cannot discuss this in any detail here. Some relevant examples are given here without much comment:

(iii) Waar heeft hij er   vaak over   gesproken
    where has   he there often about spoken
    'Where did he often talk about it?' but not 'What did he often talk about there?'

Both *er* and *waar* could either originate inside the PP or be interpreted as an independent locative. Hence, in principle (iii) should be ambiguous, but it is not, the only acceptable interpretation being the one in which there is no intervention. This is the case from Van Riemsdijk 1978. But consider now the interaction of R-pronouns and *wat voor*–split:

(iv) ?Wat$_i$ heb je   waar$_j$ [e]$_i$ voor flessen [e]$_j$ op gelegd?
    what have you where   for bottles   on put
    'What kind of bottles did you put on what?'

Here we have only a weak effect. I conclude from such facts (similar lines of argument can be established for German and French) that relativized locality is a much more fine-grained phenomenon than generally acknowledged.

22. See also Adger and Ramchand (2005) for an extension of the antiagreement idea to the syntax of Celtic languages. They argue that the morphological effects found in the complementizer system under long dependencies should be interpreted as anti-identity of certain features.

23. See Freidin and Vergnaud 2001 for enlightening discussion.

24. A case in point is Grimshaw's (1997) analysis of *XX effects in clitic clusters. Her account relies heavily on the general constraint types FILL and PARSE, but each of these is thought to be individuated to the features REFLexive, PERSon, NUMber, CASE, GENDer, at least. This alone yields ten different constraints.

25. A more extensive discussion of what an OT analysis might be like was included in an earlier version of this chapter, but it had to be cut to comply with length requirements.

References

Ackema, Peter. 2001. Colliding complementizers in Dutch: Another syntactic OCP effect. *Linguistic Inquiry* 32:717–726.

Adger, David, and Ramchand, Gillian. 2005. Merge and move: *Wh*-dependencies revisited. *Linguistic Inquiry* 36:161–193.

Bader, Thomas, and Penner, Zvi. 1988. A Government-Binding account of the complementizer system in Bernese Swiss German. Arbeitspapier 25. Bern: Universität Bern, Institut für Sprachwissenschaft.

Bayer, Josef. 1984. COMP in Bavarian syntax. *The Linguistic Review* 3:209–274.

Bayer, Josef. 2004. Decomposing the left periphery: Dialectal and cross-linguistic evidence. In *The Syntax and Semantics of the Left Periphery*, ed. Horst Lohnstein and Susanne Trissler, 59–95. Berlin: Mouton de Gruyter.

Besten, Hans B. den. 1981. On the interaction of root transformations and lexical deletive rules. *Groninger Arbeiten zur Germanistischen Linguistik* 20:1–78.

Besten, Hans B. den. 1983. On the interaction of root transformations and lexical deletive rules. In *On the Formal Syntax of the Westgermania: Papers from the 3rd Groningen Grammar Talks*, ed. Werner Abraham, 47–131. Amsterdam: John Benjamins.

Besten, Hans B. den. 1989. On the interaction of root transformations and lexical deletive rules. In *Studies in West Germanic Syntax*, ed. Hans B. den Besten, 14–100. Amsterdam: Rodopi.

Bošković, Željko. 2002. On Multiple *Wh*-Fronting. *Linguistic Inquiry* 33:351–384.

Bromberger, Sylvain, and Halle, Morris. 1989. Why phonology is different. *Linguistic Inquiry* 20:51–70.

Chomsky, Noam. 1981. *Lectures on Government and Binding*. Dordrecht: Foris.

Chomsky, Noam. 2004. *The Generative Enterprise Revisited: Discussions with Riny Huijbregts, Henk van Riemsdijk, Naoki Fukui and Mihoko Zushi*. Berlin: Mouton de Gruyter.

Chomsky, Noam. 2005. Three factors in language design. *Linguistic Inquiry* 36:1–22.

Chomsky, Noam, and Lasnik, Howard. 1977. Filters and control. *Linguistic Inquiry* 8:425–504.

Chung, Chan, and Kim, Jong-Bok. 2003. Differences between externally and internally headed relative clause constructions. In *The Proceedings of the 9th International Conference on HPSG*, ed. Jong-Bok Kim and Stephen Wechsler. Stanford, CA: CSLI.

Dayal, Veneeta. 1994. Scope marking as indirect *wh*-dependency. *Natural Language Semantics* 2:137–170.

Dayal, Veneeta. 1996. *Locality in Wh-Quantification: Questions and Relative Clauses in Hindi*. Dordrecht: Kluwer.

Fanselow, Gisbert. 2006. Partial *wh*-movement. In *The Blackwell Companion to Syntax*, eds. Martin Everaert and Henk C. van Riemsdijk, 437–491. Oxford: Blackwell.

Freidin, Robert, and Vergnaud, Jean-Roger. 2001. Exquisite connections: Some remarks on the evolution of linguistic theory. *Lingua* 111:639–666.

Fukui, Naoki, and Takano, Yuji. 2000. Nominal structure: An extension of the symmetry principle. In *The Derivation of VO and OV*, ed. Peter Svenonius, 210–254. Amsterdam: John Benjamins.

Gärtner, Hans-Martin. 2002. *Generalized Transformations and Beyond: Reflections on Minimalism*. Berlin: Akademie Verlag.

Grimshaw, Jane. 1997. The best clitic: Constraint conflict in morphosyntax. In *Elements of Grammar*, ed. Liliane Haegeman. Dordrecht: Kluwer.

Grosu, Alexander. 2002. Strange relatives at the interface of two millennia. *Glot International* 6:145–167.

Haeberli, Eric. 2003. Categorial features as the source of EPP and abstract case phenomena. In *New Perspectives on Case Theory*, ed. Ellen Brandner and Heike Zinsmeister, 89–126. Stanford, Calif.: CSLI.

Horvath, Julia. 1997. The status of "*Wh*-Expletives" and the Partial *Wh*-Movement Construction of Hungarian. *Natural Language and Linguistic Theory* 15:509–572.

Kaye, Jonathan, Lowenstamm, Jean, and Vergnaud, Jean-Roger. 1990. Constituent structure and government in Phonology. *Phonology* 7:305–328.

Keer, Edward, and Bakovič, Eric. 1997. Have FAITH in syntax. In *Proceedings of the Sixteenth West Coast Conference on Formal Linguistics (WCCFL)*, ed. E. Curtis, J. Lyle, and G. Webster, 255–269. Stanford, Calif.: CSLI.

Kuno, Susumu. 1973. *The Structure of the Japanese Language*. Cambridge, MA: MIT Press.

Lakoff, George. 1970. Irregularity in syntax. New York: Holt Rinehart and Winston.

Leben, William. 1973. Suprasegmental phonology. Unpublished ms., Linguistics Department, MIT.

Li, Wentian. 1999. Large-scale patterns in DNA Texts. Unpublished ms.

Lutz, Uli, Müller, Gereon, and Stechow, Arnim von. 2000. *Wh-Scope Marking*. Amsterdam: John Benjamins.

McCarthy, John. 1986. OCP effects: Gemination and anti-gemination. *Linguistic Inquiry* 17:207–263.

Ning, Chunyan. 1993. The overt syntax of relativization and topicalization. Unpublished ms., Department of Linguistics, University of California at Irvine.

Ouhalla, Jamal. 1993. Subject-Extraction, Negation and the Anti-Agreement Effect. *Natural Language and Linguistic Theory* 11:477.

Penner, Zvi, and Bader, Thomas. 1995. Issues in the syntax of subordination: A comparative study of the complementizer system in Germanic, Romance, and Semitic languages with special reference to Bernese Swiss German. In *Topics in Swiss German Syntax*, ed. Zvi Penner, 73–289. Bern: Peter Lang.

Pesetsky, David. 1998. Some optimality principles of sentence pronounciation. In *Is the Best Good Enough?*, ed. Pilar Barbosa, Danny Fox, Paul Hagstrom, Martha McGinnis, and David Pesetsky, 337–383. Cambridge, MA: MITWPL/MIT Press.

Piattelli-Palmarini, Massimo, and Uriagereka, Juan. 2004. The immune syntax: The evolution of the language virus. In *Universals and Variations in Biolinguistics*, ed. Lyle Jenkins, 341–377. London: Elsevier.

Pinker, Steven, and Jackendoff, Ray. 2004. The faculty of language: What's special about it? Unpublished ms., Harvard University and Brandeis University.

Pittner, Karin. 1995. The Case of German relatives. *Linguistic Review* 12:197–231.

Riemsdijk, Henk C. van. 1978. *A Case Study in Syntactic Markedness: The Binding Nature of Prepositional Phrases*. Lisse: Peter de Ridder Press. Later published by Foris Publications, Dordrecht, and currently by Mouton de Gruyter, Berlin.

Riemsdijk, Henk C. van. 1984. On pied-piped infinitives in German relative clauses. In *Studies in German Grammar*, ed. Jindrich Toman, 165–192. Dordrecht: Foris.

Riemsdijk, Henk C. van. 1988. The representation of syntactic categories. In *Proceedings of the Conference on the Basque Language, 2nd Basque World Congress*, 104–116. Vitoria-Gasteiz: Central Publication Service of the Basque Government.

Riemsdijk, Henk C. van. 1989. Swiss relatives. In *Sentential Complementation and the Lexicon: Studies in Honor of Wim de Geest*, ed. Dany Jaspers, Wim Klooster, Yvan Putseys, and Pieter Seuren, 343–354. Dordrecht: Foris.

Riemsdijk, Henk C. van. 1997. Push chains and drag chains: Complex predicate split in Dutch. In *Scrambling*, ed. Shigeo Tonoike, 7–33. Tokyo: Kurosio Publishers.

Riemsdijk, Henk C. van. 1998a. Syntactic feature magnetism: The endocentricity and distribution of projections. *Journal of Comparative Germanic Linguistics* 2:1–48.

Riemsdijk, Henk C. van. 1998b. Syntax driven (crazy) by morphology: Morphological effects in the choice of relativization strategies in Zurich German. In *Mengelwerk voor Muysken bij zijn afscheid van de Universiteit van Amsterdam*, ed. A. Bruyn and J. Arends, 67–74. Amsterdam: Algemene Taalwetenschap UvA.

Riemsdijk, Henk C. van. 2003a. Contour templates in syntax? A note on the spreading of (in-)definiteness. In *A New Century of Phonology and Phonological Theory: A Festschrift for Professor Shosuke Haraguchi on the Occasion of his Sixtieth Birthday*, ed. Takeru Honma, Masao Okazaki, Toshiyuki Tabata, and Shinichi Tanaka, 559–570. Tokyo: Kaitakusha.

Riemsdijk, Henk C. van. 2003b. East meets West: Aboutness relatives in Swiss German. In *Germania et alia: A Linguistic Webschrift for Hans den Besten*, ed. Jan Koster and Henk C. van Riemsdijk. Groningen/Tilburg: University of Groningen and Tilburg University. http://odur.let.rug.nl/~koster/DenBesten/contents.htm.

Rizzi, Luigi. 1990. *Relativized Minimality*. Cambridge, MA: MIT Press.

Salzmann, Martin. 2006. Resumptive prolepsis: a study in indirect A-bar dependencies, LUCL, Leiden University: Ph.D. dissertation.

Schmitt, Viola. 2006. Hessian headed relative clauses and the syntactic role of the relative pronoun, Department of Linguistics, University of Vienna: Master's thesis.

Tsai, Wei-Tien Dylan. 1994. On Economising the Theory of A-Bar Dependencies. Doctoral dissertation, Linguistics and Philosophy, MIT.

Vergnaud, Jean-Roger. 1974. French Relative Clauses. Doctoral dissertation, Department of Linguistics, MIT.

Vergnaud, Jean-Roger. 1985. *Dépendances et niveaux de représentation en syntaxe*. Amsterdam: John Benjamins.

Vergnaud, Jean-Roger. 2003. On a certain notion of "occurrence": The source of metrical structure, and of much more. In *Living on the Edge: 28 Papers in Honour of Jonathan Kaye*, ed. Stefan Ploch, 599–632. Berlin: Mouton de Gruyter.

Wilkins, Wendy. 1977. The Variable Interpretation Convention: A condition on variables in syntactic transformations. Unpublished ms., Linguistics Department, UCLA.

Wilkins, Wendy. 1980. Adjacency and variables in syntactic transformations. *Linguistic Inquiry* 11:709–750.

Wu, Xiu-Zhi Zoe. 2000. Grammaticalization and the development of functional categories in Chinese. Unpublished ms., Department of Linguistics, University of Southern California.

Yip, Moira. 1998. Identity avoidance in phonology and morphology. In *Morphology and Its Relation to Phonology and Syntax*, ed. Stephen G. Lapointe, Diane K. Brentari, and Patrick M. Farrell, 216–246. Stanford, CA: CSLI.

10 Ellipsis and Missing Objects

Joseph Aoun and Yen-hui Audrey Li

Language is a system pairing sound and meaning. However, this pairing is not always perfect. Crosslinguistically, it is quite common to find instances that have sound without meaning or meaning without sound. The former include expletives. The latter can be illustrated by empty categories (traces) that are derived by movement, empty pronouns, and nonnominal empty elements such as those in the "ellipsis" or "deletion" structures: VP-deletion, Gapping, Sluicing, and Stripping, among others. The questions raised repeatedly in the literature are how to represent and interpret silent but meaningful elements, and what is the status of empty elements in the organization of grammar?[1]

Since the 1960s and 1970s, there have been continuous debates on how to interpret deletion/ellipsis structures[2] and how to represent them syntactically.[3] Regarding the syntactic representations, two possibilities exist to derive the empty part: an empty element is empty throughout the derivation, or deletion applies to a fully represented structure under certain conditions. For the sake of convenience, we will refer to the latter option as the *deletion approach* and the former as the *interpretive approach.* Many works have argued for the deletion approach or the interpretive approach. A combination of both approaches has also been argued for.[4]

Our work attempts to provide further insight into this perennial subject of interest. Mandarin Chinese will serve as the main empirical basis for our work, a language that has not been as prominent as some others in the relevant literature. We will focus narrowly on the varieties of constructions in this language that have been regarded as the counterpart of a typical VP-ellipsis construction in English—the V construction (construction with a stranded V) and the Aux construction (construction with a stranded auxiliary).[5] The relevant generalizations will demonstrate that the missing part is always a subcategorized element (see Oku 1998; Goldberg 2005).[6] A null category in "ellipsis" structures comes into existence only to satisfy the subcategorization properties of a head. That is, the syntactic notion of subcategorization must be relevant in "ellipsis" structures. In addition, we will illustrate with the interaction of object relativization and the structures containing a null VP to show that the object of the missing VP is not visible for syntactic processes, providing support for an approach that includes empty elements in syntactic representations—an interpretive approach. To further explore the properties of empty elements, we will show that an empty element must be subject to some well-formedness condition (a Visibility condition). Such a condition captures the contrast between English, which does not allow the subcategorized phrase of a verb to be empty, and Chinese, which does.

10.1 "VP-Ellipsis" in Mandarin Chinese

Let us begin with the main properties of the recognized VP-ellipsis structures, illustrated by these examples from English:

(1) a. John likes the gift that you gave to him. Mary does, too.
    b. John will like the gift that you gave to him. Mary will, too.

VP-ellipsis in English is characterized by a clause containing *do* or an auxiliary without an overt verb phrase. The missing verb phrase must be interpreted. When a pronoun is present in the antecedent VP, both strict and sloppy interpretations are available. For instance, *Mary does, too* in (1a) can have the sloppy reading (2a) and the strict reading (2b).

(2) a. Mary$_i$ likes the gift that you gave to her$_i$.   Sloppy reading
    b. Mary likes the gift that you gave to him.   Strict reading

Hoji (1998) further argues that a more reliable test for VP-ellipsis constructions should be based on the (im)possibilities of various mixed readings. A true VP-ellipsis construction exhibits the following patterns (see Fiengo and May 1994; Li 2002):

(3) Max said he saw his mother; Oscar did too.
    a. Max$_i$ said he$_i$ saw his$_i$ mother; Oscar$_j$ said he$_i$ saw his$_i$ mother.
    b. Max$_i$ said he$_i$ saw his$_i$ mother; Oscar$_j$ said he$_j$ saw his$_j$ mother.
    c. Max$_i$ said he$_i$ saw his$_i$ mother; Oscar$_j$ said he$_j$ saw his$_i$ mother.   Mix 1
    d. *Max$_i$ said he$_i$ saw his$_i$ mother; Oscar$_j$ said he$_i$ saw his$_j$ mother.   Mix 2

(4) Max said his mother saw him; Oscar did too.
    a. Max$_i$ said his$_i$ mother saw him$_i$; Oscar$_j$ said his$_i$ mother saw him$_i$.
    b. Max$_i$ said his$_i$ mother saw him$_i$; Oscar$_j$ said his$_j$ mother saw him$_j$.
    c. Max$_i$ said his$_i$ mother saw him$_i$; Oscar$_j$ said his$_j$ mother saw him$_i$.   Mix 1
    d. Max$_i$ said his$_i$ mother saw him$_i$; Oscar$_j$ said his$_i$ mother saw him$_j$.   Mix 2

The patterns of mixed readings in (3) and (4) are the results of conditions applying copying/reconstruction at LF to create full-fledged representations at LF (see Fiengo and May 1994).

In many other languages, there is no counterpart of *do*; a pattern corresponding to the *do* VP-ellipsis structure in (1a) is not found. Mandarin Chinese is an example of such a language. As a possible counterpart to the VP-ellipsis construction (1a) in English, Chinese uses a lexical verb. For convenience, we refer to this construction as the "V construction."

(5) Ming hen xihuan ni gei ta de liwu. Han ye hen xihuan.
    Ming very like   you give him De gift Han also very like
    'Ming likes the gift you gave to him; Han also likes (the gift you gave to Han/
    Ming).'

It has been proposed that the V is raised to I and that the V construction is a typical VP-ellipsis structure (VP being elided; see Huang 1988). In addition, the English pattern in (1b) has a direct counterpart in Chinese. An auxiliary appears and the VP that should have followed the Aux is missing. We refer to this pattern as the "Aux construction."

(6) Ming hui xihuan ni gei ta de liwu. Han ye hui.
    Ming will like   you give him De gift Han also will
    'Ming will like the gift you gave to him; Han also will.'

The literature has mainly focused on whether the V construction in (5) is a VP-ellipsis structure, particularly with respect to the availability of a true sloppy reading and the relevance of a locality condition on sloppy readings (see, for instance, Hoji 1998; Huang 1988, 1991; Kim 1999; Li 1998, 2002; Otani and Whitman 1991; Pan 1998; Paul 1996, 1999; Tomioka 1996, 1997, 1999; Xu 2003; Wu 2003a, 2003b). Recently, more attention has been paid to the significance of the interpretation of sentences like (7a–b) (see Li 1998, 2002; Xu 2003; also see Goldberg 2005 and the references cited there for works on many other languages). These sentences contain an adjunct within the VP in the antecedent clause.

(7) a. wo jian-guo ta san-ci;   tamen ye jian-guo ____ (tamen zhi jian-guo
       I see-ASP him three times they also see-ASP   (they   only see-ASP
       yi-ci).
       one-time)
       'I have seen him three times, they have seen (him), too. (They only saw
       (him) once.)'
    b. wo renshi ta hen jiu le, wo baba ye renshi ____. (zhishi meiyou
       I know him very long Le I father also know   only not-have
       renshi hen jiu)[7]
       know very long
       'I have known him for a long time; my father knew (him), too. (Just not
       very long.)'

The missing element in the second clause (the elliptical clause) does not have an interpretation containing the frequency phrase 'three times' or the duration phrase 'a long time'. That is, (7a–b) cannot be interpreted as (8):

(8) a. wo jian-guo ta   san-ci   le; tamen ye   jian-guo ta   san-ci   le.
       I see-ASP him three times Le they   also see-ASP him three times Le
       'I have seen him three times; they have seen him three times, too.'
    b. wo renshi ta   hen jiu le, wo baba ye   renshi ta   hen jiu le.
       I   know him very long Le I   father also know him very long Le
       'I have known him for a long time; my father has known him for a long time too.'

Moreover, (7b) and (8b) should be contrasted with the following sentence, which has the interpretation indicated in the English translation.

(9) wo renshi ta   hen jiu le, tamen ye   renshi le
    I   know him very long Le they   also know Le
    'I have known him for a long time; they also have come to know (him).'

Le generally expresses an event ended, an action terminated (perfective), or a change of state taken place. It is possible with a stative verb like *renshi* 'know' to express a change of state ('My father didn't know him before; he has come to know him'). When the predicate contains a duration phrase, *le* is used in the perfective sense.

(10) a. wo baba   renshi ta   le.
        my father know him Le
        'My father has come to know him (he did not know him before).'
     b. wo baba   renshi ta   hen jiu le.
        I   father know him very long Le
        'My father has known him for a long time.'

The fact that the second clause in (9)—*wo baba ye renshi le*—only has the interpretation like the one in (10a), not (10b), indicates that the duration phrase is excluded from the missing part. Similar evidence can be found in the negative counterparts of (9)–(10). The negative marker *mei* is perfective and *bu*, imperfective, roughly speaking. A bare stative verb *renshi* only accepts *bu* and uses *mei* for negation when a duration phrase appears:

(11) wo bu/*mei renshi ta.
     I   not   know him
     'I don't know him.'

(12) wo mei/*bu renshi ta   ji   nian.
     I   not   know him several year
     'I have not known him for several years.'

However, the use of *mei* is not possible in the corresponding V construction:

(13) tamen yijing   renshi ta   ji   nian le. wo bu/***mei** renshi.
     they   already know   him several year Le I   not   know
     'They already knew him for several years. I don't know.'

If the duration phrase were included in the missing part, the unacceptability of *mei* and the acceptability of *bu* in (13) would not be accounted for.

Other adjuncts behave alike: they are not included in the missing part of the V construction. The exclusion of adjuncts in the V construction is reminiscent of the null object construction in Japanese/Korean (see Oku 1998, for instance). On the other hand, the V construction allows a true sloppy interpretation, like a VP-ellipsis structure:

(14) a. John shuo-guo ta xihuan tade laoshi
        John say-ASP   he like   his   teacher
        'John$_i$ said he$_i$ liked his$_i$ teacher.'
     b. Bill ye   shuo-guo [e]
        Bill also say-ASP
        'Bill$_j$ also said he$_i$ liked his$_i$ teacher.'
        'Bill$_j$ also said he$_j$ liked his$_j$ teacher.'
        'Bill$_j$ also said he$_j$ liked his$_i$ teacher.'   Mix 1
        '*Bill$_j$ also said he$_i$ liked his$_j$ teacher.'   Mix 2

(15) John shuo-guo tade laoshi   xihuan ta,   Bill ye   shuo-guo [e]
     John say-ASP   his   teacher like   him Bill also say-ASP
     'John$_i$ said his$_i$ teacher liked him$_i$; Bill$_j$ also said his$_i$ teacher liked him$_i$.'
     'John$_i$ said his$_i$ teacher liked him$_i$; Bill$_j$ also said his$_j$ teacher liked him$_j$.'
     'John$_i$ said his$_i$ teacher liked him$_i$; Bill$_j$ also said his$_j$ teacher liked him$_i$.' Mix 1
     'John$_i$ said his$_i$ teacher liked him$_i$; Bill$_j$ also said his$_i$ teacher liked him$_j$.' Mix 2

The possibility of true sloppy interpretations for Chinese V constructions contrasts with the absence of such interpretations in Japanese null object constructions (Hoji 1998; Li 2002). While leaving to a separate work the issue of why these two constructions differ, the presence of true sloppy interpretations in the V construction indicates that it has a full-fledged representation at LF, even though it cannot include adjuncts. Note that it is not the case that Chinese always excludes an adjunct from the missing phrase of the various types of "VP-ellipsis"-like constructions. The Aux construction behaves just like its counterpart in English.

(16) wo yao tanwang ta   san-ci;   tamen ye   yao.
     I   will visit   him three-times they   also will
     'I will visit him three times, they will (visit him three times), too.'

10.2 Deriving the Null Elements

The V construction cannot include adjuncts. Only objects are possible. What are such empty objects? To answer these questions, we should first note an important subject/object asymmetry in the interpretation of empty elements in the patterns (17a–b), illustrated by (18)–(20).

(17) a. [Subject...[$_{clause}$ [$_{subject}$ e_1] V [$_{object}$ e_2]]....]
e_2, not e_1, can be interpreted with some prominent entity in the previous discourse:

b. [[$_{clausal\ subject/topic}$ [$_{subject}$ e_1] V [$_{object}$ e_2]] (subject)....]]
Both e_1 and e_2 can be interpreted with some prominent entity in the previous discourse:

(18) a. wo$_1$ yinwei [Zhangsan$_2$ bu xihuan e_3] you diar shiwang.
    I   because Zhangsan not like   have slight disappointment
    'I am somewhat disappointed because John does not like e_3.'

b. *wo$_1$ yinwei [e_2 bu   xihuan Zhangsan$_3$] you diar   shiwang.
    I   because Zhangsan not   like   have slight disappointment
    'I am somewhat disappointed because e_2 does not like Zhangsan.'

Cf. c. wo$_1$ yinwei [e_1 bu xihuan Zhangsan$_3$] you diar   bu-hao-yisi.
    I   because   not like   Zhangsan have slight not embarrassment
    'I am somewhat embarrassed because (I) do not like Zhangsan.'

(19) a. Zhangsan$_1$ dui [wo$_2$ mei kanjian e_3] meiyou   zeren
    Zhangsan to I   not see   not-have responsibility
    'Zhangsan does not have responsibilities on (the fact that) I didn't see e_3.'

b. *Zhangsan$_1$ dui [e_2 mei kanjian wo$_3$] meiyou   zeren
    Zhangsan to   not see   I   not-have responsibility
    'Zhangsan does not have responsibilities on (the fact that) e_2 didn't see me.'

Cf. c. Zhangsan$_1$ dui [e_1 mei kanjian wo$_3$] meiyou   zeren
    Zhangsan to   not see   I   not-have responsibility
    'Zhangsan$_1$ does not have responsibilities on (the fact that) (he$_1$) didn't see me.'

(20) ta$_1$ zhao-bu-dao yige [[e_2 bu renshi e_3] de ren$_2$]
    he look-not-find one   not know   De person
    a. 'He$_1$ can't find a person$_2$ that does not know e_3.'
    b. '*He$_1$ can't find a person$_2$ that e_3 does not know e_2.'
    c. 'He$_1$ can't find a person$_2$ that e_1 does not know e_2.'

These sentences all illustrate an asymmetry in the possibility of an empty element referring to some entity in the discourse: doing so is much harder for a subject than an object. Why is there such a contrast? Without elaborating much on details, we will briefly show that the contrast is due to the interaction of the general properties of movement and the morphosyntactic properties of empty pronouns in Chinese.

What is an empty category? In the framework of Government and Binding, an empty category can be an NP trace, a variable, or a *pro/PRO*. Because the structures in question do not involve NP movement, we will disregard the option of NP traces. What about variables? Variables are generally the result of topicalization or relativization. Huang 1982 and many subsequent works such as Li 1990 and Ning 1993 argue that topicalization and relativization are movement operations and are subject to island conditions in Chinese. That is, a variable cannot be separated from its antecedent by island boundaries. However, apparent island violations are possible in some cases. Huang 1982 argues that such apparent island violations involve instances of *pro*, which is identified with the closest potential antecedent (Generalized Control Rule, GCR). For instance, the empty subject in the following sentences, when it is a *pro*, can be bound across an island by the closest potential antecedent, the topic in (21) and the matrix subject in (22).

(21) Lisi$_1$, [[e$_1$ chang ge   de] shengyin] hen haoting.
     Lisi   sing song DE voice   very good
     'Lisi$_1$, the voice with which [he$_1$] sings is very good.'

(22) Zhangsan$_1$ zhao-bu-dao [[e$_1$ renshi e$_2$ de] ren$_2$].
     Zhangsan seek-not-arrive   know   De person
     'Zhangsan$_1$ cannot find [people$_2$ [that (he)$_1$ knows e$_2$]].'

The GCR and the general characteristics of pronouns conspire to disallow an empty pronoun (*pro/PRO*) in the object position. According to the GCR, an empty pronoun must be identified with the first potential antecedent. At the same time, a pronoun is sensitive to a disjointness requirement: it must be free within a domain containing a subject (Binding Principle B). An empty pronoun in an object position must be identified by the subject of the clause according to the GCR. However, it must also be free from the subject because of the disjointness requirement on a pronoun. These conflicting requirements rule out an empty pronoun in the object position. In other words, the empty object element in (18)–(20) cannot be a variable because of the islands. Nor can it be an empty pronoun because of the conflicting requirements. Moreover, recall that the V construction is not the result of VP-ellipsis, even though it has full representations that yield the patterns of true sloppy interpretations. Nor is it clear what a deletion process should be in these cases such that the subject/object asymmetry is accommodated. Then, what is the missing element in the V construction?

We suggest that what is missing is an object and the object is truly empty in the sense that no item from the lexicon is present in the object position. It is interpreted after copying from the antecedent or the discourse context. More precisely, we claim that such a truly empty position exists only because of the subcategorization requirement of the head. This position contains categorial features to satisfy the subcategorization requirements and nothing else. The categorial features are present simply because of the subcategorization properties. In other words, this is the copying theory of ellipsis along the lines of Williams 1977, according to which ellipsis involves base generation of empty positions and subsequent copying/reconstruction of the antecedent to those empty positions at LF. For simplicity, let's refer to such a true null element with only categorial features as a TEC. A TEC exists because of the following requirement:

(23) *Subcategorization requirement on true empty categories*
 a. If a head is subcategorized for a phrase E, E must be present in the syntactic structure.
 b. An E can be generated as null (without lexical materials) only in subcategorized positions.

According to (23), a transitive verb requires an object. When no lexical items appear overtly after a transitive verb, an empty object must be present. The subcategorization requirement is fulfilled. Nothing other than the subcategorized category is present. That is, the missing element in the V construction $[V_{transitive} \underline{\quad}]$ can only be the object of a transitive verb.

The Aux construction follows from (23) as well. It has a head Aux. The property of an Aux is that it is subcategorized for a VP: [Aux + VP]. Accordingly, a VP must be present. A VP may consist of a verb and its subcategorized complements, as well as VP-modifiers. For instance, everything following the Aux *hui* 'will' and *neng* 'can' in (24a–b) is part of a VP subcategorized by an Aux.

(24) a. Ming hui hen bu gaoxing. Han ye hui ____.
  Ming will very not happy   Han also will
  'Ming will be quite unhappy; Han will (be quite unhappy), too.'
 b. Ming neng mashang   zuo-wan; Han ye   neng ____.
  Ming can immediately do-finish Han also can
  'Ming can finish the work immediately; Han also can (finish the work immediately).'

The content of the missing VP, including the lexical materials and their structures, is recovered by copying the linguistic antecedent or from the discourse context. These two constructions are represented here:

(25) a. The Aux construction

Subject + Aux + [_VP ____]   Aux subcategorized for a VP
   b. The V construction
Subject + V + [_object ____]   V subcategorized for an object

These two patterns differ in whether an adverbial modifier is included in the missing part. It is excluded in the V construction because the subcategorization frame of a transitive verb is [____ object], not [____ (object) Adjunct]. In contrast, an adjunct is included in (25a) because an Aux is subcategorized for a VP, which may contain an adverbial modifier.

In brief, the empty elements in (25a–b) exist only because of the subcategorization requirement of a head. The interpretation of the empty category is obtained at the interpretive level after copying from the antecedent or discourse context.[8]

10.3 Deletion

Our proposal is essentially an "interpretive approach." This contrasts with many works arguing for a PF deletion approach to ellipsis. The limited space precludes a substantial discussion of the relevant issues. We would like to just briefly mention two points that might provide support for the approach advocated here. The first concerns a deletion alternative to the facts discussed in this work; the second, the interaction between the Aux construction and object relativization.

10.3.1 A PF Deletion Alternative

To determine if a PF deletion approach can be extended to accommodate the Chinese patterns in (25a–b), we briefly describe what a deletion alternative might be.

What are the mechanisms of a deletion approach? Because of the limited space, we will simply consider the most advanced version: the one by Merchant (2001) based on a combination of semantic interpretation and PF deletion. In this analysis, a feature E is generated with a head. The semantics of E is to ensure that "the deleted constituent satisfies what is traditionally known as parallelism or identification of the elided material" (Merchant 2004, 671).

Details aside, what is pertinent to our discussion is that a head designated by an E feature is allowed not to pronounce its complement (the sister node to the head) at the post-PF phonological interpretative component. That is, a head licenses its sister node (complement) to be empty. To see how such an approach might apply to (25a–b), let us illustrate with an example containing a duration/frequency phrase. In the literature, various structures for those with duration/frequency phrases have been proposed (see, for instance, Huang 1982; Li 1990; Tang 1990; Soh 1998; Ernst 2001). Nonetheless, it has been recognized by many that the duration or frequency phrase should be able to occupy a position lower than the object. Briefly put, Soh (1998, 36–40) observes that when the order is [V + Object + Duration/Frequency phrase (DFP)], the object can have scope over the DFP. That is, in an example like (26), 'all students' can have wide scope with respect to 'twice'.

(26) wo qing-guo [quanbu de xuesheng] [liang ci]
        I   invited   all   De student   two times
        'I invited all students twice.'

Soh argues that the object must occupy a position c-commanding the DFP and that the node dominating both the object and the DFP, expressed as FP in (27), is sister to the verb that occupies the *v* position.

(27) [$_{vP}$ V [$_{FP}$ Object . . . DFP]]

To accommodate the V construction in Chinese by a deletion approach sketched above, one would need to restrict deletion to the contexts where the complement contains merely the subcategorized element. Then, when the FP in (27) contains a DFP, it cannot be deleted. However, such an added restriction on deletion at PF would face challenges in accounting for the fact that a nonsubcategorized adjunct can be included in interpreting the missing part of the Aux construction, in addition to the necessity of relying on a syntactic notion (subcategorization) at PF.

10.3.2 The Absence of an Object

Moreover, there is support for the emptiness of the missing part syntactically. Because a detailed discussion would involve more careful presentations of various types of relativization constructions in Chinese (Aoun and Li 2003, chaps. 4–7), we will only mention a pair of structures indicative of the emptiness of the relevant structure, while deferring the details to a separate work.

As argued for in Aoun and Li 2003, chaps. 5–6, at least two different types of relativization should be distinguished in Chinese: relativization of an argument by directly raising the phrase to be relativized (promotion analysis) or relativization of an adjunct by generating a relative operator at the periphery of the relative clause. The relative operator agrees in features with the NP modified by the relative clause, referred to as the head of a relative construction (*place where, time when, person who,...*). If a relative construction is to be derived by the promotion analysis, the head of the relative construction should originate from within the relative clause. Under an interpretive approach to the Aux construction, the Aux is followed by a null verb phrase, in contrast to a deletion approach, which allows a verb phrase fully represented syntactically.[9] If the relative clause contains a null verb phrase, there would be no object to be relativized. That is, object relativization should not be possible in a structure with a null VP syntactically. In contrast, the relativization process should not be affected by a null verb phrase when the relativized phrase does not originate from within the VP. This contrast holds quite well. For instance, sentence (28) is an instance of "why" relativization. The verb phrase expressing *qu xuexiao* 'go to school' can be empty. Similarly, the relativization of the subject argument also allows the verb phrase to be missing, as in (29). In contrast, (30) relativizes the object and a null VP is not possible, even though there is an antecedent verb phrase in the relative clause 'that he will not attend'.

(28) [[ta bu hui qu   xuexiao de] liyou] gen [[women bu hui (qu   xuexiao)
       he not will attend school De reason and we   not will attend school
    de] liyou] shi yiyang de.
    De reason be same   De
    'The reason why he will not attend school is the same as the reason we will not
    (attend school).'

(29) [[e hui qu   xuexiao de] ren]   gen [e bu hui (qu   xuexiao) de] ren]   shi
       will attend school De person and   not will attend school   De person be
    yiyang de.
    same   De
    'The people that will attend school are the same as the people that will not
    (attend school).'

(30) [[ta bu hui qu   de] xuexiao] gen [[women bu hui *(qu   de] xuexiao] shi
       he not will attend De school and we   not will   attend De school be
    yiyang de.
    same   De
    'The school that he will not attend is the same as the school we will not
    (attend).'

The contrast in the acceptability of a null VP between (28) and (29) on the one hand and (30) on the other is suggestive of the emptiness of the null verb phrase syntactically.[10]

10.4   The Case Requirement on Empty Categories

The previous section demonstrated that a null element is empty syntactically, not the result of deletion at PF. The syntactic presence of a null element is not random. It exists only when it is subcategorized by a head—that is, the existence of an empty category fulfills the subcategorization requirement (23). This captures the interpretive possibilities of the various "VP-ellipsis" constructions in Chinese (25a–b). English seems to share only some of the properties. Consider, again, the Chinese patterns in (25a–b). We mentioned that English has the Aux pattern, as illustrated in (1b). As

for the V construction, English does not allow it at all. The English sentences in
(31a–b), for instance, are unacceptable, in contrast to the acceptable Chinese (32a–
b):

(31) a. John saw him. *Mary saw, too.
     b. I like him. *She doesn't like.

Compare the following examples:

(32) a. John jian-le ta; Mary ye jian-le.
        John see-Le him Mary also see-Le
        'John saw him; Mary also saw.'
     b. wo xihuan ta;; ta bu xihuan.
        I   like   him he not like
        'I like him; he doesn't like.'

Clearly, the subcategorization requirement is a necessary but not sufficient condition
to license an empty element. The contrast between (31) and (32) is an instance of a
more general distinction between English and Chinese: Chinese, not English, allows
an object to be empty generally.[11]

(33) wo kan-le.
     I   read-Le

(34) I read *(it).

Note that an important property of (32) and (33) is that the accusative Case[12] is not
overtly realized. There is no lexical item bearing the accusative Case. As argued for
in Travis 1984, Koopman 1984, and Li 1985, 1990, nominal expressions in Chinese
are assigned Case, as in the languages with overt morphological Case markings. This
is so in spite of the fact that Chinese does not exhibit morphological cases. The
assignment of Case is also in conformity with the Visibility Condition and the θ-
criterion in the theory of Government and Binding: an argument must be assigned a
θ-role and θ-role assignment is possible only when the argument has Case (Chomsky
1981).[13]

   In contrast, there are no instances in English where an abstract Case fails to be
realized overtly. This distinction can be summarized below (see the Inverse Case Filter discussed in Bošković 1997, 134–142).

(35) English, not Chinese, requires Case to be realized on a lexical item.

Further note that the occurrence of an empty nominal element is restricted. It generally appears in an argument position (see Saito 1985, regarding a *pro* being a nominal category only). A nominal phrase in an argument position is always assigned
Case. Lobeck (1995, 1999) argues that empty elements need to be licensed by some
formal feature(s) of a specific head. Briefly, some of her examples are the licensing of

an empty VP by the [tense] feature of I, an empty IP by some appropriate features in C. Along the same line, we propose (36) below.

(36) An empty nominal element must be Case-marked.[14]

The Case requirements in (35) and (36) capture the contrast in (31)–(34). An accusative Case is assigned to an object by a verb. In Chinese, Case need not be realized by an overt lexical item. However, English must realize the accusative Case; therefore, the object cannot be empty. (31) and (34) are unacceptable.

  (36) prohibits an object not assigned Case from being empty. This is true in both English and Chinese. First, consider clausal complements. It has been claimed that a clause is not assigned Case in English (see Stowell 1981).

(37) a. Mary was afraid (*of) that the idea wouldn't work. Cf. Mary was afraid *(of) it.
   b. I suppose that he will come. Cf. *I suppose it. vs. I suppose so.

(37a–b) show that the subcategorized clause is not in a Case position. The lexical head *afraid, suppose* does not assign Case. According to (36), the object position of such a lexical head should not be empty. This is illustrated by the unacceptability of (38a–b):[15]

(38) a. *Mary was afraid that the idea wouldn't work and Bill was [$_{AP}$ happy [$_{CP}$ e]].
   b. *I suppose that he will come and they suppose [$_{CP}$ e], too.

(35)–(36) conspire to disallow an empty object in English. If Case is assigned, it must be overtly realized by a lexical object. If Case is not assigned, an empty nominal element is not licensed.

  Next, consider the corresponding cases in Chinese. A very common perception about this language is that an object can always be empty. However, if (35) and (36) are correct, we should predict that only those verbs assigning Case allow their object to be empty. When Case is assigned, the subcategorized object can be empty and (36) is satisfied. When Case is not available, the object should be just like its counterpart in English and cannot appear in the null form. This prediction is borne out. An empty object is unacceptable when the verb subcategorizes for a clausal object only. The following correlation exists:

(39) a. If a verb is subcategorized for a nominal object, the object can be empty.
   b. If a verb is subcategorized for a clausal object only, the object cannot be empty.

When the clausal object is not overt in (38b), the verb must occur with *so* in English and *zheme, zhemeyang,* or *zheyang* in Chinese, words that may be regarded as the *pro*-form of a clause.[16] The correlation is demonstrated below.

(40) *Verbs allowing a nominal object and a null object*
    a. wo tingdao-le na-jian shi.
       I   hear-Le   that-Cl matter
       'I heard that matter.'
    b. wo tingdao ta de-le da jiang le; ta ye tingdao-le.
       I   heard   he get-Le big prize Le he also hear-Le
       'I heard that he got a big prize; he also heard.'

(41) *Verbs disallowing a nominal object and a null object; zheme(yang) 'so' must*
    appear
    a. *wo renwei/yiwei na-jian shi.
       I   think/ think that-Cl matter
       'I thought/thought that matter.'
    b. wo renwei/yiwei ta hen congming; tamen ye *(zheme(yang))
       I   think/ think he very smart   they   also so
       renwei/yiwei.
       think/ think
       'I thought that he was smart; they also thought.'

(42) a. *wo cai   na-jian shi.[17]
       I   guess that-Cl matter
       'I guess that matter.'
    b. wo cai   ta hen congming; tamen ye *(zheme(yang)) cai.
       I   guess he very smart   they   also so   guess
       'I guess that he is smart; they also guess.'

(43) a. *wo dasuan na-jian shi.
       I   plan   that-Cl matter
       '*I planned that matter.'
    b. wo dasuan mingtian qu; tamen ye *(zheme(yang)) dasuan.
       I   plan   tomrrow go   they   also so   plan
       'I planned to go tomorrow; they also planned.'

Moreover, the Case requirement (35) and the subcategorization requirement (23) predict that an element should not be null when it is assigned Case by a verb but not subcategorized by it. This prediction is borne out. It has been argued that duration/frequency phrases in Chinese, being nominal expressions, are assigned Case by the verb (Li 1990).[18]

(44) wo zuo-le san-tian/san-ci   le.
      I   do-Le three days/three times Le
      'I did (it) (for) three days/three times.'

The following V construction does not have an interpretation including a duration/frequency phrase:

(45) a. wo zuo-le san-tian   le; ta ye   zuo-le. (zuo yixia hou, jiu   zou-le)
       I   do-Le three days Le he also do-Le (do a-bit after, then leave-Le)
       'I did (something) (for) three days; he did (something), too (did for a short
       while and left).'
    b. wo zuo-le san-tian   le; keshi ta mei zuo.
       I   do-Le three days Le but   he not do
       'I did (it) (for) three days; but he did not do (it).'

(46) a. wo zuo-le san-ci   le; ta ye   zuo-le (erqie zuo-le henduo-ci.)
       I   do-Le three times Le he also do-Le (and do-Le many-times)
       'I did (it) (for) three times; he did (it), too (and he did (it) for many times).'
    b. wo zuo-le san-tian   le; keshi ta (genben) mei zuo.
       I   do-Le three days Le but   he simply   not do
       'I did (it) (for) three days; but he simply did not do (it).'

In brief, the difference in the possibility of an empty complement between English
and Chinese is traced back to different requirements on the manifestation of Case.

   Before concluding this section, we would like to clarify the issue of CP deletion in
English. It has been claimed that English has the so-called null complement anaphora (Grimshaw 1979). Grimshaw noted that some predicates are acceptable with
a null complement (the following examples are Grimshaw's (38) on p. 289).

(47) Statement: John is telling lies again.
     Response: It's too bad.
               I agree.
               I'm flabbergasted.
               I'm surprised.
               It can't be true.

However, according to Lobeck (1995) and Merchant (2001), CP deletion is not
possible in English. Indeed, Lobeck (1995, 48) makes a more general statement that
"elliptical complements of the lexical heads V, P and A are ungrammatical in English." Some of the examples are listed here (Lobeck's (35) and (37) on pp. 48–49):

(48) a. *Mary doesn't expect Bill to win, but she [VP wants [CP e]]
    b. *Even though Mary [VP said [CP e]], John knows that Bill isn't going to be
       there.
    c. *John is anxious to leave, and Mary is [AP eager [CP e]] too.

According to Lobeck's generalization, the "null complement" in (47) cannot truly be
an empty complement represented syntactically. Then, why does it seem that the interpretation includes a CP complement? We would like to suggest that this is due to
the information provided by the discourse context. The CP is not present structur-
ally. The absence would lead us to predict that the patterns regarding true sloppy

interpretations (Mix 1 and Mix 2 readings) would not be exactly like (3)–(4), which were argued to be indicative of the presence of the relevant structures at LF. This seems to be true. The informants we consulted had difficulties agreeing with the relevant patterns listed below:

(49) John was surprised that he would see his father. Bill was surprised, too.
    a.   John$_i$ was surprised that he$_i$ would see his$_i$ father. Bill$_j$ was surprised that he$_j$ would see his$_i$ father, too.   Mix 1
    b.   *John$_i$ was surprised that he$_i$ would see his$_i$ father. Bill$_j$ was surprised that he$_i$ would see his$_j$ father, too.   Mix 2

(50) John was surprised that his father would see him. Bill was surprised, too.
    a.   John$_i$ was surprised that his$_i$ father would see him$_i$. Bill$_j$ was surprised that his$_j$ father would see him$_i$, too.   Mix 1
    b.   John$_i$ was surprised that his$_i$ father would see him$_i$. Bill$_j$ was surprised that his$_i$ father would see him$_j$, too.   Mix 2

Some speakers do not like these readings at all. Some others have different judgments (such as accepting (49b) but rejecting (49a), or rejecting one of the two in (50a–b)). Such variations may be due to the vagueness of the expression 'Bill was surprised, too.' Syntactically, the sentence only says that Bill was also surprised. However, the discourse context allows Bill to be surprised at something.[19]

10.5 Deletion vs. Base Generation

This work has presented an interpretive approach to the V and Aux constructions in Chinese. Many issues need to be explored further, especially with respect to the status of the true empty category in the V construction, the properties of phrase structures when an element is null syntactically, and the consequences of this approach. Because of space limitations, we will only touch on the issue of phrase structures and the prediction on the categorial types of elided elements.

Recall that an empty element is required to meet the subcategorization requirement. It only has categorial features as determined by the head. To illustrate, a transitive verb *see* must have the subcategorization frame [____ DP]. Thus, a DP must be present. The DP object simply contains the feature [+D]. The contents will be recovered for interpretation at LF.

Such a conception of empty elements raises the question of how a set of phrase markers is established when true empty categories are involved. This question is especially relevant if a "bare phrase structure" approach is adopted (Chomsky 1994). Under this approach, the computational system takes two objects (two lexical items from a Numeration) and merges them to form a new object. One of the two projects; the one that projects is the head of the phrase.

(51)

What happens when the tree structure contains a true empty category, as in (52)?

(52)

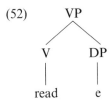

An option that might conform to the spirit of the bare phrase structure approach is to allow Numeration to contain an item "e" with only formal features (such as the categorial feature). For instance, a Numeration may contain {read, e [+C]} ([+C] representing the appropriate categorial features). "Read" is a lexical item and "e [+C]," an item with a categorial feature [+C]. The two merge and the verb projects, creating a VP. When the V projects, the "e [+C]" is labeled as a maximal category, a DP in this case (a nominal category in an argument position).[20] Alternatively, one may assume that empty elements are not in the Numeration. The computation system builds up phrase structures in the following manner: a transitive verb—e.g., *read*—has the subcategorization frame [_____ DP]. Accordingly, a node DP must be merged with the verb. This DP does not dominate lexical materials (i.e., no lexical item is selected from the Numeration). An empty element is simply a node not containing any lexical material (see note 8).

Regardless of which option is adopted, a head determines the existence of an empty element. That is, a subcategorized element, an XP, can be a true empty category.

Next, consider the possibility of an empty head. For instance, what is the status of an empty V in [vp [v ____] YP], where YP is a subcategorized element? Under an interpretive approach advocated here, an empty element is present syntactically to meet the subcategorization requirement. It is a category without lexical materials. If this conception is correct, an empty element does not contain subcategorization features. An empty V would simply be [+V], without further specification on whether it is [+transitive] or [−transitive]. It does not have the subcategorization frame such as [____ DP], [____ CP]. Thus, we would not expect an empty V to force the presence of a subcategorized complement. Following Chomsky 2000 and Collins 1997, we may assume that every merger takes place to fulfill some requirement, such as Spec-head agreement or head-complement subcategorization requirement. When a head does not have a subcategorization feature, it does not merge with a subcategorized element. In other words, we should not expect the structure [xp [x __] YP] to be generated. That is, X-ellipsis should not be possible. This derives the observation in Lobeck 1995 and Merchant 2001 that it is an XP, not an X, that is elided.

Notes

We would like to thank Candice Cheung, Tom Ernst, Jim Huang, Grace Li, Yafei Li, Yan Li, Bingfu Lu, Patricia Schneider-Zioga, Jim Tai, Dylan Tsai, Niina Zhang, and Maria Luisa Zubizarreta for their judgments, comments, and help with earlier drafts of this chapter. The feedback from the audience at Chung Cheng University and IACL 12 at Tianjin is greatly appreciated. Jean-Roger Vergnaud's Case theory and its relevance for overt and nonovert nominal categories guided our understanding of missing objects.

1. See, among many others, Hankamer and Sag 1976, Williams 1977, Winkler and Schwabe 2003, as well as the references cited there.

2. We use the terms *deletion* and *ellipsis* interchangeably, which do not necessarily mean the process of deletion or ellipsis.

3. The relevant literature has been extensive and illuminating (see an insightful and detailed review in Winkler and Schwabe 2003). Beyond those reviewed in Winkler and Schwabe, more works have been produced, such as the series of dissertations from the University of Connect-icut (Matsuo 1998; Oku 1998; Stjepanović 1999) and others from many more programs. Numerous works are included in journals, books, and conference proceedings. Indeed, a subject search produced such long lists of works that we decided against attempting even a short survey here. We plead guilty to the charge of inadequacy regarding the literature reviewed here.

4. There have been many variations of the deletion and the interpretive approaches. For the approaches and the representative works, see Winkler and Schwabe 2003, 5. There have also been proposals arguing for the need for both approaches. Hankamer and Sag's (1976) deep and surface anaphora and Williams's (1977) discussion of syntax and discourse may be considered forerunners. More recently, Matsuo (1998) provides an interesting example.

5. A third construction has also been analyzed as the equivalent of the VP-ellipsis structure: the *shi* construction (see, for instance, Wu 2003a), as in (i).

(i) Zhangsan xihuan ta;   Lisi ye   shi.
    Zhangsan like   him Lisi also be
    'Zhangsan likes him; so is it with Lisi.'

Shi is a copula and can be used as a focus or emphatic marker or to confirm what has been said in the previous discourse. The function of *shi* puts special syntactic constraints on the distribution. We discuss this structure in a separate work.

6. Goldberg presents important tests to help determine if a certain construction with a stranded verb is a "null object" construction (construction with a null object only) or a "VP-ellipsis" construction. The latter includes a nonsubcategorized adverbial interpretation in the missing part.

7. *-Le* can be suffixed to a verb as an aspectual marker or function as a sentence-final particle denoting change of state. Because the distinction of the two *le*'s is not important in this work, we gloss all occurrences of *le* as Le.

8. Oku (1998) notes that the Japanese counterpart of the Chinese V construction, the null object construction, excludes adverbials from the missing part. He proposes that a null object

construction does not have an object in derivation. An object is merged with the verb later at LF (late merger). In a work in progress, we argue that late merger is not adequate to account for the behavior of the null object constructions and that the different behavior of null objects in Chinese and Japanese can be traced to their differences in the properties of empty pronouns.

9. Goldberg (2005) discusses cases of verb raising when a VP is empty. The contrast between the possibility of raising a verb and the impossibility of raising an object from within an empty VP may be due to the same subcategorization requirement discussed in the text: an Aux determines the presence of a VP, which must be headed by a V. However, whether it has an object or not is not determined by the presence of the Aux.

10. This raises the question of how sentences like the following in English (from Lasnik 2001, 318) should be analyzed:

(i) I know what I like and what I don't.

The acceptability of (i) may be related to the fact that English, not Chinese, allows pseudogapping constructions. We propose in a separate work that such differences may be traced to the presence/absence of agreement projections in these two languages.

11. We focus on objects here. The subject can also be empty, when it is a variable bound by a topic or a *pro* identified by the subject of a higher clause.

12. The capitalized "Case" denotes the abstract Case in the Case module of the Government and Binding theory and the small "case" expresses the morphological case.

13. The Visibility requirement raises the question of what the Case property of PRO is. Chomsky and Lasnik (1993) argue that PRO is assigned a null Case. See further works by Martin (1996, 2001). However, see Cecchetto and Oniga 2004 for a different view. We leave the issue of PRO for further research (see Hornstein 2001 for a movement approach to deriving obligatorily controlled PRO).

The requirement also raises questions concerning sluicing, VP-ellipsis, and so on, which have an empty IP sister to C and an empty VP/vP sister to I. In what sense are these empty categories "visible"? Note that there is a very close relation between V and I, and I and C. Speculatively, I is always related to a V (inflected verbs, abstractly or morphologically) and C, I (see, for instance, Grimshaw 1997). The presence of a functional projection is an indication that the relevant lexical node exists. We may follow Lobeck's (1995, 1999) suggestion regarding the appropriate features in I, and C licensing an empty VP/IP.

14. (36) also raises questions regarding NP-traces, which are not Case-marked. Under a Copy and Merge approach to movement, a trace is simply the result of deletion at Spell-Out (Chomsky 1995, chap. 3). An NP-trace, then, does not involve an empty nominal element syntactically. Alternatively, one may claim that it is the notion of chains that is relevant. An NP-trace is always in a chain with a copy that is Case-marked.

15. If a verb assigns Case, the object can be empty in Chinese, regardless of whether the antecedent is a clause or a DP, as illustrated in (40) in the text. However, this need not be regarded as an instance of CP deletion. When the antecedent is a clause, what is missing can still be a DP, as in (i).

(i) wo zhidao zhejian shi/ta   lai   le; tamen ye   zhidao (zhejian shi).
    I   know this   matter/he come Le they also know this matter
    'I know this matter/that he came; they also know (this matter).'

16. These words are not nominal and are not assigned Case.

17. *Cai* is ambiguous. It may have a meaning like 'think' or a meaning close to 'guess at/take a guess at'. In the latter case, it can be followed by a nominal object, which can be empty:

(i) ta cai-le   nage miyu. wo mei cai.
    he guessed that riddle I   not guess
    'He guessed at that riddle. I didn't guess.'

18. Among other supporting evidence, Korean provides morphological indications: duration/frequency phrases are assigned an accusative Case.

19. Takahashi (2006) shows that Japanese allows an AP predicate to be null. This deserves further study.

20. If we follow Chomsky's (2000) claim that each instance of Merge must be motivated by feature matching (also see Hornstein 2001 and Collins 1997, among others), the merger of a V and an "e" with formal features (the categorial feature, for instance) is necessary when V is a transitive verb subcategorizing a nominal object.

References

Aoun, Joseph, and Yen-hui Audrey Li. 2003. *Essays on the Representational and Derivational Nature of Grammar: The Diversity of Wh-Constructions*. Cambridge, Mass.: MIT Press.

Bošković, Željko. 1997. *The Syntax of Nonfinite Complementation: An Economy Approach*. Cambridge, Mass.: MIT Press.

Cecchetto, Carlo, and Renato Oniga. 2004. A challenge to null Case theory. *Linguistic Inquiry* 35:141–149.

Chomsky, Noam. 1981. *Lectures on Government and Binding*. Dordrecht: Foris.

Chomsky, Noam. 1994. Bare phrase structure. *MIT Occasional Papers in Linguistics* 5, Department of Linguistics and Philosophy, MIT. Also in *Government and Binding Theory and the Minimalist Program*, ed. Gert Webelbuth, 383–439. Oxford: Blackwell, 1995.

Chomsky, Noam. 1995. *The Minimalist Program*. Cambridge, Mass.: MIT Press.

Chomsky, Noam. 2000. Minimalist inquiries: The framework. In *Step by Step*, ed. R. Martin, D. Michaels, and J. Uriagereka, 89–155. Cambridge, Mass.: MIT Press.

Chomsky, Noam, and Howard Lasnik. 1993. The theory of principles and parameters. In *Syntax: An International Handbook of Contemporary Research*, ed. Joachim Jacobs, Arnim von Stechow, Wolfgang Sternefeld, and Theo Vennemann, 506–569. Berlin: Walter de Gruyter.

Collins, Chris. 1997. *Local Economy*. Cambridge, Mass.: MIT Press.

Ernst, Thomas. 2001. *The Syntax of Adjuncts*. Cambridge: Cambridge University Press.

Fiengo, Robert, and Robert May. 1994. *Indices and Identity*. Cambridge, Mass.: MIT Press.

Goldberg, Lotus. 2005. Verb-Stranding VP Ellipsis: A Cross-Linguistic Study. Doctoral dissertation, McGill University, Montreal.

Grimshaw, Jane. 1979. Complement subcategorization and the lexicon. *Linguistic Inquiry* 10:279–326.

Grimshaw, Jane. 1997. Projection Heads and Optimality. *Linguistic Inquiry* 28:373–422.

Grinder, John, and Paul M. Postal. 1971. Missing antecedents. *Linguistic Inquiry* 2:269–312.

Hankamer, Jorge, and Ivan Sag. 1976. Deep and surface anaphora. *Linguistic Inquiry* 7:391–428.

Hoji, Hajime. 1998. Null Object and Sloppy Identity in Japanese. *Linguistic Inquiry* 29:127–152.

Hornstein, Nobert. 2001. *Move! A Minimalist Theory of Construal.* Cambridge, Mass.: Blackwell.

Huang, C.-T. James. 1982. *Logical Relations in Chinese and the Theory of Grammar.* Doctoral dissertation, MIT. New York: Garland Press, 1997.

Huang, C.-T. James. 1984. On the distribution and reference of empty pronouns. *Linguistic Inquiry* 15:531–574.

Huang, C.-T. James. 1987. Remarks on empty categories in Chinese. *Linguistic Inquiry* 18:321–337.

Huang, C.-T. James. 1988. Comments on Hasegawa's paper. In *Proceedings of Japanese Syntax Workshop Issues on Empty Categories*, ed. Tawa Wako and Mineharu Nakayama, 77–93. New London: Connecticut College.

Huang, C.-T. James. 1991. Remarks on the status of the null object. In *Principles and Parameters in Comparative Grammar*, ed. Robert Freidin, 56–76. Cambridge, Mass.: MIT Press.

Johnson, Kyle. 2003. In search of the English middle field. Unpublished ms., University of Massachusetts, Amherst.

Kennedy, Christopher. 2003. Ellipsis and syntactic representation. In *The Interfaces: Deriving and Interpreting Omitted Structures*, ed. Kerstin Schwabe and Susanne Winkler, 29–54. Amsterdam: John Benjamins.

Kennedy, Christopher, and Jason Merchant. 2000. Attributive comparative deletion. *Natural Language and Linguistic Theory* 18:89–146.

Kim, Soowon. 1999. Sloppy/strict identity, empty objects, and NP ellipsis. *Journal of East Asian Linguistics* 8:255–284.

Koopman, Hilda. 1984. *The Syntax of Verbs: From Verb Movement in the Kru Languages to Universal Grammar.* Dordrecht: Foris.

Lasnik, Howard. 2001. When can you save a structure by destroying it? *NELS* 31:301–320.

Li, Hui-ju Grace. 1998. Null object and VP ellipsis in Chinese. In *Proceedings of the 9th North American Conference on Chinese Linguistics*, ed. Lin Hua, 151–172. Los Angeles: University of Southern California, GSIL.

Li, Hui-ju Grace. 2002. Ellipsis Constructions in Chinese. Doctoral dissertation, University of Southern California, Los Angeles.

Li, Yan. 2003. Issues on the Chinese Null Object Construction. Unpublished ms., University of Southern California, Los Angeles.

Li, Yen-hui Audrey. 1985. Abstract Case in Chinese. Doctoral dissertation, University of Southern California, Los Angeles.

Li, Yen-hui Audrey. 1990. *Order and Constituency in Mandarin Chinese.* Dordrecht: Kluwer Academic Publishers.

Lobeck, Anne. 1995. *Ellipsis: Functional Heads, Licensing and Identification*. Oxford: Oxford University Press.

Lobeck, Anne. 1999. VP ellipsis and the Minimalist Program: Some speculations and proposals. In *Fragments: Studies in Ellipsis and Gapping*, ed. S. Shalom and E. Benmamoun, 98–123. Oxford: Oxford University Press.

Martin, Roger. 1996. A Minimalist Theory of PRO and Control. Doctoral dissertation, University of Connecticut, Storrs.

Martin, Roger. 2001. Null Case and the distribution of PRO. *Linguistic Inquiry* 32:141–166.

Matsuo, Ayumi. 1998. A Comparative Study of Tense and Ellipsis. Doctoral dissertation, University of Connecticut, Storrs.

Merchant, Jason. 2001. *The Syntax of Silence*. Oxford: Oxford University Press.

Merchant, Jason. 2003. Subject-auxiliary inversion in comparatives and PF output constraints. In *The Interfaces: Deriving and Interpreting Omitted Structures*, ed. Kerstin Schwabe and Susanne Winkler, 55–78. Amsterdam: John Benjamins.

Merchant, Jason. 2004. Fragments and ellipsis. *Linguistics and Philosophy* 27:661–738.

Ning, Chunyan. 1993. The overt syntax of topicalization and relativization in Chinese. Doctoral dissertation, University of California, Irvine.

Oku, Satoshi. 1998. A Theory of Subcategorization and Reconstruction in the Minimalist Perspective. Doctoral dissertation, University of Connecticut, Storrs.

Otani, Kazuyo, and John Whitman. 1991. V-raising and VP-ellipsis. *Linguistic Inquiry* 22:345–358.

Pan, Haihua. 1998. Null object constructions, VP-Ellipsis, and sentence interpretation. Paper presented at the Workshop on Ellipsis in Conjunction, the Social Sciences Centre of Berlin, Germany, 1998. http://www.zas.gwz-berlin.de/mitarb/homepage/webfest/Pan.PDF.

Paul, Waltraud. 1996. Verb Raising in Chinese. *NACCL* 1:260–276.

Paul, Waltraud. 1999. Verb Gapping in Chinese: A Case of Verb Raising. *Lingua* 107:207–226.

Ross, John R. 1967. *Constraints on Variables in Syntax*. Doctoral dissertation, MIT. Published as *Infinite Syntax*. New York: Ablex, 1986.

Ross, John R. 1969. Guess who? In *Papers from the 5th Regional Meeting of the Chicago Linguistic Society*, ed. Robert Binnick, Alice Davison, Georgia Green, and Jerry Morgan, 252–286. Chicago: Chicago Linguistic Society.

Sag, Ivan. 1976. *Deletion and Logical Form*. Doctoral dissertation, MIT. New York: Garland Press, 1980.

Saito, Mamoru. 1985. Some Asymmetries in Japanese and Their Theoretical Implications. Doctoral dissertation, MIT.

Sauerland, Uli. 1998. The Meaning of Chains. Doctoral dissertation, MIT.

Sauerland, Uli. 2003. Unpronounced heads in relative clauses. In *The Interfaces: Deriving and Interpreting Omitted Structures*, ed. Kerstin Schwabe and Susanne Winkler, 205–226. Amsterdam: John Benjamins.

Soh, Hooi Ling. 1998. Object Scrambling in Chinese. Doctoral dissertation, MIT.

Stjepanović, Sandra. 1999. What do Second Position Cliticization, Scrambling, and Multiple Wh-Fronting Have in Common? Doctoral dissertation, University of Connecticut, Storrs.

Stowell, Tim. 1981. Origins of Phrase Structure. Doctoral dissertation, MIT.

Takahashi, Daiko. 2006. Apparent parasitic gaps in null arguments in Japanese. *Journal of East Asian Linguistics* 15:1–35.

Tang, Chih-Chen Jane. 1990. Chinese Phrase Structure and the Extended X'-Theory. Doctoral dissertation, Cornell University.

Tomioka, Satoshi. 1996. The laziest pronouns. *Japanese and Korean Linguistics* 7, UCLA.

Tomioka, Satoshi. 1997. Property anaphora and the typology of *Pro*. Paper presented at Theoretical East Asian Linguistics Workshop, UC-Irvine.

Tomioka, Satoshi. 1999. A sloppy identity puzzle. *Natural Language Semantics* 7:217–241.

Travis, Lisa. 1984. Parameters and Effects of Word Order Variation. Doctoral dissertation, MIT.

Williams, Edwin. 1977. Discourse and logical form. *Linguistic Inquiry* 8:101–139.

Winkler, Susanne, and Kerstin Schwabe. 2003. Exploring the interfaces from the perspective of omitted structures. In *The Interfaces: Deriving and Interpreting Omitted Structures*, ed. Kerstin Schwabe and Susanne Winkler, 1–26. Amsterdam: John Benjamins.

Wu, Hsiao-hung Iris. 2003a. Ellipsis and focus. Unpublished ms., National Tsing Hua University, Hsinchu.

Wu, Hsiao-hung Iris. 2003b. Gapping in classical and modern Chinese. Unpublished ms., National Tsing Hua University, Hsinchu.

Xu, Liejiong. 1986. Free empty category. *Linguistic Inquiry* 17:75–93.

Xu, Liejiong. 2003. Remarks on VP-ellipsis in disguise. *Linguistic Inquiry* 34:163–171.

11 Tokenism and Identity in Anaphora

Edwin Williams

In work from the 1970s VP ellipsis was understood to be governed by a condition of "identity"—a deleted VP must be identical to its antecedent VP. More recent work has retreated to a weaker condition of "parallelism"—a deleted VP must be "similar" to its antecedent. The retreat is motivated by supposed empirical facts. The similarity or parallelism condition is clearly inferior to the identity condition, all else being the same, identity being the limiting case of parallelism. In this chapter, I will review the arguments favoring the parallelism condition and suggest reanalyses that allow the identity condition to be maintained. Among other things, the nature of bound pronouns and variables must be rethought.

11.1 Identity

At first blush "sloppy Identity" cases suggest that identity is too strong, since in (a) Bill likes himself, not John:

(1) a. John likes himself and Bill does too.
   b. John [likes himself$_i$]$_{VP_i}$ and Bill does $\langle\ \rangle$ too.[1]

But in fact once one sees that the pronoun in (1) functions as a variable bound to the subject function, independent of what the subject is, the problem is resolved: the antecedent VP is not "likes John," but rather, "is an x such that x likes x." This can be notated as in Williams 1994, or in the more usual lambda notation:

(2) λ(x likes x)

The notion of "identity" is delicate. In the following, we see that two traces bound to different WH words do not count as identical, whereas traces bound to the same WH word do count as identical (a,b):

(3) a.   I know who$_i$ you wanted to [see t$_i$] and did $\langle$see t$_i\rangle$

   b.   ??I know who$_i$ you wanted to [see t$_i$] and who$_j$ you did $\langle$see t$_j\rangle$

   c.   wh ... t$_i$ ... wh$_j$ ... t$_j$ vs wh$_i$ ... t$_i$ ... t$_i$

(c) schematizes the difference between (a) and (b).

On the basis of this conclusion, Williams (1977) offered an explanation of the difference between (a) and (b) in the following:

(4) John is [hard OP$_i$ to [talk to t$_i$]] but Mary isn't [hard OP$_j$ to [talk to t$_j$]]

   a.   but Mary isn't $\langle$hard OP$_i$ to [talk to t$_i$]$\rangle$

   b.   *but Mary isn't hard OP$_j$ to $\langle$talk t$_j\rangle$

In (a), the ellipsis contains the OP binding the trace, and so the antecedent also contains OP binding trace, and the two count as identical; in (b), however, the OP is exterior to the ellipsis, and is different from the OP exterior to the antecedent, so the two traces are different, and so ellipsis in (b) does not meet the condition of identity. For such cases parallelism seems too weak—any sort of parallelism that (a) meets is also met in (b), and vice versa, and yet they are have different ellipsis possibilities.

In what follows, I will review the cases which seem to support parallelism over identity. I will first look at ACD cases that in most analyses involve a parallelism condition. I will argue that the problem posed by ACD has nothing to do with ellipsis, but is rather present in all relative clauses, and once that problem is understood, the way is paved for an identity condition for ACD cases. Next I will look at sloppily bound pronoun cases that resist the classical analysis of sloppiness already mentioned in connection with (1). I will suggest that the result obtained for the ACD cases can be extended to these as well. Finally I will examine the "Hirschbuhler" inverse scope cases and will suggest and defend a view of how these are to be analyzed that is consistent with an identity condition.

11.2   Parallelism for ACD

Antecedent-contained deletion examples like (5a) seem to present a problem for ellipsis—trying to find the antecedent of the deleted VP leads to infinite regress. Most researchers (May and Larson, Fiengo and May, Kennedy, Lasnik, Hornstein, Baltin, Fox) have invoked movement, either overt or covert, to resolve the regress. Two kinds of movement have been appealed to: movement of the relative clause containing the ellipsis (extraposition), or movement of the NP containing the ellipsis (Quantifier Raising (QR), A-movement, or Object Shift):

(5) a. John ate everything which Mary did

   b.

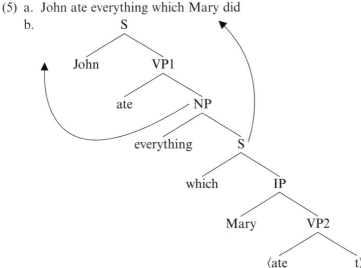

The movements have the virtue of removing the ellipsis site from its antecedent and so appearing to eliminate the regress.

Fiengo and May (1994) have given argument that the movement is indeed Quantifier Raising (QR). Their argument is that there is a difference between tensed and infinitival contexts for ACD, and that this parallels the well-known difference between raising quantifiers out of tensed and infinitival clauses:

(6) a. John believed everyone you did ⟨__⟩ to be a genius
    b. *John believed everyone you did ⟨__⟩ was a genius

However, it *is* in fact possible to force certain focused quantifiers to scope out of tensed clauses (a), without improving ACD for such cases (b):

(7) a. Someone or other believes that EACH of those men is incompetent
    b. *Someone or other believes that EACH of those men that I do ⟨__⟩ is
       incompetent

So there seems to be a reluctance for ellipsis to breach tensed S boundaries that is independent of QR.[2]

We must readdress the question of why ACD is problematic in the first place. In fact, as Williams (1994) suggests, the ACD problem is inherent in relative clauses themselves, independent of ellipsis; if we try to fill in the value of the trace in (6a) below with its "antecedent," where the antecedent is understood to be the matrix containing NP, we again get an infinite regress. Since this occurs independent of ellipsis, and ellipsis here would not add to the problem already present, if we solve the problem with relatives the ACD problem itself will evaporate.

(8) a. I read [the books [that George read t_i]]$_{NPi}$ →
   b. I read the books that George read the books that George read t

What happens in the case of relatives must be distinguished from what happens with truly vicious circularity, as the following "antecedent contained anaphors" illustrate:

(9) a.   *[His$_i$ own enemy]$_i$ would behave that way.
   b. Cf. [A man who is [his own enemy]] would behave that way
   c.   *[A picture of itself$_i$]$_i$ arrived
   d.   *A picture arrived of itself

In (b) the antecedent of *his own* is *a man* and so not a circular case. Note that the extraposition in (d) does not remedy the circularity, suggesting that the role of movement in resolving the ACD paradox is probably not correct.

Fox (2002) presents an extraposition/QR style solution to ACD that crucially relies on parallelism. In detail: an invisible copy of QP is moved to the right for purposes of scope assignment, and subsequently the relative clause is adjoined to it as an adjunct (a–c). Thus the ellipsis site in the relative is never in the antecedent VP. Subsequently, ellipsis is licensed on the basis of parallelism: x is the same as y in (d) because the binding of x by λx is parallel to the binding of y by λy:

(10) a. John likes every boy →
   b. John [likes every boy] every boy →
   c. John [likes every boy] every boy that Mary [⟨likes boy⟩] →
   d. Every boy λx Mary does like (the) boy xλy John likes (the) boy y

The first question to raise about Fox's solution is whether overt extraposition is required; Fox cites (11a,b) below as evidence for overt extraposition, on the assumption that the infinitive in (a), but not the tensed VP in (b), can be itself extraposed beyond the relative in extraposition:

(11) a.   I expect everyone [that you do ⟨__⟩] to visit Mary
   b.   *I expect everyone that you do ⟨__⟩ will visit Mary (??)
   c.   John [gave t_{NP} t_{PP}]$_{VP}$ [everything that I had planned to ⟨__⟩]$_{NP}$ [to Mary]$_{PP}$
   d.   More people than I thought ⟨__⟩ arrived.

Fox's solution requires that such further extraposition take place, but without explaining why it must. Furthermore, some clear cases of ACD (c,d) clearly do not require overt extrapolation.

But the more serious problem with Fox's solution to the ACD problem arises with the parallelism condition illustrated in (d). In Williams (1994) it is shown that there are cases that satisfy such parallelism cases but fail to provide what ellipsis needs:

(12) a. *I saw several pictures of the man who you did ⟨__⟩
     b. *I saw everyone whose mother you did ⟨__⟩
     c. [several pictures of the man]$_i$ [I saw t$_i$] who$_j$ [you did ⟨see t$_j$⟩]
     d. Several [pictures λx you did ⟨see the man x⟩] λy I did see the pictures y
     e. *John read every book and I saw the book that Sam did ⟨read t⟩
        Matrix: Every book λx (I [read the book x])
        Relative: λy(Sam ⟨read the book y⟩)

(a) is to be understood in such a way that I saw pictures and you saw a man. As (c) shows, these meet the condition of parallelism—(d) is the same as (c) but with lambdas put in. Cases of this sort were also identified by Kennedy (1994) (as reported in Heim 1997). (e) is a different kind of case that makes the same point—parallelism would license the ellipsis in such cases.

   Clearly what is wrong with such cases is that the relative clause and the "Nuclear Scope" of the quantifier are unrelated to each other—they must in some sense be related to the same quantifier for the ellipsis to work. In view of this, I would propose the following principle, which I call "Tokenism":

(13) *Tokenism*
     x and y count as the same variable not by parallelism or by alphabetic variance, but rather because x and y are the variables that define the predicates that are the restrictor and nuclear scope arguments of the same token of the same quantifier.

The problem is to identify the two variables in an ACD construction, or for that matter in a normal relative, as the same—the variable occupied by the modified NP itself, and the variable inside of the relative bound to the head of the relative. What we need is a representation like (b) below, where in some sense Q$_I$ binds *both* x and y. The normal syntax of WH, however, gives us representations like (c), where two different operators bind the variable in the restrictor and the variable in the nuclear scope. The WH must be understood not as an operator in its own right, but as simply mediating the relation between the matrix quantifier and the trace it binds, perhaps by defining the restrictor predicate, as suggested in Williams 1994, or perhaps some other way. In the "generalized quantifier" way of thinking of things, we are accustomed to thinking of the matrix quantifier as relating two sets as in (d); we might instead think of the quantifier "every" as relating its Restrictor and its Nuclear Scope as in (f), where "x/y" is any instance of x or y, where y is the variable introduced by WH, and x is the variable that the modified NP occupies. See Williams 1994 for a suggestion of how to do this, and see Heim 1997 for much relevant discussion.

(14) a. [Every boy$_i$ that Mary wanted to see t$_i$]$_i$ John wanted to see t$_i$
     b. Q$_i$ [... x$_i$ ...]$_{Restrictor}$ [... y$_i$ ...]$_{Nuclear Scope}$

c. Q_i [wh$_k$ ... x$_k$ ...]$_{Restrictor}$ [... y$_i$ ...]$_{Nuclear Scope}$
d. EVERY (A,B)
e. MORE (A,B)
f. every: for every value of x/y, R→NS

For some other constructions there is an obstacle to saying that x and y are the same variable. In the comparative construction, which ACD is also found, it would seem counter to the meaning of the comparative to say that the restrictor and nuclear scope variables were the same variable in the classical sense, since the point of the comparison is that the values are different. What we are compelled to say instead is that although they are not the same variable in the classical sense, they are *bound to the same quantifier*, and in fact to *the same token of the same quantifier*.

(15) John saw more people than Pete thought he would ⟨see t⟩
     More: Amt1 such that [λx ... [V x]](Amt1) >
             Amt2 such that [λy ... [V y]](Amt2)

The meaning of *more* is that Amt1 is greater than Amt2, so of course x and y are not the same classical variable. What we mean by the same now is that they are the variables that define the restrictor and nuclear scope of the same token quantifier, respectively.

The difference between the token-identity theory proposed here and parallelism can be seen from the following: in the first, there are two WHs but they are ultimately related to the same quantifier, the *the* on the subject; whereas in (b), there are likewise two *whos*, but related to different quantifiers (different tokens of *the*) and so do not support ellipsis.

(16) a.   The man who I like who Mary doesn't ⟨like t⟩ arrived today
     b.   *The man who I like killed the man who Mary doesn't ⟨like t⟩

Once we have arrived at this understanding of what the condition on ellipsis is, it is not necessary to invoke movement to resolve the "paradox"—the paradox is resolved by our understanding of what matters for two variables to count as the same. Summarizing:

(17) a.   One VP can take another VP as its antecedent if it is nondistinct from it.
     b.   A phrase is nondistinct from another phrase if its parts are nondistinct from the other's parts.
     c.   An empty lexical item is nondistinct from a lexical item of the same category.
     d.   A variable is nondistinct from another variable bound by the same token quantifier.

The definitions of quantifier, variable, and so on, that are needed are the following:[3]

(18) [John ate everything$_i$]$_{S;i}$
　　Q is *every*
　　Restrictor is *thing*
　　Scope is S
　　Variable is [everything]$_i$

We can see then in the following that the conditions in (16) are met without movement:

(19) John [ate [every thing [that George did [[ ]$_{E-V}$ t$_{every-restrictor}$]$_{E-VP}$]]$_{M-NP}$]$_{M-VP}$
　　a. [ ]$_{E-V}$ is nondistinct from [ate]
　　b. t$_{every-restrictor}$ is nondistinct from [everything that George did]
　　　　[Everything that George did] is the nuclear-scope variable of *every*)

Because the two conditions (a,b) are met, E(llided)-VP can take M(atrix)-VP as its antecedent and so the ellipsis in (19) is grammatical.

　　If this conclusion is correct, then it is not surprising that ACD does not require overt movement, as noted in (11), any more than relative clauses in general require overt extraposition

11.3　Parallelism for Sloppy Pronouns

As mentioned in section 11.1, certain cases of sloppy pronouns can be reconciled with an identity condition on ellipsis by regarding pronouns as taking as their antecedent the subject function, rather than to the subject itself:

(20) a. John likes himself and Bill does too.
　　b. John [likes himself$_i$]$_{VP_i}$ and Bill does ⟨ ⟩ too.
　　c. λ(x likes x)

　　However, some cases of sloppy identity cannot be understood in this way, and therefore remain a challenge to the identity condition; Fiengo and May (1994) (F&M) cite the following kind of example:

(21) a. John's mother thinks that he will win, and BILL's mother does ＿＿ too
　　b. [X's N ⟨V [C X...]⟩ (F&M, 108)

F&M suggest that the identity condition is too strong, and that the sloppy pronoun is licensed by a weaker parallelism condition: the pronoun in the ellipsis site and the antecedent pronoun must be bound similarly. Specifically, they propose that the structural path from antecedent to pronoun must be the same for the pronoun in the ellipsis antecedent and the pronoun in the ellipsis site. (b) specifies the path that the two share. The parallelism condition will work for the cases like (20) as well, so there is no need in this theory for the sloppy pronoun to be bound to the subject function independent of the subject—all that is required is that the binding of the elided pronoun be parallel to the binding of the pronoun in the antecedent.

But in fact sloppy pronouns that do happen to be bound to the subject behave differently from the other sloppy pronouns, such as the one in (21). In the case below, sloppy antecedence does not work—the second conjunct cannot mean that Bill's father thinks that Bill will win. The difference between (21) and (22) is that the antecedent of the elided pronoun is not a focus in (22), whereas it is in (21). The father/mother contrast in the following draws the focus off of *Bill's* and that apparently eliminates the sloppy reading:

(22) John's mother thinks that he will win, and Bill's FATHER does ⟨ ⟩ too.

But in the special case that the sloppy pronoun takes a subject antecedent, the position of the focus is irrelevant; in the following, the elided pronoun can be understood sloppily despite the fact that its antecedent (*my mother*) is not the focus:

(23) John's mother thinks she will win, and MY mother does too.

Furthermore, for the non-subject-based sloppy cases, the kind of structural parallelism required by F&M is not necessary; rather, a common Focus structure is required:

(24) a. John's father gave him his sense of justice, but in BILL's case, Mary did
        ⟨give him his sense of justice⟩
    b. [John's N] V him his ...
    c. [P BILL's N], NP did V him his ...
    d. 1. Second clause:
          Primary Focus F_1: Mary
          Secondary Focus F_2: Bill
          Residue: F_1 gave F_2 his$_2$ sense of justice
       2. First clause:
          Primary Focus F_1: X's father
          Secondary Focus F_2: John
          Residue: F_1 gave F_2 his$_2$ sense of justice

In (a), sloppy antecedence is possible, despite the fact that the structural relation of pronoun to antecedent is different between the ellipsis site (c) and the ellipsis antecedent (b). (d) sketches the Focus structure for (a). As one can see, the Focus structure for the two clauses are the same[4]—the embedded pronouns are bound to the corresponding secondary Focuses in their respective clauses.

In sum, then, for subject-based sloppy antecedence, focus is irrelevant; but for other cases, it appears that the antecedent of the sloppy pronoun must be the focus of its clause.

But it still seems that one needs parallelism of binding, rather than identity of ellipsis and antecedent; we may have only shown that the parallelism needed for such cases involves Focus, rather than syntactic structure. However, some further observations suggest that it is much closer to identity that this suggests:

(25) John$_i$'s mother thinks that he$_i$ will win, and
    a. ∼&... and Sam's father thinks that BILL's father does too
    b. ∼&... and Sam$_i$'s father thinks that his$_i$ MOTHER does too
    c. &... and Sam$_i$'s father thinks that HIS$_i$ MOTHER does too[5]

Since the nonsloppy reading is always available, the sloppy reading gives rise to ambiguity. In these, we see that *for nonsubject cases, the pronoun can be sloppy if its antecedent is contrasted with the antecedent of its image-under-ellipsis*; (b,c) are a minimal pair in this regard—*his* is the antecedent of the sloppy pronoun (*he*), and only when it is contrastive (c) can it be sloppy; below is the focus analysis of (c) that allows this interpretation:

(26) Antecedent: F=John, X's mother ⟨thinks that x will win⟩
    Ellipsis: F=HIS, X's mother ⟨thinks that x will win⟩

(a) is not ambiguous because *BILL* is not contrasted with the antecedent of the pronoun in the ellipsis-antecedent, but rather with the more local *Sam's father*. In (b) his is not a focus, and so is not contrasted with anything. Only in (c) where HIS is a focus (separate from the focus on MOTHER) does the sloppy reading come through.

What do these last observations have to do with tokenism? To get a sloppy Focus-based pronoun, we see that it is not enough for the antecedent of the elided pronoun to be focused; that antecedent must be contrasted with the antecedent of the pronoun in the ellipsis-antecedent. Put this way, it is quite similar to what was said in the previous section about ACD—ACD can occur when two variables count as the same, and they can count as the same when they can both be traced back to the same token quantifier (even if one is in the Restrictor and the other in the Nuclear Scope of that quantifier). In the case of Focus-based sloppy identity, we want to say that two pronouns "count as the same" when they can be traced back to the same *focus contrast pair*. The following is meant to bring out the similarity between the two cases:

(27) a. $[\ldots F \ldots] \rightarrow F, P = \lambda x[\ldots x \ldots]$
    b. $F1, \lambda x [\ldots x \ldots]_{P1} \ldots F2, \lambda y [\ldots y \ldots]_{P2}$
    c. $F1,P1 \ldots F2,P2 \rightarrow F1/F2: P1, P2$
    d. $[F1/F2]_i [\ldots x_i \ldots]_{P1} [\ldots y_i \ldots]_{P2}$
    e. Q R NS

In (a), a sentence with a focus is factored into the focus (F) and "presupposition" (P). In (b), two such sentences are factored, and in (c) the two focuses are gathered together as a "focus contrast pair" (F1/F2). That focus contrast pair is related to two expressions, the two presuppositions derived from them; as such, the focus contrast pair and its two related presuppositions are parallel to a Quantifier and its Restrictor and Nuclear Scope. Conceived of this way, the Focus-based sloppy identity cases involve the same kind of tokenism as the quantifier cases.

We may contrast the account here with other similar accounts. Rooth's (1992) account also relates the possibility of ellipsis to focus structure. This is accomplished by requiring that phrases containing the ellipsis site and the antecedent must be related in terms of their focus structure:

(28) a. in $[\ldots VP_A \ldots]_{XPA} \ldots [\ldots VP_E \ldots]_{XPE}$
       XP_A must be an instance of the XP_E focus-set[6]
       (Rooth 1992, as reported in Merchant 2002)

The focus set is analogous to the presupposition described above. The analysis of (25b,c) proceeds as follows:

(29) a. 25b: $XP_E = his_i$ MOTHER does ⟨think that he_i will win⟩
     b. 25b XP_E focus set = his_i X does ⟨think that he_i will win⟩
     c. 25c: XP_E focus set = $Y's_i$ X/MOTHER does ⟨think that he_i/Y_i will win⟩[6]

The first clause of (25) (*John's mother thinks that he will win*) is an instance of (c), and so (c) is correctly predicted to have a sloppy reading.

However, Rooth's theory falls down in that it predicts that the subject-based cases will be focus-sensitive as well, and we have seen that this is not so:

(30) John's mother thinks she can win, and MY mother does too.

(30) has a sloppy reading despite the fact that the antecedent of the pronoun is not the focus of its clause (but rather, merely contains the focus). In addition, Rooth's theory fails to make the following discrimination cited earlier:

(31) a. *Mary is hard to please and Bill is hard OP to ⟨please t⟩ as well
     b. Mary is hard to please and Bill is ⟨hard OP to please t⟩ as well

It would seem that the focus structure is the same in these two cases. But, as mentioned earlier, (a) is bad because the trace in the ellipsis site and the trace in the antecedent are bound by different OPs, whereas in (b) the OPs are part of the ellipsis and so are irrelevant.

So focus structure is relevant for a narrow set of cases of sloppy identity. This most likely is not because focus structure is a part of the theory of ellipsis, but rather because focus provides some conditions of identity of elements in addition to other identities, identities provided by quantifier binding and subject-function binding, and perhaps other sources as well. Focus in general is not framed in logical terms, such as "follows from," and so on, even if some applications can be framed in this way—this can be seen from the obligatory contrasts one finds in, for example, phone numbers with repeated digits: 452-3141. Given this, there is no particular reason for focus to interact with VP-ellipsis in a way that is framed in logical terms.

11.4 Wide Scope Quantifiers

A final kind of challenge to an identity condition on ellipsis are the "Hirschbuhler" cases (Hirschbuhler 1982):

(32) a. A Canadian flag stood in front of every embassy, and an American flag did too.

b. [every embassy$_i$ [a Canadian flag [... t$_i$ ...]$_{VP}$] and
[every embassy$_k$ [an American flag $\langle$ ... t$_k$ ... $\rangle_{VP}$]

(a) can be understood as in (b), where the quantifiers in the VP are understood to have scope over their respective subjects. The VPs themselves cannot be understood as identical in any reasonable sense—the two traces are bound by different (tokens of) quantifiers. The best that can be said is that the two traces are bound in parallel

(33) Q_{1i} —$_1$ [... t$_i$ ...]$_{VP}$ ... and Q_{2k} —$_2$ $\langle$ ... t$_k$ ... $\rangle_{VP}$
where —$_1$ is similar to (or identical to) —$_2$

My strategy for eliminating this kind of counterexample to identity will be scope reconstruction, and in particular the kind that involves subjects. It has long been observed that certain quantifiers in subject position of raising verbs can be construed as subordinate to the raising verb itself, and one mechanism for this scope subordination has been called "scope reconstruction":

(34) &Someone seems to have left $\rightarrow$ seems [someone to have left]

I would suggest that in addition to the raising-verb cases, some subject quantifiers can be "scope reconstructed" to a position inside of their own VP, regardless of whether the verb is a raising verb or not. I provide a mechanism for this reconstruction at the end of this section. Ordinarily this will make no difference in interpretation, but it will just in case an object quantifier has been assigned VP-scope:

(35) a. Someone [saw everything]$_{VP}$ $\rightarrow$
b. Someone [everything$_i$ [saw t$_i$]$_{VP}$]$_{VP}$ $\rightarrow$
c. [everything$_i$ [someone saw t$_i$]$_{VP}$]$_{VP}$

The utility of subject scope reconstruction for understanding the Hirschbuhler cases is clear: the VPs in the case of (32) will be

(36) [every embassy$_I$ [stood in front of t$_I$]$_{VP}$]$_{VP}$

This VP can then be applied to two different subjects, to give the Hirschbuhler case:

(37) An American flag VP and a Canadian flag VP

Then scope reconstruction can be applied in each case to derive the observed meanings. What remains to be done is first to give evidence that this is the right treatment, and then to rationalize the operation of scope reconstruction in these cases, and especially the idea that VP-deletion in some sense applies "before" it, which contradicts the generally held notion that VP-ellipsis is based on fully derived LF representations.

First the evidence. One kind comes from varying the size of ellipsis:

(38) a. At least one doctor tried to get me to arrest every patient, and at least one nurse did—too.
   b. ~&At least one nurse tried to get me to ⟨ ⟩ as well

(a) is ambiguous, while (b) is not. The only other difference between them is that the size of the ellipsis in (a) is larger than the size in (b). The scope reconstruction theory, with the identity condition, explains this difference, but the parallelism theory does not.

Under the parallelism theory, the structure of (a) and (b) are the following:

(39) a. Every patient$_i$ [at least one doctor [try to get me to arrest t$_i$]]
       Every patient$_i$ [at least one nurse ⟨try to get me to arrest t$_i$⟩]
   b. Every patient$_i$ [at least one doctor [try to get me to arrest t$_i$]]
       Every patient$_i$ [at least one nurse try to get me to ⟨arrest t$_I$⟩]

As inspection shows, any parallelism that holds in (a) also holds in (b), since only the size of the ellipsis site is different, and yet only (a) supports the reading in which the subject has narrow scope. Apparently the narrow scope subject reading is allowed only when the subject is adjacent to the extraction site.

But that generalization follows from the reconstruction theory. In the scope reconstruction theory, the antecedent VP in the (a) and (b) cases are, respectively:

(40) a. [Every patient [try to get me to arrest t]$_{VP}$]$_{VP}$
   b. [Every patient [to arrest t]$_{VP}$]$_{VP}$

When (a) is put together with its subject (*at least one doctor, at least one nurse*) scope reconstruction will give the desired readings. For (39b), however, the subject is too remote from the quantifier to be scope-reconstructed under it:

(41) At least one doctor [tried to get me [every patient [to arrest t]]]

If scope reconstruction applies to (41), it will not be able to subordinate the subject to the direct object, which is too far away. If the direct object in (41) is instead assigned scope in the matrix, so that scope reconstruction would give a different interpretation, then the VPs will not meet the identity condition for ellipsis:

(42) a. At least one nurse [every patient$_I$ [try to get me to arrest t$_I$]]
   b. At least one doctor [every patient$_i$ [try to get me to ⟨arrest t$_I$⟩]]

Here, under the identity theory, the ellipsis site and its antecedent contain free variables (t_I), and so cannot count as identical. Thus there is no way to get narrow scope for the subject when the ellipsis site is the small VP. Thus the identity theory predicts the exact outcomes for such cases, while the parallelism view incorrectly predicts the same outcomes for (38a) and (42b).

Another kind of evidence comes from the fact that quantifiers differ in whether they undergo scope reconstruction. We have seen that indefinites do scope-reconstruct, but universals seem not to:

(43) ∼&Every boy seems to be here

(43) is marked unambiguous because the universal cannot be construed as subordinate to *seems*. For reasons not immediately relevant (but see Williams 2003 and below) scope reconstruction does not affect universals. Given this fact, we then expect that the Hirschbuhler cases will not arise when the subject is a universal.

The following sentence is ambiguous, but in only two ways, not three ways, and the absence of the third way can be attributed to the failure of scope reconstruction to apply to universals.

(44) Every boy read six books, and every girl did too.

The two readings that are available are represented as follows:

(45) a. E6 books$_1$ [[every boy read t_I] and [every girl read t_I]]
    b. Every boy$_1$ [E6 books$_2$ [t_1 read t_2]] and
       Every girl$_1$ [E6 books$_2$ [t_1 read t_2]]

In the first reading, there are six books, and the boys read those six and the girls read the same six. As indicated, that reading has the indefinite with scope over both conjuncts. The two traces count as the same by the classical definition—two instances of a variable bound to the same token quantifier. In the (b) reading, each person, boy or girl, read a different set of six books; that reading derives from the indefinite having VP scope, and so the ellipsis site contains both the quantifier and the variable it binds.

The third possible reading, which does not exist, would have the following form:

(46) E6 books [every boy [...] ... E6 books [every girl did ⟨ ⟩ too]

Under this reading, there are two sets of six books, one set read by the boys, another read by the girls. Under a scope reconstruction theory, this could arise if the VP had the following form:

(47) [E6 books$_i$ [read t_I]]

This VP applied to the two subjects (every boy, every girl) would derive the scope-reconstructed readings if scope reconstruction could apply to universals. But since it cannot apply that reading is excluded, and so of three possible readings, exactly the right two are predicted to occur.

The scope reconstruction model is, I think, strongly confirmed by the two considerations just enumerated, and allows us to say that the antecedent and elided VP in the Hirschbuhler cases are the same VP:

(48) [Every embassy$_i$ [x$_k$ ... t$_i$.]]$_{VP}$

But why is scope construal in the form of subject scope reconstruction allowed to follow the conditions that determine ellipsis, especially when we know that other instances of scope construal are known to determine the possibility of ellipsis in the first place, and thus to precede it? A related question is, since scope reconstruction is optional, why is it not possible for it to apply to the first conjunct of a Hirschbuhler case but not the second, giving a difference in interpretive order between the two clauses:

(49) Every embassy [an American flag [...] and
     A Canadian flag [every embassy [...]]

This is not a possible meaning of (32). This is a massively false prediction, and on this point the parallelism theory would seem to at least get the facts right.

The answer must lie in the mechanism for scope reconstruction. It must be the case that scope reconstruction is not an optional process. Rather, we must suppose that the VPs in the scope-reconstructing and non-scope-reconstructing cases have different structure. I offer the following suggestion on how to achieve this.

Let us suppose that indefinite NPs are really predicates, and that an ordinary VP can be interpreted either as (a) below, or like (b), with existential closure on its subject (à la Heim 1982); the indefinite subject then supplies the value for P, and so the whole thing must be preceded by λP as in (c):

(50) a. die(x)
     b. Ex (Px $^\wedge$ die(x))
     c. λP(Ex(Px $^\wedge$ die(x))

When (c) is combined with an indefinite subject, like "a man," we get

(51) a man λP(Ex(Px $^\wedge$ die(x)) → Ex(man(x) $^\wedge$ die(x))

Now, if the VP contains a real quantifier inside of it, the scope of that quantifier can be construed between the λP and Ex of (50c), giving (52), which is exactly the structure required for the Hirschbuhler examples:

(52) λP([every embassy$_y$ Ex (Px $^\wedge$ [x stands in front of y]$_{VP}$)])

(52) is the common VP that can now be applied to the two subjects (*an American flag, a Canadian flag*) to give the right interpretation. In this conception, scope recon-

struction is not a rule reassigning scope to an element in surface structure. Rather, it is the choice of (50c) over (a) as the meaning of VP.

This account explains why scope reconstruction must either apply in both conjuncts or neither. In this account, scope reconstruction arises from the choice of (50c) as the meaning of the VP, instead of the form based on (50a). If (a) is chosen, we will get strictly wide scope for the subject; for the Hirschbuhler case, this would be

(53) λx (every embassy$_y$ (x stood in front of y))

This sort of VP combines only with a quantifier expression, and will give strictly wide scope for the subject. Since the elided VP must be identical to the antecedent VP, it will either be (52) or (53), and the scopes in the elided VP will be completely determined, so no opportunity for divergence from the antecedent can arise.

The account also explains, at least in a weak sense, why it is only existentials that appear to scope-reconstruct.

We now have answers to both of the problems raised for the scope reconstruction theory of the Hirschbuhler examples. Scope reconstruction is not really scope assignment, but rather a choice of subject/predicate relation different from the normal one, and so ellipsis can still be understood to follow all scope assignment. It follows, too, that the scope in the antecedent and the ellipsis site must match as well, under the identity condition on ellipsis.

11.5 Conclusion

In this chapter I have presented three answers to three separate challenges to the identity condition on anaphora. I suggested that the variables in the nuclear scope and the restrictor of quantifiers were to be considered identical, I suggested that that should be extended to "focus contrast pairs," and I suggested that scope reconstruction was the means of understanding some scope judgments. So, the work presented here has been piecemeal, ad hoc, and unheroic. Why bother? Because identity is a better idea than parallelism. If one's working notion is parallelism, then one asks, what kind of parallelism, or parallel in what ways? But if the working notion is identity, the only question is what does it take to make it work?

Notes

I would like to thank audiences at MIT, University of British Columbia, University of Vienna, and University of Wraclaw for hearing me out.

1. Angle brackets will be used to indicate ellipsis sites. They will be empty, or filled with the elided words.

2. Williams (2003) presents a theory from which it follows that Gapping (but not Sluicing) cannot bridge Tensed S boundaries; that explanation can extend straightforwardly to VP-deletion

3. See Williams 1996 for further discussion of this issue.

4. Here "Secondary Focus" refers to what is often called the *Topic*; see Williams 1996 for a discussion of why a Topic may be considered to be a Focus embedded under another Focus. Thanks to an anonymous reviewer for clarification of this discussion.

5. An ampersand (&) means ambiguous, and ∼& not ambiguous.

6. Subscript A = antecedent; subscript E = ellipsis site.

7. In Williams 1994, 1995, and 1996, however, it is argued that the "strict" reading of a pronoun in an ellipsis site arises from a condition on ellipsis just slightly different from identity.

References

Baltin, M. 1987. "Do Antecedent-Contained Deletions Exist?" *Linguistic Inquiry* 18(4):579–595.

Fiengo, R., and R. May. 1994. *Indices and Identity*. Cambridge, Mass.: MIT Press.

Fox, D. 2002. "Antecedent Contained Deletion and the Copy Theory of Movement." *Linguistic Inquiry* 33(1):63–95.

Heim, I. 1982. The Semantics of Definite and Indefinite NPs. Doctoral dissertation, University of Massachusetts.

Heim, I. 1997. "Predicates or Formulas? Evidence from Ellipsis." *Proceedings of Salt VII*, 197–221. Ithaca, N.Y.: Cornell University.

Hirschbuhler, P. 1982. "VP Deletion and Across-the-Board Quantifier Scope." In J. Pustejovsky and P. Sells, eds., *Proceedings of NELS 12*. Amherst: GLSA, University of Massachusetts.

Hornstein, N. 1994. "An Argument for Minimalism: The Case of Antecedent-Contained Deletion." *Linguistic Inquiry* 25:455–480.

Kennedy, C. 1994. *Argument Contained Ellipsis*. Linguistics Research Center report series. Santa Cruz: Cowell College, University of California at Santa Cruz.

Larson, R. K., and R. May. 1990. "Antecedent Containment or Vacuous Movement: Reply to Baltin." *Linguistic Inquiry* 21:103–122.

Lasnik, H. 1993. "Lectures on Minimalist Syntax." *UConn Working Papers in Linguistics: Occasional Papers Issue 1*.

Merchant, J. 2002. *The Syntax of Silence*. Oxford: Oxford University Press.

Rooth, M. 1992. "Ellipsis Redundancy and Reduction Redundancy." In S. Berman and A. Hestvic, eds., *Proceedings of the Stuttgart Ellipsis Workshop*. Heidelberg: IBM Heidelberg.

Williams, E. 1977. "Discourse and Logical Form." *Linguistic Inquiry* 8:101–139.

Williams, E. 1993. *Thematic Structure in Syntax*. Cambridge, Mass.: MIT Press.

Williams, E. 1994. "Ellipsis." Unpublished ms., Princeton University.

Williams, E. 1995. "Review of R. Fiengo and R. May, *Indices and Identity*." *Language* 71:572–576.

Williams, E. 1996. "Blocking and Anaphora." *Linguistic Inquiry* 28:577–628.

Williams, E. 2003. *Representation Theory*. Cambridge, Mass.: MIT Press.

12 Some Preliminary Comparative Remarks on French and Italian Definite Articles

Richard S. Kayne

What we call the definite article does not have consistent behavior even across a set of languages/dialects as relatively homogeneous as the Romance ones. In this chapter, I will try to bring intra-Romance comparative evidence to bear on the question of how best to understand the differences in question (having to do with interrogatives, superlatives and partitives/bare plurals). I will argue that these differences are to be understood in terms of whether or not a given language/dialect pronounces its definite article in a given context, much as in Kayne 2005a for French versus English unpronounced nouns.

The comparative evidence discussed will also bear on questions of analysis and theory for each of the domains considered. For example, unpronounced N (or NP) will be seen to move past (the counterparts of) *which* in sentences like *Which do you prefer*? Romance postnominal superlatives will be seen to involve a derivation like that proposed for Greek by Alexiadou and Wilder (1998). And Romance bare plurals will arguably contain a definite article of the sort seen overtly in French partitives.

12.1 Interrogatives

English has both:

(1) Which student did you just see?

and

(2) What student did you just see?

In (2) the *wh*-word is the same as the one in

(3) What have you done?

The French counterpart of bare interrogative *what* is either *que/qu'* or *quoi*:

(4) Qu'as-tu fait?
    'What have you done?'

(5) Tu as fait quoi?
   'You have done what?'

depending on various factors. However, neither *que/qu'* nor *quoi* can mimic *what* in (2):

(6) *Qu'étudiant as-tu vu?
   'What student have you seen?'

(7) *Quoi étudiant as-tu vu?

French does have:

(8) Quel étudiant as-tu vu?
   'Which student have you seen?'

with a *wh*-word *quel* that seems (although the interpretation of (8) may cover that of (2), too) to be a relatively close counterpart of English *which* as in (1).

Of central interest in this chapter is the fact that French does not allow the lexical noun to be unpronounced in sentences that are otherwise exactly like (8):[1]

(9) *Quel as-tu vu?

Similarly in the plural:

(10) Quels étudiants as-tu vus?
   'Which students have you seen?'

(11) *Quels as-tu vus?

The lexical noun can remain unpronounced in French only if *quel(s)* is preceded by the definite article (written as one word with *quel*[2]):

(12) Lequel as-tu vu?
   'The which have you seen?'

(13) Lesquels as-tu vus?

The Italian counterparts of (8) and (10) are the following:

(14) Quale studente hai visto?
   'Which student have-you seen?'

(15) Quali studenti hai visto?
   'Which students...'

in which Italian *quale/quali* is parallel to French *quel/quels*. Yet Italian differs from French in that Italian allows the lexical noun to be unexpressed without a definite article appearing, in contrast to (9) and (11):

(16) Quale/quali hai visto?

Moreover, Italian does not allow the definite article to appear in (16), as opposed to French (12) and (13):

(17) *Il quale hai visto?
     'The which…'

(18) *I quali hai visto?
     'The which (plural)…'

We can note in passing that English is more like Italian here:

(19) Which would you prefer?

(20) *The which would you prefer?

On the other hand, English differs from Italian in relative clauses with *quale* or *which*:

(21) the reason for (*the) which John…

(22) la ragione per *(la) quale Gianni…

English relative *which* is incompatible with *the*, while Italian relative *quale* must be preceded by the definite article, here *la*.[3] In relatives, French *quel* is like Italian *quale*, despite differing from it in interrogatives in the way just discussed. In relatives, French *quel* requires the definite article, as in Italian:

(23) la raison pour laquelle Jean…

(24) *la raison pour quelle Jean…

The question why English differs in relatives in this way from both French and Italian will not be pursued in this paper.[4] (Nor will I pursue here the Italian-internal contrast between (17)/(18) and (22).[5])

Returning to the central theme of French vs. Italian, we can ask whether the contrast discussed in (9)–(18) between French *quel* and Italian *quale* in interrogatives without a pronounced lexical N (whereby *quel* requires and *quale* disallows a preceding definite article) correlates or clusters with any other difference between the two languages.

12.2 Superlatives

Cross-Romance comparative evidence suggests a link to postnominal superlatives. English superlatives have the superlative adjective prenominal:

(25) You should give the smartest student an A.

(26) *You should give the student smartest an A.

This is also true with *most*:

(27) You should give the most intelligent student an A.

(28) *You should give the student most intelligent an A.

Plausibly, this falls under the generalization that English adjectives are (almost) always prenominal.[6]

French and Italian share the property that their adjectives can readily be postnominal, in contrast to English:

(29) *John has read a book interesting.

(30) Jean a lu un livre intéressant.   French

(31) Gianni ha letto un libro interessante.   Italian

Similarly with superlatives:

(32) L'étudiant le plus intelligent est Jean.   French
     'The student the most intelligent is J'

(33) Lo studente più intelligente è Gianni.   Italian

French and Italian also share the property of lacking a morphological distinction corresponding to *most* versus *more*. French *plus* and Italian *più* appear both in the superlatives of (32)/(33) and in comparatives:

(34) Marie est plus intelligente que Jean.   French
     'M is *plus* intelligent that/than J'

(35) Maria è più intelligente di Gianni.   Italian
     'M is *più* intelligent of/than G'

However, French and Italian differ sharply in that French (32) contains a definite article *le* immediately before *plus*, whereas Italian *più* in (33) is not preceded by a definite article. In French, this definite article is obligatory with postnominal superlatives:

(36) *L'étudiant plus intelligent est Jean.

In Italian it is impossible:

(37) *Lo studente il più intelligente è Gianni.

The fact that French has, in postnominal superlatives, an obligatory definite article that Italian cannot have is reminiscent of the fact discussed earlier that French has, with interrogative bare *quel*, an obligatory definite article (see (9)–(13)) that Italian *quale* cannot have (see (16)–(18)).

That there is a significant linkage here is supported by the fact that the following cross-Romance generalization appears to hold:

(38) If a Romance language obligatorily has an overt definite article preceding (its equivalent of) bare interrogative *quel*, then it obligatorily has a definite article preceding (its equivalent of) postnominal superlative *plus*.

12.3   Greek

We can (and must) now ask why this linkage should hold and how best to express it. (A specific answer will be proposed beginning in section 12.6.) As a first step, note that the pre-*plus* definite article in (32) is less exotic than it looks. Although in French it does not appear with nonsuperlative postnominal adjectives:

(39)   *l'étudiant l'intelligent
        'The student the intelligent'

DPs that look like (39) are possible in Greek,[7] as discussed by Alexiadou and Wilder (1998). I will attempt to adapt their analysis to French.

Alexiadou and Wilder look at the (grammatical) Greek counterpart of (39) in the following way. From the observation that Greek allows a postnominal adjective to be preceded by an "extra" definite article only if that adjective can occur in predicate position (as opposed to adjectives like *former*), Alexiadou and Wilder conclude that the postnominal adjectives in question should in fact be analyzed as predicative, originating within a small clause, in effect a kind of reduced relative clause. Their proposal adopts a raising approach to (these) relatives, approximately along the lines of Kayne (1994, §8.4), in which the relative clause is a complement of D. But Alexiadou and Wilder diverge from that analysis in one crucial way (see in part Bianchi 1999, 49; also Zwart 2000, Zribi-Hertz 2003, note 16, as well as Zribi-Hertz and Glaude 2003, 32). Whereas I had assumed that the phrase that was raised/promoted in relative clauses (to a position just below D) could never itself be a DP, Alexiadou and Wilder argue that it can be, and that that is precisely what underlies Greek having two Ds in cases like (39).

For reduced relatives, I had a derivation (for English cases like *the recently arrived letter*) essentially as follows (abstracting away from the head of the small clause) (see Kayne 1994, 98). The small clause, which was taken to have a subject NP (or QP, but not DP), is merged with (an unpronounced) C, yielding:

(40) C [$_{SC}$ letter [recently arrived]]

Preposing of the predicate phrase to SpecCP yielded:

(41) [recently arrived]$_i$ C [$_{SC}$ letter t$_i$]

followed by merger of D:

(42) the [[recently arrived]$_i$ C [$_{SC}$ letter t$_i$]]

This derivation produces an output in which the predicate phrase (whether participial or adjectival[8]) precedes the noun.

Alexiadou and Wilder argue that the small clause subject in this kind of derivation must be allowed to be a DP. Continuing for convenience with English morphemes (and using a simple adjective), their proposal leads to derivations (in Greek) like the following, in which the subject of the small clause is the DP "the student":

(43) C [$_{SC}$ [the student] [intelligent]] → preposing of predicate
      [intelligent]$_i$ C [$_{SC}$ [the student] t$_i$] → merger of D
      the [[intelligent]$_i$ C [$_{SC}$ [the student] t$_i$]]

Alexiadou and Wilder then propose that the derivation shown in (43) can be extended,[9] in the sense that the DP subject of the small clause can itself be preposed to the specifier of the higher D. Starting from and repeating the last line of (43), we have

(44) the [[intelligent]$_i$ C [$_{SC}$ [the student] t$_i$]] → DP-preposing
      [the student]$_j$ the [[intelligent]$_i$ C [$_{SC}$ t$_j$ t$_i$]]

The result is of course ungrammatical in English (and French, as in (39), and Italian):

(45) *the student the intelligent

but is grammatical in Greek.

A (remnant movement) variant of the partial derivation in (44) would have the whole small clause containing "the student" preposed to SpecD (rather than just "the student"):

(46) the [[intelligent]$_i$ C [$_{SC}$ [the student] t$_i$]] → small clause preposing
      [$_{SC}$ [the student] t$_i$]$_j$ the [[intelligent]$_i$ C t$_j$]

in which case there is significant parallelism with the derivation of prenominal relatives of the Japanese and Amharic type proposed in Kayne 1994, 93.

Both (44) and (46) attribute to (45) an initially nonobvious property, namely that it is the second definite article that is hierarchically the higher one (the one merged later)—since the first definite article is embedded within the preposed phrase containing "student."

As far as the choice between (46) and (44) is concerned, the link to Japanese and Amharic favors (46). In addition, (46) has movement to SpecD of a constituent (the small clause) that is hierarchically closer to D than what is moved in (44) (the subject of that small clause).[10] This, too, favors (46), which I will from now on take to be the correct choice for the derivation of (45) in Greek.

12.4   French Postnominal Superlatives

Since the "extra" definite article seen with French postnominal superlatives as in (32) recalls the Greek pattern of (45), let me in fact propose that French postnominal superlatives have a derivation similar to (43)+(46). Thus a French example such as

(47) le livre le plus court
       'The book the most short'

will have a derivation containing the following steps, starting from a small clause with a full DP subject:

(48) C [$_{SC}$ [le livre] [plus court]] → preposing of predicate
       [plus court]$_i$ C [$_{SC}$ [le livre] t$_i$] → merger of higher D
       le [[plus court]$_i$ C [$_{SC}$ [le livre] t$_i$]] → small clause preposing
       [$_{SC}$ [le livre] t$_i$]$_j$ le [[plus court]$_i$ C t$_j$]

Again, it is the *le* immediately preceding *plus* that is the hierarchically higher D (the one merged later).[11]

Any analysis of (47) must account for the fact that French does not allow this higher D to appear with postnominal nonsuperlative adjectives (as we had previously seen in (39)):

(49) *le livre le court
       'The book the short'

(50) le livre court

What I would like to propose is that in French (and also Italian) the predicate preposing step in (48) is limited to superlatives. In effect, this amounts to saying that in French (and Italian), when the subject of the small clause in (48) has a definite article, predicate preposing is not available at all, in any general sense. The correct way to think of the first step in (48) is rather as:

(51) C [$_{SC}$ [le livre] [plus court]] → superlative preposing
       [plus court]$_i$ C [$_{SC}$ [le livre] t$_i$]

   That French can have superlative preposing here in the absence of any more general predicate preposing should be interpreted in terms of (obligatory) pied-piping. The superlative *plus* in (51) raises across DP to SpecC and in so doing pied-pipes the adjective. Unlike Greek in its counterpart of (43), French does not allow adjective phrases per se to raise to SpecC in such structures—in French they only raise as a side effect of the raising of superlative *plus*.[12] The idea that superlatives in French (and Italian) can raise in a way that ordinary APs cannot of course recalls the fact that interrogative *wh*-phrases (in English, for example) raise in a way that ordinary DPs do not; similarly, negative phrases in some languages (very visibly in Icelandic, for example[13]) raise in a way that ordinary DPs do not. Pied-piping of the AP by *plus* is to be considered parallel to the pied-piping of NP (or QP or NumP) by the *wh*-morpheme or by the negative morpheme (see Hendrick 1990).

I note in passing that there is evidence that, even in English, superlatives raise in a way that ordinary APs do not. This is not apparent in *the most interesting book*, which appears to be parallel to *the interesting book*, but it is seen, I think, in the sharp contrast between the following:

(52) That's not the shortest/most interesting of books.

(53) *That's not the short/interesting of books.

and also in

(54) (?)Of all the students, John's the one who's written the fewest number of
     papers this year.

(55) John is the author of the few (*number of) papers that are good.

The adjective *few*, as seen in (55), normally cannot directly modify the overt noun *number*, but it can (to varying extents) is *few* is raised—as shown, I would claim, in (54). This raising is seen more transparently in:

(56) ?(?)John has written too few a number of papers to qualify for a grant.

in which *too few* has been raised past *a*, just as *fewest* has been raised (I claim) in (54).[14] In (56) *few* has clearly been pied-piped by *too*:

(57) *John has written few a number of papers.

and in (54), by extension, by *-est*. (Similarly, in (52) *short/interesting* has plausibly been pied-piped by *-est/most*.[15])

Let me repeat the contrast that holds within French:

(58) le livre le plus court
     'The book the most short'

(59) *le livre le court

The proposal is that this contrast is due to French having raising of *plus* (similarly to raising of *wh*) that pied-pipes the adjective *court*. This leads to the intermediate stage:

(60) [plus court]$_i$ C [$_{SC}$ [le livre] t$_i$]

seen in (51), which in turn leads to (58) via the merger of the higher D *le* and the preposing of (the small clause containing) *le livre* to Spec,*le*:

(61) [plus court]$_i$ C [$_{SC}$ [le livre] t$_i$] $\rightarrow$ merger of *le*
     le [[plus court]$_i$ C [$_{SC}$ [le livre] t$_i$]] $\rightarrow$ small clause preposing
     [$_{SC}$ [le livre] t$_i$]$_j$ le [[plus court]$_i$ C t$_j$]

A parallel derivation for (59) is not available in French (as opposed to Greek) because, by hypothesis, the "bare" adjective *court* cannot be raised in French in the same way that *plus court* has been in (60).

This picture of French takes *plus court* in (58) to be a constituent that excludes the definite article *le*, as shown in (61). Put another way, (58) contains no constituent of the form "le plus." That the definite article and the superlative morpheme do not form a constituent is supported to a certain indirect extent by English:

(62) That is a most interesting book.

which at the very least shows that *most* need not occur with *the* at all.[16]

Closer to present concerns, there is evidence within French itself that superlative *plus* and preceding definite article need not form a constituent:[17]

(63) les quatre plus belles femmes
     'The four most beautiful women'

(64) la quatrième plus belle femme
     'The fourth most beautiful woman'

In these examples *plus* is not immediately preceded by a definite article. I conclude that the dissociation of *le* and *plus* shown in (61) is plausible and I take it to be correct.

In (63) and (64) the superlative is prenominal rather than postnominal. In such prenominal cases in French there cannot be a definite article directly preceding *plus* at all:

(65) *les quatre les plus belles femmes

(66) *la quatrième la plus belle femme

The contrast between these and (58), with a well-formed postnominal superlative and two definite articles, can be understood as follows. As we have seen, in (58) the first definite article originates as part of the subject of the small clause; the second corresponds to the higher definite article of a relative clauselike structure. At the point in the derivation of (58) (given in (48)) just after the merger of the higher definite article we have:

(67) le [[plus court]$_i$ C [$_{SC}$ [le livre] t$_i$]]

If we were to have a numeral (cardinal or ordinal) within the small clause subject, we would have (adjusting to plural in the first of these):

(68) les [[plus courts]$_i$ C [$_{SC}$ [les quatre livres] t$_i$]]

(69) le [[plus court]$_i$ C [$_{SC}$ [le quatrième livre] t$_i$]]

Small clause preposing would then yield:

(70) [$_{SC}$ [les quatre livres] t$_i$]$_j$ les [[plus courts]$_i$ C t$_j$]

(71) [$_{SC}$ [le quatrième livre] t$_i$]$_j$ le [[plus court]$_i$ C t$_j$]

corresponding to:

(72) les quatre livres les plus courts
     'The four books the most short'

(73) le quatrième livre le plus court
     'The fourth book the...'

These are well formed, but they still have the superlatives postnominal.

Put another way, the type of derivation proposed earlier for the well-formed (58) has the (welcome) property that it does not lead us to expect (65)/(66) to be available. If it were possible in French to stop the derivation at the point shown in (67), we would get, switching back to *belle*:

(74) *la plus belle la femme

which is ill-formed in French (even with an adjective like *belle* that lends itself to being prenominal). I conclude that when the derivation reaches (67) (or (68) or (69)) it must continue on, with the small clause obligatorily moving to SpecD, yielding (58) (or (72) or (73)).[18]

There remains the question of how to allow for the well-formed prenominal superlatives of (63) and (64), as well as for the corresponding case with no numeral:

(75) les plus belles femmes
     'The most beautiful women'

in all three of which there is only one definite article. A possible answer is that French, in addition to (67), also allows the small clause subject to contain no overt article:

(76) la [[plus belle]$_i$ C [$_{SC}$ [femme] t$_i$]]

yielding (75) or its singular counterpart directly. If a numeral can be merged above CP but below D in this kind of derivation, we can derive (63) and (64), for example for (63):[19]

(77) les [quatre [[plus belles]$_i$ C [$_{SC}$ [femmes] t$_i$]]]

A question that arises is why small clause preposing applied to (76) yields a deviant result:

(78) *femme la plus belle

Adapting an idea of Alexiadou and Wilder's (1998, 327), let me say that (small clause) movement to Spec,*la*—that is, to the Spec of the higher D in (76)—is subject to a strong agreement effect, namely that the subject of the small clause must itself be preceded by (overt) definite D, as in

(79) la femme la plus belle

with the representation:

(80) [$_{SC}$ [la femme] t$_i$]$_j$ la [[plus belle]$_i$ C t$_j$]

in which the preposed small clause matches the higher D *la* in definiteness.[20]

Note that this matching requirement cannot be met in French by an unpronounced definite article that would precede *femme* in (76), otherwise (78) could incorrectly be generated. Nor, not unexpectedly, by an indefinite article:[21]

(81) *une femme la plus belle
       'A woman the most beautiful'

On the other hand, one sees no definite article per se in the well-formed:

(82) ton livre le plus court
       'Your book the most short'

Either the possessive must itself count as fulfilling the matching requirement imposed by *le*, or there must be an unpronounced *le* specifically licensed by that possessive.

Although French does not permit (81), it does have

(83) une femme des plus jolies
       'A woman of-the most pretty'

with an interpretation akin to that of *a most beautiful woman*. In French this is not possible with a nonsuperlative:

(84) *une femme des jolies

suggesting that superlative raising plays a role in (83) (though I will not pursue the analysis of (83) here).

12.5 French Superlatives vs. Italian Superlatives

The central contrast is (cf. the discussion of (36) and (37) earlier):

(85) le livre le plus court   French
       'The book the most short'

(86) il libro più corto   Italian

With a postnominal superlative, French must have a definite article preceding *plus*, while Italian cannot have one preceding *più*. To exclude the word-for-word French counterpart of (86):

(87) *le livre plus court

as a superlative in French,[22] we need to ensure that the higher definite article in:

(88) [$_{SC}$ [le livre] t_i]$_j$ le [[plus court]$_i$ C t_j]

is overt, i.e. French must not allow the equivalent of (88) with an unpronounced definite D.

We can now ask in what way Italian is different. Let me propose that Italian is only minimally different from French, in that (86) has a structure identical to (85)/(88), except that Italian leaves its definite D there unpronounced:

(89) [$_{SC}$ [il libro] t_i]$_j$ D [[più corto]$_i$ C t_j]

The unpronounced definite D of (89) is not allowed in French.

Before going on to make this proposal more precise, let me note that the unpronounced (definite) D that Italian has in (89) shares with the pronounced definite D of French (88) the property that the (specifier of the) small clause that it attracts to its Spec must match in definiteness (in the superlative interpretation; see note 22). Italian (90) is parallel to French (78), and Italian (91) (as a superlative) is parallel to French (81):

(90) *libro più corto

(91) *un libro più corto

Italian (89) and French (88) are thus strongly parallel, yet with a sharp difference concerning whether the higher D is pronounced or not.

12.6 French vs. Italian Bare Arguments

Distinguishing French (85) from Italian (86) (with the corresponding representations (88) and (89)) in terms of the pronounced versus unpronounced character of the higher D (rather than via recourse to an ad hoc distinction between French *plus* and Italian *più*) makes it possible, I think, to relate these superlative facts to another difference between French and Italian (in a way that an ad hoc distinction between *plus* and *più* would not have).

Let us ask, then, why French and Italian should differ here at all, and secondly, why it is French whose higher D must be pronounced in (85) and Italian whose higher D must not be pronounced in (86), rather than the other way around. The answer that I will now propose will rest in part on the fact that this French/Italian difference is one that is in essence already familiar from work on bare plurals and bare mass nouns (for example, Delfitto and Schroten 1991, Longobardi 1994, and Chierchia 1998).

Italian allows bare plurals, but French does not:

(92) *Jean achetait livres.   French
     'J bought (was buying) books'

(93) Gianni comprava libri.   Italian
     (Same)

Bare mass nouns/NPs show a parallel difference:

(94) *Jean buvait bière.   French
     'J drank beer'

(95) Gianni beveva birra.   Italian
     (Same)

To express (92) and (94) French has what I will, partly following the French grammatical tradition, call the "partitive":

(96) Jean achetait des livres.

(97) Jean buvait de la bière.

in which the direct object is preceded by the preposition *de* ('of') and the definite
article. (This is clearly so in (97), with definite article *la*; in (96) the expected *de les*
is reduced to *des*, in a way that is fully general in French and not limited to these
partitives.[23])

The presence of *de* in these partitives is related to the presence of an unpronounced
noun akin to overt nouns like *number*, *amount* and *quantity*—that is, we should think
of (96) and (97) as[24]

(98) ... NUMBER de les livres

(99) ... AMOUNT de la bière

with capitals indicating nonpronunciation, and *de* akin to the *de* and *of* of

(100) un certain nombre de livres

(101) a certain number of books

It is important to see that the syntax of this *de* and the syntax of the definite article
that follows it in (96)–(99) are at least partially independent. A simple indication in
this direction comes from Piedmontese, which is like French in rejecting exact counterparts of (93) and (95), and like French in having a partitive preposition akin to *de*.
However Piedmontese lacks the definite article that French partitives have; the following examples have been provided by Luigi Burzio:

(102) Maria a-l'a cata' d' sucher.
      'M she has bought of sugar'

(103) *Maria a-l'a cata' d'l sucher.
      '... of the sugar'

(In what follows, I will use the term "bare plural/mass" in such a way as to cover (102), as well as (93) and (95)—that is, 'bareness' will pick out absence of overt determiner and will be indifferent to the presence of a preposition. The French (96)/(97) are not "bare," since they contain a (reduced) definite article following the preposition.)

Within French itself, one sees this independence of *de* and the definite article in at least two ways. First, the definite article can fail to appear in cases like (96) where the plural noun is preceded by an adjective:

(104) Jean achetait de bons livres.
      'J was-buying of good books'

Yet the *de* continues to be present. Second, there is an alternation concerning quantity elements like *beaucoup* ('a lot'), which in simple cases corresponding to *a lot of friends* are followed by *de*-NP, with no definite article:

(105) Jean a beaucoup d'amis.
      'J has a lot of friends'

Yet under right-dislocation, *beaucoup* can for many speakers co-occur either with or without the definite article:

(106) Jean en a beaucoup, d'amis.
      'J of-them has a lot, of friends'

(107) Jean en a beaucoup, des amis.
      (Same, with the definite article)

Granting, then, that *de* and the definite article of partitives are independent of one another (even if they interact in important ways), we can return to (92)–(95) and conclude that French and Italian actually differ there in two separate ways. French (like Piedmontese) must have *de* where Italian does not have to have it. And, second, French has a definite article (in (96)/(97)) where Italian does not have to have one (in (93)/(95)). (On Italian partitives, see the discussion of (122) later.)

This second conclusion is very similar to what we have seen in the syntax of superlatives. More specifically, assume that I have been correct in arguing that the superlative difference has to do, not directly with the superlative morphemes *plus* and *più*, but rather with French necessarily having an overt higher definite article in certain DPs (containing postnominal superlatives), as opposed to Italian necessarily having an unpronounced higher definite article in the same (superlative) context.

Then both differences now under consideration (superlatives on the one hand, bare plurals/mass on the other) have something to do with the pronunciation (in French) versus the nonpronunciation (in Italian) of the definite article in certain contexts.

The structures given for the two French cases now under discussion are

(108) [$_{SC}$ [le livre] t$_i$]$_j$ le [[plus court]$_i$ C t$_j$]   (=(88))

(109) AMOUNT de la bière   (=(99))

Their Italian counterparts are, in the superlative case, with unpronounced D:

(110) [$_{SC}$ [il libro] t$_i$]$_j$ D [[più corto]$_i$ C t$_j$]

and in the bare mass noun case (95):

(111) AMOUNT D birra

In (111) I have attributed to Italian the same structure (but with D unpronounced) that we have in (109), less the *de*.[25]

Assume that AMOUNT in (111) is in SpecD (in all likelihood having gotten there by movement—and similarly for (109), with respect to SpecP). Then we can formulate two generalizations:

(112) In Italian, a definite D with a filled Spec can and must be unpronounced.

(113) In French, a filled Spec does not license nonpronunciation for a definite D.

The formulation in (112) allows both (110) and (111), while prohibiting (cf. (37)):

(114) *il libro il più corto   Italian
      'The book the most short'

It also allows (111)/(95), while prohibiting:

(115) *AMOUNT la birra

with a pronounced D. That (115) is impossible translates into the fact that the interpretation of (95) is distinct from that of

(116) Gianni beveva la birra.
      'G drank the beer'

As far as French is concerned, (113) excludes the counterpart of (88) in which D would be unpronounced, thereby correctly excluding as a superlative (cf. (87)):

(117) *le livre plus court

In the case of partitives, (113) is compatible with the well-formedness of (109)/(97), but excludes (the Italianlike):[26]

(118) *AMOUNT D bière

with an unpronounced D, and thereby prohibits French from having (the Italianlike) (94), repeated here:[27]

(119) *Jean buvait bière.
      'J drank beer'

The pair of generalizations (112)/(113) thus allows bringing together the difference between French and Italian superlatives with the difference between French and Italian bare plurals/mass nouns. (From the present perspective, bare plurals and bare mass nouns/NPs (at least those with an indefinite interpretation[28]) must contain NUMBER/AMOUNT, and are therefore less "bare," strictly speaking, than has been thought.)

Taking singular count nouns not to be compatible either with NUMBER or with AMOUNT, this gives us a way of understanding the assymmetry within Italian between the widespread character of bare plurals and bare mass nouns, and the much more limited character of bare singulars:

(120) *Gianni comprava libro.
          'G bought book'

The status of (120) follows from the impossibility of having an argument be a simple NP,[29] combined (since (120) has neither NUMBER nor AMOUNT in SpecD) with the limited possibilities for licensing a null D. (In Italian, a null D can perhaps only be licensed via (112).[30]

Of interest is the fact that (112) does not exclude an Italian counterpart of (109) (since in (109) AMOUNT is, given the presence of the (overt) preposition,[31] not in SpecD)—that is, Italian is not prohibited from having

(121) AMOUNT de la birra

which arguably corresponds to the well-formed *della birra* in sentences like[32]

(122) Gianni beveva della birra.
          'G drank of-the beer'

Somewhat similarly (112) does not prevent Italian from having a counterpart to French (83):[33]

(123) Ho parlato con un impiegato dei più gentili.   Italian
          'I-have spoken with an emplyee of-the most nice'

since the definite article -*i* is 'protected' by the preposition from having a filled Spec. The same holds for

(124) due dei ragazzi   Italian
          'Two of-the boys'

A question concerning (112) is, what exactly is meant by filled Spec, in particular in cases in which some phrase might have moved through SpecD, landing in some still higher position. Passage through SpecD has been proposed in at least two kinds of cases. One involves extractions from NP/DP of the sort discussed by Giorgi and Longobardi (1991, chap. 2); the other involves extraction of a dative possessor in

Hungarian (Szabolcsi 1983), which can plausibly be transposed to Italian (and French) sentences with dative inalienable possessors, for example, in Italian:[34]

(125) Gli hanno rotto la gamba.
      'To-him they-have broken the leg'

If there is in fact movement through SpecD, then, given the pronunciation of the definite article in many such cases (e.g., *la* in (125)), movement through SpecD must not count as producing a filled Spec in the sense of (112).

12.7 Back to *Lequel* and *Quale*

Consider again (38), repeated here:

(126) If a Romance language obligatorily has an overt definite article preceding (its equivalent of) bare interrogative *quel*, then it obligatorily has a definite article preceding (its equivalent of) postnominal superlative *plus*.

The relevant interrogative sentences are

(127) Lequel as-tu vu?   French
      'The which have you seen'

(128) *Quel as-tu vu?

and

(129) *Il quale hai visto?   Italian
      'The which have-you seen'

(130) Quale hai visto?

Why should the correlation stated in (126) hold?

The correlation expressed in (126) brings together interrogative *lequel/quale* and superlatives. The discussion of section 12.6 brought together superlatives and bare plurals/mass nouns. It is therefore of interest that the following seems to hold:

(131) If a Romance language has an obligatory overt definite article preceding bare interrogative *quel*, then it does not allow bare plurals/bare mass nouns any more than French does.

The fact that the *lequel* versus *quale* difference between French and Italian correlates both with a difference having to do with bare plurals/mass nouns and with a difference having to do with (postnominal) superlatives suggests folding *lequel/quale* into the perspective of (112)/(113). What we want to say, then, is that interrogative *quel/quale*, in the absence of an overt noun, enters into structures that are in fact similar to those proposed for postnominal superlatives, repeated here for French and Italian, respectively:

(132) [$_{SC}$ [le livre] t_i]$_j$ le [[plus court]$_i$ C t_j]

(133) [$_{SC}$ [il libro] t_i]$_j$ D [[più corto]$_i$ C t_j]

as well as to those proposed for bare plurals/mass nouns (possible only in Italian):

(134) NUMBER D libri

(135) AMOUNT D birra

The key question then is, where is the missing noun in (127)–(130)? Although its presence in the structure is virtually certain, its exact position is less immediate. Let me propose that the unpronounced noun (or NP) in such interrogatives precedes, rather than follows, *lequel/quale*. In all likelihood, it does so as the result of movement. The structures corresponding to the grammatical sentences (127) and (130) are thus:[35]

(136) N$_i$ le quel t_i . . .

(137) N$_i$ D quale t_i . . .

where N is unpronounced in both languages, and D is unpronounced in Italian.[36]

Taking N (or NP) in Italian to be in SpecD makes (137) immediately compatible with (112). In the same way, taking N (or NP) in French to be in SpecD makes (136) immediately compatible with (113). We consequently have a way of understanding the triple linkage across superlatives, bare plural/mass nouns and *lequel/quale*.

12.8   A Digression to English Possessors

A question that arises is, why does N(P) here move to SpecD? There would appear to be a link to Rizzi's (2000, 316) discussion of null topics in German and to Chomsky's (2001, 13) Phase Impenetrability Condition. An unpronounced category, here N (see note 35), that is not locally licensed by another category must arguably move up to the Spec of an appropriate phase (here perhaps DP), presumably to the nearest such Spec (thinking of the discussion of (125)). (This would not apply to the unpronounced D itself of (135), which is locally licensed by the phrase in its Spec.)

There is a curious set of English facts that bears on the principles regulating the syntax of unpronounced categories. These facts concern possessives with unpronounced nouns (or NPs), as in

(138) John's car is bigger than Bill's.

The possessor of the unpronounced noun can be pronominal:

(139) John's car is bigger than yours.

In these examples, the unpronounced noun clearly has an antecedent *car*. Somewhat different is:

(140) Why don't we go over to Bill's tonight?

which is perfectly natural in an out-of-the-blue context, with no feeling of an antecedent in the sense of (138)/(139). The interpretation of (140) in an out-of-the-blue context is very close, if not identical, to that of:

(141) Why don't we go over to Bill's place tonight?

a fact that (among others) led me to propose (see Kayne (2004)):

(142) ... Bill's PLACE ...

as (part of) the structure of (140). In (142), PLACE is an unpronounced noun that differs from the ones in (138) and (139) in not (necessarily) having an antecedent.

Trudgill and Hannah (1994, 76) have noted in effect that in American English (and this is certainly true for mine) the possessor in (140) cannot be pronominal:[37]

(143) *Why don't we go over to yours tonight?

To me, this sentence in clearly impossible in an out-of-the-blue context, contrary to (140). Similarly, in a contrastive context, I have a clear difference between non-pronominal and pronominal possessors, with unanteceded PLACE:

(144) Why should we go over to Bill's tonight? We should all go over to John's/
       *yours, instead.

Why should this be? The answer depends in part, I think, on the fact that in a sense, (138) and (139) are misleading—the parallel behavior of pronominal and nonpronominal possessors that those two examples display breaks down if we reinstate the lexical noun and simultaneously keep the -s:

(145) Bill's house

(146) *yours house

and similarly for *hers house, *theirs house, *ours house (and for the less regular possessive of *mine house).[38]

A natural hypothesis is that (143) is out for the same reason as (146). But if that's true, how can we distinguish these two from (139)? Assume that, parallel to (142), we have, for (143):

(147) *... yours PLACE

but that for (139) we have, rather:

(148) ... N_i yours t_i

with N-raising approximately as in (136) and (137). Let me, more specifically, adopt the approach to (145) versus (146) put forth by Bernstein and Tortora (2005), who have pronominal possessors lower in the DP structure than lexical ones (cf. Nilsen

2003 on object shift; also see Cardinaletti 1997). In particular, pronominal possessors are lower than the position in which *'s* is found, so that *your* in the simple case cannot precede *'s*, as seen in (146). To allow for:

(149) a friend of yours

they propose that when *a friend* raises to Spec,*of* (cf. Kayne 1994, 86) *your* in fact can raise to the position normally reserved for lexical possessors. In their note 30, they suggest looking at predicative:

(150) This book is yours.

in the same way, with raising of an unpronounced (pronominal) counterpart of *book* licensing the raising of *your* past *'s*.

If we generalize further to all argument positions, we in effect reach (148) as part of the analysis of (139). If the raising of *your* (and other pronominal possessors) to Spec,*'s* is dependent on such N-raising (in a way that recalls Chomsky (1995, 185) on equidistance) and if no such raising takes place with PLACE in (143)/(144)/(147), then we can draw the desired distinction.

This leads in turn to the question why unpronounced PLACE would fail to raise in (147) while unpronounced N does raise in (148), which corresponds to (139) and (150). A likely initial answer is that N raises in (148) precisely because it has an antecedent, which PLACE in (147) does not have.[39]

This might then be related to the proposal in Kayne 2002a, §9, to the effect that every antecedent-pronoun pair originates in a doubling constituent that subsequently raises (a movement induced by a property of the pronominal subpart).

12.9 Conclusion

Examples (127)–(130), with *lequel* and *quale*, have in common with (150) and (139) that there is an unpronounced noun understood to have an antecedent. Therefore, the suggestion just made as to why there should be N-raising carries over, and provides an account of why (136) and (137) are the correct structures.[40] Those structures in turn allow linking *lequel/quale* to the question of postnominal superlatives (and via (131) to the question of bare plurals).

That these three phenomena are each to be seen as reflecting a (differential) property of definite D is not self-evident. To look at *lequel* versus *quale* in that way is straightforward, less so no doubt are the other two. For postnominal superlatives, one might have thought that what was at issue was some property of the superlative morpheme itself. For bare plurals, one might have thought that the absence of any definite D in bare plurals in Italian would make the approach argued for here unlikely to be on the right track. But that consideration is overridden if it is correct to take French partitives (which do contain a definite article) to be a true French counterpart of Italian bare plurals.[41]

Moreover, the fact that within Romance there is a partial correlation/clustering across these three properties (as stated in (131) and (126)) constitutes additional evidence (especially in the case of (131)) that the syntax of definite D is central to an understanding of indefinite bare plurals/bare mass nouns across Romance.

This is of course not entirely a surprise, since we can readily see through French partitives that phrases that are globally interpreted as indefinites (similarly to bare plurals in Italian) can and do contain a definite D. The comparative evidence discussed here suggests (in a way, that recalls Cheng and Sybesma (1999, 529; 2005) on Chinese) that the same holds for Italian (cf. Chomsky's (2001, 2) uniformity principle), even though Italian bare plurals do not give their definite D any pronunciation.[42]

It goes without saying that additional Romance languages need to be examined to test the validity of the cross-Romance correlations that I have suggested, and that additional morphosyntactic properties of French and Italian (and other Romance languages) need to be looked into with an eye to seeing how widespread (and how consistent) the ramifications are of (112)/(113).[43]

The present conclusion shares with Longobardi (1994, 618) and Chierchia (1998, 386) the idea that Italian bare plurals/mass nouns[44] contain an unpronounced determiner. But I have been led to think that that determiner is an unpronounced counterpart of the definite article (see note 28), with the indefinite reading (again recalling Cheng and Sybesma 1999, 2005) depending rather on the additional presence of an unpronounced NUMBER/AMOUNT.

Notes

For helpful comments on an earlier draft of this chapter, I am indebted to Guglielmo Cinque and Jean-Yves Pollock.

1. (9) differs from:

(i) Quelle est-elle? ('Which is it(fem.)')

in which we have a (nonsubject) predicative *quelle*. (9) is representative of all cases in which *quel* is part of an argument. In (i), *quelle* is arguably not part of a DP.

The contrast:

(ii) *Quel de ces livres est le plus intéressant? ('Which of those books is the most interesting?')

(iii) Lequel de ces livres est le plus intéressant?

suggests that (iii) contains an unpronounced noun in addition to overt *livres*, as in the Turkish construction mentioned by Kornfilt (1997, 237), in which the "extra" (pronounced) noun corresponds to a classifierlike *item* (or *person*).

2. As far as I can tell, this orthographic convention is not of importance to the syntax; see Julien 2002.

3. Except, as brought to my attention by Guglielmo Cinque, when predicative:

(i) Da gentiluomo quale era . . . ('from gentleman which he-was . . . '),

recalling note 1.

4. Possibly, (21) can be linked to the fact that *the* is incompatible with plural generics in cases like (cf. Longobardi 1994, 631):

(i) Cats are smart.

and/or to the fact that *the* is incompatible with possessives, as in

(ii) (*the) your books

and/or to *the* being incompatible with inalienable possession in cases like (see Guéron 1983 as well as Vergnaud and Zubizarreta 1992):

(iii) John raised the arm.

and/or to *the* being incompatible with sentential complements as in:

(iv) John erred in (*the) telling us a lie.

and/or to the fact that *the* is morphologically related to demonstratives (see Bernstein 2004), and/or to Sportiche's (1995, §4.2) suggestion that *the* might be a specifier.

5. Which recalls Kuroda 1968. The obligatoriness of the definite article with Italian relative *quale* may suggest an analysis in which *quale*+NP is the double of an unpronounced resumptive (cf. Perlmutter 1972), yet in which NP is raised much as in Kayne 1994, 89. (The raising of a double would be similar to Kayne 2002a.)

Indirectly relevant is the fact that Italian CLLD is possible with idiom chunks. See Cinque 1977, 402, and Bianchi 1993.

6. Both with superlatives and with ordinary adjectives there are exceptions when the adjective is accompanied by a complement, as in

(i) The student most capable of solving that problem is Mary.

(ii) any student capable of solving that problem

Similarly, although for me a bit less easily, with *-est*:

(iii) (?)The student strongest in mathematics is Mary.

It may be that the preposition (*of*, *in* in these examples) is playing a crucial role, in a way related to Cinque's (2005, note 34) and perhaps to the facts mentioned in Kayne (1975, chap. 3, note 82).

7. And in Hebrew; see Alexiadou 2003 for discussion of differences between Greek and Hebrew (and Scandinavian).

Relevant also (but coming to my attention too late to be taken into account here) is Campos and Stavrou 2004.

8. It might be that adjectives have two possible sources, one within a relative clause and one not—see Alexiadou and Wilder 1998, 313, as well as Cinque 2005, note 2.

9. For them (p. 322), the derivation can alternatively stop at that point, yielding:

(i) *the intelligent the student

the equivalent of which is possible in Greek, though not in English or French, or in Italian (unless prenominal *begli* ('beautiful—m.pl.') is 'be+gli', with *gli* a (second) definite article).

10. For a notion of "closeness" that does not depend on feature-checking, see Kayne (2005a, §5.6); also Cinque 2005.

11. This conclusion and derivation differ from Matushansky 2003, whose general hypothesis that all superlatives are associated with a noun (sometimes unpronounced; cf. also Martinon 1927, 103) looks correct.

In (48) (and similarly for (44) or (45), in Greek) the Spec of overt *le* is itself overt, in a way incompatible with Koopman and Szabolcsi's (2000, 40) formulation of their Generalized Doubly Filled Comp Filter.

12. As for the question why Greek allows the equivalent of (49), with a nonsuperlative adjective, as opposed to French and Italian, I do not have a clear proposal to make. Alexiadou and Wilder (1998, 330), citing Anagnostopoulou (1994), note that (49) in Greek has something in common with clitic doubling. That may well be a promising linkage, in particular thinking of the fact that Greek has clitic doubling with nonprepositional accusatives in a way that even Spanish (which lacks (49)) does not.

For example, it might be that in order for an ordinary AP to be able to cross "D NP" in (43) on its way to SpecC, the D in question (the one within the small clause subject) must have some property that accusative clitics have when they are compatible with doubling of a non-prepositional object, especially if the relevant D c-commanded the initial position of the AP (allowing D in Greek, but not in French, to act as a successful probe for AP), thinking of Sportiche 2002. (If the (adjectival) predicate in the first line of (51) is a nonsuperlative, the derivation will not converge.) Pursuing the implications here of Sportiche's approach to D is beyond the scope of this chapter.

13. See Kayne 1998; on Icelandic, see also Svenonius 2000. Probably also related is the raising in French and Italian of *tout/tutto* ('everything')—Kayne 1975, chap. 1, and Cinque 1995, chap. 9.

14. For relevant discussion, see Hendrick 1990 and Kayne 2005b.

The fact that *a* cannot appear in (54):

(i) *... the fewest a number of papers ...

is perhaps related to the presence of *the*, in a way that would need to be clarified. Possibly (i) is related to:

(ii) *That's not the shortest of a book (that I've ever seen).

(iii) *?That's not the most interesting of a book.

Degree modifiers other than superlatives are not compatible with an 'extra' definite article in French:

(iv) *les hommes les trop/si riches ('the men the too/so rich')

recalling the contrast between (52) and

(v) *the too/so/more interesting of books

Cf. also, to a lesser extent:

(vi) the most/*too/*so intelligent of the students

   Possibly, in (61), *le* can be merged with a CP containing a degree phrase in its Spec only if the degree element is superlative *plus*, and similarly for English *the*.

15. Consider also the fact that in Persian (cf. Moshiri 1988, 24) superlatives end up prenominal, while ordinary adjectives and even comparatives are generally postnominal; also the contrast within Italian:

(i) una bellissima/*bellina donna ('a most-beautiful/a-little-beautiful woman')

   Plausibly parallel to (52) versus (53) is

(ii) That's not the shortest/most interesting of his books.

(iii) *That's not the short/interesting of his books.

   More similar, still, to the Persian facts is the contrast:

(iv) the blackest two dogs that I've ever seen

(v) *the black two dogs that I saw yesterday

16. French lacks an exact counterpart of (62), for reasons that remain to be elucidated. As is well known, English does not allow this with *-est*:

(i) *That is a shortest book.

In addition, there is for me a clear contrast between (62) and:

(ii) *?That is a most short book.

Similarly:

(iii) She is a most intelligent woman.

(iv) *?She is a most smart woman.

suggesting that the almost certainly related:

(v) *?She is a more smart linguist than he is.

is not simply due to 'competition' from *smarter*.
   The interpretation of (62) is close to that of

(vi) That is a very interesting book.

but the two differ sharply in various ways:

(vii) a very very/*most most interesting book

(viii) a not very/*not most interesting book

(ix) very/*most few books

(x) so very/*most interesting; such a very/*most interesting book

suggesting that (62) might be related to:

(xi) That is a book of the most interesting sort/kind.

with *most* a true superlative.

17. From Sportiche's (2002) perspective, they would not be expected to.

Left open is how to integrate Genoese *a ciù cösa bella* ('the most thing beautiful') (Toso 1997, 76).

If definite article and *plus* formed a constituent, the obligatory agreement shown by the second *la* in

(i) la fille la plus intelligente ('the girl the most intelligent')

would not be expected.

For some cases of nonagreement with adverbial superlatives (which fall outside the scope of this chapter), see Martinon 1927, 104.

18. Whether this obligatory continuation is due more to a property of the higher *le* or more to a property of the small clause is left an open question here.

19. The presence of a numeral between CP and D appears to interfere with small clause preposing, however, if we return to (67). Adding a numeral above CP to (67) gives us (with a plural):

(i) les [quatre [[plus courts]$_i$ C [$_{SC}$ [les livres] t$_i$]]]

Doing nothing further is not possible (just as we saw with (74)):

(ii) *les quatre plus courts les livres

But in this case, as opposed to (58), small clause preposing is not possible, either:

(iii) *les livres les quatre plus courts

20. If Sportiche (2002) is on the right track, the *la* preceding *femme* might be the head of the small clause, rather than the head of the specifier of the small clause.

A reviewer makes the interesting suggesting that (78) might be related to the definiteness requirement on Icelandic object shift.

21. Sentences corresponding to (81) are found, however (perhaps they are akin to (83), or, thinking of Martinon's (1927, 101) discussion, to a reduced relative—see also Chenal 1986, 415, 417, and Grevisse 1993, §950). Martinon also mentions as a (probable) superlative:

(i) ce qu'il y a de plus beau ('that which there is of most beautiful')

which needs to be looked into.

22. Possible as a comparative is:

(i) le seul livre plus court que... ('the only book more short than...')

23. Roodenburg (2003) suggests that with *des* the *l-* is not syntactically present at all. On bare nominals with coordination, see Longobardi 1994, 619n, and Roodenburg 2004. Cf. also Bouchard 2003.

24. Cf. the (undeveloped) suggestion in Kayne 1975, §2.9, in terms of the noun *part*; on NUMBER/AMOUNT, see Kayne 2002b, 2005a, 2005b.

The unpronounced NUMBER/AMOUNT of these partitives is not subject to the restriction concerning Italian bare plurals/mass nouns as subjects discussed by Longobardi (1994, 616). Why Italian hanging topics (cf. Cinque 1977, 406, and Benincà and Poletto 2004, 64) are (contrary to French) not subject to that restriction remains to be understood.

25. It might be that an unpronounced preposition could not be licensed by unpronounced AMOUNT.

26. The fact that no language has (as far as I know):

(i) *Jean a les amis. ('J has the friends')

with a partitive/indefinite interpretation means that the presence of an overt definite article induces for some reason to be determined the need for an overt preposition.

27. As for (104), it might be that the plural morpheme following the prenominal adjective counts as a pronounced definite D—see Pollock 1998, note 24.

28. The definite article *la* in (109)/(97) (and its unpronounced counterpart in (111)/(95)) may have something significant in common with the definite article found in generic sentences, as noted by Gross (1968, 30). The global indefinite interpretation of (111) and (109) is comparable to that of

(i) a certain amount of beer

(ii) a number of people

The presence of an overt preposition (like) *of* is not essential:

(iii) a hundred people

(iv) ein Liter Wein (German 'a liter wine')

Left aside here is any discussion of French negative sentences like

(v) Jean n'a pas d'amis. ('J NEG has not of friends')

with no definite article. It may be that Italian bare plurals match both (v) and French partitives; see note 30.

Like (ii), French partitives seem to be positive polarity items.

29. See the discussion in Longobardi 1994, 620. The possible counterexample having to do with (Italian and French) infinitives mentioned in Kayne 1999, §4 might dissolve if, as suggested to me by Viviane Déprez, their prepositional complementizer (*di/de*) reflects the presence of an unpronounced head noun—see Kayne 2003, §4.6.

30. Which would amount to saying that there are no null indefinite determiners per se in Italian. On Brazilian Portuguese, which differs from Italian in productively allowing bare singulars, see Schmitt and Munn 2002; on the relevance of French-based creoles, see Déprez 2005.

Italian allows bare singulars in negative contexts like:

(i) Non ho mai visto gatto che fosse... ('neg I-have never seen cat that was...')

as discussed by Benincà (1980).

31. See note 25. It remains to be understood why Italian partitives with *di* require an overt definite article—as opposed to Piedmontese (102) and also (in the special case of prenominal adjectives) as opposed to French (104):

(i) *Gianni comprava di buoni libri. ('G bought of good books')

32. There are differences in behavior between Italian partitives as in (122) and French partitives as in (97) that fall outside the scope of this chapter.

33. Example provided by Paola Benincà, who notes that the construction is literary in Italian, and who finds the exact counterpart of (83) less than perfectly natural.

34. See Landau 1999. Similarly, perhaps, for clitic doubling and for antecedent-pronoun relations; see Kayne 2002a.

A reviewer notes the potential relevance here of Bošković's (2002) approach to successive cyclicity.

35. If the agreement requirement discussed at (78) holds with *quel/quale*, too, then the unpronounced phrase in Spec,D in (136)/(137) should be taken to be DP.

The text proposal means that (i) (cf. note 1)

(i) Lequel de ces livres...? ('the which of these books...')

must be

(ii) N$_i$ le quel t$_i$ de ces livres...

36. Left open here is the contrast within Italian between (137) and possessive *il mio* ('the my') (also *l'altro* ('the other') and relative *il quale*—(22)), which has an unpronounced noun together with a pronounced D. One possibility is further movement of the unpronounced noun (cf. Bianchi 1999, 79, on relatives), with a link to (125); another is that the unpronounced noun in *il mio*, and so on, need raise no higher than just past *mio* itself.

With an overt noun, French and Italian do not differ, in cases like

(i) Marie a gagné le concours. (French—'M has won the competition')

(ii) Maria ha vinto il concorso. (Italian—same)

Given (112), (ii) must not have a filled Spec.

37. I have come across one speaker of American English who accepts (143). Although this leads to interesting questions, it does not bear on the text discussion.

38. Possible is *his house*, because *his* is (irregularly) the form that occurs both with and without an overt lexical noun.

39. This approach to (147) differs from the suggestion made in Kayne 2004, §1.1.

Trudgill and Hannah (1994, 76) state that, in English English, sentences like (143) are possible, contrary to (most—see note 22) American English. (Possibly there is a link to *The soup has carrots in*, which they (p. 81) also give as possible in English English.) The implication here is that for such speakers, either PLACE is being taken to have an antecedent, or else PLACE is raising for a distinct reason—cf. Longobardi 1996, §1.4, on Italian *casa* ('home').

40. If the antecedent relation underlies raising in the case of *lequel/quale*, then the motivation for raising (to SpecD) is distinct from the case of postnominal superlatives.

41. See Spector 2001 and references cited there, emphasizing the parallelism. Possibly, French partitives can in addition have an analysis corresponding to that of Italian partitives (on which, see Storto 2001).

42. Cf. also the fact that, according to Harrell 1962, 206, Moroccan Arabic, with the numerals between 2 and 10 inclusive, has the possibility of a definite article within what corresponds to indefinite *two books*, and so on.

43. For example, Delfitto and Schroten (1991) suggest a link between bare plurals and postnominal number morphology, though as noted by Chierchia (1998, note 32) their proposal does not extend to mass nouns. Nor can the presence of (pronounced) suffix number morphology be a sufficient condition for licensing bare plurals, given the apparent absence of bare plurals in Genoese (Toso 1997, 66) and Pavese (Andrea Moro, personal communication). Déprez

(2005) argues that it is not a necessary condition for bare nominals, on the basis of various creole languages.

A reviewer makes the interesting suggestion that despite (apparent—cf. Bernstein 1997) complications in French it might be that (112) is also what underlies the absence of an overt definite article following prenominal demonstratives in Italian (vs. Greek; Holton et al. 1997, 97, 317), thinking of Giusti's (1993) and Brugè's (2002) analysis of demonstratives as raising to SpecDP.

Ultimately many other language families will need to be brought into the discussion in a systematic way.

44. And by plausible extension English indefinite bare plurals. Chomsky (2000, 139) argues against bare plurals having a semantically null D; that would lead to the (plausible) conclusion that the unpronounced definite D proposed here (like the one visible in French partitives) is not semantically null.

References

Alexiadou, A. 2003. "On Double Definiteness." In L.-O. Delsing, C. Falk, G. Josefsson, and H. A. Sigurdhsson, eds., *Grammar in Focus. Volume II. Festschrift for Christer Platzack*, 9–16. Department of Scandinavian Languages, Lund University, Sweden.

Alexiadou, A., and C. Wilder. 1998. "Adjectival Modification and Multiple Determiners." In A. Alexiadou and C. Wilder, eds., *Possessors, Predicates and Movement in the Determiner Phrase*, 305–332. Amsterdam: John Benjamins.

Anagnostopoulou, E. 1994. *Clitic Dependencies in Modern Greek*. Doctoral dissertation, Salzburg University, Austria.

Benincà, P. 1980. "Nomi senza articolo." *Rivista di grammatica generativa*, 5, 51–63.

Benincà, P., and C. Poletto. 2004. "Topic, Focus, and V2: Defining the CP Sublayers." In L. Rizzi, ed., *The Structure of CP and IP: The Cartography of Syntactic Structures*, vol. 2. New York: Oxford University Press.

Bernstein, J. 1997. "Demonstratives and Reinforcers in Romance and Germanic Languages." *Lingua*, 102, 87–113.

Bernstein, J. 2004. "English *th-* Forms." Handout of paper presented at the Copenhagen Symposium on Determination, August 26–28.

Bernstein, J., and C. Tortora. 2005. "Two Types of Possessive Forms in English." *Lingua*, 115, 1221–1242.

Bianchi, V. 1993. "An Empirical Contribution to the Study of Idiomatic Expressions." *Rivista di Linguistica*, 5, 349–385.

Bianchi, V. 1999. *Consequences of Antisymmetry: Headed Relative Clauses*. Berlin: Mouton de Gruyter.

Bošković, Z. 2002. "A-Movement and the EPP." *Syntax*, 5, 167–218.

Bouchard, D. 2003. "Les SN sans déterminant en français et en anglais." In P. Miller and A. Zribi-Hertz, eds., *Essais sur la grammaire comparée du français et de l'anglais*, 55–95. Saint-Denis: Presses Universitaires de Vincennes.

Brugè, L. 2002. "The Positions of Demonstratives in the Extended Nominal Projection." In G. Cinque, ed., *Functional Structure in DP and IP: The Cartography of Syntactic Structures*, vol. 1, 15–53. New York: Oxford University Press.

Campos, H., and M. Stavrou. 2004. "Polydefinite Constructions in Modern Greek and in Aromanian." In O. M. Tomic, ed., *Balkan Syntax and Semantics*, 137–173. Amsterdam: John Benjamins.

Cardinaletti, A. 1997. "Subjects and Clause Structure." In L. Haegeman, ed., *The New Comparative Syntax*, 33–63. London: Longman.

Chenal, A. 1986. *Le franco-provençal valdôtain*. Aoste: Musumeci.

Cheng, L. L.-S., and R. Sybesma. 1999. "Bare and Not-So-Bare Nouns and the Structure of NP." *Linguistic Inquiry*, 30, 509–542.

Cheng, L. L.-S., and R. Sybesma. 2005. "Classifiers in Four Varieties of Chinese." In G. Cinque and R. Kayne, eds., *Handbook of Comparative Syntax*, 259–292. New York: Oxford University Press.

Chierchia, G. 1998. "Reference to Kinds across Languages." *Natural Language Semantics*, 6, 339–405.

Chomsky, N. 2000. "Minimalist Inquiries: The Framework." In R. Martin, D. Michaels, and J. Uriagereka, eds., *Step by Step: Essays in Minimalist Syntax in Honor of Howard Lasnik*, 89–155. Cambridge, Mass.: MIT Press.

Chomsky, N. 2001. "Derivation by Phase." In M. Kenstowicz, ed., *Ken Hale: A Life in Language*, 1–52. Cambridge, Mass.: MIT Press.

Cinque, G. 1977. "The Movement Nature of Left Dislocation." *Linguistic Inquiry*, 8, 397–412.

Cinque, G. 1995. *Italian Syntax and Universal Grammar*. Cambridge: Cambridge University Press.

Cinque, G. 2005. "Deriving Greenberg's Universal 20 and Its Exceptions." *Linguistic Inquiry*, 36, 315–332.

Delfitto, D., and J. Schroten. 1991. "Bare Plurals and the Number Affix in DP." *Probus*, 3, 155–185.

Déprez, V. 2005. "Morphological Number, Semantic Number and Bare Nouns." *Lingua*, 115, 857–883.

Giorgi, A., and G. Longobardi. 1991. *The Syntax of Noun Phrases. Configuration, Parameters and Empty Categories*. Cambridge: Cambridge University Press.

Giusti, G. 1993. *La sintassi dei determinanti*. Padua: Unipress.

Grevisse, M. 1993. *Le bon usage*. 13th ed., by André Goosse. Duculot, Paris.

Gross, M. 1968. *Grammaire transformationnelle du français: Syntaxe du verbe*. Paris: Larousse.

Guéron, J. 1983. "L'emploi 'possessif' de l'article défini en français." *Langue Française*, 58, 23–35.

Harrell, R. S. 1962. *A Short Reference Grammar of Moroccan Arabic*. Washington, D.C.: Georgetown University Press.

Hendrick, R. 1990. "Operator Binding in NP." In A. Halperin, ed., *Proceedings of the Ninth West Coast Conference on Formal Linguistics*. Chicago: University of Chicago Press.

Holton, D., P. Mackridge, and I. Philippaki-Warburton. 1997. *Greek: A Comprehensive Grammar of the Modern Language*. London: Routledge.

Julien, M. 2002. *Syntactic Heads and Word Formation*. New York: Oxford University Press.

Kayne, R. S. 1975. *French Syntax: The Transformational Cycle*. Cambridge, Mass.: MIT Press.

Kayne, R. S. 1994. *The Antisymmetry of Syntax*. Cambridge, Mass.: MIT Press.

Kayne, R. S. 1998. "Overt vs. Covert Movement." *Syntax*, 1, 128–191. (Reprinted in R. S. Kayne, *Parameters and Universals*. New York: Oxford University Press, 2000.)

Kayne, R. S. 1999. "Prepositional Complementizers as Attractors." *Probus*, 11, 39–73. (Reprinted in R. S. Kayne, *Parameters and Universals*. New York: Oxford University Press, 2000.)

Kayne, R. S. 2000. *Parameters and Universals*. New York: Oxford University Press.

Kayne, R. S. 2002a. "Pronouns and Their Antecedents." In S. Epstein and D. Seely, eds., *Derivation and Explanation in the Minimalist Program*, 133–166. Malden, Mass.: Blackwell. (Reprinted in R. S. Kayne, *Movement and Silence*. New York: Oxford University Press, 2005.)

Kayne, R. S. 2002b. "On Some Prepositions That Look DP-internal: English *of* and French *de*." *Catalan Journal of Linguistics*, 1, 71–115. (Reprinted in R. S. Kayne, *Movement and Silence*. New York: Oxford University Press, 2005.)

Kayne, R. S. 2003. "Antisymmetry and Japanese." *English Linguistics*, 20, 1–40. (Reprinted in R. S. Kayne, *Movement and Silence*. New York: Oxford University Press, 2005.)

Kayne, R. S. 2004. "Here and There." In C. Leclère, E. Laporte, M. Piot, and M. Silberztein, eds., *Syntax, Lexis & Lexicon-Grammar: Papers in Honour of Maurice Gross*, 253–273. Amsterdam: John Benjamins. (Reprinted in R. S. Kayne, *Movement and Silence*. New York: Oxford University Press, 2005.)

Kayne, R. S. 2005a. "Some Notes on Comparative Syntax, with Special Reference to English and French." In G. Cinque and R. Kayne, eds., *Handbook of Comparative Syntax*, 3–69. New York: Oxford University Press. (Reprinted in R. S. Kayne, *Movement and Silence*. New York: Oxford University Press, 2005.)

Kayne, R. S. 2005b. "On the Syntax of Quantity in English." In R. S. Kayne, *Movement and Silence*. New York: Oxford University Press.

Kayne, R. S. 2005c. *Movement and Silence*. New York: Oxford University Press.

Koopman, H., and A. Szabolcsi. 2000. *Verbal Complexes*. Cambridge, Mass.: MIT Press.

Kornfilt, J. 1997. *Turkish*. London: Routledge.

Kuroda, S.-Y. 1968. "English Relativization and Certain Related Problems." *Language*, 44, 244–266. (Reprinted in D. A. Reibel, and S. A. Schane, eds., *Modern Studies in English*. Englewood Cliffs, N.J.: Prentice-Hall, 1969.)

Landau, I. 1999. "Possessor Raising and the Structure of VP." *Lingua*, 107, 1–37.

Longobardi, G. 1994. "Reference and Proper Names." *Linguistic Inquiry*, 25, 609–665.

Longobardi, G. 1996. "The Syntax of N-Raising: A Minimalist Theory." *OTS Working Papers*, Utrecht University.

Martinon, P. 1927. *Comment on parle en français*. Paris: Larousse.

Matushansky, O. 2003. "Is "The Best" Like "Good Enough"?" Handout of paper presented at the Journée syntaxe-acquisition, École Normale Supérieure, Paris, May 21.

Moshiri, L. 1988. *Colloquial Persian*. London: Routledge.

Nilsen, Ö. 2003. *Eliminating Positions: The Syntax and Semantics of Sentence Modification*. Doctoral dissertation, University of Utrecht.

Perlmutter, D. M. 1972. "Evidence for Shadow Pronouns in French Relativization." In P. M. Peranteau et al., eds., *The Chicago Which Hunt: Papers from the Relative Clause Festival*, 73–105. Chicago: Chicago Linguistic Society.

Pollock, J.-Y. 1998. "On the Syntax of Subnominal Clitics: Cliticization and Ellipsis." *Syntax*, 1, 300–330.

Rizzi, L. 2000. *Comparative Syntax and Language Acquisition*. London: Routledge.

Roodenburg, J. 2003. "Nouvelles remarques sur *de+s*." Unpublished ms., University of Amsterdam and University of Paris 8.

Roodenburg, J. 2004. "French Bare Arguments Are Not Extinct: The Case of Coordinated Bare Nouns." *Linguistic Inquiry*, 35, 301–313.

Schmitt, C., and A. Munn. 2002. "The Syntax and Semantics of Bare Arguments in Brazilian Portuguese." In P. Pica and J. Rooryck, eds., *Linguistic Variation Yearbook*, vol. 2, 185–216. Amsterdam: John Benjamins.

Spector, B. 2001. "Plural Indefinite DPs as PLURAL-Polarity Items." Abstract of paper presented at the Workshop on Determiners (Going Romance 2001), University of Amsterdam.

Sportiche, D. 1995. "Sketch of a Reductionist Approach to Syntactic Variation and Dependencies." In H. Campos and P. Kempchinsky, eds., *Evolution and Revolution in Linguistic Theory*, 356–398. Washington, D.C.: Georgetown University Press. (Reprinted in D. Sportiche, *Partitions and Atoms of Clause Structure: Subjects, Agreement, Case and Clitics*. London: Routledge, 1998.)

Sportiche, D. 2002. "Movement Types and Triggers." *GLOW Newsletter*, 48, 116–117.

Storto, G. 2001. "On the Status of the 'Partitive Determiner' in Italian." Abstract of paper presented at the Workshop on Determiners (Going Romance 2001), University of Amsterdam.

Svenonius, P. 2000. "Quantifier Movement in Icelandic." In P. Svenonius, ed., *The Derivation of VO and OV*, 255–292. Amsterdam: John Benjamins.

Szabolcsi, A. 1983. "The Possessor that Ran Away from Home." *Linguistic Review*, 3, 89–102.

Toso, F. 1997. *Grammatica del genovese—varietà urbana e di koinè*. Le Mani, Genoa.

Trudgill, P., and J. Hannah. 1994. *International English: A Guide to Varieties of Standard English*, 3rd ed. London: Edward Arnold.

Vergnaud, J.-R., and M. L. Zubizarreta. 1992. "The Definite Determiner and the Inalienable Constructions in French and in English." *Linguistic Inquiry*, 23, 595–652.

Zribi-Hertz, A. 2003. "La syntaxe de l'article défini: De la structure à l'interprétation." *Actes du colloque Modèles syntaxiques*, De Boeck/Duculot, Louvain.

Zribi-Hertz, A., and H. Glaude. 2003. "Bare NPs and Deficient DPs in Haitian and French: From Morphosyntax to Referent Construal." In M. Baptista and J. Guéron, eds., *Bare Nouns in Creole Languages*. Amsterdam: John Benjamins.

Zwart, J.-W. 2000. "A Head Raising Analysis of Relative Clauses in Dutch." In A. Alexiadou, P. Law, A. Meinunger, and C. Wilder, eds., *The Syntax of Relative Clauses*, 349–385. Amsterdam: John Benjamins.

II Phonology

13   Reduplication

Morris Halle

This chapter attempts to illustrate a formalism for expressing the main types of reduplication that have been noted in the languages of the world. The formalism is an amalgam of ideas in Raimy 2000 and Frampton 2004, with my own attempts to deal with various aspects of reduplication. Explaining the formalism and showing how it accounts for the three different kinds of reduplication that are now known turned out to require more text than I had originally expected. Because of the great length of this part of the study, the chapter does not include a critical discussion of my differences with Raimy and Frampton, or with many of the other studies of reduplication, including Marantz 1982, Broselow and McCarthy 1983, McCarthy and Prince 1986, Steriade 1988, McCarthy and Prince 1995, Hume 2004, Fitzpatrick and Nevins 2004, and Fitzpatrick 2004. It is my plan to deal with these matters in a separate study.

The most important conclusion of the present study is that there are three (and only three) kinds of reduplication: simple reduplication, partial reduplication, and augmented reduplication. Simple reduplication (discussed in section 13.1) involves the copying of a sequence of contiguous segments in a word. Partial and augmented reduplication (discussed in sections 13.2–13.3 and 13.4–13.6, respectively) are, basically, instances of simple reduplication with end corrections. Partial reduplication can be viewed as simple reduplication in which a terminal (beginning or end) subsequence is omitted, whereas augmented reduplication is simple reduplication with the pre- or postposing of a terminal subsequence of the reduplicated string.

To distinguish these three reduplications I make use of special junctures that are inserted into the segment sequence by readjustment rules. Since these junctures are formal objects that are beyond the interpretive capabilities of the machinery that runs the human vocal tract, these junctures have to be eliminated in the course of the derivation of the output sequence. The proposal below is that these uninterpretable elements are eliminated by special rules that also relinearize the segment sequence (rules (7), (20), and (45)). Although the relinearization rules are strikingly similar, I am unable at this point to express this similarity in an appropriate formal

way. One of the main aims of my further study of reduplication phenomena is to fill
this crucial gap.

13.1 About Reduplication

Like parts of a piece of music, parts of a word can be repeated, and this fact, called
reduplication in the technical literature, is used in languages the world over to signal
differences among grammatically related forms. Some examples of this process—
taken from Raimy 2000—are given in (1).

(1) a. *Mangyarrayi (p. 135)*

gabuji	g-ab-ab-uji	old person(s)
jimgan	j-img-img-an	knowledgeable one(s)
yirag	y-ir-ir-ag	father(s)
waŋgij	w-aŋg-aŋg-ij	child(ren)

   b. *Agta (pp. 127–128, stresses omitted)*

pusa	pus-pus-a	cat(s)
kaldiŋ	kal-kal-diŋ	goat(s)
jyanitor	jyan-jyan-itor	janitor(s)
takki	tak-tak-ki	leg(s)
uffu	uf-uf-fu	thigh(s)
bari	bar-bar-i	(my whole) body

In Mangyarrayi (1a) the plural is signaled by repeating the substring beginning with
the vowel of the first syllable and ending with the consonant(s) preceding the vowel
of the second syllable. In Agta (1b) the plural is signaled by repeating the substring
that starts at the beginning of the word and ends with the consonant that follows the
first vowel of the word. What is especially noteworthy in the examples in (1) is that
the repeated material is always a contiguous subsequence; except for being contiguous, however, the substrings do not possess well-recognized linguistic properties. For
example, in both sets of examples in (1), the substrings are not coextensive with
either the morphemes or the syllables that make up the word.

It is assumed below that words and morphemes are sequences of discrete segments
(phonemes) and that each segment is a complex of distinctive features. Following the
widely accepted practice introduced in Goldsmith 1976, the phonetic features of a
segment are formally distinguished here from its timing slot. This is illustrated in (2)
with the Agta word /bari/ 'body'.

(2) Feature complexes   b   a   r   i

                      | | | |

     Timing slots x_1 x_2 x_3 x_4

Each of the letters in the top line of (2) stands for a complex of features, whose internal structure will not be further analyzed here. As indicated in (2), the x's in the bottom line stand for the timing slots to which the feature complexes in the top line are linked.

It is widely assumed in phonology, usually without discussion, that segments are concatenated into sequences, and this fact is reflected in the left-to-right order of the letters that represent the segments in the usual phonological representation. Hence a sequence such as /kæt/ is not identical to the sequence /tæk/, although the two sequences are composed of the same segments. To make explicit the conventions that distinguish /tæk/ from /kæt/ Raimy 2000 introduces a formal device for concatenating two segments in a sequence. This device is represented here by an arrow, and the notation "a → b" means "a precedes b." In this notation, the string /b → a → r → i/ differs from the strings /i → b → r → a/ or /b → r → i → a/, and so on, in the obvious way. Implicit in representation (2) is the assumption that the concatenators are placed not between consecutive feature complexes but rather between their timing slots.

In the familiar phonological transcription, a given segment is preceded and/or followed by at most one other segment. In the formalism illustrated in (2), this means that the timing slot linked to a given feature complex can have no more than two concatenators: one on its left and the other on its right. This restriction is, of course, quite natural for surface representations of speech events because the vocal tract—the machinery that humans with intact hearing use for producing the acoustic speech signal—is so constructed that it can pronounce only one phoneme at a time. While this restriction must hold of the output representations of the phonology, that is, of the representation that the vocal tract uses to articulate the words, there is no reason to suppose that this restriction must also hold of representations other than the surface representation—in particular, of the representations that figure in the internal (mental) computations of the output string.

Raimy's crucial innovation was to admit phonological representations where a phoneme has more than the two concatenators in (2). Specifically, Raimy admits phonological representations that, in addition to the "linear" concatenators in (2), also include what might be called "extralinear" concatenators, illustrated in (3).

(3)   b   a   r   i
      | | | |
      x_1 → x_2 → x_3 → x_4

The extralinear concatenator shown below the sequence of timing slots in (3), which Raimy has called LOOP, has a direction opposite that of the linear concatenators.

As noted, such extralinear concatenators cannot appear in the surface representation—that is, in the bottom line of the computation—because the human speech machinery (our lips, tongue, velum, glottis, and so on) cannot handle representations where a given segment is followed (or preceded) by more than one other segment. As noted, however, this restriction does not apply to the representations at other stages in the computation of an utterance, and Raimy's work has demonstrated the utility of this enrichment of the phonological notation.

The existence of uninterpretable elements in intermediate representations raises the question of how such uninterpretable elements are removed from the representation. The answer adopted here, following Raimy's and Frampton's lead, is that such uninterpretable elements are removed at the same time that the string is relinearized. Specifically, to remove the uninterpretable LOOP it is necessary to produce two copies of the string delimited by the LOOP. This is illustrated in (4).

(4) b   a   r   i   b   a   r   b   a   r   i
     | | | | >>>> | | | | | | |
     $x_1 \rightarrow x_2 \rightarrow x_3 \rightarrow x_4$ $x_1 \rightarrow x_2 \rightarrow x_3 \rightarrow x_1 \rightarrow x_2 \rightarrow x_3 \rightarrow x_4$

The *relinearization* rule responsible for the transformation in (4) is of the form (5).

(5) $x_1 \rightarrow x_2 \rightarrow \cdots x_{n-1} \rightarrow x_n \ggg x_1 \rightarrow x_2 \rightarrow \cdots x_{n-1} \rightarrow x_2 \rightarrow \cdots x_{n-1} \rightarrow x_n$

Rule (5) is the device made available by Universal Grammar (UG)—the human language capacity—to ensure that the sequences in the output of the phonology include no uninterpretable configurations. Rule (5) converts an "unreadable" sequence on its left into the one on its right that is fully legible by the output device. It is the particular way in which the uninterpretable LOOP concatenator is eliminated by the relinearization rule (5)—that is, by repeating (copying) the subsequence enclosed by the LOOP—that makes the LOOP a suitable notation for reduplication.[1] It is shown below that (5) is ordered with respect to particular phonological rules and also with respect to other relinearization rules. Additional relinearization rules are given below (see (20) and (45)).

The graphic means employed to this point to represent concatenators of various sorts have resulted in sequences of considerable typographic complexity. To simplify the representations and to make them clearer, I have replaced Raimy's concatenators and LOOPs utilized above with a set of junctures, following here in many respects the lead of Frampton 2004. Specifically, below I have systematically omitted the linear concatenators and reflected the order of elements by their left-to-right position in the line. The extralinear LOOP concatenator was represented above by an arrow pointing in a direction opposite that of the linear concatenators. All LOOPs share this property of pointing in a direction opposite that of the linear concatenators. LOOPs differ from one another in where they begin and where they end. These terminal points can be marked by a pair of junctures inserted into the sequence at appropriate points. I have chosen to use square brackets ([,]) to mark the terminal points of the LOOPs. Given these conventions, the representation in (4), reproduced on the left-hand side of (6), can be replaced by the one on the right-hand side of (6).

(6) b   a   r   i   b a r i
   | | | | | | | |
   $x_1 \rightarrow x_2 \rightarrow x_3 \rightarrow x_4$ $[x_1\ x_2\ x_3]\ x_4$

In (7) I have restated the relinearization rule (5) in the junctural notation.

(7) $x_1\ [x_2 \ldots x_{n-1}]\ x_n\ \ggg\ x_1\ x_2 \ldots x_{n-1}\ x_2 \ldots x_{n-1}\ x_n$

In both sets of examples in (1) there is no reduplication in the singular; in Mangyarrayi and Agta reduplication serves to signal the plural of the different words. This implies that there are no junctures in the singular form of these nouns, and that the junctures are inserted by special readjustment rules. Specifically, it is supposed here that in both Mangyarrayi and Agta, the exponent of the plural morpheme is phonetic zero, but that notwithstanding its lack of phonetic substance, the plural morpheme in both languages triggers readjustment rules that insert square-bracket junctures (i.e., our notational equivalents of Raimy's LOOPs) into the underlying junctureless segment sequence of the stems when these are in construction with a plural morpheme. The effects of the readjustment rules of the two languages are illustrated in (8), with some forms from (1).

(8) a. g a b u j i   j i m g a n   Mangyarrayi
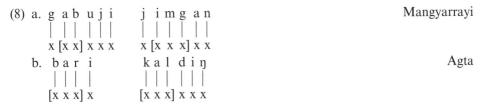
     x [x x] x x x   x [x x x] x x
  b. b a r i   k a l d i ŋ   Agta
     [x x x] x   [x x x] x x x

The readjustment rules for the plurals in Mangyarrayi and Agta respectively are stated in (9).[2]

(9) a. *Mangyarrayi (1a)*
    i. Insert a [juncture to the left of the timing slot linked to the first vowel of the word.
    ii. Insert a] juncture to the right of the timing slot linked to the consonant directly preceding the second vowel of the word.
  b. *Agta (1b)*
    i. Insert a [juncture to the left of the first timing slot of the word.
    ii. Insert a] juncture to the right of the timing slot linked to the consonant directly following the first vowel of the word.

It is worth noting at this point that segment length is not one of the phonetic features in the universal set. Vowel length and consonant gemination are expressed formally by linking a feature bundle to two consecutive timing slots. This fact explains why in Agta geminate consonants in the underlying representation appear ungeminated in reduplicated forms. By inserting a] juncture after the timing slot following the first vowel in the word, rule (9bii) ensures that an ungeminated consonant will appear in the output. This is shown in (10).

(10) Feature complexes

Timing slots

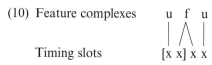

The relinearization rule (7) applies to (10) and converts it into (11), from which the square-bracket junctures, which are illegible to the output device, have been removed by relinearization.[3]

(11) Feature complexes

Timing slots

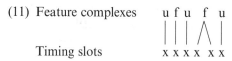

The output form (11) is atypical in that in (11) it is possible to determine that the initial two timing slots are the result of relinearization. This is generally not the case. As illustrated in (4) with the Agta example *barbari* 'my whole body' (which is a plural and therefore subject to reduplication), elimination of the square-bracket junctures makes it impossible to detect which of the repeated substrings represents the original bracketed sequence ("the base") and which is the one generated by the rule ("the reduplicant"). This distinction between base and reduplicant, which is central in many theories of reduplication, plays no role in any of the examples below and, as far as I know, is not needed in order to account for reduplication and similar processes elsewhere. The theory developed here thus has fewer means to characterize the data, yet, as shown below, produces adequate accounts of all relevant facts. I take this outcome as support for the theory of this study.

In most cases discussed below the timing slots are copied together with the feature complexes to which they are linked. In these representations the distinction between timing slot and the features linked to it can be eliminated without the representations losing any of their perspicuity. The simplified representations in (12), where each of the alphabetic letters is assumed to stand both for a feature complex and for its associated timing slot, therefore commonly appear in place of the more complex representations in (8).

(12) a. g[a b] u j i   j [i m g] a n
     b. [b a r] i   [k a l] d i ŋ

13.2 Partial Reduplication

The examples reviewed to this point were all cases of full reduplication, where a contiguous substring of a phoneme sequence was repeated. In intermediate representations fully reduplicated strings are delimited by pairs of square-bracket junctures of opposite direction, as shown on the left in (13). The surface string on the right is then generated by relinearization rule (7).

(13) A[BCD]E >>>> A-BCD-BCD-E

In addition to full reduplication, there exist, as noted, also partial reduplication and augmented reduplication. The latter share in common the fact that they are instances of full reduplication, with modifications that affect terminal substrings in the fully reduplicated sequence.

In partial reduplication, illustrated in (14), a terminal (initial or final) subsequence of the fully reduplicated string is deleted. In intermediate representations the deleted subsequence is delimited by an angle-bracket juncture that is paired with the square bracket of opposite direction at the end of the reduplicated string. Special relinearization rules to be discussed below generate the surface string shown on the right.

(14) A[B>CD]E >>>> A-CD-BCD-E
     A[B<CD]E >>>> A-BCD-B-E

In the case of augmented reduplication, which is discussed in sections 13.4 through 13.6, a terminal subsequence is repeated outside the reduplicated string, as shown in (15), where in the intermediate representations on the left the repeated subsequence is delimited by a square-bracket juncture in boldface paired with the square bracket of opposite direction at the end of the reduplicated string.

(15) A[B]CD]E >>>> A-B-BCD-BCD-E
     A[B[CD]E >>>> A-BCD-BCD-CD-E

The readjustment rules (see (9)) that insert the different kinds of juncture responsible for reduplications are subject to the prohibition in (16).

(16) Between a juncture internal to a reduplicated string and the square-bracket
     juncture of opposite direction that terminates the reduplicated string, there
     may be no intervening juncture of the same direction as the terminal juncture.

The restriction (16) rules out intermediate representations such as those in (17a), while allowing those in (17b).

(17) a. A[B<C>D]E   A[B[C]D]E   A[B<C]D]E
    b. A[B]C>D]E   A[BC>[D]E

In this and the following section I focus on partial reduplications, where only a part of the original string is reduplicated. I begin the discussion with the two cases in (18): those in (18a) are examples of reduplication in the plural formation of certain nouns and of a class of adverbs in Madurese from Marantz 1982, while those in (18b) are examples of intensive or pejorative verb formation in Levantine Arabic from Broselow and McCarthy 1983.

(18) a. *Madurese*

estre	tre-estre-an	'wives'
buwa?	wa?-buwa?-an	'fruits'
maen	en-maen-an	'toys'
garadus	dus-garadus	'fast and sloppy'

    b. *Levantine Arabic*

barad	bar-ba-d	'shaved unevenly'
marat	mar-ma-t	'cut unevenly'
laff	laf-la-f	'wrapped (intensive)'
hall	hal-ha-l	'untied, undid'

In the examples in (18a) from Madurese, reduplication is triggered by the noun plural suffix /-an/ as well as by the adverb-forming morpheme whose exponent is phonetic zero. The reduplication does not result in the entire stem /garadus/ 'fast' being copied; instead, only the *final* syllable /dus/ is copied, and the copied syllable appears *before* the base sequence. Similarly, in the Arabic examples in (18b), again, not the entire initial CVCV or CVC portion of the stem is copied, but only its *initial* CV part, and here the reduplicated substring appears *after* the initial CVC. In summary, in partial reduplication an abstract sequence ABC becomes either BC-ABC or ABC-AB. Significantly, it is always a terminal—initial or final—subsequence that is missing from the reduplicated form. It is as though the terminal subsequences were deleted from the fully reduplicated string (i.e., A̸BC-ABC or ABC-AB̸C̸).

To deal with partial reduplications of this kind, a new type of juncture is introduced. These new junctures, which are the counterpart of Raimy's JUMP concatenators, are represented below by angle brackets, and they are subject to further restrictions. First, an angle bracket may appear only inside a substring marked for reduplication (i.e., inside a substring delimited by a pair of square brackets). Second, an angle bracket is always paired with the nearest square-bracket juncture of opposite direction. In particular, a right angle bracket is paired with the nearest left square bracket, and a left angle bracket is paired with the nearest right square bracket. This is shown in (19) with two examples from (18).

(19) a. [gara>dus] >>> dus-garadus
    b. [b<ar]ad >>> bar-b-ad

The relinearization rules for strings containing angle brackets are given in (20).

(20) a. x_1 [x_2 x_3> x_4] x_5 >>> x_1 − x_4 x_2 x_3 x_4 − x_5

   b. x_1 [x_2 <x_3 x_4] x_5 >>> x_1 − x_2 x_3 x_4 x_2 − x_5

As suggested in Harris and Halle 2005, a good way of visualizing partial reduplication is to view it as a two-step procedure: in the first step the string delimited by the (external) square brackets is copied in its entirety, and in the second step the substring delimited by the angle bracket is deleted. This is illustrated in (21).

(21) a. x_1 [x_2 x_3> x_4] x_5 >>> x_1 − x_2 x_3 x_4 − x_2 x_3 x_4 − x_5 >>> x_1 x̶₂ x̶₃ x_4 x_2 x_3 x_4 x_5

   b. x_1 [x_2 <x_3 x_4] x_5 >>> x_1 − x_2 x_3 x_4 − x_2 x_3 x_4 − x_5 >>> x_1 x_2 x_3 x_4 x_2 x̶₃ x̶₄ x_5

In the enriched notation just introduced, the facts from Madurese in (18a) are the result of the readjustment rules (22a), and their effects are illustrated in (22b).

(22) a. i. Insert a] juncture to the right of the (timing slot linked to the) last stem segment.

   ii. Insert a [juncture to the left of the (timing slot linked to the) first stem segment.

   iii. Insert a > juncture to the right of the (timing slot linked to the) onset of the last stem syllable.

   b. [g a r a> d u s] >>> g̶a̶r̶a̶ d u s g a r a d u s /dus-garadus/
      [m a>e n] − an >>> m̶a̶en-maen-an /en-ma-en-an/

The Levantine Arabic examples are accounted for by the readjustment rules in (23a), with the effects illustrated in (23b). These rules are triggered by a special intensive/pejorative affix (represented in (23b) as I/P), which is adjoined to the stem in the morphology. Because its phonetic exponent is zero, it does not appear in the output, but the morpheme triggers the rules in (23a).

(23) a. i. Insert a [juncture to the left of (the timing slot linked to) the first stem segment.

   ii. Insert a] juncture to the right of (the timing slot linked to) the penultimate stem consonant.

   iii. Insert a < juncture to the left of (the timing slot linked to) the penultimate stem vowel, and, in the absence of such a vowel, to the penultimate stem consonant.

   b. barad − I/P >>> [b <a r] a d >>> bar-b̶a̶r̶-ad /bar-b-ad/
      laff − I/P >>> [l a <f] f >>> laf-laf̶-f /laf-la-f/

13.2.1 The Perfect in Attic Greek and a Note on Kolami Echo Words

An interesting example of partial reduplication is the perfect formation in Attic Greek, as discussed in Steriade 1982, 195–208, which is also the source of the

examples in (24). Steriade remarks that "the perfect reduplication pattern breaks up
into four subclasses" as shown in (24). The sets in (24a–b) illustrate the perfect of
consonant-initial verbs, whereas those in (24c–d) show the perfect of vowel-initial
verbs.

(24) a. sper   e-sper-m-ai   'sow'
        strep^h   e-strop^h-a   'turn'
        kten   e-kton-a   'kill'
        gno: e-gno:-k-a   'know'
        blasta   e-blaste-k-a   'sprout'
     b. lu: le-lu:-k-a   'untie'
        klep   ke-klop^h-a   'steal'
        tla: te-tla-men   'endure'
        pneu   pe-pneu-k-a   'breathe'
        grap^h   ge-grap^h-a   'write'
        bri:t^h   be-bri:t^h-a   'be heavy'
     c. angel   a:ngel-k-a   'announce'
        et^hel   e:t^hele:-k-a   'want'
        op^hel   o:p^he:le:-k-a   'owe'
     d. od   odo:d-a   'smell'
        ager   aga:ger-k-a   'collect'
        eger   ege:ger-m-ai   'awaken'

As (24a) shows, in certain consonant-initial verbs the perfect stem takes the /e/ prefix, which in Greek grammars is known as the Perfect Augment. In a second class of
consonant-initial verbs, shown in (24b), the perfect stem is formed by reduplication
of the first stem consonant and infixation of the /e/. Thus the perfect everywhere is
marked by the /e/ augment, but the verbs in (24b) are subject, in addition, to /e/
infixation, which, as shown below, is a simple case of partial reduplication. Verbs of
the latter class are therefore subject to a readjustment rule, which inserts the junctures shown in (25b).

(25) a. e-sperm-ai   e-kton-a
     b. [e>-l] u: -k-a   >>>>> ∅ – lelu: -k-a
        [e> – p]neu-k-a >>>>> ∅ – pepneu-k-a

Steriade 1982 argued that the difference between the two sets of consonant-initial
stems is phonetically predictable: stems beginning with a single consonant and those
beginning with a [voiceless stop] + sonorant and [voiced stop] + /r/ undergo reduplication, whereas stems beginning with other consonant clusters do not. She connected
this fact with the Greek syllabification of word-initial consonant clusters and found

supporting evidence for this in the treatment of verbs with stem-initial /bl/ and /gl/ of which many have perfect forms with or without reduplication. According to Steriade, the word-initial clusters of these verbs are ambiguous metrically in Greek poetry, suggesting that before /l/ the initial voiced stop may or may not have been syllabified as a syllable onset. Generalizing this to the treatment of /gl/- and /bl/-initial verbs, Steriade proposed that the /e/ augment undergoes partial reduplication in verbs where the consonant is in the onset of the syllable following the /e/ augment, but not where the consonant and /e/ are tautosyllabic.

The readjustment rules for the Greek perfect are given in (26a) and their effects are illustrated in (26b).

(26) a. i. Insert a [juncture before (the first timing slot of) the augment.
     ii. Insert a] juncture after (the timing slot linked to) the first consonant of the root, provided that augment and stem consonant are heterosyllabic.
     iii. Insert a > juncture after (the timing slot linked to) the augment /e/.

   b. e – (V)C X >>>> [e > – (V) C] X^4

To account for the perfect forms of the vowel-initial verbs in (24c,d), we need to add the well-supported assumption that Attic Greek is subject to a phonological rule that replaces a sequence /e+V/ by a long version of the second vowel, as shown in (27).

$$(27) \quad e - [-\text{cons}] >>>>> [-\text{cons}]$$

$$
\begin{array}{cccc}
| & [+\text{son}] & & [+\text{son}] \\
| & | & & \wedge \\
x_1 & x_2 & x_1 & x_2
\end{array}
$$

Rule (27) accounts for what Sihler (1995, 485) has called the "quantitative augment." According to Sihler, this augment "entailed the lengthening of a word-initial vowel. It arose by imitation of paradigms in which the usual augment *e-* contracted with the initial vowel of the root (or a laryngeal) to make the corresponding long vowel."

The vowel-lengthening rule (27) alone accounts for the forms in (24c). It clearly fails to account for the behavior of the vowel-initial verbs in (24d). The forms in (24d), however, need no additional machinery beyond that introduced above, for they fall out directly once it is seen that, like the verbs in (24b), the verbs in (24d) are subject to partial reduplication due to the application of the readjustment rules (26a). This is shown in (28).

(28) [e> -od] -a >>> od-e-od-a >>>> od-o:d-a
    [e> -ag] er-k-a >>> ag-e-ager-k-a >>> ag-a:ger-k-a

In sum, the /e/ augment is the exponent of the perfect in all Greek verbs, with a subset of these undergoing partial reduplication in (26a). The surface effects of partial reduplication in consonant-initial stems are strikingly different from the surface effects in vowel-initial verbs, but that is fully accounted for by (26a) and (27).[5]

There is thus a single unified treatment of the augment in Greek for both vowel-initial and consonant-initial verbs. This result, however, is available only if the facts are represented in the notation that has been introduced here; without this notation, the result is not expressible or even conceivable, and one is forced to adopt unhelpful, opaque accounts like that of Sihler 1995, 488–489. The unified account of the Greek augment above thus provides important empirical support for the theory introduced here.

I conclude this section with a brief look at the echo words in Kolami (29a), a case of partial reduplication that is the mirror image of the Greek augment, and was also discussed by Steriade 1988, 89. Whereas in Greek the augment is a prefix that is partially reduplicated, in Kolami it is a suffix, the echo suffix /gi/, that is subject to partial reduplication. I have stated the Kolami readjustment rules in (29b) and have illustrated their effects in (29c) with two of the examples from (29a).

(29) a. pal   pal-gi-l   'tooth'
         kota   kota-gi-ta   'bring it'
         iir   iir-gi-ir   'water'
         maasur   maasur-gii-sur   'men'
         saa   saa-gii   'go' (cont. ger.)

  b. i.   Insert a < juncture before the suffix /g i/
      ii. Insert a [juncture after the first timing slot linked to a vowel
      iii. Insert a] juncture at the end of the word

  c.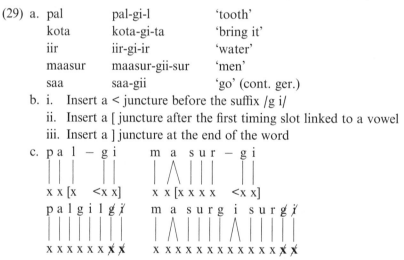

As shown in (29c), in Kolami it is necessary to make explicit the fact that reduplication junctures are inserted on the tier of timing slots rather than among the feature complexes of the segments. Like the reduplication in Greek, that of Kolami affects a contiguous sequence of timing slots. In Greek the string consisted of the augment plus timing slots of the stem up to and including the first consonant; in Kolami the affected string is the suffix plus the timing slots preceding it, up to (but not including) the first vowel slot of the stem. In both languages the affix appears only once in the output (and hence is delimited by an angle-bracket juncture).[6]

13.3 Metathesis

As the examples in section 13.2 showed, a string of the form AB can be subject to partial reduplication of two kinds, for in a string AB either A or B may undergo partial reduplication:

[A > B] >>> BAB   [A < B] >>> ABA

In the former case, exemplified by the Greek augment, the output is of the form BAB; in the latter, that of the Kolami echo words, the output is of the form ABA. The question to be investigated next is what output is produced by a string where both A and B are subject to partial reduplication. Such a sequence is subject to both relinearization rules (20a) and (20b), and, as shown in (30), this produces as output the sequence BA.

(30) [A> <B] >>> A̸BAB̸ >>> BA

This is a result of the greatest interest because it shows that implicit in the notation for partial reduplication is also a treatment of metathesis, a widely attested phonological process. As observed by Hume (2004, 204), there is at this time "no unified, explanatory account of why metathesis occurs, why it favors certain sound combinations and why we obtain the outputs that we do." In this section I show that Hume's questions are answered by the theory developed here.

The first thing to be noted about metathesis is that it affects contiguous sequences of segments and never involves noncontiguous sequences.[7] Thus, while there are metathesis operations with the effect of AB >> BA or AB-C >>> C-AB or A-BC >>> BC-A, there are no instances of metathesis of the form ABC >>> CBA (setting aside the special cases mentioned in note 7). This follows directly from the notation. As mentioned earlier, angle brackets can be inserted only inside a sequence enclosed in square brackets. As a result, the only well-formed sequences of a sequence ABC containing a pair of angle brackets are those in (31), and as shown there, none of the three results in the output CBA.

(31) a. [A> <BC] >>> A̸BC-AB̸C̸ >>> BC-A
     b. [AB> <C] >>> A̸B̸C-ABC̸ >>> C-AB
     c. [A> B <C] >>> A̸BC-AB̸C̸ >>> BC-AB

(31c) is of particular relevance, for it shows that when a pair of angle brackets are inserted between elements that are not contiguous, the result is something other than metathesis.

Many of the examples cited by Hume are triggered by loss of an intermediate element. This is true of her examples from Balangao (1), Hungarian (2), Basaa (4), Udi (10), Elmolo (9), and Hixkaryana (28). The obvious reason for this correlation is that deletion in these cases generates the required contiguity of the elements without which metathesis cannot occur. Although contiguous subsequences of segments figure in almost every metathesis example in Hume's paper, this striking fact is not even mentioned.

As illustrated in (31a,b), a subsequence of two (or more) elements may metathesize with a single elements. An example of this type in Hume's paper is that of the Mutsun plural suffix /mak/ in (15) (p. 224), which surfaces as /kma/ after stems ending with a vowel. By contrast, the locative suffix /tak/ surfaces—in the same context—as /tka/. These differences are accounted for by positing for these two suffixes the slightly different readjustment rules shown in (32).

(32) a. [m a><k] >>> k-ma
     b. t [a><k] >>> t-k-a

On the account proposed here, metathesis is a special case of partial reduplication. A well-known example that also supports this consequence is the treatment of vowel-liquid sequences in the Slavic languages. A strong tendency, to which all Slavic languages were subject at one stage in their history, is the replacement of closed syllables with open syllables. One aspect of this general development was the replacement of word-medial midvowel + liquid rimes. As shown in (33), in Russian (and other East Slavic languages) these closed syllables were converted into open syllables by partial reduplication (termed pleophony, Russ. *polnoglasie* in the handbooks), while elsewhere (e.g., in Polish) the rimes were subject to metathesis. (For more discussion, see Bräuer 1961, 78ff.)

(33) IE *berz-a   Russ. berez-a   Pol. brzoz-a   'birch'
       IE *golv-a   Russ. golov-a   Pol. głow-a   'head'
       IE *gʰord   Russ. gorod   Pol. grod   'town'
       IE *vols   Russ. volos   Pol. włos   'hair'

In the present formalism the two rules have the respective forms in (34), where C stands for consonant, V for [−high] vowel, and R for liquid.[8]

(34) a. Pleophony C [V <R] C X >>> C V R V C X   East Slavic
     b. Metathesis C [V > < R] C X >>> C R V C X   South/West Slavic

The historical relatedness of these development is reflected in the obvious similarity of the notations in (34a) and (34b).[9]

13.3.1 Kaingang

A particularly instructive example of the relation between total and partial reduplication is provided by the plural formation of Kaingang, as discussed by Steriade 1988 on the basis of data in Wiesemann 1972.[10] In Kaingang, the plural is signaled in a variety of ways—in particular, by final-syllable reduplication (35a), insertion of /g/ in the penultimate rime (35b), and raising of penultimate vowel to [+hi] (35c). Each of these three changes alone is a sufficient signal of the plural, but a given change may also co-occur with one or both of the other changes. Thus, penult /g/ insertion may co-occur with penult V raising, as shown in (35d); or reduplication may co-occur with /g/ insertion as shown in (35e), or with penult raising, as shown in (35f); and all three of these stem changes may co-occur, as shown in (35g). At the end of each set of examples in (35) I have given the formula for the type of reduplication the set undergoes.

(35) a. *Final-syllable reduplication*

kry	kry-kry	'irritate'	
jengag	jengag-gag	'roasted meat'	jen[gag]

    b. */g/ insertion*

kavi	ka-g-vi	'stretch'	
juryn	ju-g-ryn	'sharpen'	ju[ryn><-g]

    c. *Penult V raising*

kagje	kygje[11]	'knot'

    d. *Raising and /g/ insertion*

jakajen	jaky-g-jen	'turn, twist'	
pafam	py-g-fam	'quiet'	
pefam	pi-g-fam	'quiet'	pe[fam><-g]

    e. *Reduplication and /g/ insertion*

ne	ne-g-ne	'bury'	
tav	ta-g-tav[12]	'turned'	[tav<-g]

    f. *Reduplication and penult V raising*

gon	gun-gon	'swallow'	
ʔog	ʔug-ʔog	'drink'	[ʔog]

    g. *Reduplication, /g/ insertion, and penult V raising*

tav	ty-g-tav	'turned'	
tam	ty-g-tam	'cover'	
pov	pu-g-pov	'divided'	
kavej	kavi-g-vej	'dirty'	ka[vej><-g]

I assume that in Kaingang the plural has two exponents: /g/ and zero, and both of these exponents may trigger reduplication and/or penult V raising. If /g/ is chosen as plural exponent it automatically triggers the readjustment rules in (36d), which as shown in (38) produces Penult /g/ insertion

(36) a. Insert] at the end of the word—that is, after the /g/ exponent of the plural.

    b. Insert [before the onset of the last syllable.

c. Insert < before the /g/ exponent of the plural.
d. Insert > before < (optional).

After relinearization the sequences are subject to the phonological rules of the language, among which the two rules in (37) are of special importance.

(37) a. V >>> [+high] in env. ____ σ ## penult raising (opt).
b. Glides are deleted in env. ____ C.

In the derivations in (38) I have shown the effects of applying these rules to some of the plural forms cited in (35). In the derivations below, the top line shows the underlying form, where the plural exponent is ∅ (phonetic null) in /jengag/, but /g/ elsewhere. The different rules are listed on the left, and the abbreviation "dna" means that the rule does not apply.

(38)	jengag	tav-g	kavej-g	kavi-g	pafam-g
(36)	jen[gag]	[tav<-g]	ka[vej<-g]	ka[vi><-g]	pa[fam><-g]
(20)	jengag-gag	tav-g-tav	kavej-g-vej	ka-g-vi	pa-g-fam
(37a)	dna	ta-g-tav	kave-g-vej	dna	dna
(37b)	dna	dna	kavi-g-vej	dna	py-g-fam
	'roasted meat'	'turned'	'dirty'	'stretch'	'quiet'
	(35a)	(35e)	(35g)	(35b)	(35d)

In all examples in (38) the plural morpheme /g/ is infixed before the last stem syllable. In the second and third examples there is partial reduplication, whereas in the fourth and fifth examples there is metathesis. Formally the difference between these two sets of forms results from the absence versus presence of a right angle bracket inserted by the optional application of rule (36d). The perspicuous character of the derivations must be taken as empirical support for the notations introduced above and for the theory that underpins them.

13.4 Augmented Reduplication in Tigre with a Digression on Tigre Syllabification

The intricate facts of Tigre reduplication discussed in this section indicate the need for further enrichment of the theoretical machinery. In Rose 2003, my main source of Tigre data, all verbal forms are cited in the third-person masculine perfective (see her note 1). Most of her examples therefore end with the phonetic exponent of this suffix, short or long /a/. Because this suffix plays no role in what follows, I have systematically omitted it in the forms I cite. Moreover, in citing Tigre forms below I have also omitted surface syllabification and have given the forms without the many schwa vowels that appear in Rose's paper. These schwa vowels are inserted by the syllabification algorithm discussed in section 13.4.1, which while straightforward, is intricate in a way that seems worth the digression below.

13.4.1 Digression on Tigre Syllabification

The most important fact about surface forms of Tigre words is that the appearance of (most) schwas in surface strings is readily predictable from a metrical analysis of schwaless strings, utilizing to this end the theory of footing of Idsardi 1992, 2004. The utility of the Idsardi formalism for purposes of the computation of word stress has been documented in a series of papers, some of which are listed in the references to Halle and Idsardi 2000. The Idsardi formalism has been shown by Purnell 1997 to serve correctly for the computation of the tone contours of words in many tone languages in Africa and elsewhere. The analysis in this section is one of the first to show that footing and metrical structure of the Idsardi theory also account for complicated facts of syllabification.

The sequences of timing slots that constitute words are grouped into feet and then syllabified by means of the rules in (39). The insertion of parentheses into a sequence of timing slots divides the sequence into feet; in particular, a left parenthesis foots all elements on its right, and a right parenthesis foots all elements on its left. The feet are thus defined by single unpaired parentheses. Timing slots that are neither to the right of a left parenthesis nor to the left of a right parenthesis remain unfooted. Each foot has a head, which is either its leftmost or its rightmost element.

(39) a. Insert a right parenthesis **)** (boldface) juncture after a timing slot projecting from a vowel.[13]

    b. Insert right parentheses) iteratively from left to right, starting at the left edge and skipping two timing slots after each insertion. (No insertion between the timing slots of a long vowel.) Feet are left-headed.

    c. Insert /ə/ (schwa) after the head of a foot if no vowel follows the head.

I have illustrated the application of these rules in the syllabification of Tigre words in (40a).

(40) a.   ktb   >>> kt)b   >>> kət)b   'write'
         mssl   >>> ms)sl)   >>> məs)səl)   'resemble'
         ma:sl   >>> ma:)sl)   >>> ma:)səl)   'be diplomatic'
         dna:gs >>> dn)a:)gs) >>> dən)a:)gəs) 'become scared'
         kta:tb >>> kt)a:)tb) >>> kət)a:)təb) 'write a little'

    b.   gfr-ko 'I whipped' >>> g)fr-ko) >>> gə)fər)-ko)
         But gfr-a:'he whipped' >>> gf)r-a:)   >>> gəf)r-a:)
         dnga:gs 'become a little scared' >>> d)ng)a:)gs) >>> də)nəg)a:)gəs)

The footing of the forms in (40b) does not follow directly from the rules in (39). To obtain the footings in (40b) it is necessary to posit an additional rule, which like (39a) is ordered before (39b). This rule inserts a right parenthesis *after* the leftmost timing slot. I have represented this juncture, like the junctures inserted by rule (39a), with a boldface parenthesis. According to Rose (2003, 110, note 2), this additional rule is needed to handle forms with consonant-initial suffixes; it therefore does not apply in /gəfr-a:/ 'he whipped', where the suffix begins with a vowel. As the last example in (40b) shows, this special rule also applies to some forms without consonant-initial suffix, but my understanding of Tigre phonology is too rudimentary to propose a plausible formulation of the extended rule.[14]

Since the rules in (39), supplemented by the rule in the paragraph above, account for all schwas in Tigre words, schwas have been omitted in the transcriptions of Tigre words below. This makes it possible to state the various reduplication and metathesis processes of Tigre in their most perspicuous form, especially since schwa insertion applies to the outputs of the reduplication and metathesis processes discussed below.

13.4.2 Tigre Reduplications

Setting aside the semantic/morphological functions of the different verb forms in which they figure, Tigre stems are of three basic types, which, following Rose (and Raz 1983), I designate as A, B, C. As illustrated in (41a), type A is a pure triconsonantal stem. Types B and C are also triconsonantal, but they are subject to special readjustment rules. As shown in (41b), in type B stems the penultimate consonant is doubled, and in type C (see (41c)) a long /a:/ is infixed before the penultimate stem consonant. This long /a:/ is a suffix in the morphology, but is infixed into the stem by metathesis. This long /a:/ is distinct from the 3sG suffix, which, as noted, has been systematically omitted in the examples cited here.

(41) a. ktb   'write'
        grf   'whip'
        dgm   'tell, relate'
        sbr   'break'
     b. mssl   'resemble'
        grrm   'be beautiful'
        mzzn   'weigh'
        9ddm   'invite'
        mzz-   'give responsibility'
     c. sa:kr   'praise'
        sa:rH   'send away'
        ma:sl   'be diplomatic'
        ka:tb   'write repetitively'
        ma:sl   'give many examples'

I propose to account for these three types of stems by positing the purely consonantal stem as underlying, with syllabification being supplied by the rules in (39). The stem appears in its underlying shape in forms of class A, but is subject to the readjustment rules in (42) in forms of class B and C. In (42a,b) I have stated the effects of the readjustment rules first, and below the statement I have given the formal rules inserting the appropriate junctures. Directly underneath each set of rules I have illustrated their effects with an actual Tigre word.

(42) a. Reduplicate the penultimate stem consonant.
Insert a [juncture before and a] juncture after the penultimate consonant of the stem.
msl >>> m[s]l >>> mssl 'resemble, be an example of'
   b. Metathesize the last two consonants of stem with the /a:/ suffix.
Insert [juncture before the penultimate stem consonant.
Insert] juncture after the /a:/ suffix.
Insert > juncture after the last stem consonant.
Insert < juncture before the /a:/ suffix.
msl >>> m[sl>-<a:] >>> ma:sl 'give many examples of'

This brings us to the so-called frequentative aspect, which in Tigre, "consistently expresses diminutive action" (Rose 2003, 112). This verbal aspect is signaled by a suffix /a:/, which, though homophonous with the "intensive" /a:/ suffix, is distinct from the latter, in that it triggers both reduplication of the penultimate consonants and metathesis (of the /a:/) with the directly preceding two-consonant sequence.

I have illustrated this in (43). (43a) shows the base verb /dngs/ meaning 'to be scared'. The "intensive" variant of this verb undergoes only metathesis and surfaces as /dna:gs/ (see (43b)). The "frequentative" shown in (43c) undergoes both reduplication of the penultimate consonant and metathesis.

(43) a. dngs   'become scared'
    b. dna:gs   'become very scared'   Intensive
    c. dnga:gs   'become slightly scared'   Frequentative

We obtain the intensive form /dna:gs/ (43b) from the intermediate representation /dn[gs><-a:]/, where /a:/ is the exponent of the intensive morpheme. Formally this form is generated by the readjustment rule (42b), which metathesizes the /a:/ with the last two stem consonants. The same metathesis operation is involved in the frequentative in (43c), but the form is subject in addition to rule (42a), which results in the reduplication of the penultimate stem consonant. Applying the two readjustment rules in (42) to the underlying string /dngs-a:/, we obtain the sequence

dn[[g]s><-a:]

where the pair of square brackets generated by (42a) is internal to the pair of square brackets generated by (42b). This violates the prohibition (16) since the second square-bracket juncture is of the same direction as the first square-bracket juncture and intervenes between it and the internal right square-bracket juncture. Since no empirical consequences of this violation are known, it is assumed here that when two identical junctures abut, one of the two abutters is deleted by the notational conventions in (44), and its (undeleted) mate is printed in bold type.

(44) a. A [[B] C] D >>> A [**B**]C] D
     b. X [Y [Z]] W >>> X [Y[**Z**] W

This bit of tidying up the notations has two effects. First, it eliminates the violation of prohibition (16). Second, the output strings in (44) include an unpaired square-bracket juncture, printed in boldface in (44), and to this point no suggestion has been made as to how this "unreadable" juncture is to be eliminated from the representation. We will assume that like the rest of the "unreadable" junctures, the unpaired square-bracket juncture is eliminated by relinearization rules, which are given in (45), where the sequences of dots . . . stand for junctures that may appear in these positions.

(45) a. x_1 [x_2] . . . x_3 . . . x_4] x_5 >>> $x_1 - x_2$ [x_2 . . . x_3 . . . x_4] $- x_5$
     b. x_1 [x_2 . . . [$x_3 x_4$] x_5 >>> $x_1 -$ [x_2 . . . $x_3 x_4$] $- x_3 x_4 - x_5$

The junctures in the output of the rules (45) are eliminated by the subsequent application of the relinearization rule (7) or (20).

As illustrated in (46), the first step in deriving the surface form of (43c) is the elimination of the boldface square bracket by the application of the relinearization rule (45a). The remaining junctures are eliminated in the next step by application of the relinearization rule (20).

(46) a. dn[g]s><-a:] >>> dn-g-[gs><-a:]
     b. dn-g-[gs><-a:] >>> dn-g-a:-gs

The order in which the relinearization rules apply is crucial, for as shown in (47), if (20) is applied first, an uninterpretable string is generated.

            (20)
(47) dn[g]s>-<a:] >>> dn-a:-g]s ***

It is to be observed, moreover, that in the first step of the derivation in (46), the reduplicated consonant /g/ must be placed outside the left square bracket. This technical detail is crucial, for as shown in (48), placement of /g/ inside the square-bracket juncture produces an incorrect result:

(48) dn[g]s><-a:] >>> dn[g-gs><-a:] >>> dn-a:-g-gs ***

I close this discussion of the Tigre facts with Rose's (2003, 113) interesting observation that Tigre has "the ability to form verbs with up to three reduplicative syllables," where "with each reduplication, the meaning is [further] attentuated." Rose illustrates this with the examples in (49).

(49) dgm   'tell, relate'
      dga:gm   'tell stories occasionally'
      dga:ga:gm   'tell stories very occasionally'
      dga:ga:ga:gm   'tell stories infrequently'

The underlying string of the longest form in (49) and the derivation of its surface
string are shown in (50) (Rose 2003, 124). The multiple affixation of the frequentative morpheme is specifically ruled out in the other Ethiopic languages (see Rose
2003, section 13.1). The parentheses in (50) delimit the different cyclic constituents
of the word. The first step in each cycle is the insertion of reduplication junctures by
a readjustment rule; the next two steps show the effects of the application of the relinearization rules (45a) and (16).

(50) UR: (((dgm-a:)-a:)-a:)
      1st cycle: (dgm-a:) >>> d[g]m>-<a:] >>> dg[gm><-a:] >>> dga:gm
      2nd cycle: (dga:gm-a:) >>> dga:[g]m>-<a:] >>> dga:g[gm>-<a:] >>>>
                  dga:ga:gm
      3rd cycle: (dga:ga:gm-a:) >>> dga:ga:[g]m>-<a:] >>>> dga:ga:g[gm>-<a:]
                  >>>> dga:ga:ga:gm

The underlying representation (UR) in (50) indicates the morphological composition
of the forms; each additional intensive /a:/ suffix is directly reflected in the meaning
of the form. And each /a:/ suffix also triggers exactly the same readjustment rules—
that is, augmented consonant reduplication and /a:/ infixation. However, the read-
justments are not part of the underlying representation; they are rather steps in the
derivation of the form, instituted on each cycle. I regard the naturalness of this analysis as a significant argument in favor of the account presented here.

13.5   Augmented Reduplication in Mokilese

Additional support for the relinearization rules in (45) is provided by the interesting
fact that double reduplication of a string W results in a sequence of three rather than
of four W's. As shown in (51), this follows automatically if the strings in question are
relinearized by the rules in (44) and (45).

(51) a. [[W]]U >>> [W]]U >>> W [W] U >>> W W W U
      b. X [[Y]] >>> X [[Y] >>> X [Y] Y >>> X Y Y Y

Actual examples of this kind of triplication are provided by the Mokilese progressive
reduplication discussed by Blevins 1996.

(52) a. pɔdok/pɔdpɔdok   'plant/ing'   [pɔd]ok
      b. kasɔ/kaskasɔ   'throw/ing'   [kas]ɔ

   c. andip/andandip   'spit/ting'   [and]ip
   d. sɔɔrɔk/sɔɔsɔɔrɔk   'tear/ing'   [sɔɔ]rɔk
   e. caak/caacaacaak   'bend/ing'   [caa]]k

Examples (52a–d) show that in forming the progressive aspect the first three segments of a verb stem are reduplicated, and, as shown in the right-hand column of (52), this is notated by enclosing the first three segments of the string in (paired) square-bracket junctures.

Example (52e) differs from the rest in that the root here is monosyllabic. As Blevins (1996, note 1) points out, monosyllables "must undergo triplication in the progressive." In terms of the theory developed here, progressive forms of monosyllabic roots are subject to the insertion of an additional pair of square brackets. Because of the convention (44) and the relinearization rules (45), this results in triplication, as shown in (53).

(53) [[caa]]k >>> [caa]]k >>> caa[caa]k >>> caa-caa-caak

The Mokilese example thus shows that given the formalism developed here, triplication rather than quadruplication is the output of doubly reduplicated sequences. The fact that formalism and observed behavior go so neatly together constitutes further evidence in support of the theory developed here.

13.6   Reduplication in Sanskrit

The most intricate examples of reduplication that I am aware of are those of the Sanskrit conjugation.[15] As I attempt to show below, all Sanskrit reduplications, like those of the Tigre frequentative (see section 13.4), involve simultaneously both partial reduplication (represented here with unpaired angle-bracket junctures) and augmented reduplication (represented here with an unpaired square bracket in boldface).

13.6.1   Preliminaries and Obstruent Modifications in Reduplication

The possibility of the reduplicating junctures],[appearing inside other junctures, in particular inside an > juncture, has the consequence that simple reduplication of the type ABABC can be derived in two ways, as shown in (54).

          (7)
(54) a. [AB]C >>> ABAB-C
        (44)   (45)   (20)
    b. [[A]>BC] >>> [A]>B]C >>> A[A>B]C >>> A-BAB-C

At first glance, the fact that the theory provides two distinct ways of accounting for a given output sequence might appear to reflect a shortcoming. However, the facts of Sanskrit reduplication, to which I now turn, indicate that this is an incorrect conclusion and, that in order to do justice to these facts, the formally simpler alternative based on the underlying representation [AB]C must be replaced by the formally more complex [A]>B]C, even in those cases where the simpler account might seem adequate.

MacDonnell (1916, 122) writes: "Five verbal formations take reduplication: the present stem of the third conjugational class, the perfect (with the pluperfect), one kind of aorist, the desiderative, and the intensive. Each of these has certain peculiarities which must be treated separately." The five reduplications are illustrated in (55) below with examples from Whitney 1885. (Below, the digraph C!—where C stands for consonant—represents a retroflex C.)

(55) a. *tap* 'heat': perf. *tata:pa*; aor 3. *a-ti:tapat*; int. *ta:tapyate*; desid. *titapsa*;

   b. *bʰi:*'fear': pres. *bibʰyati*; perf. *bibʰa:ya*; aor 3. *bi:bʰayat*; int. *baibʰi:*; desid. *bibʰi:s!a*

   c. *kam* 'love': perf. *cakame*; aor 3. *a-cakamata*; int. *cañkam*; desid. *cikamis!a*

   d. *stambʰ* 'prop': perf. *tastambʰa*; aor 3. *a-tastambʰat*; int. *tasta:bʰ-* ; desid. *tis!tambʰis!a-*

   e. *ks!aip* 'throw': perf. *ciks!aipa*; aor 3. *ciks!ipat*; int. *caiks!ip*; desid. *ciks!ipsa*

In all five kinds of reduplication the initial stem obstruent(s) are subject to the same set of modifications. These modifications illustrated in the examples (55b–e) are deaspiration (55b), palatalization (k >>> c) (55c,e), and obstruent cluster simplification (55d,e). These consonantal modifications are the subject of this section. Two of the five kinds of reduplication are discussed in sections 13.6.2 and 13.6.3.

Although these three processes are totally distinct, all three affect the initial obstruent(s) of a reduplicated form. This environment is difficult to characterize, given the means available to phonological rules. Forms such as *ka:kud* 'palate' and *gagan!a* 'sky' show that one of the three processes, palatalization, does not take place in all cases where a word-initial onset is followed by an identical onset in the next syllable. At the very least, the rule of palatalization must therefore be limited to reduplicated forms.

The notation introduced here provides a simple solution to this difficulty. As noted above, the underlying representation [A]>B] is relinearized in two separate steps. As shown in (56), the first step (rule (45)) generates the sequence A[A>B] (augmented reduplication), and the second step (rule (20)) turns it into ABAB (partial reduplication). This is shown in (56).

(56) [A]>B] >>>> A [A>B] >>> A – BAB

The output of the first step in the derivation (56) allows us to refer to the obstruents affected by the three modifications as the segments directly preceding the [juncture. Since the segments following this juncture are guaranteed to be identical with those

that precede it, there is no need to mention this identity in the rule; it is sufficient to
refer to the fact that the segments subject to change are followed by the [juncture.

In (57) I have shown the effects of the readjustment rule for the five verbs in (55),
followed by the first step of the relinearization process (rule (45)).

(57) tap >>> [t]>a]p >>> t [t>a]p   Perf. *tata:pa*
      bʰi >>> [bʰ]>i] >>> bʰ [bʰ>i]   Perf. *bibʰaida*
      kam >>> [k]>a]m >>> k [k>a]m   Perf. *cakame*
      stambʰ >>> [st]>a]mbʰ >>> st[st>a]mbʰ   Perf. *tastambʰa*
      ks!aip >>> [ks!]>ai]p >>> ks! [ks!>ai]p   Perf. *ciks!epa*

It is the obstruents directly preceding the [juncture that are subject to deaspiration,
palatalization, and/or obstruent cluster simplification. Correct outputs are obtained
by assuming that all three of these rules are ordered after the relinearization rule
(45) and before the relinearization rule (20).

The three obstruent modification processes are not the only argument supporting
the proposition that reduplication in Sanskrit needs to be of the complex form
[A]>B], rather than of the less cumbersome form [AB]. As shown in sections 13.6.2
and 13.6.3, in a number of additional cases the complex intermediate representation
is required in order to obtain the correct segment sequences in the reduplicated
forms.

I conclude this section with a brief discussion of the three processes that affect initial obstruents in reduplication. The first of these, deaspiration, is a reflex of Grass-
mann's law. Deaspiration in Sanskrit could be formulated as a process applying to
an obstruent when followed by an aspirated segment in the next syllable, and this
formulation would obviate the need to stipulate that the latter segment is identical
with the one undergoing deaspiration. The alternative proposed above, however, is
no more complicated, and it takes advantage of the fact that its environment is identical with that of the other two obstruent modifications, for which an alternative similar to that available for deaspiration is not available.

Palatalization turns the dorsal obstruents [k,g] into coronal affricates [c, j]. Histor-
ically palatalization was triggered by a following [−back] vowel. As pointed out by
Steriade 1988, the palatalization encountered in reduplicated forms frequently occurs
before [+back] vowels, where the historical process could not ever have applied. A
typical example of this kind is the root /kup/ 'be angry' whose perfect is /cu-kaupa/;
aorist /a-cu:kupat/; intensive /caukup-/; desiderative /cukupis!a-/. The only (correct)
environment for palatalization in Sanskrit is therefore before the [juncture.

Like palatalization, the third modification, obstruent cluster simplification, also
takes place in the environment before the [juncture. In this environment a sequence
of two obstruents like /st sk sp/ or /ks!/ loses the obstruent that is [+cont]. As a result

/s/ is lost in /st sk sp/, and /s!/ in /ks!/. Cluster simplification thus affects the [+continuant] segment regardless of its position. The rule is stated in (58).

(58)   x >>> ∅ in env. _____   x [or   x _____ [
        | | |
        +cont   −cont   −cont

13.6.2 Perfect Reduplication

As remarked in section 13.6.1, Sanskrit has reduplication in five morphologically distinct contexts. Because of limitations of space, only the perfect and the intensive reduplications are discussed here.

As above, it is assumed here that every reduplication process is the consequence of a readjustment rule inserting reduplication junctures into the timing slot sequence of the word. These junctures are subsequently eliminated by the relinearization rules (20) and (45).

The most important factor governing juncture insertion in Sanskrit is the syllable structure of the sequence; the distinction between timing slots belonging to the onset and to the rime of the stem syllable, in particular, is of basic importance here. Sanskrit has only three vowels in underlying representations: [−high] /a/ and [+high] /i,u/. The vowel /a/ is always rime-initial, but its location in a syllable is not predictable: "*a* ... occur[s] root-initially (in *ais, auc*), root-medially (in *yaj, vac*), after two segments (in *vraç*) or just after one (*vardh*)" (Steriade 1988, 94).

In the perfect, junctures are inserted by the readjustment rules (59).

(59) a. Insert a [juncture before the initial timing slot of the root.
   b. Insert a matching] juncture after the rightmost timing slot in the rime that is linked to a [−cons] segment.
   c. Insert the > juncture in the env. __x] (i.e., before the timing slot marked in step (b)).
   d. Insert an (additional)] juncture in the env. [x____ (i.e., after the timing slot marked in step (a), provided the segment is in the onset of the syllable). If the root begins with a sequence of two obstruents, insert the] juncture in env. [xx__ (i.e., after the second obstruent).

The effects of (59) are illustrated below with the root *snih* 'be sticky', whose full-grade form is *snaih* and whose perfect is *sis!neha (= sis!naiha)*. (All forms below are from Whitney 1885 or Steriade 1988.) In (60a) I have shown the junctures inserted by (59); (60b) shows the changes wrought by the relinearization rule (45); and (60c), those of the second relinearization rule (rule (20)).[16]

(60) a. s n a i h a
         | | | | | |
        [x] x x> x] x x

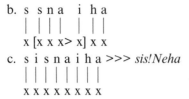

b. s s n a   i h a
   | | | | | | |
   x [x x x> x] x x

c. s i s n a i h a >>> *sis!Neha*
   | | | | | | | |
   x x x x x x x x

In (61) I have given the derivation of the perfect form of a number of additional verbs.

(61) a. ks!aip 'throw' [ks!]a>i]p-a >>> ks!-[ks!a>i]pa >>> c-[ks!a>i]pa >>>
        c-iks!ai-pa >>> *ciks!epa*
        ks!am 'endure' [ks!]>a]m-e >>> ks!-[ks!>a]m-e >>> c-[ks!>a]m-e >>>
        c-aks!a-m-e

In (61a) rule (59b) inserts a] juncture after the /a/, the rightmost [−cons] segment in the rime. In roots beginning with two obstruents, the boldface] juncture is inserted after the second obstruent (59d). The cluster is simplified and the /k/ palatalized to /c/ before the [juncture (see the discussion in section 13.6.1).

     b. suar 'sound' [s]u>a]r-a >>> s-[su>a]ra >>> s-asuar-a >>>> *sasva:ra*

(61b) shows that in view of (59b) the right] juncture may not follow the rime liquid /r/, but, as shown in (60) and (61a), it follows a [−cons] glide, which is part of the syllable rime. This form also shows that the > juncture is inserted before the slot preceding the right] juncture (cf. (59c)).

     c. sarj 'send forth' [s]>a]rj-a >>>> s [s>a]rja >>> *s-asa-rj*
     d. pat 'fly, fall' [p]>a]t-a >>> p[p>a]ta >>> *p-apa-ta*

In (61c,d) the > juncture is placed one timing slot before the second] juncture, as required by (59c).

     e. iat 'stretch' [i]>a]t-a >>> i [i>a]t-a >>> i-aia-ta >>> *yayata*

In (61e) the] juncture is placed to the immediate right of /i/ as required by (59d), in spite of the fact that the initial segment is [−cons], for /i/ is the onset of the syllable. This does not happen when the root begins with the [−high] /a/, because /a/ is always part of the rime and can never be part of the onset (cf. (59d)).

     f. ai 'go' [a>i]-a >>> iai-a >>> **yaya *iyaya*
     g. auc 'pleased' [a>u]c-a >>> uau-c-a >>> **woca *uwoca*

Since the roots in (61f,g) begin with a [−high] vowel, rule (59d) cannot apply to them. The other three rules of (59) should apply normally. This, however, would generate the incorrect outputs **/yaya/ and **/woca/. The correct outputs are obtained by positing an additional rule Glide Insertion (following Steriade 1988, 93), which converts /i-a/ to /iy-a/ and /u-a/ to /uw-a/, as shown below.

i-ai-a >>> iy-ai-a >>> *iyay-a*
u-auc-a >>> uw-auc-a >>> *uwoca*

Steriade's rule of Glide Insertion is specifically limited to applying only before roots beginning with /a/. As shown below, Glide Insertion also applies exceptionally in other roots.

Exceptions to (59) are represented here by the examples in Steriade 1988, 122.

(62) a. suap 'sleep' [s]>u]ap-a >>> s [s>u]ap-a >>> s-usu-ap-a >>>> *sus!vapa*
b. miaks! 'glitter' [m]>i]aks!-a >>> m [m>i]aks!a >>> m-imi-aks!-a >>>
mimyaks!a

In (62a,b), unlike in (61b), the right] juncture is inserted not after the rightmost [−cons] segment of the rime, but after the rightmost [−cons] segment of the onset (cf. (59b)). The other three rules in (59) apply regularly.

In (62c,d) I have given the derivations of additional exceptional verb forms cited by Steriade (1988, 122). Unlike the forms in (62a,b), these begin with vowels, in fact, with [+high] vowels. I assume that, as in (62a,b), rule (59b) applies in these forms and inserts a] juncture to the right of the initial high vowel. The next rule—(59c)—cannot apply here meaningfully, since there is no timing slot to the left of the env. _____ x]. I assume that in such cases the > juncture is inserted to the right of the only timing slot preceding the] juncture inserted by rule (59b). The remaining rule (59d) completes the juncture insertion. The resulting rather heavily junctured forms are shown below as the input stage of the derivations.

c. uas 'shine': [u]>]as-a >>> u-[u>]as-a >>> u-u-as-a >>> u-w-as-a >>>
uvas-a
d. iaj 'offer' [i]]>aj-a >>> i-[i>]aj-a >>> i-i-aj-a >>> i-y-aj-a >>> *iyaj-a*

In the first step of the two derivations shown in (62c,d), the relinearization rule applies and generates the output sequences. These, however, raise a question as to the proper application of the linearization rule (20). The proper treatment of a string of the form [A>] parallels that of [A>B] where B=0. On this reasoning, since [A>B] is relinearized as BAB, if B=0, then BAB = A. The forms /u-[u>]as-a/ and /i-[i>]aj-a/ are therefore turned into /u-u-as-a/ and /i-i-aj-a/, which are subject to Glide formation (Steriade 1988, 93). The derivations (62c,d) are thus minimally different from those of /iat/ 'stretch' in (61e), just like those in (62a,b) are minimally different from the regular /suar/'sound' in (61b).

The derivations in (62) approach the limits of the notational system developed here. That these derivations terminate in the correct output sequences was somewhat surprising to me, in spite of the fact that any other outcome would have revealed a fundamental inadequacy in the proposed theory. The fact that no such inadequacy has been discovered must therefore be taken as evidence in support of the theory presented here.

13.6.3   The Intensive

The readjustment rules for the Sanskrit intensive are given in (63). They obviously are very similar to those of the perfect (59), but the differences are not to be overlooked.

(63) *Intensive*
   a. Insert a [juncture before the initial timing slot of the root.
   b. Insert a matching] juncture after the rightmost timing slot in the rime that is linked to a [+son] segment (i.e., a liquid or a nasal).
   c. Insert > juncture at the end of the syllable onset of the verb root.
   d. Insert a] juncture in the env. [x____ (i.e., after the timing slot marked in step (a), provided the segment linked to x is not [−high] /a/). If the root begins with a sequence of two obstruents, insert the] juncture in env. [xx__ (i.e., after the second obstruent).

The first difference between the rules in (63) and those in (59) is that in the perfect (59), the reduplicated material of the rime excludes liquids or nasals, whereas in the intensive these are included (cf. (63b)). A root such as /kam/ 'love' reduplicates as /ka-kama/ >>> *cakama** in the perfect, but as /kamkam-/ >>> *cañkam*- in the intensive. As (64) shows, the difference is due to the different insertions of the right] junctures, by (59b) and (63b) respectively.

(64) [k]>a]m >>> k [k>a]m >>> c[k>a]m >>> *c-aka-m*   Perfect
      [k]>am] >>> k [k>am] >>> c[k>am] >>>> *c-amkam*   Intensive

A second difference concerns (63c). This rule differs from its perfect counterpart (59c) in that in the perfect the > juncture is inserted directly before the last reduplicated rime slot, whereas in the intensive the > juncture is inserted after the last onset slot. This is illustrated in (65) with the forms of the root /tuais/ 'be stirred up'.

(65) [t]ua>i]s >>> t [tua>i]s >>> t-itvai-s-a >>> *titvesa*   Perfect
      [t]u>ai]s >>> t [tu>ai]s >>> t-aitvai-s >>> *tetves**   Intensive

The intensive form of roots that end with a short vowel followed by an obstruent requires further comment. As (66) shows, the rules developed to this point generate systematically incorrect output forms.

(66) grab^h 'grab' [g]r>a]b^h-a >>> g [gr>a]b^h-a >>> j [gr>a]b^h-a >>> *j-agra-b^h-a*
      *** correct form *ja:grab^{h}a*
      pac 'cook' [p]>a]c-yate >>> p [p>a]c-yate >>> *p-apa-c-yate* *** correct form *pa:pacyate*
      tij 'be sharp' [t]>i]j-te >>> [[t]>i]k-te >>> t [t>i]k-te >>> *t-iti-k-te* *** correct form *tetikte* from taitikte
      bud^h 'know, wake' [b]>u]d^h-i:ti >>> b [b>u]d^h-i:ti >>> *b-ubu-d^h-i:ti* *** correct form *bobud^{h}i:ti* from baubud^{h}i:ti

The difference between the correct forms and those generated by the rules developed so far concerns the short root vowel. In the correct forms we find in place of a short vowel, either long /aː/ (if the root vowel is short /a/) or the diphthongs /ai/ or /au/, which surface as /e/ or /o/ respectively, if the root vowel is short /i/ or /u/ respectively. We therefore obtain the correct outputs by a readjustment rule that inserts /a/, which applies after the first step in the linearization process (the same environment where palatalization, deaspiration, and cluster simplification apply) and inserts the vowel /a/ before the [juncture (see (67a)). This rule applies to intensive forms of roots that end with a short vowel followed by an obstruent. Its effects are shown in (67b).

(67) a. Insert /a/ in env. -son _____ [

    b. bud^h 'know, wake' [b]>u]d^h-iːti >>> b [b>u]d^h-iːti >>> ba [b>u]d^h-iːti >>> ba-ubu-d^h-iːti >>> *bobud^{h}iːti*

MacDonnell (1916, 202) describes the fourth (and final) difference between intensive and perfective reduplications as follows: "Over twenty roots with final or penultimate nasal, **r** or **uː** interpose an **i:** (or **i** if the vowel would be long by position) between the reduplicated syllable and the root; e.g., ... **han** *slay*: **ghan-iː-ghan**; **krand** *cry out*: **kan-i-krand** and **kan-i-krad** (from /kan-i-krnd/ mh), **skand** *leap*: **kan-i-skand** and **can-i-skand**."

I assume that these twenty roots are subject to a special readjustment rule in addition to those of (63), which is stated in (68). This rule is ordered directly after (63), but before any of the rules of the phonology.

(68) In intensive forms of the roots listed below, insert /<iː/ before the right] juncture.

    /gam, g^{h}an, krand, skand, b^{h}ar, uart, nau ... /

I have illustrated the effect of this rule in (69).

(69) [sk]>an]d >>> [sk]>an<iː]d >>> sk [sk>an<iː]d >>>> k [sk>an<iː]d >>> opt >>> c [sk>an<iː]d >>> c-aniːskan-d >>> *caniskad*

The shortening of the long /iː/ is due to a general rule of Sanskrit phonology that applies in closed syllables and that is ordered after all relinearization rules.

Steriade observes that most of the intensive forms in (68) are also exceptions to palatalization, and attempts to account for both by noting that in the relinearized form the consonant failing to be palatalized is two syllables removed from its trigger. This account is, of course, not available here since I have argued that palatalization affects obstruents before the [juncture (see section 13.6.1). Since on both accounts the insertion of the /iː/ extension affects only a small list of twenty or so roots, it does not seem that the small gain in generality achieved by Steriade's alternative makes up for the loss resulting from the need to express palatalization by a rule that depends on the appearance of an identical obstruent later in the string.

13.7 Conclusions

Above I have attempted to present in detail the transformations in the linear order of segments that are observed in different types of reduplication. My main findings are:

First, there are (exactly) three kinds of reduplication: simple reduplication (copying), partial reduplication, and augmented reduplication.

Second, metathesis is a special case of partial reduplication (see section 13.3), which interacts in surprising—yet predictable—ways with other kinds of reduplication (see sections 13.4 through 13.6).

Third, the Greek augment /e/ is a prefix that undergoes partial reduplication not only with certain consonant-initial stems (as shown by Steriade 1982) but also with certain vowel-initial stems (as shown in section 13.2.1). This result has further—as yet unexplored—consequences for the treatment of the augment in other Indo-European languages, especially in Gothic.

Fourth, augmented reduplication is a distinct type of phonological operation with varying effects in different languages explored above for Tigre (section 13.4), Mokilese (section 13.5), and Sanskrit (section 13.6).

Fifth, all three kinds of reduplication are triggered by special extralinear concatenators that are inserted by readjustment rules.

Sixth, the widely varying transformations in segment sequences that have been observed in reduplications in different languages are all due to the application of the three relinearization rules (7), (20), and (45). The first of the three relinearizations—that is, (7)—reflects the transformation resulting from simple copying of a substring; the latter two rules, (20) and (45), express more complex transformations, where the copied sequences are modified at their edges, either by subtracting a terminal subsequence (20) from, or by adding such a subsequence (45) to, a reduplicated substring. Further complexities found in the data are consequences of the fact that a given form may be subject simultaneously to two or even all three of the relinearizations. What is lacking at this point is a proper grasp of the computational power implicit in the relinearization operations.

Seventh, the accounts above of facts from the phonology of different languages crucially involve derivations with numerous intermediate representations. Such derivations are specifically excluded in the different versions of Optimality Theory (OT) that of this writing (August 2005) are the predominant approaches in phonology. This study therefore constitutes a direct challenge to OT phonology to offer viable alternative accounts for the facts discussed above. Unless and until such alternative accounts are advanced, the data and the analyses in this study stand as blatant counterexamples that invalidate all versions of OT.

Notes

As noted in the text this study developed under the direct influence of Raimy 2000 and Frampton 2004. I am especially indebted to John Frampton for our many discussions, without which this chapter would not have been written. I am grateful to Julie Sussman, Jerry Sussman, and Donca Steriade, as well as to two anonymous reviewers for numerous corrections and improvements in the text and argumentation of this chapter. Any remaining inadequacies are my sole responsibility.

1. In Wilbur 1973 attention was drawn to the fact that in reduplication there are instances of both overapplication and underapplication of particular phonological rules. These exceptional applications of rules were serious counterexamples to every phonological theory. One of the important discoveries of Raimy's study was that all cases of overapplication and underapplication affect segments that are multiply linked like x_1 and x_3 in (4). This discovery provided Raimy with the basis for an extension of the theory of rule application that properly solves all problems connected with over- and underapplication of phonological rules (see Raimy 2000, section 2.2.1). Since this result crucially depends on the existence of segments with multiply linked concatenators, it must be considered additional support (additional to the reduplication facts discussed in this chapter) for Raimy's concatenator notation. As explained below, the aspects of Raimy's notation that are crucial to reduplication, the subject of this chapter, are expressed here formally by a set of junctures.

2. Readjustment rules are not the only source of reduplication in languages. It has been shown that Manam has words with reduplicated syllables in underlying representations. For some discussion, see Fitzpatrick 2004.

3. I assume that (7) is a rule, rather than a convention, because it is ordered with respect to other rules. (For discussion, see section 13.6.1.)

4. In (26b) the symbol (V) stands for a vowel that may optionally occur in this position; see discussion below.

5. Note that the pluperfect (= past + perfect) /e-lelu-k-a/ derives from an underlying representation where the past prefix /e/ precedes the perfect prefix, which is also /e/, but which in addition triggers reduplication (i.e., /e-[e> -l] u-k-a/). The simple aorist (past) is /e-lu-a/, with the e augment, but without partial reduplication.

6. It may be noted here that the well-known English example of partial reduplication *table-shmable* is, like that of Kolami (see (29)), an instance of suffixation, as suggested by Raimy 2000, 78. For additional discussion, see section 13.7.

7. The attested cases of noncontiguous metathesis involve metatheses of consecutive consonants (skipping intervening vowels), or of consecutive syllable onsets, or of consecutive syllable rimes—that is, metatheses of elements that are contiguous on special projections of the base string. For additional discussion, see Halle 2001.

8. An example of metathesis quite similar to that of Slavic is cited by Hume from the Dravidian language Kuvi (Hume's example (23), 225), which metathesizes vowel-sonorant rime sequences.

9. In Harris and Halle 2005, we discuss examples from Spanish where the plural imperative suffix /-n/ undergoes either metathesis or (partial) reduplication.

10. I thank an anonymous reviewers of this chapter for suggesting the analysis of the Kaingang data in this section.

11. /y/ stands for a [+high, +back −round] vowel.

12. The glides /v/ and /j/ are deleted before consonants by a rule of the phonology of Kaingang. /tam/ >>> /ty-g-tam/ from /[tam]<g]/ 'cover' in (35g) is not an instance of deletion, but of nasal assimilation. This process turns /m+g/ into a dorsal nasal, which is represented as /g/ in Wiesemann's transcription. (See Steriade 1988.)

13. This parenthesis is distinguished typographically from the parentheses inserted by rule (b) by being printed in bold type.

14. I thank Andrew Nevins for drawing my attention to the forms in (40b).

15. The following discussion of the Sanskrit reduplication is heavily indebted to Steriade 1988. Although my theory of reduplication and the accounts I offer of particular reduplication processes in Sanskrit differ from those of Steriade, the treatment of the complex body of data that I offer below would not have been possible without Steriade's study.

16. The retroflex coronals are the result of the so-called *ruki* rule of Sanskrit, and the mid-vowels e and o are surface realizations of the diphthongs ai and au, respectively.

References

Blevins, Juliette. 1996. Mokilese reduplication. *Linguistic Inquiry* 27:523–530.

Bräuer, Herbert. 1961. *Slawische Sprachwissenschaft*. Berlin: de Gruyter.

Broselow, Ellen, and John McCarthy. 1983. A theory of internal reduplication. *Linguistic Review* 3:25–98.

Fitzpatrick, Justin. 2004. The representation and linearization of nonlinear precedence. Unpublished ms., MIT.

Fitzpatrick, Justin, and Andrew Nevins. 2004. Phonological occurrences: Relations and copying. http://ling.auf.net/lingBuzz/00051.

Frampton, John. 2004. Distributed Reduplication. Northeastern University.

Goldsmith, John. 1976. *Autosegmental Phonology*. Doctoral dissertation, MIT. New York: Garland Press, 1979.

Halle, Morris. 2001. Infixation vs. Onset Metathesis in Tagalog, Chamorro, and Toba Batak. In Michael Kenstowicz, ed., *Ken Hale: A Life in Language*, 153–168. Cambridge, Mass.: MIT Press.

Halle, Morris, and William J. Idsardi. 2000. Stress and length in Hixkaryana. *Linguistic Review* 17:199–218.

Harris, James W., and Morris Halle. 2005. Unexpected plural inflections in Spanish: Reduplication and Metathesis. *Linguistic Inquiry* 36:195–222.

Hume, Elizabeth. 2004. The indeterminacy/attestation model of metathesis. *Language* 80:203–237.

Idsardi, William. 1992. The Computation of Prosody. Doctoral dissertation, MIT.

Idsardi, William. 2004. Calculating metrical structure. In Raimy, E. and C. Cairns, eds. Forthcoming. *Contemporary Views on Architecture and Representation in Phonological Theory*. Cambridge, Mass.: MIT Press.

MacDonnell, Arthur. 1916. *A Vedic Grammar for Students*. Reprint New Delhi: Motilal Banarsidass, 1993.

Marantz, Alec. 1982. Re reduplication. *Linguistic Inquiry* 13:435–482.

McCarthy, John, and Alan Prince. 1986. Prosodic morphology. Unpublished ms., University of Massachusetts.

McCarthy, John, and Alan Prince. 1995. Faithfulness and reduplicative identity. In Jill Beckman, L. Dickey, and S. Urbanczyk, eds., *UMASS Occasional Papers* 18:249–384.

Purnell, Thomas C. 1997. Principles and Parameters of Phonological Rules: Evidence from Tone Languages. Doctoral dissertation, University of Delaware, Newark.

Raimy, Eric. 2000. *The Morphology and Phonology of Reduplication*. Berlin: Mouton de Gruyter.

Raz, Shlomo. 1983. *Tigre Grammar and Texts*. Malibu: Undena Publications.

Rose, Sharon. 2003. Triple Take: Tigre and the case of internal reduplication. *San Diego Linguistics Papers* 1:109–128 (UCSD).

Sihler, Andrew. 1995. *New Comparative Grammar of Greek and Latin*. Oxford: Oxford University Press.

Steriade, Donca. 1982. Greek Prosodies and the Nature of Syllabification. Doctoral dissertation, MIT.

Steriade, Donca. 1988. Reduplication and syllable transfer in Sanskrit and elsewhere. *Phonology* 5:71–155.

Whitney, William D. 1885. *The Roots, Verb-Forms and Primary Derivatives of the Sanskrit Language*. Reprint New York American Oriental Society, 1988.

Whitney, William D. 1889. *Sanskrit Grammar*. Reprint Cambridge, Mass.: Harvard University Press, 1941.

Wiesemann, Ursula. 1972. *Die phonologische und grammatische Struktur der Kaingang Sprache*. The Hague: Mouton.

Wilbur, Ronnie. 1973. The Phonology of Reduplication. Doctoral dissertation, University of Illinois, Urbana.

14 The Logic of Contrast

B. Elan Dresher

14.1 Introduction

Jean-Roger Vergnaud has always advocated formal rigor in linguistic theory as a way of making theoretical notions precise. This is especially needed in phonology, where what he has called "recreational diagrams" have sometimes taken the place of formally explicit theoretical underpinnings. I will argue that the history of the notion of contrast in phonology provides a series of illuminating case studies of the dangers of leaving key notions vaguely defined.

Since Saussure it has been a fundamental premise of linguistic theory that contrast is central to understanding the nature of linguistic inventories: an element is defined not only by its substance but by the elements it is in contrast with ("dans la langue il n'y a que des différences"). In phonology contrast is informally understood as applying to phonemes, but at least since the work of Trubetzkoy and Jakobson it has been understood that phonemes are made up of distinctive features, and that the significant oppositions in a language involve features. It is one thing to say that two phonemes, say /z/ and /l/, are in contrast in a given language; it is another thing to determine which particular features are contrastive in these phonemes. Are /z/ and /l/ distinguished by the feature [sonorant], or [lateral], or [continuant], or [strident], or by some or all of these?

As I will show, this question has rarely been asked, let alone answered, in the phonological literature, even in work that would appear to presuppose it. In this chapter I will consider a few such examples, drawing on work from widely separated time periods. Though the terminology and theoretical frameworks may differ, I will try to show that all are hindered by the same problem: the lack of an explicit and adequate means of identifying contrastive and redundant feature values.

14.2   Two Approaches to Assigning Contrastive Feature Specifications

14.2.1   Contrast Based on an Ordering of Features

In the case of phonemes viewed as primitive elements, every phoneme is in contrast
with every other one, and there is no further structure to the set. When phonemes are
analyzed as complexes of features, however, it is necessary to specify the structure of
the contrastive set. I have argued (Dresher 1998, 2002, 2003a, 2003b), following
Jakobson, Fant, and Halle 1952 and Jakobson and Halle 1956, that contrast must
be established by setting up an *ordering*, or *hierarchy*, of features, where the first feature divides an inventory, and successive features divide the subsets in turn until all
phonemes have been distinguished. As Vergnaud has put it (personal communication), the logic of contrast is the logic of "given that": determination of whether or
not a feature is contrastive in any particular phoneme depends on what contrastive
features have already been specified.

Consider an inventory with the phonemes /p/, /b/, and /m/, and suppose for the
sake of this example that they are specifiable for the features [voiced] and [nasal].[1]
This inventory is given in (1).

(1) *A simple inventory*

	p	b	m
[voiced]	−	+	+
[nasal]	−	−	+

If [voiced] is ordered ahead of [nasal] (henceforth, [voiced] > [nasal]), then /p/ is
contrastively [−voiced] and /b, m/ are contrastively [+voiced]; then the latter two
are distinguished by [nasal], which is contrastive only in the [+voiced] set. If, on the
other hand, the features are ordered [nasal] > [voiced], then /m/ is contrastively
[+nasal] and /p, b/ are contrastively [−nasal]; now, the feature [voiced] only distinguishes between the phonemes in the [−nasal] set. The two orderings can be drawn
as in (2).

(2) *Two orderings of the features [voiced] and [nasal] applied to /p b m/*

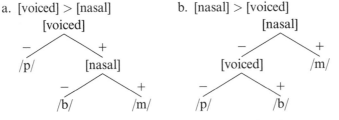

The phonemes in (2a) and (2b) are thus specified for the contrastive features in (3a)
and (3b), respectively.

(3) *Contrastive specifications derived by (2)*

a. [voiced] > [nasal]   b. [nasal] > [voiced]

	p	b	m
[voiced]	−	+	+
[nasal]		−	+

	p	b	m
[voiced]	−	+	
[nasal]	−	−	+

Notice that although the inventories and features in both the (a) and (b) orders are identical, the contrastive specifications differ: in each order, one redundant specification is left out, though it is a different specification in each order. This discrepancy underlines the fact that on this view, contrast must be evaluated relative to an order of features; without an order, the notion remains undefined. Let us call this the Contrastive Hierarchy (CH) approach to determining contrastive feature values.

14.2.2 Contrast Based on Logical Redundancy

The above procedure for determining contrastive feature specifications is not the only one that has been employed in the linguistic literature, nor is it even the predominant approach. More usually, contrastive specifications have been assigned by removing all the specifications that are *logically redundant*. We can define logical redundancy as in (4).

(4) *Logical redundancy*

If Φ is the set of feature specifications of a member, M, of an inventory, then the feature specification [F] is *logically redundant* iff it is predictable from the other specifications in Φ.

A feature that is logically redundant is predictable from the other features. In example (1), there are two logically redundant specifications: since /p/ is the only [−voiced] member of the inventory, its feature value [−nasal] is predictable; similarly, the value [+voiced] for /m/ is predictable given [+nasal], since /m/ is the only [+nasal] phoneme. By this reasoning, we arrive at the contrastive specifications in (5); just such specifications are proposed by Martinet (1964, 64) for Standard French.

(5) a. *Contrastive specifications by removing logically redundant values*

	p	b	m
[voiced]	−	+	
[nasal]		−	+

b. *Redundancy rules*

i. [−voiced] → [−nasal]   ii. [+nasal] → [+voiced]

Logical redundancy is defined in (4) with reference to specification over the full set of features. For it is only by first specifying all segments for every feature that we can determine which features are redundant. Let us then call this the Full Specification (FS) approach to determining contrastive values.

As demonstrated by Dresher (2002, 2003b), this procedure is seriously flawed, because it may not be possible to remove all the logically redundant feature specifications while retaining enough specifications to differentiate the phonemes. To take a simple example, suppose inventory (1) lacked /b/. In an inventory consisting only of /p/ and /m/, the phonemes differ with respect to both the features [voiced] and [nasal]. Therefore, each specification is predictable from the others and every specification is logically redundant in terms of the definition in (4). Obviously, they cannot all be removed. In such cases, the FS procedure for determining contrast fails, and must be supplemented by another procedure. For example, we may decide that [voiced] is a more important feature than [nasal] (or vice versa), but that is tantamount to ordering them, as in the CH approach.

Such situations arise rather commonly. Consider a familiar inventory with the five vowels /i e a o u/, which have at least the specifications in (6).

(6) *Five-vowel system, features [high], [low], [back], [round]*

	i	e	a	o	u
[high]	+	−	−	−	+
[low]	−	−	+	−	−
[back]	−	−	+	+	+
[round]	−	−	−	+	+

A contrast in the feature [high] is all that distinguishes /i/ from /e/ and /u/ from /o/, therefore these values of [high] are contrastive. The value [−high] of /a/ is predictable from [+low], and so is logically redundant. The same is true of all values of the feature [low]: for the high vowels, [+high] predicts [−low]; all the other vowels are distinguishable without [low], whose value is thus predictable from the features [back] and [round]. In particular, [+back, −round] predicts [+low] (/a/); all other combinations of [back] and [round] predict [−low]. At the same time, each of [back] and [round] is predictable from the other together with the feature [low]: [−low, −back] predicts [−round] and [−low, −round] predicts [−back] (/i e/); [−low, +back] predicts [+round], and [−low, +round] predicts [+back] (/u o/); and [+low] predicts [+back, −round] (/a/).

Therefore, combinations of any two of [low], [back], and [round] make the third feature logically redundant. It follows that they are all logically redundant, but clearly cannot all be omitted. This situation arises as a consequence of trying to determine contrast simultaneously for all features, rather than using the logic of "given that": feature F is redundant given G, and G is redundant given F, but these logical situations do not apply at the same time.

The particular problem here is that there are too many features for the number of vowels, given their distribution in the feature space. Reducing the number of features to three will allow the FS method to yield a result, but then another theory is needed to decide which feature is dispensable. For example, without the feature [round] in (6), [low] is required to distinguish between /a/ and /o/, and [back] is the only feature that distinguishes between /i e/ and /u o/. Removing the logically redundant features results in the contrastive specifications in (7).[2]

(7) a. *Contrastive specification by FS: Features [high], [low], [back] only*

	i	e	a	o	u
[high]	+	−		−	+
[low]			+	−	
[back]	−	−		+	+

b. *Redundancy rules*

    i. [+low] → [−high]   iii. [−back] → [−low]

    ii. [+high] → [−low]   iv. [+low] → [+back]

Even reducing the number of features will not always give good results for the FS method, depending on the way members of an inventory are dispersed over the space defined by the feature set. An example of such an inventory is the vowel system of Maranungku (Tryon 1970), given in (8).

(8) *Maranungku: Features [high], [low], [back]*

	i	æ	ɑ	ə	ʊ
[high]	+	−	−	−	+
[low]	−	+	+	−	−
[back]	−	−	+	+	+

Removing the logically redundant values results in the contrastive specifications in (9). As is evident, these specifications fail to distinguish between /i/ and /æ/.[3]

(9) a. *Maranungku: Contrastive specification by FS*

	i	æ	ɑ	ə	ʊ
[high]			−	+	
[low]		+	−		
[back]	−	−	+		+

b. *Redundancy rules*

    i. [+low] → [−high]   iv. $\begin{bmatrix} -\text{high} \\ -\text{back} \end{bmatrix}$ → [+low]

    ii. $\begin{bmatrix} -\text{low} \\ -\text{back} \end{bmatrix}$ → [+high]   v. $\begin{bmatrix} -\text{high} \\ -\text{low} \end{bmatrix}$ → [+back]

    iii. [+high] → [−low]

We can model the space corresponding to the inventories in (7) and (8) with diagrams as in (10). The lines connect neighbors that are distinguished by only a single feature. In the typical five-vowel inventory in (10a), every phoneme except /a/ has two such neighbors; the configuration shown results in sufficient contrastive features to uniquely characterize each phoneme.[4] In (10b), however, /i/ and /æ/ occupy parallel positions in a contrast based on [back], but have no other neighbors that could further differentiate them; thus, they are assigned the same contrastive specifications, and cannot be distinguished.

(10) *Distribution of phonemes in the space of features*
    a. /i e a o u/, features [high], [low], [back]

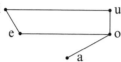

    b. Maranungku, features [high], [low], [back]

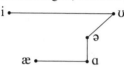

Whether or not an inventory has paths that make its members distinguishable by FS is an accidental property, and should not be the basis of a theory of contrastiveness.[5] CH does not depend on the members of an inventory having any particular pattern of distribution in the space of features, and does not succumb to these difficulties.

It is clear, then, that the two methods for determining contrast reviewed above are incompatible. They give different results even in simple cases, such as the example above with only two features and an inventory of three members. They also differ with respect to full specification (unnecessary in the hierarchical method, necessary in the logical redundancy method). The CH approach is additive, assigning contrastive features in succession, whereas the FS approach is subtractive, removing redundant features where possible. Further, the CH approach can give different contrastive representations for the same inventory and the same set of features, depending on ordering of the features; the FS approach, where it gives an answer, will always give the same contrastive representations for a given inventory and set of features. Most important, the FS approach does not work in many cases, whereas the CH procedure is guaranteed to give a result in every case.

Despite the clear differences between these methods of determining contrast, they have not been adequately differentiated in the literature. Sometimes we find both approaches apparently coexisting in the same work, with paradoxical results.

14.3   Some Pregenerative Approaches to Contrast

14.3.1   Trubetzkoy

Trubetzkoy was the first phonologist to treat contrast formally. He did this in terms of the notion of *opposition*, where an opposition is the relation between any pair of contrasting members of an inventory (in our case, phonemes in a language). Though he contributed many insightful ideas and analyses, his discussion in the *Grundzüge* (1939, translated into English as Trubetzkoy 1969) suggests that he did not have a single approach to distinguishing between contrastive and redundant values, but rather oscillated between the two incompatible approaches sketched above.

As part of his analysis of the logical basis of the concept of an opposition, Trubetzkoy (1969, 68) calls attention to the properties common to the members of an opposition, what he calls their "basis for comparison." In a *bilateral* opposition the sum of the properties common to both opposition members is common to them alone; in a *multilateral* opposition, the set of common properties are shared also by at least one other member of the inventory. According to Trubetzkoy (p. 69), bilateral oppositions "are the most important for the determination of the phonemic content of a phoneme." By *phonemic content* he appears to mean the set of contrastive (possibly only marked) specifications that characterizes a phoneme.

But how does one determine if an opposition is bilateral or multilateral? Trubetzkoy does not give a clear answer to this question. Consider again the miniature example in (1). If we adopt a hierarchical approach and limit oppositions to contrastive features, then on the ordering [voiced] > [nasal] (2a), /b/ and /m/ form a bilateral opposition because they are the only phonemes that share the common contrastive feature [+voiced]. However, /b/ and /p/ do not form a bilateral opposition, since /p/ shares no contrastive features with /b/ that it does not also share with /m/. In the ordering [nasal] > [voiced] (2b), it is /p/ and /b/ that form a bilateral opposition based on [−nasal], whereas *b:m* and *p:m* both form multilateral oppositions. That is, on the CH approach, determining that an opposition is bilateral or multilateral depends on the feature ordering.

In the FS approach, we must decide whether oppositions are to be evaluated on the basis of full specifications (1) or contrastive ones (5). If it is the former, then *p:b* and *b:m* are both bilateral oppositions, whereas *p:m* is multilateral; if the latter, then there are no bilateral oppositions in this inventory.

We thus have at least four different classifications of the oppositions in (1), depending on which analysis we use: the CH approach gives two answers (depending on which feature ordering we choose), and the FS approach gives two more (depending on whether we use fully specified or contrastive feature values). So which approach does Trubetzkoy take?

Trubetzkoy's remarks on the subject do not add up to any one consistent approach, though he appears to presuppose the FS approach, at least in the earlier sections of the book. The statement that bilateral oppositions are important in determining phonemic content suggests that bilateral oppositions are in some sense prior to determination of contrastive values, as in the FS approach. On the one hand, he writes (p. 68) that "only the phonologically distinctive properties are to be considered" in deciding if an opposition is bilateral or multilateral. But he goes on, "some nondistinctive properties may be taken into consideration as well" if these can contribute to making an opposition bilateral.

To illustrate, Trubetzkoy (1969, 68–69) presents an example from Standard French. In this language, he observes, *d* and *n* "are the only voiced dental occlusives." He observes further that "neither voicing nor occlusion is distinctive for *n*, as neither voiceless nor spirantal *n* occur as independent phonemes." This notion of contrastiveness is consistent with the FS approach: if *n* is the only dental nasal, any other features it may have are predictable, hence not contrastive. Assuming that contrasts are established by FS, the status of selected oppositions in French is as in (11). Specifications that are redundant on this approach are italicized. In keeping with Trubetzkoy's observation, *d:n*, and even *t:d*, do not form bilateral oppositions unless at least one redundant specification is taken into account.

(11) *Determination of bilateral oppositions in French: FS approach*

Pair	In common	Shared with	Opposition
t:n	[dental]	d	multilateral
t:d	[dental, *−nasal*]	–	bilateral
d:n	[dental, *+voiced*, *−continuant*]	–	bilateral
d:b	[+voiced, −nasal]	g	multilateral

Trubetzkoy provides no argument that *d:n* in fact *do* constitute a bilateral opposition in French. No empirical consequences to support this claim are adduced. In a hierarchical approach to contrastive specification, it is not at all obvious that voicing is redundant for /n/, or that *d:n* or *t:d* participate in bilateral oppositions. For example, if [voiced] is ordered above [nasal], then the voicing contrast will include in its purview the nasal consonants as well, as shown in (12a). In this ordering, *d:n* participate in a bilateral opposition, but *t:d* do not. On the other hand, the features could be ordered as in (12b), in which case nasals are not specified for voicing, *d:n* do not form a bilateral opposition, but *t:d* do.

(12) *Determination of bilateral oppositions in French: CH approach*

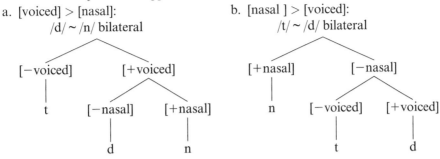

a. [voiced] > [nasal]:
   /d/ ~ /n/ bilateral

b. [nasal] > [voiced]:
   /t/ ~ /d/ bilateral

Though the discussion of bilateral oppositions in French presupposes an FS approach to contrast, Trubetzkoy takes a rather different tack in later sections of the *Grudzüge*, one consistent with what I have been calling the CH approach. Returning to French later in the book (1969, 126), he considers whether the consonants /p b f v/ should be analyzed as occurring at a single place designated as "labial," or whether the labial series should be split into two places, bilabial and labiodental. He argues for the latter, because "in the entire French consonant system there is not a single phoneme pair in which the relation spirant : occlusive would occur in its pure form." Indeed, he follows this analysis to its logical conclusion (note 93) and disputes that there is an opposition between occlusives and spirants in French, because degree of occlusion cannot be regarded independently of position of articulation. His analysis of the contrastive differences in the French obstruents can be summarized in (13).[6]

(13) *French obstruents (based on Martinet 1964, 65)*

	Bilabial	Labiodental	Apical	Alveolar	Prepalatal	Dorsovelar
Voiceless	p	f	t	s	š	k
Voiced	b	v	d	z	ž	g

This result cannot be achieved by a FS theory that begins with full specification, because there would be no way to decide that the contrast in terms of [continuant] should be suppressed in favor of the place distinction. Nor is this always the case, in Trubetzkoy's view. He observes that a similar issue arises in Greek, which has a bilabial stop /p/ and labiodental fricatives /f v/, and a postdental stop /t/ and interdental fricatives /θ ð/. Is the primary contrast one of stop versus fricative or of place? Here Trubetzkoy appeals to "parallel" relations between stops and fricatives at different places. In the sibilant and dorsal series (/ts s z/ and /k x ɣ/, respectively), the contrast is unambiguously one of stop versus fricative, since stops and fricatives occur at exactly the same place of articulation. By parallelism, Trubetzkoy proposes that the same contrast should apply to the ambiguous cases, which leads to the conclusion that the minor place splits are phonologically irrelevant. The inventory would thus be presented as in (14).

(14) *Greek: major place, voicing, occlusion > minor place*[7]

	Labial	Apical	Sibilant	Dorsal
Voiceless stops	p	t	ts	k
Voiceless fricatives	f	θ	s	x
Voiced fricatives	v	ð	z	ɣ

The difference between the treatment of the place contrasts in Greek and French is consistent with a CH approach that assigns a different ordering of the continuant feature relative to minor place features in the two languages.

It is interesting that when he has empirical reasons for assigning contrastive features, Trubetzkoy tends to assume CH. For example, he observes (1969, 102–103) that a "certain hierarchy existed" in the Polabian vowel system whereby the back ~ front contrast is higher than the rounded ~ unrounded one, the latter being a subclassification of the front vowels. Trubetzkoy's rationale for this analysis is that palatalization in consonants is neutralized before all front vowels (and before "the maximally open vowel *a* which stood outside the classes of timbre"). Also, the oppositions between back and front vowels are constant, but those between rounded and unrounded vowels of the same height are neutralizable (after *v* and *j* to *i* and *ê*). The vowel system, according to Trubetzkoy's contrastive distinctions, is given in (15). The diagram suggests that the feature [back] has wider scope than [round].

(15) *Polabian (Trubetzkoy 1969, 102–103): [back] > [round]*

		back
front		
(unround)	round	
i	ü	u
ê	ö	o
e		ɑ
a		

14.3.2   Martinet and Jakobson on French Contrastive Features

Though Trubetzkoy did not follow any consistent procedure in determining contrastive specifications, his discussion of the French labial obstruent oppositions at least makes clear that one has to decide whether the contrast is based on place of articulation (bilabial /p b/ versus labiodental /f v/) or continuancy (stop /p b/ versus fricative /f v/). This issue was revisited a number of times by linguists in the Prague School tradition. Here I will consider two analyses, one by Martinet (1964) and the other by Jakobson and Lotz (1949). These analyses do not clarify the procedure for determining which features are contrastive. On the contrary, they are even less transparent than Trubetzkoy's discussion.

14.3.2.1 Martinet (1964): Contrasts Based on Place

Martinet's *Éléments de linguistique générale*, first published in 1960 and translated into English by Elisabeth Palmer (Martinet 1964), follows in the Prague School tradition of phonological analysis. Martinet's analysis of the Standard French consonantal inventory appears to draw on Trubetzkoy's, though the theoretical basis for it is if anything even more obscure. This despite the fact that Martinet (1964, 62–64) goes to some lengths to provide a method of determining what the relevant features are that characterize the set of contrasting phonemes for French. He does not, however, provide an algorithm or any general method, and his discussion leaves unanswered a series of questions as to why he makes the choices he does. His approach, as far as I can see, is consistent with neither FS nor CH.

Martinet (p. 64) proposes the contrastive specifications shown in (16). He puts the names of the features in quotation marks to emphasize that these are not intended as exhaustive phonetic descriptions, but rather as phonological contrastive categories.[8]

(16) *Contrastive sets of French consonants (Martinet 1964, 64)*

"unvoiced"	/p f t s š k/	"voiced"	/b v d z ž g/
"nonnasal"	/b d j/	"nasal"	/m n ɲ/
"bilabial"	/p b m/	"labiodental"	/f v/
"apical"	/t d n/	"lateral"	/l/
"hiss"	/s z/	"hush"	/š ž/
"palatal"	/j ɲ/	"uvular"	/r/
"dorsovelar"	/k g/		

The contrastive features for voicing and nasality appear at first to follow from FS: the segments listed as contrastively "unvoiced" or "voiced" are those that have a direct counterpart in the other category; phonemes that are not contrastively voiced or voiceless include /m n ɲ l r j/, all of which lack voiceless partners. Similarly, only voiced /b d j/ are listed as contrastively "nonnasal." But the method is not consistently applied: /j ɲ/ are treated as a minimal pair with respect to "nasal/nonnasal" on a par with /b m/ and /d n/, despite the fact that /j/ is not an obstruent or a stop, and hence is distinguished from /ɲ/ by several other features. It is not explained why these features are suppressed here but not in other cases.

The remaining features do not fall into binary plus and minus groupings, and thus require some further interpretation. It is evident that Martinet is following Trubetzkoy's approach in favoring place distinctions over occlusion: no feature like "continuant" is listed in (16), though minor place distinctions, such as "bilabial" and "labiodental," are. Unlike Trubetzkoy, Martinet does not make explicit his reason for favoring place over continuancy distinctions. This aspect of his analysis cannot be reconstructed in terms of a FS approach, because /b v/ are not distinguished only by place.

The lack of negative place designations such as "nonlabial," and so on, suggests that Martinet conceives of place as a multivalued feature, with values including "bilabial," "labiodental," "apical," "palatal," "uvular,"[9] and "dorsovelar." Despite their names, which suggest a connection with stridency, the features "hiss" and "hush" can be interpreted as being values of this place feature as well; otherwise, we might have expected some segments to be contrastively "nonhiss" or "nonhush." The same considerations hold for the feature "lateral."

Martinet represents some of these features and phonemes in tabular form, shown in (17).[10] With the feature "nonnasal" omitted, this table begins to look more like the result of a CH approach to contrast, with the ordering [place] > [voiced] > [nasal].

(17) *French consonants (Martinet 1964, 65)*

	"Bilabial"	"Labiodental"	"Apical"	"Hiss"	"Hush"	"Palatal"	"Dorsovelar"
"Voiceless"	p	f	t	s	š		k
"Voiced"	b	v	d	z	ž		g
"Nasal"	m		n			ɲ	
						j	

14.3.2.2 Jakobson and Lotz (1949): Contrasts Based on Manner Jakobson and Lotz (1949) take a different approach to French consonant contrasts than do Trubetzkoy and Martinet. They propose that French stops and fricatives are distinguished by manner rather than by place. They do not explicitly indicate how they arrive at their contrastive specifications, but their results are consistent with CH. Based on their representations, we can reconstruct their analysis in terms of the tree in (18).

(18) *Contrastive Hierarchy for French consonants (Jakobson and Lotz 1949)*[11]

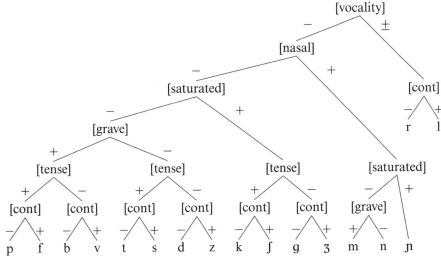

   Though a hierarchical approach to contrast is only implicit in Jakobson and Lotz 1949, in the 1950s Jakobson and his collaborators explicitly proposed what I have been calling the CH approach and presented a number of arguments in favor of it (see Jakobson, Fant, and Halle 1952; Cherry, Halle, and Jakobson 1953; Jakobson and Halle 1956; Halle 1959). Jakobson, Fant, and Halle (1952) go so far as to state that the "dichotomous scale" "is the pivotal principle of the linguistic structure." Nevertheless, their use of it was inconsistent, perhaps because they were unable to arrive at a single universal hierarchy that could apply to all the languages they studied. Nor did they present empirical arguments that would connect it to phonological activity. Therefore, there was no defense when the use of "branching diagrams" (i.e., contrastive feature hierarchies) was challenged on various grounds by Stanley (1967); they do not appear in Chomsky and Halle 1968, which replaced CH and the underspecification of redundant features with full specification in the phonology combined with the beginnings of a theory of markedness.
   Despite the arguments of Stanley (1967), underspecification began to reappear in generative phonology in the 1980s. However, CH, which could have given underspecification a principled rationale, did not reappear with it. Once again, the basis for distinguishing between contrastive and redundant specifications remained largely unstated and fatally vague, undermining a number of otherwise insightful proposals.

14.4 Some Generative Approaches to Contrast

14.4.1 Structure Preservation (Kiparsky 1985)

Another example where an important theoretical proposal is undermined by a lack of an explicit theory of contrast concerns the development of theories of underspecification in the 1980s. Kiparsky (1982, 1985) observes that voicing in English is distinctive for obstruents but not sonorants.[12] He proposes that this fact suggests that there exists a marking condition that prohibits voicing from being marked on sonorants in the lexicon (19a). He proposes further to extend this prohibition throughout the lexical phonology, a constraint he calls *Structure Preservation* (19b).

(19) *Underspecification and Structure Preservation (Kiparsky 1985, 92)*
    a. Marking condition: *[αvoiced, +sonorant] in the lexicon
    b. Structure Preservation: Marking conditions such as (19a) must be
       applicable not only to underived lexical representations but also to derived
       lexical representations including the output of word-level rules.

The marking condition in (19a), together with Structure Preservation (19b), accounts for the fact that English lexical voicing assimilation is triggered by and applies to obstruents, not sonorants.

    The term "Structure Preservation" is taken from syntax (Emonds 1976). Emonds's initial definition is given in (20).

(20) *Structure-preserving transformation (Emonds 1976, 3)*
    A transformation... that introduces or substitutes a constituent C into a
    position in a phrase marker held by a node C is called "structure preserving."

More informally, "a transformational operation is structure-preserving if it moves, copies, or inserts a node C into some position where C can be otherwise generated by the grammar." In the syntactic theory assumed by Emonds 1976, Structure Preservation is reasonably well defined, because it can be assessed against the set of phrase structure rules.

    In the theory of phonology assumed by Kiparsky (1985), however, there is no analogue to the phrase structure rules to provide a set of structures against which Structure Preservation can be assessed. The lack of an independent source of "structures" creates a serious ambiguity in the notion of Structure Preservation.

    In the English example mentioned above, Kiparsky assumes that the relevant domain within which voicing is distinctive is that of the obstruent consonants. While this choice of relevant domain is quite plausible and perhaps correct, it is by no means self-evident. The domain relevant to a contrast is never simply given by the system. Failure to specify the principles that motivate conditions like (19a) causes Structure Preservation to be ill-defined.

One language in which this question arises in dramatic fashion is Russian. Maddieson (1984) presents the consonantal inventory of Russian as in (21).[13]

(21) *Russian consonantal inventory (Maddieson 1984)*

	Bilabial	Labiodental	Dental	Dental/alveolar	Palatoalveolar	Palatal	Velar
Voiceless plosive	p		t				k
Voiced plosive	b		d				g
Voiceless sibilant affricate				ts	tš		
Voiceless nonsibilant fricative		f					x
Voiceless sibilant fricative			s		š		
Voiced sibilant fricative			z		ž		
Voiced nasal	m		n				
Voiced trill			r				
Voiced lateral approximant			l				
Voiced central approximant						j	

In what class of segments is voicing contrastive in this language? Because of the existence of unpaired voiceless segments /f ts tš x/, there is no single answer to this question: the domain can be assigned in various ways, depending on how features are ordered. Proceeding from widest to narrowest, we can say that voicing is contrastive in any of the domains in (22).

(22) Domains within which voicing is potentially contrastive
  a. The language: [voiced] > all other features
  b. The obstruents: [sonorant] > [voiced] > other features
  c. The (obstruent) plosives and fricatives: [sonorant] > [continuant], [delayed release] > [voiced]
  d. The nonfricatives and coronal fricatives: [sonorant] > [continuant] > place features > [voiced]
  e. The stops and coronal fricatives: all other features > [voiced]

Each of these domain specifications is correct, in the sense that we can specify the domain so that voicing can indeed be said to be contrastive over that domain. Admittedly, some domain specifications are more natural than others. More particularly, each domain specification implies some hierarchy of features, as in (22).

Other scenarios are possible. For example, [voiced] can intervene between the place features dividing labial from velar fricatives. In that case, one of /f/ or /x/ will be contrastively voiceless, the other will not.

Observe how the notion of a "counterpart" changes with the ranking of the features. Thus the question "does /ts/ have a voiced counterpart?" has no single answer. In (a), every voiced segment is a counterpart to /ts/ with respect to [voiced]; in (b), all the voiced obstruents {b, d, g, z, ž} are its counterparts; in (c) it has no voiced counterpart; in (d), the voiced counterpart of both /ts/ and /tš/ is /d/; in (e), it again has no voiced counterpart.

By the same token, Structure Preservation requires an ordering of features against which it may be evaluated. To put the question concretely, is it a violation of Structure Preservation if /ts/ is voiced in the lexical phonology?

In the case of Russian, we must look to empirical evidence for information on what the actual patterning of the consonant system is. Voicing assimilation does not affect sonorants, nor do sonorants trigger it. Therefore, we conclude that voicing is noncontrastive for sonorants. However, all the obstruents participate in voicing assimilation, including the affricates and noncoronal fricatives.[14] This fact suggests that, unlike the sonorants, these phonemes are contrastively [−voiced].

Establishing a contrastive hierarchy for Russian would play the same role with respect to Structure Preservation that the phrase structure rules played in Emonds's original syntactic formulation. Constraints such as (19a) could then be derived from the feature hierarchy in a systematic way.

14.4.2   Contrastive Underspecification (Steriade 1987)

Steriade (1987) argues that we must distinguish between two rule types. First, there are redundancy, or R-rules, which introduce a redundant value within a class for which that value is fully predictable. The familiar voicing on sonorants provides her prototypical example of an R-value introduced by an R-rule. The second class of rules, D-rules, introduce D-values—that is, contrastive feature values that distinguish between segments. In a language with voicing contrasts among obstruents, the feature [voiced] is distinctive in the obstruent inventory, and so is a D-value for the obstruents. Steriade proposes that only R-values are underspecified; contrary to Kiparsky (1985), she proposes that both D-values (+ and −) are specified underlyingly. Thus, in a language with both voiced and voiceless stops, the voiced stops are specified as [+voiced] and the voiceless stops as [−voiced].

Steriade's proposal puts the notion of contrast at the center of underspecification theory, by making a basic distinction between contrastive and redundant values. It thus becomes absolutely crucial to know whether a feature value is redundant or contrastive in any particular instance. Like Kiparsky, however, Steriade does not supply an explicit formal mechanism for determining contrasts, but relies on analyses that are plausible-looking and yield the desired results.

The Pasiego dialect of Montañes Spanish has five vowels. Steriade (1987, 343) argues that /a/, which neither triggers nor blocks a rule of height harmony, has no marking for the feature [high]. This is because "the impossibility of simultaneous [+high, +low] specifications establishes that the height of low vowels is a R-value" (p. 342). This analysis appears to be unproblematic, especially when the vowel system is diagrammed as in (23), where /a/ is the obvious odd person out with respect to the feature [high]:

(23) *Pasiego (Steriade 1987)*

```
    i           u   +high
                         D-class of [high]
    e       o       −high
```
_____

```
        a               R-class of [high]
```

However, these cases are deceptively simple looking: the basis according to which D-values are determined is not self-evident. The values in (23) correspond to (24a), and require [low] > [high]. If [high] > [low], as in (24b), [high] would be a D-value for /a/. Notice also that in the former case, the high vowels are specified [−low].

(24) *Pasiego Spanish vowels: Possible orderings of [high] and [low]*

a. low > high						b. high > low				
i	e	a	o	u		i	e	a	o	u
+	−		−	+	high	+	−	−	−	+
−	−	+	−	−	low		−	+	−	

Similarly, Steriade (1987) argues that the low vowel /a/ is unspecified for [back] in triangular five-vowel systems such as those of Ainu and Tamil. Again, though she does not state this explicitly, the analysis relies on a contrastive feature hierarchy whereby [low] > [back]. A similar point can be made for the other cases she discusses.

Although Steriade (1987) makes no mention of the contrastive hierarchy as a general principle for determining if feature values are contrastive or redundant, she does propose a hypothesis that translates into a constraint on possible hierarchies. Dividing features into *stricture features* (essentially manner features for consonants and height features for vowels) and *content features* (place features for consonants and timbre features for vowels), she proposes that in a redundancy rule $[\alpha F] \rightarrow [\beta G]$, F may be a stricture feature and G may be a content feature, but not vice versa. Thus, we may have a redundancy rule $[+\text{low}] \rightarrow [+\text{back}]$, but not $[+\text{round}] \rightarrow [+\text{high}]$. This is tantamount to claiming that stricture features must always have wider contrastive scope than content features—that is, they are ordered higher in the contrastive hierarchy.[15]

14.4.3 Arguments against Underspecification

The lack of formal contrastive underpinnings for the underspecification theories of the 1980s led to a backlash against underspecification in the 1990s. The main arguments, however, really concern the lack of a theory of contrast, rather than underspecification per se.

Thus, it has been argued (Steriade 1995; Kirchner 1997) that underspecification is applied inconsistently. For example, in most languages there are no voiceless sonorants and no nasal obstruents. In the first case, [+voiced] is typically omitted from sonorants because it is predictable. By the same token, in the second case, [+sonorant] is predictable given [+nasal]; nevertheless, this specification is rarely omitted. Numerous such cases can be adduced, and many analyses that have appealed to underspecification have indeed been inconsistent in this way.

The answer to the charge of inconsistency is that the contrastive feature hierarchy decides which features are omitted. In the above example, [sonorant] is a major class feature that is typically high in the order. Assuming [sonorant] > [voiced], the inventory is divided into sonorant and nonsonorant sets before it is divided by [voiced]; since there is no voicing contrast in the [sonorant] set, [voiced] is redundant in that set, hence underspecified. Similarly, it is more common for [sonorant] to take scope over [nasal] than it is for [nasal] to take scope over [sonorant]. Therefore, [+sonorant] must be specified even where it is made logically redundant by [+nasal]. The hierarchy [nasal] > [sonorant] is less likely and could lead to an unusual set of contrasts in an inventory.[16]

The problem of inconsistency is thus not inherent in contrastive (under)specification itself, but rather in implementations of underspecification theory (such as that of Steriade 1987) that provide no principled rationale for distinguishing between contrastive and redundant feature values. The contrastive hierarchy provides such a rationale.

Notes

I am honored to dedicate this chapter to Jean-Roger Vergnaud, who has been a source of inspiration to me for many years. The example sentence used by Jakobson and Lotz (1949), which doubles as their dedication to Henri Muller, is appropriate here as well: *Cher Maître, voulez-vous nous permettre de vous présenter nos hommages et nos meilleures voeux de santé, de parfait bonheur et de tranquillité d'âme!*

This research was supported in part by grant 410-2003-0913 from the Social Sciences and Humanities Research Council of Canada. The chapter has benefited from comments by two reviewers.

1. It is not obvious that these are the operative features, or if they are, that they apply to these segments—see note 12 for some alternatives. In this chapter I will generally use the features as found in my sources.

2. The specifications in (7a) violate the Distinctness Condition (Halle 1959, 32), which holds that two phonemes are distinct (in contrast) if and only if at least one feature that is contrastive in both has a different value in each—that is, plus in the former and minus in the latter, or vice versa, but not zero.

3. Similar arguments hold against the procedure for contrastive specification discussed by Archangeli (1988). The failure of this class of algorithms does not constitute an argument against contrastive specification in general; for further discussion, see Dresher 2002, 2004.

4. This discussion assumes a space of only the three features [low], [high], and [back]. As shown above, adding even one feature, [round], enlarges the feature space in such a way that there are insufficient near neighbors to distinguish the members of the inventory.

5. Hall (2004, 2007) argues that the existence of phonetic enhancement (Stevens, Keyser, and Kawasaki 1986), which heightens phonetic contrasts by increasing the number of featural distinctions between phonemes, dooms FS to failure. That is, any method relying on phonetic minimal pairs distinguished by only one feature is based on the wrong intuition about how segments in an inventory are distributed in the space of features.

6. Because Trubetzkoy does not give a chart, I adapt this one from Martinet 1964, whose analysis is clearly influenced by Trubetzkoy.

7. I substitute phonetic transcription for Trubetzkoy's Greek letters.

8. "Hiss" is the translator's rendering of Martinet's term *sifflant*, and "hush" translates *chuintant*. I use ɲ in place of Martinet's ñ.

9. The representation of /r/ as "uvular" is unexpected, because Martinet asserts elsewhere (p. 54) that /r/ does not always have a uvular pronunciation in French. According to Trubetzkoy's criteria, variation in place of /r/ indicates that [uvular] is not the defining characteristic of the phoneme. Features such as "rhotic" or "liquid" and "nonlateral" would appear to be more obvious choices, but these are not considered by Martinet, for reasons left unexplained.

10. Martinet comments that not all the phonemes and features listed in (16) appear in the table. Note that /j/ is listed in an unlabeled row.

11. In the feature system assumed by Jakobson and Lotz (1949, 152), "the liquids *l* and *r* are complexes combining the consonantal characteristic with a vocalic one." The full feature names are "vowel/consonant," "nasal/oral," "saturated/diluted," "grave/acute," "tense/lax," and "continuous/interrupted." They consider the French *r* flap articulation to be interrupted, in contrast to the continuous lateral opening of *l*.

12. The example of [voiced] being predictable given [sonorant] is perhaps the oldest and most common example of underspecification in the literature (Stanley 1967; Kiparsky 1982, 1985). Nevertheless, it may not be a good example if, as has been argued, sonorants do not have the same voicing feature as voiced obstruents (Piggott 1992; Rice 1993; Avery 1996; Boersma 1998). For purposes of this discussion, we will assume for the moment that sonorants do potentially bear a feature [voiced] that is also carried by voiced obstruents. What is crucial here is the logic of the argument, whether or not sonorant voicing is in fact a good exemplar of it.

13. Maddieson's sources are Jones and Ward 1969 and Halle 1959. I omit the palatalized/velarized distinction from the chart. Following Calabrese 1995, I also omit /v/ from the

underlying inventory. Russian is language 008 on the UPSID database. I have left off Maddieson's dental diacritics from dentals (*ţ*, etc.), and substituted *š* for *ʃ*, *ž* for *ʒ*, and *ts* for "*ts*."

14. This fact was famously taken by Halle (1959) to argue against the post-Bloomfieldian taxonomic phonemic level. In post-Bloomfieldian theory, the voicing of /k/ to [g] changes one phoneme to another, and hence is a morphophonemic rule, whereas the voicing of /ts/ to [dz] is an allophonic rule.

15. Ghini (2001), however, proposes that place contrasts precede height contrasts.

16. Other theories have been proposed that posit dependency relations among features: markedness theory (Chomsky and Halle 1968; Kean 1975), feature geometry (Clements 1985; Clements and Hume 1995; Sagey 1986; Halle 1995), Government Phonology (Kaye, Lowenstamm, and Vergnaud 1986), Dependency Phonology (Anderson and Ewen 1987), and Radical CV Phonology (van der Hulst 1996). The relationship of these theories to the Contrastive Hierarchy is complex, and cannot be discussed here, but all of them, in different ways, impose hierarchical relations among distinctive features.

References

Anderson, John, and Colin Ewen. 1987. *Principles of Dependency Phonology*. Cambridge: Cambridge University Press.

Archangeli, Diana. 1988. Aspects of underspecification theory. *Phonology* 5, 183–207.

Avery, Peter. 1996. The Representation of Voicing Contrasts. Doctoral dissertation, University of Toronto.

Boersma, Paul. 1998. *Functional Phonology: Formalizing the Interactions between Articulatory and Perceptual Drives (LOT International Series 11)*. The Hague: Holland Academic Graphics.

Calabrese, Andrea 1995. A constraint-based theory of phonological markedness and simplification procedures. *Linguistic Inquiry* 26, 373–463.

Cherry, E. Colin, Morris Halle, and Roman Jakobson. 1953. Toward the logical description of languages in their phonemic aspect. *Language* 29, 34–46.

Chomsky, Noam, and Morris Halle. 1968. *The Sound Pattern of English*. New York: Harper & Row.

Clements, G. N. 1985. The geometry of phonological features. *Phonology Yearbook* 2, 225–252.

Clements, G. N., and Elizabeth V. Hume. 1995. The internal organization of speech sounds. In John A. Goldsmith, ed., *Handbook of Phonology*, 245–306. Oxford: Blackwell.

Dresher, B. Elan. 1998. On contrast and redundancy. Paper presented at the annual meeting of the Canadian Linguistic Association, Ottawa. Unpublished ms., University of Toronto.

Dresher, B. Elan. 2002. Determining contrastiveness: A missing chapter in the history of phonology. In Sophie Burelle and Stanca Somesfalean, eds., *Proceedings of the 2002 Annual Conference of the Canadian Linguistic Association*, Département de linguistique et de didactique des langues, Université du Québec à Montréal, 82–93.

Dresher, B. Elan. 2003a. Contrast and asymmetries in inventories. In Anna-Maria di Sciullo, ed., *Asymmetry in Grammar, Volume 2: Morphology, Phonology, Acquisition*, 239–257. Amsterdam: John Benjamins.

Dresher, B. Elan. 2003b. The contrastive hierarchy in phonology. In Daniel Currie Hall, ed., *Toronto Working Papers in Linguistics (Special Issue on Contrast in Phonology) 20*, Department of Linguistics, University of Toronto, 47–62.

Dresher, B. Elan. 2004. On the acquisition of phonological contrasts. In Jacqueline van Kampen and Sergio Baauw, eds., *Proceedings of GALA 2003, Volume 1 (LOT Occasional Series 3)*, 27–46, LOT, Utrecht.

Emonds, Joseph E. 1976. *A Transformational Approach to English Syntax: Root, Structure-Preserving, and Local Transformations*. New York: Academic Press.

Ghini, Mirco. 2001. *Asymmetries in the Phonology of Miogliola*. Berlin: Mouton de Gruyter.

Hall, Daniel Currie. 2004. Pairwise, pound foolish: Adjacency and contrast in inventories. Paper presented at the MOT Phonology Workshop, University of Ottawa, February. Unpublished ms., Department of Linguistics, University of Toronto.

Hall, Daniel Currie. 2007. The Role and Representation of Contrast in Phonological Theory. Doctoral dissertation, University of Toronto.

Halle, Morris. 1959. *The Sound Pattern of Russian: A Linguistic and Acoustical Investigation*. The Hague: Mouton.

Halle, Morris. 1995. Feature geometry and feature spreading. *Linguistic Inquiry* 26, 1–46.

Hulst, Harry van der. 1996. Radical CV Phonology: The segment-syllable connection. In Jacques Durand and Bernard Laks, eds., *Current Trends in Phonology: Models and Methods*, 333–361. Salford, Manchester: European Studies Research Institute, University of Salford.

Jakobson, Roman, and Morris Halle. 1956. *Fundamentals of Language*. The Hague: Mouton.

Jakobson, Roman, C. Gunnar M. Fant, and Morris Halle. 1952. *Preliminaries to Speech Analysis*. MIT Acoustics Laboratory, Technical Report, No. 13. Reissued by MIT Press, Cambridge, Mass., 1976.

Jakobson, Roman, and J. Lotz. 1949. Notes on the French phonemic pattern. *Word* 5, 151–158.

Jones, D., and D. Ward. 1969. *The Phonetics of Russian*. Cambridge: Cambridge University Press.

Kaye, Jonathan, Jean Lowenstamm, and Jean-Roger Vergnaud. 1986. The internal structure of phonological elements: A theory of charm and government. *Phonology Yearbook* 2, 305–328.

Kean, Mary-Louise. 1975. The Theory of Markedness in Generative Grammar. Doctoral dissertation, MIT. Reproduced by the Indiana University Linguistics Club, Bloomington, 1980.

Kiparsky, Paul. 1982. From cyclic to Lexical Phonology. In Harry van der Hulst and Norval Smith, eds., *The Structure of Phonological Representations (Part I)*, 131–176. Foris: Dordrecht.

Kiparsky, Paul. 1985. Some consequences of Lexical Phonology. *Phonology Yearbook* 2, 85–138.

Kirchner, Robert. 1997. Contrastiveness and faithfulness. *Phonology* 14, 83–111.

Maddieson, Ian. 1984. *Patterns of Sounds*. Cambridge: Cambridge University Press.

Martinet, André. 1964. *Elements of General Linguistics*. With a foreword by L. R. Palmer. Translated by Elisabeth Palmer. Chicago: University of Chicago Press.

Piggott, Glyne. 1992. Variability in feature dependency: The case of nasality. *Natural Language and Linguistic Theory* 10, 33–77.

Rice, Keren. 1993. A reexamination of the feature [sonorant]: The status of "sonorant obstruents." *Language* 69, 308–344.

Sagey, Elizabeth. 1986. The Representation of Features and Relations in Non-linear Phonology. Doctoral dissertation, MIT.

Stanley, Richard. 1967. Redundancy rules in phonology. *Language* 43, 393–436.

Steriade, Donca. 1987. Redundant values. In Anna Bosch, Barbara Need, and Eric Schiller, eds., *CLS 23: Papers from the 23rd Annual Regional Meeting of the Chicago Linguistic Society. Part Two: Parasession on Autosegmental and Metrical Phonology*, 339–362. Chicago: Chicago Linguistic Society.

Steriade, Donca. 1995. Underspecification and markedness. In John A. Goldsmith, ed., *Handbook of Phonology*, 114–174. Oxford: Blackwell.

Stevens, Kenneth N., Samuel Jay Keyser, and Haruko Kawasaki. 1986. Toward a phonetic and phonological theory of redundant features. In Joseph S. Perkell and Dennis H. Klatt, eds., *Symposium on Invariance and Variability of Speech Processes*, 432–469. Hillsdale: Lawrence Erlbaum.

Trubetzkoy, N. S. 1969. *Principles of Phonology*. Berkeley: University of California Press. Translated by Christiane A. M. Baltaxe from *Grundzüge der Phonologie*. Göttingen: Vandenhoek & Ruprecht, 1939.

Tryon, D. T. 1970. *An Introduction to Maranungku (Pacific Linguistics Series B, 14)*. Canberra: Australian National University.

Index

A′-Movement, 34, 150, 168, 174, 175, 177, 180, 188, 207
A/A Condition, 8, 9, 11
A-A′ distinction, 144, 148, 150
Abels, K., 145, 146
A′-binding, 168
Abney, S. P., 73, 88
A′-chain, 149, 150, 152
A-Chain, 19, 20, 32, 149–153
Ackema, P., 242, 244
A′-dependency, 170, 172
Adger, D., 204–207
Adverbial, 74, 77, 82, 85, 86, 87, 96, 259
Agr, 94, 95–98, 99, 101
Agree, 64, 169–174, 176–179, 187
Agreement, multiple, 142, 159
  Object-Verb, 87, 91, 95
  Subject-Predicate, 11, 111
  Subject-Verb, 8, 11, 97, 213, 243
AgrO, 26–28, 84, 87, 90, 101
AgrS, 25, 101
Agta, 326, 329, 330
Albanian, 43
Alexiadou, P., 291, 295, 296, 300
Algonquin, 51
Allomorph, 84, 95
A-movement, 22, 30, 31, 32, 149, 150, 153–156, 210, 211, 213, 276
Anagnostopoulou, E., 145
Anand, P., 212, 213
Anaphor, 6, 12, 27, 28, 31, 32, 33, 64
Antecedent Contained Deletion (ACD), 276–283
Antiagreement, 207, 210, 212, 214, 219, 243

Antireconstruction, 210–214
Aoun, J. , 21, 167, 185, 197, 199, 200–205, 109, 210–212, 217–219, 251, 252, 254, 256, 258, 260, 262, 264, 266
A′-position, 150–152
A-position, 150
Appositive, 29
Arabic, 106, 107, 108, 114, 116, 117, 119, 123
  Egyptian Arabic, 116, 117
  Lebanese Arabic, 167, 185, 197, 200, 202, 207, 213, 216–219
  Levantine Arabic, 332, 333
  Moroccan Arabic, 109, 124
  Palestinian Arabic, 220
  Standard Arabic, 109, 112, 113, 118, 121
Argument structure, 138, 140, 141
Armenian (Eastern), 77, 79, 81, 82, 84–89, 93, 94–96, 98, 99, 100
Armenian (Western), 95
Aspect, 73, 86
Aspect Phrase (AspP), 88, 90
  predicate, 85, 86
  progressive aspect, 88
  VP aspect, 74, 75, 76, 86, 88, 91, 93, 100
Avoid Pronoun Principle, 229, 240, 245
Awbery, G., 168

Baker, M., 119–121, 126, 156
Bakir, M., 111, 126
Balangao, 337
Baltin, M., 276
Basaa, 337
Basque, 209

Benmamoun, E., 105, 106, 108, 110, 112, 114, 116, 118, 120, 122, 124, 199
Bhatt, R., 199
Bhattacharya, T., 89
Bianchi, V., 295
Big DP, 208, 209
Binding Theory (BT), 141, 145, 149
Biolinguistic, 133–135
Blevins, J., 345
Bobaljik, J., 119, 211
Boeckx, C., 168, 188, 197, 198, 200, 202, 204–210, 212–220
Borer, H., 73, 76, 88, 90, 100
Boskovic, Z., 29, 30, 146, 262
Boundedness, 73, 88, 91, 92, 95, 99, 100, 198
  predicate, 75, 76, 85, 87
  verb phrase, 76, 77, 86, 90 (see also Verb Phrase Aspect)
Bresnan, J., 10
Breton, 185
Bricolage, 138
Bridge adjunct, 236–240
Brody, M., 199, 204
Broselow, E., 325, 332
Bulgarian, 198
Butt, M., 84

Case position, 20, 23, 24
  abstract case, 18, 53, 262
  accusative, 22, 25, 30, 43–46, 49, 51–56, 58, 61, 74–87, 90, 95–99, 112–114, 262, 263
Case assignment, 18, 20, 24, 59, 75, 94, 99, 109
Case marking, 4, 7, 4, 76–81, 84, 85, 93, 95, 98–100, 263
Case transmission, 24–25
  checking, 18, 84, 87, 107
  dative, 43–47, 52, 54, 56
  ergative, 212, 213
  genitive Case, 3, 18, 77, 234
  governed Case, 3–4, 5, 18
  inherent Case, 54, 213
  nominative, 19, 25, 107, 108, 110, 112, 113, 114, 143, 209, 212, 213
  null case, 22

partitive, 74, 77, 99
structural Case, 54, 92, 98, 107, 142, 148, 154, 155
subject Case, 3, 18
Causative, 54, 60
C-command, 8, 26, 27, 31, 33, 141, 142, 146, 169, 179, 182, 184, 185, 198, 203, 212, 218, 220, 260
Cecchetto, C., 155
Celtic, 168
Chamorro, 207
Cheng, L., 198, 311
Chierchia, G., 88, 302, 311
Chinese, 232, 251–253, 255, 257, 260–266, 311
Chomsky N. 13, 15, 17, 18, 19, 20, 21, 22, 23, 24, 32, 46, 54, 59, 60, 64, 87, 106, 110, 114, 115, 133, 134, 136, 137, 138, 140–144, 146, 150, 152, 154, 156, 157, 169, 174, 175, 177, 179, 180, 183, 197, 199, 204, 205, 208–210, 214–220, 227, 229, 245, 262, 266, 308, 310, 311
Choueiri, L., 167, 185, 199, 200, 217, 218
Chung, C., 232
Chung, S., 207
Cinque, G., 47, 105, 311
Classifier (Cl), 78, 89, 91, 92
Clitic, 43, 46, 47, 48, 50, 97, 107, 171, 174, 212, 220, 229, 238, 240, 244
  accusative, 58, 61, 62
  pronoun, 44, 45, 122
Clitic-Left Dislocation (also CLLD), 212
  enclitic, 84, 97, 116, 117, 122
  proclitic, 116, 117, 123
  subject, 46, 54, 62, 63
Collins, C., 141, 212, 267
Comparative construction, 12, 145, 280
Complementizer, 6, 20, 35n.2, 83, 92, 109, 110
  declarative, 174, 175
  for, 6, 7, 11
  nominal CP, 29
  relative, 170, 171, 172, 174, 175, 179
  resumptive, 175, 177
Conceptual-intentional interface (C-I), 136, 138, 139, 141, 142, 144, 146, 148, 151, 215

Consonant, 84, 85

Control, 22, 23, 157, 257

Coordination, 110

Copula, 111, 112, 113, 114, 119, 122, 124, 233
  null, 110–113
  verbal, 110–112, 114, 115, 116, 119, 120,
    121, 123

Copy, 140, 145, 146, 149, 150, 152, 180, 182,
  186, 187, 199, 201, 202, 205, 210–214, 217,
  220, 242, 258, 259

Corte, 49, 50, 55–58

C-T, 144, 148, 149, 150, 152, 153

Dative-nominative experiencer construction,
  152

Dativity, 44

Davis, H., 51

Davis, L, 20

Dèchaine, R.-M., 51

Declarative, 171, 174, 175, 178, 241

Defective intervention, 209, 210, 219

Definiteness, 44, 45, 47, 48, 55, 57, 61, 74, 75,
  77, 78, 80, 81, 84, 85, 87, 125
  definite description, 169, 182, 183, 186, 187,
    188
  definite pronoun, 183–185

Deletion
  category, 8
  Complementizer, 10, 12, 265
  recoverability, 9
  subject pronoun, 9, 10
  VP-deletion, 12, 251
  wh-deletion, 12

Delfitto, D., 302

Demirdash, H., 198

Demonstrative, 80, 126

Den Dikken, M., 28

Descriptive adequacy, 134

Determiner, 81, 89, 91, 94
  definite, 301, 302, 305, 310
  null, 89
  strong/weak, 80–82

Deviance, 144, 145, 151

Di Domenico E., 47

Discourse, 78, 79, 82, 140, 141, 144, 256–259,
  265, 266

Discrete infinity, 137

Distributed Morphology (DM), 49, 61, 63,
  64, 93

Distributive (also distributivity, also
  distributive reading), 44, 45

D-Linked, 82

Donati, C., 145

Donkey anaphora (also E-type anaphora),
  182

Doron, E., 123–126

Double object construction, 73

Dresher, E. , 359, 360, 362, 364, 366, 368,
  370, 372, 374, 376

D-Structure, 137, 139

Dutch, 234–236, 243

Elbourne, P., 182

Elmolo, 337

Emonds, J., 12, 372, 374

Enç, E., 78, 80, 81, 82, 84

English, 9, 18, 20, 47, 48, 82, 88, 106, 108,
  111, 114, 115, 119, 138, 152, 156, 167, 185,
  199, 201, 206, 230, 232–234, 251–255,
  261–265, 293–299, 308, 309

EPP, 22, 29, 30, 33, 34, 46, 107, 114, 140,
  149, 153, 156, 157, 173, 178, 213, 243

Ernst, T, 259

Evans, G., 182

Event, 75, 76, 85, 87, 90, 92, 93, 94

Evolution, 135–139

Exceptional Case Marking (ECM), 22, 25,
  26, 27, 28, 30, 31, 32, 34, 54, 62, 143, 148,
  153, 154, 155, 156, 157

Existential Construction, 80

Explanatory adequacy, 134, 135, 138, 197

Expletive, 20, 24, 25, 28, 34, 106, 106–108,
  110, 152, 156, 157, 251

Extended Standard Theory (EST)/Y-model,
  137, 142

Extended X-bar Principle, 91

External argument, 143, 144, 147, 148

Extraposition, 276, 278, 281, 286

Faculty of language (FL), 133, 134–136,
  138–140

Fant, G. M., 360, 371

Fassi Fehri, A., 111, 126
Feature, 139
  activation, 173, 174
  Agree, 148–154
  case, 151
  Edge (EF), 139, 148–154
  inheritance, 144, 145, 147–150, 154, 156
  interpretable, 151, 154
  P-, 174, 177
  Tense, 143
  uninterpretable, 144, 149, 150–152, 154,
    155, 169, 178, 213
  wh-, 151, 152
Ferguson, S., 198
Fiengo, R., 252, 276, 277, 281
Filter, 4–5, 7–10, 11, 12
  Case, 18, 19–22, 24, 25, 28, 29, 53, 54
  Doubly Filled COMP (DFC), 227, 231, 237,
    240, 241
  Inverse Case, 30, 31, 33, 36, 262
Finite, 107, 109, 110, 171, 176, 177, 209,
  245
Finnish, 74–78, 85, 87, 88, 90, 92, 95, 99
Fitzpatrick, J., 325
Focus, 277, 282–285, 289
Fox,. D., 185, 186, 199, 214, 276, 278
Frampton, J., 325, 328
Free relative, 145
Freidin, R., 20, 21, 157, 169, 183
French, 10, 11, 115, 291–309, 361, 366–371
Fukui, N., 30

Garden path, 136
Gartner, H-M., 242
Gender, 43, 44, 45, 47, 50, 51, 57, 124, 125.
  See also Phi-features
Generalized Quantifier, 279
Georgian, 51
German, 152, 211, 308
  Swiss German, 227–230, 233, 240, 242, 244,
    245
Glaude, H., 295
Goldberg, L., 251, 253
Goldsmith, J., 326
Governing Category, 31, 32
Government-Binding Theory, 18, 168, 197,
  257, 262

Greek, 291, 295–297, 299
  Attic Greek, 334, 335
Grewndorf, G., 198
Grimshaw, J. , 105, 110, 111, 114, 126, 242,
  244, 265
Groat, E., 198
Grohmann, K., 198, 199
Grosu, A., 232
Guilliot, N., 185

Haeberli, E., 243
Hale, K., 73
Halle, M., 49, 61, 73, 93, 325, 326, 328, 330,
  332–334, 336, 340–342, 344, 346, 352, 354,
  360, 371
Haplology, 227, 230, 237, 238, 240, 242
Harlow, S., 168, 174
Harris, J.W., 47, 333
Head-raising, 167, 171
Head-raising relative, 152
Hebrew, 105, 106, 111, 114, 116, 123–127
Heim, I., 182
Hidden locative, 233–235
Hindi, 84, 87, 90, 94, 95, 99, 212, 213
Hiraiwa, K., 142, 143, 146
Hirschbuhler, P., 276, 285, 287–289
Hixkaryana, 337
Hoji, H., 252, 253, 255
Holmberg, A., 152
Hornstein, N., 168, 185, 197–200, 202, 204,
  206, 208, 210, 212, 214, 216, 276
Hroarsdottir, T., 152
Huang, J. C-T, 146, 147, 253, 257, 259
Hume, E., 325, 337, 338
Hungarian, 337

Iatridou, S., 145, 212
Icelandic, 142, 143, 152, 209, 297
Identity Avoidance, 227–229, 231, 233, 235,
  237, 239, 241–243, 245
Identity effects, 205–208
Idsardi, W., 341
I-Language, 133–136, 142, 144, 154
Inclusiveness Condition, 138, 145, 183, 199
Indefiniteness, 47, 74, 77–79, 81, 83, 84, 86,
  87, 89, 93, 98, 100
Infinite Regression, 276, 277

Infinitival, 3–4, 18, 19,27, 31, 32, 36, 143, 153, 157
  complement, 17, 27, 29, 34, 243
  indirect question, 13
  interrogative, 6
  relative, 6, 7
Infl, 22, 24, 25, 30
Inflectional morphology, 48
Instrumental, 83
Intervention, intervention effect, 142, 143, 151, 152, 153, 203, 209, 210, 243
Irish, 168, 171, 172, 174, 206
Ishihara, S., 155
Island violation, 146, 167, 168, 171, 179, 228, 230, 231, 233, 236, 238, 239, 257
  adjunct-island, 146, 147
  subject-island, 147, 151, 153, 154, 156
  CED-islands, 204
  islandhood, 202, 204, 209
  strong island, 205, 208
Italian, 43, 48, 50, 51, 52, 53, 54, 57, 58, 59, 61, 62, 207, 244, 291–301, 303–310
Izvorski, R., 145

Jackendoff, R., 227
Jakobson, R., 359, 360, 368, 369–371
Johnson, K., 212

Kahnemuyipour, A., 84
Kaingang, 338, 339
Karimi, S., 84, 89
Kayne, R., 31, 46, 51, 57, 138, 146
Keer, E., 244
Kennedy, C., 276, 279
Keyser, S. J., 73
Kim, J-B., 232
Kim, S., 199, 253
Kiparsky, P., 74, 75, 76, 87, 372, 374
Kitagawa, Y., 29
Kolami, 334, 336, 337
Korean, 232, 255
Krifka, M., 75
Kuno, S., 232

Label, 141, 143, 145, 148, 151, 155, 267
Làconi, 44, 45
Lakoff, G., 244

Lambda Calculus, 275, 279
Landau, I., 146
Larson, R., 73, 94, 276
Lasnik, H., 19, 20, 21, 22, 31, 137, 141, 146, 149, 198, 199, 210, 211, 227, 276
Late Insertion, 49, 147
Latin, 11, 58
Lebeaux, D., 185
Leben, W., 227
Left-dislocation, 107
Left periphery, 143, 151
Lexical Categories, 47, 105, 114, 119
Lexicon, 139, 143, 145, 154, 253
Li, Y.-H. A., 167, 197, 200–204, 217, 251–253, 255, 257, 259
Linear Correspondence Axiom (LCA), 138, 159, 216
Lobeck, A., 213, 262, 265
Locality, 142, 147, 167, 168, 171, 172, 179, 204, 228, 243, 253
Locative, 51, 52, 54, 83, 126
Logical Form (LF), 1, 12, 21, 58, 98, 137, 139, 142, 168, 181, 183, 184, 186, 188, 204, 214, 216, 242, 252, 255, 258, 261
Long-distance Agree, 144, 151, 155, 156
Long-distance resumption, 174–175, 229
Longobardi, G., 302, 306, 311
LOOP, 327–329
Lotz, J., 369–371

McCarthy, J., 227, 325, 332
McCloskey, J., 168, 172, 177, 205
MacDonnel, A., 347
Madurese, 332, 333
Mahajan, A., 84, 87, 90
Mangyarrayi, 326, 329
Manzini, M. R., 43, 44
Marantz, A., 47, 49, 59, 61, 73, 93, 143, 325, 332
Maranungku, 363, 364
Martinet, A., 361, 367–370
Mass noun, 75, 88, 89, 93
Mass/count, 88, 91, 92, 302–308, 311
May, R., 212, 252
M-command, 146, 159
Megerdoomian, K., 74, 76, 78, 80, 82, 83, 84, 86, 88, 90, 92, 94, 96, 98

Merchant, J., 199, 208, 213, 284
Merge,
  External (EM), 140, 141, 144, 212
  Head, 160
  Internal (IM), 140, 141, 143, 144, 145, 146, 155
  Iterated, 139, 142
  Pair, 147
  Set, 147
  Unbounded, 137–139
Metathesis, 337, 338, 342, 343, 354
Middle English, 6, 11
Milsark, G., 80
Minimal Link Condition (MLC), 202, 204
Minimal Match Condition, 203–205, 210, 212
Minimal Move, 203, 210
Minimalist Program, 133, 135, 197, 211, 217
Minimality effect, 179, 202–205, 209, 210, 217
Miyagawa, S., 156
Mood, 176–178
Morphological merger, 118
Murasugi, K., 213

Narrow syntax, 136, 138, 139, 143, 168, 169, 188, 227, 242
Nash, L., 51
Negation, 108, 112, 113, 114, 116, 118, 119, 121, 122
  Sentential, 108, 116, 117, 118, 124
Negative Polarity Item (NPI), 27
Nested dependency, 136
Neural networks, 136
Nevins, A., 212, 213, 325
Nissenbaum, J., 143, 155, 175
Nominal class, 44, 45, 47–51, 55–57, 58, 60, 61, 251, 262–264, 267
Nonfinite, 109
No-Tampering Condition (NTC), 138–141, 144, 146
NP movement, 19, 106, 108, 110, 257, 260
Null operator, 168, 172, 173, 177
Number, 73, 105, 122, 124, 125, 303, 306
Number Phrase (NumP), 88, 89
Numeral, 299, 300

Object Shift (OS), 276
Obligatory Contour Principle (OCP), 227, 228, 231, 235, 237, 240–242
Ochi, M., 204
of- insertion, 17, 19
Oku, S., 251, 255
Operator, 233, 241, 242, 245, 260, 276, 279, 284, 286. *See also* Variable
Optimality Theory (OT), 244, 354
Otani, K., 253
Ouhalla, J., 118, 243
Ozark English, 6

Pan, H., 253
Parameter, 135, 156, 244, 245
Parenthetical Interpretation, 10
Participle, 110, 142, 144, 156
Particle, 109, 116, 117
Partitive, 74–77, 79, 81, 82, 99, 291, 303–305, 311
Passive, 95–97, 143, 147, 155
Passive verb, 19, 169
Paul, W., 253
Perlmutter, D., 201
Persian, 84, 87, 89, 94, 99
Person, 43, 44, 47, 51–53, 57, 61, 65, 122, 124, 125. *See also* Phi features
Pesetsky, D., 82, 176, 198, 199, 214
Phase, 142, 143
  head, 143, 144, 148, 150–153, 156, 174, 176
  level, 143, 148, 151, 155, 156
Phase Impenetrability Condition (PIC), 143, 152, 169, 170, 171, 173, 176, 179–181, 184
Phi-features, 43, 45, 47, 114, 142, 143, 144, 148, 172–178, 184, 188, 207–209, 212
Phrase structure rules, 17, 266, 267
Piatelli-Palmarini, M., 242, 243
Pied-piping, 297, 298, 303, 304
Pinker, S., 227
Pleonastic nominal, 23–24
Plural, 43–45, 46, 55, 56, 75, 77, 88
Plurality, 44–46
Pollock, J., 25
Possessive, 231, 234–236
Postal, M. , 26, 31, 149
Potsdam, E., 83
PP-extraposition, 136, 154

Pred, 119–121
Predicate
  nominal, 73–74, 92, 112
  nonverbal, 106, 110, 112, 119, 120, 121, 126
  unbounded, 74, 85
  verbal, 73–74, 90, 92, 109, 110, 116, 118, 126
Predicative, 47, 48, 295–297
Preference Principle, 180, 184, 186, 187, 188
Prepositional Phrase, 83, 106
  locative PP, 235, 238, 239
Prince, A., 325
Principle A (Condition A), 28, 31, 32, 142, 180, 181
Principle B (Condition B), 32, 33, 257
Principle C (Condition C), 21, 141, 145, 180–188
Principle of Minimal Compliance, 177, 178
Principles and Parameters (P&P), 107, 135, 137, 189
PRO, 6, 7, 12, 19, 21–23, 257
Probe-goal, 138, 141, 142, 151, 155
Proper names, 80
Propositional Island Condition, 6
Purnell, T. C., 341

Quantification, 45, 75
  Universal Quantifier, 81
Quantificational, 44, 45, 49, 55, 57
Quantified Indefinites, 78, 79, 81, 83, 86, 87, 89, 93, 98
Quantifier float, 208
Quantifier Raising (QR), 276–278
Quantifier Variable Binding, 12, 185, 186
Quantitative Determinacy, 75, 77, 87, 90
Quantization, 75
Quirky agreement, 209, 210

Raimy, E., 325–329, 332
Ramchand, G., 76, 204–207
Readjustment rules, 325, 329, 331, 333–336, 338, 339, 342, 343, 345, 348, 349, 352–354
Reconstruction effect, 167–169, 180, 181, 182, 187, 188, 197, 199, 201, 202, 210, 211–213, 252, 258
Recursive system, 136, 139, 144

Reduplication
  augmented, 325, 331, 340, 345, 354
  partial, 325, 331–338, 340, 347, 354
  simple, 325, 346, 354
Reflexive, 142, 199
Reinhart, T., 139
Relative clause, 6, 20, 21, 260, 261, 276–279, 293, 295
  aboutness relative, 231–134, 238, 240
  direct gap relative, 170
  free relative, 12
  locative relative, 229, 231, 233, 237, 238, 240
  long-distance relative, 171, 173, 188
  restrictive relative, 12, 167
  resumptive relative, 167–169, 171–175, 181
  such that relative, 233–235
Relativized Minimality, 204, 205
Remnant movement, 296
Restrictor, 279–281, 283, 284, 289
Resumptive pronoun, 107, 124, 167, 168, 172, 175–178, 182–185, 187, 188, 201, 203, 205, 208–213, 215, 228, 231, 236, 238, 240
Reuland, E., 142, 157
Richards, N., 141, 176, 177, 198, 208
Right-branching, 91
Ritter, E., 73, 88, 125
Rizzi, L., 138, 143, 151, 158, 199, 204, 207, 213, 242, 308
Romero, M., 199
Rooth, M., 284
Ross, J. R., 33, 201, 214, 216
Roussou, A., 210
Rouveret, A., 53, 54, 59, 167, 168, 170, 172, 174, 176, 178, 179, 180, 182, 184, 185, 186, 188, 189
Rudin, C., 198

Safir, K., 199
Sag, I., 12
Saito, M., 26, 149, 198, 262
Salem, M., 211
Salish, 51
Sanskrit, 346, 348, 349, 352–354
Sauerland, U., 182, 199
Savoia, L. M., 43, 44
Schroten, J., 302

Schwa, 77, 84, 85

Scope, 47, 149, 212, 216
  nuclear, 279–281, 283, 284, 289
  reconstruction, 285–289

Scottish Gaelic, 76, 77, 87, 99, 100, 206

Sensorimotor interface (SM), 136–138, 141, 142, 144, 154, 155

Sentential adverb, 83, 141, 142, 143, 147, 148, 149, 150, 151, 153, 154, 155

Shlonsky, U., 118, 124

Sigurdsson, H., 156

Sihler, A. , 335, 336

Sloppy reading (Bound-variable reading), 252, 253, 255, 257, 265, 275, 281, 282–284

Small clause, 295–302

Soh, H. L., 259, 260

Spanish, 9, 64, 61, 244

Speas, M. , 30

Spec-Head, 25, 26, 46, 90, 91, 99, 146, 213, 267

Specificity, 77, 78, 79, 81–84, 87, 88, 91, 93–96, 98–100

specific NP, 79, 86, 89

Specifier-Complement distinction, 146

Specifier-of relation, 92

Spell-Out, 125, 142, 146, 154, 155, 156, 172, 174, 175, 209, 213

Split-vP, 73, 83

Sportiche, D., 199, 208, 210

SQA, 75, 76, 77, 87, 88, 89

S-structure, 137, 139, 140, 142

Starke, M., 47

Steriade, D., 325, 334–336, 338, 348–351, 353, 354, 374–376

Stowell, T., 29

Stress, main, 96, 98
  phrasal, 83, 96, 97
  word-level, 84, 85

Strict reading (Coreferential reading), 252, 260, 262

Strong Minimalist Thesis (SMT), 135–138, 140, 142, 143, 144, 146

Subcategorization, 251, 252, 258–264, 266, 267

Subjacency, 168, 169, 179

Successive-cyclic movement, 146, 150, 151, 153–156, 168, 169, 173, 174, 177, 178, 186, 187, 208

Superiority effects, 197, 201, 209, 212

Superlative preposing, 295, 297

Svenonious, P., 143

Swiss, 43

Tagalog, 88

Tallerman, M., 168

Tamrazian, A., 83, 96

Tang, C-C. J., 259

Telicity, 73, 77, 88

Tenny, C., 76

Tensed-S Condition, 8, 9, 277, 278

that-trace effect, 207

there-replacement, 24, 26, 27

Theta-Criterion, 21

Theta-role, 21, 23, 51, 119, 140, 144

Tigre, 340–344, 346

Timing slot, 326, 327, 329, 330, 333, 335, 336, 341, 349–352

Tokenism, 277, 279–281, 283–285, 287, 289

Tomioka, S., 212, 253

Topicalization, 107, 151

Trace, 4, 6, 7, 8, 9, 19, 21, 25, 31, 34, 47, 53, 54, 59, 138, 148, 150, 199, 201, 205–207, 214, 216

Transitive verb, 97, 143, 169, 258, 259, 267

Travis, L., 73, 88, 89, 262

Trubetzkoy, N. S., 359, 365–370

Tryon, D. T., 363

Tucking in, 141

Turkish, 78, 84, 87, 94, 99, 100

Udi, 337

Unaccusative, 95, 96, 97, 98, 142, 143, 147, 155, 169

Unergative, 97, 169

Urdu, 84, 87

Uriagereka, J., 242, 243

v*, 143, 144, 147, 148–150, 152, 153, 155

v*-V, 148, 149, 157

Vagli Sopra, 44–46, 48, 49, 50, 51, 55, 56, 57, 62

Valois, D., 73, 88, 89

van Riemsdijk, H., 228–230, 232, 234, 236, 238, 240, 242–245

Variable, 228, 231–234, 236, 257. *See also* Operator
Vaux, B., 84, 85
Vergnaud, J. R., 18, 73, 91–94, 133, 154, 156, 227, 242, 245, 350, 360
Verkuyl, H. K., 73, 75, 87, 93, 100
Vowel, 77, 84, 85
VP ellipsis, 33, 251–253, 255, 257, 261
VP-shells, 73, 90

Wallace, A. R., 139
Wasow, T., 21
Weak crossover, 149, 218
Weisemann, U., 338
Welsh, 168–172, 174, 179, 181, 185, 187
wh-complement, 106, 107
wh-feature, 151, 152
wh-fronting, 198
wh-in-situ, 199, 213
wh-movement, 7, 20, 21, 106, 109, 145, 147, 151, 152, 177, 183, 186, 201, 213, 229–231, 233, 237
wh-NP, 19, 32, 82
wh-operator, 167
wh-phrase, 4, 5, 14, 82, 126, 147–152, 168, 174, 175, 198, 200, 208–210, 212, 213, 217, 228, 233, 241, 297
Whitman, J., 253
Whitney, W., 347, 349
Wilder, C., 291, 295, 296, 300
Williams, E., 12, 97, 258, 275–280, 282, 284, 286–289
Willis, D., 168
Witkos, J., 199
Wu, X., 232
Wurmbrand, S., 211

X-bar Theory, 17, 91
Xu, L., 253

Yip, M., 242

Zero Morpheme, 4
Zribi-Hertz, A., 295
Zubizarreta, M. L., 91, 92, 93, 94, 99

Current Studies in Linguistics

Samuel Jay Keyser, general editor

1. *A Reader on the Sanskrit Grammarians*, J. F. Staal, editor

2. *Semantic Interpretation in Generative Grammar*, Ray Jackendoff

3. *The Structure of the Japanese Language*, Susumu Kuno

4. *Speech Sounds and Features*, Gunnar Fant

5. *On Raising: One Rule of English Grammar and Its Theoretical Implications*, Paul M. Postal

6. *French Syntax: The Transformational Cycle*, Richard S. Kayne

7. *Panini as a Variationist*, Paul Kiparsky, S. D. Joshi, editor

8. *Semantics and Cognition*, Ray Jackendoff

9. *Modularity in Syntax: A Study of Japanese and English*, Ann Kathleen Farmer

10. *Phonology and Syntax: The Relation between Sound and Structure*, Elisabeth O. Selkirk

11. *The Grammatical Basis of Linguistic Performance: Language Use and Acquisition*, Robert C. Berwick and Amy S. Weinberg

12. *Introduction to the Theory of Grammar*, Henk van Riemsdijk and Edwin Williams

13. *Word and Sentence Prosody in Serbocroation*, Ilse Lehiste and Pavle Ivic

14. *The Representation of (In)definiteness*, Eric J. Reuland and Alice G. B. ter Meulen, editors

15. *An Essay on Stress*, Morris Halle and Jean-Roger Vergnaud

16. *Language and Problems of Knowledge: The Managua Lectures*, Noam Chomsky

17. *A Course in GB Syntax: Lectures on Binding and Empty Categories*, Howard Lasnik and Juan Uriagereka

18. *Semantic Structures*, Ray Jackendoff

19. *Events in the Semantics of English: A Study in Subatomic Semantics*, Terence Parsons

20. *Principles and Parameters in Comparative Grammar*, Robert Freidin, editor

21. *Foundations of Generative Syntax*, Robert Freidin

22. *Move α: Conditions on Its Application and Output*, Howard Lasnik and Mamoru Saito

23. *Plurals and Events*, Barry Schein

24. *The View from Building 20: Essays in Linguistics in Honor of Sylvain Bromberger*, Kenneth Hale and Samuel Jay Keyser, editors

25. *Grounded Phonology*, Diana Archangeli and Douglas Pulleyblank

26. *The Magic of a Common Language: Jakobson, Mathesius, Trubetzkoy, and the Prague Linguistic Circle*, Jindrich Toman

27. *Zero Syntax: Experiencers and Cascades*, David Pesetsky

28. *The Minimalist Program*, Noam Chomsky

29. *Three Investigations of Extraction*, Paul M. Postal

30. *Acoustic Phonetics*, Kenneth N. Stevens

31. *Principle B, VP Ellipsis, and Interpretation in Child Grammar*, Rosalind Thornton and Kenneth Wexler

32. *Working Minimalism*, Samuel Epstein and Norbert Hornstein, editors

33. *Syntactic Structures Revisited: Contemporary Lectures on Classic Transformational Theory*, Howard Lasnik with Marcela Depiante and Arthur Stepanov

34. *Verbal Complexes*, Hilda Koopman and Anna Szabolcsi

35. *Parasitic Gaps*, Peter W. Culicover and Paul M. Postal

36. *Ken Hale: A Life in Language*, Michael Kenstowicz, editor

37. *Flexibility Principles in Boolean Semantics: The Interpretation of Coordination, Plurality, and Scope in Natural Language*, Yoad Winter

38. *Phrase Structure Composition and Syntactic Dependencies*, Robert Frank

39. *Representation Theory*, Edwin Williams

40. *The Syntax of Time*, Jacqueline Guéron and Jacqueline Lecarme, editors

41. *Situations and Individuals*, Paul D. Elbourne

42. *Wh-movement Moving On*, Lisa L.-S. Cheng and Norbert Corver, editors

43. *The Computational Nature of Language Learning and Evolution*, Partha Niyogi

44. *Standard Basque: A Progressive Grammar*, 2 Volumes, Rudolf P. G. de Rijk

45. *Foundational Issues in Linguistic Theory: Essays in Honor of Jean-Roger Vergnaud*, Robert Freidin, Carlos P. Otero, Maria Luisa Zubizarreta, editors